EDUCATION IN A FREE SOCIETY

Bill Conrad
317 Maple
Elmhurst, Il.
60126

seventh edition

EDUCATION IN A FREE SOCIETY

An American History

S. Alexander Rippa
University of Vermont

Longman
New York & London

Education in a Free Society:
An American History, Seventh Edition

Copyright © 1992, 1988, 1984, 1980, 1976, 1971, 1967 by Longman Publishing Group.

Longman, 95 Church Street, White Plains, N.Y. 10601

Associated companies:
Longman Group Ltd., London
Longman Cheshire Pty., Melbourne
Longman Paul Pty., Auckland
Copp Clark Pitman, Toronto

Senior editor: Naomi Silverman
Production editor: Ann P. Kearns
Cover design: Joseph DePinho
Production supervisior: Richard C. Bretan

Library of Congress Cataloging in Publication Data

Rippa, S. Alexander.

    Education in a free society : an American history / by S.
Alexander Rippa.—7th ed.
       p.   cm.
    Includes bibliographical references and index.
    ISBN 0-8013-0606-X
    1. Education—United States—History. I. Title.
LA212.R57 1992
370'.973—dc20
                                            90-22283
                                             CIP

1 2 3 4 5 6 7 8 9 10-HA-9594939291

To Barbara, Frances Frogel, Diane, Joel,
David, and Benjamin,
a wise and loving family,
and the memory of
Paul; my parents, Hinda and Guss;
and Reuben H. Frogel, M.D.

Contents

Preface to the Seventh Edition

In writing a history of American education, I have adhered to a chronological approach, which is one of the distinctive values of the historical method. I have also studied educational history as a vital aspect of social history, because education at any given time or place is a reflection of the society of which it is an integral part; indeed, to be understood adequately in the light of up-to-date historical evidence, educational ideas and practices should be reexamined in their social settings from time to time. Maintaining this view, I have undertaken a new synthesis reflecting my own critical interpretation.

My synthesis is selective rather than encyclopedic, with topics organized around dominant patterns of educational thought. I have focused on those ideas that continue to provide a strong foundation for education in a free society. While the chapters present the material chronologically, the topics in some instances overlap, especially when I had to trace a single theme across several decades for purposes of analysis and clarity.

Certainly no synthesis as sweeping as the history of education in American society could be written without the monographs produced in the past by imaginative and scholarly writers. The research of others is gratefully acknowledged. Nevertheless, a historian's approach is still evident in his or her own work: in the very selection of materials and data, the interpretation of conflicting views, the point of anchor in the mainstream.

I have tried to give serious attention to certain historical forces underestimated and even overlooked in their impact on American education. A fresh look, for example, at some powerful ideas from psychology, at the changing concepts of the status of women, at the growing influence of the business creed, and at the impact on the school of the new "information society" is long overdue.

I have included materials based on my research from primary-source documents and recently published monographs. I have tried to offer balanced presentations of contemporary developments: for example, the turmoil over court-ordered school busing; the drive to establish alternative education systems; the legal debates over school finance reform; the controversies in colleges and universities over campus unrest and open admissions; the growing fiscal crisis in education; the continuing struggles for equality of opportunity, the education of the handicapped, and the legal mandate for "mainstreaming" (especially Public Law 94-142); the drive for affirmative action with a focus on the historic *Bakke* case; and the growing Hispanic influence and the issue of bilingual education. I have included additional material on Jean Piaget's contributions to the areas of learning and human development and have discussed changes in the education of Native Americans. Also highlighted are the successes and problems of the Asian Americans, especially the refugees from Southeast Asia who fled after the withdrawal of the United States from Vietnam and the fall of Saigon in 1975. Additionally, I have called the reader's attention to revisionist historians, who have clearly raised important issues for careful study and have stimulated valuable research.

For the seventh edition, more attention is given to John Dewey's contributions to the history of educational thought. I have also discussed some of Ralph Waldo Emerson's major essays; his nineteenth-century ideas seem especially relevant to life in the computer age of the twentieth century. In this edition, there is more attention given to the impact of modern media of communication, especially television, during the post–World War II decades. I have underscored the significance of Howard Gardner's theory of multiple intelligences (MI) and have examined the swiftly moving developments in computer technology, with specific attention to the creation and uses of artificial life. A discussion is included of the impact on educational policy of former President Ronald Reagan's "New Federalism" during the 1980s. I have also underscored the courage and efforts of women in educational history whose lives and accomplishments capture the imagination— for example, Mary Wollstonecraft and Abigail Adams in the eighteenth century; Emma Willard, Mary Lyon, Harriet Tubman, Jane Addams, and Mary Harris Jones in the nineteenth century; and Maria Montessori, Eleanor Roosevelt, and Carol Gilligan in the twentieth century. I have highlighted a central tragedy of the 1980s and 1990s—the crisis of the American family and the growing problem of homeless and neglected children in America.

I have updated my bibliographic essay with many important publications. At the end of each chapter, I have included questions that I hope will encourage the readers to think critically and to engage in an ongoing dialogue on many issues and topics presented throughout the book. I hope that my work will offer suggestions to other educators and historians who are stimulated to explore more intensively some research areas and will help all readers to achieve a deeper appreciation of America's rich heritage in educational history.

I have also discussed the Carnegie Commission and the Holmes Group reports of 1986. I have called the reader's attention to the numerous reports, studies, and scholarly books about American schools that emerged during the early 1980s. The recommendations often overlap and conflict. Will the spate of national reports over education policy help bring about fundamental reforms and remedy serious problems? The challenge confronting the American people is to find constructive remedies from the many prescriptions offered through the various studies and reports.

I believe that a study of the history of education will enable educators, students, and other citizens to reappraise more carefully those forces from the past that are still at work in the present and to solve more successfully some of the crucial problems that confront American education in a changing world. There is considerable advantage in gaining a perspective on the current scene through understanding our heritage. A knowledge of the past is indispensable to a clear analysis of conflicting educational points of view. We should understand our heritage, know our goals, and reorder our scale of national priorities.

One of the goals of a free nation is to encourage the development of human potential. Indeed, the whole concept of individual liberty and freedom of thought is based on the conviction that such freedom nurtures human abilities and that this in turn will lead men and women toward enlightenment. It is this faith that a free nation seeks to fortify. It provides justification for the familiar argument that opportunities must be open to all, because unused human abilities at any level deprive a free society of the mainspring of its vitality. There is no guarantee, of course, that fallible human beings will win over all obstacles or that justice will triumph in the end. But a free society provides the best means for nurturing human gifts at every level and putting reason and goodwill to work.

A brief part of Chapter 5 and sections of Chapter 10 are an outgrowth of research for my doctoral dissertation at Harvard University, written under the supervision of Bernard Bailyn, Adams University Professor. In modified forms, some of this material previously appeared as articles in the *History of Education Journal, The History of Education Quarterly, The School Review, The Social Studies,* and *The Ball State University Forum.*

My obligations in this project are manifold. I am deeply indebted to my colleagues and students who posed some searching questions during the course of this study in the hope that I might come up with more persuasive explanations. I want to express special acknowledgment to the staff of the University of Vermont Library, who helped to facilitate my research in every possible way. I appreciate, too, the many courtesies extended to me by the Harvard University Libraries during the past four decades, the Schlesinger Library at Radcliffe College, the San Diego State University Library, and the Bodleian Library at Oxford University during a sabbatical year abroad.

No one engaged in a work of such comprehensive scholarship can fail to be aware of the infinite patience and cooperation of those who contributed to the success of his enterprise. Archivists and librarians at several research centers in the United States and England were helpful with my many bibliographical inquiries. In particular, I wish to thank Monica Racine, circulation librarian, and her staff at the University of Vermont, who were always helpful and cooperative. Julio A. Martinez, director of the Chicano collection at the San Diego State University Library, was helpful during my research on Mexican Americans. To these people and others I owe a great deal for whatever success this book has achieved during the past twenty-five years.

My greatest debt is to my beloved wife, Barbara Frogel Rippa, and our children, Diane, Joel, David, and Benjamin who have encouraged me with their love and confidence. My wife has helped me with this book from beginning to end. Without her devotion it might never have been started, and without her advice, its completion would have been long delayed.

PART ONE

The Formative Period
1607–1865

CHAPTER 1

The Colonial Tradition

Americans are the western pilgrims, who are carrying along with them that great mass of arts, sciences, vigor, and industry which began long since in the east; they will finish the great circle. The Americans were once scattered all over Europe; here they are incorporated into one of the finest systems of population which has ever appeared, and which will hereafter become distinct by the power of the different climates they inhabit.

DE CREVECŒUR, *Letters from an American Farmer*, 1782

The study of colonial education is of great importance and interest and has become a vital and exciting field in American historical research. Perhaps this resurgence of interest and fascination lies in the basic theme of colonial history: the building of diverse societies in the wilderness of the New World. The relative simplicity of colonial society makes it easier to examine important relationships among social elements—for example, political structures, family ties, and educational patterns—than is possible in more developed and complex societies.

Sometimes this preoccupation with the colonial period has overemphasized the uniqueness of the American experience and obscured a European culture that the settlers inherited from the Old World. It has also led to erroneous notions of historical development as simple processes through which social institutions such as schools slowly evolved into their present form. Historical scholarship has revealed the inadequacy of this idea of American uniqueness and such simple evolutionary conceptions of social change.

The colonists who settled along the coasts of New England and Virginia during the early years of the seventeenth century transplanted to American soil the old institutions of a European culture. Their intellectual heritage was similar to that of the Old World from which it was mainly derived. They were bound together in countless ways by deeply rooted traditions and customs. There was the important bond of a common language forged by England in establishing an Anglo-Saxon civilization. On both sides of the Atlantic Ocean there were the basic postulates of Western thought. English in its essential elements, the result of converging streams of influence, colonial society reflected an ideology deeply rooted in a European way of life.

It would be naïve, however, to assume that patterns of thought were transplanted unchanged to colonial America and developed in the same way as in the Old World. The early settlers, weary and often ill after perilous ocean voyages, encountered problems of survival on a raw continent far from their homeland. Vast in area, with a small population confined to widely scattered settlements, the New World in the seventeenth century became a haven for varied nationalists. Colonial attitudes represented by such ethnic diversity were modified by a new physical environment and by contact and assimilation with Native American, other Caucasian, and African American elements. These two geographic and social forces—environmental survival and racial interaction—had a selective influence on European ideas. In conquering a strange wilderness and in devising new patterns of social relationships, the colonists soon found their old modes of thinking changed, their family ties weakened, and their attitudes and hopes altered. Surely one cannot fully understand the development of American education without taking into account how the New World changed the European Heritage.

The thirteen original colonies not only differed from Europe in geography and social life. There were sectional contrasts, too, in the New World. For example, the land in the South, so different from the soil of New England, encouraged a rural, agricultural economy that inhibited the growth of publicly supported schools. Southern economy, predominantly extractive, made extensive slaveholding profitable in the tobacco and rice colonies and led to the establishment of an agricultural aristocracy, profoundly affecting social relationships for generations to come. On the other hand, unlike the sparsely settled, isolated plantations and homesteads in the southern colonies, the complex economy of New England was conducive to compact communities and growing mercantile interests. There were differences, too, between the settled regions along the Atlantic seaboard and the frontier regions farther inland. The inhabitants of the back country had little in common with the planters or merchants in the more settled coastal regions. Cultural differences were more striking than common features, and the varied societies that emerged in the New World affected the number and nature of schools and, more indirectly, colonial attitudes toward civic and social institutions.

THE SOUTHERN COLONIES

The colonial South was profoundly affected by an agrarian economy and a strong leadership that played an important role in American history. New settlers, duped by propaganda about the New World and unprepared for conditions in the wilderness, quickly learned to farm and to cope with reality. Even the coastal towns were close to the frontier back country, and city inhabitants were always in contact with the farmers who fed them. After the first settlement at Jamestown in 1607, rural isolation and an agrarian way of life were basic determinants of southern society.

In 1614 John Rolfe shipped a cargo of tobacco to London and paved the way for a one-crop agricultural system that coincided with the European mercantilist theory. A raw product could be transported to England, processed there, and distributed in the colonies and Europe at a profit. By accident the colonists had discovered a money crop leading to prosperity. The need for a cash crop and a credit system devised by English merchants in the seventeenth century tied the tobacco growers to the mother country. By 1617 the settlers were planting tobacco everywhere in the Chesapeake Bay region, even in the streets of Jamestown. Its growth spread so rapidly that the governor soon ordered that no settler should be permitted to plant the weed until he had first planted two acres of corn. It was soon discovered that tobacco exhausted the soil in approximately seven years, and planters eagerly acquired a succession of fresh land. The southern planter also required a plentiful supply of cheap labor to cultivate the crop and increase his profits. The opening of the African slave market after the Treaty of Utrecht in 1713, together with an abundance of cheap land, had a tremendous impact on southern society.

A plantation system based on slavery soon dominated most of the coastal plain from the Chesapeake Bay region to Florida. Then, as now, the African American was a common human element against a southern rural background. Large plantations clustered along the estuaries and rivers that threaded the coastal plain. Along the banks of navigable rivers, seagoing vessels docked at the plantation wharves. The inland waterways of Virginia and Maryland became focal points for the commercial interests of the tobacco planters, who were dependent on English shippers for their merchandise and compelled to trade with Bristol and London. Here, then, was a rural society sparsely settled over a large area, led by a planter aristocracy, and obsessed with the importance of land, a key to social status in a section where agriculture was the primary interest.

The Leadership of the Landed Aristocrats

During the first half of the eighteenth century, the Atlantic coastal plain of eastern Virginia was transformed from a dense wilderness to a well-ordered civilization of large estates and plantations. An influential landed aristocracy emerged before the American Revolution, overshadowing the community around them and impressing their ideas and attitudes on the people. In Virginia and Maryland these wealthy planters constructed large estates along the Potomac, the James, the Rappahannock, and the Patuxent rivers. Most of these families, such as the Carters, the Fitzhughs, and the Byrds, had a strong sense of duty to society. Imitators of the English country families, they were a hard-working ruling class and contributed able leadership at the time of the American Revolution. Throughout the colonial period, they maintained political control. These wealthy landed proprietors acted as church wardens in their parishes, served as county sheriffs, and sat as justices in the local courts. From their group came other county officers, the colonels of the militia, and members of the House of Burgesses and the Council of State. Because of their education and wealth, they exerted a remarkable influence out of all proportion to their numbers. Unfortunately, few sustained attempts have been made to depict this fascinating period of southern history before the American Revolution, for historians have tended to concentrate instead on the Civil War and Reconstruction eras.

Most of these landed aristocrats were of English lower-class or middle-class background. Those who were in titled positions of influence in England were not likely to emigrate to America, haven for the poor and the social heretics. About one-half of the white immigrants in the colonial South had arrived in the New World as indentured servants.

Family fortune and great wealth were accumulated by land acquisition and tobacco growing. In an expanding economy these were the quickest ways to prosperity. Since the aristocrats filled all offices from the vestry to the governor's council, political power paved the way for the easy purchase of large tracts. With wealth came status, privilege, and power. Possessing great wealth in land and slaves, the planters automatically succeeded to positions of great influence. They were chosen as justices of the county courts by the governor's commission; they were selected for membership in the Assembly; and they succeeded to vacancies on the vestry. Probably the most sustaining forces perpetuating the status of the landed aristocracy were the laws of primogeniture and entail, which passed the estate on to the eldest son. In all this, the local people acquiesced and apparently approved, for most of the immigrants were accustomed to the English concept of social stratification.

The aristocrats were colorfully dressed, wearing long coats, knee breeches, yellow or scarlet waistcoats, ruffled shirts, silk stockings, and shoes with bright buckles. They wore expensive oiled periwigs dusted with powder. Wigs were abandoned toward the end of the eighteenth century, and the aristocrats wore their powdered hair in a queue, adorned with triangular-shaped cocked hats. The ladies appeared with elaborate coiffures and wore silk or satin hoop skirts and high-heeled shoes. The children were dressed as miniature adults.

Perhaps the most interesting of all the wealthy landed proprietors of the early eighteenth century was William Byrd II of Westover, who kept detailed diaries of life on his Virginia plantation.[1] There were other founders of family dynasties in the colonial South: William Fitzhugh, Richard Lee II, and Robert Carter, of Nomini Hall, to mention a few.[2] Although individualistic in temperament, they all lived according to the same general social pattern. Byrd was typical of this ruling class.

William Byrd was a remarkable American of the early eighteenth century. Educated in England and later in Holland, he enjoyed English plays, the friendship of nobles in the coffeehouses, and the companionship of women. Apparently England was always Byrd's nostalgic "home." At Westover, he acquired one of the largest libraries in the colonies. He imported portraits of his famous acquaintances in England. In fact, Byrd was always busy: he supervised all the details of his plantation from early morning until late at night; he speculated in land and real-estate schemes; he continued his father's slave-trading activities; he prospected for copper and coal; he personally attended sick slaves or neighbors; and he studied like a monk, often reading Hebrew, Latin, or Greek from three o'clock in the morning until breakfast. He usually read a portion of Homer or Petronius and a Hebraic passage before breakfast. In addition to current English works, he also read in the original versions Dutch, French, and Italian literature. Although Byrd allowed little time for fun, he openly flirted with women, even in the presence of his wife. He attended meetings of the Council of State in Williamsburg, where he stayed afterward with other planters, drinking heavily and playing dice and often losing at cards.

The preoccupation of Byrd and other wealthy planters with mundane affairs did not mean that they lacked upper-class ideals. On the contrary, more than anything else, they were determined that they and their families should not become barbarians in the hostile wilderness. At no time did they overlook family stability and forget their English heritage. Insofar as colonial conditions allowed, they copied the English gentry, following the manners of the country gentlemen of the mother country. On that pattern they modeled their homes and their way of life; in a similar manner they sought to educate their sons in all knowledge deemed essential for an English gentleman.

The wealthy aristocracy of the colonial South, then, were determined, forceful personalities, carving from the wilderness the genesis of a great nation. They were a diligent class, spending long working hours in personal and civic affairs and in the management of their own plantations. Of course, no one will deny that some selfishness and indolence prevailed among the upper class. But by and large these wealthy planters were in a real sense men of business, merchant capitalists, concerned with managing their estates and making a profit through trade in the world market. Their correspondence reveals their business acumen, their foresight, and their boundless energy. Overly ambitious, perhaps, and greedy for land, they were, nevertheless, an independent, fearless group who rarely made wealth a goal in itself. Land they sought for prestige and family tradition: these they enjoyed. But more important, they linked the prerogatives of power with responsibility and a deep sense of obligation to others. The wealthy planters were imbued with a belief that in return for their privileged position they were duty-bound to serve the state and to govern well. George Washington, for example, personified this code of dedication and service when he accepted command of the Continental Army. This ruling aristocracy of the early eighteenth century produced Washington, Jefferson, Marshall, and other great statesmen destined to lead a new democracy.

Isolated from other families by great distances, the wealthy planters developed a spirit of hospitality that prevailed for generations. Plantations were separated by heavily wooded tracts, and overland roads were difficult and hazardous. As a result, waterways became the main travel routes. For transportation purposes, the estates were usually located near the riverbanks. Rural living far from the nearest neighbor in virtual human isolation except for slaves induced an avid interest in social activity among the plantations. There were at times an unrestrained gaiety and social whirl. Guest rooms were seldom empty, for celebrations and visitors were frequent. Even strangers passing by were entertained hospitably and welcomed as guests. Secluded from public view and shielded by stately trees, the planters and their families were able to enjoy a life greatly valued by the English gentry and to participate eagerly in outdoor sports like the country squires of the mother country.

In Charleston, South Carolina, the planter aristocracy developed a notable center of culture and business activity. In 1776 Charleston was approximately one-third as large as Philadelphia, which had about 35,000 inhabitants. In many cases the South Carolina planters were wealthier than the tobacco elite. Like the ruling class in Virginia, they were self-made, enterprising businessmen. Instead of tobacco, they grew rice and indigo and engaged in a lucrative slave trade. In Charleston they built large ocean-front summer homes to escape the heat and mosquitoes on their inland rice plantations. By the end of the eighteenth century, Charleston had become the wealthiest city in colonial America.

Contrary to romantic legend, the plantations were frequently noisy, filthy, and trouble-filled due to servant problems. At Byrd's Westover, servants were a constant problem. Upper-class manners were not so polite as one might expect in such aristocratic elegance. Quarrels were loud and often bitter, and both men and women imbibed sufficiently to be drunk in public. Profanity in everyday speech by both sexes was quite common.

At least plantation routine was fairly stable. Dinner was served in the hot afternoon, usually at three o'clock. In the warm, humid climate, numerous flies were brushed away with large fans by African American children. At nine o'clock the planter usually retired in a high canopied bed. It is unlikely that he slept soundly, for bedbugs were common. Byrd washed his feet every day, apparently an unusual habit in a period when baths were rarely taken by anyone.

It would be a mistake to assume that all planters were aristocrats imitating the English gentry. It is true that the wealthy planters held the reins of political control. But the vast majority of planters were farmers owning from fifty to a hundred acres. Yeomen and small farmers, mainly Presbyterian Scots from Ulster, were distant neighbors to the aristocrats. They lived in the back country on the fringe of civilization, up the rivers and beyond the swamps, where a different southern society evolved.

Social activity was not confined to upper-class plantation life. In the colonial South the local church was a weekly focal point of wide social interest. In fact, the Anglican Church was a primary social institution. It was legally established and supported by local taxes. Its vestry was actually an instrument of local government. The Anglican vestry established tax rates and even collected local taxes. It officially disseminated provincial news and laws every Sunday from the pulpit. If many attended church once a week, it was not only for religious purposes. Perhaps more important was the chance to socialize, to gossip, to transact business. Notices of all kinds were posted on the church doors. Few would dare miss the social opportunity afforded by church attendance in the Anglican South.

While the early settlers in the New World shared a common religious background, life in the wilderness soon brought about marked contrasts. Religion in the South did not serve as an instrument of civic discipline as it did in New England. The Virginia planters were no less religious than the settlers of Massachusetts. But the South lacked the cohesive strength of the New England town and the religious force of Calvinism. Weak and unstable, undistinguished by piety, the Anglican Church established few local roots. There was, in fact, widespread southern apathy toward religious obligations. The Virginia pattern was typical outside New England: in Maryland, for example, the Roman Catholic priests could not sustain a religious unity and obedience. In the South neither religion nor family could induce people to conform in the frontier wilderness.

The most striking difference between the coastal region and the back country was the prevalence of free labor in the interior. The frontiersmen were handicapped by lack of transportation and were compelled to depend on self-sufficient farming. Slavery was never adapted to this small-scale system of agriculture based chiefly on growing potatoes, wheat, oats, barley, and hay. Large families afforded abundant labor in the back country. Free land was highly attractive and easily accessible, and settlers could not be held in a position of quasi serfdom. The rapid settlement of the back country thwarted any attempt to transplant feudal ideas to America and introduced into southern society a vigorous, independent group of yeoman farmers destined later to play leading roles in the rise of the common people.

THE MIDDLE COLONIES

On the eve of the Revolution the presence of non-English-speaking groups on the Atlantic seaboard reinforced the belief that the New World was a haven for the world's oppressed. Collectively, these diverse elements inter-acted and partially fused, modifying ideas and social institutions and paving the way for the rise of an American nationality. Toward the end of the colonial period, J. Hector St. John (de Crèvecœur), a naturalized American from France, referred to a great melting pot from which emerged a new man, an American: "What then is the American, this new man? He is either an European, or the descendant of an European; hence that strange mixture of blood, which you will find in no other country."[3] The metaphor used by de Crèvecœur and repeated by many writers underscores the assimilative process prevalent in the New World. This idea of the United States as a melting pot of races and nationalities has been a recurring and frequently overworked theme in American history. Social historians have shown a continuing interest in examining the different ores that entered into this melting pot, pointing out that not all of it melted completely. If a melting pot fused a heterogeneous mass into something different, these new Americans retained, nevertheless, a definite impress of their national origins.

Quakerism
One of the most successful Englishmen to found a colony in the New World was William Penn. As a young man he enjoyed many advantages, including a college education. His father was a prominent admiral in the Royal Navy, and Penn seemed destined for a career in the life of the English court. Then suddenly, in 1667, at the age of twenty-three, he heard a Quaker sermon based on the theme "There is a faith that overcometh the world." Apparently the sermon converted him, for Penn gave up the gayest court in Europe to serve among the Society of Friends, often called Quakers.

Distressed at the persecution of religious sects in England and Europe, William Penn viewed his proprietary grant in the New World as a haven for oppressed Quakers and other harassed peoples. He called his proprietary colony on the Delaware, which King Charles II named Pennsylvania, the

"Holy Experiment." Penn also hoped to rebuild his declining wealth through an investment for his family. To attract settlers to his colony he published a short description of Pennsylvania, citing with Quaker honesty the positive and negative features of the new land. Penn's promotional tracts were translated into German and distributed in the villages and towns of the Rhine Valley. The land was in ruins and the Germans impoverished from the Thirty Years' War. Internal religious conflicts started by princes who sought to impose their religion upon the people had left Germany a devastated battleground. Penn appealed especially to the European pietist sects. To dispose of his 28 million acres held by the charter, he offered generous terms for land purchases. To every settler who would establish his home and family in the colony, Penn promised five hundred acres of free land, with the right to buy additional land at one shilling an acre. Even more important, he also offered, in addition to cheap land, religious toleration and representative government.

The first Germans arrived in Pennsylvania in October 1683. Led by Francis Daniel Pastorius, a lawyer from Frankfurt, these pioneers settled just north of Philadelphia in Germantown. No one should come who does not want to labor long and hard, Pastorius warned prospective immigrants. "Hic opus, hic labor est," he wrote. Through his leadership and writings, Pastorius helped to build a self-sustaining, flourishing village. Economic stability, based on family solidarity, industry, and hard work, created prosperous German settlements.

The Germanic culture in the New World displayed unusual vitality. From eastern Pennsylvania the Germans moved into southern New York, western Maryland and Virginia, and even the Carolinas. From the Rhineland and Switzerland, German-speaking groups also settled in the southern colonies. In fact, the German contribution to the civilization of the colonial South has not been fully explored. By the outbreak of the Revolution, German settlers had moved into every English colony. The heaviest concentrations were in Pennsylvania, particularly Lancaster County, where the German language predominated.

The tolerant attitude of the Quakers encouraged others to settle in the colony. Businessmen in particular were attracted to Philadelphia, which enterprising Quakers transformed into a leading center of local and international trade. First settled by Quakers, Philadelphia became the most diverse city in religion among the colonies, a port of entry for immigrants attracted by the promise of fertile land and freedom of conscience. From other colonies and from various parts of the British empire, shipmasters, craftsmen, and traders of various merchandise came there to share in the business wealth that Quaker tolerance helped to establish. Prosperous Quaker merchants built commodious houses and furnished them luxuriously, tempering to some extent the Quaker determination to adhere to a simple life. By the end of the colonial period, Philadelphia surpassed New York and Boston as a center of commerce.

Paradoxically, despite certain ideas of religious freedom, the Quakers, like the Puritans, were strict moralists and censors of human behavior. They discouraged all worldly vanities. For example, they regarded theatrical plays as temptations to evil and banned performances in Philadelphia. Painting, too, was considered a form of idolatry forbidden by the Bible, and music was condemned for its sensuality. The Quakers were strong pacifists and viewed Pennsylvania as a land of peace untrammeled by war and armies. They considered themselves as a separate people and developed a social isolation that has persisted with varying degrees of intensity to the present time.

Quaker individualism in biblical interpretation was based on a belief in the guidance of an "Inner Light." To Quakers the Divine Presence was a guide and a confider, manifesting Himself directly to each of His children. There was part of God in every person, Quakers believed, and ritual and sermon were unnecessary. Twice a week the Quakers went to their meeting-house and awaited in silent meditation the Light Within. They dressed in absolute simplicity, abhorred class distinction, and rebelled against war, oaths of any kind, and capital punishment.

This religious core of Quakerism was reflected in the writings of John Woolman, devout teacher, tailor, and farmer. He believed that personal communication with God enabled people to revise and supplement what they learned on secular or spiritual matters. Woolman and his fellow Quakers rejected the need for learned ministers to interpret religious truths and believed that even the most humble person could speak with God. In the most literal expression of the Reformation search for a simple Christianity, Quakerism reduced theology to a primary belief in the supremacy of the human conscience. The Bible was considered no substitute for intuitive values revealed by an Inner Light, a personal communion with God.

New Netherland and New York

The settlement of New Netherland reflected the pervading influence of a Dutch culture that persisted for over a century. The liberal religious policy there attracted inhabitants with diverse views. Indeed, the doors of the colony were open to so many non-Dutch that it became an unusual haven for religious freedom in the New World. Nevertheless, long after 1664, when New Netherland passed under the control of the British, Dutch influence remained dominant. Dutch culture, for example, was seen in the architecture of the Hudson Valley. The picturesque legends and folklore of the fun-loving and superstitious Dutch Americans were vividly preserved by Washington Irving and other New York writers who created from memories of irascible governors and doughty burghers a distinctive segment of American literature. Only the English were able to counteract the Dutch in sufficient numbers to supersede Holland's rich contributions to the New World.

In New York a small, powerful aristocracy emerged that rivaled in wealth and landholdings the upper class of the southern colonies. There were, however, striking contrasts between the two groups. Unlike the Virginia planters, the New York landlords were more interested in trade and law than in agriculture. For New Yorkers land was merely a capital investment acquired while one pursued other interests. New York society was too heterogeneous to permit the development of a paternalistic upper class like that which emerged in the southern colonies. The wealthy landlords symbolized a conservative element in New York politics, a group primarily concerned with commerce and finance.

While the influence of diverse nationalities during the seventeenth and eighteenth centuries has sometimes been underestimated, it should be remembered that education in colonial America owed more to England than to any other nation. At no time were the non-English-speaking groups in a majority. In Pennsylvania, for example, where Benjamin Franklin thought that the Germanic culture might supplant the British, the Germans outnumbered other nationalities only in a few sections. The fact that the Swedes, the Dutch, and the Germans tended to ostracize themselves from their British neighbors and to live separately in contiguous communities also helps to explain why their influence was overshadowed by that of the English. Indeed, the Germans willingly surrendered political control to their English-speaking neighbors representing the mother country. The Germans had fled from an impoverished land overrun by war, persecution, and famine. Their tie with Europe was primarily a religious bond. These factors, then—numerical majority, closer ties with the motherland, and political leadership in the New World—explain in large measure the far more influential role played by England in the subsequent educational development of the United States.

NEW ENGLAND

The New England colonists were confined to a small area with physiographic conditions that limited agricultural expansion. New England was about one-eighth the area of the southern colonies; yet by 1700 its population was about equal to that of the South. Massachusetts alone comprised about two-thirds of the total population of New England. Traversed by two mountain ranges, New England's glacial soil was thin and stony, with only a few fertile areas from alluvial deposits along the riverbanks. The Green Mountains and the Berkshire Hills extended north and south from Canada to Connecticut; and the White Mountains formed a group nearer to the coast. The seashore north of Cape Cod was rugged and forbidding with deep inlets from the Atlantic Ocean. South of the Cape along a wide beach were natural harbors interspersed with treacherous shoals. Originally one vast forest, New England was subject to severe climatic variations. Long and harsh winters added immeasurably to the severe obstacles encountered by the Puritan colonists.

On the other hand, these environmental limitations were compensated to some extent by certain important advantages. Some natural isolation and forced seclusion provided an element of protection from the powerful Indian tribes in the West. Abundant timber for shipbuilding, numerous bays and harbors for commerce and trade, and adjacent waters teeming with herring, cod, and whale beckoned New Englanders to the open sea. Encouraged by easy access northward to the Grand Banks of Newfoundland, fishing became a basic part of the Yankee commerce. The fisheries also stimulated the shipbuilding industry. By 1675 no less than six hundred vessels and four thousand men were engaged in the fishing industry. The following year as many as thirty Yankee-built ships a year were being sold to the mother country. Other industries, too, sprang up: extraction and exportation of raw materials, especially forest products; manufacturing, such as textiles; and trading, particularly the fur trade. This industrial diversification encouraged the growth of compact settlements and towns and deeply influenced the pattern of New England's social and economic life.

The township system of local government was indigenous to American soil and ideally suited to the New England communities. Established in Massachusetts after 1635 by the General Court, the town was a geographical entity covering about forty square miles. The town meeting was the primary agency for control of the community. At the town meeting taxes were levied, economic measures approved, and various social services provided. The meeting enforced the will of the majority, who were empowered to tax citizens for measures designed to promote the welfare of the total group. To prevent dispersion of the population and effect cohesion among local congregations, the leaders of the Massachusetts Bay Colony strongly supported the township type of settlement.

Puritan Thought

Perhaps the most significant force in shaping colonial intellectual life was a religious tradition inherited from the Protestant Reformation. Begun by Martin Luther in 1519, the Reformation had a profound impact on the colonization of the New World. Internal religious strife in the Protestant camp and deep struggles between the Catholic and Protestant leaders were major factors in the European settlement of North America. Protestantism was dominant in the New World, and the social institutions of American life evolved in the shadow of Protestant religious beliefs.

Few leaders exerted a greater influence on the settlement of colonial America than did John Calvin, sometimes referred to as the "Protestant Pope." Unlike Lutheranism, Calvinism left an indelible mark on American thought.

Born in France in 1509, Calvin was educated in both theology and law. To escape persecution he left France and went to Basel, Switzerland, where he wrote the *Institutes of the Christian Religion,* one of the most famous works of the Reformation. After 1536 Calvin lived in Geneva, which he controlled as a city-republic. By 1630 there were seventy-four editions and nine translations of the *Institutes.* His prolific writing, numerous speeches, and voluminous correspondence strongly affected the course of the Protestant Reformation.

Calvin's ideas infiltrated the major countries of Europe and upset the internal affairs of all between 1560 and 1650. In England his followers were the Puritans; in Scotland, the Presbyterians; in France, the Huguenots; and in Holland, the members of the Dutch Reformed Church. From these religious groups came the majority of the emigrants to the thirteen colonies. Most important in the settlement of America were the Puritans, whose religious singularity in the Massachusetts Bay Colony gradually conditioned all other ideas in colonial New England.

The Puritans, who settled in the Massachusetts Bay Colony in the 1630s, considered the Church of England to be a true, although corrupt, church. They wanted to reform the church from within. The Puritans forged ahead with wealth, numbers, and rank, posing a direct challenge to the English government.

The ideas of the Pilgrims, who came over on the *Mayflower,* differed sharply from those of the Puritans. The Pilgrims were Separatists. They rejected the authority of the state over the church and believed that a man should be allowed to worship according to the dictates of his own conscience. Unlike the Puritans, the Separatists were simply a small and humble band who merely wanted to retreat to a remote area where they could set up their own church. Despised because of their views, the Separatists fled England and took refuge at Plymouth Rock, where they became known as the Pilgrim Fathers.

The Pilgrims actually influenced American history out of all proportion to their contemporary importance or small numbers. The *Mayflower* weighed anchor on September 16, 1620, and reached Cape Cod late in November. The long voyage to the New World was hazardous in the face of terrible odds. The months ahead at Plymouth were even more difficult. By 1637 the little group of settlers numbered only 549. Scurvy, smallpox, and winter storms had taken a heavy toll. The Pilgrims' faith and courage, especially that of William Bradford, the historian, and that of John Carver, the governor, became a symbolic force in American life.

Within a decade after the Pilgrims landed at Plymouth, Puritan leader John Winthrop was approaching the New England shore in the early summer of 1630 on the *Arbella,* a ship of 350 tons, 28 guns, and a crew of 52. The *Arbella* was one of eleven ships, carrying a total of about 700 passengers, 240 cows, and 60 horses. The ship had sailed on March 29 from Cowes in the Isle of Wight and reached Massachusetts in late June. Winthrop kept a journal from Easter Monday 1630 until his last illness in 1649.[4] A primary source of early Massachusetts history, the journal was filled with entries of the Puritan leader's hopes, sorrows, and vindications. During the long ocean crossing, Winthrop often preached to his fellow passengers to propitiate God. He urged more unity and stricter conformity in the New World. One of his oft-quoted sermons dramatized Winthrop's divine aspirations for the Puritan venture in Massachusetts: "Wee shall be as a Citty upon a Hill, the eies of all people are uppon us; soe that if wee shall deale falsely with our god in this worke wee have undertaken and soe cause him to withdrawe his present help from us, wee shall be made a story and a by-word through the world."[5] A city upon a hill was also to be a place for old England to notice, a model to copy, a divine mission, a covenant with God. How different was Winthrop's ambition from that of the Pilgrims who had landed at Plymouth ten years before!

Having spent more than seventy days at sea on the *Arbella,* Winthrop sailed near Maine along the New England coast in June 1630, describing in glowing terms his first impressions. As a site for this covenant with God, for this Puritan mission, Massachusetts, Winthrop believed, had been specially selected by God. Despite the drowning of his son soon after landing, his initial zeal and hope seldom waned. Later journal entries described the bitter winter storms, the discontent, the lingering deaths from smallpox. He was impatient with those who complained: for Winthrop all this was part of God's grand scheme.

From 1630 to 1634 Winthrop was governor of the Massachusetts Bay Colony. The embodiment of New England Puritanism, caricatured in drawings with a long nose and a somber expression. Winthrop was a fanatic, a religious enigma of conglomerate qualities. His journal and private letters are interspersed with details, descriptions, and narrow-minded views revealing a self-disciplined and intensely religious man. "My trust is in his mercy, that, upon faith of his gracious promise, and the experience of his fatherly goodness, he will be our God to the end," Winthrop wrote in a letter to his wife on April 28, 1629. "Only the fruition of Jesus Christ and the hope of heaven can give us true comfort and rest."[6] Born in 1588, he had embraced Puritanism at an early age. Religion had become his total obsession: he was unyielding, crusading, completely possessed with a deep evangelical responsibility to others. Winthrop's religious crusade soon established in Massachusetts a rigid conformity far exceeding the original Puritan goal. Under his leadership the Massachusetts colonists set up a theocracy quite different from the church-state system in England.

Unlike Plymouth, the Massachusetts Bay Colony developed into a powerful center for American Puritanism. Between 1629 and 1642, about twenty thousand colonists settled in New England, mainly in the Bay Colony. A crusading faith, Puritanism extended its evangelical zeal throughout New England. Not all the settlers, however, possessed the religious drive of the ruling group who sought to create a "Bible Commonwealth."

A cardinal principle of Puritan faith was the acceptance of the Bible as the inspired word of God, granting to humankind a divine rule of conduct and an approved form of worship. Every aspect of the church required authorization of the Scriptures. The Puritan had to support every proposition by chapter and verse.

Calvinist theology was a matter of supreme importance in the everyday life of the New England Puritans. Man, in their view, was a sinner and the world a habitation of evil and temptation. Man's chief concern was not earthly pleasure, but the welfare of his soul. The Puritan doctrine of salvation or regeneration was based on the omnipotence of God and the impotence of man. Man's earthly mission was the glorification of God, omnipotent ruler of the universe, who decreed the destiny of His creatures and by means of His providences warned, rewarded, and punished His saints on earth. Man had no power of his own to cleanse his life, to attain mastery over the evil within himself. His only hope of salvation or regeneration was the grace of God.

Fundamental in Puritan theology was the doctrine of predestination. Adam's sin had separated man from his Creator and had implanted a corrupt love of self and material gain in the sons of man. However, the Son of God in His compassion for man's suffering had entered into a covenant with God for the salvation of a chosen few among the descendants of Adam. Thus the sacrifice of Christ on earth had conferred everlasting salvation upon the elect. Others were condemned to an afterlife of eternal suffering.

> Your wickedness makes you as it were heavy as lead, and to tend downwards with great weight and pressure towards hell; and if God should let you go, you would immediately sink and swiftly descend and plunge into the bottomless gulf, and your healthy constitution, and your own care and prudence, and best contrivance, and all your righteousness, would have no more influence to uphold you and keep you out of hell, than a spider's web would have to stop a falling rock.[7]

Such was the preaching of Jonathan Edwards in a frequently published sermon. This doctrine of predestination cast a dark shadow over the lives of the colonists.

Man could do nothing on earth to achieve his own salvation. Born in sin, he could be liberated only by God's grace, hopefully by faith instead of by deeds. If by chance he were among the elect, his fortune was due to the love of Christ and the grace of God. Upon the elect God had placed His approval: they were the exalted, the ardent Calvinists, confident, aggressive, determined to assert their ordained right to rule.

Although the Puritans recognized man's inability to achieve perfection in this world, they were not completely fatalistic in their outlook toward life. Believing intensely in the glory and grandeur of God, undaunted by a transitory existence, the Puritans merely accepted with unquestioned faith the sinfulness of man.

Puritanism was an articulate philosophy, reflecting the intellectual climate of seventeeth-century England. Although man was an inherently evil creature, he was also a rational being, capable of understanding his own actions and accepting responsibility for them. Human life, moreover, had value insofar as man had the freedom to choose between good and evil. Drawing upon the traditions and ideas of the Reformation and the Renaissance, the Puritans stressed the harmony of faith and reason, insisting that one strengthened the other. In the Puritan mind, there was no conflict between the revealed truth of God and the natural world of man. The Puritan could even accept scientific knowledge as an adjunct faith. The Puritans adopted an intellectual rather than an intuitive approach to life and sought to unify faith and reason into a coherent ideology.

This synthesis was a cornerstone in the intellectual life of colonial New England. It produced, first of all, political intolerance and led to the suppression of dissent; and in this respect, it was an inhibiting force on the mind. Toleration to any extent had no sanction in the Puritan creed. Those who opposed the Puritan oligarchy were obviously not among the elect. If God had condemned them to hell, then His saints could not tolerate their evil ways. Indeed, toleration was a flagrant defiance of the will of God.

Puritan thought also led toward a relatively high educational level. The Puritans who settled in the Massachusetts Bay Colony in the 1630s strongly believed that they were a people chosen by God to establish His kingdom in the New World. Preachers and historians throughout the seventeenth century reiterated this idea of New England's divine mission. Because the Puritans were so convinced that they were a peculiar people exemplary of God's elect, they displayed a deep sense of responsibility to God. It was mainly this determination and hope to be accepted in the eyes of God that made work and education such primary concerns in the Puritan mind: to achieve nobility and attain salvation, man must transcend his physical surroundings by education, work, and great personal struggle. Almost immediately after setting foot on American shores, the Puritans erected a printing press, established schools, and founded a college. With its rigorous stress on work and learning, Puritanism evolved into a system of thought admirably suited to a frontier way of life.

Social distinctions in New England were almost as sharply drawn as in the southern colonies. There was a powerful aristocratic group, but it was not a class of leisure. In Puritan New England everyone worked. In fact, de Crèvecœur observed with approval "that restless industry which is the principal characteristic of these colonies." To maintain rigid social lines, the Puritans were seated carefully in church according to status. Until 1772, even the catalogue for Harvard College arranged the students in the order of social rank, listing the Winthrops and the Saltonstalls near the top. Although slaves were few in number, the New England colonists were not morally opposed to the system. The first public denunciation of slavery in Massachusetts occurred in 1700 in a pamphlet written by Judge Samuel Sewall, in which he criticized "the wicked practice." The African American people were generally despised and in church sat in the "slaves' gallery." Drawn from a semifeudal social structure in the Old World, the early leaders of the Massachusetts Bay Colony were as determined to establish a society of class distinctions as to maintain a rigid conformity in religious belief.

Religion, then, was the most pervasive influence in colonial New England. While the colonists differed profoundly, perhaps vindictively, concerning the most effective path to salvation, all sects agreed, at least, that the Bible was the ultimate source of God's revelation. There were, of course, wide differences in interpreting the Bible. Minority groups from Europe yearned to interpret the Scriptures free from political interference.

It should be clearly understood, however, that religious toleration was a concept neither recognized nor approved. The emigrants in the seventeenth and early eighteenth centuries had little patience for toleration. Those who sought refuge in the strange forests of New England and Virginia really wanted freedom from interference by opposing sects or political authorities. They were land-hungry, too: to throngs of unemployed inhabitants in an overpopulated Jacobean England wracked by periodic financial depressions, the vision of landed proprietorship led even the poorest servant to sell himself into a four-years' bondage to pay for passage to an unsettled New World. Once in America, those who had been persecuted in Europe soon began feverishly to expel the heretics from their own political domain.

The Growth of Towns

The growth of town life on the eastern seaboard accentuated the contrasts between the northern and southern colonies and made commercial New England a focal point of intellectual activity. Except for Williamsburg and Charleston, urban life developed north of the Potomac. The northern towns maintained closer contacts with Europe. In the larger towns printers published books, almanacs, and newspapers. The towns attracted leading figures in law, medicine, and to some extent theology. In the towns were also the homes of the merchant aristocrats whose contribution to intellectual life accelerated the dissemination of ideas from abroad.

While Maryland and Virginia were establishing an agrarian aristocracy, New England was building a commercial civilization of merchants and masters of shipping. In the span of only two generations, enterprising traders in Boston and other port towns had accumulated enormous wealth and established family dynasties. A number of merchants flourished in New England after emigrating to Massachusetts Bay from London during the depression years of Charles I. Fortunes were built on the fur trade, land speculation, and, most of all, commerce and shipping. A proud and powerful group, these aristocrats developed a sense of family pride that equaled, and perhaps surpassed, that of the planter aristocracy in the South.

The merchant-capitalists adhered to a creed of success that emphasized qualities similar to the ascetic characteristics extolled by Puritan ministers. Apprentices heard from their masters on weekdays and from ministers on Sundays commendations of thrift, sobriety, diligence, and sincerity. In their sermons preachers emphasized over and over again the evils of idleness and the gospel of work. Diligence and work became intertwined with salvation, on which, the fate of one's soul hinged. A moral code blocking so-called wasteful activities and keeping its followers faithfully toiling was surely conducive to material gain. Thus the prudential creed of Puritanism with its glorification of work as a goal in itself bolstered the efforts of a rising mercantile class in America. God would favor the earnest and pious worker who with hard labor could also become a wealthy merchant and then lead other apprentices along the same path to success. In Puritan New England social status and fortune gradually merged with divine election, and wealth and class became important signs of divine justification.

By the end of the colonial era, frontier society had gradually wrought a transformation in modes of behavior. Life in the colonies was basically fluid and flexible: neither the Virginia planters nor the merchant aristocrats of New England were able to stratify society in any lasting way. Men could acquire cheap land on the frontier for homesteads and enter new occupations with comparative ease, casting off traditional restraints of family and class. Colonial America, of course, did not understand the meaning of democracy. In the modern sense of the term, there was no such thing in the colonies. Yet, as men strove against nature, they disregarded inherited ideas concerning family loyalties, religious establishments, and class distinctions.

The influence of the frontier on colonial society was all pervasive. In exploring new terrain and in fighting its native inhabitants, the settlers achieved a new outlook on life, instilling both independence and practicality. Vastly different from those settlers remaining on the Atlantic seaboard, these western pilgrims lived constantly in the shadow of Native American groups, with the dubious protection of their cabins, their weapons, and their own sharp eyes. Conditions in a frontier wilderness were rigorous at best; and in each succeeding settlement west, the colonists became imbued with a spirit of freedom and self-reliance. Those in the back country believed that the road to power, prestige, and wealth should be open to youth and ambition and ability regardless of inheritance or religious conviction. Certainly more than any other force, the colonial frontier vital-ized the liberal elements in an emerging American ideology. As men, women, and children struggled to convert an unknown wilderness to a civilized way of life, centuries-old traditions gradually lost their binding force, and colonial society manifested a color and spirit distinctly different from that of the Old World.

FOR DISCUSSION AND CRITICAL THOUGHT

1. With reference to social and religious attitudes, compare and contrast the three cultures that evolved in colonial America.
2. Discuss the impact of slavery and the plantation system on family life and society in the southern colonies.
3. Obviously there have been many complex changes in American society since the colonial era. Nevertheless, do you note any attitudes prevalent in contemporary society that might be rooted in colonial culture? Com-ment critically.

NOTES

1. Louis B. Wright and Marion Tinling, eds., *The Secret Diary of William Byrd of Westover, 1709–1712* (Richmond, Va.: Dietz Press, 1941); Maude H. Woodfin, ed., and Marion Tinling, trans. and collator, *Another Secret Diary of William Byrd of Westover, 1739–1741, with Letters and Literary Exercises, 1696–1726* (Rich-mond, Va.: Dietz Press, 1942); and Louis B. Wright and Marion Tinling, eds., *William Byrd of Virginia: The London Diary (1717–1721) and Other Writings* (New York: Oxford University Press, 1958).
2. See, for example, Richard Beale Davis, ed., *William Fitzhugh and His Chesapeake World, 1676–1701: The Fitzhugh Letters and Other Document*, vol. 3 of the Virginia Historical Society Documents (Chapel Hill: University of North Carolina Press, 1963).
3. J. Hector St. John (de Crèvecœur), *Letters from an American Farmer; Describing Certain Provincial Situations, Manners, and Customs . . . of the British Colonies in North America* (London: Printed for Thomas Davies and Lockyer Davis, 1782), p. 51.
4. *Winthrop's Journal, "History of New England," 1630–1649*, ed. James Kendall Hosmer, 2 vols., Original Narratives of Early American History (New York: Barnes & Noble Books, 1946).
5. John Winthrop, "A Modell of Christian Charity" (1630), *Winthrop Papers* (Mas-sachusetts Historical Society, 1931), 2:295.
6. Letter dated 28 April 1629, from John Winthrop to his wife, Margaret, as reprinted in John Winthrop, *The History of New England from 1630 to 1649, from*

His Original Manuscripts, ed. James Savage (Boston: Printed by Phelps and Farnham, 1825), 1:356.

7. Jonathan Edwards, *Sinners in the Hands of an Angry God,* "A Sermon Preached at Enfield, 8 July 1741, at a Time of great Awakenings; and attended with remarkable Impressions on many of the Hearers" (Boston: Reprinted and sold by J. Kneeland, 1772), pp. 14–15.

CHAPTER 2

Education in the Seventeenth and Eighteenth Centuries

But I thank God, there are no free schools *nor* printing, *and I hope we shall not have these (for a) hundred years, for* learning *has brought disobedience, and heresy, and sects into the world, and* printing *has divulged them, and libels against the best government. God keep us from both!*

SIR WILLIAM BERKELEY's *Report on Virginia*, 1671

After God had carried us safe to New England, *and wee had builded our houses, provided necessaries for our livli-hood, rear'd convenient places for Gods worship, and setled the Civill Government: One of the next things we longed for, and looked after was to advance* Learning *and perpetuate it to Posterity; dreading to leave an illiterate Ministery to the Churches, when our present Ministers shall lie in the Dust.*

From *New England's First Fruits*, 1643

THE COLONIAL FAMILY

No formal structure, certainly no "system" of public schools, was ever envisioned by the early settlers in the English colonies. The family was the only binding social institution in a land of uncertainty and struggle.[1] The Scriptures underscored the family as the main social unit; and the general biblical design for family relationships was indeed a serious matter for all settlers. Whether on large estates, in towns, or in frontier cabins, the colonists knew the meaning of a benevolent patriarchal family.

The family was the most important element in colonial life: it was the primary unit of enterprise and production and the principal agency for human socialization in a wilderness. The husband was the legal master of the family, and women were placed in a dependent role. Nevertheless, women were scarce and highly valued, for immigration always brought to the colonies more men than women. In fact, women were so scarce in Virginia in 1619 that the Virginia Company sent to the colony a shipload of marriage-able girls who were traded to planters for 120 pounds of tobacco each. Girls were usually married by the age of sixteen, and men by twenty. Because of numerous children, the colonial family was a large social unit with servants and many relatives usually living under the same roof. Families with twelve children were commonplace. Patrick Henry, for example, was one of nine-teen children. Not all children survived, for the death rate was very high.

The family, then, was a social institution common to all. In a civilized family life, education of the young was generally accepted.

Children in the family were valued for their labor in the home and in the fields. The girls helped with all the household tasks while the boys tilled the soil, sowed seed, chopped wood, and fed and cared for the horses and livestock. For colonial children, life meant obedience and incessant work. Make your children obey, advised "Poor Richard," and you can teach them anything.

In a New World of busy parents, numerous children, and endless chores, obedience and work became cardinal virtues. "For God's sake," wrote John Adams to his wife, Abigail, in 1774, "make your children *hardy, active, and industrious;* for strength, activity and industry will be their only resource and dependence."[2] Industry and obedience were also considered vital deter-rents to savagery in a frontier wilderness: more than anything else, colonial families sought to prevent their children from lapsing into barbarism.

There was always a deep fear of the strange wilderness. Before John Winthrop and the first Puritans sailed from England, John Cotton admon-ished them in a departing sermon on the importance of educating the children in order to prevent a degeneration in the New World. This persistent fear was shared by other religious denominations, too: the Angli-cans in Virginia and the Carolinas, the Quakers in Pennsylvania, and the Catholics in Maryland. Of all the influences that shaped colonial society, none had deeper roots than the determination of the settlers to perpetuate a civilized way of life in a primitive environment.

In this respect, the Puritans of the Massachusetts Bay Colony had a decided advantage in the theocratic government controlled by those with preconceived views regarding education. The Puritan leaders imposed reli-gious unity and encouraged compact settlements in order to attain cultural solidarity. Significant, too, was the emergence of a closely knit town life that accelerated New England's educational growth. The Puritan clergy were determined that every child should have a chance to learn to read the Scriptures. Except for Rhode Island, the New England colonies followed the Puritan leadership. Massachusetts Bay was fortunate from another vantage point as well: of all the colonies none had more university graduates among its leadership. Of the eighty ministers in New England in 1643, at least half held degrees from Oxford or Cambridge. The Puritan leaders of the Bible Commonwealth knew the meaning of an education and sought immediately to transplant to American soil the educational traditions of England. In the sparsely settled southern colonies, however, especially in Virginia and Maryland, there was extreme difficulty in educating all children.

THE ATTITUDES OF THE SOUTHERN COLONISTS

Education in the southern colonies was considered to be a private and individual concern instead of a civil or religious matter. The Anglican Church, to which the southern colonists officially adhered, was not indifferent toward education. But unlike the Puritans of New England, the Anglicans in the South did not view the state as an agency for establishing schools. The church furnished schooling on a charity basis only to the children of those settlers who could not afford to pay for it. As in England, the Anglican Church in the New World considered education to be a primary obligation of the parent and home.

Significant, too, was the attitude of the wealthy planters who occupied a dominant place in the social structure. Able to provide an education for their own youth, they were little disposed to champion the cause of educating all children. The plantation families of Virginia sometimes sent their sons back to the mother country for an education, but more frequently they employed tutors who lived at the manors, avoiding the hazards and dangers of the long ocean voyage. The diseases of childhood, especially smallpox, took a heavy toll, and many children did not survive the dreaded voyage to England on a tobacco ship.

Education in the colonial South, then, was chiefly a private matter, rather than a public concern of the state. Those characteristic patterns that emerged in the South reflected this dominant attitude. Tutors were used on the plantations by the wealthy aristocracy, charity schools were founded by religious and philanthropic societies, such as the Society for the Propagation of the Gospel in Foreign Parts (the SPG), and private schools were slowly established in the southern towns.

The Transmission of a Renaissance Culture

The planter aristocrats were determined to acquire a Renaissance culture for their sons. Their zeal for contact with traditional learning was reflected in the libraries they maintained on their isolated plantations. The planters somehow managed to obtain titles covering the widest range of interests: translations of Greek and Latin classics, histories, treatises on government and law, and books on music, science, and medicine.

In order to perpetuate this type of learning, they employed tutors. Sometimes two planters not too widely separated shared the cost and hired one tutor, usually an indentured servant, for their children. The tutors drilled the planters' sons in Lilly's *Latin Grammar,* Hodder's *Arithmetic,* the *English Rudiments,* and *Euclid.* The daughters of the aristocrats learned French and once in a while other subjects from the plantation tutor; more frequently, they learned appropriate social graces from their mothers. In some cases, the tutor served in other posts, too, such as overseer or steward on the planter's manor. In Charleston and Savannah there were fewer tutors, and private schools offering a conglomeration of subjects were promoted through advertisements.

The journal and letters of Philip Fithian vividly describe how a tutor tried to educate children on a plantation. A Princeton graduate preparing to become a Presbyterian minister, Fithian was hired as a tutor by Robert Carter, of Nomini Hall, from 1773 to 1774. He was paid a salary of forty pounds a year to teach seven of the surviving Carter children and a nephew English, Latin, Greek, English history, and mathematics. The children were also taught to dance and to play a musical instrument by masters who traveled the countryside on regular routes. Usually an informal dance was held after the master had given a lesson. Fithian was often annoyed by the children's extracurricular interests in frequent social affairs and horseback riding. "The education of children requires constant unremitting attention," he wrote.[3]

Apprenticeship

The apprenticeship system marked the first legal attempt by the colonies to enforce a child's education. The laws stated the terms under which an apprenticeship could be arranged. The typical apprenticeship between a child and a master specified that the child would serve faithfully and that the master would care for the boy and teach him his trade. One type of apprenticeship was primarily for orphaned children. The other pattern was for all children who wanted to learn a trade. As the years passed and the demand for skilled labor increased, each colony sought to provide some kind of apprentice training for orphans, the destitute, and the illegitimate.

The children of poor families usually had no formal education, for the farms and plantations of Virginia and Maryland were too widely separated for the establishment of any type of community school. Occasionally, "free schools" were specially created for orphans and the children of very poor parents. These free schools were usually provided through the wills of Virginia planters, who bequeathed land, food, and miscellaneous supplies. Small fees were collected if the parents were able to pay, and orphans and those too poor to pay their own way were admitted free. In Virginia the first free school was founded in 1635 by Benjamin Symmes, a planter, who endowed it with two hundred acres of land and the milk from eight cows. In

1659 Thomas Eaton established another free school through a bequest of five hundred acres, some cattle, and two slaves. Both schools provided some instruction in reading, writing, and arithmetic. The Eaton Free School and the Symmes Free School continued until 1805, when they merged and became the Hampton Academy.

The College of William and Mary

By the end of the seventeenth century, the College of William and Mary was founded at Williamsburg. Students entered the college after having learned Latin and Greek. In their three college years they studied logic, rhetoric, mathematics, ethics, and some classical works.

Established in 1693, the second college to open in colonial America, the College of William and Mary was not a very notable institution in its earliest years. In 1712 William Byrd II wrote in his diary that there were only twenty-two students and that the headmaster had been dismissed for being a "sot." Philip Fithian noted on February 12, 1774, that the professors played cards all night in the public houses and were often seen drunk in the streets. In later years, however, the college earned considerable prestige and attracted some eminent professors. For example, George Wythe became the first professor of law in America. The first Phi Beta Kappa Society was founded at William and Mary on December 5, 1776. Thomas Jefferson, John Marshall, James Monroe, and other prominent southern statesmen were educated there.

SECTARIANISM IN THE MIDDLE COLONIES

The growth of education in the Middle Colonies was slow. Several barriers slowed the establishment of schools: the various nationalities of the immigrants, the lack of social cohesion in the sparsely settled areas, the diverse religious sects in the population, and the absence of a common tradition in language and political theory. Each religious group sought to educate its own children in its parishes as a matter of denominational interest. There were a few charity schools, too, for children of the poorer classes. At the end of the seventeenth century, private schools began to appear, mostly in Philadelphia and the larger towns. Unlike the Puritans in Massachusetts, the denominational groups did not use the civil authority to help establish and maintain schools. Lacking state support, education in the Middle Colonies generally followed sectarian lines.

Pennsylvania

In the colonial schools of Pennsylvania, both the Quakers and the Germans stressed the importance of a practical education and the inculcation of religious beliefs. William Penn's first and second Frames of Government for Pennsylvania, passed by the colonial legislature in 1682 and 1683, provided for a system of public schools stressing the values of religious training for all children and a utilitarian education in some skill or trade for those twelve years of age. These acts never went into effect because of so many diverse interests in the heterogeneous religious structure. Penn's ideas, nevertheless, influenced the Quakers' schools, which remained under the jurisdiction of the Society of Friends. Although the Quaker communities did not make education a civil responsibility, they did provide the parochial elementary schools in which the children were at least taught the rudiments of reading and writing. The pupils learned to read from the Bible or Pastorius' *New Primer,* a scriptural text, which was also used by the Mennonites.

One of colonial Pennsylvania's most famous teachers was Christopher Dock, a Mennonite, whose *Schul-Ordnung* (1770) was the first book on pedagogy printed in America. Dock arrived from Germany about 1710 and opened a school among the Mennonites of Montgomery County. For a while he taught six days a week in two schools, alternating with three days in Skippack and the other three in Sallford.

In *Schul-Ordnung* (or "School-Management"), Dock discussed methods, morals, and manners.[4] He recognized individual differences in children and stressed love and human understanding as bases for all discipline. He told how he taught his pupils at different ability and age levels and how he tried to appeal to each child's need for love and praise. Famous for his own piety and gentle disposition, Dock insisted that the teacher should patiently remedy the causes of moral infractions, instead of treating merely the symptoms. The shy pupil should be taught with gentleness and much love, never with harshness and physical punishment. Such a liberal conception of methodology and child nature stood in striking contrast to the Puritan view and reflected the changing outlook of the European Enlightenment.

While denominational schools founded by the Quakers, Mennonites, and other religious groups were the most numerous in colonial Pennsylvania, private schools without sectarian interests were also established, especially in Philadelphia. These were more secular and offered a variety of utilitarian courses. With its growing population and its widening commercial interests, Philadelphia soon attracted a number of private-venture schools during the first half of the eighteenth century.[5]

The Influence of New Netherland

Like other settlers in the southern colonies and in New England, the Dutch wanted to preserve the essentials of a European culture and a civilized way of life in the wilderness of the New World. Holland was traditionally concerned with education as a means of perpetuating the creed of the Dutch Reformed Church. In New Netherland the colonists transplanted to American soil this religious interest of the Old World and sought to reproduce a close church and school relationship.[6] The Dutch control of New Netherland lasted from only 1621 until the English conquest in 1664; but the early Dutch settlers clung tenaciously to their language and customs long after the English occupation.

In fact, there is no more vivid illustration in colonial history of such a persistent attempt to transmit through education the cultural patterns of the Old World. The Dutch school was viewed as a strong social instrument for bolstering the work of the church. However, amid the harsh realities of frontier life, the school was forced to become more than a supportive institution. For Dutch settlers in the New World, it became a fortress against acculturation.

Dutch parents and church leaders vigorously resisted the adoption of the English language. They refused to introduce English into the church services. They bitterly opposed innovation and strove to preserve Dutch customs. As Kilpatrick wrote: "All the strength of the Dutch character seemed rooted in opposition."[7]

In New York, despite "their utmost efforts," complained a Dutch official in 1754, "parents have found it in a degree impossible to transmit" the Dutch language to the children. The following year the local consistory refused to employ a schoolmaster with a knowledge of English. "A man who knew no English would not surreptitiously spread that commercial language, and certainly he would not favor loosening church ties with Holland." Instead, the church officials doubled the salary that "any one in this service has ever before enjoyed" and paid all the travel expenses for a Dutch schoolmaster who emigrated with his entire family from Amsterdam. So overjoyed was the consistory with obtaining a native master's services that an additional bonus of twenty pounds was given, "considering the loss which Mr. Welp suffered in the sale of his goods, in consequence of his removing from Amsterdam at short notice."[8] Even this effort was largely ineffectual, for, as time passed, the Dutch children, growing up in a new English-speaking setting, would not continue exclusively along traditional family paths.

The sectarian nature of the schoolmaster's work reflected the close church-school relationship that was so characteristic of Dutch education in colonial America. To begin with, the master was an officer of the church. While teaching in the school, he also served the church by participating in regular services. On Sundays, for example, he would open the church and arrange the benches and stools. After ringing the bell, he would return to his home (which was also the schoolhouse), where the children had assembled, ready to march with him to church. During services, the schoolmaster was responsible for the behavior of the children and for making certain that everyone paid attention. In addition to these duties, he assisted the minister with virtually every phase of the religious service, ranging from baptisms to funerals.

The daily school routine was infused with a variety of prayers, starting with the early morning prayer and concluding with the evening prayer at the close of the day. In fact, the entire curriculum strongly emphasized religious training. Both the schoolmaster and the parents were specifically charged with training children in the catechism. The school day began at eight o'clock in the morning, with a recess from eleven to one, and ended at four o'clock. In remuneration for his school and church services, the master usually received, in addition to certain tuition fees, "four hundred guilders in wheat, of wampum value."[9]

Occasionally, too, according to the records, the masters engaged in certain extralegal activities. In 1660, for example, schoolmaster Jan Juriae-sen Becker read "the sermon on Sundays," then sold "liquor to the Indians," and was subsequently indicted and "fined 500 guilders." A few months later, Becker was again "fined thirty guilders because 'he entertained people [in his tap house] after nine o'clock, and tapped during the sermon.'"[10]

After the English conquest in 1664, the Anglican attitude toward education replaced previous Dutch attempts to maintain schools. The Anglican Church was much less interested in education than was the Dutch Reformed Church. "Besides the establishment of two Latin grammar schools at different periods in New York City, and the legislation connected with the founding of King's College (Columbia University)," declared Kilpatrick, "absolutely nothing was done by the general assembly with intent to influence the schools of the Province. The laissez-faire policy, so far as elementary education was concerned, reigned supreme."[11]

The colonial authorities in New York did encourage the work of the Society for the Propagation of the Gospel in Foreign Parts, which sponsored from five to ten charity schools between 1710 and 1776. Nevertheless, despite the missionary zeal of the SPG, the conflict of diverse cultures and the confusion wrought by two dominant languages interfered with the establishment of schools. Educational efforts in New York lagged far behind those of the Massachusetts Bay Colony.

THE IMPACT OF NEW ENGLAND PURITANISM

Within a decade after the Puritans landed on the shores of the New World in the 1630s, two types of schools emerged in colonial New England: the earliest primary schools,[12] such as the dame schools and the reading and writing schools for the children of the lower classes, and the Latin grammar school for the sons of the elite.[13]

The Primary Schools
Copied from England, the dame schools provided the first instruction for boys and sometimes the only schooling for girls. They were private-venture

schools supported by small fees from parents and maintained by widows or spinsters in their own homes, usually in the kitchen where household chores were performed. The reading and writing schools in the larger towns actually deemphasized writing and stressed reading, which was more important for religious instruction. These schools were available for beginners, too, and for those who wanted to learn more than could be obtained from parents or accomplished in the dame schools.

In colonial New England the whole idea of education presumed that children were miniature adults possessed of human degeneracy. The daily school routine was characterized by harshness and dogmatism. Discipline was strict, and disobedience and infractions of rules were often met with severe penalties meted out by quick-tempered, poorly qualified instructors. All teaching and learning revolved around the Puritans' interpretation of the Bible. In religion-dominated New England the Puritan leaders were determined that children should be taught to read in order to have immediate access to the Bible. In the primary schools, only the rudiments of reading, some writing, and a little arithmetic were taught. In some cases children attended a dame school or a reading and writing school for no more than a few weeks; rarely, if ever, did they attend for more than a year.

In addition to memorizing the catechism, the children were taught the alphabet from the hornbook. This device had a wooden handle and a single sheet of paper mounted on a carved board. The paper was covered by a piece of transparent cow's horn to keep it clean and intact. From the hornbook the children proceeded to the *New England Primer,* a catechistic reflection of the Puritan ideology.[14]

The New England Primer

Like the hornbook, the *Primer* began with the letters of the alphabet and certain combinations of letters, such as "ab eb It," called the "syllabarium." The most famous part of the *Primer* was a series of rhymed couplets illustrated with woodcuts for each letter of the alphabet. The first couplet began with the religious assertion:

> In Adam's fall
> We sinned all.

and closed with a scriptural note:

> Zaccheus he
> Did climb the Tree
> His Lord to see.

Also included in the *Primer* were several prayers and hymns and "The Shorter Catechism." A few editions included another catechism written by John Cotton apparently in 1641 entitled "Spiritual Milk for American Babes, drawn out of the Breasts of both Testaments for their Souls Nourishment."

There was also a woodcut of John Rogers, a Protestant martyr burned at the stake in 1555, with his wife and children viewing the spectacle, to illustrate Rogers's poem "Exhortation to His Children." In Puritan New England, it seemed, the devil was lurking everywhere ready to seize the souls of children already predisposed to sin and eternal damnation. The last feature of most editions of the *Primer* contained an allegory of Youth yielding to the temptations of the Devil.

The *New England Primer* first appeared in 1690 and was reprinted over and over again. It was estimated that at least 3 million copies were distributed in the colonies over a period of 150 years. The *Primer* was the most frequently used schoolbook in colonial New England. With its Puritan tone, its dour outlook, and its rigorous stress on moral pessimism, the *New England Primer* dominated the children's first schooling.

Probably more memorable than the *Primer* in the minds of Puritan children was a lengthy poem describing in vivid and horrifying terms the Last Judgment. *The Day of Doom,* written by Michael Wigglesworth in 1662, was the first best-seller in the New World. Educated at Harvard, intensely consumed by religion, Wigglesworth personified the most austere form of New England Puritanism. The first eighteen hundred copies of *The Day of Doom* were sold immediately. The poem was quickly reprinted and widely sold, even by peddlers on the street. Apparently everyone who could read owned a copy. For over a century, *The Day of Doom* was one of the best-known American poems.

Children were forced to memorize and repeat the warnings of this gloomy description of man's punishment for innate depravity stemming from Adam's sin. How much vicarious terror Wigglesworth induced in both children and adults no one can say. A poetic statement of the Puritan creed written in a short, rhyming meter, *The Day of Doom* told of an avenging Judge sitting on the Throne of God. A frequently quoted section of the poem, which must have caused some relentless torment in the minds of any sinful Puritans, pointed to all the innocent infants who died at birth pleading before the Judge not to be thrown into Hell:[15]

> You sinners are, and such a share
>   as sinners may expect
> Such you shall have, for I do save
>   none but mine own elect.
> Yet to compare your sin with their
>   who liv'd longer time,
> I do confess yours is much less,
>   though ev'ry sin's a crime:
> A crime it is; therefore in bliss
>   you may not hope to dwell;
> But unto you I shall allow
>   the easiest room in hell.

Even the Elected Saints who felt so certain of a place in Heaven must have pondered the theme of this terrifying poem.

The Latin Grammar Schools

In the spring of 1635, the colonists of Boston held a mass meeting, elected Philemon Pormort as schoolmaster, and established a grammar school that was later called the Boston Public Latin School. The Boston Latin School, which is considered to be the oldest secondary school in America, was public in the sense that it was under public control and was partly supported by public funds. The Latin grammar schools flourished in the compact settlements of New England and were the only type of secondary education in colonial America until the rise of private schools and academies in the eighteenth century.

There is no exact description of the program of the Latin schools of seventeenth-century New England; however, judging from the entrance requirements of Harvard College in 1642 and from the offerings of the Boston Latin School in 1712, the curriculum was modeled, not surprisingly, after that of the Latin schools of Europe and especially England, in which classical study and religious instruction prevailed. The content of the curriculum was dominated by a belief that the study of the classics, and of Latin in particular, constituted the main work of the school.

In Europe a mastery of both written and spoken Latin was often considered the mark of a well-educated man. In the Old World the curriculum of the Latin grammar schools provided a humanistic education for only a small element of the population preparing for leadership roles in church and state. In colonial New England the Latin grammar schools also catered to the needs of a small upper class. The primary schools were usually terminal and mainly for the common people. Whether a boy attended a Latin grammar school was determined chiefly by the socioeconomic standing of his parents in the town. In general, only a select group of youth from educated families attended the Latin grammar schools. Girls were almost never admitted to a grammar school, although some teachers gave them private instruction when the school was not in session. After a child had learned to read from his hornbook and the *New England Primer,* he either worked as an apprentice or attended a reading and writing school. Those boys destined for college enrolled in the Latin grammar schools at the age of seven or eight. These schools were designed to prepare boys for entrance into Harvard College and, after that, for leadership in the church.

The curriculum of the Latin grammar schools tried to prepare boys to meet the following entrance requirements of Harvard:

> 1. When any Schollar is able to read Tully or such like classicall Latine Authour ex temporare, and make and speake true Latin verse and prose *Suo (ut aiunt) Marte,* and decline perfectly the paradigmes of Nounes and

verbes in the Greeke tounge, then may hee bee admitted into the
Colledge, nor shall any claim admission before such qualifications.

The program of instruction in the Boston Latin School in 1712 also gives
some indication of the classical content of the curriculum during the seventeenth and eighteenth centuries. According to Morison, the seven-year
course stressed the teaching and learning of Latin:

> The three first years were spent in learning by heart an "Accidence," as
> beginning Latin books were then called, together with the *Nomenclator,* a
> Latin-English phrase-book, and vocabulary called *Sententiae Pueriles.* For
> construing and parsing, the *Distichia* attributed to Dionysius Cato, a
> collection of maxims popular since the early Christian era, was used.
> Corderius' *Colloquies* and Aesop's *Fables* were also read, in Latin. Fourth
> year began Erasmus' *Colloquies,* continued Aesop, studied Latin gram-
> mar, and read Ovid *de Tristibus.* Fifth year continued Erasmus and Ovid,
> including the *Metamorphoses,* and began Cicero's *Epistolae,* Latin prosody,
> and Latin composition with Garretson's *English Exercises for School-Boys to
> Translate.* Sixth-year scholars began Cicero's *de Officiis,* Lucius Florus,
> Virgil's *Aeneid,* and Thomas Godwyn's excellent English treatise on
> Roman history and antiquities, which had been used at the University of
> Cambridge in John Harvard's day; they continued the *Metamorphoses,*
> made Latin verse, dialogues, and letters, and began Greek and Rhetoric.
> During the seventh and last year, the boys, now fourteen to sixteen years
> old, began Cicero's *Orations,* Justin, Virgil, Horace, Juvenal, and Per-
> sius, made Latin dialogues, and turned "a Psalm or something Divine"
> into Latin verse, with a Latin theme every fortnight. For Greek, they
> read Homer, Isocrates, Hesiod, and the New Testament.
>   All in all, a pretty stiff and thorough classical course.[16]

Furthermore, Middlekauff points out:

> Had a Boston lad of 1712 reappeared in Boston Latin School in the
> 1790s, about all that he would have noticed amiss was that the scholars
> now spent four years instead of seven in the school, a change made in
> 1789. This four-year stint could not match the colonial seven in the
> number of authors read, but it managed to provide rigorous training in
> several of the classics.[17]

Perhaps the most noticeable feature of the Latin-school program was its
similarity to the curriculum of the Latin grammar schools of England.
Obviously, the main purpose was to teach boys to read, write, and speak
Latin and to instruct them in the elements of Greek.

> Learning the rules, reciting them, parsing and construing, translating
> from Latin to English and back again, "making Latin," translating

Greek, and puzzling over its rules—this was the course the scholar followed until his master declared him ready for college.[18]

Like instruction in Latin and Greek, some elementary arithmetic and occasionally algebra, geometry, and trigonometry were obtained from textbooks which with rare exception were written and printed in England. Geography, too, was taught from textbooks, not globes and maps. Those texts used for occasional instruction in astronomy adhered to the Copernican thesis, although a few still retained Ptolemaic ideas. Most of the textbooks in astronomy described the universe of Newton without the mathematics to make the Newtonian conception understandable. The law of gravitation was seldom mentioned. "Despite this omission," states Middlekauff, "the books convey the most important point their writers wished to make: the universe has a divine purpose."[19]

Instruction in religion was basic in the Latin grammar schools. The teacher was selected and licensed by the church. Each day began with religious exercises, with each boy reading a verse aloud from the Bible. After reading and singing a Psalm, the boys then recited a prayer. On the second morning of the week each pupil had to repeat one passage or sentence from the sermon of the preceding Sabbath. Every Friday from one to three o'clock the boys were catechized.

In most of the Latin schools, the course of study lasted for seven years. Apparently school was in session six days a week and continued throughout the winter and summer. The school day was usually from six to eleven o'clock in the morning and from one to four or five o'clock in the afternoon. The boys sat on benches for long hours. Great faith was placed in the *memoriter* method of drill and rote learning. Through repeated recitations the students were conditioned to respond with a definite answer to a particular question. Class discussions were not permitted. The Latin schools inherited the English tradition of severe discipline. It was not unusual for a quick-tempered schoolmaster to hit a pupil for an unsatisfactory recitation. School regulations designated the punishments that should be meted out for fighting, lying, cursing, and playing cards or dice.

Few men made a career of teaching in the Latin grammar schools. Most of the teachers were either indentured servants, students preparing for the ministry, or transients passing through the community. Generally the salaries of the teachers varied in amount, depending on the colony and the town. Interesting ways were used to pay the schoolmasters, if they were paid at all. For example, salaries were sometimes paid in tobacco, peas, corn, barley, wheat, or other commodities. Teachers were often required to keep the church clean and to assist the ministers at baptisms and funerals, which even included digging graves.

A famous exception to the poor quality of itinerant teachers in the colonies was Ezekiel Cheever, who taught in the Latin schools of New

England from 1638 until his death in 1708. Cheever became master of the Ipswich Grammar School in 1650. Twenty years later, he moved to the Boston Latin Grammar School, where he served for thirty-eight years and established a noted reputation. At the Boston Latin School he was paid an annual salary of sixty pounds. Cheever's name appears frequently in colonial literature. With his long white beard, a birch rod, and an uncontrollable temper, he apparently etched a God-fearing image in the minds of his pupils. The author of a Latin *Accidence,* he drilled his boys not only in correct Latin but also in manners and religion. When Cheever died in his nineties, Cotton Mather, one of his former pupils, declared in a funeral oration:

> Do but name Cheever, and the echo straight
> Upon that name good Latin will repeat.

So great was Cheever's fame that the governor and other notables attended his funeral.

The Acts of 1642 and 1647

Perhaps the most significant concept of the New England tradition in education was a legal assertion that schools were a civil responsibility of the state. In the beginning, attendance in the primary schools was not compulsory. Education, either from parents or in a school (if one was available), was a discretionary matter for the family to decide. This was a deeply rooted English belief. In the frontier society of the New World, however, this traditional system broke down, and schooling could no longer remain on a voluntary basis at parental discretion. In the Massachusetts Bay Colony both church and civil authorities were especially dissatisfied with the inadequate training that children were receiving. Then, too, in a theocratic community the Puritan leaders must have viewed an organized school as a strong instrument for the preservation of religious orthodoxy.

Only twenty-two years after the settlement of the Bay Colony, the Puritans sought to give some legal sanction to education. In 1642 the Massachusetts General Court passed a law requiring the selectmen of each town to inquire into the literacy of the children and to fine those parents and apprentices' masters who refused to account for their children's ability "to read and understand the principles of religion and the capital laws of the country." While the Act of 1642 did not force towns to establish schools, the government expressed concern and centered the responsibility for seeing that children were taught. If a child's education was being neglected, the children could be removed from custody and the parents and masters fined. This act was the first educational law in the colonies. Although it did not guarantee the establishment of schools, the Massachusetts Act of 1642, nevertheless, marked a significant milestone in the history of American education.

In 1647 the General Court of Massachusetts, in an unprecedented move, passed the famous "Old Deluder Satan" Act which required the establishment and support of schools.[20] After stating in the preamble the religious motive for requiring the establishment of schools, the act provided that towns of fifty householders shall appoint someone to instruct "all such children as shall resort to him to write and read," the teacher to "be paid either by the parents or masters of such children, or by the inhabitants in general." The act also required every town of one hundred families or householders to establish a Latin grammar school to prepare youth for Harvard College. Failure to obey the law was punishable by a fine of five pounds.

The Act of 1647 was the first legal basis of a public-school system in Massachusetts. It also became a model for legislation in other colonies where similar laws were enacted. In general, there was noncompliance with the law, and in order to force reluctant communities to establish grammar schools, additional acts increasing the amounts of the fines were passed.

While this act requiring the maintenance of schools was indeed important in colonial history, the dominant motive behind the law was far from democratic. The Puritan leaders would have been deeply disturbed if they thought that their schools would ever contribute to a free society; to them a democratic state was the worst form of political organization. John Winthrop, in particular, was an outspoken opponent of equalitarianism; to him a democracy was "the meanest and worst of all formes of Government."[21]

The Puritans in the seventeenth century were concerned with maintaining a way of life, and it is not surprising that they used the schools as a means to that end. In the Massachusetts Bay Colony, where the reins of social control were tightly held by the theocratic officials, it would have been strange indeed if no attempt had been made to use the classroom to inculcate in youth the fundamentals of the Puritan creed. The schools were designed, not to open the paths to social opportunity, but rather to develop in the pupils a passive acceptance of the existing political and religious patterns. In colonial New England, as everywhere, education was rooted in the society of which it was an integral part.

The American public schools of today should not be viewed as sole legacies of Puritan New England. The establishment of universal, tax-supported elementary and secondary schools was a distinctive achievement of the American people. Evolving from a different way of life in the New World, education in the United States changed and gradually expanded to meet the needs of a dynamic society.

The Early Years at Harvard College

The first college established in the colonies, Harvard College was founded in the fall of 1636 to provide the Puritan Church with a trained ministry. The first years were difficult ones for the new college. Nathaniel Eaton, who was appointed head of the institution and the first professor, apparently beat his students excessively, even for colonial times. Mrs. Eaton was in charge of feeding the students, but the food was scanty and often spoiled. Eaton once hit his assistant with a walnut cudgel for about two hours. Before fleeing to Virginia after being dismissed, he embezzled college funds from Harvard's first endowment.

Four years after opening its doors, the college began to make some progress. Appointed president on August 27, 1640, Henry Dunster, a young Cambridge graduate, taught all the courses himself and extended the program for a bachelor's degree to four years. At this time Harvard was a small institution with an enrollment that rarely exceeded twenty. In 1650 the college was granted corporate autonomy by the General Court. With a capable president, a new building, and a program similar to that of the English universities, Harvard College was finally on a firm basis. With the exception of William and Mary, no other college was established in the English colonies before 1700.

At the beginning of the eighteenth century, the traditional position that religious orthodoxy held in the lives of the colonists was being challenged in every quarter by strong forces. In their refusal to conform in matters of faith and in their pleas for religious freedom, Roger Williams and Anne Hutchinson had been among the first to oppose the Puritan stronghold; their voices of dissent, however, were not the last to be heard in the colonies. The very fact that different religious ideas were vying for expression on American soil tended to break down the power of the predominant faith. Some degree of toleration became a daily imperative. Those who had emigrated to the New World to escape religious control were not likely to exchange one brand of authoritarianism for another and acquiesce willingly to new restrictions imposed by church leaders. Beginning about 1734, the Great Awakening struck every colonial hamlet and community with an outburst of amateur preaching, prayer meetings, and hysterical conversions. Church leaders with tenaciously held ideas did not share the religious enthusiasm engendered by this religious upheaval. The vehemence with which James Davenport and other impassioned evangelists preached to the common people, denouncing the rich and the upper classes and urging direct communion with God, disturbed conservatives and threatened the prevailing social structure. In the burgeoning commercial centers along the seacoast, a rising middle class needed a freer environment conducive to trade and prosperity; they were receptive, also, to an education different from that which served the Puritan ministers and the southern aristocrats. All in all, by the turn of the century, the country was witnessing the dawn of a new age in which natural science and a whole range of ideas from European philosophies were capturing the imagination of people everywhere and contributing to the growing secularization of American education. But this is part of another story.

FOR DISCUSSION AND CRITICAL THOUGHT

1. In what ways did education reflect the attitudes and mores of society in colonial America?
2. Can some of today's problems (for example, religion in the public school and the use of corporal punishment) be traced to the colonial period? Explain.
3. Why was the system of education that evolved in the southern colonies more of a private matter than an issue of community concern?
4. What were the educational consequences of cultural diversity in the Middle Colonies?
5. How did religious doctrine in colonial New England influence school practices?

NOTES

1. Contemporary studies of the colonial family have added fresh interpretations to a traditional topic of historic interest. Two important contributions are Edmund Morgan's *The Puritan Family: Religion and Domestic Relations in Seventeenth-Century New England* (rev. ed.; New York: Harper & Row Torchbook, 1966) and Bernard Bailyn's *Education in the Forming of American Society: Needs and Opportunities for Study* (Chapel Hill: University of North Carolina Press, 1960; reissued in 1972 in a Norton paperbound edition), pp. 15–29. Morgan and Bailyn argue that educational developments in colonial American cannot be understood fully apart from the history of the family in the New World. For Bailyn the decline of the colonial family is of primary importance; for Morgan its emergence and power describe the Puritan experience. European scholars have also been studying the history of the family and are challenging some standard interpretations. The most important investigation has been carried out by Philippe Ariès. His results have been published in English under the title *Centuries of Childhood: A Social History of Family Life*, trans. Robert Baldick (New York: Random House [Vintage Books], 1965; originally published in France in 1960). Ariès shows that vital changes affected the European family between the medieval and early modern period. His work has important implications for the history of the colonial family and underscores the need for additional research.
2. Letter dated 7 July 1774, from John Adams to Abigail Adams, as reprinted in *Familiar Letters of John Adams and His Wife Abigail Adams, During the Revolution, with a Memoir of Mrs. Adams,* ed. Charles Francis Adams (New York: Hurd & Houghton, 1876), p. 21. Italics in original.
3. Letter to John Peck, 12 August 1774, as reprinted in Hunter Dickinson Farish, ed., *Journal and Letters of Philip Vickers Fithian, 1773–1774: A Plantation Tutor*

of the Old Dominion (new ed.; Williamsburg, Va.: Colonial Williamsburg, Inc., 1957), p. 165.

4. Martin G. Brumbaugh, "The Translation of *The Schul-Ordnung,*" in *The Life and Works of Christopher Dock, America's Pioneer Writer on Education* (Philadelphia and London: Lippincott, 1908), pp. 91–156.

5. See pp. 62–64.

6. The most complete study is William Heard Kilpatrick's *The Dutch Schools of New Netherland and Colonial New York,* U.S. Bureau of Education Bulletin No. 12, Whole Number 483, 1912 (Washington, D.C.: Government Printing Office, 1912).

7. Ibid., p. 152.

8. Ibid., pp. 154–155.

9. For an interesting "contract" issued by Dutch officials in October 1682, see Alice Morse Earle, *Colonial Days in Old New York* (New York: Empire State Book, 1938), pp. 31–34.

10. Kilpatrick, *Dutch Schools of New Netherland and Colonial New York,* pp. 116–117.

11. Ibid., p. 18.

12. In this context "primary schools" mean the first schools in the historical order of development.

13. Robert Middlekauff points out that this "hierarchy of schools" or "system" was similar to the structure found in a city of England and, in the New World, was especially prevalent in large towns like Boston and Newport. See Robert Middlekauff, *Ancients and Axioms: Secondary Education in Eighteenth-Century New England,* Yale Historical Publications *Miscellany* 77 (New Haven and London: Yale University Press, 1963), p. 54.

14. See Paul Leicester Ford, ed., *The New England Primer,* Classics in Education No. 13 (New York: Bureau of Publications, Teachers College, Columbia University, 1962; reprinted from the 1897 edition).

15. Michael Wigglesworth, *The Day of Doom: or A Description of the Great and Last Judgment, with A Short Discourse about Eternity* (London: Printed by W.G. for John Sims, 1673), pp. 54–55.

16. Samuel Eliot Morison, *The Intellectual Life of Colonial New England* (2nd ed.; New York: New York University Press, 1956), pp. 105–106.

17. Middlekauff, *Ancients and Axioms,* p. 154.

18. Ibid., p. 84.

19. Ibid., p. 102.

20. Historians disagree regarding the basic purpose of the "Old Deluder, Satan" Act. For conflicting views, see, for example: Morison, *Intellectual Life of Colonial New England,* p. 17; and Charles A. Beard and Mary R. Beard, *The Rise of American Civilization,* vol. 1, *The Agricultural Era* (New York: Macmillan, 1927), pp. 179–180.

21. "John Winthrop's Defense of the Negative Vote" (June 1643), *Winthrop Papers* (Massachusetts Historical Society, 1944), 4:383.

CHAPTER 3

Age of the Enlightenment: The Impact of Secular Thought

Let us then suppose the Mind to be, as we say, white Paper [tabula rasa], *void of all Characters, without any Ideas; How comes it to be furnished? Whence comes it by that vast Store, which the busy and boundless Fancy of Man has painted on it, with an almost endless Variety? Whence has it all the Materials of Reason and Knowledge? To this I answer, in one word, from* Experience: *in that, all our Knowledge is founded, and from that it ultimately derives itself.*

JOHN LOCKE, *An Essay Concerning Human Understanding,* 1690

Reason and free inquiry are the only effectual agents against error.

THOMAS JEFFERSON, *Notes on the State of Virginia,* 1781

Let there be free schools established in every township.

BENJAMIN RUSH, "A Plan for the Establishment of Public Schools," 1786

From the mid-eighteenth century to the eve of the Revolutionary War the ideological foundations of American life were profoundly affected by a changing intellectual climate in Europe. In subtle and various ways a stream of ideas from the Enlightenment swept into the colonies from abroad, gradually uprooting centuries of superstitions and inherited traditions and paving the way for a new educational outlook in the United States. New conceptions emerged concerning the structure of the universe, the methodology of science, and the nature of man.

41

THE ENLIGHTENMENT

The Enlightenment, sometimes called the Age of Reason or the *Aufklärung,* refers to a profound intellectual revolution in world history that rejected theology as the final arbiter and sought instead to interpret the universe in terms of logical analysis. It was a rational movement, extending from about 1650 to 1800, in which faith in science and human reason was substituted for dogma based on religious belief and supernatural revelation. During this period philosophers began to view mankind's problems in a different light, discarding many preconceived ideas founded on doctrine. Believing mathematics to be the ultimate key to universal problems, these men adopted a mechanical approach to their surroundings and built a new world view to explain the secrets of nature. Medieval theologians and philosophers had interpreted man and the universe in terms of the Scriptures; for the new philosophers the path to understanding was mathematics, logic, and human reason. With historical roots deep in the Middle Ages, the Enlightenment was one of the few movements that led to such a fundamental change in human thought, freeing the minds of people from centuries of dogma and myth and preparing the way for a dynamic world perspective. This new spirit of inquiry led to great scientific advances that had important implications for education at every level.

New Views of the Universe

In the sixteenth century the Copernican thesis of a heliocentric universe revolutionized astronomy and marked a great advancement in human thought. Nicolaus Copernicus, a Polish astronomer, completed his famous treatise *De Revolutionibus Orbium Coelestium* in 1530, although the work was not published until 1543. Contradicting the Ptolemaic system, Copernicus denied that the earth was the center of the universe. Instead, he disclosed an inverted astronomical pattern: the planets, including the earth, revolved around a stationary sun.

Here was a daring revolt posing a threat to both Catholic and Protestant theologians, who bitterly opposed the Copernican theory and denounced it as hypothetical and false. The Christian tradition held the view that God had created the universe with the earth at the center, surrounded by the sun and stars. The *De Revolutionibus* was listed on the *Index* from 1616 to 1757 as undermining truth.[1] Copernicus died before his beliefs were publicized. Giordano Bruno was excommunicated and burned at the stake in 1600 for his attempts to popularize the Copernican conception of the universe; and Galileo Galilei was condemned to abjure on his knees the truth of his own scientific views in support of the Copernican theory. By the time that Copernicus, Bruno, Galileo, Brahe, and Kepler had completed their scientific investigations in the sixteenth and early seventeenth centuries, the grand design of a limitless, heliocentric universe had become an epoch-making milestone in human history, demolishing the basis of medieval science and paving the way for Isaac Newton's historic synthesis.

Newton's application of mathematics to astronomy produced a startling revelation of the physical universe. Born in 1642, Newton conducted his first experiment at the age of sixteen, when he computed the force of the wind during a storm in England. Before the age of thirty, he discovered the binomial theorem, fluxional calculus, and the method of tangents. In *Philosophiae Naturalis Principia Mathematica,* published in 1687, Newton stated his most important discovery: every particle of matter is attracted by or gravitates to every other particle with a force inversely proportional to the squares of their distances.[2] Newton's universal law of gravitation was a supreme achievement of the seventeenth century. Building on the great scientific advances of Galileo and Kepler in the Reformation period and elaborating on his own law of gravitation, Newton constructed a world-machine: instead of a group of planets, each operating independently of the others, the universe became a great machine, an orderly, mechanical whole, bound together by the force of gravity. This mechanical orderliness of the universe was not subject to caprice or divine intervention but was proved by rational deductions from mathematical laws. Thus mathematics had furnished the instrument for uncovering natural phenomena; and natural law became the intellectual foundation for all scientific explanations.

Deism

In addition to a radically different approach to science, the Enlightenment also evolved a new view of religion known as Deism. If, as Newton theorized, the Deity had designed a world-machine, then perhaps His existence was no longer essential. Because of new scientific discoveries, some men turned to reason and to natural law, instead of to tradition and ecclesiastic authority, for criteria of human thought and behavior. This interest in science soon led to the primacy of human reason in religious belief. As reason became the dominant principle of the human mind, religion, too, was viewed in the light of rational thought. For those adhering to Deism, the stress in theology shifted from the Scriptures to nature as a source of divine revelation.

The ideological roots of this conflict between the new science and religious orthodoxy lay in the works of such seventeenth- and early eighteenth-century English deists as Anthony Collins and the Third Earl of Shaftesbury. From Newton's conception of the universe, they deduced the corollary that God as a supreme architect had created a perfect, self-regulated world-machine. Mechanical laws alone were deemed insufficient to explain the origin and continuation of the universe. Dissatisfied with a cosmology that seemed to eliminate God from the world order, these English writers adopted instead a belief in God as a First Cause or Intelligent Agent responsible for the creation and design of the Newtonian universe.

The Emergence of a Scientific Methodology

In the history of American education, one of the most important outcomes of the intellectual ferment in Europe during the seventeenth and eighteenth centuries was the emergence of a radically different philosophy of learning. A new scientific method challenged the traditional theory of learning that had dominated Western thought for at least four centuries. According to the traditional view, people were born with a faculty of reason that needed to be formed by the proper methods of study; and the best mental training for this purpose was the mastery of the classics, philosophy, and mathematics. Essentially, this traditional theory of the way people acquired knowledge about the external world held that "true" ideas either existed apart from man in a separate realm, waiting to be understood by the mind when it had been trained to grasp them, or were innately acquired or implanted at birth in the mind of the infant. The scientific methodology of Descartes, the French mathematician and philosopher, and Francis Bacon, the renowned Lord Chancellor of England, rejected the authority of the ancient writers and attacked this traditional view of learning.

Born in Touraine, France, in 1596, René Descartes was a great pioneer in mathematics. He founded analytical geometry, and through his mathematical concepts he helped scientists state their conclusions with greater clarity and accuracy. Descartes discovered in mathematics a certainty and a clearness for which he had been searching; for him mathematics was the only area of human thought in which there were no doubts and disputes. He was bitterly dissatisfied with the formalism of the medieval scholasticism that characterized his own early Jesuit schooling. Descartes sought instead to find what he considered to be the right method for obtaining knowledge. The result of this search and the method he proposed for the discovery of truth was presented in his *Discourse on Method,* first published in 1637.

Descartes assumed that the fundamental postulates of all knowledge were inherent in the nature of the human mind. He believed that certain primary ideas were innate and that the growth of knowledge consisted in drawing out their implications. "When I say that an idea is innate in us (or imprinted in our souls by nature)," explained Descartes, "I do not mean that it is always present to us. This would make no idea innate. I mean merely that we possess the faculty of summoning up this idea."[3] The faculty of reason that distinguished truth from error was the guiding element in human life. Thus, according to Descartes, the true method of science was deductive in its approach, and the basic process of learning required rational thinking. For the first time since the days of ancient Greece, human reason, long subdued by religious authoritarianism, was recognized with dignity and philosophically defended.

Francis Bacon, later Lord Verulam, was born in 1561 in London. Unlike Descartes, he made no distinctive contribution to mathematics or to the analysis of concepts. Bacon was, however, greatly impressed with the possibilities of science and became an outstanding proponent of a new scientific method in the seventeenth century. He was a subtle, magnificent thinker, at times amazingly modern in his conceptions and outlook. In his *New Atlantis,* for example, he described a Utopia on an imaginary South Sea island where scientific experimentation had invented strange machines that skimmed beneath the water and flew in the air. Through his scientific writings and his position as Lord Chancellor in England, Bacon exerted great influence throughout Europe.

Like Descartes, Bacon proposed a new method of science; but unlike Descartes, his method did not involve a priori reasoning from primary ideas. Bacon believed that people relied too much on tradition and superstitions. He was profoundly dissatisfied with Aristotle and the medieval scholastics. He repudiated the traditional authorities and advocated instead the study of nature by the scientific method. Bacon's name became synonymous with the inductive method in science.

In *Novum Organum,* or *True Suggestions for the Interpretation of Nature,* first published in 1620, Bacon recommended the use of systematic observation, experimentation, and inductive reasoning. Observation of nature, he believed, was the only medium through which we obtained knowledge about the world around us: "Man, being the servant and interpreter of Nature, can do and understand so much and so much only as he has observed in fact or in thought of the course of nature: beyond this he neither knows anything nor can do anything."[4] In calling for the study and interpretation of all aspects of nature, he advocated an experimental procedure that would begin with observations of particular things and move toward broader generalizations.

Bacon's main interest, then, was in an inductive method. The principal elements of this new scientific method were observing nature, collecting facts, and generalizing from individual facts to their common features. Most important in the history of education were Bacon's emphasis on a controlled method of investigation and his assertion that knowledge and "truth" came through observation and experience rather than through accepted ideas derived from religion or traditional authority.

Here was a beginning step in what was no doubt the most important intellectual revolution of the seventeenth and eighteenth centuries: an assertion that humankind could, through reason and by a controlled method of investigation, obtain knowledge without reliance on supernatural revelation or traditional authorities. Here, indeed, was the formulation of a new method of thinking, a new way of acquiring knowledge and seeking truth.

The development of this scientific method soon attracted the attention of thoughtful men in both Europe and America. In the seventeenth century it led to a new theory of human learning.

John Locke and the Doctrine of Empiricism

The assumption that all ideas were innate—that is, hereditary parts of the rational faculty of the human mind—was the chief basis of the traditional philosophy of rationalism. These innate ideas related to a variety of fields, such as religion, mathematics, and morality. An innate religious idea, for instance, was the existence of God, with which Descartes was so deeply concerned. Original mathematical axioms were also deemed beyond empirical experience. This assumption of rationalism blocked experimentation and constituted a major barrier to the promotion of scientific knowledge. It was, in fact, this fundamental assumption that John Locke (1632–1704) dared to question and examine.

John Locke possessed a genius for interpreting in an understandable way some of the explosive ideas of the Enlightenment. His writings cover a wide range, dealing with problems in philosophy, education, government, religion, and economics. Locke's ideas, for example, had a great impact on American political traditions. According to Locke, governments were instituted for the welfare and happiness of people and were not designed to perpetuate the rights of the ruling class. In a state of nature, he pointed out, all men were free and equal. The people had a right to rebel when the ruler became a tyrant. His two *Treatises on Civil Government,* issued in 1690, provided the American leaders for independence a philosophical justification for their rebellion in 1776 against an absolute king.

Locke made his most noteworthy contribution in his famous *Essay Concerning Human Understanding,* completed in 1687 and published three years later. This philosophical treatise had considerable influence on educational thought first in Europe and later in America. He also completed a series of letters entitled *Some Thoughts Concerning Education,* published in 1693.

Locke attacked the notion that all ideas in people were innate at birth. As a physician, he concluded that the infant was not born with a preformed mind containing ideas concerning morality, God, and other values. In fact, according to Locke, there was not one idea in the human mind that could be called innate.

Instead, according to Locke, the mind at first was a sheet of "white paper," a tabula rasa, or smooth tablet, upon which sensory perceptions were impressed in the brain and images formed in the mind. Locke asserted that there were only two sources of ideas: "External, material Things, as the Objects of SENSATION, and the Operations of our own Minds within, as the Objects of REFLECTION."[5] Sensations came from experiences in the external world through the sense organs and led to simple ideas. The other source of ideas, the power of reflection, came from the ability to acquire knowledge in one's own mind through such abstract workings as reasoning, doubting, believing, and knowing. Through analysis, discrimination, and association, the mind worked over the simple ideas derived from sensory perception and recombined them into such complex patterns as principles, concepts, and relations. While all ideas and knowledge originated in sensory perception, reason was still the highest faculty of the mind: for Locke, rational judgment synthesized into higher mental abstractions the raw materials provided by the five senses.

Locke's empirical approach had some important implications for education. His denial of innate ideas helped to destroy the theological doctrine of innate human depravity so tenaciously held by Puritan leaders. Since the mind was a tabula rasa at birth, then there could be no innate depravity in children. Locke also implied that all people were alike at birth, or "born equal," and that human differences emerged from experiences and education. Thus he assumed that human nature was not set at birth but developed from the impact of the environment on the individual. Among leaders of thought in the seventeenth century, John Locke was preeminent. His writings had a widespread and profound effect, especially on Jean Jacques Rousseau, philosopher and writer, whose own eighteenth-century ideas revolutionized contemporary social theories and led to a new view of human nature.

Rousseau and a New View of Human Nature

Brilliant, erratic, and suspicious of rational ideas, Rousseau exhibited two personalities: a genius, first and foremost, with a remarkable intellect, he had an extraordinary talent developed with little formal education; at the same time, he was unstable, sensitive, devoid of emotional maturity, and uprooted and alienated from the stabilizing influence of all social institutions. In his *Confessions* he revealed with unusual candor the story of his life, which is difficult both to understand and to describe in any clear terms. He was born in 1712 in Geneva. His mother died when he was born, and his father and relatives could not care for him. He was apprenticed to an engraver, who treated him cruelly. He ran away at the age of sixteen and eventually tried all sorts of occupations. He apparently loved only the natural beauty of the mountains, valleys, and pastures. Both church and state condemned his works. Alienated from the society around him, Rousseau had a persecution complex so severe that he accused even one of his close friends, David Hume, of plotting against him. He died in 1778, eleven years before the beginning of the French Revolution, which was instigated and sustained to some extent by his political ideology.

As a writer Rousseau first attracted public attention in 1750 through his *Discourse on the Arts and Sciences,* for which he won a prize offered by the Academy at Dijon. His second *Discourse,* published four years later, on *The Origin of Inequality among Men* profoundly affected the dominant ideas of Europe. Rousseau concluded in the second *Discourse* that in a state of nature people were more nearly equal than they were in a civilized society. Both essays were concerned with reforming society, which Rousseau believed could be accomplished through a return to a state of nature. He maintained that in such a state man lived in peace, untouched by greed and avarice and unencumbered by convention and artificial conveniences. According to Rousseau, the natural savage was good; he became selfish in a civilized society that judged life by material standards. Voltaire, a literary foe, remarked cynically that he was almost tempted to walk on his hands and feet because Rousseau had glorified savagery so much. While Voltaire stressed the benefits of civilization, Rousseau maintained that progress was an illusion and emphasized instead a primitive life.

Rousseau's enthusiasm for the idea of equality and his faith in the natural nobility of man deeply impressed eighteenth-century Europe. First France and soon other nations were fascinated by Rousseau's simple words: man was by nature good, but society corrupted him. To this great thinker, a new political order and a new way of education were the keys to man's fulfillment. In 1762 these ideas were expressed with considerable force in the *Social Contract,* a political treatise, and *Émile, ou Traité de l'Éducation,* a conglomeration of treatise and story in five books.

Thus Rousseau had rebelled against the traditional idea that human nature was inherently evil and man was born in original sin. Here he broke with Calvinism. According to Rousseau, the child was born with inherent tendencies that were good; social institutions made him evil. As he wrote in the beginning of *Émile:* "God makes all things good; man meddles with them and they become evil."[6] This belief in the inherent goodness of human nature was the most important element in his educational philosophy.

The fact that Rousseau's vision of a new education underestimated the importance of reason in human development apparently did not detract from its great influence on modern education. Reason is a unique possession of man, who, in the course of human history, has sometimes failed to utilize his rational potential. Nevertheless, by shifting the center of education from the church to the child, Rousseau accomplished a Copernican revolution in the eighteenth century.

His educational ideas cast children in a new light and gave them a central role in the educative process. His main idea in *Émile* was simple and yet compelling in its appeal: to develop good men and through them a better society, education must consider the child. And to teach the child, you must understand him. Begin by studying the child, Rousseau urged; and this he tried to do himself in *Émile*. For the first time, a child's life was not viewed as an inferior counterpart of adulthood. Children no longer dressed and were no longer forced to act as miniature adults. A prophet of freedom, Rousseau stressed naturalism in education and laid the basis for a new curriculum.

Johann Heinrich Pestalozzi (1746–1827)

Pestalozzi has often been called a disciple of Rousseau. His educational ideas and the school he eventually established at Yverdon in Switzerland in 1805 attracted widespread attention. His famous writings, *Leinhard und Gertrud* ("Leonard and Gertrude"), *Wie Gertrud ihre Kinder lehrt* ("How Gertrude Teaches Her Children"), and *Schwanengesang* ("Swansong"), have been translated into many languages. Applying Locke's empirical principles and Rousseau's ideas of naturalism, Pestalozzi emphasized sense realism or the utilization of sensory experiences in developing a child's perceptive powers. In teaching children, Pestalozzi associated actual objects, models, and pictures with their symbols and meanings. For older youth there was greater stress on practical activities and the study of science and nature. Pestalozzi also believed that the teacher should gear instruction to the child's various stages of natural development. Above all, his new views of teaching and learning underscored the importance of educating teachers to understand children in order to coordinate the development of the child with the curriculum of the school.

Deeply religious, Pestalozzi had great compassion for the underprivileged and downtrodden masses in Europe. Reproduced paintings portray him with an expression of sympathy and devotion on an unattractive, wrinkled face as peasants' children clad in rags gather around him in a schoolroom. He was convinced that society could be improved only by helping each individual to develop his own inherent power and self-respect. Profoundly distressed by the devastation to family life in Switzerland after the French wars, Pestalozzi established orphanages at Stanz and Neuhof and boarding schools first at Burgdorf in 1799 and six years later in an old castle at Yverdon, where he acquired lasting fame. In the history of education, few men possessed greater faith in the school as a social instrument for uplifting people from misery and degradation.

THE TRANSMISSION OF SECULAR IDEAS TO THE UNITED STATES

The predominantly sectarian nature of colonial society, distant and remote from European intellectual centers, deterred to some extent the spread of secular ideas from abroad. But the media for transmission did exist and slowly increased: in addition to books, pamphlets, and newspapers, there were personal contacts through correspondence and travel. Before and during the American Revolution, there were politically active leaders who not only were aware of European thought and writings but also sought to use those enlightened ideas in an effort to change the institutional structure of colonial society.

With the influx of new ideas, the Puritan clergy found it increasingly difficult to maintain control in New England. The tight hold by John Cotton and John Winthrop began to loosen under sharp criticism and attack. Outspoken controversies emerged concerning the type of church-state relationship that should prevail. John Wise, for example, favored a more liberal idea of the church in a democracy. He advocated separation of church and state and wrote persuasively in favor of a democratic control within the church. He advanced the idea of congregationalism as a type of church organization in which the church members themselves would be the ultimate authority. The old theocratic church-state system in Massachusetts could not withstand the onslaughts of criticism or hold back the swiftly moving currents of change.

Throughout the eighteenth century the ideas of the Enlightenment answered new demands springing from changing ways of American life. The approaching conflict with England marked the end of an era and called for new patterns of social relationships. A growing urban society in the flourishing seacoast towns and the increase of trade and commerce were transforming America. The mercantile activities of a new middle class called for a freer environment and some degree of religious toleration as a practical necessity.

Those ideas that gave people the power to control their own destiny— for example, a belief in reason and natural law instead of predestination, and a faith in science and progress instead of supernaturalism—especially appealed to a rising middle class of independent tradesmen who wished to be free, enlightened, and successful. American merchants wanted to acquaint themselves with new knowledge in more practical areas. It was necessary for them to be familiar with modern languages, accounting, geography, and current economic conditions. Almost every town in the eighteenth century advertised private schools for evening instruction in subjects useful in commerce and trade. Lectures on mechanics, electricity, astronomy, and other subjects were available to those seeking new information. The growing number of newspapers also accelerated the dissemination of new knowledge. In addition to political letters and items on recent happenings at home and abroad, there were shipping news, essays, moral advice, and bits of interesting and often useful information. From 1753 to 1755 Benjamin Franklin improved the postal services by lowering the rates and simplifying the procedure for mailing newspapers through the government post office. Those improvements also facilitated the communication of ideas. The postrider with his familiar pouch of newspapers and letters became a more frequent sight, even in the rural communities. Thus American society on the eve of the Revolution contained elements conducive to change and provided a fertile soil for the growth of basic ideas of the Enlightenment.

Spread of Deism

The impact of science on theology was a major force in changing American patterns of thought during the late eighteenth century. The Newtonian view of the universe as a rational world-machine appeared to deny important aspects of orthodox Calvinism. Not all American statesmen of this period came under the spell of Deism; but many were attracted by the Deist's attempt to reconcile the Scripture with the ideas of the new science. "The Creator of man is the Creator of science," wrote Thomas Paine in 1796, "and it is through that medium that man can see God, as it were, face to face."[7] Only science, Paine believed, could reveal the true doctrines of Christianity. In his famous *Age of Reason,* Paine explained his scientific approach to religion. Just as a scientist seeks truth from nature's laws, so, too, must people find religious faith through rational thought. Nature, in the light of reason, is the only true source of God's revelation. Thomas Jefferson, also viewing God as a "Great Architect," prepared his own Bible from rational passages that agreed with nature's laws. Similarly, Benjamin Franklin depended on the "sacred book of nature." To those who studied seriously the Newtonian universe, nature revealed a Deity unlike the Calvinist God.

Benjamin Franklin

The secular ideas of the Enlightenment had a great effect on Benjamin Franklin, whose span of life, 1706–1790, was completely within the eighteenth century. In the opinion of most historians, he ranks as the first American of his time. Franklin's life in many ways personified the interests and ideals of an emerging middle class in colonial America.

One of the great statesmen of the Revolutionary era, Franklin possessed a unique capacity for observing the human ways and thoughts of others. Nowhere is this talent more evident than in his *Poor Richard's Almanack,* which was first published in 1732 under the pseudonym of "Richard Saunders" and continued for twenty-five years. His worldly, down-to-earth, and witty sayings appealed to American farmers and a busy, commercial middle class: "Early to bed and early to rise makes a man healthy, wealthy, and wise." "Creditors have better memories than debtors." "Eat to live; live not to eat." "A little House well fill'd, a little Field well till'd, and a little Wife well will'd, are great riches."[8] Franklin's wit and wisdom came from a variety of printed and popular materials, including the works of Bacon, Pope, Dryden, Swift, and other famous writers. There were translated sayings, too, from Spanish, French, German, and Latin sources. For a new group of diligent, working Americans, Franklin's *Almanack* undoubtedly offered a welcome note of relief from the gloomy sermons of colonial preachers. The *Almanack* itself was a cohesive educational force in eighteenth-century America, binding together into a general character many diverse and scattered national types.

Franklin practiced what he advised and strove intensely for self-improvement. In a chapter of his *Autobiography* (written near Paris in 1784), he said:

> I wished to live without committing any fault at any time, and to conquer all that either natural inclination, custom, or company might lead me into. As I knew, or thought I knew, what was right and wrong, I did not see why I might not *always* do the one and avoid the other.[9]

He listed thirteen virtues, each with a brief precept, which he tried to practice in his daily life: temperance, silence, order, resolution, frugality, industry, sincerity, justice, moderation, cleanliness, tranquillity, chastity, and humility. Through rigorous self-examination, Franklin methodically checked his own progress every day toward what he described as this "arduous project of arriving at moral perfection." He frequently extolled such secular traits as thrift and industriousness, which reflected to some extent the economic goals of merchant capitalism with its growing stress on moneymaking and profit. Versatile and utilitarian, he was forever interested in practical problems, always trying to invent something new or seeking to solve some mundane difficulty. In his personality and practical achievements, Franklin was the first to attain the ideal of a rising middle class in America: above all, a self-made man, boldly independent and financially successful.

Franklin's ideas on education were closely related to his utilitarian outlook on life and were designed to promote the interests of an ambitious middle class. Strongly influenced by the writings of John Locke, Franklin believed that knowledge should be both meaningful and useful. Indeed, for him education was a part of life aimed chiefly at improving society. At sixteen, while working as an apprenticed printer on his brother's newspaper, he had criticized Harvard College for what he called its social injustice and uselessness. Later in life, he worked successfully on his "first project of a public nature," a subscription library for Philadelphia. In 1743, at the age of thirty-seven, he issued his "Proposal for Promoting Useful Knowledge among the British Plantations in America," another attempt to foster learning and disseminate information to the people. His educational interests spanned the gamut of available scientific knowledge, for more than anything else he enjoyed intensely the applied sciences, which he valued and respected. Through Franklin the secular thought of the Enlightenment flowed into American education, striking at the core of colonial classicism and planting the seeds for a new type of secondary school.

Franklin first suggested the establishment of an academy in Philadelphia as early as 1743. Six years later he asserted his views more vigorously by circulating his *Proposals Relating to the Education of Youth in Pensilvania*[10] and soliciting funds to implement his plan. The academy was given a charter in 1753. Two years later the government granted an additional charter for a college, from which developed the University of Pennsylvania.

Franklin's plan for a new academy differed sharply from the traditional curriculum for the Latin grammar school. There was a strong utilitarian tone in his proposals:

> As to their Studies, it would be well if they could be taught *every Thing* that is useful, and *every Thing* that is ornamental: but Art is long, and their Time is short. It is therefore propos'd that they learn those Things that are likely to be *most useful* and *most ornamental*, Regard being had to the several Professions for which they are intended.[11]

In addition to a classical department, Franklin proposed as an independent branch of his Philadelphia Academy an "English School" that would prepare youth for business and "the several offices of civil life." The method of instruction, Franklin hoped, would lead toward scientific observation and experimentation. He wanted the academy to be located, if possible, "not far from a river, having a Garden, Orchard, Meadow, and a Field or two." He also expected it to be equipped with a library, maps, and scientific and mathematical apparatus.

The most important curricular aspects of Franklin's plan emphasized the study of English, of "the most useful living foreign Languages, French, German and Spanish," and of several branches of mathematics and "natural and mechanic philosophy." Franklin thought that merchants would profit by learning to write business letters and would be better civil servants if they were thoroughly acquainted with what had been written in English. Foreign languages, he believed, had less value for a man of the business world. In line with Locke's guiding principle of a "sound mind in a sound body," Franklin also stressed the importance of health and advocated frequent physical exercise "in Running, Leaping, Wrestling, and Swimming, etc." In addition, he suggested:

> While they are reading Natural History, might not a little *Gardening, Planting, Grafting, Inoculating,* etc. be taught and practised; and now and then Excursions made to the neighbouring Plantations of the best Farmers, their Methods observ'd and reason'd upon for the Information of Youth?[12]

All in all, Franklin's proposals included a wide variety of subjects: English grammar, composition, and literature; classical and modern foreign languages; science; writing and drawing; rhetoric and oratory; geography; history (of various types); agriculture and gardening; arithmetic and accounting; and mechanics.

Franklin's ideas obviously reflected his own experiential background and utilitarian and commercial interests. His plan was also strongly influenced by empiricism and the new scientific knowledge from the Enlightenment. In his introductory remarks and in several footnotes of his text, Franklin made many references to European writers, especially to the ideas of Milton and Locke. It is important to note, too, that he completely omitted sectarian instruction, except for a course on the history of religion.

Actually, Franklin's academy did not develop as he had planned. Upon his return from abroad after a long absence, he was disappointed that the English School had been subordinated to the Classical Department of his academy, which had gradually drifted under the control of the "Latinists." In 1789 he reviewed the minutes of the board of trustees and commented in a harshly critical letter "that the original Plan of the English school has been departed from; that the Subscribers to it have been disappointed and deceived." The classical program and the college-preparatory function of the Latin grammar school remained dominant and deeply entrenched. Nevertheless, on the eve of the Revolution, Franklin's ideas were spreading as the Enlightenment began to affect the educational outlook in America.

The American Philosophical Society

In 1727 Franklin formed a Junto, a discussion club, and in 1743 the American Philosophical Society. In 1769 the two were merged into the American Philosophical Society for Promoting Useful Knowledge. From 1769 to his death in 1790 Franklin was reelected annually as president of the society. David Rittenhouse was president from 1791 to 1796, when he was succeeded by Thomas Jefferson, who held the office until 1815.

The aims of the American Philosophical Society were to promote political discussions and exchange scientific knowledge and other information on a wide scale. Apparently anything that had to do with the advancement of human happiness was considered of interest. Discussions ranged, for example, from questions of national organization and security to new discoveries in the sciences and the problem of educating children at the taxpayers' expense. By 1800 there were over 650 members, including such eminent Europeans as Condorcet, Lafayette, Lavoisier, and Du Pont de Nemours. Even exiles from the royal French court during the French Revolution were freely admitted into the organization. Because of its large European membership, the American Philosophical Society became an important medium for the transmission of ideas of the Enlightenment to America.

The organization also helped to create in American society a deepening national interest in education and other postwar problems. After the American Revolution, the Philosophical Society became interested in the subject of the role of education in the new republic. In 1795 the society offered a prize for the best essay on a "system of liberal Education and literary instruction, adapted to the genius of the Government of the United States; comprehending also a plan for instituting and conducting public schools in this country, on principles of the most extensive utility."[13] The prize was shared by two essays: Samuel Harrison Smith's *Remarks on Education* (1798) and Samuel Knox's *An Essay on the Best System of Liberal Education* (1799).

Apparently the subject was so important after the Revolution that outstanding leaders of the time were already pondering the issue by the American Philosophical Society. Before the end of the century, every prominent American leader had given some attention to the problem of building an educational system for the new republic. All seemed convinced that people must be educated in order to remain free citizens.

In their wide range of ideas, in their search for new concepts, Washington, Jefferson, Benjamin Rush, and others less known in American history surveyed the important issue of education in a free society. They foresaw educational needs at least a century before their time. To begin with, all pointed to the educational deficiencies of the colonies: poorly qualified teachers, inadequate schools, and poor equipment. On a more positive note, almost every spokesman called for a national system of popular education, supported by taxes, from the elementary school to the university. In their eyes, the main purpose of education was to uplift the well-being of the citizenry and to utilize natural science for the service of humankind. In fact, almost every leader of American thought during this period believed that science provided the best tool for discovering those basic laws in nature on which it was believed human progress depended. These statesmen also wanted to strengthen nationalism by teaching pupils republican principles and the duties of American citizenship. Education was deemed a public responsibility of the federal government, a bulwark of freedom and security. President Washington, in his Farewell Address published in 1796, urged the advancement of education for the national welfare. Of all these eighteenth-century statesmen, no one, perhaps, displayed more interest in the subject and certainly no one had more confidence in education as an instrument for the preservation of freedom than Thomas Jefferson.

Thomas Jefferson

Jefferson was born near the frontier settlement of Charlottesville, Virginia, in 1743. He received an education at the College of William and Mary and studied law in the office of George Wythe. His lifelong attainments were many and varied. His public service alone was quite remarkable: member of the Virginia legislature, delegate to the Continental Congress, governor of Virginia, minister to France, secretary of state, vice president, and two terms as President of the United States. A farmer and amateur botanist, he loved, too, the quietness and rural surroundings of his beloved home, Monticello.

Jefferson's personal life and political career reflect his rare blending of energy, patience, and unusual self-discipline. He was an American devotee of Renaissance learning, an important transmitter of European ideas, especially those from French sources. His views were influenced mainly by the philosophic works of Locke, by British ideas on constitutional law, and by French educational writings. He was fluent in Latin, Greek, and several modern languages. He wrote long letters, often quoting from books he cherished. His private library was impressive and among the finest in America.

Above all, Jefferson sought human freedom and abhorred every form of tyranny or absolutism. "I have sworn," he declared, "upon the altar of God, eternal hostility against every form of tyranny over the mind of man." While serving in Paris as American minister and successor to Franklin, he expressed to his friends in letters written in 1785 and 1786 his revulsion against "kings, nobles, or priests" as "conservators of the public happiness." He feared the temptations of his own countrymen to delegate too much power and, as a result, forfeit their rights and liberty. He had written the Declaration of Independence at the age of thirty-three; upon returning from France, he wanted to have a "Bill of Rights" added to the Constitution. Despite intense Federalist vituperation in the bitter presidential campaign and deep personal disappointment in the course of the French Revolution, Jefferson's faith in the ability and goodness of humankind never wavered. "Equal and exact justice to all men," he declared in his first inaugural address in 1801. Few statesmen in American history have so vigorously strived for an ideal; perhaps none has so consistently viewed public education as the indispensable cornerstone of freedom.

Jefferson was convinced that the primary requisite of a free society was a continuous system of public education. His Bill for the More General Diffusion of Knowledge, proposed to the legislature of Virginia in 1779, contained the basic elements of his educational ideas. In this plan for a state-controlled system of education, Jefferson would establish (1) tax-supported elementary schools, with free instruction for the first three years, for the purpose of teaching reading, writing, and arithmetic to white boys and girls; and (2) twenty state grammar schools in which a few talented poor students from the elementary schools would be taught free, at the taxpayers' expense, for varying periods up to a maximum of six years. The twenty secondary schools would teach English grammar, Greek, Latin, geography, and advanced arithmetic to white boys. The entire plan departed from the utilitarianism of Franklin and emphasized instead academic training. Jefferson elaborated on his proposal in more detail in his *Notes on the State of Virginia,* written in 1781 and slightly revised in the winter of 1782. He recommended that those boys sent from the elementary schools to the twenty secondary schools be given a chance for one or two years

> and best genius of the whole selected, and continued six years, and the residue dismissed. By this means twenty of the best geniuses will be raked from the rubbish annually, and be instructed, at the public expense, so far as the grammar schools go. At the end of six years' instruction, one-half are to be discontinued (from among whom the grammar schools will probably be supplied with future masters;) and the other half, who are to be chosen for the superiority of their parts and disposition, are to be sent and continued three years in the study of such sciences as they shall choose, at William and Mary college, the plan of which is proposed to be enlarged, as will be hereafter explained, and extended to all the useful sciences. The ultimate result of the whole scheme of education would be the teaching all children of the state reading, writing, and common arithmetic; turning out ten annually, of superior genius, well taught in Greek, Latin, geography, and the higher branches of arithmetic: turning out ten others annually, of still superior parts, who, to those branches of learning, shall have added such of the sciences as their genius shall have led them to; the furnishing to the wealthier part of the people convenient schools, at which their children may be educated at their own expense.—The general objects of this law are to provide an education adapted to the years, to the capacity, and the condition of every one, and directed to their freedom and happiness.[14]

Jefferson's plan reflects an interesting combination of aristocratic and liberal approaches: the cultivation of an aristocracy of talent to lead the nation and the recruitment of this intellectual elite from the gifted boys of Virginia, regardless of parental wealth. Girls were not afforded equal opportunities, compulsory attendance was not proposed, and the black people were completely ignored. Essentially undemocratic, his plan, nevertheless, was among the most liberal of any advanced by an American statesman in the eighteenth century. Probably the most democratic feature was Jefferson's attempt to remove the stigma of pauperism from elementary schooling. Indeed, in a society of class distinctions, the failure of the plan was undoubtedly caused by the refusal of well-to-do citizens to pay taxes for the education of the poor.

The bill was defeated by a state legislature not yet prepared to accept a concept of universal education. In 1817 the proposal was revised in the Bill for Establishing a System of Public Education, but that was also rejected. Just as Franklin's educational efforts for a more practical type of education led eventually to the establishment of the University of Pennsylvania, so, too, did Jefferson's plan end with the founding of the University of Virginia.

The University of Virginia was Jefferson's favorite project and the last great work of his life. No institution of higher learning ever bore so

completely the impress of a single mind and inspiration. Jefferson created the
project in every way. As the architect, he planned the campus and directed
all the details: he mapped out the landscape, arranging every tree and shrub
and outlining every door, window, and fireplace. He even bought the bricks
and picked the trees to be used for lumber. He also chose the library books,
selected the students, appointed the faculty, and developed the courses of
study. Then he carried the whole idea through the Virginia legislature and
lived to see the university open with a total of forty students in March 1825,
a month before his eighty-first birthday. Jefferson died the following year on
July 4, exactly fifty years after the adoption of the document that made his
name immortal in American history.

Not one of the plans for public education advanced by American leaders
during the latter part of eighteenth century had any real measure of success in
terms of actual adoption in the new republic. After the Revolution there was
still a widespread suspicion of a powerful central government. Then, too,
education still carried strong popular connotations from the colonial era of
dominant theological support. Vested religious interests were still influential, and defense of the status quo actually increased under Jefferson because
of conservative fears of passing control of the schools on to a liberal administration. Although there was widespread interest among national leaders for
improved public enlightenment, serious discussions of the idea of a tax-
supported system of education were not heard again until the early decades of
the nineteenth century.

TRADITION AND CHANGE
IN AMERICAN EDUCATION

The Role of the National Government

Despite the concern for education expressed by the more liberal statesmen of
the time, neither the Articles of Confederation nor the new Constitution
recognized education as a strong national interest. In most of the states from
which the delegates to the Constitutional Convention in Philadelphia came,
the citizens did not consider education to be in the province of any government. Indeed, when the Constitution was drafted in 1787, education was
not regarded as an undertaking of either the state or federal government. The
failure of the Constitution to deal with education in more than residual terms
no doubt reflected the general view that the teaching of youth was primarily
a religious or private matter. Because the Constitution provided that all
powers not conferred upon the federal government were retained by the
states, education was viewed as a state function. Thus when popular interest
later developed in support of public schools, the chief proponents turned to
the state governments to provide them.

While the government, under the Articles of Confederation, lacked the power to act in major areas of national interest, it did, however, formulate an important land policy that was to affect American education. Soon after the Revolution large numbers of settlers moved into the territory north of the Ohio River and west of the Appalachian Mountains and demanded the right to buy these new lands. The states along the Atlantic seaboard had renounced their title to this countryside and ceded their claims to the national government. Until new states were formally admitted from these domains, the regulation of new land was a national responsibility, but a survey was needed before sales could be made to settlers. Even before the adoption of the Constitution, Congress enacted the Land Ordinance of 1785, which provided for a rectangular survey of the Northwest Territory. The lands were divided into townships six miles square, and each township was further divided into sections one mile square. The words in the official Ordinance of 1787, which incorporated the Northwest Territory, reflected the prevailing views of American statesmen during the early national period: "Religion, morality, and knowledge being necessary to good government and the happiness of mankind, schools and the means of education shall be forever encouraged."

In each township the sections were numbered from one to thirty-six, with the sixteenth section being reserved for the support of education. This provision did not require that schools be built on the sixteenth section, but the proceeds from its rental or sale by the state were to be applied to education. In 1787 and 1788 two tracts were sold to land companies. As part of the sale agreement, Congress granted each company a township for a future college with the sixteenth section reserved for the maintenance of schools. This precedent of section grants of every township for the support of schools was followed first in 1802 with the admission of Ohio and then in the admission of all other states except Texas, Maine, and West Virginia. After 1850, beginning with the admission of California, more than one section was granted by the federal government for the support of education. While the revenues derived from these section grants certainly offered incentives and extended educational opportunities in the new nation, it soon became clear that much more support would be needed from the states in order to provide tuition-free public schools for all children.

Toward Secularization of Elementary Education

After the Revolution the traditional view of the child as a miniature adult possessed of unregenerate human nature was still prevalent, especially in New England. Puritan discipline, imposing order by fear and physical abuse, did not suddenly disappear in the new nation. As late as 1800, whips, ferules, and whipping posts were still used in some one-room schools.

The "little red schoolhouse" of rural America is nostalgically preserved in literature. It was usually a poorly heated and ventilated rectangular structure with its once white or red paint weather-ravaged and faded. Some one-room schools, even those that had never been painted, withstood the elements amazingly well and lasted for years.

With its Puritanical outlook toward human nature, the United States lagged far behind Europe, where a harsh view of the child was outmoded by the middle of the eighteenth century. Pestalozzi's influence on European education had been far-reaching. The schools of Prussia, for example, were completely reorganized to incorporate Pestalozzi's ideas and approach, and the cantons of Switzerland had established normal schools to prepare teachers to use his methods in public instruction. Philipp Emanuel von Fellenberg's institute at Hofwyl, modeled on Pestalozzi's ideas in *Lienhard und Gertrud*, emphasized vocational training in tailoring, printing, shoemaking, and other trades. Fellenberg's influence in popularizing Pestalozzi's ideas both in Europe and in the United States was quite extensive.

During the early years of the nineteenth century, the educational ideas of Rousseau and Pestalozzi began to appear in the United States. A deliberate effort to introduce the latter's approach into American elementary schools was made by William Maclure, who, after amassing a fortune in Philadelphia, devoted the remainder of his life to geological study and educational reform. In 1804, while on a diplomatic mission to France, he became interested in Pestalozzi's ideas. On several occasions he visited Pestalozzi at Yverdon and Fellenberg at Hofwyl. He asked Pestalozzi to come to the United States to establish a school. Because of age and personal problems, Pestalozzi declined the invitation, suggesting instead Joseph Neef, who had formerly taught under him and had established an orphanage in Paris. Neef accepted Maclure's invitation, arrived in Philadelphia in 1806, and three years later opened a successful school demonstrating Pestalozzi's methods and principles. Pestalozzianism was more widely publicized in the United States through articles and reports and through Edward A. Sheldon's application of Pestalozzi's system during the early 1860s at the Oswego Normal School in New York.[15]

Despite a brief period of popularity in some quarters, Pestalozzianism failed to gain widespread acceptance in the United States. Nevertheless, an enlightened theory had begun to affect American educational thought. Teachers were slowly beginning to view children in a new light and to recognize that the learning process was far more complex than that suggested by faculty psychology with its stress on rote memorization and mental training. Mainly dormant during the early decades of the nineteenth century, the ideas for a new education did not disappear completely. With different leaders in another social setting, Rousseau's educational theories were destined to make a more significant impact upon American elementary schools.

The gradual secularization of elementary education was also reflected in the changing content of reading books. For example, editions of the *New England Primer* began to appear with substitutions and revisions in the rhymes. The religious tone in the *Primer* was somewhat softened as more secular material was added. Punishments for wicked children no longer meant eternal damnation, but involved instead withholding of rewards. Other changes also indicated a different mood. The tendency to praise England ended, and pictures or descriptions of the British monarch gradually disappeared. Rhymes like the following were inserted:

> Great Washington brave
> His country did save.
>
> Queens and kings
> Are gaudy things.

With the exception of the *New England Primer* and a few texts in limited editions, the books used in American schools during the first half of the eighteenth century were either imported from England or reprints of British texts.

After the Revolutionary War, a number of different school texts were published in the United States. Spurred by patriotism and eager for profits, American textbook writers and publishers sought cultural independence from England. Their efforts were part of a larger postwar drive in the new nation to perpetuate democracy through public enlightenment. The chaos in Europe after the French Revolution was a source of deep concern among American leaders, who hoped to inculcate loyalty to the United States by instilling in boys and girls a knowledge of democratic precepts and a strong patriotic commitment. In line with this nationalist sentiment, most American schoolbooks in one way or another were filled with repetitious, patriotic motifs. The United States became, as Ruth Elson points out, "the best of all possible worlds."[16] Another important purpose of the new readers was to foster a middle-class morality. The most widely circulated textbooks reflecting these aims were Noah Webster's *Elementary Spelling Book* and William Holmes McGuffey's *Readers*.

Noah Webster's widely adopted *Elementary Spelling Book* was a famous primer for at least a century after its publication in 1783. The speller was really the first of three parts of the complete text. A grammar was published the following year, and a reader appeared in 1785.[17] Of the three parts, the speller was the most successful. It was often called the "blue-backed speller" because of the color of the binding. In sixty years, about 20 million copies were sold, with many books used repeatedly as copies were passed down in

families. In 1828 alone approximately 350,000 copies were sold; two decades later the sales had approached a million copies a year. According to
Commager, "The demand was insatiable. . . . No other secular book had
ever spread so wide, penetrated so deep, lasted so long."[18]

Emphasizing patriotic and moralistic exercises, this popular speller
translated Webster's own views into short, easy-to-remember maxims incul-
cating contentment with one's economic status and respect for honest work
and property rights. Children were admonished in several aphorisms to know
the value of money, which should be wisely spent, and to avoid the dangers
of drinking, which led to ruin and poverty. Webster placed great stress on
such virtues as industry and thrift and urged acquiescence to life's poverty
and distress. In a post-Revolutionary era when extremes of wealth and
poverty coexisted in vivid contrasts, Webster's social views no doubt influenced many American children who read and reread the maxims and memorized their lessons from the famous "blue-backed speller."

The school texts that far exceeded in sales all others commonly used in
the elementary schools after the Revolution were the famous McGuffey
Readers. It was estimated that 122 million copies were sold after 1836.
Compiled by William Holmes McGuffey, the six readers in the series were
graded in difficulty from the first level to the sixth grade. In content these
readers also replaced the moral pessimism of the Puritan texts with a strong
secular tone emphasizing middle-class morality. The selections in the *Readers*
were a collection of pieces from American folklore and other sources that
children in one-room schoolhouses read aloud over and over again. Each piece
was selected because it supposedly taught a moral lesson or condemned
unsatisfactory behavior. Like Franklin's *Almanack* and Webster's *Speller,* the
McGuffey *Readers* stressed the familiar virtues of honesty, truth, reliability,
charity, temperance, and obedience.

The Growth of Private Schools and Academies

At the beginning of the eighteenth century, the dominant pattern of secondary education was confined to the Latin grammar school. Circumscribed in
both goals and curricula by college-entrance requirements, these schools
were basically aristocratic, catering to a small group of select youth. In the
town schools of New England, boys were taught by public instructors, and
in the Middle Colonies and in the South, by religious teachers and private
tutors. One of the main reasons most Latin grammar schools were resistant to
change was their limited financial support. In New England these institutions, as town schools, were supported chiefly from public funds. To expand
the curriculum or establish additional schools in order to meet new social
pressures would have exceeded existing tax limits or placed a heavy tax
burden on local citizens who were not yet convinced that secondary education
was a legitimate responsibility of local government.

After the Revolution, the swiftly moving tempo of social change led to increasing demands for a more practical secondary education. This secular trend toward utilitarianism was characteristic of an expanding commercial society. The aftermath of war offered dissatisfied individuals a better chance for change and helped to pave the way for a new type of secondary school. In the new nation Franklin's proposals for a *"more useful"* course of study were relevant to the educational demands and interests of growing numbers of merchants and artisans in Boston, New York, Charleston, and other urban centers.

At first the need for a different secondary education was met by private schools usually conducted in the master's home. It was a simple matter: all the master required was a space in his study, a few books, and some willing students. There were no controls and no records to keep. Anyone who paid the fee was accepted for instruction in any vocational or academic subject offered on demand. A few masters referred to their private ventures as "public schools" because classes were open to any person willing to pay the fee.

Colonial newspapers often carried advertisements announcing the opening of a school, the hours of day and evening classes, and the fees charged for instruction in a variety of subjects. In a single advertisement a teacher might offer to teach up to twenty-five different subjects. The following advertisement of a private school in New York City in 1723 is typical of many that appeared in colonial newspapers before the Revolution:

> There is a School in New York, in the Broad Street, near the Exchange, where Mr. John Walton, late of Yale Colledge, Teacheth Reading, Writing, Arethmatick, whole Numbers and Fractions, Vulgar and Decimal, The Mariners Art, Plain and Mercators Way; Also Geometry, Surveying, the Latin Tongue, the Greek and Hebrew Grammers, Ethicks, Rhetorick, Logick, Natural philosophy and Metaphysicks, all or any of them for a Reasonable Price. The School from the first of October till the first of March will be tended in the Evening. If any Gentlemen in the Country are disposed to send their Sons to the said School, if they apply themselves to the Master he will immediately procure suitable Entertainment for them, very Cheap. Also if any Young Gentlemen of the City will please to come in the Evening and make some Tryal of the Liberal Arts, they may have opportunity of Learning the same things which are commonly Taught in Colledges.[19]

The subjects most frequently offered were in response to any need for which young men were willing to pay. In all private schools the basic language taught was English, not Latin or Greek. Because the expanding trade of the new nation had created a demand for men with skills in navigation, accounting, and foreign languages, these subjects were often in demand and advertised in the newspapers.

,   While most private schools were open exclusively to boys, some offered instruction to girls, usually at different hours and on a part-time basis. A master's wife, for example, added to her husband's advertisement in the *New York Mercury* in 1765 the following notice:

> N.B. Mrs. Carroll Proposes teaching young Ladies plain work, Samples, French Quilting, Knotting for Bed Quilts, or Toilets, Dresden, flowering on Cat Gut, Shading (with Silk, or Worsted) on Cambrick, Lawn, and Holland.[20]

Schools designated "for the instruction of YOUNG LADIES only" were sometimes established in the larger towns. For example, the following advertisement of a school of this type appeared in 1770:

> As I have discovered sundry inconveniences to result from teaching YOUTH of both sexes, and having been frequently solicited by several respectable families in this city, to establish a school, for the instruction of YOUNG LADIES only, in READING, WRITING, ARITHMETIC, and ACCOMPTS; I have opened a school for said purpose in LAETITIA-COURT; contiguous to Front, Second and Market streets. As the utility of such an undertaking (properly conducted) is undeniably evident, I hope for the encouragement of the public, which I shall endeavour to deserve, by a constant assiduity to promote the improvement of my pupils in the aforesaid branches, as also in having the strictest regard to their morals—Such misses as are obliged to attend other schools, I shall take for half days.
>
> MATTHEW MAGUIRE[21]

Thus the private schools were responsive to the changing social climate of the United States in the eighteenth century. Unlike the Latin grammar schools, they catered primarily to a rising middle class of merchant capitalists. All courses were judged in terms of their vocational value. Anyone could attend to take any courses that were considered worthwhile. The quality of instruction was dubious; class hours, variable; and admission standards, practically nonexistent.

While the private schools met a transitional need in the colonies, they were small, usually unstable and insolvent, and unable to cope with the growing demands of a new clientele. During the eighteenth century, some private schools began to use the terms "Academy," "English School," or "English Grammar School" in local advertisements to denote different or broader programs. After the Revolution, more schools followed this procedure. At the same time, the idea of a more practical course of study, which deviated from the traditional curricula of the Latin grammar schools, was spreading.

There soon arose a new type of institution similar to the academy Franklin had proposed. In the beginning, the academies coexisted with the Latin grammar schools and provided a more utilitarian education. Gradually, however, these institutions multiplied in number, and toward the end of the eighteenth century the academy became the dominant pattern of secondary education in the United States.

There were many variants, for not all academies developed in the same way. The first academies were for young men; later, separate schools for girls were founded. In sparsely settled areas where nonboarding academies could not be successfully financed, two schools were sometimes merged into a coeducational institution that included a "female department." In New England a number of academies for young men were primarily college-preparatory schools and have maintained that function to the present day. In the South there were some military academies for boys and "finishing schools" for girls. Adopting such various titles as seminaries, female academies, college institutes, and public academies, these institutions grew rapidly and by 1860 flourished throughout the country.

The academies differed significantly from the Latin grammar schools and the small private schools. They were often boarding schools supported from a variety of sources: church or philanthropic endowment, tuition and fees from parents, or, as in New York, limited state funds. Their internal organization was more complex, and the curriculum was broad and quite diversified.

An academy was usually founded by a group, instead of by an individual, and was larger than a private-venture school that a master operated to suit himself. Those academies that petitioned for and received charters of incorporation from the state were administered by boards of trustees who had wide discretionary powers. The board controlled the budget, hired the staff, and made all the rules for both teachers and students. In nonincorporated academies, the same situation prevailed: sometimes called committees or proprietors, these officers still made all the decisions. They hired and fired themselves and proliferated into endless committees of all sorts. At Philips Andover, for example, where the trustees divided themselves among numerous committees, a special group was even appointed to consider a request to construct outhouses.[22]

The problem of financial support continually plagued the trustees. Sometimes there were serious restrictions on the amount of income academies were allowed to hold. Teachers' salaries, then as now, were always a major item in the budget. Obtaining funds, however, was only part of the problem; to open and operate an academy, the officers, of course, had to recruit students. Like the masters in the private schools, these men relied chiefly on newspaper advertisements and often made extravagant claims to entice the most gullible parents and students.

Beginning in 1784, the academies in New York were given a strong financial incentive to cooperate and work closely with the state government. The New York legislature specified the terms academies had to meet in order to obtain a charter of incorporation. Most important were the requirements concerning control and financial support. To become incorporated, the academy had to contribute more than half of the money needed for its own support, and there had to be at least twelve and no more than twenty-four trustees. By meeting the terms of its charter and reporting annually its financial status to the Regents, an academy obtained state grants. As a double check, the Regents maintained supervision over the academies through periodic reports, examinations, and visitations. In no other state were academies so liberally supported from state funds.

The various curricula of the academies appeared to be an attempt to combine into one institution the classical elements of the Latin schools and the more utilitarian content proposed by Benjamin Franklin. In catering to the popular demands of a new middle class in the United States, a wide range of subjects was offered. In New York, for instance, over a hundred different subjects were available at one time or another between 1787 and 1900. Programs generally revolved around the study of English grammar and literature, the core of the curriculum. English classics by such men as Milton and Pope were frequently added to the more formalized programs stressing Latin and the study of Caesar and Cicero. Geography became a popular subject, along with American history, which attracted great interest as a part of patriotic nationalism. The curricula of many academies reflected the newer scientific interests of the early nineteenth century by offering "natural philosophy" (a combination of all the natural sciences), along with astronomy, chemistry, and botany. Algebra and geometry, too, received increased attention. Also stressed were such commercial subjects as navigation and surveying, while some academies advertised business courses comprising penmanship, bookkeeping, and public speaking. Of course, not every academy offered all these subjects at the same time.

As more subjects were added to the curriculum, there was a corresponding increase in the number of textbooks. Jedidiah Morse's *Geography Made Easy,* printed in 1784, stressed geography of the United States (not Britain or Europe) and was widely read and memorized. In 1795 Morse's condensed *Elements of Geography* appeared for use in the lower grades. Like Webster and McGuffey, Morse also sought to inculcate loyalty to the new nation. With no illustrations and only a few maps, Morse's *Geographies* were quite different from later texts published in this field. New texts also appeared in English grammar, the commercial subjects, foreign languages, and practical mathematics.

The chief significance in this broad range of offerings was that it indicated rather clearly a strong popular willingness to direct the secondary school along more practical and democratic channels. These schools frequently offered a terminal education for persons not planning to attend college. As transitional institutions between the single-purpose Latin schools and the comprehensive public high schools, the academies vividly demonstrated the value and success of secondary education. Here was a broader program that helped the common people prepare for life in a swiftly changing commercial and business world. The academies, of course, were tuition-charging institutions, "public" but not "free," and as a result many boys and girls could not afford to attend. Nevertheless, in expanding the curricula to attract non-college-bound youth and in broadening the entrance requirements to include people of all denominations, the academy movement constituted an important step forward in the democratization of American secondary education.

Developments in Higher Education

The first colleges in colonial America were founded primarily for religious purposes. Like the Puritans in the Massachusetts Bay Colony, other denominations also wanted to provide for a literate clergy. This desire to perpetuate a Christian tradition in the New World explains in large part the colonial proliferation of colleges before the American Revolution. Founded in 1701, Yale was under sectarian control, and, like Harvard, its primary educational aim was to prepare ministers. With a similar view, Rhode Island College (later Brown University) was founded in 1764 to provide a formal training for Baptist ministers. Indeed, the aim of training students for the ministry was stated in the charters of all the colonial colleges founded before 1776 except the College of Philadelphia, which was not specifically under church control. Even King's College, while chiefly nondenominational, was chartered in 1754 only after a controversy between Presbyterian and Anglican forces; as a compromise measure, the college's charter provided for the election of clergy from four different Protestant denominations to the board of control. Reinforcing this primary religious aim, the colonial colleges usually appointed clergymen as instructors. (See the table on page 68 for the original name, founding date, and sectarian control of nine colonial colleges founded before the American Revolution.)

There was another motive, too, in establishing these colonial colleges in the wilderness. Their charters underscored the need for loyal college-trained civil leaders to bolster the work of the orthodox ministers. The first colleges, then, were founded to perform this twofold function of training both church and state leaders.

The early colleges were modeled after Oxford and Cambridge as these two universities existed in the seventeenth century. In matters involving administration, curriculum, and degree requirements, Harvard was a virtual prototype of Emmanuel College at Cambridge, a Puritan stronghold. Yale,

NINE COLONIAL COLLEGES FOUNDED BEFORE
THE AMERICAN REVOLUTION

Present Name	Original Name	Founding Date	Sectarian Control
Harvard University	Harvard College	1636	Congregational
College of William and Mary	College of William and Mary	1693	Anglican
Yale University	Collegiate School, and Yale College	1701	Congregational
Princeton University	College of New Jersey	1746	Presbyterian
Columbia University	King's College	1754	Nondenominational
University of Pennsylvania	College of Philadelphia	1755	Nondenominational
Brown University	Rhode Island College	1764	Baptist
Rutgers, The State University of New Jersey	Queen's College	1766	Dutch Reformed Church
Dartmouth College	Dartmouth College	1769	Congregational

too, borrowed heavily from the examples set by the British universities. There was also some influence from Scotland, especially in the establishment of William and Mary, Princeton, and the College of Philadelphia. Like Cambridge and Oxford, the colonial colleges in the beginning were essentially upper-class institutions, rigidly adhering to Renaissance ideals and aristocratic traditions.

About the middle of the eighteenth century, the colleges were forced to deviate from their Old World examples because of new and changing conditions in America. Most evident in colonial society was the growing religious diversity that called for modifications in the English patterns. For instance, unlike the collegiate systems of control in England, the colonial colleges established interdenominational boards. There were some very practical reasons for the development of more liberal practices. There were obvious needs to broaden the base of financial support and to attract more students in the face of increasing collegiate competition. The most striking example of a more tolerant outlook was seen in the charter of Rhode Island College, which prohibited doctrinal tests for admission and forbade sectarian bias in classroom instruction.

There were other signs, too, of the changing social climate. After 1750, more laymen like Benjamin Franklin were instrumental in founding the colleges. There was less stress on ministerial training and a corresponding decrease in the number of students entering the clergy. Harvard developed a broader approach toward sectarianism, which contrasted sharply with the earlier narrowness of Puritan leaders. In 1760, for example, Harvard permitted Anglican students to attend Christ Church in Cambridge, instead of the customary Congregational meeting place. This secular trend was also evident at Yale during the administration of Thomas Clap, who was head of the College from 1739 to 1766, first as rector and then under a revised charter of 1745, as president. Although its main purpose was still training students for the ministry, Yale added a program for those interested in other professions. Clap personally lectured on a number of topics in this program, ranging from politics and law to agriculture and anatomy. He had a favorite theory of "terrestrial comets" which led to some interesting secular research and discussion at Yale during his presidency.[23] In 1770 the College of William and Mary declared that its aim was not only to prepare Anglican ministers but also to train future physicians and lawyers. Toward the end of the colonial period, a large percentage of college students were sons of merchants and middle-class professional laymen who were more interested in secular matters than in religious training.

Throughout the colonial period the college curriculum was dominated by a study of the classical languages and literature. Copied from the English universities, Harvard's first course of studies remained virtually the same for almost a century. Other colonial colleges followed Harvard's lead, stressing the medieval arts, sciences, languages, and literature. During the first year, students studied the core of the four-year program — Latin, Greek, Hebrew, rhetoric, and logic. This was continued the second year by emphasizing again Greek, Hebrew, and logic and beginning "natural philosophy." In the third year, metaphysics and "moral philosophy" were added, while the fourth year was devoted to a review of Latin, Greek, logic and "natural philosophy" and an introduction to mathematics. The chief difference between the college curriculum in the colonies and the program at Oxford or Cambridge was the greater colonial significance attached to the study of Hebrew, which some colonial leaders regarded as the divine language of the saints in heaven. Although his proposal was defeated, President Ezra Stiles at Yale, for example, wanted to require Hebrew for all students during the first year. The sequence of courses varied at Yale, but the subjects taught were the same as those required by Harvard. In fact, this basic type of classical curriculum prevailed at all the colonial colleges.

During the eighteenth century the intellectual ferment from the great scientific discoveries of the Enlightenment gradually wrought important changes in the American college curricula. These developments were facilitated to some extent by examples of the Scottish universities, which were more strongly affected by Newtonian science than were Oxford and Cambridge. As early as 1711 the College of William and Mary appointed a professor of natural philosophy and mathematics, and in 1779 Jefferson suggested that the professorship of divinity and oriental languages be replaced by courses in medicine, chemistry, law, and modern foreign languages. Harvard founded the Hollis Professorship of Mathematics and Natural Philosophy in 1728 to encourage scientific teaching through demonstrations and laboratory experiments. At Yale the curriculum was substantially modified by 1750 with the introduction of Newtonian science and other material. Both presidents Clap and Stiles were greatly interested in science, especially astronomy, and helped to build a strong scientific tradition at Yale. By 1766, mathematics was not only required for admission to Yale but also taught in each year of the curriculum. In 1754 King's College advertised that its program would stress "everything *useful*," including surveying, geography, navigation, commerce, mineralogy, husbandry, and government. In 1756, at the College of Philadelphia, Provost William Smith established an interesting three-year program that included some science, mathematics, and utilitarian courses. All these changes indicated the growing importance of an urban middle class in America and clearly revealed the secular spirit of the Enlightenment.

Of great importance in the history of higher education was the *Dartmouth College* decision handed down in 1819 by John Marshall, chief justice of the United States Supreme Court. The litigation stemmed from an attempt by the state legislature to assume control of Dartmouth, a private college. The main issue, in brief, was whether New Hampshire could retroactively alter the college charter.[24] For five hours, Daniel Webster (1782–1852), a then unknown Dartmouth alumnus, argued eloquently before the Court on behalf of the college. *"This, Sir, is my case!"* pleaded Webster, reportedly in tears. "It is the case, not merely of that humble institution, it is the case of every College in our land. It is more." Chief Justice Marshall, also in tears, leaned forward to hear every word of the young lawyer's closing remarks. "Sir, you may destroy this little Institution; it is weak; it is in your hands!" continued Webster. "I know it is one of the lesser lights in the literary horizon of our country. You may put it out. But if you do so, you must carry through your work! You must extinguish, one after another, all those greater lights of science which, for more than a century, have thrown their radiance over our land! It is, Sir, as I have said, a small College. And yet, *there are those who love it.*"[25] On February 2, 1819, the Court ruled that the Dartmouth College charter, granted in 1769 by King George III, was a contract within the meaning of the federal Constitution and was therefore protected by the Constitution against legislative alteration. Dartmouth College was a private agency subject to the policies of its board of trustees and not to the control of the state. New Hampshire's attempt was ruled illegal; and Dartmouth, with its colonial charter, remained a private college. This decision, vital for the protection of corporate business in the states, became a milestone in American jurisprudence.

The *Dartmouth College* case is also a landmark in American education. On the eve of the Jacksonian movement, the decision guaranteed to private colleges a necessary right to exist, free from expropriation and popular pressures. A vast number of new colleges with little or no financial support entered into an open arena of intense, and often bitter, competition for survival. Over seven hundred, in fact, were forced to close their doors before 1860. By encouraging the growth of small sectarian colleges and by preventing the legislatures from transforming existing foundations, the decision delayed the development of state universities for several years.

The emergence of industrial capitalism during the early decades of the nineteenth century had profound implications for the history of American education. The factory system began to lure people from farms to urban centers and to beckon Europeans to leave home and emigrate to the seaboard cities. This same system also created a rising tide of labor discontent, arousing the fears of wealthy manufacturers and merchants who wanted to force the new working class to acquiesce more willingly in the established political and economic order. There were growing demands also to assimilate the immigrants with Old World traditions into the American mainstream. Slowly at first, but with increasing tempo during the nineteenth century, the currents of change spread from the Northeast to other parts of the country as new and powerful forces reshaped American society.

By aggravating a whole new set of social problems, the rise of industrialism was accompanied by a wave of humanitarian agitation to alleviate new human miseries and evils. Living conditions in the urban slums were revolting. Factory working hours were long; wages, low; and job conditions, deplorable. Child labor was exploited, while throngs of unemployed clustered in coastal towns. Family life was deteriorating and crime was increasing. At the same time, examples of enlightened European thought and experimentation were reaching American shores. Rousseau's eighteenth-century conception of the inherent goodness of man and Pestalozzi's humanitarian ideals and devotion to education gave credence to the growing conviction among reformers that extremes of human misery and poverty were both unnecessary and improvable. The social impact of the Industrial Revolution was first felt in New England, where educational statesmen channeled humanitarian strength into the public-school movement.

FOR DISCUSSION AND CRITICAL THOUGHT

1. Discuss the educational implications of the Enlightenment ideology.
2. Tell briefly how Pestalozzi's famous school at Yverdon (established in 1805) might differ from a Latin grammar school in Boston at the beginning of the nineteenth century.
3. What forces contributed to the secularization of American education after 1750? What impact did the new secular outlook have on schooling?
4. The Age of the Enlightenment witnessed a change in the content of reading material for children. What brought about this change? How did

this change in literature reflect some of the historical changes during the eighteenth and nineteenth centuries?

5. Library shelves abound with volumes about Thomas Jefferson's ideas and accomplishments. Point to some central themes in Jefferson's educational views and assess their crucial significance for the United States today. Discuss, in particular, the relevance of Jefferson's educational ideology for the 1980s and 1990s, indicating some of its strengths and inadequacies.

6. In what way do you think Benjamin Franklin's ideas on education influenced the development of secondary schools? Explain your response in the light of important trends in secondary education.

7. Discuss the significance of the *Dartmouth College* case in the history of higher education.

NOTES

1. This official church ban on *De Revolutionibus* was not changed until 1822, when formal sanction was given to the fact that the sun was the center of the planetary system.

2. *Definitions and Axioms or Laws of Motion,* in *Sir Isaac Newton's Mathematical Principles of Natural Philosophy and His System of the World,* trans. Andrew Motte in 1729, with a historical and explanatory appendix by Florian Cajori (Berkeley: University of California Press, 1960), pp. 1–28.

3. René Descartes, "The Third Set of Objections: Reply to Objection X," *The Philosophical Words of Descartes,* trans. Elizabeth S. Haldane and G.R.T. Ross (New York: Dover, 1955), 2:73. The Cartesian theory of "innate ideas" soon conflicted with the principle of sensory experience as the source of knowledge and sparked a long and profound controversy in education and philosophy.

4. Francis Bacon, *Aphorisms Concerning the Interpretation of Nature and the Kingdom of Man,* bk. 1, in *Novum Organum,* trans. R. Ellis and James Spedding (London: George Routledge and Sons, n.d.), p. 60.

5. John Locke, *An Essay Concerning Human Understanding* (10th ed.; London: Printed for Arthur Bettesworth and Charles Hitch. . . ., 1731), vol. 1, bk. 2, chap. 1, nos. 2–4, pp. 67–69.

6. Jean Jacques Rousseau, *Émile,* trans. Barbara Foxley (New York: Dutton, 1911), bk. 1, p. 5.

7. Thomas Paine, *Age of Reason: Being an Investigation of True and Fabulous Theology* (New York: Peter Eckler, n.d.; originally published in 1794 [pt. 1] and 1796 [pt. 2], pt. 2, p. 183.

8. Benjamin Franklin, *Poor Richard's Almanack, Being the choicest Morsels of Wisdom,* written during the Years of the Almanack's Publication (Mount Vernon, N.Y.: Peter Pauper Press, n.d.).

9. Benjamin Franklin, *Autobiography* (New York: Macmillan, 1909), p. 79. Italics in original.

10. Benjamin Franklin, *Proposals Relating to the Education of Youth in Pensilvania*

(Philadelphia, 1749), as reprinted in *The Papers of Benjamin Franklin*, ed. Leonard W. Labaree and Whitfield J. Bell, Jr. (New Haven, Conn.: Yale University Press, 1961), 3:395–421.

11. Franklin, *Proposals*, p. 404.
12. Franklin, *Proposals*, p. 417.
13. Quoted in Allen Oscar Hansen, *Liberalism and American Education in the Eighteenth Century* (New York: Macmillan, 1926), p. 110.
14. Thomas Jefferson, *Notes on the State of Virginia, with an Appendix* (8th American ed.: Boston: Printed by David Carlisle, 1801), query 14, pp. 216–217.
15. See Will S. Monroe, *History of the Pestalozzian Movement in the United States* (Syracuse, N.Y.: C.W. Bardeen, 1907).
16. Ruth Miller Elson, *Guardians of Tradition: American Schoolbooks of the Nineteenth Century* (Lincoln: University of Nebraska Press, 1964), p. 166.
17. The complete title of the three parts was *A Grammatical Institute of the English Language, Comprising an Easy, Concise, and Systematic Method of Education, Designed for Use of English Schools in America.*
18. Henry Steele Commager, "Noah Webster, 1758–1958," *Saturday Review* 41 (18 October 1958): 12.
19. Reprinted in Robert Francis Seybolt, *The Evening School in Colonial America*, Bulletin No. 24 (Urbana: Bureau of Educational Research, University of Illinois 1925), pp. 29–30. Interestingly enough, in a subsequent "Bulletin" in this series Seybolt states that this particular private school offered the first "academy curriculum" in America, antedating Franklin's Philadelphia Academy by twenty-eight years. See Robert Francis Seybolt, *Source Studies in American Colonial Education: The Private School*, Bulletin No. 28 (Urbana: Bureau of Educational Research, University of Illinois, 1925), p. 99.
20. Reprinted in Seybolt, *The Evening School in Colonial America*, p. 63.
21. Reprinted in Seybolt, *Source Studies in American Colonial Education: The Private School*, p. 71.
22. Middlekauff, *Ancients and Axioms*, p. 142.
23. Louis W. McKeehan, *Yale Science: The First Hundred Years, 1701–1801*, Yale University School of Medicine Publication No. 18 (New York: Henry Schuman, 1947), pp. 17–42.
24. Timothy Farrar, *Report of the Case of the Trustees of Dartmouth College against William H. Woodward, Argued and Determined in the Superior Court of Judicature of the State of New-Hampshire, November, 1817, and on Error in the Supreme Court of the United States, February, 1819* (Portsmouth, N.H.: John W. Foster, and West, Richardson, & Lord, 1819).
25. This description, of course, and these particular remarks were not included in the *official* report of the case. Dr. Chauncy A. Goodrich, a Yale professor who witnessed the courtroom scene, later wrote a detailed description in a letter to Rufus Choate. See Rufus Choate, "A Discourse Commemorative of Daniel Webster" (Delivered at Dartmouth College on 27 July 1853), *Addresses and Orations of Rufus Choate* (3rd ed.: Boston: Little, Brown, 1879), pp. 273–74. Italics in original. A handwritten excerpt from this famous letter is reproduced by Carroll A. Wilson in "Familiar 'Small College' Quotations: I. Daniel Webster and Dartmouth." *The Colophon 3*, New Series (Winter 1938): 18.

CHAPTER 4

The Common School Movement

A large majority of our fellow-creatures are slaves, serfs or poor hired laborers, toiling from fear of the lash or fear of want to obtain a miserable subsistence, or to produce the means of supporting a favored few in luxury and idle ease. Discords and hatreds are rife among them, and the darkest selfishness benumbs their hearts and renders them indifferent to each other's misery.

ALBERT BRISBANE, *Association; or A Concise Exposition of the Practical Part
of Fourier's Social Science,* 1843

What is a man born for but to be a Reformer . . . ?

RALPH WALDO EMERSON, "Man the Reformer," 1841

If then, education be of admitted importance to the people under all forms of governments; and of unquestioned necessity *when they govern themselves, it follows, of course, that its cultivation and diffusion is a matter of* public *concern; and a duty which every government owes to its people.*

THADDEUS STEVENS, from an address to the Pennsylvania House
of Representatives, 11 April 1835

THE BREAKDOWN OF TRADITIONAL
WAYS OF SOCIAL LIFE

On March 4, 1829, Andrew Jackson of Tennessee came to Washington to take the oath of office as President of the United States. His devoted admirers followed wearily behind, traveling from far and near, to view the spectacle (and in some cases to stay and scramble hopefully for jobs in the new administration). The quiet city of Washington was jammed beyond capacity

74

with thousands of wildly enthusiastic people. "A monstrous crowd of people is in the city," wrote Daniel Webster in a letter to his sister-in-law. "I never saw anything like it before . . . . They really seem to think that the country is [to be] rescued from some dreadful danger."[1] Jackson walked form his hotel to the inaugural ceremonies, bowing to the cheering spectators. With a long, wrinkled face and a thick shock of straight white hair pushed back from his forehead, the general, not quite sixty-two years of age, was tall and erect. Dressed in a black suit, his gaunt figure dominated the throngs of onlookers gathered to hear his inaugural address. Then, after taking the oath of office, he rode in impressive military style to the White House. When vast crowds surged forward, following their idol past the front doors and into the presidential home, Jackson's political foes viewed the whole affair with utter consternation. The noisy people, according to observers, behaved abominably, breaking glasses and bowls and standing in dirty shoes on fine furniture in order to catch a fleeting glimpse of their new leader. With the ascension of Andrew Jackson to the presidency, all the decorum that had characterized the White House in the past suddenly disappeared.

Born in South Carolina in 1767 of poverty-stricken parents, Jackson was orphaned at fourteen and had no formal schooling. The presidents before him had had wealth and, except for Washington, a college education. In striking contrast to his predecessors in the White House, Jackson lacked urbanity and refinement in clothes and personal appearance. He chewed quantities of tobacco, spitting regularly even during conversations on affairs of state, smoked an old bowl pipe, and occasionally told unprintable tales. On the Tennessee frontier, he had been a shrewd politician, horse trader, and land speculator, amassing a small fortune in real estate and slaves. Rough in manner, he relished wrestling matches and fist fights; after killing a man in a duel, he saved the pistol as a trophy for personal display. Above all, "Old Hickory" was a frontier farmer and had come to the nation's capital from the West.

The dramatic inauguration of Andrew Jackson in 1829 symbolized some of the profound social and political changes occurring in American life. Since the election of George Washington, eight new states had been formed between the original thirteen and the Mississippi River—Kentucky, Tennessee, Ohio, Louisiana, Indiana, Mississippi, Illinois, and Alabama. In fact, in 1829 there were more people in Tennessee and Kentucky than in the combined area of Massachusetts, Rhode Island, and Connecticut. A flood of land-hungry people was moving steadily westward, accelerating the shift of political power away from the Northeast. Streaming in from the old seaboard states, the frontier settlers became imbued with a rugged independence and a new liberalism in politics that flourished in the backwoods climate. Unopposed by religious- and private-school traditions, the idea of public education also took root and slowly grew, paralleling the westward migrations into the territories beyond the Allegheny Mountains. In the beginning, however, the western pioneers were far more concerned with the immediate problems of building a material way of life than with establishing public schools.

The antebellum South was also affected by swiftly moving events. Indeed, no section underwent a more profound transformation of its entire economic life. Eli Whitney's invention, patented in 1794, and the subsequent demand for cotton by mill owners in New England and Great Britain revitalized slavery and a plantation economy. The rise of the Cotton Kingdom, with its stratified society and rural agrarian life, sharply restricted the development of public education in the southern states.

In the Northeast, as was previously noted, a great technological revolution and the emerging power of industrial capitalism precipitated a host of new social problems. Building on a factory system and creating a new labor force, industrialism profoundly influenced the course of the public-school movement. It is significant to observe that the growing sentiment for public education followed very closely the industrial expansion of the United States.

Before the Civil War, no aspect of American culture could escape the impact of the great transformations that occurred in the West, the South, and the East. In the political arena, each section sought to expand its influence and to direct the national destiny in conformity with its own interests.[2] On the social scene, these changes accelerated the breakdown of traditional ways of life and set the stage for the rise of the free public school. For clarity and depth of understanding, this period of educational history must be studied in the light of these important socioeconomic developments.

An Economic Transformation of the South

After graduating from Yale College in 1792, Eli Whitney sailed to Savannah, Georgia, to become a tutor on a plantation. While en route aboard ship, he accepted an invitation to visit Mulberry Grove, a plantation near Savannah, where he overheard the planters discussing the importance of a practical gin to separate the cotton fibers from the green seed. Because the fiber adhered tightly to the seed, it required a slave an entire day to gin a pound of lint. For that reason, few planters grew cotton in the southern states. At the same time, great interest in cotton production had been stimulated by the inventions of spinning and weaving machinery in England, which had become a vast market for cotton fiber. With a warm climate and a slave system of labor, the South was perfectly suited for cotton cultivation to supply this overseas demand. Only a practical machine was needed to expedite the ginning of the cotton fiber. Within ten days Whitney made a cotton gin, operated by a hand crank, which was nothing more than a cylinder with wire teeth that drew the seed through a wire screen, tearing the seed from the fiber. A revolving brush removed the lint from the teeth of the cylinder.

Rarely in human history has such a simple technological breakthrough so materially affected an entire society. The impact of the new invention was immediate and widespread. It unleashed a tremendous potential for cotton growing, creating an unbalanced, one-crop economy. It stimulated a series of westward migrations from the depleted lands of the seaboard states to the fertile soils of the Mississippi Valley. As William E. Dodd points out:

> The ease with which one might raise a crop of cotton and the relatively large returns which it brought drew men of all classes to the lower South. Thousands of square miles of rich lands within easy distance of navigable rivers gave the people of the region a sense of new opportunity, a feeling that the world belongs to him who can exploit it, and a restless craving for a new life and wide acres—all of which influenced profoundly not only the lower South but the whole course of American history.[3]

In August of each year, as cotton cultivation increased, the flowering green bolls burst open and the matured plants transformed the land into long white carpets.

It was estimated that southern cotton in 1850 was worth $102 million. "Cotton is king," boasted Senator James Henry Hammond of South Carolina in 1858. With the expansion of cotton exports, the southern states by 1859 were supplying 75 percent of the world's cotton supply.

About two-thirds of the white people in the antebellum South were in a middle socioeconomic group between the wealthy planters at the top of the scale and the poor whites at the bottom. Research has shed some light on this large segment of the population.[4] The middle class comprised many independent yeomen who owned small farms next to the large plantations. These people usually consumed what they produced, while the planters concentrated on exportable goods for profit making. The middle class also included overseers, artisans, and traders. There was a high rate of illiteracy in this group, owing in part to the rural conditions of the Cotton Kingdom.

Yet, despite the preponderance of "plain folk of the Old South," economic power and political leadership were still vested in approximately four thousand families holding the most fertile lands. The fact that a large middle class was so completely obscured by the wealthy and politically dominant planters was, according to Avery Craven, "the great tragedy of the ante-bellum South."[5] By 1850, about a thousand southern families at the top of the social structure received an income of over $50 million annually, which was almost as much as the combined income of all the other families in the Old South. It was this relatively small upper class who held the reins of political power and represented the South in federal councils.

The invention of the cotton gin and the subsequent rise of the Cotton Kingdom led to the revival of slavery in the South. The cultivation of cotton in the warm southern climate was ideally suited to the slave system. The low cotton plants were picked by slave gangs of men, women, and children, working across the wide plantation fields. By 1860 the slaves constituted more than one-third of the total southern population of about 12 million. With few exceptions, African Americans remained illiterate because efforts to teach them to read were discouraged. In fact, most of the southern states did not permit the instruction of reading to slaves. The whites especially feared those slaves who could read, since insurrections in the 1820s and 1830s were led by literate people. More than any other factor, the existence of approximately 4 million illiterate slaves differentiated the antebellum South from the West and the North.

Harriet Tubman (1815?–1913)

For slaves like Harriet Tubman (born around 1815 in Dorchester County, Maryland) the quest for freedom was a powerful goal. In 1849 when she learned she was soon to be sold, she ran away alone through the "underground railroad" to Philadelphia. "Dere's *two* things I've got a *right* to, and dese are, Death or Liberty—one or tother I mean to have," she exclaimed. "No one will take me back alive; I shall fight for my liberty, and when de time has come for me to go, de Lord will let dem kill me."[6] After obtaining her own freedom, she helped other slaves to escape. Her first objective of bringing her own family out of bondage was later broadened to include other slaves whom she guided North, traveling by night and hiding by day.

Harriet Tubman returned repeatedly to the plantations and guided more than three hundred slaves from bondage to freedom, taking some as far as Canada. Carrying the babies herself in a basket on her arm, she led bands of fugitives, constantly alert to the pursuers. During the 1850s she became the most successful conductor on the "underground railroad." To African Americans of eastern Maryland, she became "Moses," the redeemer of her people from the Egypt-land slave system of the South. Ann Petry describes the "Moses" legend in vivid terms:

> They said, voices muted, awed, that she talked with God everyday, just like Moses. They said there was some strange power in her so that no one could die when she was with them. She enveloped the sick and the dying with her strength, sending it from her body to theirs, sustaining them.[7]

Harriet Tubman's concept of freedom extended beyond the abolition of slavery and included recognition of all the rights of citizenship for African Americans. In 1862, encouraged by abolitionist governor John Andrew of Massachusetts, she went to Beaufort on Port Royal, one of the South Carolina Sea Islands recently captured by Union forces, where she helped the fugitive slaves to develop educational skills. The following year, in 1863, Beaufort became the center of the famous Port Royal "experiment," a humanitarian enterprise largely composed of northern volunteers who went South to assist the freed slaves.[8] Tubman organized special classes, including one in home-making, designed to provide marketable skills for women who had been field hands on the plantations. She herself was an exemplary model for her students, because every day she made gingerbread, pies, and root beer which she sold to meet her own living expenses. She also worked in the freedman's hospital, caring for African Americans suffering from malnutrition and various diseases of the swampy area. She was even called upon to dispense her own herbal remedy for dysentery and was sent at one time to Fernandina, Florida, were many soldiers were dying from the disease. The accomplishments of this remarkable woman, and the legends surrounding her, constitute a poignant chapter in American history.

Repression of Creative Thought

The most important, and probably the most enduring, effect of the slave system was the repression of creative thought in southern society. Slavery produced a climate of fear, an inhibiting force on any creative mind. Within the slave regime, there were animosities among the African Americans and potential danger for the whites. The hatred generated by indifferent and sometimes cruel overseers and the anguish wrought by family separations in the slave market led to increasingly rigid precautionary measures by the master class.[9] Recent studies of slavery do not support Ulrich B. Phillips's benevolent portrayal of the plantation system of labor. The recurring theme in his works is that antebellum slavery was far from a cruel system. Phillips stressed instead a paternal relationship between the kind master and the childlike slave.[10] Nevertheless, the frequency and number of runaways indicate that the slaves were not quite so content and submissive as was generally believed. For instance, the insurrection led by Nat Turner, an African American preacher, in Southampton County, Virginia, in August 1831, alarmed the entire South. While there were no other major slave insurrections in the southern states, the masters and their families were still plagued by rumors of uprisings and plots.

The slave regime not only produced tensions and fears but also consumed a great deal of energy that might otherwise have been channeled into intellectual activity. Frederick Law Olmsted, a northern journalist who reported his southern travels in the 1850s,[11] attributed the limited creative output of the Old South to the slave system. This hypothesis is not unique; it has been reiterated by subsequent writers. Yet Olmsted's observation seems plausible. It was no easy task to contrive a continuous proslavery defense against the growing hostility and frequency of the abolitionist attacks.[12] For instance, all the time and effort expended in devising, writing, and publicizing a proslavery argument might have been diverted into the public-school movement that, except in North Carolina under Calvin H. Wiley's leadership, failed to materialize in any substantial way in the South.

The slave system was indeed a formidable obstacle to the development of public schools. Viewing the issue from a somewhat different point of view, Edgar W. Knight, a famous historian of southern education, also underscored the negative impact of the slave barrier:

> In the Southern States several factors and influences especially served to retard the force of the revival spirits which was so effectively felt in some other sections. Chief among these factors was the institution of slavery, which tended to produce class and social distinctions and to widen the line which separated the independent from the dependent part of the community.[13]

Whether the delay of public education in the antebellum South was due more to the rigid class society, fortified by the slave system, or to the rural character of the southern states, the fact remains that by the time of the Civil War, the South lagged far behind the North in the establishment of public schools.

An indirect outcome of the southern defense was even more significant in terms of its impact on subsequent educational developments. Fearful of the rising power of northern industrialism, southern leaders resisted social change and used repressive means in an effort to safeguard a way of life inexorably bound to a slave system of labor. Those in the South who did not concur with proslavery views found it increasingly difficult to speak out against the southern leadership, especially after 1840. There emerged, as Clement Eaton said, "an intolerant spirit in regard to the discussion of certain sensitive subjects, notably slavery and heterodox religious ideas."[14] Nowhere were the debilitating effects of slavery more vividly seen than in this determination of the white South to maintain a caste society: censorship and repression became important weapons in the defensive tactics of the proslavery battle against increasingly belligerent abolitionist attacks.[15] Thus, on the eve of the Civil War, freedom of thought, so characteristic of the eighteenth-century South during the Enlightenment and so vital to any substantial creative output, began to disappear in southern society.

The Rise of Industrialism

From the inauguration of Jackson to the election of Lincoln, a more significant transformation occurred in the North. During the colonial period almost all articles were made by the family in the home or in small workshops of the rural villages, where smiths built hammers, farm implements, and wagons. Traveling craftsmen made shoes for entire families or pointed nails for the scattered households. Under the impact of the Industrial Revolution, domestic manufacturing moved out of the village homes and workshops into hastily built factory towns that sprang up near the sources of water power.

First centered near the falls of the Pawtucket River in Rhode Island, the factories shifted northward into Massachusetts, which maintained a supremacy in the cotton-spinning industry. In 1813, at Waltham, Massachusetts, Francis Lowell and a group of stockholders from Boston invested their capital in the first large-scale factory operation in the United States. Ten years later they built the city of Lowell on the Merrimack River for their cotton-mill plants. The system spread: first cotton, then woolens and paper, went into production as factories arose and flourished in other towns throughout the North.

While the embargo of 1807, the War of 1812, and the interferences from Napoleon curtailed imports and encouraged the rise of American industrialism, the protective tariff of 1828 was even more instrumental in stimulating the growth of manufacturing in the Northeast. In 1804, for example, there were only 4 cotton mills in New England; three years later 15 were in operation; and by 1831 there were 801 mills employing about 70,000 factory workers. Before 1820 almost all wool was handmade into cloth; in 1830 most of the wool was sent to the New England mills, whose finished product was sold to the nation. In 1820 the woolen and cotton mills in the North produced over $8 million in cloth. Ten years later the annual output from the iron-manufacturing industries in Pennsylvania and the woolen and cotton mills in New England had increased to about $58.5 million. In 1860 the products of textile factories and iron-mill operations alone were valued at $330 million. Thus, for every cotton magnate in the South there was a wealthier businessman in the Northeast, commanding a whole crew of factory workers.

New modes of transportation accelerated this vast industrial growth, greatly affecting the intensity and direction of social change. In 1807 Fulton's small *Clermont* puffed slowly up to the Hudson River, inaugurating a colorful travel era in American history. In a manner vividly depicted by Mark Twain, steamboats were soon churning upstream on the Mississippi, carrying passengers and cargo to the northern cities. American engineers built elaborate canal systems like those in Europe. In 1825 the opening of the famous Erie Canal cut the travel time from Albany to Buffalo from twenty to ten days and linked New York City with the Great Lakes. The success of the Erie Canal spurred other canal-digging operations in Pennsylvania and Maryland.

In a different venture business leaders quickly launched a far more ambitious project. The first railroad tracks were laid in 1830. Within three decades at least thirty thousand miles of railroad tracks fanned out across the nation from leading commercial areas. The development of the New York

Central, the Baltimore and Ohio, and the Pennsylvania Railroad systems
shortened the transportation time between the rising industrial cities of the
Midwest and the older manufacturing centers on the eastern seaboard. In
1838 the National Turnpike to Vandalia, Illinois, was completed at a cost of
over $4 million. The immediate effect of this vast transportation network
was to increase the movements of people and goods to the West and to
expand enormously the national market.

Significant, too, were the contributions of other Americans whose
inventions helped to complete this industrial revolution in the North. For
example, in 1846 Elias Howe, a manufacturer of cotton-mill machinery at
Lowell, Massachusetts, patented the first sewing machine. Samuel F. B.
Morse, a painter and sculptor, invented the electromagnetic telegraph,
which spanned the settled parts of the nation by 1850. In their endeavors, of
course, American inventors were not alone, for much pioneer work had
already been accomplished by others in England. As forerunners, for instance, there were Watt's steam engine, Arkwright's and Crompton's spinning machinery, and Stephenson's locomotive. Nevertheless, Americans
showed great resourcefulness in adapting to new conditions and improving
upon those inventions that had already been introduced abroad.

The industrial development of the North soon made Boston, New
York, Philadelphia, and other coastal cities into national banking centers of
great economic wealth. By the time Jackson was elected President, almost all
the financial resources of the nation had become concentrated in a small
geographic area of the Northeast. New York City alone, for example, had
banking resources of $28 million, and the National Bank in Philadelphia had
capital resources of $35 million, with $40 million in loans. By 1860 the
industrial investments of the Northeast far exceeded in monetary wealth the
value of all the farms and cotton plantations in the South.

The Importance of Organized Labor

In the history of American education, one of the most significant outcomes of
the Industrial Revolution was the gradual emergence of a new, public-
school-minded working class in the northern cities. Indeed, the rapid growth
of manufacturing depended on a readily available source of labor for the new
factories. The early textile mills in Massachusetts, averaging about 150
employees, drew upon the local New England countryside for their labor
supply. The workers were mainly young girls who came in from the farms to
work for a few years. At the Lowell Manufacturing Company the workers had
to live in carefully managed boardinghouses where strict rules were maintained for the protection of their health.

These initial efforts at Lowell, however, were not typical of working
and living conditions that developed in other mill towns. As competition in
the textile industry increased, wages were cut and hours lengthened. With-

out legal restrictions, the working day began at five o'clock in the morning and ended at six-thirty in the evening. The workers earned less than $1.50 for a six-day week, exclusive of board, tending four looms for thirteen to fourteen hours a day. In the middle states and in southern New England, where the factories were smaller and frequently operated on an individual rather than on a corporate basis, whole families were hired to tend the looms and spindles. In 1833 the New England Association of Farmers, Mechanics, and other Working Men reported that two-fifths of the factory workers in New England were children between seven and sixteen who toiled at least fourteen hours daily except on Sundays. The workers were employed as long as needed, by the hour or day, and then dismissed.

Thus, the new lords of the loom controlled the destiny of the urban workers in a manner strikingly different from the socioeconomic patterns of colonial America. In contrast to the economic independence of the subsistence farmers in the eighteenth century, the new wage earners in the rapidly growing cities had become linked to a productive system in which they owned little or nothing. "From the earliest hour in the morning till late at night, the streets, offices, and warehouses of the great cities are thronged by men of all trades and professions, each following his vocation like *per petuum mobile*, as if he never dreamed of cessation from labor, or the possibility of becoming fatigued," wrote Francis J. Grund, an Austrian immigrant who described American society during the Jacksonian era.[16] More devastating, perhaps, in terms of human morale were the shocking housing conditions of the factory workers. It was not uncommon for entire families to crowd into a single room after a day of twelve to fourteen hours at the mill.

To this urban social setting was added another element that sharply altered the supply and demand of factory workers. A rising tide of immigrants augmented the ranks of the workers in the mills. Irish, Germans, English, and Scandinavians flocked to the United States. Between 1815 and 1845 a million Irish came over. From 1846 to 1855 almost 3 million emigrants left Europe for the United States.

An orderly departure at first, emigration by the 1840s had swelled into a mass exodus. In Europe it was becoming increasingly difficult for the Irish and the Germans to earn a livelihood on the farms and in the factories. In Norway and Sweden social discrimination and religious prejudice added to the general discontent. In the late 1840s there was widespread famine in Ireland due to the potato-crop failures. The United States, on the other hand, was being favorably publicized abroad by shipping companies and in newspapers and travel guidebooks. Emigrant literature in the form of handbills and posters, for example, advertised opportunities available in Iowa and Wisconsin. More impressive were the glowing reports from friends and relatives who had already settled in the United States. Lured by news of prosperity in the United States, dispirited Europeans packed their belongings and departed hopefully for the New World. Families and even entire villages abandoned their old homes. In crowded quarters aboard unsanitary and foul-smelling freighters, most of the bewildered emigrants, weary from the long six-week passage, came through the port of New York.

In a very significant way, the hordes of immigrants arriving on American shores were destined to affect the public-school movement. The mass influx from Europe created new social tensions in the United States. The Irish and most of the Germans were predominantly Catholic. Old religious arguments flared anew as natives and aliens clashed in daily human relations. With each shipload of European newcomers, fears increased among the resident population that the foreign-born, with different customs and backgrounds, might fail to assimilate into American society. Perhaps worse, they might even jeopardize the republican experiment of a young nation. Hence, their very presence in such large numbers added strong support to an argument advanced with some force by the educational reformers: more than any other social institution, the common school would help to "Americanize" the immigrants.

Often destitute upon arrival and willing to work for any sum, the aliens drifted to the factory towns and competed with the native workers for jobs and housing. The infusion of cheap labor had adverse effects on working and living conditions. Low wages and overcrowded tenements in the late 1840s led to a "cellar population" in New York City, where families huddled together in cold, unlighted, disease-ridden quarters. Such a congested aggregation of people forced the city to assume new public responsibilities. New York, for example, installed gaslights on the city streets as early as 1830. Sanitation and fire and police protection also became municipal functions.

Apparently this was the social pattern Jefferson foresaw and feared when he referred to "the mobs of great cities" contributing to the basis of government "as sores do to the strength of the human body." New groups of workers, totally dependent on a wage system, had arrived in the United States.

Thus the whole social setting at this time was conducive to some widespread group action on behalf of the workers. The precedent for collective bargaining by workers' unions was established as far back as 1799, when the Federal Society of Journeymen Cordwainers ordered a strike to combat wage cuts by the masters. As the population increased in the flourishing industrial cities, labor organizations grew and multiplied. In 1827 the first city central union of wage earners was founded in Philadelphia, and seven years later the National Trades' Union was formed. By the time of Jackson's election, artisans in almost every trade had organized into unions. Before the panic of 1837, for example, there were sixteen labor unions reported in Boston and fifty-three in Philadelphia. However, the attitudes of the courts toward strikes and the growing hostility of employers toward unionization thwarted any further consolidation of labor ranks. Not until the 1850s was there any large-scale resumption of unionist activities.

The surge of immigration also deterred any significant organization in the labor class. More concerned with improved personal status than with political power or unionization, the new workers turned instead to the massive reform movement that swept across the North from about 1830 to 1860. During this period, confused and splintered by the impact of strange new forces, the workers' groups pursued short-range goals and sought outlets for social protest. The avalanche of prolabor propaganda published during the reform era was a reflection of this discontent. It was, in fact, an important determinant of the kinds of social issues with which the new workers would immediately concern themselves. One of the problems attracting the greatest interest was the creation of a system of free public schools.

SUPPORTING FORCES IN THE PUBLIC-SCHOOL MOVEMENT[17]

The Early Demands of the Workers' Organizations

The growth of poverty and slums in the cities and the execrable working conditions in the mills and factories led to new demands for equality of educational opportunity for all members of American society. Labor leaders and reformers spoke out in favor of free public schools as the only sensible approach toward ameliorating the abuses of the factory system and the social evils of urbanism. "In some districts, no schools whatever exist!" exclaimed a Philadelphia Working Men's Committee in 1830. "No means whatever of acquiring [an] education are resorted to; while ignorance, and its never failing consequence, crime, are found to prevail in these neglected spots."[18] In a vigorous campaign for political and educational equality, the ranks of the newly formed workers' associations were augmented by a diverse group of journalists, intellectuals, and professional people.

Specifically, the workers wanted higher wages, shorter hours, and, above all, an improved educational system for their children. They criticized the "pauper" common schools and rejected the idea of education as a charity. The workers demanded instead a system of schools open without charge to all children in the state. This demand for a free public-school system was a recurring theme in the early labor literature and became a major plank in the workers' political parties from 1828 to 1832.

Robert Dale Owen, an early leader in the New York Workingmen's party, voiced these demands of the wage earners with much force and enthusiasm. One of the most versatile figures in the early history of the American labor movement, Owen grew up in the shadow of England's textile mills. His father was one of the most successful industrialists in the United Kingdom. On tours of the textile mills, young Owen saw firsthand the human misery of the English factory system, which he later condemned as worse than American slavery. According to his biographer:

> He encountered child labor in its most appalling form. He witnessed boys and girls five years his junior toiling from fourteen to sixteen hours a day, kept at machines only through fear of the lash. In antiquated, ill-lighted, and poorly ventilated buildings he found working conditions intolerable. He felt for himself the hot air that registered seventy-five degrees and breathed the damp atmosphere laden with fiber and dust. From the lips of surgeons he learned that more than a fifth of these children were crippled by excessive toil or brutal punishment. [19]

For the rest of his life, Owen abhorred the employment of children in the mills and factories.

Owen considered a better educational system to be a prerequisite for all other reforms. In six essays on the subject of public education, first published anonymously in the *New York Daily Sentinel* in April 1830 and later copied by other newspapers, Owen called for a system of education at public expense that would eliminate the growing stratification in American society. Owen believed that in a republican society the state should be the educational guardian of all its children. He pointed to the shortcomings of the common-school system and urged that public education be placed on a solid, tax-supported basis. He recommended a broad curriculum beyond the usual three R's that would offer history, modern languages, drawing, chemistry, and music. In addition, he demanded that the program include courses in agriculture and industrial arts. A militant reformer, Owen kept the issue of public education alive and at the top of the workers' party platform.

A long-time friend of Owen, Frances Wright, a Scottish reformer, came to the United States in 1819 and also launched a personal campaign on behalf of the working classes. Born into wealth, she was an arresting personality in the early years of the labor movement. She supported practically every humanitarian cause. She advocated free boarding schools, supported by the state governments, for children of the common people. Denouncing the ancillary role of women in American society, Frances Wright advanced the idea of birth control, demanded feminine equality before the law, and led a colorful crusade for women's education.

It is true that labor support for free public education was important, as Philip R. V. Curoe points out. [20] In educating their own membership on the importance of public education, the leaders of the trade unions and workers' political parties counteracted to a considerable extent the complacency of apathetic parents. However, contrary to the exaggerated claims of early labor historians, the contribution of the workers' organizations to the public-school movement was only one among many supporting forces and should be viewed in a balanced perspective. The demands of Owen, Frances Wright, and other articulate spokespersons for educational equality were a part of the widespread agitation for reform during the 1830s. In a broad sense, the leaders of the workers had joined forces with those humanitarian reformers who attacked the moral and social problems of urbanism and the factory system and who saw in public education a key to self-realization for the common people.

THE EMERSONIAN CONCEPTION: INDIVIDUALISM AND REFORM

The movement for free public schools was part of a widespread humanitarian crusade characterized by a faith in the perfectibility of humankind. "The power which is at once spring and regulator in all efforts of reform is the conviction that there is an infinite worthiness in man," declared Ralph Waldo Emerson (1803–1882) in a lecture entitled "Man the Reformer."[21] The idea was not new; it had been voiced before during the Enlightenment. But Emerson's speeches and writings gave it new strength and conviction, inspiring one of the greatest reform movements in American history.

Emerson's main goal of education was "commensurate with the object of life, to teach self-trust." Respect for the individual and for oneself is the secret of education. "Cannot we let people be themselves, and enjoy life in their own way?" asked Emerson in his essay on *Education*. "You are trying to make that man another you. One's enough."[22]

In "Self-Reliance," Emerson enhances the individual's importance by suggesting to people: "Trust thyself: Every heart vibrates to that iron string" and "whoso would be a man, must be a nonconformist." Emerson espouses the virtues of originality, accepting oneself, and working with what one possesses. Essentially, one must accept who one is and discover the talents that lie within oneself, instead of observing what others do well and trying to emulate them. As Emerson wrote, "Insist on yourself; never imitate."

This is powerful advice: through an understanding of Emerson's thought-provoking ideas, people should learn that they have power within themselves waiting to be released if only they would allow themselves to express it. In addition, Emerson asserts that one is who one is and one can run but cannot hide from oneself. The sooner one realizes that one must work from within oneself to have any chance of becoming what one wants to be, the sooner one can begin that work and the sooner one's goals will be reached.

According to Emerson, everything in nature was a part of a transcendent God; and every person, too, shared a "spark of the divine." From this pantheistic relationship of humans to nature and to God emerged an amorphous body of ideas called Transcendentalism. Emerson lectured at lyceums about nature, spoke of a benevolent Creator, and described to audiences "the currents of the Universal Being [that] circulate through me." In the eyes of a benevolent God, Emerson believed, man is divine and mankind perfectible. Thus he reiterated the romantic belief in the inherent goodness of people. We are "not minors and invalids in a protected corner, not cowards fleeing before a revolution, but guides, redeemers and benefactors, obeying the Almighty effort and advancing on Chaos and the Dark," wrote Emerson in "Self-Reliance."[23] In assuming that both people and their social institutions could be infinitely improved, Emerson provided the basic philosophical tenet for the entire reform movement.

It was, perhaps, the most sweeping humanitarian crusade in history, inspiring a motley group of men and women to united action along the most diverse channels: antislavery, temperance, women's rights, and education were only a few of the reform issues. Apparently nothing escaped the zeal of the crusader. According to Henry Steele Commager:

> *Every* institution was called upon to show its credentials, and to justify its course of conduct—the great and the trivial alike, the institution of the State or the practice of shaving, the institution of the Church, or the eating of meat, the institution of marriage or the wearing of beards! In our day most reformers are content with a single crusade, but the reformers of the 'thirties were, most of them, "universal" reformers.[24]

This great wave of humanitarianism was, to a large extent, an outgrowth of the increased social tensions and economic disorders paralleling the rise of industrialism. The panic of 1837 itself was a vivid stimulus for social reform. In New York alone the debacle left one-third of the working people without jobs; indeed, one citizen of every eight was classified a public pauper. In the wake of economic collapse, the closed factories and mills and the thousands of hungry, penniless, and unemployed gave concrete evidence of human suffering and must have stirred many potential reformers from complacency to action.

In general, the people most oppressed and in need of social reform neither instigated nor led the crusades. Of course, the workers' interest in educational reform was evident, especially in the urban centers before 1840. The labor classes were particularly anxious for a better education for their children and, more than anything else, wanted to remove the stigma of charity from public education. However, the prolabor leaders during the early years of the Jacksonian period usually came from outside the ranks of organized workers. The most active standard-bearers of the New York Workingmen's party, for example, were enthusiastic reformers with non-labor backgrounds.

Most of the reform leaders during the Jacksonian period were from the older middle classes, from the clergy and the merchants, and not from the labor masses nor from the rising aristocracy of industrial entrepreneurs. These middle-class reformers with commercial and ministerial backgrounds excoriated the new factory system, blaming it for the depression, for the city slums, and indeed for almost every social distress. They attacked the new business leaders, the owners of the textile mills, and they vigorously defended labor rights. With enthusiasm and missionary zeal, they readily turned to other humanitarian causes for social betterment. It is not surprising that such an array of reforming talent was channeled into the public-school movement, for, like Pestalozzi, each leader shared in common a deep belief in the power of education to remedy society's new evils and to uplift people from poverty and hardship. In an era of great social reform, the cause of publicly supported schools had a strong appeal and drew substantial support from prominent humanitarians.

In addition to the humanitarian influence of the times, a number of other important forces helped to pave the way for free public schools. Among the more pervasive attempts to stimulate interest in the idea of public education were the reports on European education, and the activities of the American lyceum. However, the most important force of all was the able leadership of James G. Carter, Horace Mann, Henry Barnard, and others, who through their personal dedication, their official positions, and their important reports and journals directed and greatly strengthened the public-school movement.

American Reports on European Education

An important factor that helped to create some general interest in public education was the descriptions of European schools disseminated in the United States by interested officials. Apparently American travelers were deeply impressed by the work of Pestalozzi and Fellenberg and the educational reforms in Prussia and other German states. Archibald D. Murphey, of North Carolina, for example, described his impressions in a report to the state legislature in 1817. Victor Cousin's report to the French government in 1831, describing public education in Prussia, was translated and reprinted in London and New York in 1834 and widely used by American reformers. Calvin Stowe's report to the legislature of Ohio in 1837, praising the Pestalozzian reforms of Prussian education, also made a deep impression in the United States.

Parts or all of these reports were also printed in several educational periodicals, which began to appear in growing numbers during the reform period and vigorously supported the public-school campaigns. Among the most important state organs were the *Common School Journal,* published biweekly from 1839 to 1852 and edited by its founder, Horace Mann, for the first ten years of its publication; and the *Connecticut Common School Journal,* published from 1838 to 1842 and edited by Henry Barnard. Thus reprinted and publicized more extensively, the ideas in the American reports on European schools helped to strengthen considerably the arguments of the educational reformers in the United States.

The American Lyceum

During the common school movement, there were hundreds of educational societies and associations that sought to mold public opinion in favor of free schools. Among the most effective were the American Lyceum, the Pennsylvania Society for the Promotion of Public Schools, the Western Literary Institute and College of Professional Teachers, and the American Institute of Instruction. Of these, the most influential and best known was the American Lyceum.

The first local units of the American Lyceum were established by Josiah Holbrook in 1826. The son of a wealthy Connecticut farmer, Holbrook studied under Benjamin Silliman at Yale, where he acquired a lifelong interest in applied science. His demeanor apparently belied his humanitarian warmth. "He looks like a fanatic in his pictures. Lips compressed and brows bent, he stares sternly at the beholder," writes Carl Bode. "What fails to show is Holbrook's deep humanity."[25] At thirty-eight, Holbrook's enthusiasm for scientific knowledge was reflected in his suggestion for a national hierarchy of lyceums. Published in the *American Journal of Education* in October 1826, Holbrook's plan called for an organization of local societies for mutual instruction in science and utilitarian subjects. He believed that these local associations, if established according to some general plan, would multiply quickly and help to enlighten the American people. Holbrook envisioned a federation of lyceums, beginning at the grass-roots level of the local village and extending across the United States.

Holbrook devoted much time to his project. He promoted his idea through lectures and magazine and newspaper articles. Under his leadership the first lyceum was organized in Millbury, Massachusetts, in November 1826. Within a year several nearby villages formed lyceums and joined together at Leicester in a county association. By 1828 Holbrook had helped to organize at least a hundred lyceums. As he had predicted, the idea of voluntary associations for mutual instruction spread swiftly across the nation.

Advertised at first as "associations for mutual instruction and information in the arts and sciences," the early lyceums charged dues of one dollar for the purchase of books and scientific equipment. In villages and farming communities, interested citizens collected materials and conducted forums on popular subjects. "All declare, by joining a Lyceum, that they wish to extend their knowledge," wrote Henry Barnard in 1838. "And, from the manner in which they associate, each may become, by turns, a learner and a teacher."[26] Spurred by Holbrook's scientific interest, the members enthusiastically collected plants and geological specimens. There were extensive displays of scientific materials and apparatus, including some made by Holbrook himself. In later years the range of discussion topics cut across other scientific areas, such as "Meteorology" and "The study of physiology as a branch of general education." Eager for knowledge, the more ambitious members began to invite prominent figures to lecture before them. Horace Mann, Benjamin Silliman, Daniel Webster, Ralph Waldo Emerson, and others seized the opportunity to espouse their ideas or promote their favorite crusades. The first meetings of the Boston Society for the Diffusion of Useful Knowledge were so crowded after it opened in 1828 that the lyceum manager frequently asked each speaker to repeat his lecture the following night. Emerson was probably the most popular lyceum speaker of all. "My pulpit is the lyceum platform," he once remarked. For a fee of fifty dollars the townspeople heard him lecture on material that was later published in his *Essays*.

Most important of all, the lyceums enthusiastically supported the movement for free public schools. In 1831 the state and local lyceums united in a national federation. On May 4 delegates from Maine, Massachusetts, New York, and several local lyceums convened in New York City and organized the American Lyceum. The avowed purpose of the newly formed national organization was "the advancement of education, especially in common schools, and the general diffusion of knowledge."[27] Among its very first resolutions in 1831, the delegates declared:

> That we regard the school teachers of our country (who are now estimated at 50,000) as a body on whom the future character and stability of our institutions chiefly depend; that they are therefore entitled to our highest consideration, and that whatever may be their faults or deficiencies, the remedy for both is in the hands of the society at large.[28]

Most of the other resolutions of the American Lyceum from 1831 to 1838 dealt with education issues.[29] So, too, did the numerous lectures presented before its meetings; for example, "School discipline" (1832), "Learning to read and write the English language" (1832), "The general principles of instruction" (1833), "Raising the standards of female education" (1833), "Missionaries of education" (1836), "The education of the blind" (1836), and "Religious instruction in common schools" (1838).

While the national body exerted a positive force on public education, the most effective programs were carried out by hundreds of smaller lyceums scattered across the nation. By 1839 there were approximately four thousand to five thousand local lyceums in the United States. In the small villages and towns the lectures presented before lyceums in favor of school improvements were voiced and heard in a meaningful social context. Equally as important, the lyceum, through its educational programs, kept the issue of school improvement alive in the minds of local townspeople. It is significant to note that wherever a local lyceum sprang up, a growing concern for public education developed in the community. "The increase of active and well conducted Lyceums in this State, and at this season, is much to be desired, as one of the most direct and effectual means of directing the attention of the people to the importance of improving the schools," declared Henry Barnard in December 1838.[30] By creating a social climate favorable to public education, the lyceums stirred the townspeople from apathy and became a powerful bulwark against those elements in the community opposed to tax-supported schools.

THE IDEOLOGY OF THE EDUCATIONAL REFORMERS

The Revisionist Point of View

In 1968 Michael B. Katz questioned Horace Mann's motives and offered a different interpretation of the common school movement.[31] The reformers, argues Katz, were trying to develop a common school system that would train young workers for the new factories and inculcate into the new immigrants the moral and ethical values of the ruling class—in short, a system that would provide a sense of stability and order in the expanding cities. The aim, according to Katz, was to discipline a growing population to serve the needs of a new industrial and urban society. Thus, according to the revisionist stance of Katz and others, Horace Mann and the common school reformers were not motivated solely by humanitarian desires but instead were trying to protect their own socioeconomic status and provide a new industrial system with trained, docile workers.

A controversial aspect of the revisionist position is their argument that the new common school was forced on an unwilling working class. The revisionist interpretation means that the majority of the American people during the nineteenth century did not favor the traditional organization of public schooling that evolved by the twentieth century. Thus Katz's interpretation not only questions the motives of Mann and other leaders of the common school movement, but also challenges the traditional view that underscored the importance of the working class in support of the common school concept.

These various interpretations indicate the complexity of the common school movement. No separate interpretation is sufficient. The common school movement reflects a complex pattern of conflicting social and financial factors: the desire of the ruling elite to guard their own social and economic status; the eagerness of factory owners to have a properly trained and disciplined work force; the wishes of the working groups to use the common school to climb up the socioeconomic ladder in the United States; and certainly not least, the driving force of Horace Mann and other reform leaders to improve American society through public schooling.

Continuing Opposition to Public Education

Despite the humanitarian zeal of the reformers and the favorable atmosphere engendered by the work of the lyceums, it was not an easy task to overcome the resistance to free public schools. The arguments were strong and deeply entrenched. As might be expected, some individuals wondered why the wealthy should be required to pay for the education of the workers' children. The idea that education was a family matter instead of a public concern was still strong, and there was stubborn opposition to the payment of property taxes for school support. Editorial remarks in the press were particularly hostile to the idea of tax-supported public schools. For example, on July 10, 1830, the *Philadelphia National Gazette* criticized editorially the equalitarian demands of the workers.

> Universal opulence, or even competency, is a chimera, as man and society are constituted. There will ever be distinctions of conditions, of capacity, of knowledge and ignorance, in spite of all the fond conceits which may be indulged, or the wild projects which may be tried, to the contrary. The "peasant" must labor during those hours of the day, which his wealthy neighbor can give to the abstract culture of his mind.

Those opposed to public schools argued along other lines, too. Some appealed to religious prejudices, asserting that public education would conflict with parochial schools. Others contended that if the children of the poor were educated at the taxpayers' expense they would grow up lazy and with no initiative. Educated workers were not essential, the argument ran; indeed, if the children of the poor were forced to attend school, they would not be free to work. In fact, *Niles' Weekly Register,* published for businessmen, reported how much wealth could be made for American manufacturers if all the children could be employed full time in the mills. The strongest opposition came from those conservative interests who argued over and over again that the wealthy ought not to be taxed to educate the children of the poor.

In countering these arguments and in overcoming the resistance to tax-supported public schools, the most powerful element in the common school movement was the quality of educational leadership. In the history of American education, it is doubtful that a more dedicated and able group of statesmen has ever labored with such vigor and zeal for better public schools. At the helm were such famous men as James G. Carter, Horace Mann, and Henry Barnard. There were others, too, who gave much time and energy for educational service.

James G. Carter (1795–1849)

One of the first educational leaders in the reform movement, James G. Carter, of Massachusetts, paved the way for the outstanding work of Horace Mann. After graduation from Harvard College in 1820, Carter launched a campaign to improve the common schools. He wrote two widely publicized series of newspaper articles on education that appeared in pamphlet form in 1824 and 1826.[32] In commenting on the educational scene, Carter deplored the current neglect of the common schools, which had received virtually no legislative support for almost forty years. Although Carter commended the earlier educational efforts of the Massachusetts Bay Colony, he noted the gradual decline of free schools. He decried the prevalent system that condoned untrained teachers, irregular attendance, and short terms. In fact, he warned that the common schools would disappear within twenty years unless some legislative action were taken. In 1826, according to Carter, only a small percentage of the children in Massachusetts had a chance to attend school.

Turning to methodology, Carter stressed the importance of the inductive method of Bacon and expressed views similar to those of Pestalozzi. He pointed out that quality education would be costly. Good schools must be graded, furnished with uniform textbooks, and supplied with competent teachers. Carter proposed the establishment of a normal school for the preparation of qualified teachers.

A former district schoolteacher, Carter leveled his most trenchant criticism against the district system of school organization and control. Over the years, the state had passed the responsibility for maintaining public schools onto the towns which, in turn, had shifted it to the local districts. The first school law, passed by the Massachusetts legislature in 1789, had legalized the district system, which evolved during the preceding century, by authorizing the towns to divide themselves into autonomous districts for the organization and control of local schools. In 1800 the districts were granted the power to tax the local community for the support of public schools. In 1827 the system became firmly entrenched when the legislature empowered the districts to appoint school trustees, who were authorized to select textbooks and to employ teachers. The annual salary for male teachers in the district schools was about $185; however, women were usually paid $64 a year, if they were employed for the entire year. In contrast to the schoolteachers' wages, mechanics in the early 1830s were sometimes paid $300 a year. This pattern of district organization was soon copied by other states where, as in Massachusetts, the system degenerated into local political feuds leading to chaotic school conditions.

Continuing his campaign for educational reforms, Carter worked for more effective state support and control and urged legislative action for school improvements. He condemned the law of 1789 for encouraging what he termed lax standards. In 1826, under his leadership, the state finally vested in town school committees the powers that the local school districts had exercised so unsuccessfully for thirty-seven years. In 1834 he was instrumental in establishing a state school fund to assist towns in maintaining a higher level of public education. The following year Carter was elected to the Massachusetts legislature. Two years later, in 1837, as chairman of the House Committee on Education, he skillfully persuaded a reluctant legislature to create the first really effective state board of education in the United States.

The law of 1837 was the culmination of Carter's years of dedicated efforts. In establishing a framework for more efficient state control, the law deviated from the usual practice of providing for an elected state superintendent of schools. Instead, a small state board was created, with the power to appoint a secretary. As the chief state school official, the new secretary would be responsible directly to the board. Without power to enforce its polices and recommendations, the new board had no real authority over the public schools. The secretary's task was merely to investigate school conditions, collect information, and enlighten the people of the state. The secretary and the board would make recommendations for action to the legislature. Thus, much depended on the educational leadership exercised by the new secretary and the members of the board.

On May 6, 1837, Horace Mann was asked by Edmund Dwight, a close friend who had worked with Carter for the creation of a state board of education, to consider the secretaryship. As president of the state senate, Mann had also helped Carter to secure passage of the new law. On May 18, Dwight tried again to persuade Mann to consider the appointment. Governor Edward Everett also wanted Mann for the new position and had written a letter nominating him for the post. Dwight showed the letter to Mann, who at first was not at all enthusiastic over the idea. "Whoever shall undertake that task," he wrote in his private journal after talking with Dwight, "must encounter privation, labor, and an infinite annoyance from an infinite number of schemers. He must condense the steam of enthusiasts, and soften the rock of the incredulous."[33] Apparently no one really expected Mann to consider the offer seriously. Some of his friends argued with him not to give up a promising political future for a poorly paid and unrewarding position. Nevertheless, to the surprise of those who thought Carter was better suited for the post, Horace Mann, a young, highly respected lawyer and senator, accepted the appointment on June 30, 1837, and became the first secretary of the newly formed State Board of Education. "Henceforth, so long as I hold this office, I devote myself to the supremest welfare of mankind upon earth," wrote Mann after accepting the office. " . . . *Faith* is the only sustainer. I have faith in the improvability of the race—in their accelerating improvability."

Horace Mann (1796–1859)

Surely Horace Mann's decision to accept the secretaryship came as no surprise to his family and closest friends. More than anyone else, Mann embodied the humanitarian spirit sweeping across the North. He was a true reformer, always generous in thought and action, forever yielding to social needs. His humanitarian interests spanned far and wide, touching on every crusade in the reform movement. For example, he welcomed the oppressed immigrant arriving in the United States; he was a friend of Samuel G. Howe, educator of the blind; he supported Dorothea Dix, a pioneer in the humane treatment of the mentally ill, and secured a law establishing the first mental hospital in the United States; he sponsored legislation regulating the traffic in lottery tickets and the sale of alcoholic beverages; he worked for separation of church and state and defended freedom of the press; and he later participated in the abolition of slavery. Yet, of all the social issues of the times, none appealed to him more strongly than the cause of public education. "Men are cast-iron; but children are wax," Mann wrote two days after accepting the secretaryship. Thus, Mann's decision in 1837 to embark on a new career in education was merely another reflection of his humanitarian faith.

To understand more clearly Mann's important work during his twelve-year tenure as secretary to the state board, it is important to review first the early forces in his life that helped to shape his later outlook on education. Indeed, almost everything he did and wrote from 1837 to 1848 bore the impress of his early environment.

Born on a New England farm near Franklin, Massachusetts, on May 4, 1796, Mann complained most of his life of poor health, which resulted in part from overwork and poverty. His father died when he was thirteen. Mann's boyhood struggles and privation furnished a harsh background for his formative years. From the gloomy sermons of Nathaniel Emmons, the village preacher, Mann endured great mental anguish and developed a lifelong and bitter hatred for Calvinism. He wrote that Emmons "not only preached to his people, but ruled them, for more than fifty years." Sensitive, frail, and nervous, Mann reacted sharply to the preacher's words: "To my vivid imagination, a physical hell was a living reality, as much so as though I could have heard the shrieks of the tormented, or stretched out my hand to grasp their burning souls, in a vain endeavor for their rescue," he recalled. "Such a faith spread a pall of blackness over the whole heavens, shutting out every beautiful and glorious thing." Although Mann renounced Calvinism for Unitarianism, he never escaped completely from the fear and discipline instilled by the Reverend Mr. Emmons' preaching.

The pressures and demands of his early environment struck deep and lasting roots. He remained forever opposed to dogma and orthodoxy in religion. Despite a limited education, he acquired from his parents a lifelong respect for knowledge. Until the age of fifteen, Mann's only formal schooling amounted to brief periods of eight to ten weeks a year. "An inward voice raised its plaint forever in my heart for something nobler and better," he wrote. "And, if my parents had not the means to give me knowledge, they intensified the love of it." He eagerly read the few books in his native village, named for Benjamin Franklin, who, in appreciation of the compliment, gave the town a library instead of a church bell because, according to Mann, "he thought that they would prefer sense to sound." At the age of twenty, with ferverish intensity and moral drive, he prepared in six months, with the help of private instruction, for entrance to Brown University. "All my boyish castles in the air had reference to doing something for the benefit of mankind," Mann remembered. "The Early precepts of benevolence, inculcated upon me by my parents, flowed out in this direction; and I had a conviction that knowledge was my needed instrument." Graduating with honors from Brown in 1819, Mann spoke at commencement on the topic, "The Gradual Advancement of the Human Species in Dignity and Happiness."

Horace Mann served as secretary of the State Board of Education from 1837 to May 1848. From the moment that he accepted the secretaryship in 1837 until he resigned eleven years later, Mann wrote that he worked for the cause of public education an average of at least fifteen hours a day; furthermore, during these years he spent no time for diversion and rarely, if ever, visited friends in the evening. His salary was only $1,500 a year, with no travel or expense allowances. He had no clerical help, doing his own writing and corresponding. Mann worked until, according to his wife, "his strength was seen to be nearly exhausted."

Upon assuming his new post, Mann began immediately to campaign for educational reform. In the 1830s the media of communication were slow and frustrating, but Mann surmounted these and other obstacles. He resorted to all kinds of propaganda techniques to enlighten the people. To present the facts and overcome popular apathy, he first obtained information and disseminated reports describing the sad plight of the district schools. Then he traveled up and down the state, carrying his message directly to the people. A shrewd and tactful politician, Mann knew his audiences well, and, as Howard Mumford Jones points out, he appealed to the self-interests of every public group.[34] For instance, in his widely publicized *Fifth Report*, printed in 1841, Mann told the conservative propertied classes that adequate taxes for the support of the common schools were "the cheapest means of self-protection and insurance." Where else, asked Mann, could you find "any police so vigilant and effective, for the protection of all the rights of person, property and character, as such a sound and comprehensive education and training, as our system of Common Schools could be made to impart?" He expounded his views before lyceums, teachers' institutes, and open meetings and conventions. He founded and edited the *Common School Journal* to inform teachers and to sway public opinion. He set up and administered normal schools to improve the quality of teacher preparation. In the spring of 1843, Mann traveled abroad to observe educational methods and then described with glowing terms in his *Seventh Report* what he had witnessed in Europe. "How weary a life this would be if my soul were not in it!" Mann exclaimed.

Most effective of all were Mann's twelve annual reports,[35] which greatly influenced public opinion not only in the United States but also in Europe and later in South America. Mann was a skillful and imaginative writer. His official reports are still pertinent to educational problems that have recurred with disturbing frequency through the years. For example, in his *First Report* (1837) he pointed to certain basic requirements for quality education. He discussed the importance of adequate and sufficient school buildings, capable and dedicated school-committee members, qualified teachers, and a strong popular commitment to free public education. In this Mann was particularly concerned with the local community's lack of interest in "the education of *all* its children." Subsequent reports touched on a wide range of vital issues: the necessity for adequate financial support, the advantages of school-district consolidation, the supervision of the teaching-learning process, the need for higher teacher salaries, and the improvement of teacher and administrative preparation.

Mann's preference for women teachers in the early grades of the common schools was ahead of the prevailing attitudes of the times. "I believe there will soon be an entire unanimity in public sentiment in regarding female as superior to male teaching for young children," he declared in 1838. Mann was no doubt influenced by Pestalozzi, who also held women teachers in high esteem for the early school years.

Of course, the battle in Massachusetts for adequate public support of the common schools was not easily won. Despite his sincerity and steadfast devotion, Mann was bitterly attacked by those opposed to his philosophy and his work. Local politicians and preachers resented Mann's interference in school affairs and attacked him in the press and in weekly sermons.

Sectarian bias was especially strong in Massachusetts, where the influence of the church in civic affairs still posed a formidable barrier to religious liberty. Mann's liberal views were well known, and apparently his earlier speech to the Massachusetts legislature in defense of religious freedom was long remembered by church officials. Although deeply religious, Mann warned against efforts to teach sectarian creeds in the common schools, for this, he feared, would jeopardize public education. He believed that the Scriptures were valuable for instilling moral values, and he contended that the King James Version of the Bible should be read without comment in the schools.

For his advocacy of nonsectarianism, Mann was assailed as Godless. For example, Frederick A. Packard, secretary of the American Sunday School Union in Philadelphia, called Mann an atheist. Through anonymous magazine and newspaper articles and through bitter denunciations at public meetings, he repeatedly attacked Mann. Matthew Hale Smith, a Calvinist preacher, harshly criticized the state board of education for "allowing an individual, under the sanction of its authority, to disseminate through the land crude and destructive principles, principles believed to be at war with the Bible and with the best interests of the young for time and eternity." Packard and Smith insisted that local citizens could have religious instruction in the schools if they wished; furthermore, if the townspeople were deprived of this decision-making power, then they could withdraw their financial support of public education. The fight became so intense that a legislative attempt was made in 1840 to destroy the state board of education. "What have I done that has brought upon me this contumely and bitterness?" cried Mann in a letter to his friend, the Reverend Mr. S. J. May, in 1845. "What have I done that renders me thus worthy of the extreme of ridicule and opprobrium?" Not until 1855 was the religious issue in Massachusetts finally settled with the adoption of a constitutional amendment.

The most widely publicized controversy was Mann's running battle in 1844 with the Boston schoolmasters. The disagreement was sparked by comments in Mann's *Seventh Report* in 1843, praising the Pestalozzian methods of the Prussian schools. Mann was particularly impressed with the classroom rapport and the mutual respect and love between the teacher and pupil. "I heard no child ridiculed, sneered at, or scolded, for making a mistake," Mann wrote. "I wonder," he continued, "whether a visitor could spend six weeks in our own schools without ever hearing an angry word spoken, or seeing a blow struck, or witnessing the flow of tears." The report was initially received with enthusiasm. It was translated into French and German and widely read in foreign circles.

However, thirty-one Boston principals resented Mann's innuendoes and issued a 144-page reply, followed later by two additional rejoinders, the last of which was entitled "Penitential Tears; or a Cry from the Dust, by 'the Thirty-one,' Prostrated and Pulverized by the Hand of Horace Mann." Their response was based on a traditional view of human nature and a defense of the

existing social order. The schoolmasters, for instance, demanded the reten-
tion of corporal punishment, which Mann deplored. Indeed, their whole
argument was essentially a plea for recognized authority, an appeal for, in the
words of the schoolmasters, "stern virtue, and inflexible justice, and scorn-
despising firmness of the Puritan founders of our free schools." Mann, on the
other hand, wanted to inculcate a more humane respect for the pupil by
emphasizing self-discipline and self-control. Although he never advocated
the complete elimination of corporal punishment, he believed that obedience
and respect could be obtained through understanding and kindness.

There ensued an angry and widely circulated exchange of views between
Mann and the Boston schoolmasters. In his reply Mann suggested that the
traditional methodology of the Puritans was as rough and rocky as the
Atlantic shores on which they had first set foot. Mann had the last word in
the long and bitter controversy, and his 124-page "Answer to the Rejoinder
to the Reply to the Remarks on the *Seventh Report*" finally ended some of the
criticism and brought to a close the bitter argument.

In this famous controversy and on other issues, Mann vividly demonstrated his persuasiveness and debating skill. Josiah Quincy, John Greenleaf
Whittier, Charles Sumner, and other leaders came to his defense; indeed,
throughout the dispute the weight of public opinion was on Mann's side.
Although the controversy irked and disappointed him, nevertheless it increased public confidence in his ability and greatly strengthened his stand as
a vigorous supporter of free public schools.

When Mann resigned from the secretaryship in 1848, the common
schools in Massachusetts were on a solid foundation and the victory for which
he had labored so hard was secure and permanent. During Mann's twelve
years of educational leadership, Massachusetts led the nation in the movement for free public schools. The financial support of the common schools in
the state was doubled, three normal schools were founded, and the professionalization of teaching was greatly enhanced. What is sometimes accepted
without question today was during the early decades of the nineteenth
century a radically new idea. For example, Mann's plea in the late 1830s that
teachers should be professionally trained was a novel approach. One of his
outstanding accomplishments was the opening of the first public normal
school in the United States at Lexington, Massachusetts, on July 3, 1839.

Moreover, Mann's persuasive influence on education extended beyond
Massachusetts into New York and other northeastern states and into the
West. His ideas also promoted the cause of public education in South
America. Domingo Faustino Sarmiento, who visited the United States from
August to November 1847, became so inspired by Mann's work and writings
that he sought to reform the schools in Chile and Argentina upon his return
home. *De la Educación,* published by Sarmiento in 1849, was the first of
several important writings that interpreted Mann's ideas for South America.

More than anyone else, Horace Mann had stirred the American conscience with his pleas for a tax-supported system of common schools. As elementary as the proposition might seem, his Jeffersonian argument is worth restating, for in a different social context the theme is just as important today as it was during the first half of the nineteenth century: the foundation for a free society is a universal system of public education. Mann elaborated frequently upon the unique system of common schools he sought to build. "In a social and political sense, it is a *Free* school system," explained Mann in his *Twelfth Report* (1848).

> It knows no distinction of rich and poor, of bond and free, or between those, who, in the imperfect light of this world, are seeking, through different avenues, to reach the gate of heaven. Without money and without price, it throws open its doors, and spreads the table of its bounty, for all the children of the State. Like the sun, it shines, not only upon the good, but upon the evil, that they may become good; and, like the rain, its blessings descend, not only upon the just, but upon the unjust, that their injustice may depart from them and be known no more.[36]

In the history of American education, few state leaders have ever risen to such a noble conception of their task.

Henry Barnard (1811–1900)

Henry Barnard's educational leadership in Connecticut and Rhode Island was as important as Horace Mann's work in Massachusetts. Barnard did not have to struggle in early life with hardship and poverty. He was sent to private schools, and, at the age of fifteen, to Yale, where he was graduated in 1830. He taught for a year in Pennsylvania, and, like Mann, he studied law and was admitted to the bar in 1834. While at Yale he interrupted his studies to journey through the South. In 1835 he went abroad, where he spent much of his time on a two-year tour studying European education and practices of school supervision. He visited Fellenberg at Hofwyl and observed Pestalozzian methods. Barnard was obviously impressed with the possibilities of educational reform.

Soon after his return from Europe, Barnard began a long and noteworthy career in education. Elected by the Whigs in 1837 to a term in the Connecticut legislature, he sponsored legislation sympathetic to humanitarian causes and consistently supported the lyceum movement. Like Mann, he favored the education of women. In 1838 Barnard introduced a bill, passed unanimously by the legislature, that established a state board of education similar to that created a year before in Massachusetts. At a salary of three dollars a day and traveling expenses, Barnard became the board's first secretary. When he switched at the age of twenty-eight from a law career to service in education, Barnard remained forever dedicated to his work; and, unlike Mann in 1848, he never went back to politics. His school reforms in Connecticut were similar to those effected by Mann in Massachusetts. In the beginning, however, Barnard met with less success. The sweeping changes he proposed, entailing new taxes, angered the conservative forces in the state who, in 1842, removed Barnard from office and abolished the board of education.

Greatly discouraged after four years of service, Barnard went to Rhode Island, where he accepted a similar post as the first commissioner of education. He remained there until 1849. Like Mann in Massachusetts, he promoted the cause of education and inspired a deep faith in the public schools. With the Whigs in political power again, Barnard was invited back to Connecticut in 1851 to become principal of the newly formed normal school at New Britain and ex-officio secretary of the state board of education. Until he resigned in 1855 because of ill health, Barnard rewrote the Connecticut school laws and worked for efficient supervision of public education. From 1867 to 1870 he served as the first United States commissioner of education.

While Barnard lacked the eloquence and humanitarian drive of Horace Mann, he surpassed him in literary output and scholarly achievements. In addition to writing several educational reports, Barnard, from 1838 to 1842, edited four volumes of the *Connecticut Common School Journal* and, from 1845 to 1849, three volumes of the *Journal of Rhode Island Institute of Instruction.* His most distinctive contribution was the publishing and editing of the *American Journal of Education.*[37]

A great treasury of information about American and European education, *Barnard's Journal,* as it was sometimes called, was published between 1855 and 1882 in thirty-one volumes of about eight hundred pages each. A helpful index was published by the United States Bureau of Education in 1892. During this period, *Barnard's Journal* was the only educational magazine of national significance. A wealthy person with lucrative financial ties in New England, New York, and the West, Barnard spent so much of his own private fortune on his publications that he died in virtual bankruptcy after a long life of almost ninety years.

Other Leaders

There were other key figures who helped to pave the way for educational reform: John Swett in California, Caleb Mills in Indiana, and Calvin H. Wiley in North Carolina, to mention only a few of the most prominent leaders. In ways not quite so effective and dramatic as those of Mann and Barnard, these men also fought for common schools. For example, Swett helped to secure passage of effective school laws in California, while Mills devoted much of his time to serving Wabash College and writing articles in support of public education. In the South, too, a little progress was made, especially in North Carolina, where Wiley served with distinction as state superintendent of schools from 1853 to 1866. Wiley's educational policies in North Carolina were similar to those pursued by Mann in Massachusetts.

But the problems encountered by Wiley in North Carolina and by other educational leaders in the South were far greater than those found in New England. There were, first and foremost, the rural character of southern society and the class tensions wrought by slavery. These obstacles were great and explain in large part the resistance of the antebellum South to educational reform. These barriers, however, must not overshadow other equally strong deterrents to educational change. The idea, derived from colonial tradition, that education was a family prerogative was deeply entrenched. In fact, according to Knight, any intrusion by the state into the area of education was considered "dangerous and pagan."[38] There was also the prevalent notion that "free" public education meant charity or "pauper" schooling. These traditions persisted for years and substantially blocked any southern movement toward free public education supported by general taxation.[39]

TOWARD TAX SUPPORT AND STATE CONTROL OF THE PUBLIC SCHOOLS

During the first half of the nineteenth century, the educational reformers supplemented the district patterns of local control with more centralized systems of public schools. With the appointment of Gideon Hawley in January 1813, as state superintendent of the common schools, New York became the first state to create a state superintendency. Other states gradually followed in the path of New York and Maryland by providing for some form of unified control. While there was considerable variation among the states, the typical arrangement included a state board of education and an office of state superintendent or commissioner of schools.

Early State School Funds
The main responsibility of the first state superintendencies was to control disbursements from the public-school funds. Although school support was not yet considered in some quarters to be a state obligation, there was, nevertheless, a growing tendency before the Civil War to provide so-called permanent endowments earmarked specifically for public schools. These funds were first established by those older states that did not share in the congressional land grants. Consisting largely of miscellaneous revenues derived from escheats, liquor licenses, marriage fees, and other sources, the

earliest school funds were small and were usually allowed to accumulate before being apportioned to the schools. The interest from the permanent school fund was also used for the common schools.

The endowments stimulated some local effort for school support by requiring local tax levies, against which there was considerable resistance. The states began to provide for local participation in the revenue distributions on matching bases: before a community could receive revenue from the fund, an amount equal to its share had to be raised through local taxation. This important principle, first followed in 1805 in New York, was ultimately adopted by other states.

Unfortunately, there was widespread mismanagement of the public-school endowments. Before the Civil War there were revenue losses through bank failures and cases of outright embezzlement. There were other less glaring violations of the public trust. Although set aside for school purposes, the income from the funds was sometimes used by the states for current noneducational expenses. It was quickly discovered that the early school funds were not dependable sources of revenue.

With the collapse of the so-called permanent school funds, efforts to support the public schools through local taxation increased. At first, the states passed laws permitting the local districts to tax themselves for public schools *if* the people voted for the tax levy. But every effort toward taxation was hotly contested by local citizens. Later, most of the states found it necessary to enact laws forcing the local districts to tax themselves up to a limited point for school support. From the very beginning, then, there was stubborn resistance to the idea of taxation for schools open to all; and in every skirmish of the long campaign, there was rising opposition to taxation for educational purposes. Thus the most difficult issue of all in the common school movement was establishing the *principle* of public support.

The Issue of Public Support

To win the battle, there were two major obstacles the proponents of educational reform had to eliminate: the general belief that a "free" education was only important for "pauper" children of poor families, and the use of "rate bills" that permitted the public schools to levy a special tax, often on a per diem basis, on those parents with children enrolled in the schools. Parents were assessed according to the number of children they sent to school. These two barriers posed a major hardship for large families of low socioeconomic status who could neither afford to pay the tax nor willingly accept the stigma of charity attached to "free" schools. In an age of democratic aspirations for the common man, many argued that charity education for the poor produced a class distinction, an invidious connotation inappropriate for American society.

While the battle for public support was waged in practically every part of the nation, the bitterest and most historic struggle outside New England occurred in Pennsylvania in 1835. The outcome was significant, because it set a precedent for other states confronted with a similar issue.

Overcoming the "Pauper School" Tradition

In Pennsylvania the sectarian interests of the culturally diverse population strongly interfered with the establishment of a public-school system. The German-speaking settlers, who maintained their own parochial schools, viewed public education as a threat to their religious solidarity. Opposed to taxation, the thrifty Germans also feared that English free schools would replace their traditional medium of instruction. While the workers in the urban areas clamored for free schools, the Germans in the central part of the state voiced adamant opposition.

Even the pauper schools, which were established by the state early in the century, were largely ineffective. The pauper law required parents to declare themselves publicly as paupers before tuition for their children could be paid to the nearest private school. The expense for this free schooling was assessed against a special fund that was derived in the same manner as tax revenue collected for roads or other public needs. There were neither standards nor attendance requirements for those schools to which the poor children were sent. Although the humanitarian societies in the cities were among the first to oppose the pauper-school laws, the strongest resistance actually came from those for whom the pauper schools were intended. Most parents refused to stigmatize themselves as sufficiently indigent to warrant a charity education for their children; as a result, there were very few children enrolled in schools under the pauper law. Even worse, by 1828 over half of the estimated 400,000 children between the ages of five and fifteen throughout the state were not enrolled in any school at all.

The Pennsylvania Free School Act of 1834 was finally enacted after much agitation from educational reformers who sustained a vigorous campaign for years to eliminate the pauper law and to establish a statewide system of common schools. The new act provided for local taxation and some state aid, but it was not mandatory. Each of the 987 rural and urban school districts created by the new act was required to hold an election to determine whether or not the people wanted to accept the provisions of the law. Those districts rejecting the act were to continue under the old pauper-school law of 1809. The outcome of the school elections seemed conclusive: over one-half of the school districts voted to accept the provisions of the new Free School Act.

The issue, however, was far from settled. The school election struggles wrought intense bitterness among community factions. In some districts those favoring the new act were so harassed that church, neighborhood, and even family ties were broken.

By the time the legislature reconvened in 1835, the questions of repeal and the reenactment of the old pauper-school law had become the dominant issue. Many representatives to the legislature who had voted in favor of the law were subsequently defeated for reelection. In the opening days of the legislature, the opponents of the law bombarded the representatives with memorials and petitions for repeal of the Act of 1834. Indeed, petitions demanding repeal came in from about two-thirds of the counties in the state. In fact, so many petitions were received by the House of Representatives that a special committee was formed to handle the volume. Interestingly enough, the committee remarked "that in most of the petitions not more than five names out of every hundred are written in English, and the great mass of them are so illegibly written as to afford the strongest evidence of the deplorable disregard so long paid by the Legislature to the constitutional injunction to establish a general system of education." The Senate immediately repealed the law by an overwhelming majority. The House, however, stood firm, and under the leadership of Thaddeus Stevens refused to reconsider the Free School Act. Even more important, he finally persuaded the Senate to accept an amended law much stronger than the original bill.

A Vermonter who emigrated to Pennsylvania in 1815, Thaddeus Stevens was the key figure in the bitter legislative struggle. "Rarely an orator, yet words were his only weapons," remarked Thomas Frederick Woodley.[40] There is no doubt that Stevens's forceful and uncompromising stand helped tremendously to convince the House of the importance of free public schools. With Stevens in command, the free-school proponents marshaled their strength against the clamorous demands of the opposition. Governor George Wolf of Pennsylvania may have differed with Stevens on other issues, but in the free-school controversy he was a close ally. Governor Wolf not only favored the Free School Act but also indicated that he would veto any action to withdraw the Act of 1834. With strong gubernatorial support, Thaddeus Stevens made an eloquent plea to the House of Representatives on April 11, 1835, not to repeal the Free School Law.[41] His speech was, according to Carl Russell Fish, "one of the great orations of American history." Stevens's address and the contest that precipitated it were so important, Fish continues, that they marked "the turning point toward a public school system free to all on equal terms."[42]

Speaking from hastily prepared notes, Stevens rose to what he later described as his most important single achievement. "Mr. Speaker," he began, "I will briefly give you the reasons why I shall oppose the repeal of the school law. . . . I will attempt to show that the law is salutary, useful and important; and that consequently, the last legislature acted wisely in passing, and the present would act unwisely in repealing it." Later in his address, Stevens echoed the classic theme of the reformers' arguments:

> if an elective republic is to endure for any great length of time, *every* elector must have sufficient information, not only to accumulate wealth, and take care of his pecuniary concerns, but to direct wisely the legislatures, the ambassadors, and the executive of the nation—for *some* part of all these things, *some* agency in approving or disapproving of them, falls to every freeman. If then, the permanency of our government depends upon such knowledge, it is the duty of government to see that the means of information be diffused to every citizen. This is a sufficient answer to those who deem education a private and not a public duty—who argue that they are wiling to educate their *own* children, but not their *neighbor's* children.[43]

Apparently, Stevens's forceful argument and persuasive tone had a stunning impact upon those in the House chamber. According to contemporary reports, he "electrified" the House and "saved the common school system." Governor Wolf was so overcome with joy that he threw his arms around Stevens and embraced him.

With the passage of a stronger act, the principle of tax support for public education gradually replaced the old pauper-school idea in Pennsylvania. Although still permissive in its main stipulations, the amended law provided for local and county taxation and for state aid and supervision of the public schools. Those districts refusing to accept the provisions of the new act were denied state funds. The success of the free-school forces in Pennsylvania in eliminating the pauper-school concept set a memorable precedent, spurring reform efforts in other states. As humanitarianism swept across the North after 1835, the pauper-school idea gradually disappeared.

Abolishing the "Rate Bill"

Originating in English history, the "rate bill" system was prevalent during the colonial period in Massachusetts and Connecticut. Later the system spread to other parts of the country, especially to New York State, where it became entrenched and persisted for years as a means for supplementing school revenues. In actual practice, the system contributed more to truancy and irregular attendance than to school income because parents often kept their children out of school to avoid paying an assessment. Thus, during the reform era educational leaders voiced strong protests against a practice that ultimately defeated the whole concept of a free school open to rich and poor alike.

By the close of the Civil War, Pennsylvania, Indiana, Ohio, Illinois, and Vermont had eliminated the rate bill through legislative action. In New

York and Connecticut, however, the struggle to abolish the system was more prolonged and bitterly contested than anywhere else in the North. In those states the rural districts were less wealthy and more conservative than the cities. These less populous areas strongly resisted all efforts to replace the local rate assessments with a statewide form of adequate taxation. Finally, after much agitation and two referenda, the New York legislature abolished the rate bill in 1867. A year later, Connecticut and Rhode Island also eliminated it and created free school systems.

Except in the South, the rate-bill system was also abolished in other states without the bitter controversies that characterized the long campaigns in New York and Connecticut. At the end of a devastating war, most of the southern states continued for years to assess rates to supplement school funds. Eventually, however, after the terrible ordeal of Reconstruction, the rate-bill system was abolished throughout the United States.

The Emergence of the Public High School

During the early stages of the common school movement, the educational reformers began to argue more strongly in favor of a tuition-free secondary school that would offer the functional training for which the academies were so highly valued. In fact, demands for free secondary education often paralleled arguments advanced in favor of public elementary schooling, and for many reformers the belief that education was a public necessity instead of a private luxury applied to the secondary school as well as to elementary education. Many were distressed not only by the academies' tuition-charging practices but also by the private control of these institutions. Proponents of public secondary education pointed more frequently to the paradox of a common school system that attempted to provide equality of educational opportunity to everyone and a secondary education available only to those who could pay for it.

Largely in response to these growing demands for a tuition-free secondary education not offered by the common schools, the Boston School Committee opened the English Classical School in May 1821. Renamed the English High School three years later, this institution was probably the first public high school established in the United States. It was essentially a publicly supported academy for those boys who wanted "to become merchants and mechanics." Since Boston already had a Latin school to prepare students for the university, the curriculum of the new high school omitted the classical subjects and included those courses generally offered by the English department of an academy.

After 1821 other cities also established public high schools. For example, one was founded in Portland, Maine, also in 1821, and four years later New York City opened a public high school. Apparently Boston's venture into public secondary education was an initial success, for in 1826 a separate public high school for girls was also established. Somewhat paradoxically, the Girls' High School was so popular that it was closed two years after it opened: because of the overwhelming demand, the mayor of Boston feared that educating all the girls who wanted to attend the school would bankrupt the city! In 1852 the Girls' High School was reopened as a training institution for teachers.

Far more significant in terms of its ultimate impact upon the public high-school movement was the Massachusetts Law of 1827, enacted largely through the efforts of James G. Carter. This act required the establishment of a tax-supported high school in all towns or districts of five hundred or more families. It also required that Latin and Greek be offered in the curriculum when towns or districts with high schools had reached a population of at least four thousand.

The Massachusetts Law of 1827 was an important milestone in the history of secondary education. It set an example that was soon followed by other states. Maine, New Hampshire, and Vermont, for example, copied the Massachusetts law. At mid-century there were almost a hundred public high schools in Massachusetts alone. By 1860 the public high-school movement had spread to other parts of the nation, particularly to the cities, where secondary schools were most numerous.

After the surrender of the Confederate Army at Appomattox Court House in 1865, the drive for free secondary education began anew, following a path marked in the earlier fight for tax-supported common schools. In the first struggle, it was a battle before state legislatures to obtain passage of laws authorizing or forcing the establishment of free common or elementary schools. In the case of secondary schools, these earlier laws had already been enacted, and the chief problem was determining whether they provided a legal foundation for secondary education. If the earlier laws had given the districts the right to tax for public elementary schools, did these same districts have the right to establish public high schools? In an effort to solve this problem, the battle for free high schools was largely fought in the courts after the Civil War over issues of legal interpretation. Thus the years following the Civil War witnessed a number of state judicial decisions that ultimately laid a firm legal basis for public secondary education. The most famous case of all resulted in the important Kalamazoo decision of 1874.

In 1872 a citizen of School District No. 1 in Kalamazoo, Michigan, sued to prevent the board from collecting taxes for the support of secondary schools. This was obviously a taxpayer's move to ascertain the right of local school authorities to support free high schools. The unanimous decision, handed down two years later by the Michigan Supreme Court and written by Justice Thomas M. Cooley, affirmed the right of the school board to levy taxes for public high schools. Cooley pointed out that from the beginning the state of Michigan had intended to provide not only an elementary schooling but also an equal educational opportunity for all youth to go on to higher studies. Having already set up elementary schools and a state university, Cooley continued, the state would be inconsistent if it compelled citizens to obtain a private secondary education. This decision, affirming the power of a community to levy taxes for the support of secondary schools, supplied a significant precedent that was followed in other states whenever the issue was raised.

It is important to remember that the real triumph of the American struggle for free schools was the establishment of three vital principles on which every adequate *public*-school system would have to be based. The first principle was that education was a primary responsibility of the state instead of an obligation traditionally assumed by the family. The second principle, and a corollary of the first, was that the state had both the right and the power to raise through taxation on a citizen's property sufficient funds for school support. Finally, in spite of all obstacles, the bitter struggle for free schools established the important principle of a nonsectarian, publicly supported school system open to all youth, regardless of creed or financial status.

By 1865 the United States was rather firmly committed to these basic principles. Most of the states had established public-school systems, and a large number of children were obtaining an elementary education. In addition, some youth in Massachusetts, New York, Pennsylvania, and a few other states were receiving a free secondary education. Like the common school for which Horace Mann, Henry Barnard, and other reformers had labored so hard to build, the new public high school also stood as an integral part of a unified system of public education. "The high school must be a public school," declared George S. Boutwell, secretary of the Massachusetts Board of Education, on the eve of the Civil War. "A *public school* [is] . . . a school established by the public—suported chiefly or entirely by the public, controlled by the public, and accessible to the public upon terms of equality, without special charge for tuition."[44] More than any other single factor, this idea of a public school open to *all* is the most distinctive feature of American education. It was a nineteenth-century ideal that has endured to the present time.

FOR DISCUSSION AND CRITICAL THOUGHT

1. During the 1820s and 1830s the lyceums supported by Josiah Holbrook helped to create a social climate favorable to public education. Through the lyceums local communities took an active stand in favor of educational reform. Today some citizens are disgruntled with the costs and results

of public education. What approach do you recommend that would bring about more public support of the schools? What were some of the arguments offered by opponents to tax-supported schools? How were they refuted? Are any of these arguments relevant today? Explain.

2. Explain why Ralph Waldo Emerson's arguments for individualism and nonconformity are especially relevant for life in the 1990s.

3. Advocates of the common school idea were not torn between equality and excellence—an important issue of the twentieth century. What were the major forces behind the common school movement of the nineteenth century?

4. Discuss the common school movement in terms of Horace Mann's dream of the nineteenth century and some of the grim realities of the 1980s and 1990s.

5. To what extent were the newly established common schools in the nineteenth century instruments of social control and/or agencies of social mobility? Explain.

6. How did the urban growth of the United States and the influx of immigrants during the 1840s lead to changes in the public schools?

7. Discuss the significance of the *Kalamazoo* case of 1874 for the development of public secondary schools.

8. Discuss three basic principles on which an effective public school system should be based. Suggest another important principle essential for excellent public schools.

NOTES

1. Letter dated 4 March 1829, from Daniel Webster to Mrs. E. Webster, *The Private Correspondence of Daniel Webster,* ed. Fletcher Webster (Boston: Little, Brown, 1857), 1:473.

2. Recent Jacksonian historiography has played down the growing problem of sectional conflict and has stressed instead a theme of class struggle between "the capitalistic groups, mainly Eastern," backed by the business community and a coalition of "noncapitalist groups, farmers and laboring men, East, West, and South" supporting Jackson's rise to power. See Arthur M. Schlesinger, Jr., *The Age of Jackson* (Boston: Little, Brown, 1946), passim.

3. William E. Dodd, *The Cotton Kingdom: A Chronicle of the Old South* (New Haven, Conn.: Yale University Press, 1919), p. 5.

4. Frank L. Owsley, *Plain Folk of the Old South* (Baton Rouge: Louisiana State University Press, 1949).

5. Avery Craven, *The Coming of the Civil War* (2nd ed., Chicago: University of Chicago Press, 1957), p. 32.

6. Sarah H. Bradford, *Scenes in the Life of Harriet Tubman* (Auburn, Ala.: W. J. Moses, Printer, 1869; reissued by Books for Libraries Press, 1971), p. 21.

7. Ann Petry, *Harriet Tubman: Conductor on the Underground Railroad* (New York: Crowell, 1955), p. 130.

8. See Willie Lee Rose, *Rehearsal for Reconstruction: The Port Royal Experiment* (Indianapolis: Bobbs-Merrill, 1964).

9. See Clement Eaton, *The Freedom-of-Thought Struggle in the Old South* (New York: Harper & Row Torchbook, 1964), pp. 89–117.

10. Basing his research chiefly on plantation records, Phillips strongly influenced American attitudes toward black slavery. See Ulrich B. Phillips, *American Negro Slavery: A Survey of the Supply, Employment and Control of Negro Labor as Determined by the Plantation Regime* (New York: D. Appleton-Century, 1918; reissued in 1940), and *Life and Labor in the Old South* (Boston: Little, Brown, 1930).

11. Frederick Law Olmsted, *The Cotton Kingdom: A Traveller's Observations on Cotton and Slavery in the American Slave States,* ed., with an introduction, by Arthur M. Schlesinger (New York: Knopf, 1953).

12. In the minds of many southern planters, it must have seemed more than a coincidence that *The Liberator* was first published in Boston in January 1831, and that the Nat Turner insurrection occurred seven months later.

13. Edgar W. Knight, *Public Education in the South* (Boston: Ginn, 1922), p. 264.

14. Clement Eaton, *The Mind of the Old South* (Baton Rouge: Louisiana State University Press, 1964), p. 242.

15. See Eaton, *The Freedom-of-Thought Struggle in the Old South,* pp. 118–237, 335–352.

16. Francis J. Grund, *The Americans in Their Moral, Social and Political Relations* (Boston: Marsh, Capen & Lyon, 1837), p. 202.

17. In his classic interpretation, *Public Education in the United States: A Study and Interpretation of American Educational History* (Boston: Houghton Mifflin, 1919), Elwood P. Cubberley argued that the movement for common schools consisted of several battles to establish free school systems from 1830 to 1860. In 1968 Michael B. Katz's thought-provoking book, *The Irony of Early School Reform: Educational Innovation in Mid-Nineteenth Century Massachusetts* (Cambridge, Mass.: Harvard University Press, 1968), focused on the interrelationships among ideology, school development, and social structure, with special attention to urban school systems. During the 1970s, Katz and other scholars examined relationships between schools and class conflict and class imposition; an emerging interest in ethnicity and race produced a number of related works on different forms of conflict and subordination in public schooling.

These "revisionist" scholars cast doubt on the optimistic assumptions characteristic of the Cubbberleyan approach and focused new light on the ways in which public schools reflected and to some extent perpetuated economic and social inequalities. See, for example, Michael B. Katz, *Class, Bureaucracy, and Schools; The Illusion of Educational Change in America* (New York: Praeger, 1971); Clarence J. Karier, Paul C. Violas, and Joel Spring, *Roots of Crisis: American Education in the Twentieth Century* (Chicago: Rand McNally, 1973); Joel H. Spring, *Education and the Rise of the Corporate State* (Boston: Beacon Press, 1972); and Samuel Bowles and Herbert Gintis, *Schooling in Capitalist America: Educational Reform and the Contradictions of Economic Life* (New York: Basic Books,

1976). For a discussion of the varieties of historical interpretation concerning the common school movement, see "The Ideology and Politics of the Common School," Chapter 4 of Joel Spring, *The American School, 1642–1985: Varieties of Historical Interpretation of the Foundations and Development of American Education* 2nd ed. (White Plains, N.Y.: Longman, 1990).

18. *Working Man's Advocate* (New York, 6 March 1830, as reprinted in John R. Commons et al., eds., *A Documentary History of American Industrial Society* (Cleveland, Ohio: Clark, 1910), 5:96.

19. Richard William Leopold, *Robert Dale Owen: A Biography* (Cambridge, Mass.: Harvard University Press, 1940), p. 10.

20. Philip R. V. Curoe, *Educational Attitudes and Policies of Organized Labor in the United States,* Contributions to Education No. 201 (New York: Bureau of Publications, Teachers College, Columbia University, 1926), p. 33.

21. Ralph Waldo Emerson, "Man the Reformer" (Lecture read before the Mechanics' Apprentices' Library Association, Boston, 25 January 1841), *Nature, Addresses, and Lectures* (Boston: Houghton Mifflin, 1855), 1:237.

22. Ralph Waldo Emerson, "Education" (1876), *Lectures and Biographical Sketches* (Boston: Houghton Mifflin, 1884; Riverside Edition of *Emerson's Complete Works,* vol. X), pp. 123–156.

23. Ralph Waldo Emerson, "Self-Reliance," *Essays: First Series* (Boston: Houghton Mifflin, 1865; originally published in 1841), 2:49.

24. Henry Steele Commager, ed., *The Era of Reform, 1830–1860* (Princeton, N.J.: Van Nostrand, 1960), p. 10. Italics in original.

25. Carl Bode, *The American Lyceum: Town Meeting of the Mind* (New York: Oxford University Press, 1956), p. 16.

26. Henry Barnard, ed., "Lyceums," *Connecticut Common School Journal* 1 (December 1838): 40.

27. "Constitution and Bylaws of the American Lyceum," Article II, in Cecil B. Hayes, *The American Lyceum: Its History and Contributions to Education,* U.S. Office of Education Bulletin No. 12 (Washington, D.C.: U.S. Government Printing Office, 1932), p. 38.

28. "Resolutions of the American Lyceum,"in Hayes, *The American Lyceum,* p. 59.

29. There is no record of the meetings of the American Lyceum after 1840. Local lyceums continued mainly as sponsors of lecture series before merging into the Chautauqua movement.

30. Barnard, ed., "Lyceums," p. 39.

31. See Katz, *Irony of Early School Reform,* passim.

32. James G. Carter, *Letters to the Hon. William Prescott, LL.D. on the Free Schools of New England, with Remarks upon the Principles of Instruction* (Boston: Cummings, Hilliard, 1824), and *Essays upon Popular Education, Containing a Particular Examination of the Schools of Massachusetts, and an Outline of an Institution for the Education of Teachers* (Boston: Bowles & Dearborn, 1826).

33. Mann's private diary includes notes entered irregularly over a six-year period. In his opening entry on 4 May 1837, he referred to it as his sacred *"book of judgment."* See Mary Peabody Mann, *Life of Horace Mann* (Washington, D.C.: National Education Association, 1937). This is the Centennial ed., reproduced

in facsimile from the original publication in 1865 by Walker, Fuller and Co. in Boston.

34. Howard Mumford Jones, "Horace Mann's Crusade," in Daniel Aaron, ed., *America in Crisis* (New York: Knopf, 1952), pp. 98–99.

35. For some excerpts from Mann's *Reports* and a succinct analysis of his writings, see Lawrence A. Cremin, ed., *The Republic and the School: Horace Mann on the Education of Free Men,* Classics in Education No. 1 (New York: Bureau of Publications, Teachers College, Columbia University, 1957).

36. Horace Mann, *Annual Reports on Education,* vol. 3 of the *Life and Works of Horace Mann,* ed. Mary Mann (Boston: Horace B. Fuller, 1868), p. 754. Italics in original.

37. This famous publication by Barnard should not be confused with another periodical by the same title edited from 1826 to 1831 by William Russell.

38. Knight, *Public Education in the South,* p. 265.

39. Knight's retrospective view of the reform effort in the antebellum South was far more positive than appears warranted by the facts. "But for the Civil War and its dreadful aftermath," he concludes, "the history of public education in the South would be a different and a better story." Ibid., p. 267.

40. Thomas Frederick Woodley, *Thaddeus Stevens* (Harrisburgh, Pa.: Telegraph Press, 1934), p. 6.

41. This famous address is reprinted under the heading, "General Education—Remarks of Mr. Stevens" [before the House of Representatives], in *Hazard's Register of Pennsylvania*, vol. 15, no. 18 (Philadelphia: Printed by Wm. F. Geddes and ed. by Samuel Hazard, 2 May 1835), pp. 283–287.

42. Carl Russell Fish, *The Rise of the Common Man, 1830–1850,* vol. 6 of *A History of American Life* (New York: Macmillan, 1941), p. 217.

43. Stevens, *Hazard's Register of Pennsylvania,* p. 284.

44. George S. Boutwell, *Thoughts on Educational Topics and Institutions* (Boston: Phillips, Sampson, 1859), p. 188. Italics in original.

PART TWO

An Era of Transition
1865–1919

CHAPTER 5

Evolving Patterns
of Educational Thought

*Democracy, this most alluring record, that it alone can bind, and ever seeks to
bind, all nations, all men, of however various and distant lands, into a
brotherhood, a family. It is the old, yet ever-modern dream of earth.*

WALT WHITMAN, *Democratic Vistas,* 1871

The Problem of the Twentieth Century is the problem of the color-line.

W. E. BURGHARDT DU BOIS, *The Souls of Black Folk,* 1903

*I have undertaken to get at the facts from the point of view of the business
men—citizens of the community who, after all, pay the bills and, therefore,
have a right to say what they shall have in their schools. . . . We must bring
the work of the schools into the closest relation to the life of the people.*

CHARLES H. THURBER, from an Address at the Annual Meeting of the
National Education Association, 9 July 1897

*Hear the wail of the children, who never have a chance to go to school, but
work ten to eleven hours a day in the textile mills.*

MARY HARRIS JONES, during the march of the mill children, 28 July 1903

THE LEGACY OF WAR
AND RECONSTRUCTION

The Destruction of the Old South

The shots that rang out across Charleston Harbor from Fort Sumter on April
12, 1861, set the federal garrison aflame, and for four historic years the blaze

spread, engulfing the South in a gory holocaust. At the time there was no comprehension in either the North or the South of the full gravity of a civil war. Many did not realize that a full-scale war had even begun. President Abraham Lincoln merely sought to quell a rebellion and sounded a call for three-month volunteers, while men of Confederate sympathies followed the dictates of loyalty and tradition, dashing off to battle and expecting to return home soon. How different was the aftermath of this senseless start! In the wake of terrible devastation, those who learned to destroy also learned to hate. Through subsequent months of horrible despair and misery, desertion and disaffection became common problems as embittered civilians and battle-weary soldiers on both sides wondered why they were killing each other.[1] When at long last the flames subsided in 1865, the casualty toll was appalling; about 258,000 soldiers on the Confederate side and 359,000 on the Union side perished, littering the southern fields with dead Americans. Thousands of survivors were maimed for life. This was the first of history's modern wars, fought with such ruthlessness and brutality that the psychological wounds would take generations to heal.

The terms of peace imposed upon the South at the close of the Civil War would have to be unobjectionable to the defeated Confederacy or eventually all work toward reconstruction might be reversed. A peace settlement rarely endures through the years unless it is acceptable to both the vanquished and the victor. With foresight and great wisdom Lincoln foresaw this; unfortunately, a congressional majority did not. Unlike Lincoln, the so-called Radical Republicans in the House of Representatives and the Senate asserted that secession had suspended the federal Constitution; the southern people were defeated enemies; and hence, any reprisal was deemed permissible and necessary to crush forever the Confederate South. In fact, the mood of the Radical leaders, Thaddeus Stevens in the House, and Charles Sumner in the Senate, was like that of the earlier French Jacobins during the Reign of Terror.

Stevens's sole passion centered on a plan of ruthless punishment for the "conquered provinces." Lame from birth, now old, perilously ill, unmarried, and cared for by a devoted African American housekeeper, he sought, almost successfully, to destroy President Andrew Johnson, whose lenient terms of reconstruction he loathed. His violent temper was widely known, and congressmen feared his lashing tongue. Stevens's and Sumner's reconstructionist policies of revenge rekindled the fires of sectional hatred, even among the most temperate in the South, forestalled amity and reconciliation, and left for posterity a legacy of racial hatred and unsolved racial issues and problems.

The Radicals failed to comprehend the most elementary postwar facts. First of all, the war obliterated the South, the scene of actual battles. The total devastation wrought by generals Sherman, Sheridan, and others is incomprehensible, even to generations today who have lived through more destructive wars. Sherman, in particular, left a deliberate trail of destruction wherever he went. After burning Atlanta in November 1864, he and his troops launched their infamous drive through central Georgia to the coast, destroying everything in a path three hundred miles long and sixty miles wide. Columbia, South Carolina, was burned by Sherman's explicit orders. "It is now a wilderness of ruins," wrote a northern reporter who toured the South at the end of the war. "Its heart is but a mass of blackened chimneys and crumbling walls."[2] In the fall of 1865, an estimated half-million white people were without shelter or food in the ravaged areas of Georgia, Alabama, and Mississippi. In South Carolina and northern Georgia, the poverty and distress were equally acute if not worse. Such cities as Mobile, Jackson, Charleston, and Richmond were devastated from bombardment and fire.

Such destitution reduced a large part of the white population and thousands of liberated slaves to actual starvation. Railroads had been destroyed. Banks were in ruins, and there was no currency or credit. Because approximately half of the white men between the ages of eighteen and thirty-five had been killed or seriously maimed, there was a critical lack of manpower with which to resume farming and routine businesses. "I cannot understand the prevailing view of the war among even pious and intelligent Americans—it is simply barbaric—to whip the South and go home rejoicing, to build monuments to victory, leaving one-third of their countrymen in the depths of distress," declared General Samuel Chapman Armstrong, founder of Hampton Institute, in 1874.[3] Few societies anywhere have ever had to struggle against such fearful odds.

Such scenes of ruin and pathos in 1865 only intensified the agonizing sequel to war. The burden of defeat weighed heavily on the hearts and souls of the southern people, for this had been no war of professional soldiers. The Confederate cause was idealized into the all-absorbing passion for a separate way of life. In a real sense this had been the only motivating force for killing and dying. Thus the psychological consequences of defeat were far more disheartening to the people than the loss of a war. Crushed in spirit, they could view with only despair and bitter memories the task of rebuilding their beloved land.

The Confederate soldiers straggled home to poverty-stricken communities. Amidst havoc and devastation, they found a totally disorganized society. Their former white friends were either missing or demoralized. Worst of all, the behavior of the freed African Americans dismayed and frightened the surviving white people.

The first years of freedom were periods of great social tension, aggravated by disease, hunger, and intense suffering. The former slaves, adrift without resources, were helpless and ignorant. Unaccustomed to freedom, they spent days and nights loitering about the community. Many deserted the plantations and small farms, neglected their crops, drank quantities of liquor, and pilfered from barns whatever they could find. Others indulged in rowdy behavior, sometimes pushing the white people from the sidewalks. All were too bewildered to understand anything except the fact that they were not bound any longer by forced labor. In the postwar confusion many African American families disintegrated, as roving bands of young freedmen deserted to the towns, leaving behind the old people and the children.

The Radicals not only exhibited a callous disregard for destitution and human misery but also displayed a complete ignorance of southern mores. Above all, they failed to consider in their vindictive plan of reconstruction the attitudes of the southern people toward the former slaves. None of the South's fundamental beliefs was suddenly altered by defeat. The end of the war could not change overnight the opinions of the southern whites concerning the African American people. Those who had owned slaves or had observed them in daily associations regarded individuals with affection, occasionally mingled with fear. Regarding the mass of freed slaves, however, the southern white people viewed them as socially inferior and politically ignorant. It was expected that the ex-slaves would need considerable training in order to assume the responsibilities of freedom. It was also assumed that their former owners and friends would be the teachers.

Instead, groups of missionaries and a horde of "carpetbaggers" descended from the North upon a ravaged and embittered South. Many came on behalf of the Freedmen's Bureau, created by Congress in 1865; others, under private auspices; and some, merely to wander and loot and to exploit the newly freed people. Northern organizations such as the Boston Educational Commission and the American Missionary Association established schools for the former slaves, provided teachers, and equipped the classrooms. These missionaries greatly antagonized southern whites by teaching the freedmen Yankee war songs, by advancing equalitarian ideas, and by instilling hostile attitudes toward the former master class. In daily affairs, the oppressive and tactless manners of the bureau's agents actually generated much hostility and intensified even more the already strained relations between the white people and the African Americans.

Southern reaction to Radical intransigence persisted with varying degrees of intensity for decades. Contrary to a general impression, the movement to disfranchise African Americans did not really gain impetus until after the Populist revolt in the 1890s, which threatened temporarily the one-party system in the South. In exploiting racial prejudice for political advantage, certain agrarian factions in the South helped to create a psychological atmosphere that encouraged during the next two decades the enactment of "Jim Crow" legislation and the disfranchisement of blacks by state laws.[4] The earlier "Black Codes," the terroristic Ku Klux Klan, and some legalized schemes of disfranchisement gradually forced the southern African Americans into a state of economic peonage and soon underscored a social inferiority almost as glaring as the abolished institution of slavery.

People only recently freed from bondage were forced to acquiesce in the new social order of the white South. How did the African American citizens feel about their inferior status? Unfortunately, it is impossible to assess their view immediately after the Civil War, for they left no written record of what was in their hearts and souls during this tumultuous period.[5] There were occasional protests, to be sure, especially from a few articulate African American leaders; but, by and large, the journalistic version during the late nineteenth century of an easygoing, passive African American people went unchallenged for decades.

Toward the end of the century, the economic and social subordination of African Americans was proving far more onerous for the South than the memories of Radical Reconstructionism. The slim resources of the South were insufficient to maintain adequately two public-school systems. The price of segregation was also costly in other, less obvious, ways. The new social discipline sharply restricted innovation and change, for a stratified society can ill afford to encourage educational experimentation and reform. Every change would have to adjust to the southern biracial scheme—a heavy restriction not likely to encourage a creative thinker to move along unexplored paths. Thus the emerging pattern of race relations strengthened the status quo and reinforced a rigid conservatism in educational thought.

The Disruption of Educational Patterns in the South

The schools in the South, like other social institutions, were caught in this maelstrom of war and peace. When General Lee surrendered at Appomattox, public education was totally disorganized and the colleges and private academies closed; and for at least a generation, the harsh consequences of Radical Reconstruction destroyed any basis for southern educational reform. Human desolation, racial conflict, and political disharmony were formidable barriers indeed to the development of public schools. These obstacles consumed the time and energies of the southern people, subordinating public education to the more pressing needs of a disrupted and poverty-stricken society. Helplessly in debt from the fraudulent and extravagant spending of the Reconstructionist governments and overburdened with millions of uneducated ex-slaves, the southern states remained for decades in economic chaos.

While most of the southern whites were without any formal schooling, the illiteracy of the African Americans was far more acute. Because education of slaves was viewed as dangerous and thus was generally forbidden, there were no southern schools for African American children at the close of the war.[6] Thus, at its lowest point in history the South was faced with the belated and virtually impossible task of establishing public-school systems comparable in quality to those of the North.

There are conflicting views concerning the educational contribution made by the carpetbag governments established by the Radical Reconstructionists. The traditional interpretation of Radical domination as a travesty on state and local governments has been modified in recent years by certain scholars who point to similar excesses in the North during the Reconstruction era. However, no one has yet argued convincingly that Radical domination of the South constituted good government. There is a tendency, also, to credit a few long-term social services, especially in the field of education, to Radical rule. The issue is far from settled, for here, too, interpretations vary.

Some southern historians view with pessimism any long-range benefits allegedly derived from the Reconstruction regimes. Edgar W. Knight, for instance, asserts that the South owes nothing to the carpetbag governments. Like others, he points to the graft and looting of funds and the exorbitant debts as memorable barriers in the path of an adequate tax system for public-school support.[7] Nevertheless, despite their deficiencies, the carpetbag governments did concern themselves with two important educational ideals: the constitutional mandates for systems of common schools and the injunctions for education of African Americans. It should be remembered that these ideals were not reached immediately after 1876 either, when the southern whites seized back the reins of political control.

The roots of failures that plagued educational efforts in the South were more social than political: segregation, rural impoverishment, and southern conservatism disillusioned the most dedicated reformers, regardless of race or political affiliation.

After the restoration of Democratic rule, retrenchment became the immediate policy of the new state administrations. This is not surprising in the light of the extravagance of the carpetbag legislatures and a depression following the panic of 1873. Governmental expenditures were drastically cut.

Public education bore the greatest brunt of the stringent economies. The attitudes of the Democratic regimes toward school expenditures were especially severe and bitter. For example, one state official in Virginia believed that "it were better for the State to burn the schools," while another thought that taxation to support free schools, "imported here by a gang of carpetbaggers," was socialistic.[8] This immediate reaction to Radical Reconstruction handicapped for years the public schools in the Deep South.

The curtailment in school expenditures, along with the general impoverishment of the people, led to drastic cuts in the length of the elementary-school term. Under Radical rule, the highest average attained was a 100-day term; however, not until 1900 was this amount of schooling restored by the Democratic administrations. The amount of funds expended per pupil was also reduced. In 1890, for example, with a national average of $17.22 per pupil, state expenditures ranged from $3.38 in South Carolina to $43.43 in Colorado.[9]

The most devastating effect of the Democratic policy of retrenchment was a rising tide of illiteracy among the southern white people. In Tennessee, for example, Colonel James B. Killebrew, an assistant superintendent of schools paid by the Peabody Education Fund, discovered in 1872 "that while the white population had increased only 13 per cent during the preceding ten years, white illiteracy had increased 50 per cent."[10] In spite of these statistics, no action was taken until the turn of the century to improve the state's public schools.

The Peabody Education Fund

Despite the confusion and despair of the Reconstruction years, a significant effort was made to breathe new life into southern education. While the Radicals in Congress were passing the Reconstruction Acts, George Peabody, one of the nation's wealthiest financiers, was working to restore good will between the North and the South. A native of Massachusetts, Peabody had acquired considerable wealth in London and had already achieved an international reputation for charitable philanthropy through donations to alleviate poverty in the London slums. He had formerly lived in the South and was aware of the critical post–Civil War needs of public education.

On February 7, 1867, and on June 29, 1869, Peabody established through two grants a fund of $2 million, the interest from which was to be used for the promotion of elementary education in the South. He also donated $1.5 million in bonds of several southern states; however, the trustees did not receive a return on these repudiated bonds. Thus, contrary to some reports, it is accurate to state that the trust fund amounted to a total of $2 million. Such an early postwar manifestation of benevolence by a northerner toward the South helped to alleviate some sectional tension.

The Peabody Education Fund was directed by a distinguished Board of Trustees from both the North and the South. This in itself was conducive to postwar harmony. Those who accepted membership on the board gave much time and energy to their task. Even Ulysses S. Grant, while he was President, attended the board meetings. So, too, did Hamilton Fish during his years as secretary of state. Admiral Farragut, according to those who worked with him on the board, was as energetic in his educational service as he had been in running Union ships past the Confederate batteries. There were others on the board, too, including a South Carolinian and a Virginian who developed close friendships with their fellow trustees from the North. This leadership from the very beginning sparked public confidence in the educational work of the fund and initiated an era of better understanding between the two sections.

Under the administration of Barnas Sears, the first general agent, and later Jabez L. M. Curry, the Peabody Education Fund became a powerful stimulus to the development of state school systems and to the improvement of teacher education throughout the South. Until his death in 1880, Sears's wise policies guided the administration of the fund. A New England educator who at one time was president of Brown University, Sears tried to encourage the southern people to help themselves. Thus, in line with this policy, aid was granted to the support of the common schools, provided that a larger sum was raised by taxation than that awarded by the fund. Enthusiastic and tactful, Sears did much to win local support for the public schools. Under his guidance, the fund helped to develop in the South the idea of adequate taxation for public education and reduced considerably white hostility to black education. Sears made the slogan "Free schools for the whole people" generally acceptable to the southern people. His educational policies were well established by the time Curry, a southerner, assumed the management of the fund in 1881. When the trustees eventually decided to liquidate the fund, they established in Nashville, Tennessee, the George Peabody College for Teachers. Chartered in 1909 and opened four years later, Peabody College has played a leading role in the improvement of southern education.

The Quest of the African American

Material aid from philanthropic funds was only one aspect of the post–Civil War movement for African American education. To effect long-range benefits, racial tolerance and a strong sense of southern responsibility were also needed. Indeed, after the Civil War the whole area of African American education became an issue of growing concern.

The earliest and most highly respected educational leader of his race was Booker T. Washington (1856–1915), whose views commanded attention throughout the South and the North. Born a slave, he vividly described in *Up from Slavery* (1901) the scenes of joy and thanksgiving when former slaves heard the Emancipation Proclamation read to them. He told of the tearful happiness of his mother, who had prayed for years for freedom and feared that she might not survive to witness the event. Few slaves understood the issues of the war, and most were oblivious to the fact that their own freedom was at stake. Fewer still climbed during the turbulent Reconstruction era to positions of leadership and respect. Booker T. Washington's rise "up from slavery" and his subsequent success in education form a dramatic tale of courage and perseverance. With insight and wisdom, he rose above the level of racial hatred and viewed humankind with humility and compassion.

During a critical period in American history, Washington offered the most sensible approach to the problem of African American education. A graduate of Hampton Institute, he advocated industrial education for young African Americans. At a time when ideas of education for African Americans were confined to a few books, to dreams of mastering some Latin and Greek, he stressed instead the dignity of labor and urged manual training for useful occupations in the local community. Washington urged people to begin at the bottom, to learn how to read and write, and to acquire skills in all types of trades. He was not alone in his advocacy of industrial education,[11] but he popularized with skill and great leadership a wide range of ideas concerning economic self-advancement that coincided with the temper of the times. His persuasive arguments won friends and attracted followers from both the North and the South to the cause of black education.

In 1881 Washington founded Tuskegee Institute in an unfriendly white community in Alabama. Like Benjamin Franklin, he stressed a practical and useful curriculum. The goal at Tuskegee was to teach industrial arts and trade skills and to instill thrift and honesty in the students. More than anything else, Washington wanted to encourage in African American youth attitudes of self-respect and confidence. Following closely the policies of General Samuel C. Armstrong, his former mentor at Hampton Institute, Washington urged his students to make themselves useful and essential to the economic interests of the South in order to reduce racial enmity and eventually to win confidence and respect from the white people. Such a gospel of training and work, preached in an atmosphere of racial tension, gave southern African Americans an alternative to despair and defeat and offered some measure of hope for social betterment.[12]

Through lectures, articles, and books, Washington expounded his views, persuading philanthropists to donate funds to develop Tuskegee into the finest institution of its kind in the South.[13] An able speaker, he inspired his audiences with his eloquent and forceful arguments. He appealed to the self-interest of northern manufacturers and financiers by pointing out in dollars and cents the relationship between industrial education for the blacks and the availability of a cheap labor supply of skilled, docile workers. Then he proceeded to convince the white South that the education of the freedmen was in the best interests of the entire section. Hold African Americans down in ignorance, Washington warned, and the whole South will be chained down, too, for their services are vital to the southern economy. "No people ever had so much to gain by lifting up a race," Washington declared. "No people ever had so much to lose by the degradation of a race."[14] His argument that the community would profit and rise from the labor of African Ameri-

cans obviously pleased and appealed to the dominant white citizens. The
Peabody and Slater funds increased their grants, and contributions poured in
from such industrialists as H. H. Rogers of Standard Oil Company and
Andrew Carnegie.

Not everyone concurred with Washington's views. Other leaders, in
particular, attacked his emphasis on vocational training, asserting that the
Tuskegee program was far too restrictive. W. E. Burghardt Du Bois, an
African American scholar, was interested in fulfilling aspirations through
routes other than the industrial curriculum urged by Washington. "Mr.
Washington's programme practically accepts the alleged inferiority of the
Negro races," charged Du Bois in 1903.[15]

No two African American leaders differed more profoundly in their
philosophies of education; no two personalities stood in such striking contrast. Slight and nervous, with a neatly trimmed goatee, Du Bois resembled
a European aristocrat. Unlike Washington, whose first house had been a
slave's hut, Du Bois never approached the realities of bondage. Born in Great
Barrington, Massachusetts, shortly after the Civil War, he grew up in an
environment relatively untouched by racial prejudice. His family had long
been free. Proud and outspoken, aloof from the common masses, he never
forgot his family heritage. When he first traveled South to attend Fisk
University, he was shocked by people's way of life. Du Bois studied in
Germany, earned his doctorate from Harvard University in 1895, and wrote
extensively about southern conditions. He devoted a large part of his life to
social protest. With a brooding passion, he lucidly described the forced
peonage of his people and the harsh injustice of the southern caste system. In
1910 he became editor of *Crisis,* a journal of the newly formed National
Association for the Advancement of Colored People (NAACP). Under Du
Bois' forceful editorship, the magazine condemned proposals to establish
segregated public schools in Philadelphia, Chicago, and Columbus, Ohio.

At the very time Booker T. Washington was urging economic self-
advancement and counseling moderation in race relations, Du Bois and his
followers were castigating the whites and pointing to the sad plight of
African Americans in southern society. "All this is bitter hard," he cried.
"And many a man and city and people have found in it excuse for sulking,
and brooding, and listless waiting."[16] The erection of caste barriers and the
overemphasis on industrial training, Du Bois asserted, stifled aspirations.

Winning civic equality, Du Bois argued, requires intellectual and
professional leadership, personifying the best in the African American heritage. Furthermore, the African American citizen must demonstrate equality
with white people in culture, ability, and scholarship. This, Du Bois
declared, demanded an education far different from the manual training of
Tuskegee which, he charged, perpetuated a servile image of his race. In later

years he became more outspoken, accusing Washington and his "Tuskegee Machine" of exercising dictatorial control over people's affairs.[17] There were other critics, too, who argued in the same forceful terms that the African American should have an opportunity for self-fulfillment through the type of education and the facilities available to white children.

Instead of militant protest, Washington, who never joined the NAACP, called for patience and advocated a gradual remedy of social injustices through training and work. "Poverty and ignorance have affected the black man just as they affected the white man," he declared in the summer of 1884. ". . . But the day is breaking, and education will bring the complete light."[18] It is futile, Washington argued, to try to cross the bridge to civic equality in one leap. Do not demand political privileges, he told his people, until you are able to discharge them creditably. Listening to Washington's words, the restless young followers of Du Bois, born free and still uneducated and destitute, wondered perhaps how long they would have to wait and how hard they would have to struggle to win from the white southerner their constitutional rights of citizenship.

Thus the racial issue was joined on these and other controversial points. No problem in American history has weighed more heavily on the conscience of the southern people than that of the racial dilemma. Long a symbol of strife, the African American people appeared caught in a chasm widened by Radical vengeance. There still lurked in the mind of the white southerner the fear of African American domination. This fear alone was a heavy burden for the white people—a fear that all southerners must eventually overcome. "More and more we must learn to think not in terms of race or color or language or religion or political boundaries, but in terms of humanity," Washington urged.[19] At the dawn of the twentieth century, such faith and wisdom were wise counsel for all.

Walter Hines Page and the Southern Education Movement

By the turn of the century, southern poverty and depression had become educational issues of national concern. Prodded by a few southern leaders and some noted philanthropists from the North, the South was beginning at long last to respond to a new drive to extend public education to all citizens. Several conferences were called throughout the southern states. The most important of these was the so-called Ogden movement, or the Conference for Education in the South.[20] The first meeting was held at Capon Springs, West Virginia, in 1898, under the leadership of the Reverend Mr. Edward Abbott, from Cambridge, Massachusetts. This initial conference was organized as the Conference for Christian Education in the South. The second and third conferences, meeting in 1899 and 1900, were more secular in tone and attracted several civic and business leaders.

In 1901 the conference established the Southern Education Board. Two years later, the General Education Board, incorporated by a congressional act, was formed. Heavily supported by John D. Rockefeller, Jr., the General Education Board directed much of its talent and funds toward the South to help provide for free public schools on community-wide bases. The positive force this large-scale movement exerted in uplifting the quality of southern schools stemmed in part from the idealism and dedication of a new educational leadership.

Walter Hines Page, perhaps more than any other white southerner, personified the new leadership so desperately needed in the post–Civil War era. A native of North Carolina, Page was one of the promoters of the Conference for Education in the South. He helped to organize the Southern Education Board and was a member of the General Education Board when it was first established. When only twenty-three years of age, he wrote newspaper articles urging more schools for southern children. His repeated efforts to redeem "The Forgotten Man"[21] (the so-called poor white trash) from sickness and ignorance through a free public-school system became the dominant theme of the southern education movement. *"I believe in the perpetual regeneration of society, in the immortality of democracy, and in growth everlasting,"* Page declared in 1901.[22]

Page, who traveled widely and whose versatile interests spanned the globe, occasionally chastised the southern people for their provincialism and extreme conservatism. He ridiculed those who discussed only "before-the-war" topics, referring to them as "mummies." He labeled "little sisters of the dead" those elder women who devoted all their time writing poems about the dead and forming societies in commemoration of Confederate soldiers. He urged the people to stop living in the past and to strive now for their land and its people. "The new South cannot build up its possible civilization merely by looking backward and sighing," he declared in an article published in 1881 in the *Atlantic Monthly.*

Acutely aware of "the white man's burden," Page worried, too, about the "dark shadow" that "is visible everywhere—negroes of all shades of colour, utterly cast out of politics, yet getting on in the world in every other way; and politics itself an unspeakable degradation." The deprivation of the southern African Americans casts an "insidious gloom" over "a beautiful land," Page wrote in 1899. "The white man's caste," which is "more tightly drawn and more heavily laid on than in any other land I ever saw," is like a "smouldering volcano."[23] Denounced as a traitor, Page left North Carolina and achieved great distinction in northern journalism. "Thoughtful men were not free [in the South] because of the mass of unthinking men about them," he remarked in 1904.[24]

THE EXPANDING FORCES
OF BUSINESS ENTERPRISE

The Triumph of Northern Industrialism

While a devastated South fought and struggled to survive, the North, ironically, passed through the tragic years of war and reconstruction more prosperous than ever. The North, in fact, was experiencing a business boom unparalleled in American history. Capital was abundant for large-scale enterprise, war profits were huge, and graft was so commonplace as scarcely to draw a second glance. Jefferson's vision of a nation of small farmers faded before the startling rise of a new industrial United States.

Charles A. Beard and Mary R. Beard, in *The Rise of American Civilization,* attributed this industrial growth to a "Second American Revolution," which shifted the national hegemony from a "planting aristocracy of the South" to "the capitalists, laborers, and farmers of the North and West."[25] Undoubtedly the Civil War promoted an economic revolution in the United States and greatly accelerated the emergence of an industrial economy.

This great transformation merely accompanied and followed the war and was not caused by it. Long before secession, the North surpassed the South in urbanization and economic expansion. As northern population increased and cities, factories, and railroads expanded, the North was well on the road toward business prosperity. The chief obstacle was a southern minority that maintained control of the national government. But the South seceded from the Union and relinquished its veto in the Senate over federal policy when Abraham Lincoln was elected President in 1860. Thus, the ascension of the Republican party to political power and the secession of the South opened the way for a vast economic victory in the North. The path was clear for the implementation of an economic program that the South had so vehemently opposed; a coalition of northern industrialists and bankers and western farmers persuaded Congress to enact a high protective tariff benefiting manufacturers and to pass a Homestead Act promising free land to northern and western farmers. Economically, the war was already a northern triumph long before the bloody battle at Gettysburg.

Closely identified with the revolutionary changes occurring in the North were the refining of oil and the production of steel. Shrewd and thrifty, John D. Rockefeller decided in 1862, while other young men his age were patriotically marching off to war, that the oil industry had a profitable future. Only twenty-two when Fort Sumter was fired on, he exhibited unusual business acumen. Rockefeller invested in a refinery, and just before the end of the war he launched on a career of great expansion. By 1872, with monopoly in mind, he was well on the way toward control of a vast oil empire that would eventually comprise over 90 percent of the nation's output.

During the same years Andrew Carnegie, the son of an immigrant Scottish weaver, wisely assessed the possibilities of steel for rails and bridges, as he busily worked for six dollars a week as a telegraph operator for the Pennsylvania Railroad. His spectacular climb from an impoverished childhood to the status of multimillionaire steel magnate is one of the United States's great success stories. For Rockefeller, Carnegie, and other barons of the northern industry, war and peace proved opportune times for colossal fortune building.

Behind the great empires of the industrial giants were scores of innovations: steel girders, bridges, rails, and new industrial machines of all kinds. The United States Patent Office issued close to 62,000 patents before the end of the war. From 1865 to 1900 the number increased to over 600,000.

The business boom spiraled upward from 1865 to 1900, spurred on by an elaborate system of national communications. The 30,000 miles of railroads in 1860 had increased to 193,000 by 1900. A growing network of trunk lines, including five transcontinental routes, moved freight and passengers among the cities and across the nation. "Commodore" Cornelius Vanderbilt, for example, forced through devious means the consolidation of several small railroads between New York and Chicago into the profitable New York Central, the best route through heavily populated communities. While the railroads contributed substantially to northern wealth, Vanderbilt and other railroad owners often charged discriminatory rates and engaged in socially irresponsible practices.

Meanwhile, the recently invented telephone permitted more direct contacts in an expanding business community, encouraging enterprising manufacturers to increase their sales volumes through large-scale distribution. By the turn of the century, the Bell System operated 677,000 telephones; within two decades the number approached 6,000,000, with coast-to-coast lines in full operation. A hierarchy of wholesalers and brokers furnished the necessary credit and facilities for national exchange. Capital moved more freely than goods, as thousands of investors bought the stocks of new corporations that expanded and flourished in the free-enterprise system.

In a new social setting, old economic conflicts flared anew and became more bitter, sharpened by the intensity of a fierce competitive struggle for larger profits. As the new masters of capital and industry vied with one another in an unrestrained market, the most powerful interests formed monopolies, eliminating competition and overthrowing those of weaker economic status. In an era of no income taxes, the earnings of Rockefeller, Carnegie, Vanderbilt, and others at the top of the social structure were enormous. Carnegie, for example, had an estimated income of $10 million per year from 1894 to 1899.

To justify their actions, the multimillionaires resorted to the doctrine of social Darwinism.[26] Imported from England, this concept adapted to society

Charles Darwin's biological theory of the struggle for existence and the survival of the fittest. Herbert Spencer applied the law of the jungle to the economic system in a manner that delighted the self-made industrial giants. "While the law may be sometimes hard for the individual, it is best for the race, because it insures the survival of the fittest in every department," Carnegie declared in 1889. "We accept and welcome, therefore, as conditions to which we must accommodate ourselves, great inequality of environment, the concentration of business, industrial and commercial, in the hands of a few, and the law of competition between these, as being not only beneficial, but essential for the future progress of the race."[27] During the Enlightenment and the great reform era, acquisitive gain was viewed not so much as an exclusive goal reserved for only a few but rather as a means toward improving society in general. Now the monopolistic power of a few great titans of American industry and capital was based increasingly on materialistic values as ends in themselves. Such a rationale differed sharply from older patterns of thought and symbolized in a dramatic fashion the great transformation occurring in American society.

As business enterprise grew and flourished, the number of children employed by manufacturers reached alarming proportions. By the early 1900s, about 1.7 million boys and girls under the age of sixteen were hired for long hours of work in the fields and factories. With the growing use of machines unequipped with safety measures, industrial accidents occurred with shocking frequency. For example, exhausted children, working sixteen hours daily in the factories, would carelessly lean over a loom to catch a broken thread and, catching instead their own hair in a machine, be scalped as the machine turned again. Working conditions were just as deplorable: cold, filthy, dark sweatshops or factories were without ventilation, rest rooms, and fire escapes.

Mary Harris Jones (1830–1930) and the Struggle to Overcome the Abuses of Child Labor

Born in Cork, Ireland, on May 1, 1830, Mary Harris attended schools and the normal school in Toronto, Canada, where her father took the family while he worked as a railroad construction laborer. While teaching in Memphis, Tennessee, in 1861, she married a loyal member of the Iron Molders' Union named Jones. Her husband and four small children died in a yellow-fever epidemic that ravaged Memphis in 1867; four years later she lost all her possessions in the Chicago Fire that destroyed her home and newly established dressmaking shop. The bereft widow then dedicated her life to trade-union work for the newly organized Knights of Labor.

For five decades she was active as a labor organizer throughout the United States, speaking out eloquently in favor of higher wages and better working conditions for the workers in the steel and cotton mills, in the copper and coal mines, on the railroads, and in the garment industry. "I have espoused the cause of the laboring class in general and of suffering childhood in particular," she wrote in 1903. ". . . The children [must be] freed from the workshops and sent to school."[28]

Known as Mother Jones, she demonstrated a crusader's ability to win publicity and government attention to the plight of the children. In 1903, to dramatize the evils of child labor, she conducted a caravan of striking children on an overland march from the textile mills of Lexington, Pennsylvania, to the home of President Theodore Roosevelt at Oyster Bay, New York.

During the following two years she obtained employment in the cotton mills in Alabama, Georgia, and South Carolina to obtain personal evidence of child labor conditions. She committed herself increasingly to the workers' struggles against low wages, long hours, and depressed working conditions. A strong individualist, Mother Jones was a social activist, passionately humane, utterly fearless, and forever dedicated to improving the lives of young children in the mines and factories. She died in Silver Springs, Maryland, seven months after her centennial birthday.

The Drive for Efficiency

Despite the incredibly unsafe working conditions in the factories, business leaders at the conventions of the National Association of Manufacturers (NAM) harshly criticized "the narrow vision of the school room" and the "gross inefficiency" of the common schools. In the minds of the new leaders of industry and finance, the curricula proposed by the early school reformers could no longer meet the needs of an industrial society. Theodore Search, the second president of the National Association of Manufacturers, remarked in 1898 that "it is well to hold fast to the classical and literary studies. They have their place in all educational systems, but it is unfair to the great material interests of the land to leave out of account the obvious demands of industry and commerce." Other business leaders were less restrained in their criticisms. "You thought the school that had to do with a man above his ears educated the man—never!" exclaimed F. W. Gunsaulus, president of the Armour Institute, in 1908. "An overwrought and cruel method of brain stuffing!" asserted NAM in a reference to the public-school system. "The stupid theory that education means A, B, C. Why, the hands need just as much practice as does the brain." Other businessmen also charged the common schools with being "repressive" and with "dulling the instinct" of children to work with their hands. "Our schools have acted as if the child might as well be an idiot as be concrete-minded," remarked NAM in 1912.[29]

The shortage of vocational training courses in the public schools was deplored by the business community. "To give special training to the two millions of people engaged in the professions and to leave out educational facilities along lines of specific training for the thirty millions engaged in productive work in this country is to cast a slur upon manual labor," declared Arthur D. Dean, special supervisor of industrial education in Boston. The *Nation's Business* voiced the same idea and argued editorially that the "aim of Education must be to prepare each child for self-support and thus make every school of the nation a place for life preparation." Unless vocational training courses were firmly established in the public-school curricula, warned the National Chamber's Committee on Education in 1916, "the industrial and commercial position of the United States as a nation will be progressively impaired."[30]

In advocating vocational training in the public schools, business leaders frequently pointed out that many youngsters were forced to drop out of the schools after the elementary grades. "Half of all our children leave school by the end of the sixth grade with only he rudiments of education which, in large part, they speedily forget, and with no preparation or guidance for life work," declared the National Chamber in a resolution passed at its first meeting in 1931. "The statistics are startling, and in sad contrast to the better practice of most of the nations of northern Europe." According to the NAM Committee on Industrial Education, 60 to 65 percent of the children in the common schools in 1914 dropped out by the end of the fifth or sixth grade, "having learned nothing but a little reading, writing and arithmetic, which most of them quickly forget."[31]

NAM berated the public-school systems for what it called "gross inefficiency." Children were being sent out into the "alleys and dark ways" of an industrial world for which they had no real preparation. "As it is today, the criminal boy sent to some one of our reformatories, has a better chance of becoming a skilled workman and earning larger wages than the average boy who is not a criminal, in our public schools," remarked one NAM member. As another businessman put it: "The factory is where the school should be . . . . In that way we will get results and get something that will be a benefit to industrial America." NAM spokesman S. Parkes Cadman voiced the same idea: "It is important that we should teach our children the humanities, but it is also important that we should teach them the nobility of digging a ditch or plowing a lot or turning at the lathe." The public schools should "be systematized, thoroughly, comprehensively, and with the sole view of utmost efficiency; efficiency in every direction to the last degree, and for the last child."[32]

Efficiency might be measured in a variety of ways; and one way the business community deemed a fair measurement was the value produced by an institution in terms of dollars and cents. In the eyes of business leaders during this period, the public schools were usually considered a poor investment. NAM President Search declared in his annual report in 1898 that "we expend very large sums of money in city and county for public education that is for the most part of such a character that it avails the people little in their practical affairs." Ten years later President James W. Van Cleave of the NAM decried the number of public schools that expended tax funds on the "merely ornamental branches of learning." After World War I, a NAM official exclaimed that the nation gave "public funds, millions of dollars of the money of the taxpayers, to train anybody who wants to be a first, second, third or worse kind of a lawyer, but not a dollar to anyone who wants to serve Mr. Leland or any of the rest of you with high intelligence in your factories!"[33]

Indeed, according to the business community, this financial outlay for the public schools was a waste of the taxpayers' money. Chairman H. E. Miles of the NAM Committee on Industrial Education complained in 1911 that $450 million was being expended annually in the United States to support a common school system based upon "theories and not upon realities; upon dreams of things as they might be, not upon the actualities of things as they are, and as they will be as far into the future as man can see." The following year Miles asserted, "The Common schools of our country cost, in mere maintenance, $500,000,000 a year. They use, in addition, plants of the value of a billion dollars, and far the greater part of this expenditure is for only half the children. It is far too great an outlay for an efficient return." In 1914 Miles concluded that "the United States [was] spending a half billion dollars a year teaching nobody anything in particular." Six years later, at the twenty-fifth annual convention of the association, NAM Treasurer William P. White of the Lowell (Mass.) Paper Tube Corporation declared:

> I live in a manufacturing town. . . . We are going to spend over a million dollars for a high school to teach the children of the working people of that town white collar, starched collar jobs. . . . The expenditure that is being now made [for the public school system], and the laws that are being passed for its expenditure are as absolutely a waste as though it were thrown into the gutter. (Applause).[34]

On the eve of the Great Depression, Howell Cheney, chairman of the NAM Committee on Junior Education and Employment, charged that "industry was getting by far the prejudiced end of the selection; that more and more as this public school institution developed, the superior workers, the ablest minds went on and went beyond industry and perhaps turned their backs upon it." The business community, on the other hand, had been getting boys and girls incapable of completing minimum requirements in the public schools. Even those pupils who managed to complete a high-school education were "inefficient," as far as Cheney was concerned. In 1927 he told businessmen that "forty per cent of high school graduates haven't a command of simple arithmetic, cannot multiply, subtract and divide correctly in simple numbers and in fractions. Over forty per cent of them cannot accurately express themselves in the English language or cannot correctly write in their mother tongue."[35]

Even worse, in the eyes of business leaders, "it is for want of a measure of practical education that these abstract-minded youth develop to such an extent into impractical, overzealous, unbalanced theorists often referred to in reproach of the educated classes." In 1911 NAM President John Kirby, Jr., cautioned a group of students at Kenyon College "as to the direction in which you permit your thoughts to flow, for 'as a man thinketh so is he.' " Kirby concluded his speech by asking the graduating seniors if they planned to "go out of here brimful of theories and distorted conceptions, to help swell the great army of cranks and malcontents." The following year, in an address before the seventeenth annual convention of the NAM, Kirby declared: "I have said before, and I repeat now, that among the greatest enemies of orderly government and sound institutions are the men and women who are carried away by whimsical notions . . . , who follow leaders in society whose minds are dwarfed by illogical and impractical ideals." These "impractical" idealists, he continued, "would make a kaleidoscope of the Constitution and a football of our Courts, simply because the Constitution acts as a balance wheel to their emotional tendencies and because the Courts, being consti-tuted of human intelligence, are not infallible." The Constitution represents the permanent will of the people and is not to be cast aside by the whim of the hour or the opinion of the minority, Kirby explained. It was wisely devised as a check against the "tyranny of the mob."[36]

Kirby and other leaders in the business community did not blame the student alone for any "distorted conceptions": the chief criticism for spread-ing fallacious theories was hurled at both the teachers and the textbooks. The NAM accused the colleges and high schools of being "prolific sources of socialistic recruiting" and contended that academic freedom had its limits. "The principles of Socialism are taking hold upon the minds of youth through teaching permitted, or in the name of 'academic freedom' actually encouraged, in our schools, colleges, universities, and even in theological seminaries," *American Industries* declared editorially in 1913. "The teaching of false history and false science would not be tolerated anywhere. It is less important that young men should be safeguarded against false teaching in matters that go to the very groundwork of their mortality [*sic*] and their citizenship?" Three years later *American Industries* censured those who, the editors charged, used the cloak of academic freedom to hide "subversive" teachings. "It is claptrap, sensationalism, appeal to the groundlings, the unwelcome notoriety they give the institution, that forces at last the hand of the trustees. Then the other rises about 'academic freedom,' freedom to cheapen the reputation of the university and repel students. Academic freedom!" The high schools and the colleges were helping to create "a condition of distrust in our American institutions, which threatens the stability of the nation," NAM declared in 1912. These schools and colleges are full of educators "whose heads are laden with all sorts of 'isms' and falacious [*sic*] theories, which they are instilling into the minds of young men who are sent to them to be educated," NAM continued.

> We are working to counteract this condition through the dissemination of literature tending to operate as an antidote for such teachings, to remove the weeds which have grown up in the heads of some college professors and students, and to set them to thinking on straight and practical lines. It is a slow, tedious and expensive undertaking, but it must be done if future generations are to be made up of clear thinking, practical men.

Local manufacturers were urged to investigate what was being taught their own sons and to find out how much money was being spent by taxpayers to spread doctrines the business community abhorred.[37] Apparently this concern over textbook content has never been far from the minds of business leaders.[38]

Growing Business Influence on Education

It is significant to note how quickly American educators absorbed the business creed and responded to repeated demands for "efficiency." During the early decades of the twentieth century, the schools slowly adopted a business ideology that stressed the need for efficient workers and citizens. School administrators, in particular, applied the values and techniques of an industrial order to public schooling in a democracy. According to Raymond E. Callahan, "the wholesale adoption of the basic values, as well as the techniques of the business-industrial world [from 1910 to 1929] was a mistake in an institution whose primary purpose was the education of children."[39] By introducing new administrative techniques and devising all sorts of tests and evaluative instruments, educators sought to eliminate "waste," accelerate "promotions," and increase "efficiency" in the public schools. This development had profound consequences: it narrowed the function of the public school by teaching specific skills and attitudes that mirrored the business world and molded the individual to fit into an industrial society.

FOR DISCUSSION AND CRITICAL THOUGHT

1. Read Chapter 10, "An American Tragedy in Education," of Raymond E. Callahan, *Education and the Cult of Efficiency* (University of Chicago Press, 1963). Was the movement for "accountability" and retrenchment during

the mid-twentieth century rooted in the "efficiency" drive of the business community? Comment critically.

2. Compare and contrast the views of Booker T. Washington and W. E. Burghardt Du Bois regarding the education of African Americans during the post–Civil War period. Which approach do you feel would have been more beneficial in advancing the status of African Americans? Explain.

3. Does Martin Luther King's idea of social change through nonviolence reflect Booker T. Washington's conservative philosophy? Explain.

4. What were the effects of the Civil War on public schooling in the southern states?

NOTES

1. See Bruce Catton, *A Stillness at Appomattox* (New York: Doubleday, 1953), p. 189. "There were so many deaths that affected the outcome of the war not a particle—deaths that had nothing to do with the progress of the campaign or with the great struggle for union and freedom but that simply happened, doing no one any good." The battles were, continues Catton, "a madman's business."

2. Sidney Andrews, "Scenes in the Track of Sherman's Army, Columbia [South Carolina], September 12, 1865," as reprinted in Louis M. Hacker, ed., *The Shaping of the American Tradition* (New York: Columbia University Press, 1947), 2:656.

3. From a letter to his class at Williams College in 1874, as quoted in Charles William Dabney, *Universal Education in the South* (Chapel Hill: University of North Carolina Press, 1936), 2:462.

4. See C. Vann Woodward, *The Strange Career of Jim Crow* (3rd rev. ed.; New York: Oxford University Press Galaxy Book, 1974).

5. Nevertheless, the lives of some were filled with infinite courage. For a remarkable "autobiography of an illiterate man," see Theodore Rosengarten, *All God's Dangers: The Life of Nate Shaw* (New York: Knopf, 1974). "What happens to the history of a people not accustomed to writing things down?" asks Rosengarten. "To whom poverty and illiteracy makes wills, diaries, and letters superfluous?" (p. xxiii).

6. There was an interesting northern attempt during the war to educate about ten thousand slaves deserted by the southern white inhabitants of the Sea Islands of South Carolina. See Willie Lee Rose, *Rehearsal for Reconstruction: The Port Royal Experiment.*

7. Edgar W. Knight, *Education in the United States* (3rd rev. ed.; Boston: Ginn, 1951), p. 468.

8. C. Vann Woodward, *Origins of the New South, 1877–1913, A History of the South,* vol. 9, ed. Wendell Holmes Stephenson and E. Merton Coulter (Baton Rouge: Louisiana State University Press, 1951), p. 61.

9. Ibid., pp. 61–62.

10. Dabney, *Universal Education in the South,* 1:302.

11. See August Meier, *Negro Thought in America, 1880–1915: Racial Ideologies in the Age of Booker T. Washington* (Ann Arbor: University of Michigan Press, 1963), pp. 85–118. Meier asserts that "Washington, in fact, showed little or no originality in his program" (p. 97).

12. For some of Washington's most important ideas, see Booker T. Washington, *Character Building: Being Addresses Delivered on Sunday Evenings to the Students of Tuskegee Institute* (New York: Doubleday, Page, 1902).

13. At one time, during a lecture tour, Washington even traveled from Boston to Atlanta specifically to present a five-minute address to a southern white group. See *Up from Slavery: An Autobiography* (Boston: Houghton Mifflin, 1901; reissued by Doubleday in 1953), pp. 204–205.

14. "The Negro and His Relation to the Economic Progress of the South" (Address delivered before the Southern Industrial Convention at Huntsville, Alabama, 12 October 1899), in E. Davidson Washington, ed., *Selected Speeches of Booker T. Washington* (Garden City, N.Y.: Doubleday, Doran, 1932), p. 78.

15. W. E. Burghardt Du Bois, *The Souls of Black Folk: Essays and Sketches* (2nd ed.; Chicago: A.C. McClurg, 1903), p. 50.

16. Ibid., p. 76.

17. Du Bois died on 28 August 1963. For a vivid characterization, gleaned from a personal interview with Du Bois shortly before his death, see Ralph McGill, "W. E. B. Du Bois," *Atlantic Monthly* 216 (November 1965): 78–81. Du Bois's bitterness never waned, writes McGill. Mincing no words, Du Bois revealed, as before, his deep hatred for what he had earlier called "The White World's Vermin and Filth" (a verse from *Darkwater* [1920]). He renounced his native land, adopted communism, and at the age of ninety-four became a citizen of Ghana.

18. "The Educational Outlook in the South" (Address delivered before the National Education Association, Madison, Wisconsin, 16 July 1884) in E. D. Washington, ed., *Selected Speeches of Booker T. Washington*, p. 10.

19. Quoted in Samuel R. Spencer, Jr., *Booker T. Washington and the Negro's Place in American Life* (Boston: Little, Brown, 1955), p. 201.

20. This movement is discussed in Dabney, *Universal Education in the South*, vol. 2, "The Southern Education Movement," passim. See also Edwards Jenning Carter, "The Educational Awakening in the South" (Ph.D dissertation, University of North Carolina, 1943), pp. 34–93.

21. "The Forgotten Man" is the title of a commencement address that Page delivered at North Carolina State College at Greensboro in June 1897. See Walter Hines Page, *The Rebuilding of Old Commonwealths, Being Essays Towards the Training of the Forgotten Man in the Southern States* (New York: Doubleday, Page, 1902), pp. 1–47.

22. Walter Hines Page, "The School That Built a Town" (Commencement address delivered at the State Normal School at Athens, Ga., 11 December 1901), in ibid., p. 102. Italics in original.

23. Letter dated 2 March 1899, from Walter Hines Page to Alice Wilson Page, as reprinted in Burton J. Hendrick, ed., *The Training of an American. The Earlier Life and Letters of Walter H. Page, 1855–1913* (Boston and New York: Houghton Mifflin, 1928), pp. 393–395.

24. Walter Hines Page, "The Unfilled Ambition of the South," in *Proceedings of the Conference for Education in the South, The Seventh Session, Birmingham, Ala., 26–28 April 1904,* p. 107.

25. Charles A. Beard and Mary R. Beard, *The Rise of American Civilization* (New York: Macmillan, 1930) 2:52–121.

26. See Richard Hofstadter, *Social Darwinism in American Thought* (Boston: Beacon Press, 1955; originally published in 1944 by the University of Pennsylvania Press).

27. Andrew Carnegie, "Wealth," *North American Review* 148 (June 1889): 653–64.

28. Letter to President Theodore Roosevelt dated 30 July 1903, as reprinted in Philip S. Foner (ed.), *Mother Jones Speaks: Collected Writings and Speeches* (New York: Monad Press for the Anchor Foundation, 1983), p. 555.

29. National Association of Manufacturers, the following: *Circular No. 21,* "Annual Report of the President" (Philadelphia, 1898), p. 20; *Pamphlet No. 4,* "The Next Step in Education" (New York, n.d.; Address delivered on 15 April 1908, by Dr. F. W. Gunsaulus, president of the Armour Institute, Chicago), pp. 21–22; *Pamphlet No. 5,* "The Boy and the Law" (New York, 1908), p. 18; *Proceedings of the Seventeenth Annual Convention Held at New York City, 20, 21, and 22 May 1912* (New York, 1912), pp. 151, 156–58; *Pamphlet No. 28,* "Industrial Education" (New York, n.d.; Report of the Committee on Industrial Education Submitted at the Seventeenth Annual Convention in New York City on 21 May 1912, pp. 4–5, 14.

30. National Association of Manufacturers, *Proceedings* (1907), p. 131; *Nation's Business* 1 (15 April 1913): 2; ibid. 1 (15 September 1913): 12; H. E. Miles, "Training the Children for Efficient Lives," ibid. 2 (15 April 1914): 14–15; "Commerce in the Month's News, " ibid. 4 (June 1916): 2; and Chamber of Commerce of the United States, *Report of the Committee on Education* (Washington, 1916), p. 4.

31. Chamber of Commerce of the United States, *Policies of the Chamber of Commerce of the United States* (Washington, 1929), p. 27; and National Association of Manufacturers, *Proceedings of the Nineteenth Annual Convention Held at New York City, 19 and 20 May 1914* (New York, 1914), pp. 99–100.

32. National Association of Manufacturers, the following: *Pamphlet No. 22,* "Industrial Education" (New York, n.d.; Report of the Committee on Industrial Education at the Sixteenth Annual Convention in New York City on 16 May 1911), p. 11; *Proceedings* (1914), p. 101; *Pamphlet No. 5* (1908), p. 28; *Proceedings* (1907), pp. 111–12; *Proceedings of the Twenty-fifth Annual Convention Held at New York City, 17, 18, and 19 May 1920* (New York, 1920), p. 104; *Pamphlet No. 8,* "The Open Door" (New York, 1908), p. 13; *Proceedings* (1912), p. 151; and *Pamphlet No. 28* (1912), p. 5.

33. National Association of Manufacturers, the following: *Circular No. 21* (1898), p. 19; *Pamphlet No. 9,* "Industrial Education as an Essential Factor in our National Prosperity," by James W. Van Cleave (New York, n.d.; Address before the National Society for the Promotion of Industrial Education, Chicago, 23 January 1908), p. 10; and *Proceedings of the Twenty-fourth Annual Convention Held at New York City, 19, 20, and 21 May 1919* (New York, 1919), p. 177.

34. National Association of Manufacturers, the following: *Pamphlet No. 22,* (1911),

p. 5; *Proceedings* (1912), p. 155; *Proceedings* (1914), p. 101; and *Proceedings* (1920), pp. 103–104.

35. Howell Cheney, "The Relations of Industry to Public Education," *American Industries* 30 (October 1929): 81–82; and National Association of Manufacturers, *Proceedings of the Thirty-second Annual Convention Held at Chattanooga, Tenn., 25, 26, and 27 October 1927* (New York, 1927), p. 269.

36. National Association of Manufacturers, the following: *Pamphlet No. 28,* (1912), p. 14; *Circular No. 39,* "Proceedings of the Fifth Annual Convention" (Philadelphia, 1900), pp. 91–105; *Pamphlet No. 20,* "Cruel Unionism" (New York, n.d.; Address delivered by John Kirby, Jr., at Kenyon College, Gambier, Ohio, 3 February 1911), p. 21; and *Pamphlet No. 25,* "An Address of John Kirby, Jr." (New York, n.d.; delivered at the Seventeenth Annual Convention of the National Association of Manufacturers, Waldorf-Astoria Hotel, New York City, 21 May 1912), pp. 12–19.

37. National Association of Manufacturers, Report of the Committee on Readjustments After the War, *Proceedings* (1919), p. 107; *Open Shop Bulletin,* 7 February 1921, No. 4; *American Industries* 13 (July 1913): 11; ibid. 16 (February 1916): 22; and ibid. 12 (February 1912): 43.

38. See pp. 254–257.

39. Raymond E. Callahan, *Education and the Cult of Efficiency: A Study of the Social Forces That Have Shaped the Administration of the Public Schools* (Chicago: University of Chicago Press, 1962), p. 244. See also Merle Curti, *The Social Ideas of American Educators, with New Chapter on the Last Twenty-five Years* (Paterson, N.J.: Littlefield, Adams, 1959; published originally in 1935 by the American Historical Association), pp. 230–232.

CHAPTER 6

Toward a New Pedagogy

The democratic ideal demands of the school that it shall give the child's own experience a social value; that it shall teach him to direct his activities and adjust them to those of other people.

JANE ADDAMS, *Democracy and Social Ethics*, 1902

The public school has done its best for us foreigners, and for the country, when it has made us into good Americans.

MARY ANTIN, *The Promised Land*, 1912

THE SOCIAL SCENE

The Impact of Urbanism

The rise of the urban United States after the Civil War was inextricably linked to the triumph of industrialism. As factories expanded, the rural townspeople swarmed into the bustling cities in rising numbers to escape the growing depression and drudgery of the farm and to seek new jobs and opportunities. Steadily and quickly, business enterprise became a vital part of a new configuration, dominated by the great metropolis.

The growth of cities was phenomenal. After 1900 one of every three Americans lived in a city with a population of eight thousand or more. For example, in 1860 New York had a population of 850,000 and was next in size to London and Paris. By 1914, New York's population had increased to about 4 million. Philadelphia, with a population of about 563,000 in 1860, had grown to more than 1,500,000 by 1914. At the same time, rural life everywhere, depleted by this exodus to the cities, was poverty-stricken and filled with despair.

Unlike the small homogeneous town of the rural United States, the city of the new industrial age contained a highly mobile and impersonal human aggregation, pushed and pulled by competing interests that hastened a breakdown in traditional values and ways of life. In the rural communities the family and the church were the most important social forces in the lives of the people. However, in the large cities these institutions became less influential: the teeming cities, in fact, were vast collections of uprooted human beings, usually strangers, sometimes unfriendly and even hostile toward one another. This inhospitable environment, devoid of such cohesive elements as the family and the church, added immeasurably to the social distresses of urbanism.

The "New" Immigration and the Issue of Americanization

The urban growth of American society was also accelerated by a vast influx of non-English-speaking immigrants who crowded into the cities. While the stream of newcomers from northern and western Europe continued unabated, another tidal wave began about 1882. Approximately ten million Russians, Poles, Bohemians, Hungarians, Slovaks, Greeks, and Rumanians emigrated to the United States from southern and eastern Europe between 1880 and 1914. In 1905 alone, over one million new immigrants arrived on American shores. Many were Jewish refugees and impoverished peasants from Polish and Russian ghettos. Their patterns of life differed sharply from those of the native-born Americans and of immigrants coming from northern and western Europe.

Unlike the rural Americans who migrated from the farms to the cities, most of the Europeans drifted to the slums and congested tenements. "The tenement districts of New York are places in which thousands of people are living in the smallest space in which it is possible for human beings to exist—crowded together in dark, ill-ventilated rooms, in many of which the sunlight never enters and in most of which fresh air is unknown," reported a state-sponsored Tenement Housing Commission in 1903. "They are centres of disease, poverty, vice and crime, where it is a marvel, not that some children grow up to be thieves, drunkards, prostitutes, but that so many should ever grow up to be decent and self-respecting."[1] Each nationality resisted assimilation and segregated itself, clinging tenaciously to Old World languages, mores, and political orientations. Industrial railway officials, who were usually responsible for importing the new immigrants, hired the willing and naïve foreigners for menial and underpaid jobs. Only with good fortune and great perseverance could immigrants from eastern and southern Europe climb immediately above the low status to which they were at first consigned upon arrival in the United States.

The infusion into a free society of new citizens with such diverse customs and ideologies created a host of social problems and added new dimensions to the old issue of Americanization. Jammed into the cities, the new immigrants succumbed to the squalor and disease-breeding conditions of tenement housing into which poverty forced them. Others, bewildered by a strange environment, simply congregated with relief in ghettos that simulated Old World societies. Some with funds traveled immediately west to work in the mines, on farms, or on the railroads. But the great mass of newcomers could not possibly have moved to the agricultural frontier on arrival because they were completely penniless. Most of the immigrants remained near the port of entry, working in the cities or wandering along the streets seeking jobs or diversion. "It is impossible to describe the mud, the dirt, the filth, the stinking humidity, the nuisances, the disorder of these streets," commented an Italian dramatist who toured the immigrant quarters in New York City in 1898. "The saddest sight of all is that of the children, thrown half naked into the open streets. . . . I visited those streets in the middle of November and the little creatures had nothing but shirts to their backs."[2] For thousands of native and immigrant workers, separated from family and divided by religion and national origin, rootless and anonymous, the city was no more than an industrial jungle marked by extremes of poverty and wealth. By 1900 the crowded, filthy tenement conditions of the poor, laboring classes were as bad as those of the worst European slums.

The immigrants not only alarmed the native-born Americans by their foreign ways but also shocked the dominant Protestant citizens by their rigid devotion to Judaism or Catholicism. The newcomers of foreign birth clung together in racial groups and worshiped in synagogues and churches like those in their homelands. Some erected tabernacle booths to the rear of the tenements or paraded in front in honor of the saints. Others organized fraternal orders and printed newspapers in their native tongues. There were formed, for instance, such associations as the Polish National Alliance (1880) and the Order of Sons of Italy (1905). Even more significant, by establishing their own foreign-language parochial schools and refusing to send their children to the common schools, a small segment of the new immigrants threatened to impede the most hopeful process of assimilating the immigrant into American society.

Changing from the rural life of the European village to the complex ways of a vast city, from a homogeneous setting to a tense milieu of cultural diversity, the immigrants faced a grave dilemma. On the one hand, they were challenged to adjust their life to a totally new environment. This they had to do to some degree in any case, in order to earn a livelihood in American society. Had they foreseen the unemployment and social distresses that awaited them in the United States, many would never have ventured in the first place the long trip across the Atlantic Ocean. At the same time, each national group wanted desperately to retain those folkways and religious values that gave meaning and warmth to family life. In the minds of the older immigrants, acculturation meant a destruction of a priceless heritage. Caught in the middle of this cultural tug-of-war were the immigrant children who were far more willing to conform, even to risk family separation, in order to climb the economic ladder to American success. "Why should that chasm between fathers and sons, yawning at the feet of each generation, be made so unnecessarily cruel and impassible [*sic*] to these bewildered immigrants?" asked Jane Addams.[3] The futile efforts of immigrant parents and grandparents to resist acculturation and to hold the young within the family fold constitute a poignant chapter in American social history.

Because of this general reluctance to interact with American culture, there developed among the native-born citizens a deliberate attempt to "Americanize" the immigrants as quickly and completely as possible. This effort was based in part on an assumption that the growing social problems of the cities stemmed directly from the changing character of immigration. "These southern and eastern Europeans are of a very different type from the north Europeans who preceded them," Ellwood P. Cubberley remarked in 1909. "Illiterate, docile, lacking in self-reliance and initiative, and not possessing the Anglo-Teutonic conceptions of law, order, and government, their coming has served to dilute tremendously our national stock, and to corrupt our civil life."[4]

But "Americanization" is an elusive term that defies definition, for its meaning varies with the changing social context. During the early decades of the twentieth century, it meant far more than teaching a new language to new citizens. The approach of World War I focused attention on the question of national loyalty and added a new sense of urgency to the problem. The intent was, as Cubberley urged,

> to break up these groups or settlements, to assimilate and amalgamate these people as a part of our American race, and to implant in their children, so far as can be done, the Anglo-Saxon conception of righteousness, law and order, and popular government, and to awaken in them a reverence for our democratic institutions and for those things in our national life which we as a people hold to be of abiding worth.[5]

Cubberley's view reflected a growing militancy among social workers and political leaders to abolish the ghettos, to enact more stringent immigration laws, and to superimpose upon the European immigrants a new system of values. To carry out the latter mandate directly involved the public schools in a difficult task that soon became an expected social role of education.

The schooling of immigrant children was almost guaranteed through compulsory attendance laws. By 1890, twenty-seven states and territories required parents or guardians to send their children to school. Not unexpectedly, Massachusetts had led with a historic compulsory school attendance law in 1852, requiring that children from eight to fourteen years of age be sent "to some public school" in the town or city where they resided.[6] Some unanimity among the states on this issue was reached toward the end of World War I. By 1918, each legislature had enacted such a law.[7] The upper age limits ranged theoretically from twelve to sixteen years. Some states permitted children to leave school on completion of a stipulated number of grades, regardless of age. Immigration authorities during this period helped to enforce the law by reporting the arrival of children to the public-school officials.

The main classroom effort was to inculcate in the immigrant children certain "American" attitudes and values. In 1910 Jane Addams observed that "the public schools in the immigrant colonies deserve all the praise as Americanizing agencies which can be bestowed upon them."[8] During the slow process children were gradually being taught by the teachers, and learning more quickly from their native-born peers, a whole new pattern of life that in many ways replaced that instilled by the family.[9] At times, the public-school teacher was forced to become a parent substitute for the immigrant children. In New York City, for example, the teachers had to bathe hundreds of children every week. As Lawrence A. Cremin (1925–1990) remarks: "The syllabi said nothing about baths, and teachers themselves wondered whether bathing was their charge. But there were the children and there were the lice!"[10] The task was enormous. By 1911 over half of the pupils in the public schools of thirty-seven of the most heavily populated cities were children of immigrant parents. The problem was too complicated to be solved overnight. At the beginning of the century the public schools' staffs and facilities for such a responsibility were meager and grossly inadequate.

Assimilating the adult alien into American society was a different aspect of the same educational problem and implied an enormously expanded concept of the public school. But it should not be assumed that educators willingly accepted this new responsibility. On the contrary, at the turn of the century the schools adhered tenaciously to the narrower view of Americanzation as solely a mastery of the English language. All that the public schools offered to the older aliens was evening English classes, which the immigrants refused to attend anyway. Berger describes the frustrating attempts to teach the adult immigrants "meaningless words" and criticizes the "shortsightedness" of educators before 1918.[11] Only after World War I did educators approach the problem from a broader vantage point and revise the curricula to meet more successfully the manifold needs of the immigrant in American culture.[12]

The Rise of Progressivism

The problem of Americanizing the immigrant children was only one aspect of a larger movement for social betterment which gathered momentum in the years from Appomattox to World War I. Progressivism,[13] enlisting the support of such political leaders as William Jennings Bryan, Theodore Roosevelt, and Woodrow Wilson, was characterized by a great surge of public interest in social amelioration. All the old ideas of social reform were again advanced with renewed vigor. Indeed, the times echoed with panaceas for alleviating society's ills.

What differentiated the new ideology from that of the antebellum years was the depth and range of the proposed reforms. The social problems attacked by the progressivists were old; the proposed solutions, however, were broader and more complex, reflecting the changing social and economic conditions. There was, for example, more action for slum clearance and better schools and less talk about social welfare and charity.

Certainly not all the reformers during the progressive era shared precisely the same views, but there was a common base for their ideological outlook. The influence of evolutionary thought was profound: could humankind, accepting the tenets of Darwinism, direct the evolutionary process into socially desirable channels? The progressivists not only shared a firm belief in the worth and dignity of the individual but also assumed that humans through science and critical intelligence could control their own destiny. There was a growing respect for the method of science that, the progressivists believed, justified human intervention in the affairs of an increasingly complex society. All envisioned a better world amenable to human control. Progressivism, then, was a cluster of ideas emphasizing deliberate and directed social change: above all, the new reformers shared a vision of progress toward a more humane and rational society of the future.

The "muckrakers," surely the most popular agitators for social change, were themselves powerful reformers: their choice of subject alone was often a weapon eagerly used not only for selling journals but also for curbing vice and urban evils. Lincoln Steffens's first installment on city corruption, "Tweed Days in St. Louis," written with Claude H. Whetmore, was published in *McClure's Magazine* in October 1902. The following month Ida Tarbell's first report on the Standard Oil Company appeared in the same magazine. Both journalists started a new trend by deliberately revealing through factual reporting the dishonesty and graft in politics and business.

As the movement gained momentum, the muckrakers abandoned their initial efforts toward strictly objective reporting. They became instead fierce crusaders: searching, exposing, even indicting, and writing verdicts. They sought relentlessly to stir the American people from apathy to action for social reform. Never before in the nation's history had there developed so swiftly such a spontaneous and fearless critique of the social order.

Around the turn of the century, Jacob A. Riis, a police reporter and crusading journalist, described the physical squalor and the stark poverty in the New York City tenement houses. Appalled by what he saw, Riis called public attention to the overcrowded, ramshackle dwellings and the parental neglect of children who roamed in the streets half naked in the wintry climate. "The problem of the children is the problem of the State," Riis declared. "The immediate duty which the community has to perform for its own protection is to school the children first of all into good Americans, and next into useful citizens."[14]

Riis was not alone in underscoring the importance of public education in fighting what he called "the battle with the slum."[15] Every humanitarian proposal reflected a belief in social regeneration through educational reform. "To grasp this relationship between progressive education and progressivism," Cremin states, "is to sharpen significantly our understanding of both."[16]

Jane Addams (1860–1935) and Hull House: Cultural Pluralism in Action

Jane Addams, for example, called for an expanded school curriculum that would add "human significance" to a person's life. "We are impatient with the schools which lay all stress on reading and writing," she wrote in 1902.[17] Ten years later, voicing the same criticism, she asked: "Are the educators, like the rest of us, so caught in admiration of the astonishing achievements of modern industry that they forget the children themselves?"[18] From the day that Addams and Ellen Gates Starr, a close friend and former classmate at the Rockford (Illinois) Female Seminary, opened its doors in September 1889, Hull House, located on South Halsted Street in Chicago, was an educational force in the lives of the impoverished immigrants of the surrounding area. Through the vigor and appeal of her speeches and writings, Jane Addams made her Chicago center into one of the most important settlement houses.

Although Addams traveled all over the world, Hull House remained her home and the reflection of her personality and ideas. Originally built by a Chicago businessman as a country residence, Hull House in the 1890s was located in the heart of the crowded Nineteenth Ward with about five thousand Greek, Italian, Russian, German, Sicilian, and other immigrants—a vital part of a foreign population that comprised three-fourths of Chicago's million inhabitants. By 1893 Hull House had become a major center for about forty clubs and activities, including a day nursery, dispensary, playground, gymnasium, sewing and cooking courses, and a cooperative boardinghouse for working girls. About two thousand people were crossing its threshold each week.

A major element in the success of Hull House was Jane Addams's talent for attracting outstanding people and putting them to work. For example, she was a close friend of John Dewey and was very much interested in his theories of education. Dewey occasionally worked at Hull House and believed that Addams was a personification of his educational idea that one learned by doing.[19] Williams James also admired her work and told her: "You utter instinctively the truth we others vainly seek."[20]

As a result of her experience at Hull House, Jane Addams became a student of democracy and of education. To gain support and to explain the work of Hull House to the community, she devoted much time to writing and public speaking. Basic to the broad philosophy of education that Addams developed during the forty-four years she lived at Hull House was a vision of a society in which all people, regardless of race, gender, or socioeconomic status, would have a chance to develop individual talents and interests. She believed that personally enriching experiences for the immigrants were vital in a society based on democracy as a way of life. At the settlement house, she tried to solve the daily problems of new citizens. The result was a humane institution in which the immigrants were able to grow and eventually contribute to community affairs.

Jane Addams's writings and lectures reflected her deep love for children. She was told in 1882 after an operation on her spine that she could never bear a child of her own. James Weber Linn, her nephew and biographer, called this her greatest grief. She spoke frequently about woman's "long historical role of ministration to basic human needs" and strived personally to fulfill this important role, acting, for example, as a midwife for an illegitimate baby whom the scandalized immigrant housewives in the Hull House neighborhood would not touch. Some of the most important activities of Hull House were classes and clubs for children, especially the nursery and kindergarten. It was the dangers of child labor that first drew her into politics, and her battle against child labor consumed her energy and effort almost completely until later in her life when she worked intensely for peace and international understanding.

When World War I began in 1914, her whole attention was focused on the issue of international peace. On December 10, 1931, she was awarded the Nobel Peace Prize, which she shared with Nicholas Murray Butler of Columbia University. During the ceremony at Oslo she was described as "the foremost woman of her nation" and a "spokesman for all peace-loving women of the world."

Felix Adler, a humanitarian leader and the son of a German rabbi, opened in 1878 the first "free kindergarten" in the slums of New York City. Two years later he added an elementary school called the Workingman's

School, later renamed the Ethical Culture School, which stressed manual training. For Adler, who was president of the Ethical Culture Society, a practical education meant more than preparation for a job. "Work instruction . . . is an organic part of the regular instruction," Adler declared. "It becomes the means of making the hand a wise and cunning hand by putting more brain into it."[21]

The work of Jane Addams and Felix Adler reflected the humanitarian zeal and intensity of purpose that characterized the new reform era. The scope of the movement was nationwide and the programs educationally diverse. In Biloxi, Mississippi, for instance, Wesley House, situated near the oyster canneries to which Bohemians and other immigrants were transported from Baltimore by the factory owners, maintained night schools and boys' clubs for the workers. At the Ann Street Settlement of Baltimore, Maryland, the reformers worked among the immigrants in the Polish quarter of the city. And in San Francisco the People's Palace was opened in 1898 for the benefit of a large Italian ethnic community.[22] In working with young children, the reformers organized neighborhood preschools; for the teenager, they developed manual-training programs, with apprenticeships in carpentry, plumbing, printing, and tailoring; and for the adult immigrants, they established evening classes in English and other subjects. At Hull House, in fact, the immigrants eagerly attended lectures in sociology, economics, and political science. During the process of education, the reformers understood and respected the language and culture of the immigrant learners.

Here, then, was a deliberate educational attempt to improve the quality of American life. In general, the movement was external to the public school and alien to the traditional purpose and scope of public education.

The teaching profession— confused, weak, overwhelmed—could not resist all the social pressures for change powered by such crusading zeal. The significant factor, of course, is that the schools did respond, unwillingly perhaps, to these and other social forces and soon absorbed different activities and programs into an expanded conception of public education.

Influenced by new ideas and leaders, the public schools changed radically. Walter Hines Page, Robert Ogden, and Seaman A. Knapp, for example, promoted the cause of education in the South; William T. Harris's work in St. Louis and Washington, while injecting a conservative spirit into education, added greatly to the professional stature of classroom teaching and school administration; and Francis Wayland Parker "revolutionized" the school system of Quincy, Massachusetts, and helped to modify the philosophy of American education.[23] At the helm, of course, would ultimately stand John Dewey, whose faith in democracy and science embodied the progressivist hope that intelligent social action would generate among the American people critical thought and individual self-determination.

Thus, by the turn of the century new forces were transforming American society. There was the legacy of war and Radical Reconstruction, with such vivid reminders as racial prejudice and segregated school systems. The expansion of business enterprise, the social impact of urbanism, and the changing character of immigration were bringing to bear tremendous pressures on the public schools.

Most of these new pressures, in one way or another, were finding expression in a growing ideology of humanitarian protest. As the progressivist movement gained momentum, the varied proposals for social change aimed directly toward the good society through educational channels.

While this torrent of protest during the decades following the Civil War helped to stimulate some progress in education, there was still much work to be done. In the prostrate South alone new systems of dual schooling were being erected, and every step of the painful process was overshadowed by the heightening issue of racial equality. The drive to establish public high schools, interrupted by the Civil War, was also being renewed. Meanwhile, an emerging and newly powerful business class was voicing discontent and demanding curricular changes at a time when thousands of immigrant children in the cities—the "slum children," in the words of Jacob Riis— were crowding into public schools and creating a virtual nightmare for an underpaid and poorly prepared teaching staff. Surely these problems alone were sufficient to tax and frustrate professional educators for years, if nothing else had intervened.

But this was not the case. During the post–Civil War years, new scientific points of view, and above all the theory of evolution, revolutionized the field of psychology, sharply affecting the outlook of educational leaders. At the same time, an influx of European ideas began to modify the conception of the American school itself. The cumulative effect of these new intellectual currents was to alter significantly traditional theories concerning the society in which people live and the whole process of education.

THE IMPACT OF
EVOLUTIONARY THOUGHT

The publication of Charles Darwin's *Origin of Species* in 1859 marked a momentous turning point in the history of ideas. With its doctrine of evolutionary change and progress, Darwinism stressed the power of people to control their environment and coincided perfectly with the spirit of the reform era. It offered a new approach to the study of nature and expanded the concept of development. In fact, the appearance and gradual assimilation of the *Origin of Species* led to such a dramatic shift in the history of science that the following century became for the most part an account of extended variations on Darwin's major themes.

The indirect influence of Darwinism on American education was long range and profound. First of all, Darwinism brought about a sharp change in biological inquiry, giving the new biology a firm place in the school curriculum. Before Darwin introduced the concept of evolutionary process, the main emphasis was on the study of biological structure. For example, such terms as "cell" and "protoplasm" were of primary importance as the anatomist and the physiologist tried to comprehend the structure of living tissue. However, with the advent of Darwinism, biologists became less interested in how the living tissue was built and more concerned with how it functioned. The increasing importance of such terms as "metabolism" and "maturation" was indicative of the functional approach in the new biological outlook.

With its stress on evolutionary growth, Darwinism also emphasized individual differences and encouraged the study of child development. It cast the child in a new light, breaking with the Calvinistic dogma of original sin. Thus the theory of biological evolution helped to undermine the rigidity of the traditional classroom organization, with its harsh approach to pupil discipline and its unchanging curriculum.

The theory of evolution also repudiated the old idea of an immutable social order and supported the classroom study of current problems in a *changing* world.

Finally, the theory of biological evolution struck at the very core of traditional theology, which unleashed the most virulent attacks not only upon Darwin's work but also on anything even remotely associated with or attempting to explain the new doctrine.[24]

Through analogies and Darwinian ideas, people applied the theory of evolution to fields other than biology, particularly to the study of society. Indeed, Darwinism profoundly influenced the study of people and society. The idea of species evolution gave a scientific rationale for certain eighteenth-century views of perfectibility. Of course, the biological struggle for survival did not coincide exactly with the traditional idea of humans as rational organisms in a free society, but at least the result held out endless hope for a superior human being. Just as animal life grew naturally from protozoan to rational being, so society, too, evolved from the primitive jungle to a sophisticated state. Instigated by the social Darwinians, the thesis was widely held that evolution, spurred on by industry and science, would propel society naturally along the path toward infinite progress.

William Graham Sumner (1840–1910)

Theories of social evolution were not restricted to any one American school of thought. There were, in fact, fundamentally diverse points of view. William Graham Sumner, for example, espoused a strong laissez-faire doctrine. A professor at Yale University from 1872 to 1910, Sumner was the principal

American exponent of social Darwinism. He warned repeatedly against governmental interference with the social order. In a competitive society, the survival of the fittest, Sumner asserted, was essential for social progress. "It may shock you to hear me say it, but when you get over the shock, it will do you good to think of it: a drunkard in the gutter is just where he ought to be," Sumner told a group at the Brooklyn Historical Society in 1883. "Nature is working away at him to get him out of the way, just as she sets up her processes of dissolution to remove whatever is a failure in its line."[25] In Sumner's doctrine, great wealth was a necessary inducement for efficiency and social selection. "In no sense whatever does a man who accumulates a fortune by legitimate industry exploit his employés, or make his capital 'out of' anybody else," Sumner declared. "The wealth which he wins would not be but for him. . . . It is a necessary condition of many forms of social advance."[26]

Although skeptical of any value derived from *public* education, Sumner, nevertheless, favored compulsory schooling in order to protect the social status quo. "The faith in book-learning is one of the superstitions of the nineteenth century and it enters for a large part into the bequest which the nineteenth century is about to hand over to the twentieth," he remarked at a dinner on January 25, 1897, honoring Henry Barnard.[27] The school, he believed, should help to assure stability and order by instilling industry, perseverance, and other economic virtues in American boys and girls. "True education," Sumner declared, develops "intelligent men with minds well-disciplined and well under control, who are able to apply their full force to any new exigency, or any new problem, and to grasp and conquer it."[28]

Sumner, however, rejected the popular argument that universal suffrage in a democratic state demands a tax-supported system of public schools. "This doctrine is politically immoral and vicious," he declared. Sumner believed that "liberty, and universal suffrage, and democracy are not pledges of care and protection, but they carry with them the exaction of individual responsibility." In granting the right to vote, the state gives this privilege and nothing more and expects each citizen in return to "take upon himself the responsibility for his own success or failure."[29]

Lester Frank Ward (1841–1913)

Basically opposed to Sumner's laissez-faire social theories were the views of Lester Frank Ward, author of *Dynamic Sociology*, the first general sociological treatise published in America. Ward's two-volume work appeared in 1883, the same year that Sumner's *What Social Classes Owe to Each Other* was published. Ward also studied social institutions from an evolutionary point of view, but his conclusions were vastly different from those of Sumner.

Ward accepted the framework of Darwinism, but he opposed a deterministic view of human evolution: within the genetic process, a new and potent factor emerges with the development of the human mind. "In animals, the mind-force is low, and progress is correspondingly slow. In man, it presents a series, and we find degrees of social development and elevation proportionate to the increment as we rise from the lowest to the highest of the human races."[30] This "mind-force" directs human actions, interferes with and controls the natural processes, and makes the evolution of man telic and humanly directed. The social system should not be allowed to drift blindly according to nature but must instead be guided along progressive channels by human intelligence. This social direction is the primary concern of education.[31] Thus, repudiating Sumner's conservative approach, Ward placed his whole faith in education as an instrument of social progress.

Herbert Spencer (1820–1903)

Of all the new syntheses of evolutionary development, Herbert Spencer's writings were by far the most widely read in the United States. His general philosophy of education reflected to a large extent the new evolutionary doctrine of Darwin and the growing importance of science in the post–Civil War era. Spencer was, in fact, the great popularizer of the theory of evolution and of social Darwinism. His influence on the American people increased steadily after the Civil War, culminating in a visit to the United States in 1882 to deliver a series of lectures and to attend the banquets and celebrations in his honor.

Spencer was interested in the whole range of evolutionary phenomena. Unlike Darwin, who confined his theory of evolution to animals and plants, Spencer applied his own principles of evolution and dissolution to vast areas, ranging from biology to psychology, sociology, and even the planetary systems. *First Principles*, published in 1862, set forth the fundamentals of his evolutionary naturalism. His most ambitious achievement was the formulation of his "system of synthetic philosophy," which appeared in a series of ten volumes. Spencer regarded his philosophy as "synthetic" because it attempted to establish a set of universal principles that could be verified empirically by science. When advance subscriptions to the first volumes of the *System of Synthetic Philosophy* were being solicited in the United States, Spencer's fame among New Englanders was already well established. "Mr. Spencer represents the scientific spirit of the age," stated the *Atlantic Monthly* in 1864. "From profound generalizations upon society, he rises to make the duty of the individual most solemn and imperative."[32]

Of his many works, Spencer's treatise on education was probably most widely distributed in America. His educational views were expressed in four separate essays published originally in England between May 1854 and July 1859.[33] In this work Spencer's style is forceful and clear. His critical remarks on certain educational practices have a distinctly modern tone.

The general aim of education, according to Spencer, is moral training.

All aspects of education are concerned with "the right ruling of conduct in all directions under all circumstances." How does one learn to live morally? "That is the essential question for us," declared Spencer. "Not how to live in the mere material sense only, but in the widest sense." For Spencer there were five important activities to be stressed: (1) those leading to self-preservation, (2) those essential for self-support, (3) those concerned with child rearing and parenthood, (4) those necessary for good citizenship, and (5) those relevant to leisure time. In the pursuit of knowledge, students should be trained in all five areas; in this way, Spencer believed, these practical activities would provide for a general "intellectual education." In essence, then, Spencer's aim of education "in the widest sense" was really preparation for life.

In the light of this goal, Spencer considered formal education as grossly deficient. He bitterly assailed current practices. "So overwhelming is the influence of established routine!" he exclaimed. "So terribly in our education does the ornamental override the useful!"[34]

And what knowledge is of most worth for this practical education? Science, answered Spencer in his classic statement.

> This is the verdict on all counts. For direct self-preservation, or the maintenance of life and health, the all-important knowledge is—Science. For that indirect self-preservation which we call gaining a livelihood, the knowledge of greatest value is—Science. For the due discharge of parental functions, the proper guidance is to be found only in—Science. For that interpretation of national life, past and present, without which the citizen cannot rightly regulate his conduct, the indispensable key is—Science. Alike for the most perfect production and highest enjoyment of art in all its forms, the needful preparation is still—Science. And for purposes of discipline—intellectual, moral, religious—the most efficient study is, once more—Science.[35]

Spencer's educational ideas were in the mainstream of modern pedagogy. Like Locke, for example, he excoriated rote learning. "Children should be led to make their own investigations, and to draw their own inferences," Spencer declared. "They should be *told* as little as possible, and induced to *discover* as much as possible."[36] Spencer's experimentalism was similar to Bacon's inductive approach. His plea for health education (indicative, no doubt, of his own lifelong struggle against illness) agreed with Locke's arguments for maintaining a vigorous body. His view of the child coincided with Rousseau's naturalism; and his emphasis on object-teaching followed Pestalozzi's views. In fact, many of Spencer's astute observations on methodology and child development are consistent with current psychological studies. Thus, in his approach to an education that was both intellectual and intensely practical, Spencer ranks as one of the great pioneers of American progressivism. He underscored the tenets of progressive education so force-fully that he anticipated much of the work of John Dewey.

FOR DISCUSSION AND CRITICAL THOUGHT

1. How did Jane Addams's educational philosophy contribute to social reform?
2. In what ways do the practices of immigrant schooling during the late nineteenth century and the philosophy of cultural pluralism evident in Jane Addams's Hull House provide lessons for immigrant education today?
3. Is the lack of caring for the less fortunate that is evident in some parts of contemporary society related to William Graham Sumner's theory of social Darwinism of the late nineteenth century? Comment critically.

NOTES

1. Robert W. DeForest and Lawrence Veiller, eds., *The Tenement House Problem*, as reprinted in Otis Pease, ed., *The Progressive Years: The Spirit and Achievement of American Reform* (New York: Braziller, 1962), p. 106.
2. Giuseppe Giacosa, "The Natures of Waste," as reprinted in Oscar Handlin, ed., *This Was America: True Accounts of People and Places, Manners and Customs, as Recorded by European Travelers to the Western Shore in the Eighteenth, Nineteenth, and Twentieth Centuries* (Cambridge, Mass.: Harvard University Press, 1949), pp. 402–403.
3. Jane Addams, *Twenty Years at Hull-House, with Autobiographical Notes* (New York: Macmillan, 1910), p. 236.
4. Ellwood P. Cubberley, *Changing Conceptions of Education* (Boston: Houghton Mifflin, 1909), p. 15.
5. Ibid.
6. However, after 1925, no state could legally compel attendance in a *public* school (*Pierce, Governor of Oregon, et al.* v. *Society of Sisters of the Holy Names of Jesus and Mary, 268 U.S. 510 {1925}*).
7. This record was later broken during the school segregation controversies in the 1950s. South Carolina (in 1955), Mississippi (in 1956), and Virginia (in 1959) repealed their compulsory attendance laws.
8. Addams, *Twenty Years at Hull-House*, p. 254.
9. See Mary Antin, *The Promised Land* (Boston: Houghton Mifflin, 1912), "Initiation," pp. 206–21.
10. Lawrence A. Cremin, *The Transformation of the School: Progressivism in American Education, 1876–1957* (New York: Knopf, 1961), p. 71. See also Alan M. Thomas, Jr., "American Education and the Immigrant," *Teachers College Record* 55 (February 1954): 253–67.

11. Morris Isaiah Berger, "The Settlement, the Immigrant and the Public-School: A Study of the Influence of the Settlement Movement and the New Migration upon Public Education, 1890–1924" (Ph.D. dissertation, Columbia University, 1956), pp. 108–13.

12. "By then it was too late," asserts Berger. "Restriction rather than Americanization had become the answer to the 'immigrant problem.' " Ibid., p. 108.

13. While there have been various attempts to define "progressivism," Gabriel ascribes to the movement the broadest possible connotation: "Progressivism was a mass movement which united diverse elements in American society. It transcended the agrarianism and the sectionalism of the Populists and the humanitarianism of such urban reformers as Jacob Riis and Jane Addams. It was a crusade in which farmers, wage earners, and small business men all marched shoulder to shoulder. In democratic United States the philosophy of such a movement could not be expressed in neat logical formulas. Progressivism was a potpourri of social theories and beliefs." Ralph H. Gabriel, *The Course of American Democratic Thought: An Intellectual History Since 1815* (New York: Ronald Press, 1940), p. 332.

14. Jacob A. Riis, *The Children of the Poor* (New York: Scribners, 1892), pp. 1, 8. See also Riis's earlier exposé, *How the Other Half Lives: Studies Among the Tenements of New York*, American Century Series (New York: Sagamore Press, 1957; originally published in 1890). Soon after this first book was published, Theodore Roosevelt, who subsequently became chairman of the New York City Police Commission (1893–1895), visited Riis and inquired how he could help combat the evils of tenement life.

15. Jacob A. Riis, *The Battle with the Slum* (New York: Macmillan, 1902).

16. Cremin, *The Transformation of the School*, p. 88. No one so clearly connects the progressivist movement in education with the main currents of American social history as does Cremin. Beck is also emphatic on this point: "There are those who do not know that grappled to the progressive tradition by the firmest associations is the history of progressive education. If progressive education is repudiated, progressivism as a whole is diminished." Robert H. Beck, "Progressive Education and American Progressivism: Felix Adler," *Teachers College Record* 60 (November 1958): 78.

17. Jane Addams, *Democracy and Social Ethics* (New York: Macmillan, 1902), pp. 180, 219.

18. Jane Addams, *The Spirit of Youth and the City Streets* (New York: Macmillan, 1912), p. 119.

19. See pp. 175–181.

20. James Weber Linn, *Jane Addams: A Biography* (New York: D. Appleton-Century, 1935), p. 438.

21. Felix Adler, "The Workingman's School and Free Kindergarten," *Reports and Announcements* (1879–1906), as quoted in Beck, "Progressive Education and American Progressivism: Felix Adler," p. 79.

22. Berger, "The Settlement, the Immigrant and the Public School," pp. 16–17, 33–35.

23. For a description of other innovations launched before World War I, see John

Dewey and Evelyn Dewey, *Schools of To-morrow* (New York: Dutton, 1915), passim.

24. See Richard Hofstadter, *Social Darwinism in American Thought* (Boston: Beacon Press, 1955; originally published in 1944 by the University of Pennsylvania Press).

25. William Graham Sumner, "The Forgotten Man," in the *Essays of William Graham Sumner*, ed. Albert Galloway Keller and Maurice R. Davie (New Haven: Yale University Press, 1934), 1:481.

26. William Graham Sumner, *What Social Classes Owe to Each Other* (New York: Harper & Bros., 1883), p. 54.

27. Sumner, "The Teacher's Unconscious Success," *Essays*, 1:7.

28. See Sumner, "The Teacher's Unconscious Success," "Discipline," and "Integrity in Education," *Essays*, 1:6–10, 20–35, and 38–42.

29. Sumner, *What Social Classes Owe to Each Other*, pp. 41–42.

30. Lester Frank Ward, *Dynamic Sociology, or Applied Social Science, as Based upon Statical Sociology and the Less Complex Sciences*, 2 vols. (New York: D. Appleton, 1883), 1:698.

31. See ibid., vol. 2, chap. 14, "Education," pp. 540–633.

32. "Reviews and Literary Notices," *Atlantic Monthly* 13 (June 1864): 776–777.

33. Herbert Spencer, *Education: Intellectual, Moral, and Physical* (New York: D. Appleton, 1871).

34. Ibid., p. 43.

35. Ibid., pp. 93–94.

36. Ibid., pp. 124–125. Italics in original.

CHAPTER 7

Building a Philosophy of Education

It is no dream or illusion, the realization of a common school, perfect in its appointment, with the means for the highest and best education at hand. All is ready when the people are ready to move, to demand that the methods of quantity shall go, and the methods of quality shall come in.

FRANCIS WAYLAND PARKER, "Democracy and Education," July 1891

The obvious fact is that our social life has undergone a thorough and radical change. If our education is to have any meaning for life, it must pass through an equally complete transformation.

JOHN DEWEY, "The School and Social Progress," April 1899

THE INFLUX OF EDUCATIONAL IDEAS FROM ABROAD

During the post–Civil War decade, the rapid transition from a predominantly rural and agricultural economy to an urban and industrial way of life brought about great changes in American society. By the turn of the century, these changes had had a profound effect on individuals, transforming their mode of living and challenging their means of self-realization. Almost symbolically, the closing of the frontier ended a colorful era in American history and damped the aspirations of westward-bound settlers for a stake in the rich public domain. The traditional ideals of free competition and rugged individualism came under scrutiny in the light of new and accelerating social and economic forces. The rise of monopolistic corporations, for example, which brought about new ways of producing and distributing capital and goods, had a striking impact upon labor-management relationships. At the same time, a steady stream of immigrants and the growth of cities created new social problems in such areas as sanitation and human welfare. These and other developments pointed rather urgently to the need for new approaches in dealing with more complex public issues.

During this transitional period, American thought was influenced by an influx of important educational ideas from abroad. There were, of course, the famous theories of Pestalozzi which, after 1865, continued to flow into the United States, affecting in particular patterns of teacher training in the normal schools. The ideas of Johann Friedrich Herbart enriched the methodology of teaching during an era in American education characterized too often by *memoriter* learning and pupil recitation. Friedrich Froebel's *kindergarten* (a garden where children grow), with its new respect for the young child, decreased the rigidity of the classroom atmosphere and gave new dimensions to the study of child development.

This same period of flux and change in American society also witnessed a succession of new educational leaders who extended the work of Mann and Barnard and helped to translate into practice the important theories of European educators. William Torrey Harris (1835–1909) helped Americans to adjust to the stresses and strains of a dynamic society through a Hegelian idealism that combined tradition with change. One of the primary aims of the school, Harris believed, was to preserve the laissez-faire philosophy of an industrial leadership. Indeed, according to Harris, true self-actualization first required individual acquiescence to the social status quo. In more practical ways, first as superintendent of schools in St. Louis (1868–1880) and later as United States commissioner of education (1889–1906), Harris established a high criterion of educational administration.

In sharp contrast to Harris's advocacy of social adjustment, Francis Wayland Parker (1837–1902) viewed education as an exploratory process leading to self-discovery. Influenced by Pestalozzi and especially by Froebel, Parker was opposed to a regimented education and believed that the school must help to create an environment conducive to growth and free expression. Called the "father of progressive education," Parker was a New England educator who devoted his whole career to pedagogical reform.

Finally, and certainly the commanding figure of the age, was John Dewey (1859–1952), whose philosophy in its fullest expression came to symbolize the very spirit of educational progressivism. Like Mann, he believed in universal education as the best way of achieving a more democratic society. In stressing the close interrelationships between the school and society, Dewey, more than anyone else, conceived of educational purpose in truly social terms.

Johann Friedrich Herbart (1776–1841)

Herbart, like Plato, was both a profound philosopher and a skilled educator. He was appointed to a renowned chair in philosophy made famous by Immanuel Kant at the University of Königsberg. There, for a quarter of a century, he lectured, wrote a *Text-book in Psychology* (1816) and *Psychology as a Science* (1824), and conducted a pedagogical seminar and small practice school for students preparing to teach. Herbart's other books also reflected his systematic thought on issues in education, ethics, and general philosophy.

Like Locke and Spencer, Herbart viewed moral development as the primary aim of education. For Herbart the means to this end was instruction, for, like Socrates, he believed that virtue was founded on knowledge. Education should produce good men, Herbart wrote; indeed, moral stature was the long-range goal of an educational program. This aim of moral character was equated with five types of ideas that should be inculcated through instruction: inner freedom, perfection, benevolence or goodwill, justice, and equity or retribution. Thus, in Herbart's view, morality was both the foundation and the goal of education.

As a psychologist, Herbart made his most significant contribution in the history of education. He developed a new system of educational thought based on psychological concepts. Separating pedagogy from metaphysics, Herbart helped to develop education into a distinct science with a specific content and methodology, worthy of professional study by all who planned to teach.[1] "Those . . . who have no true psychological insight," he wrote, "rarely understand anything of education."[2]

Herbart disagreed with the older psychological view of formal discipline with its stress on the separate faculties of the mind. He also refused to accept the passivity of the mind, a tabula rasa, as described by Locke. Instead, according to Herbart, the mind functioned as a unit through powerful ideas. These ideas were active forces, which made up the very substance of Herbartian psychology.

According to Herbart, learning occurred through the active assimilation of dynamic ideas. Herbart used the term *apperception* to denote the understanding of a new idea from its context. Hence we understand a new word or experience through its relationship to the context or other ideas. An *apperceptive mass*, Herbart explained, was a cluster of ideas that helped the learner to interpret and assimilate new sensory data. Herbart's stress on *correlation* of studies reflected this apperceptive approach to learning. For example, he urged that history be correlated with literature as a study technique for instilling desirable social attitudes in children.

Today, of course, educational psychologists disregard the Herbartian word *apperception* and refer instead to *mental set* or *pattern*, which recognizes the volitional and psychomotor aspects of mental phenomena. In Herbart's conception of learning, there were no creative thoughts, no essentially *new* ideas. An idea entered the mind and was assimilated. To be intellectually creative was merely to synthesize ideas on a higher level.

Herbart's famous theory of interest conflicted later with the views of American progressivists. Herbart believed that interest was an essential component of learning; indeed, if interest were not present in the learning situation, then the teacher should help to provide it through "educative instruction."[3] Herbart assumed that voluntary or spontaneous interests during the instructional process were induced through the method of association. The ideas that captured the interest of the pupil were supported by an apperceptive mass of related ideas. Thus, according to Herbart, ideas were self-activating in the learning process: in fact, without initial ideas, the pupil would have no impulse or interest to learn. Ideas, then, became active powers, stimulating interest in other ideas and experiences.

John Dewey and other educational leaders in the progressivist movement believed that interests sprang from the "felt needs" of the learner. "Herbartianism seems to me essentially a schoolmaster's psychology, not the psychology of a child," wrote Dewey in 1895.[4] Initial and spontaneous interests arose from an activity invoked during the learning process and then spread to other activities in a continuous cycle.

Herbart translated his theory into practice through four important "steps of instruction": clearness, association, system, and method.[5] He placed considerable emphasis on the instructional process, accentuating the importance of teaching skill instead of "mental discipline." Although Herbart stressed the importance of methodology, he did not restrict teaching to any formal "system." Through these four successive stages, Herbart conceived of a unified yet flexible method of teaching that would develop meaning and understanding and accelerate the learner's progress. Herbartian disciples later formalized this method into five steps: preparation, presentation, association, systematization, and application. Herbart, however, never regarded his systematic methodology as a rigid, mechanical scheme that characterized the formal five steps introduced into American normal schools.

Several years after Herbart's death, Tuiskon Ziller, of the University of Leipzig, elaborated on and publicized Herbart's work. Ziller's efforts led to the organization in 1868 of a scientific society for the study of Herbartian principles. By 1885 Wilhelm Rein, one of Ziller's disciples, had established at the University of Jena a practice school for the study and application of Herbart's ideas.

After 1885, a few Americans, most notably Charles De Garmo and Charles and Frank McMurry, traveled to Germany and observed and studied Herbartian ideas and practices at Jena. Upon returning to the United States, De Garmo and the McMurry brothers popularized Herbartianism through their own textbooks on methodology, which were widely adopted in American normal schools and colleges, especially in the Midwest. In 1892 they were instrumental in establishing a Herbart Club, later renamed the National Herbart Society, an American counterpart of the German organization. With its title changed again in 1902 to the National Society for the Scientific Study of Education, this association facilitated the spread and application of Herbartian views in the United States.

American enthusiasm for Herbartianism continued unabated during the last two decades of the nineteenth century. Charles DeGarmo's widely read *Essentials of Methods* first appeared in 1889, and *The Elements of General Method Based on the Principles of Herbart* by Charles A. McMurry was published in 1892. Five years later the publication of *The Method of the Recitation*, written by Charles and Frank McMurry, marked another addition to the growing Herbartian literature. Educators seemed intrigued by such pedagogical terms as *apperception*, *interest*, and *formal steps of instruction*.

Herbart's psychological theories were originally postulated before Darwinism, and some of his ideas were superseded by new knowledge or discarded completely. No psychologist today, for example, would seriously accept Herbart's basic thesis that emotion and interest spring from ideation. But Herbart did give new dimensions to the methodology of secondary-school teaching. He stimulated additional studies of the learning process and helped to discredit faculty psychology. Modified by new patterns of thought, Herbartianism might well mark the beginning of the scientific study of education in the United States.

Friedrich Froebel (1782–1852)

Froebel's life encompassed a tumultuous period in German history. Like Pestalozzi, he lived through all the horrors of war, with its terrible impact on the family. The ruthlessness of the Napoleonic conflicts, like all national wars, threatened the children most of all. Froebel's attention to preschool education no doubt reflected his grave concern for the welfare of small children. Introspective and quiet, a former teacher in Pestalozzi's institute at Yverdon, Froebel was long interested in the development and education of children from three to seven years of age. He recognized, too, what others in more recent times have come to accept: the significance of the early childhood years as a basis for personality development.

The Education of Man (1826) was Froebel's most significant treatise on pedagogical theory. In this work Froebel viewed education as the necessary element in a general evolutionary process by which mankind emerged from an animal state. Indeed, Froebel's whole philosophy of education was rooted in a conception of organic evolution: man was deemed a "human plant" governed by a universal law of development applicable everywhere to all stages of growth. According to Froebel, everything was a pantheistic expression of God's creative will. Education was not the transmission of the cultural heritage to posterity; neither was it considered to be an adjustment process of man to his environment. Instead, education was the evolutionary development of man to the "highest equilibrium and symmetry," to a productive organism powered by the spiritual energy of God.

For Froebel, child growth was much more than a transitory stage in this evolutionary process toward maturity. Although he often wrote in a mystical vein about "the Divine Unity" in all development, Froebel, nevertheless, underscored childhood as a separate entity in the human growth span. In fact, delineated by definite age limits, each stage of human development was vital in Froebel's theory, for successful completion of one growth span was considered essential to the full development of the next stage.[6] Thus, in Froebel's view, childhood would have to be an important stage in human development.

According to Froebel, childhood was divinely inspired and guided. Like Rousseau, he viewed the child as inherently good. Wickedness was not the result of original depravity. Evil stemmed from the "arbitrary and willful interference with the original orderly and logical course of human development."[7] Even more important, developmental retardation or divergence resulted from an incorrect educational methodology.

In demanding appropriate attention to early child development, Froebel evolved a new concept of preschool education. Childhood was not merely a preparation for adult status. In Froebel's view, the child was an important part of "the Divine Unity," with a unique and creative world of his or her own. But unlike Rousseau, Froebel believed that the young child should grow and learn through social participation. Consider, for example, Froebel's theory of play, which illustrated his profound insight into child psychology. For Froebel, the young child's world of play was never simply a form of recreation: it was, rather, a very important step in the development of the child. Play was deemed a harmonious combination of freedom with restraint and of creativity with purpose. In elaborating on the different types of play activities, Froebel emphasized the importance of self-expression in preschool education. He was, in fact, the first to recognize the significance of play in the young child's life. "Play is the highest phase of child development—of human development at this period," he wrote.[8]

Despite ridicule and great misunderstanding, few educational theories have been more widely implemented than those of Friedrich Froebel. Of course, his ideas and practices were subsequently modified in the light of new research, but the following principles remained dominant and influenced profoundly the history of American elementary education: (1) the family is the primary social institution in the life of the young child; (2) play is an essential phase of early childhood; (3) purposeful learning is derived from self-activity; and (4) the curriculum should correlate with stages in child development.

These ideas are usually associated with the kindergarten Froebel established at Blankenburg, Germany, in 1837. The founding of this institution is often cited as Froebel's most significant educational achievement. However, few kindergartens were established in Germany. In the United States, as Froebel himself had predicted, the kindergarten as a new institution attracted more favorable attention.

Froebel's ideas were transmitted to the United States by German immigrants after the Prussian Revolution of 1848. Mrs. Carl Schurz, who had studied under Froebel, opened an American kindergarten in her home at Watertown, Wisconsin, in 1855. Mrs. Shurz's small neighborhood class was conducted in German. The following year Henry Barnard published in the *American Journal of Education* a brief statement about Froebel's "infant-gardens," describing the new education as "one of the most interesting and instructive contributions to the London Educational Exhibition."[9] Within a decade, other kindergartens were opened in the densely settled German American communities. In 1860, the first private, English-speaking kindergarten was established in Boston by Elizabeth Palmer Peabody, sister-in-law of Horace Mann and Nathaniel Hawthorne. In subsequent years, especially during the early phase of the movement, most of the kindergartens were privately sponsored by interested philanthropists or church officials. Felix Adler's school in New York City, for example, was a humanitarian effort to help the worker's children.

A noteworthy development in the American movement was the incorporation of the kindergarten into the local public-school system. Under the leadership of Superintendent William T. Harris this step was initially taken in St. Louis in 1873.[10] Essentially an urban movement, the drive to establish public kindergartens gained momentum as other cities followed St. Louis's example. By the turn of the century there were about 4,500 kindergartens in the United States, most of which were privately sponsored. "Froebel's kindergarten is a great blessing to civilization, and for this and much else Froebel's name is to be celebrated as one of the great apostles of humanity," Harris declared in 1903.[11]

Nevertheless, despite the zeal and propaganda of its proponents, the status of the public kindergarten has always been somewhat insecure. While Froebel's basic ideas spread and greatly influenced the curricula and methodology of elementary education, the kindergarten itself has remained essentially a private affair, especially in those communities where school support has been a recurring issue.

AMERICAN LEADERSHIP AND INNOVATION

The Work of William Torrey Harris

A native New Englander who traveled west, William T. Harris appeared on the educational scene at a critical point in the common school movement.

After Appomattox there were few precedents for a city superintendent confronted with the overwhelming burden of educating hundreds of pupils. The pre—Civil War drive to educate at public expense all American children now posed the difficult problem of accommodating growing numbers of pupils efficiently in a city system. In the 1870s St. Louis, like other cities, had inadequate facilities and a beleaguered and poorly paid teaching staff.

Superintendent Harris met the challenge in St. Louis, established his own rules, and methodically worked out every detail of an urban school system. For example, he approached the initial problem of large-scale enrollments by instituting the graded school, organized on a quarterly system, with pupils grouped and promoted on the basis of periodic examinations. Thus, in the spirit of Mann, Harris demonstrated to observers at home and abroad that a heterogeneous population of American children could obtain an education in a public-school system.

Under Harris's leadership, the schools of St. Louis attracted widespread attention. His influence on other school officials was extended through lecture tours and voluminous correspondence. His regular *Annual Reports*, issued from 1869 to 1880, were widely publicized, even in Germany, and became models for other educational leaders. As a result, educators from other American cities and from Europe came to St. Louis during the 1870s to observe Harris's accomplishments.

In St. Louis, Harris strove constantly to improve efficiency in school management. He collected statistics on every conceivable subject, ranging from such items as school furniture and attendance records to pupil eyesight and calisthenics. He jotted down ideas on slips of paper that he filed away carefully for reference. He disseminated "guidance sheets" to principals and teachers and even specified regulations for janitors! He watched school fire drills and supervised the hanging of classroom blackboards at a particular angle.

At the same time, with a dedication bound to enlist staff loyalties, Harris raised professional standards in all phases of teaching. He expressed unusual concern during the post–Civil War period for the status and welfare of his teachers. We must, he argued, demand "the strongest safeguards to protect the teacher." Warning against overworking an already burdened teaching staff, Harris urged shorter hours, a five-day school week, and "nearly one-fifth or one-sixth of the year for vacations." His "pep talks" before the annual meetings of the St. Louis Teachers' Association became elaborate, morale-boosting affairs, complete with artistically printed programs, background music, and charity solicitations, "mainly for sick and homeless teachers." Meanwhile, always a shrewd recruiter, Superintendent Harris lured experienced teachers from other systems to St. Louis by increasing their annual salaries from $900 to as much as $1,500 or even from $800 to $2,000.[12]

Harris, the energetic and practical school administrator, was also an eminent scholar widely known in the field of philosophy. His educational views were based on the ideology of the German philosopher Hegel. In fact, Harris was the most famous Hegelian in the United States. He was a distinguished leader of the St. Louis philosophical movement.[13] He founded and edited the *Journal of Speculative Philosophy*, which appeared quarterly from January 1867 until December 1893. In 1890 he published *Hegel's Logic*.

The Hegelian doctrine of self-estrangement, to which Harris often referred with approval, sheds some light on Harris's own theory of education.[14] Indeed, he wrote, "the process of self-estrangement underlies all education."According to this doctrine, man has two selves—a natural self and a spiritual self. Man's true self is his spiritual being, which is essential for living in society but is in opposition to nature. In Harris's view, education involves the conquest of man's natural or animal self by his spiritual being. To accomplish this, education must "estrange" man from his natural self and help him to realize his true self by adopting the mores of society. This is not an easy task, for, according to Harris, there is a continual collision between the will of the individual and the demands of society. Thus, education in the final analysis becomes a process of changing man's natural inclinations and forcing him to "adjust" with much discipline and work to the environment. As Harris wrote, "Education is the process of the adoption of the social order in place of one's mere animal caprice."

Drawing upon Hegel's philosophy, Harris sought to justify the prevailing social order. He responded to criticisms of industrial capitalism by advancing his own Hegelian conception of inevitable progress. He saw nothing wrong with capitalism or the competitive spirit engendered by the pursuit and accumulation of wealth. Ignoring the tenement conditions and the urban slums, Harris pointed instead to the benefits derived from the factory system and wrote about the end products and the leisure time the machine age gave humankind. All the evils of society, Harris argued, were not signs of disintegration. On the contrary, social stresses and strains were merely aspects of a dialectical process toward a higher synthesis. The means to a more promising future, to this new synthesis, was an education that helped the pupil to identify with an evolving industrial civilization. Thus, by the dialectic process of resolving contradictions (or antitheses) into progressively higher positions (or syntheses), Harris infused American educational thought with a spirit of absolute idealism.

Harris advanced what he termed a "rational psychology" that gave priority to human reason and subordinated matter to spirit. Opposed to materialism, he stressed the superiority of mind over the physical world. The ultimate nature of reality, in Harris's view, was mind, or a creative intelligence.

For the curriculum, Harris preferred subjects he believed helped to develop "self-active" and free citizens, always in consonance with the mores of American society. For elementary education, he emphasized the mastery of five subjects or, as he described them, the "five windows of the soul": mathematics, literature and art, geography, grammar, and history. At the high-school level, he urged concentration in the humanistic studies and the social sciences. Harris's staunch defense of the traditional subjects reflected his idealistic conviction that cultural and spiritual values were of primary importance in American education.

Harris rejected the Pestalozzian concept of sense training as "false psychology" and minimized the importance of utilitarian courses. On this point he differed with Herbert Spencer. While Harris was not opposed to science in the curriculum, he believed that the school's primary concern was "education for culture."

Harris was strongly in favor of "moral training" in the public schools. The emphasis was always on training or habit formation rather than instruction. He defined morality in behavioral terms: "regularity, punctuality, silence (self-restraint), industry, and truthful accuracy." These "cardinal virtues of the school lie at the basis of every true moral character," Harris declared. "Every well-disciplined school inculcates these things."[15]

Often criticized for being too conservative, Harris never deviated from his own lockstep form of school organization. The graded system, in his view, was the best one for elementary education. Resisting curricular change, Harris defended his vertical K–8–4 plan as the only workable pattern for kindergarten through high school. He discounted as exaggerated "impulse and inclination" the Herbartian emphasis on interest as a motivating force and adhered instead to textbook instruction as the dominant methodology in teaching.

Apparently Harris saw no conflict between education as social subordination and adjustment and his own stress on pupil self-activity and human reason. Indeed, the idea of self-activity was basic in Harris's educational philosophy. He espoused with favor Froebel's concepts and even adapted to the elementary school some of the liberal methodology proposed for the kindergarten. But "self-activity" for Harris had a limited connotation: he fervently believed, for example, that the school should train the child to obey habitually, with or without understanding, and to accept at all times established authority. These and other contradictions Harris merely resolved by his own dialectical method.

Voiced from St. Louis and Washington, Harris' pedagogical ideas were a strong influence during a formative period in educational history. Discipline, authority, adjustment—these were the keynotes of his powerful ideology, which still exerts a force on the minds of American teachers and laypersons.

Francis Wayland Parker and the "Quincy Plan"

Every profession has its great pioneers who perpetually spark the imaginations of dedicated practitioners. In the years following the Civil War, Francis Wayland Parker was truly an innovator whose educational theories continue to evoke admiration (and criticism) among teachers and laymen. Unlike Harris, Parker showed none of the marks of a systematic thinker. "Temperamentally, he was a man of action," wrote Flora Cooke, one of Parker's former students, "and he left behind him few published articles to serve the uses of students of education."[16]

Francis Wayland Parker was born in a small New Hampshire village in 1837, the year that Horace Mann accepted the secretaryship of the Board of Education in Massachusetts. He worked on a farm and attended a district school for brief periods during the year. At sixteen he began his career as a village teacher in Webster, New Hampshire; five years later he moved to the Midwest, where he became principal of a school in Carrollton, Illinois. "It was probably the roughest school [in which] I ever taught," Parker recalled in his *Autobiographical Sketch*. "I remember the first speech I made to the pupils seated in a big chair. I told them that my idea of a good school was to have a first class time, and that in order to have a good time they must all take hold and work together, and then they would be sure of a good time."[17] At the outbreak of the Civil War, he enlisted in the Union Army, rose from private to the rank of colonel, and served during the entire conflict.

In 1868, Park resumed teaching in Dayton, Ohio, and began studying the leading works of European educators. He became increasingly restless with the regimented control and harsh pupil discipline he witnessed in the schools and quickly abandoned in his own classroom. "There should be no whipping or flogging" and "the switch is a clear indication of a poor teacher," he later declared.[18]

In 1872, with a legacy of five thousand dollars from his aunt, Parker followed in the path of Horace Mann (to whom he frequently referred) and went to Europe for two and a half years. He attended lectures at the University of King William in Berlin and traveled extensively on the Continent. He studied Herbart's ideas, observed the practices of Pestalozzi, and became thoroughly imbued with the pedagogical ideas of Froebel, a "never-failing source," Parker later acknowledged, for his own educational theories.

Returning to the United States in 1875, Parker accepted a superintendency in Quincy, Massachusetts, where, according to Charles Francis Adams, a member of the school committee, "the school system had fallen into a rut."[19] The teacher in Quincy, Adams declared, had "turned his scholars into parrots and made a meaningless farce of education. . . . It was, in a word, all smatter, veneering, and cram." Seeking a change, the members persuaded the town to hire a superintendent and "put the working-out of the new system in his hands." The committee then canvassed the field of potential candidates and

> chanced across one who had not only himself taught, but in teaching had become possessed with the idea that it was a science, and that he did not understand it. He had . . . made himself master of the modern German theories of common-school education. A self-educated and self-made man, with all the defects as well as the virtues of men of that class, he was now eagerly looking about for an opportunity to put his theories in practice. That opportunity was offered him in Quincy.[20]

Parker moved into his new job with great zeal and sought immediately to infuse the Quincy schools with a new spirit. "Nothing that is good is too good for the child," he believed, "no thought too deep, no toil too great, no work too arduous."[21]

To begin with, Parker abandoned the whole curriculum and introduced a completely different, experimental program. "The essence of the new system was that there was no system about it—it was marked throughout by intense individuality," Adams declared.[22] Throughout his career, much of Parker's ire was directed toward meaningless recitations of words and symbols. With no time wasted, he quickly tried to supplant *memoriter* work with understanding and more meaningful learning.[23] The teachers themselves brought in new reading material for the children and relied less and less on the traditional textbook. In geography, for instance, Pestalozzi's "object lesson" was stressed, with knowledge obtained through various classroom projects. "Go, today, into the Quincy schools and in a few moments two or three young children, standing about an earth board and handling a little heap of moistened clay, will shape out for you a continent, with its mountains, rivers, and coast indentations, designating upon it the principal cities, and giving a general idea of its geographical peculiarities," Adams bragged in 1879.[24] The effect of these reforms on both pupil and teacher was, in Adams's words, a "point of interest." The teachers experienced a new sense of accomplishment, and "the children actually went to school without being dragged there." Remembering the situation in Quincy before Parker arrived, Adams remarked: "It was certainly most pleasant to go into the rooms and feel the atmosphere of cheerfulness, activity and interest which prevaded [*sic*] them." The "revolution," as Adams described the Quincy Plan, was complete. "Nothing escaped its influence; it began with the alphabet and extended into the last effort of the grammar school course."[25]

Parker's "new departure" in Quincy and his subsequent reforms at the Cook County Normal School in Chicago reflected his deep love for children and his lifelong faith in democracy as a way of life. Integral to his own personality, both beliefs were ever present in his educational approach. "In every child he saw the image of God, and so he not only loved, but, in a sense, worshiped little children," declared E. E. White, who was state commissioner of schools when Parker worked in Dayton, Ohio.[26]

Because Parker viewed the child as naturally curious about everything, his curricular concepts were broad, covering a wide range of subjects. For example, art ("the revelation of the laws of nature and of man") became a pervasive part of the entire instructional process. He also stressed the study of grammar (to be taught and mastered "beyond doubt"). According to Lelia Patridge's "Notes," Parker believed that every lesson should be planned and presented "to evolve thought."[27] Geography, studied with the "critical eye" of a "field geologist," assumed great importance, beginning, as Parker said, "with the real earth."[28] "*Above all*," Parker urged, "*have the structure distinctly in your own mind* before you attempt to teach it. *Vagueness on the part of the teacher is generally the main fault in teaching.*"[29]

Evaluated in the light of certain criteria, Parker's Quincy Plan was an obvious success. In 1879, partly to quell the critics, the Quincy pupils were subjected to state examinations and exceeded the scores of other school children in Massachusetts. Parker's reforms were also being viewed as a bold "new departure" in American educational history and were drawing considerable attention in the late 1870s. By 1878, the number of observers visiting the Quincy schools had increased so much that the school committee had to intervene with regulations to control the situation. "The outcome was what may always be expected under similar circumstances—progressive movement," Parker later remarked in recalling his work in Quincy. "If you ask me to name the best of all in results, I should say, the more humane treatment of little folks. . . . The rod was well-nigh banished. The doctrine of total depravity will have much to answer for in the day of judgment."[30]

After achieving fame in Quincy, Parker left in 1880, spent three years as a supervisor in Boston, and then moved on to the principalship of the Cook County Normal School in Chicago. As principal, he was responsible for the teacher-training classes and a practice school that became a public school for the surrounding neighborhood. For eighteen years at Cook County, Parker had a unique opportunity to refine his educational theories and techniques. He was omnipresent in the school and on the playground, towering over the pupils, who followed and worshiped him as though he were a benevolent god. "It is impossible, in mere words, to convey the confidence which he invariably inspired in children," wrote his biographer.[31]

Parker's intense, almost naïve, devotion to the child was patterned after Froebel's ideas. Almost verbatim, his phraseology was Froebelian: "The child is the climax and culmination of all God's creations," Parker began in his first *Talk*, "and to answer the question, 'What is the child?' is to approach nearer the still greater question, What is the Creator and Giver of Life?" "The spontaneous tendencies of the child are the records of inborn divinity."

"All mental and moral development is by self-activity."[32] "God has given us every child in this world to save."[33]

In Parker, the educational theories of Rousseau, Pestalozzi, and Froebel found an avid transmitter: by the late nineteenth century no educational leader in the United States had digested so completely their romantic notions of the child. "I wish to have these words written in italics," emphasized Parker before an open session of the Herbart Club in the summer of 1895. "We do not claim that nature is the center, neither do we claim that history and literature are the center, *we do claim that the child is the center*, that this being, this highest creation of God, with its laws of body, mind, and soul, determines in itself the very nature and condition of its growth."[34] Largely through the efforts and writings of Parker, John Dewey, and G. Stanley Hall, the focus of attention in American elementary education gradually shifted from the traditional curriculum to "the child-centered school."[35]

Parker's reverence for the child was strengthened by his optimistic belief in the capacity of people for growth and change. "I have unbounded faith in the development of the human race," he stated in his "Pedagogical Creed."[36] He also believed fervently that "the goal of humanity is freedom" and that "democracy is the only form of government under which the methods of freedom can be fostered."[37] Over and over again, he told his teachers that "a school should be a model home, a complete community and embryonic democracy."

Parker's faith in democracy as a form of government never waned. In linking the school with democracy, he viewed public education as the cornerstone of a free nation. "Here in America we are bringing together all peoples from all parts of the known world, with all their prejudices born of centuries," Parker noted. "Here they come into our broad continent, and we propose to have them live together, and legislate together for the best good of the whole. No dream of the past, no vision of the progress of humanity, could ever propose such a tremendous problem as this." What is the function of the public school toward solving this problem? Simply this, answered Parker: the school eliminates prejudice and fuses diverse nationalities into a new society. "The social factor in school is the greatest factor of all; it stands higher than subjects of learning, than methods of teaching, than the teacher himself," he declared. Children in a public school, "before prejudice has entered their childish souls, before hate has become fixed, before mistrust has become a habit," learn to live and to work together. "This mingling, fusing, and blending give personal power, and make the public school a tremendous force for the upbuilding of democracy."[38] Thus, for Parker, the public school was to be the cohesive element in a free society.

It was this deep belief in the democratic process that set Parker apart from the European theorists and gave this approach its only original mark. Based on European ideas, Parker's views foreshadowed the important, and more indigenous, work of his friend, John Dewey, who arrived at the University of Chicago in 1894 and opened his own "Laboratory School" two years later.

AN AMERICAN SYNTHESIS: THE EDUCATIONAL PHILOSOPHY OF JOHN DEWEY

The Formative Years

John Dewey was born in Burlington, Vermont, in 1859, the year that Darwin's *Origin of Species* was published. He was graduated from the University of Vermont in 1879, and after teaching for short intervals in South Oil City, Pennsylvania, and in Charlotte, Vermont, he reentered the university for a year of graduate study in philosophy. He studied under Professor H. A. P. Torrey, whose philosophical teaching was based on Scottish realism.[39]

Later, at the then-new Johns Hopkins University, where he earned his doctorate, Dewey was introduced to the Hegelian idealism of George S. Morris and the experimental psychology of G. Stanley Hall. His early interest in psychology continued at the University of Michigan, where he taught for several years and worked with Morris, who was also a member of the faculty. He was also influenced by the psychological ideas of William James, whose *Principles of Psychology* (1890) was "the greatest single influence in changing the direction of Dewey's philosophical thinking."[40]

There were other forces, too, that affected Dewey's outlook: for example, George Herbert Mead's social theories, Auguste Comte's positivism, and Thorstein Veblen's socioeconomic ideas.[41] Dewey's thought was also profoundly influenced by Darwinism, with its strong experimental approach.[42] It is important to remember, too, that this formative period in Dewey's intellectual growth coincided with the rise of progressivism, with its turbulent atmosphere of militant social protest. As Dewey's own ideas gradually shifted from the study of philosophy as a strict discipline toward a broader view of social aims and a more active consideration of educational issues, these elements that affected his thinking came into sharper focus.[43]

Dewey's frequently quoted definition of philosophy indicates the changing direction of his system of ideas: "Philosophy may even be defined *as the general theory of education*," he wrote in 1916. "Unless a philosophy is to remain symbolic—or verbal—or a sentimental indulgence for a few, or else mere arbitrary dogma, its auditing of past experience and its program of values must take effect in conduct."[44] For Dewey, then, philosophy became an *instrument* of action in human affairs. Indeed, his whole doctrine of *instrumentalism* revolves around the theory that ideas are tools or instruments with which people might change (or improve) their environment; and the truth or error of these ideas is determined by whether or not they ultimately work in actual practice.

In 1894 Dewey accepted an appointment as head of the departments of philosophy, psychology, and pedagogy at the University of Chicago, where he remained for ten years. From 1904 until emeritus status, he was professor of philosophy at Columbia University. During his long career at Columbia, he wrote and published extensively, attracting a multitude of devoted followers. For at least a half century he was regarded by many as the foremost educational philosopher in the United States. Certainly no other philosopher has devoted so much attention to American education; none has influenced the schools so profoundly.

John Dewey developed his philosophy of education for two basic reasons: First, he believed that the public-school systems were in a state of degradation and could no longer adequately educate the nation's children. Second, and equally significant, Dewey was a philosopher with a vision and a strong sense of optimism and hope for the future of American education . He hoped that some day the United States would become a utopian society, strongly committed to the ideals of human compassion and brotherhood among people of different races and creeds. Dewey formulated a philosophy of education to merge these two convictions into one. He proposed a radical transformation of the existing public school systems with the implementation of progressive education, based on the premise that social reform and progress truly begins with the education of children. If the main emphasis of education is placed on the development of "social" skills and behavior, Dewey argued, society would eventually follow this goal. This was the main ideology of progressive education and explains why John Dewey assumed the leadership of the movement. The Progressive thinkers captured this idea in their philosophy and their efforts to transform an America of individualism, waste, corruption, and greed into a nation of humanism, compassion, and equality. How could the United States be described as a great society if a majority of the American people were uneducated, poor, and lacking in a sense of pride and hope for the future? Dewey's philosophy of education struck at the very core of this irony.

John Dewey detested the uniformity of curriculum, the massing of students, and the textbook learning to which children were subjected. The teachers dominated the classrooms and set rigid guidelines and goals for each child. This type of education, Dewey believed, alienated children from learning. This narrow approach to education, Dewey insisted, must be replaced with a new system that gave high priority to the interests of the child—a different approach in which learning became self-motivated, enjoyable, and child-centered.

Thus Dewey developed a viable alternative that gave children the freedom to develop and understand themselves in the context of the world around them—a practical education based on experience, participation, and hands-on exercises. Active learning became the core of Dewey's philosophy—an approach that represented learning by living, a concept Dewey held dear to his heart. No longer would children be forced to memorize information that had no practical meaning to them. Instead, they would be encouraged to investigate, experiment, and discover those things that sparked their interests. They would be given the opportunity to reach their own conclusions when participating in experiments that had a direct correlation to the world around them.

In a larger perspective, Dewey hoped that this method of teaching would help to develop the full potential of each student. If children understood their own abilities and capacities through experience, Dewey argued, as adults, they would become productive members of society. Ultimately the school would instill habits and behaviors in the children that would encourage them to control their environment, not simply adapt to it. This was the crux of progressive education, exemplifying the faith John Dewey had in the human spirit for creating a "worthy, lovely, and harmonious" society in the United States.

Dewey's arrival at the University of Chicago in 1894 was a fortuitous event in American education. In terms of historical significance, it was, as Dworkin says, comparable to Mann's appointment as secretary to the Massachusetts State Board of Education. Dewey appeared on the educational scene at a particularly appropriate time—"as if he had had an eye on a clock of destiny."[45] His early reform efforts in Chicago in the late 1890s drew sympathetic support from a vast array of disillusioned forces. Not all were fighting for the same cause, but each group viewed public education as a means toward social betterment.[46] To some extent, Jane Addams's work at Hull House and Parker's reforms at the Cook County Normal School had already paved the way for Dewey's innovations in his Laboratory School. At the University of Chicago there were numerous educational events and lectures during the 1890s, including, for example, Horace Mann's Centennial and the 150th anniversary of Pestalozzi's birth. There was, then, by the end of the nineteenth century a highly receptive audience for educational change.

It remained for John Dewey to synthesize through his work and writings the important ideas of educational reform that had been in ferment for years. Dewey, after all, was heir to a liberal tradition in Western educational thought that reached back to the theories and work of such famous predecessors as Bacon, Pestalozzi, Rousseau, Herbart, and Froebel. Like Jefferson and Mann, Dewey recognized the crucial significance of public education in a democracy. While his synthesis was obviously tempered by the unique demands of the American scene, it should, nevertheless, be viewed as a part of the mainstream of intellectual history.

The "Dewey School"

In the Laboratory School he established with his wife, Alice Chipman Dewey, at the University of Chicago, Dewey developed experimentally some of his educational ideas. The school opened in January 1896, with 2 instructors and 16 children. By 1902 the school had expanded to a maximum enrollment of 140 pupils with 23 teachers and 10 university graduate students who served as assistants. Ranging in ages from four to fourteen, the children were divided into small groups, with 8 to 10 pupils in each class. With Dewey as director and Mrs. Dewey as principal, the school pursued a course so unique that by 1904 it became, according to Cremin, "the most interesting experimental venture in American education."[47]

What was so unusual about Dewey's Laboratory School? How did it differ from other elementary schools of the 1890s? First and foremost, the Laboratory School was child-centered. Pupil interests became basic determinants of the curriculum and were followed from time to time wherever they might lead. Dewey declared in 1895:

> The ground must be traveled step by step. It is always *today* in the teacher's practice. The teacher must be able to see to what *immediate and proximate use* the child's interests are to be put in order that he may be moving along the desired line, in the desired direction. The interest to scribble must be taken advantage of *now*, not in order that ten years from now he shall write beautiful letters, or do fine bookkeeping, but that he may get some good of it now; may affect something which shall open another step in advance, and draw him on from his own crudity. This utilizing of interest and habit to make of it something fuller, wider, something more refined and under better control, might be defined as the teacher's whole duty.[48]

Thus the Laboratory School differed sharply from the traditional school in its treatment of course material. As Dewey remarked to the children's parents in February 1899, "The teachers started with question marks, rather than fixed rules."[49] Of course, an experimental school, associated with the University of Chicago, that altered so completely its traditional curriculum in the pursuit of so-called self-directed interests was a somewhat daring innovation destined to elicit some comment at the turn of the century.

The purpose of the school was twofold: "(1) to exhibit, test, verify, and criticize [Dewey's] theoretical statements and principles; and (2) to add to the sum of facts and principles in its special line."[50] The Laboratory School was linked to the University of Chicago from 1896 to 1904. During this period, Dewey and his staff tried to develop a unified system from the kindergarten to the college level.

According to Katherine Mayhew and Anna Edwards, two sisters who at one time actually taught at the school and later wrote a book about the venture, the faculty sought to relate the present to the past through a multitude of meaningful learning activities. Dewey and the teachers developed certain "experimental practices" based on "the growth stages" of the learner. There are interesting references in *The Dewey School* to "a spirit of freedom and mutual respect" throughout the school; "self-discipline" among the children; "subject matter modified to suit experience"; "alert curiosity about the keen interest in all life, both plant and animal"; and "the growth of self-directive power and judgment." Judging from the lengthy descriptions of two disciples, the "Dewey School" was truly an educational oasis at the beginning of the twentieth century.

Dewey's Educational Writings

It is noteworthy that Dewey's most important educational theories were formulated during the Chicago years when he was so involved with the realistic problems and issues of his Laboratory School.[51] Statements *about* Dewey's ideas are numerous, and no attempt will be made to add another long digest to the list. A brief and careful examination of his most famous writings will, however, indicate the range and depth of Dewey's educational thought. Of course, no abstract or analysis is a satisfactory substitute for actually reading his complete work.

The School and Society, first published in 1899, was a series of three lectures Dewey delivered to friends and parents of the Laboratory School. At the time, their purpose was to refute certain criticisms and to increase the financial support of the school. The three lectures did far more: seized upon by proponents of the "new education" as a rationale for their experimental practices, Dewey's small book became one of the most popular of his educational treatises.

In his first lecture, entitled "The School and Social Progress," Dewey elaborated on the transfer to the public school of educational functions formerly performed in the home. "This has not been done 'on purpose,' " he declared. Curricular modifications in the school, Dewey explained, reflect the changes occurring in society. "It is to this, then, that I especially ask your attention: the effort to conceive what roughly may be termed the 'New Education' in the light of larger changes in society." Dewey then proceeded to point out how the rise of industrialism had accelerated a great transformation in society. "If our education is to have any meaning for life, it must pass through an equally complete transformation," Dewey asserted.

> The introduction of active occupations, of nature study, of elementary science, of art, of history: the relegation of the merely symbolic and formal to a secondary position; the change in the moral school atmosphere, in the relation of pupils and teachers—of discipline; the introduction of more active, expressive, and self-directing factors—all these are not mere accidents, they are necessities of the larger social evolution.

It remains but to organize all these factors, to appreciate them in their fullness of meaning, and to put the ideas and ideals involved into complete, uncompromising possession of our school system. To do this means to make each one of our schools an embryonic community life, active with types of occupations that reflect the life of the larger society, and permeated throughout with the spirit of art, history, and science. When the school introduces and trains each child of society into member-ship within such a little community, saturating him with the spirit of service, and providing him with the instruments of effective self-direction, we shall have the deepest and best guarantee of a larger society which is worthy, lovely, and harmonious.[52]

From Dewey's early writings one cannot fail to sense his fresh hope and optimism at the dawn of a new century for a better society for all Americans.

In his subsequent lectures, "The School and the Life of the Child" and "Waste in Education," Dewey criticized the "traditional schoolroom" with "its passivity of attitude, its mechanical massing of children, its uniformity of curriculum and method." He pleaded for a child-centered education in which, as he put it, "the child becomes the sun about which the appliances of education revolve." Bring "nature and society" into the school and subordi-nate "the forms and tools of learning . . . to the substance of experience," urged Dewey. He illustrated his arguments with several examples drawn from practices in the Laboratory School. "The growth of the child in the direction of social capacity and service, his larger and more vital union with life, becomes the unifying aim; and discipline, culture and information fall into place as phases of his growth," he concluded.[53]

Like Rousseau, Parker, and others in the progressivist tradition, Dewey placed the child at the center of the educational process. But by 1899 Dewey was extending this point beyond the thesis of his predecessors and was arguing for an essentially political role of the school as a basic instrument for social change. This was evident, too, in *My Pedagogic Creed*, first published in 1897. "Education is the fundamental method of social progress and reform," he wrote.[54] Here, perhaps, is seen most clearly the close relationship between Dewey's social theory of education and the broader aims of the progressivist movement in which these ideas evolved.

Three years later, in another small treatise, Dewey elaborated further on his child-centered views of this educative process.[55] In *The Child and the Curriculum* (1902) he argued for a more meaningful connection between the immediate experiences of children and the organized knowledge of the disciplines. "Abandon the notion of subject-matter as something fixed and ready-made in itself, outside the child's experience," urged Dewey. "Cease thinking of the child's experience as also something hard and fast; see it as something fluent, embryonic, vital; and we realize that the child and the curriculum are simply two points which define a single process."[56] *How We*

Think was published in 1910; and six years later, *Democracy and Education*, now a classic in educational history, appeared.

Dewey wrote *How We Think* because, as he put it, of his own "conviction . . . that the native and unspoiled attitude of childhood, marked by ardent curiosity, fertile imagination, and love of experimental inquiry, is near, very near, to the attitude of the scientific mind."[57] This "attitude," Dewey explained, is characterized by "reflective thinking" that occurs only when a problem is presented. Thinking is an *active* process involving experimentation and problem solving. *"Demand for the solution of a perplexity is the steadying and guiding factor in the entire process of reflection,"* he emphasized.

> Where there is no question of a problem to be solved or a difficulty to be surmounted, the course of suggestions flows on at random. . . . But a question to be answered, an ambiguity to be resolved, sets up an end and holds the current of ideas to a definite channel. Every suggested conclusion is tested by its reference to this regulating end, by its pertinence to the problem in hand.[58]

Thus, for Dewey, problem solving was essential for mental activity; it was, in brief, the underlying factor in the thought process.

In explaining how we think, Dewey described a process of "five logically distinct steps":[59] (1) The occurrence of a problem—"a felt difficulty." (2) Analysis of the problem into its various elements *before* proceeding to solve it. "This, more than any other thing, transforms mere inference into tested inference, suggested conclusions into proof." (3) Formulation of hypotheses as to possible solutions. "Suggestion is the very heart of inference; it involves going from what is present to something absent." (4) The rational elaboration of ideas through experimentation. "As an idea is inferred from given facts, so reasoning sets out from an idea." (5) Actual corroboration of an idea. *"Conditions are deliberately arranged in accord with the requirements of an idea or hypothesis to see if the results theoretically indicated by the idea actually occur."*

In its simplest form, Dewey's process was nothing more than the time-honored method of inductive reasoning advocated in the seventeenth century by Francis Bacon. Applied to the teaching-learning process, it became the dominant methodology of experimentalism. Rejecting dogma and a closed mind, the experimental attitude gained enormous prestige under Dewey's influence and permeated American education at every level in the twentieth century.

Democracy and Education synthesized the varied aspects of Dewey's pedagogical theory. Most of the ideas had been advanced in previous writings; his social views, for example, were a reiteration of statements presented in *My Pedagogic Creed* and *The School and Society*. Nevertheless, as a single volume, *Democracy and Education* became widely accessible and thus provided in 1916 a popular summary compatible with the reform spirit of the time.[60]

Dewey argued for a type of education conducive to "the development of a democratic community" characterized by "greater freedom" and "a consciously socialized interest." His philosophy, he said, applied "to social groups which are intentionally progressive, and which aim at a greater variety of mutually shared interests in distinction from those which aim simply at the preservation of established customs." Over and over again, Dewey underscored the dynamic character of American education, requiring, he believed, a "consciously directed movement" in "a progressively developing society."[61]

Throughout his writings, Dewey referred to education as a *process*, not an end product, "a continuous process of growth, having as its aim at every stage an added capacity of growth."[62] This point of view, Dewey stated, differs sharply from the traditional conception. "Since in reality there is nothing to which growth is relative save more growth, there is nothing to which education is subordinate save more education," he declared. Education is not a *preparation* for life. Education begins when the child is born and continues throughout life. In brief, education *is* life. As Dewey wrote: "The inclination to learn from life itself and to make the conditions of life such that all will learn in the process of living is the finest product of schooling."[63]

Dewey gave high priority to the concept of "experience" in the teaching-learning process. He defined *education* as "that reconstruction or reorganization of experience which adds to the meaning of experience, and which increases ability to direct the course of subsequent experience."[64] This point of view permeated his whole educational philosophy. He considered "experience" to be the basis of all methodology.[65] "Method is a statement of the way the subject matter of an experience develops most effectively and fruitfully," he explained. Emphasizing again the main theme of *How We Think*, Dewey asserted that "thinking is the method of intelligent learning" and that one learns how to think through "*experience*."

> Hence the first approach to any subject in school, if thought is to be aroused and not words acquired, should be as unscholastic as possible. To realize what an experience, or empirical situation, means, we have to call to mind the sort of situation that presents itself outside of school; the sort of occupations that interest and engage activity in ordinary life. And careful inspection of methods which are permanently successful in formal education, whether in arithmetic or learning to read, or studying geography, or learning physics or a foreign language, will reveal that they depend for their efficiency upon the fact that they go back to the type of the situation which causes reflection out of school in ordinary life. They give the pupils something to do, not something to learn; and the doing is

of such a nature as to demand thinking, or the intentional noting of connections; learning naturally results.[66]

Not since Rousseau has anyone relied so exclusively on the *quality* of direct experience in formulating an educational theory.

In a democratic society, Dewey expected "intelligence to be the purposive reorganization, through action, of the material of experience." By teaching boys and girls how to think, the school would help them ultimately to *"control"* and change their environment. "Education is a constant reorganizing or reconstructing of experience," Dewey repeated. "It has all the time an immediate end, and so far as activity is educative, it reaches that end—the direct transformation of the quality of experience."[67]

> Men have long had some intimation of the extent to which education may be consciously used to eliminate obvious social evils through starting the young on paths which shall not produce these ills, and some idea of the extent in which education may be made an instrument of realizing the better hopes of men. But we are doubtless far from realizing the potential efficacy of education as a constructive agency of improving society, from realizing that it represents not only a development of children and youth but also of the future society of which they will be the constituents.[68]

This optimism, so characteristic during his formative years, became the mainspring for Dewey's educational argument. He hoped that a new synthesis of educational theory would resolve certain dualisms in educational thought—that old antitheses between vocation and culture, interest and discipline, activity and subject matter, and the child and society could be harmonized within a new educational framework. Then and only then, he believed, would a democracy reap the benefits promised by a new age of science and industry.

Dewey's views were disseminated everywhere through his work at Chicago and Columbia and, until his death in 1952 at the age of ninety-two, through a steady stream of articles, commentaries, and books.[69] At Teachers College, Columbia University, Dewey had direct contact through his courses with a vast number of teachers from all parts of the United States and from other nations. Many of his books passed through several editions and reprintings. *The School and Society*, for instance, was translated into several European and Oriental languages and publicized throughout the world; in recent years, no other educational work has been so widely distributed.

As early as 1904, when he moved to Columbia, Dewey was being recognized in some quarters as the chief spokesman for the "new education." He was one of the few leaders in the history of American education who lived long enough to see his own conclusions become the established doctrine of a new movement sweeping across the land. What he failed to witness, of course, was the counterrevolution in the years following his death that sought to repudiate the progressivist creed and to recast "the school and society" in a different light.

It is a grave understatement to remark that Dewey's ideas were misunderstood: few thinkers have been so severely condemned because of the feverish work and gross *mis*interpretations of their followers.[70] In fairness to everyone, however, Dewey should not be absolved from all blame for the manner in which his own beliefs were so distorted. The works of his self-appointed disciples have been widely perused by classroom teachers because their books are directly related to methodology and professional problems and are more coherent and readable. Removed from context, Dewey's vaguely defined terms—"experience," "growth," "democracy," and so on— tended to create confusion and permitted those who had read his works, or who had read *about* them, to shape the meaning to fit their own preconceived notions.[71] In disjointed and incredibly obscure prose, through thirty-six books and over eight hundred articles, Dewey built his philosophical system and led his followers along a pragmatic path toward an ideal society.

FOR DISCUSSION AND CRITICAL THOUGHT

1. What was the significance of European thought in the development of an American philosophy of education?
2. Do you agree, as Richard Hofstadter notes in *Anti-intellectualism in American Life* (Knopf, 1983), that an anti-intellectualism pervasive in American life reflects to some extent Benjamin Franklin's utilitarian philosophy and John Dewey's pragmatic outlook? Comment critically.
3. In what way is the educational philosophy of John Dewey evident in schools today? How have his ideas been modified during the past few decades? How might he change contemporary schools? Could these changes possibly affect the high dropout or "push-out" rate of students? Explain.
4. John Dewey borrowed ideas from several philosophers and reformers. Identify these leaders, and tell how Dewey synthesized their ideas into a new philosophy of education.

NOTES

1. See Johann Friedrich Herbart, *The Science of Education: Its General Principles Deduced from Its Aim*, trans. Henry M. and Emmie Felkin (Boston: Heath, 1895).

2. Johann Friedrich Herbart, *Brief Encyclopaedia of Practical Philosophy*, trans. Robert Ulich, in Robert Ulich, ed., *Three Thousand Years of Educational Wisdom: Selections from Great Documents* (2nd ed.; Cambridge, Mass.: Harvard University Press, 1965), p. 511.

3. For a provocative interpretation of Herbart's concept of "education *through* instruction," see Gabriel Compayré, *Herbart and Education by Instruction*, trans. Marie E. Findlay (New York: Crowell, 1907), pp. 46–47.

4. John Dewey, *Interest in Relation to Training of the Will*, Second Supplement to the Herbart Yearbook for 1895 (Chicago: University of Chicago Press, 1895), p. 29.

5. Herbart, *The Science of Education*, p. 126.

6. Friedrich Froebel, *The Education of Man*, trans. and annotated W. N. Hailman (New York: D. Appleton, 1887), pp. 28–29. Note the similarity between this Froebelian concept and the more recently defined term "developmental task." See Robert J. Havighurst, *Developmental Tasks and Education* (New York: Longmans, Green, 1951), p. 6.

7. Froebel, *The Education of Man*, p. 119.

8. Ibid., pp. 54–55.

9. Henry Barnard, "Froebel's System of Infant-Gardens," *American Journal of Education* 2 (1856): 449–451.

10. There is some doubt concerning the historical accuracy of the date and place of the first *public* kindergarten established in the United States. See Douglas E. Lawson, "Corrective Note on the Early History of the American Kindergarten," *Educational Administration and Supervision, Including Teacher Training* 25 (1939): 699–703. Contrary to traditional claims, Lawson credits Boston with establishing in 1870 the first kindergarten as a part of its public system.

11. William T. Harris, "The Kindergarten as a Preparation for the Highest Civilization" (Address before a meeting of the International Kindergarten Union, Pittsburgh, Pa., on 16 April 1903), p. 24.

12. Kurt F. Leidecker, *Yankee Teacher: The Life of William Torrey Harris* (New York: Philosophical Library, 1946), pp. 258–60.

13. See Charles M. Perry, "William Torrey Harris and the St. Louis Movement in Philosophy," in Edward L. Schaub, ed., *William Torrey Harris, 1835–1935* (Chicago: Open Court Publishing, 1936), pp. 28–48.

14. For a provocative discussion of Hegel's influence upon Harris's educational ideas, see John S. Roberts, *William T. Harris: A Critical Study of His Educational and Related Philosophical Views* (Washington, D.C.: National Education Association, 1924), pp. 39–46.

15. William T. Harris, "Morality in the Schools," Register Tract Series, No. 12 (pamphlet reprinted from the *Christian Register*, Boston, 31 January 1889).

16. Francis Wayland Parker, *Talks on Pedagogics: An Outline of the Theory of Concentration*, ed. Elsie A. Wygant and Flora J. Cooke (New York: John Day, 1937; published for the Progressive Education Association from the original edition), "Preface to Revised Edition," p. xv. First published in 1894, this was Parker's most important book. It is a collection of informal lectures presented to teachers in July 1891, at a Teachers' Retreat, Chautauqua Assembly, in New York.

17. William M. Giffin, *School Days in the Fifties: A True Story with Some Untrue Names of Persons and Places, With an Appendix, Containing an Autobiographical Sketch of Francis Wayland Parker* (Chicago: A. Flanagan, 1906), p. 121.

18. Francis W. Parker. "The Child," *National Education Association Journal of Proceedings, and Addresses, 1889, Held at Nashville, Tennessee*, p. 482. Nevertheless, during his long career Parker apparently did not refrain from the use of corporal punishment; at least, this appeared to be the case in Carrollton, Illinois. According to Marion Washburne, "There was one incorrigible who had to be thrashed, but the young principal (Parker) took pains to do it out of school, where he could claim no advantage from his position of teacher, and when he and the bad boy met on equal terms, as man to man." Marion Foster Washburne, "Col. Parker, The Man, and Educational Reformer: A Biographical Sketch," in *Talks on Teaching* by Francis W. Parker (reported by Lelia E. Patridge) (New York: Barnes, 1883), Appendix, p. 8.

19. Charles F. Adams, Jr., *The New Departure in the Common Schools of Quincy and Other Papers on Educational Topics* (Boston: Este & Lauriat, 1879), p. 33.

20. Ibid., pp. 33–35.

21. Francis W. Parker, *Talks on Pedagogics: An Outline of the Theory of Concentration* (New York and Chicago: E. L. Kellogg, 1894), p. 451.

22. Adams, *The New Departure in the Common Schools of Quincy*, p. 37.

23. For some lively descriptions of pupil-teacher relationships in Quincy during Parker's tenure, see Lelia E. Patridge. *The "Quincy Methods" Illustrated: Pen Photographs from the Quincy Schools* (New York: E. L. Kellogg, 1885).

24. Adams, *The New Departure in the Common Schools of Quincy*, p. 43.

25. Ibid., pp. 37–45.

26. National Education Association, *Journal of Proceedings and Addresses of the Forty-first Annual Meeting Held at Minneapolis, Minnesota* (7–11 July 1902), p. 406.

27. *Notes of Talks on Teaching* (4th ed.: New York: E. L. Kellogg, 1883; presented by Francis W. Parker, at the Martha's Vineyard Summer Institute, 17 July–19 August 1882, and reported by Lelia E. Patridge), talk 14, "Composition," p. 89.

28. Geography was obviously one of Parker's favorite subjects. He even wrote a book entitled *How to Study Geography* (New York: D. Appleton, 1889), which he dedicated "to all teachers who thoughtfully and thoroughly prepare every lesson."

29. Ibid., p. 93. Italics in original.

30. Francis W. Parker, " 'The Quincy Method' " (Address delivered on 20 April 1900) in U.S. Bureau of Education, *Report of the Commissioner of Education for the Year 1902*, 1:240.

31. Ida Cassa Heffron, *Francis Wayland Parker: An Interpretive Biography* (Los Angeles: Ivan Deach, Jr., 1934), p. 60.

32. Parker, *Talks on Pedagogics* (1894), pp. 3, 23, 25.

33. National Education Association, *Journal of the Proceedings and Addresses, Asbury Park, New Jersey, 1894*, p. 587.

34. Francis W. Parker, "Contribution to the 'Discussion' of Dr. C. C. Van Liew's Essay on 'Culture Epochs,' " National Society for the Study of Education, First

Supplement to the *Yearbook* of the National Herbart Society (1895), p. 156. Italics in original.

35. The title of only one of a score of books espousing the same point of view. See, for instance, Harold Rugg and Ann Shumaker, *The Child-Centered School* (Yonkers-on-Hudson, N.Y.: World Book, 1928).

36. Ossian H. Lang, ed., *Educational Creeds of the Nineteenth Century*. The Practical Teachers' Library, vol. 4, no. 1 (New York and Chicago: E. L. Kellogg, 1898), "The Pedagogical Creed of Col. Francis W. Parker," p. 54.

37. Parker, *Talks on Pedagogics* (1894), pp. 419–420.

38. Ibid., pp. 420–422.

39. "Biography of John Dewey," written by his daughters and edited by Jane Dewey, in Paul Arthur Schilpp, ed., *The Philosophy of John Dewey*, The Library of Living Philosophers, vol. 1 (Evanston and Chicago: Northwestern University, 1939), pp. 3–45. See also George Dykhuizen, "An Early Chapter in the Life of John Dewey," *Journal of the History of Ideas* 13 (October 1952): 563–72.

40. "Biography of John Dewey," in Schilpp, ed., *The Philosophy of John Dewey*, p. 23.

41. For a discussion of some similarities between Dewey's social ideas and Veblen's *The Theory of the Leisure Class* (1899), see Morton G. White, *Social Thought in America: The Revolt against Formalism* (New York: Viking Press, 1949), pp. 94–100.

42. See John Dewey, *The Influence of Darwin on Philosophy, and Other Essays in Contemporary Thought* (New York: Henry Holt, 1910), pp. 1–19.

43. See George Dykhuizen, "John Dewey: The Chicago Years," *Journal of the History of Philosophy* 2 (October 1964): 234–239.

44. John Dewey, *Democracy and Education: An Introduction to the Philosophy of Education* (New York: Macmillan, 1916), p. 383. Italics in original. Fourteen years later, Dewey asserted in retrospect that "the form, the schematism, of his [Hegel's] system now seems to me artificial to the last degree." John Dewey. "From Absolutism to Experimentalism," in *Contemporary American Philosophy: Personal Statements* (New York: Macmillan, 1930), 2:21.

45. Martin S. Dworkin, ed., *Dewey on Education: Selections*, Classics in Education No. 3 (New York: Bureau of Publications, Teachers College, Columbia University, 1959), pp. 8, 17.

46. See Robert L. McCaul, "Dewey's Chicago," *School Review* 67 (Summer 1959): 258–80; and Ray Ginger, *Altgeld's America: The Lincoln Ideal versus Changing Realities* (New York: Funk & Wagnalls, 1958).

47. Cremin, *The Transformation of the School*, p. 136.

48. Dewey, *Interest in Relation of Training of the Will*, p. 31. Italics in original.

49. John Dewey, *The School and Society, Being Three Lectures* (Chicago: University of Chicago Press, 1907; supplemented by *A Statement of the University Elementary School*), "Three Years of the University Elementary School," p. 116.

50. Katherine Camp Mayhew and Anna Camp Edwards, *The Dewey School: The University Laboratory School of the University of Chicago, 1896–1903* (New York: D. Appleton-Century, 1936), p. 3. As Dewey himself succinctly puts it, "Its aim was to test certain ideas which were used as working hypotheses." John

Dewey, "The Theory of the Chicago Experiment," ibid., Appendix 2, p. 464.

51. See Melvin C. Baker, *Foundations of John Dewey's Educational Theory* (New York: King's Crown Press, 1955).

52. Dewey, *The School and Society*, pp. 20, 26, 43–44.

53. Ibid., pp. 48, 51, 73, 107.

54. John Dewey, *My Pedagogic Creed* (Washington, D. C.: Progressive Education Association, n.d.), Article V, "The School and Social Progress," p. 15. In this small pamphlet, Dewey enunciated his beliefs in concise and forceful terms.

55. John Dewey, *The Child and the Curriculum and The School and Society* (Chicago: University of Chicago Press, 1956; a Phoenix Book Edition of *The Child and the Curriculum*, originally published in 1902), pp. 3–31.

56. Ibid., p. 11.

57. John Dewey, *How We Think* (Boston: Heath, 1910), p. iii.

58. Ibid., p. 11. Italics in original.

59. Ibid., p. 72–78. Italics in original.

60. Cremin describes *Democracy and Education* as "the clearest, most comprehensive statement of the progressive education movement." Cremin, *The Transformation of the School*, p. 120.

61. Dewey, *Democracy and Education*, pp. 375–77.

62. Ibid., p. 63. Of all Deweyan ideas, this conception of education as growth is perhaps the most controversial. According to Richard Hofstadter: "In the hands of some of Dewey's followers this idea became one of the most mischievous metaphors in the history of modern education. . . . The idea of growth invited educational thinkers to set up an invidious contrast between self-determining, self-directing growth from within, which was good, and molding from without, which was bad." Richard Hofstadter, *Anti-intellectualism in American Life* (New York: Knopf, 1963), p. 373.

63. Dewey, *Democracy and Education*, p. 60.

64. Ibid., pp. 89–90.

65. See, in particular, ibid., chap. 11, "Experience and thinking," pp. 163–178; 12, "Thinking in Education," pp. 179–92; and 13, "The Nature of Method," pp. 193–211.

66. Ibid., pp. 180–81, 211. Italics in original.

67. Ibid., pp. 55–57, 89. Italics in original.

68. Ibid., p. 92.

69. Dewey was certainly a prolific writer. A large number of his articles and books dealt with his fundamental philosophical theories. See Milton Halsey Thomas, *John Dewey: A Centennial Bibliography* (Chicago: University of Chicago Press, 1962). This useful publication includes a chronological list of Dewey's published writings, beginning with the earliest in 1882. Also, in a second part, are listed alphabetically by author the "writings about John Dewey."

70. For a résumé of some misconceptions of Dewey's ideas, see Harold G. Shane, "An Interpretation of John Dewey's Basic Ideas and Their Influence on Classroom Practices," *College of Education Semicentennial Addresses* (Kent, Ohio: Kent State University *Bulletin*, May 1960), pp. 13–16. In the late 1930s Dewey himself took strong issue with his disciples' work and interpretations. See John

Dewey, *Experience and Education*, Kappa Delta Pi Lecture Series (New York: Macmillan, 1939; originally published in February 1938).

71. As Ulich states, "No doubt the lack of direction and discipline, characteristic of many of the initial experiments in progressive education, is partly due to a one-sided interpretation of these concepts on the part of Dewey's followers." Robert Ulich, *History of Educational Thought* (New York: American Book, 1950), p. 335. See also Dworkin, ed., *Dewey on Education*, pp. 1–18. "Dewey wrote badly," declared Dworkin. "His style was often opaque, his terminology ambiguous" (p. 13).

CHAPTER 8

The Influence of Educational Psychology

Too many of our philosophers and psychologists have been book-ridden—content to distinguish and divide and evolve an arm-chair theory of knowledge. It is due to their lack of earnestness, their easy-going conservatism, their a-priori and scholastic ways, that we still have no philosophy of education, save only the rags and tatters of systems, and that the whole field has so long been a cave of the winds.

G. STANLEY HALL, "Child-Study and Its Relation to Education," August 1900

The school must permit the free, natural manifestations of the child if in the school scientific pedagogy is to be born. This is the essential reform.

MARIA MONTESSORI, "A Critical Consideration of the New Pedagogy in Its Relation to Modern Science," 1912

THE IMPACT OF RESEARCH
IN PSYCHOLOGY

The decades from Appomattox to World War I witnessed intensive research and a growing number of controversies in psychology. Disagreement was especially intense because of the enormous human significance of psychological concepts. Under the influence of Darwinism, new experimentation led to the development of distinct psychological systems that profoundly affected American education. Integral to these systems were an evolutionary conception of the human mind and new theories of learning.

The Background of Psychological Controversy

During the nineteenth century the most popular conception of learning was based on faculty psychology. A widely publicized theory of faculty psychology was formulated by Christian von Wolff in 1734, and a similar version was advanced by Thomas Reid, a Scottish philosopher, in 1785.[1] In line with religious orthodoxy, this psychological doctrine viewed the mind as a spiritual entity, apart from the physical body and unique to humans. It was believed that the mind could be successfully studied by "armchair" introspective methods instead of empirically by an observation of behavior. The evidence of how one felt inwardly was considered to be the chief evidence of the way the mind worked.

In the United States the most commonly accepted theory held that this unitary, single mind consisted of three separate sets of faculties or independent powers; (1) the will, or volition, which enables people to act; (2) the emotions, affections, and passions by which people love and hate and feel pleasure or pain; and (3) the intellect, or understanding which enables people to think and reason, make judgments, and comprehend meanings. Proponents of faculty psychology were chiefly concerned with scholarly knowledge and became absorbed in training the intellectual faculties.

The theoretical system of faculty psychology was especially important in the history of American education because it provided a justification for "mental discipline" as the dominant methodology in secondary and higher education. Variously defined as the ability to remember and apply, the sharpening of the wits, or an ability to rationalize, "mental discipline" assumed that the mind required a particular kind of training for its fullest development. This training meant a study of certain abstract subjects, such as the classics, philosophy, and mathematics, which were considered to be the most important content of a formal education. This schooling called for intensive drill and practice and cultivation of the memory. A mind so sharpened and so stored with knowledge was believed ready for any calling; indeed, it was considered "trained" and equipped for life. Thus, according to this doctrine, transfer of training resulted from strengthening the "faculties" or powers of the mind instead of from the specific benefits derived from a particular subject or a method of study. By the turn of the century, faculty psychology and mental discipline were still prevalent guides to methodology and curricular content. Although psychologists are not yet entirely agreed on what the mind is or how it functions, they are unanimous in rejecting this simple notion that the mind is composed of "faculties" that can be trained for effective use in all later life situations.

An Evolutionary Conception
of the Human Mind

In the years following the Civil War, the influence of Darwinism led to a radically different conception of the human mind. Instead of being viewed as a separate entity independent of the body, the mind was seen as a product of evolutionary growth. Darwin himself had included the study of the human mind within his broader evolutionary study of nature. Spencer, too, in his study of mental phenomena, had strengthened the evolutionary point of view.

According to this biological approach, the ability of humans (or any organism) to survive depended on maintaining an evershifting equilibrium or "adjustment" with surroundings. Human thoughts, which Dewey defined as plans or imaginative projections of possible action derived from previous experience in working toward an equilibrium or "adjustment," came to be viewed as a vital part of this evolutionary process. Mental activity was a behavioral *function* by which the organism adapted itself to a changing environment.

No longer, wrote William James in his monumental *Principles of Psychology* (1890), should one refer to the mind as divided into separate powers or "faculties." Each "faculty" is an essential part of human behavior. Human thoughts at any time are a total experience, a unity, changing and flowing like a river. "The transition between the thought of one object and the thought of another," declared James, "is no more a break in the *thought* than a joint in a bamboo is a break in the wood."[2] Mental activity is a continuous flow, a "stream of thought," as James called it, and any subdivision of the mind into separate elements is unwarranted.[3]

According to James, the impulses or movements by which the organism adjusts itself to its environment become fixed in "habit systems." While James believed that these "habit systems" governed human conduct, he also emphasized the human capacity to exercise initiative and to introduce novelty into the evolutionary process. The human mind is not only an instrument enabling people to adjust to their environment, as in the case of lower forms of animal life; according to James, the mind is also an instrument capable of *changing* our environment.

In the meantime, Edward L. Thorndike, one of James's students at Harvard, was conducting experiments in animal learning that provided additional support for this evolutionary concept of the mind. Using as a theoretical base the reflex arc that connected the brain and neural tissue to the organism's total behavior, Thorndike also refuted the idea of the mind as a separate entity. Instead, contended Thorndike, the mind develops as the organism responds totally to its environment. Even more significant, Thorndike, too, proclaimed the instrumentality of the human mind as a potent force that can change our environment or modify human nature for better or for worse. Human nature, Thorndike argued, is nothing but a mass of "original tendencies" to be molded by "all the forces that act upon it before and after birth."[4]

On this point, Thorndike's position was unequivocal. He denied that human nature was inherently good. He disagreed sharply with Rousseau and his child-centered followers who believed that the best schooling interferes least with the dictates of nature. Thorndike did not believe that people's "original tendencies" were good and sufficient to satisfy basic human needs. Instead, argued Thorndike, human nature should become whatever people can make of it, to the limit of one's capacity to learn. "Original nature has achieved what goodness the world knows as a state achieves order, by killing, confining or reforming some of its elements," he asserted bluntly. "It progresses, not by *Laissez faire,* but by changing the environment in which it operates and by renewedly changing itself in each generation."[5] Moreover, in stressing the social role of education, Thorndike wanted the school to *change* human behavior in line with humankind's goals. "It is a first principle of education," he declared, "to utilize any individual's original nature as a means to changing him for the better—to produce in him the information, habits, powers, interests and ideals which are desirable."[6]

Here, then was a novel and important psychological concept destined to influence American education profoundly: the human mind was a behavioral instrument that enabled people to change their own nature or modify their environment, if necessary, in order to improve the conditions of life.

The Influence of G. Stanley Hall (1846–1924)

One of the earliest psychological systems structured within the new evolutionary framework was that developed by Granville Stanley Hall. After earning Harvard's first doctorate in psychology in 1878, Hall studied experimental psychology at Leipzig under Wilhelm Wundt. In 1883 he founded at Johns Hopkins University the first psychological laboratory in the United States, only four years after Wundt had launched in Leipzig the world's first formal psychological laboratory.[7] In 1887 Hall launched the *American Journal of Psychology,* the first psychological journal in the United States. He assumed the presidency of Clark University in 1889 and soon converted that new institution into a famous center for research and study in child development. By the turn of the century, Hall had become a leading figure in American psychology and education.

Hall tried for years to reconcile human mental life with Darwin's theory of biological evolution. "As soon as I first heard it in my youth I think I must have been almost hypnotized by the word 'evolution,' " Hall wrote. He was once introduced to an audience as "the Darwin of the mind" and remarked later in his autobiography that this compliment gave him more satisfaction than any other he had ever received.[8]

Hall's fundamental thesis was that mind and body evolved in a parallel fashion through a series of stages from presavagery to civilized life. Moreover, in Hall's view, the individual "recapitulates" the evolution of the race. In formulating this "general psychonomic law," Hall borrowed extensively from others, most notably from Herbart and Spencer.

Hall concentrated his research in the field of child development. His first important contribution was a monograph entitled "The Contents of Children's Minds," which attracted widespread attention. Based on a rather unscientific questionnaire method, this study concluded that children's concepts vary greatly with each change in environment. Hall urged parents and teachers to acquaint children with "natural objects" which, he believed, would increase the conceptual range of children's minds.[9] In 1891 Hall founded the *Pedagogical Seminary,* a periodical devoted to child study. In his research, he held tenaciously to Darwinian conceptions; for example, in the "recapitulation" theory Hall and his co-workers found an explanation for the "big-injun" war games that sometimes characterize the play of preadolescent children. Evolutionary, too, was Hall's systematic study of physical growth and his attempt to explain the psychology of adolescence and early adulthood as consummations resulting from organic changes within the human body.[10]

Hall was a prolific writer, completing, among other works, two huge volumes of *Educational Problems* (1911). During his years at Clark University, more than a hundred questionnaire studies were completed. In an era already marked by unusual interest in child study, Hall's ideas became immensely popular. He was widely recognized as a national leader of the child-study movement in the United States.

Like Parker and Dewey, Hall placed the child at the center of the educational process and oriented the entire school effort around individual needs and interests. Hall wanted the school to adapt itself to the *natural* stages of human growth. His argument, of course, was old; it dated all the way back through Parker, Pestalozzi, and Rousseau to the seventeenth-century Moravian clergyman John Amos Comenius. In *The Great Didactic* (written about 1632), Comenius had asserted that human development was governed by certain laws of nature that constitute a basis for educational theory and practice.[11] However, by the end of the nineteenth century Hall was extending the traditional argument far beyond its original meaning and developing a radically new concept of a child-centered school with curricular content derived *exclusively* from the study of child development. He wanted, in brief, "to break away from all current practices, traditions, methods, and philosophies" and establish a curriculum "based solely upon a fresh and comprehensive view of the nature and needs of childhood."[12] In Hall's view, every aspect of education was to be evaluated against the criteria of the pupils' needs at each stage of human development.

This was not all. He also wanted to apply his yardstick to society. "There is really no clue by which we can thread our way through all the mazes of culture and the distractions of modern life save by knowing the true nature and needs of childhood and of adolescence," Hall declared.

> I urge, then that civilizations, religions, all human institutions, and the schools, [be] judged truly, or from the standpoint of the philosophy of

history, by this one criterion: namely, whether they have offended against these little ones or have helped to bring childhood and adolescence to an ever higher and completer maturity as generations pass by. Childhood is thus our pillar of cloud by day and fire by night.[13]

No doubt Parker enthusiastically agreed; the theme was old, and constant repetition made it familiar. By 1900 Hall's ideas were already part of a firmly entrenched doctrine.[14]

Child Growth and Development: The Work of Arnold L. Gesell (1880–1961)

In the history of child psychology, Arnold Lucius Gesell was a student of human behavior whose important work perpetuated with unusual stability the traditions of Darwin and Hall. Gesell was interested in observing and studying the growth and development of children in a laboratory setting. During his medical training at Yale University, he established a clinic of child development that became a leading research center in the United States. Gesell's monumental two-volume *Atlas* was an early publication that reflected a strong hereditarian position.[15]

According to Gesell there is a fundamental orderliness in human development that is evident in an age-behavior relationship. Gesell was greatly interested in developmental pathology, and he relied heavily on the use of tables in diagnosing and predicting potential difficulties in children.[16] His widely read lists of standards for child development were supplemented by photographs and films prepared at the Yale Clinic.

Between 1906, when he earned his doctorate, and 1948, when he retired from Yale, Gesell became the most popular spokesman for the concept of *maturation* in developmental psychology. He was a clear and forceful writer, and he presented his views with much conviction. What is the basic determinant of *growth?* Within broad limits of experiential change, Gesell answers, the child *grows* as his germ plasm dictates. Environment provides a setting for growth and development and occasionally directs the outcome of a particular developmental phase; but the actual contribution of environmental change to variation in human development is relatively unimportant. Maturation, Gesell stresses over and over again, is the essential determinant of developmental change. The tendency to *grow*—the most potent force in life—cannot be diverted by environmental variations children typically experience.

Emphasized repeatedly through several books, pamphlets, and audiovisual aids, Gesell's principles of child development became guidelines for scores of researchers, teachers, and parents. Despite the influence of psychoanalysis and the significance of the new Gestalt theory, the Gesellian view has remained virtually unchanged.

THE INFLUENCE OF EUROPEAN IDEAS

The Cognitive Research
of Jean Piaget (1896–1980)

While American interest in child study was primarily behavioral, with an emphasis on physical development, European research focused to a large extent on mental ability and the growth of thought in children. At the University of Geneva, Jean Piaget and his co-workers began in the 1920s to systematize the methods of observing children at play and to develop the clinical interview as a research tool for studying children from the ages of two to fourteen. The most distinctive features of Piaget's method were the skillful development of key questions in a laboratory setting and the experimental technique of asking the child over and over again to account for every action or possible hypothesis. Using the facilities of the Institut Jean-Jacques Rousseau, Piaget described some of the unusual difficulties the child encounters in comprehending adult concepts in logic, physics, and mathematics. He shed new light on the child's gradual comprehension of the world around him. His detailed studies of cognitive development probed deeply into unexplored areas of child psychology. "In an age of moonshots and automation," writes David Elkind, "the remarkable discoveries of Jean Piaget are evidence that in the realm of scientific achievement, technical sophistication is still no substitute for creative genius."[17]

The main theme of Piaget's *The Language and Thought of the Child,* written in 1923, revolves around the idea of egocentrism.[18] Children gradually perceive an awareness of themselves; and until they distinctly see themselves apart from their own environment, they cannot comprehend the subjectivity of their own outlook. Things exist as they *appear* to be. Piaget uses the term "realism" to convey this acceptance of reality in the child's mind. From such egocentrism follows another conception: "participation" in which children, failing to distinguish themselves from the external world, attribute mind and life to everything they encounter. Piaget then views the whole span of intellectual growth in terms of the gradual release of the child from this egocentric pattern of thought.[19] Step by step, from the point of early egocentrism to the child's gradual emancipation and maturity, Piaget and his staff studied the symbolic meaning of words, the comprehension of nature's forces, the foundations of moral judgment, and other important aspects of cognitive development. Such intensive observations and laboratory work at Geneva posed new hypotheses in psychology and provoked some stimulating investigations in the United States on perception and intelligence in children.[20]

Piaget's approach to the genesis and development of human knowledge is novel and provocative. In later publications, he postulates the intriguing principle of "equilibration" in the cognitive process. The child, Piaget explains, is an active, self-regulating organism whose mental growth is characterized by progressive changes through adaptation. This mental development tends toward order: it represents a constant progression from a less to a more stable "equilibrium." Thus, according to Piaget, the growth of thought in children is a manifestation of the organism's steady tendency toward a new and more complete "equilibrium," toward a progressively higher form of intellectual development. By adding this new factor of "equilibrium" to cognition, Piaget has extended the developmental theory that explains the child's mental growth solely in maturational and experiential terms.

Piaget's Developmental Stages

Piaget viewed the course of intellectual growth in terms of progressive changes in cognitive structures. All children do not go through the stages at the same time; however, all children pass through the stages in the same order. The attainments in earlier stages are essential for those in later stages, and some of the earlier intellectual processes may continue into later periods of development. The stages are not definite. Gradual and continuous changes occur throughout the growth period.

Piaget identified four main periods of intellectual development: (1) the sensorimotor period (age zero to two); (2) the preoperational period (age two to seven); (3) the concrete operational period (age seven to eleven or twelve); and (4) the period of formal operations (age eleven or twelve on). As the child passes through these periods, he or she changes from an individual with little cognitive development and who is dependent on his or her senses or motor activities to an individual capable of greater flexibility of thought and abstract reasoning. Piaget believed that every child must pass through these periods in a fixed sequence, since the cognitive changes of one stage depend on the intellectual attainments of the past.

The sensorimotor period extends from birth to about age two. During this period the first organized patterns of behavior occur. At first the infant is completely egocentric and does not distinguish between his or her own body and outer reality. At about eight months the infant begins to become aware of his or her environment as separate from himself or herself. The beginnings of symbolic play also occur during this period, starting at about eighteen months.

During the period of preoperational thought that extends from ages two to seven, the child gradually prepares for the period of concrete operations. At the beginning of this period, the child responds to external appearances, such as the learning of the concept of conservation. The preoperational child believes that a row of four objects tightly grouped contains fewer items than a longer row of four objects loosely grouped. Only after much experience can the child go beyond surface appearances. After counting both rows of items many times, the child will come to understand the equivalence of both rows. During this period, the child also learns to use language and to form mental images.

The period of concrete operations extends from age seven to eleven or twelve. The term "concrete operations" refers to mental acts that the child can perform on objects at hand. Dramatic changes in the characteristics of thought occur during this period. Logic and objectivity increase and the child now begins to think deductively. The child is also able to conserve quantity and number, to form concepts of space and time, and so classify or group objects if the objects are present. The child is still tied to the concrete operations of the immediate world. He or she can solve problems only if the objects necessary for the solution of the problem are physically present.

The period of formal operations begins in early adolescence at about age twelve. During this period the child's thought becomes increasingly flexible and abstract. To solve problems the child uses logical processes where all possibilities in a solution are considered. The adolescent can also imagine what might occur if a situation were changed. He or she can also consider a number of possible alternatives in a problem-solving situation, whereas the concrete operational child can only solve problems in a real situation with the objects actually present. The child entering this stage begins to "operate on operations" where he or she can think about himself or herself as well as about concrete things.

Children learn best when they are actively manipulating materials in their environment. Piaget confirms this belief through his theory of conservation. After manipulating objects, a child of the preoperational level can learn to conserve quantity between two sets of objects. This statement is further emphasized through the work of Maria Montessori, who states that "play is a child's work." In play the child is practicing the various actions that will eventually be internalized as thought.

The Montessori Method

For over half a century the work of Maria Montessori (1870–1952) has generated enthusiasm among European educators and reformers. For anyone interested in compensatory education for disadvantaged children, her famous method is still considered timely and useful. Yet little is known in the United States about the genesis of her method or even the actual ideas behind the recent movement associated with her name.[21] Some of her American disciples today are unaware that the Montessori method originated in a slum district of Rome in 1906 as part of an experiment in the education of preschool children from the culture of poverty.

Born in the town of Chiaravalle, Italy, Maria Montessori is one of the great pedagogues of modern times. She studied mathematics and engineering on the secondary-school level, and later, in defiance of local prejudice, enrolled as a medical student at the University of Rome. She was the first woman in Italy to earn the degree of Doctor of Medicine.

In 1897 Montessori was appointed to the Psychiatric Clinic of the University of Rome, where she came into contact with mentally defective children who at this time were institutionalized in the city's insane asylums. As she worked with these children, she gradually took issue with the prevailing opinion on how best to help them. She soon concluded that mental deficiency was an educational instead of a medical problem. The following year, in a speech that aroused great interest, she voiced her position before 3,000 members of the first congress of the Associazione Pedagogica Italiana. Impressed by her views, Guido Baccelli, minister of education, asked her to present a series of lectures to Roman teachers on the education of mentally defective children, and later appointed her to head the newly established Orthophrenic School.

Montessori was director of the Orthophrenic School from 1898 to 1900. Here she worked with "hopelessly deficient" children from Rome's primary schools. For two years she devoted time and energy to teaching these children, training teachers, and consulting with other physicians in Paris and London. She combined her own theories with those of Jean Itard and Eduard Séguin, two nineteenth-century French doctors to whom she often refers in her writings.

She taught the children of the Orthophrenic School to read and write and then gained much recognition at a public school examination when her "hopelessly deficient" pupils successfully competed with other children of "normal" intelligence. Some called her accomplishment "miraculous"; Montessori, however, brushed aside such references and attributed her success instead to the superiority of her own methods, which were based on a different, *"more rational"* idea. "Little by little," she wrote, "I became convinced that similar methods applied to normal children would develop or set free their personality in a marvellous and surprising way."[22]

In 1901 Montessori went back to the University of Rome where she studied experimental psychology under Giuseppe Sergi, whose strong recommendation led to her appointment in 1904 as Professor of Pedagogical Anthropology.[23] During this period she also taught a course on pedagogy for teachers in Rome and maintained a small private practice. It was an important stage in her life—a transitional stage marked by hard work ("studying, repeating, working experimentally") and a strong determination "to test the truth of [her] idea."

In 1906, after five years of advanced study, Montessori had a chance to verify some of her theories. She was asked by Edoardo Talamo to develop a new type of infant school in a slum district of Rome, known as the San Lorenzo quarter. Talamo's plan was to establish a school for children of the poor—a school located in a section of San Lorenzo that was being remodeled as part of a housing reform project. For Montessori, Talamo's offer provided, as she remarked, "a great opportunity."

The new school was called "Casa dei Bambini" (The Children's House). The first Casa opened its doors at 58 Via dei Marsi on January 6, 1907.

When she first entered San Lorenzo, Montessori was appalled at the "spectacle of genuine misery. . . . We enter here a world of shadows," she declared. Without supervision children from the ages of three to six, too young for the public school, were left unattended to run wild in the streets, destroying property and defacing the walls of buildings. "They grow among the poisonous shadows which envelop over-crossed humanity." Rough and crude in manner, eyes dull and vacant, faces blank except for whining and crying—all in all, observed Montessori, the children appear absolutely wretched. For these children, she continued, "home means a straw pallet thrown down in the corner of some dark hovel. . . . In speaking of the children born in these places, even the conventional expressions must be changed, for they do not 'first see the light of day'; they come into a world of gloom." There all sorts of crimes flourished unchecked. The dilapidated tenements were filthy and unsanitary. "It was as if I found myself in a city upon which some great disaster had fallen," exclaimed Montessori as she walked through the streets of San Lorenzo for the first time.

After years of study at the University of Rome, Montessori understood the social roots of failure among children of the poor. She realized that all children are not ready for school at the same time, and she believed moreover that children of the poor are at a special disadvantage. For the San Lorenzo child, the public school did not provide equality of opportunity: the culture of poverty, with "poisonous shadows" and "dark dens of vice and wretchedness," militated against the kind of progress that was expected of children in the classroom. The young boys and girls of San Lorenzo were not only unprepared for school, but after entering the classroom, they then began to lag further and further behind. "The down-trodden of society," wrote Montessori, "are also the down-trodden in the school."[24]

Her dream was to launch "a great reform in the school," a reform that would bring about "a great regeneration" of "the very poor." The "soul of the people," she said, must be "set free from the torpor of vice, from the shadows of ignorance."

Thus Montessori expands the whole concept of compensatory education. In developing a program for the Casa dei Bambini, she did not start by asking what "uncultured children" need for success in the first grade. Rather, she asked: What do all children need for self-realization as human beings? A student of anthropology, she was convinced that each person possesses a strong potential for self-fulfillment. During the early years of childhood, it is important to encourage this human potential which might be stifled or blocked by environmental forces. Hence, in the Montessori method, the teacher has a strategic role: to encourage the development of each child toward full self-realization.

Assisted by Talamo, she created a new kind of school for young children. Her immediate aim was to plan an educational program that would compensate for some of the deficiencies of slum conditions. San Lorenzo, emphasized Montessori, "is the Quarter of the *poor*" with all "the misery of deep human poverty." An obvious defect is the lack of intellectual stimulation. One cannot "establish circulating libraries that the poor may read at home" or "send among these people books which shall form their domestic literature—books through whose influence they shall come to higher standards of living. . . . For many of them have no light by which to read! . . . Here, there can be no privacy, no modesty, no gentleness; here, there is often not even light, nor air, nor water!"[25] To compensate for such conditions, Montessori believed that some form of environmental "nourishment" was essential.

At the Casa dei Bambini, she tried to change each child's sensory impressions in ways that would strengthen the powers of perception. This approach, she thought, would foster mental growth, would, in fact, help to improve "intelligence."[26] Furthermore, she urged, "it is necessary to begin the education of the senses in the formative period, if we wish to perfect this sense development with the education which is to follow." Sensory education, then, is the basis of the Montessori method.

To translate her ideas into practice, Montessori invented some ingenious and varied educational "games." The "didactic apparatus" for these games consisted of twenty-six separate items (for example, cylinders, geometric insets, rectangular blocks, and colored tablets). Each piece of material was carefully graded and self-corrective. In addition, she designed and had manufactured lightweight, movable furniture: small chairs and tables, for example, replaced the then customary large stationary desks. (Montessori especially disliked stationary furniture because it hindered the child's freedom of movement.) She also planned special activities to develop auditory skills (the "game of silence") and to encourage vocabulary enrichment and the use of correct and fluent speech. "If one considers the charm of human speech one is bound to acknowledge the inferiority of one who does not possess a correct spoken language," declared Montessori, in her lengthy discussion on the importance of language.[27] The appeal of her approach lies in the fact that it "nourished" the development of mental structures through the use of new materials meaningful to the child.

The didactic apparatus served two purposes. First, it permitted Montessori to individualize teaching to an extraordinary degree. "It is our duty to understand the individual," she told her followers over and over again. With her new material and educational "games," she proceeded to revolutionize the learning situation.

She was harshly critical of the tradition classroom where children were forced to sit immobile and silent, where, she remarked bitterly, they "are repressed in the spontaneous expression of their personality till they are almost like dead beings." It is not surprising, therefore, that she abandoned the typical group arrangement. Instead she encouraged freedom to progress at one's own pace. Her conception of freedom, however, did not mean that children could do as they pleased. There were limits—a point worth underscoring: the restrictions were established in the interests of the group, and whatever annoyed or offended other people was to be "suppressed." There was freedom to learn in her carefully prepared environment, and every aspect of this freedom had a didactic purpose. The children were free to use the learning materials, but in ways planned by the teacher.[28]

Second, the didactic material enabled Montessori to introduce important compensatory stimuli into the teaching-learning situation. The exercises with the "games" encouraged the San Lorenzo preschoolers to redirect their behavior along new channels. At first erratic and wild, whining and crying, the children were slowly taught to pattern their conduct differently, to behave, in brief, like other, more advantaged schoolchildren.

Montessori had a tremendous exuberance and joy for life, and she believed that young children possessed this same eagerness and energy. She loved to see her preschoolers intrinsically motivated and active, and in her carefully prepared environment, the children found lessons that were helpful and gratifying. Through practice in language and poise and through exercises in motor coordination, they gradually learned to listen, concentrate, and become self-controlled.

Compassionate and concerned about less fortunate people in society, Montessori pleaded for "higher standards of justice," a "spirit of love which is essential to the teacher," and a greater understanding of the individual. "What really makes a teacher," she wrote in 1913, "is love for the human child." The teacher, she believed, is "truly an educator of humanity." During her long career, she often talked about "the teacher's mission" which, she said, "is the mission of reforming the school" and the larger world in which we live. "Through the redeeming and protective labours of pedagogy, the lowest human manifestations of degeneration and disease will disappear."[29] Since the dawn of the twentieth century, few leaders have expressed such faith in education as a force for elevating humankind to new hope and dignity.

Psychoanalysis

Another European conception that has had tremendous implications for the study of human behavior is psychoanalysis. Stemming from the work of the eminent Viennese Sigmund Freud (1856–1939), this approach strives to reveal the innermost depths of the psyche. It points to the role of sex in human life and emphasizes through introspective methods the unconscious determination of behavior.

The psychoanalytic approach has directly influenced medicine more than education. It has lured a long line of dedicated followers in psychiatry and, beginning in the 1940s, in guidance and counseling. Concerned with human drives, motivations, and instincts, Freud's almost exclusively biological theories have been modified in recent years by Karen Horney, Erich Fromm, Harry Stack Sullivan, and others, who stress the social nature of the individual and find anxieties and frustrations rooted more in cultural pressures and conflicts. Perhaps the most significant impact of Freudian psychology on American education has been to stimulate new research in mental hygiene and to draw increasing attention to the crucial preschool years in personality development.

Alfred Binet (1857–1911) and
the Measurement of Intelligence
Of Darwin's immediate followers in the field of psychology, Francis Galton was the first to contribute some ingenious experimental studies on individual differences among people. In *Hereditary Genius,* Galton applied a statistical method to genetics and related individual differences to hereditary factors.[30] Galton's point of view in scientific inquiry greatly influenced Alfred Binet and other psychologists who were also interested in the complex human mental processes.

Throughout his life Binet, a French physician, was concerned with problems of intelligence and reasoning. By 1890 he had begun some empirical studies on the origins of intelligent behavior that gradually led to his famous intelligence scale.

In 1904 the French minister of public instruction appointed Binet to an educational commission on special classes. The work of the commission was to differentiate between the lazy or indifferent pupil and the mentally deficient child. Paris school officials were concerned about feeble-minded children and wanted to place them in institutions with simplified programs. Working with Théodore Simon, Binet tried to devise suitable tests of intelligence that would detect and measure mental defects.

In 1905 Binet and Simon proposed a set of tests arranged from the simplest to the most difficult. In this first series were questions calling for the repetition of digits, the naming of designated objects, the completion of sentences, and the comprehension of questions and reading material. Three years later this scale was revised, with the tests progressively arranged according to age levels of three to twelve years inclusive; these levels, experimentally determined, were the ages at which an "average" child performed the tests successfully. A pupil's *mental age* was the level which he or she attained on the scale.

Meanwhile, Louis William Stern, in Germany, made a significant contribution by suggesting a change in the calculation of the intelligence-test scores. He recommended the use of an "intelligence quotient" (IQ) to be obtained by dividing the mental age by a child's chronological age. Stern tried to show that the IQ for most children is usually constant from year to year.

During this period there was considerable demand in the United States for more objective methods of investigating psychological development. Research was dominated by introspection and Hall's questionnaire techniques, which were fallible and unscientific. Binet's approach was enthusiastically viewed by American psychologists as a new research method for studying the subnormal child. In 1910 the revised Simon-Binet Scale was translated and adapted for American use. At the same time Lewis M. Terman began experimenting with Binet's test.

In 1916 Terman produced the Stanford Revision of the Binet Scale, which extended Binet's method to the average and superior child. Terman's Revision was based on work with a thousand subjects and standardized in the form of tests for age levels from three to eighteen years. Measures for the sixteen-year-old testee were supposed to be for adults, and tests for the eighteen-year-old were designed for "superior" adults.

The Stanford-Binet Scale attracted widespread attention. With its rapid use and extension throughout the world, the measurement of human abilities became an important concern of American education and psychology. The 1916 edition was replaced in 1937 with the publication of Forms L and M of the Stanford-Binet. The latest revision (1960), which combined certain tests of the 1937 edition into a single Form L-M, is one of the most frequently used individual intelligence tests in the United States. Despite some criticism, the Stanford-Binet conception of mental ability is still the main criterion against which all other mental tests are evaluated.

The more recently developed Wechsler Adult Intelligence Scale (1955), for ages sixteen and above, and WISC (the Wechsler Intelligence Scale for Children [1949]), for ages five to sixteen, are also of great importance as individual tests of mental ability. The original Wechsler Scale, prepared in 1939, was of great value in military hospitals during World War II. The revised scales are major tools of the clinical psychologist.

Changing Views of Human Intelligence

Human intelligence is no longer perceived simply as a narrow cluster of mental abilities measurable by an IQ test. A new definition of intelligence has been gaining acceptance during the twentieth century—one that includes a broad range of human abilities among the components of human cognition. This conceptual change is of profound significance with some major educational and social consequences.

The concept that intelligence is only one *thing,* a type of brainpower that can be measured by a test, was dominant during the first half of the twentieth century. Although Alfred Binet viewed intelligence as the exercise of several mental abilities, English psychologist Charles Spearman, his disciple, added an important principle that gradually became widely accepted. He tried to identify a single factor common to all diverse mental facilities. Spearman called this single factor "general intelligence," symbolized by the letter '*g.*' All cognitive ability, according to Spearman, demanded access to the *g* factor. From the beginning there has been serious disagreement regarding the *g* factor as being basically innate or susceptible to environmental forces. In 1912 Louis William Stern invented the idea of the IQ, and four years later Terman developed the Stanford Revision of the Binet Scale, setting the stage for wide-scale intelligence testing in the United States.

By 1990 the *g* factor idea of intelligence no longer dominated scientific research. Major controversy centered around the observation that there was little connection between how individuals scored on IQ tests and their subsequent success in life. Thus, what the standard IQ test measured was only a small part of the intricate combination of factors that made up human intelligence or that had anything to do with those cognitive abilities that encouraged people to function successfully in adult life. Instead, a more pluralistic view of human intelligence emerged as an important and overriding concept.

Toward the end of the twentieth century, the most widely accepted of various approaches was Howard Gardner's theory of multiple intelligences, or MI theory. Drawing on data from various disciplines such as anthropology, psychology, neurology, and pathology, Gardner eventually focused on seven areas of intellectual ability—various intelligences, as he refers to them—that are apparently independent of one another. He provides physiological evidence that each of the seven intelligences exists as a separate entity.[31] The seven intelligences and the careers that each might lead toward, with prominent persons suggested to exemplify each of the seven areas, are as follows:

1. *Linguistic:* a sensitivity to the order and meaning of words; writer, poet (for example, Jean-Paul Sartre and T. S. Eliot).
2. *Musical:* exceptional sensitivity to rhythm, pitch, and melody; singer, composer (for example Luciano Pavarotti and Aaron Copland).
3. *Logical-Mathematical:* the ability to recognize patterns and order, to understand significant problems and to solve them; scientist, mathematician (for example, Isaac Newton and Albert Einstein).
4. *Spatial:* the capacity to perceive the visual world accurately and to

re-create or modify parts of that world; sculptor, architect (for example, Michelangelo and I. M. Pei).

5. *Bodily-Kinesthetic:* the ability to handle objects adroitly and to use the body skillfully; dancer, athlete, and surgeon (for example, Isadora Duncan, Jack Nicklaus, and Michael DeBakey).

"THE PERSONAL INTELLIGENCES"

6. *Interpersonal:* The capacity to understand other human beings and their relationships and to make distinctions among individuals, especially among their moods, motivations, and intentions; religious leader, politician, teacher (for example, Mahatma Gandhi, Lyndon B. Johnson, and John Dewey).

7. *Intrapersonal:* an individual's examination and knowledge of one's own feelings and the capacity to draw upon one's emotions as a means of understanding oneself and others; therapist, novelist (for example, Sigmund Freud and Marcel Proust).

As Gardner points out, spatial, logical-mathematical, and bodily-kinesthetic are *object-related* and are controlled by the structure and function of the particular objects with which one comes in contact. Language and music, on the other hand, are *object-free* forms of intelligence and depend on the structure of particular languages and music. The personal forms of intelligence depend on powerful and competing constraints—for example, the existence of the individual and of other persons; the interpretations of people. "My methodological principle is to look at the mind through a lot of lenses—development, breakdown, cross-cultural material, evolutionary data," explained Gardner. "And these different lenses all support the existence of multiple intelligences."[32]

NEW THEORIES OF LEARNING

In describing general behavior, two major schools of thought evolved during the early decades of the twentieth century: connectionism, or modern associationism, and Gestalt, or "field," interpretations. In modified form, these are still basic to current systems in psychology. Connectionism is the older of these views; as an American theory of learning, it stems from Edward L. Thorndike's original experimentation in animal psychology.

Thorndike's Psychology of the Learning Process

The concept that pleasure and pain as consequences of human actions are determiners of general behavior has a long history in psychology. It formed the basis of psychological hedonism developed in the eighteenth century by

Jeremy Bentham (1748–1832) and later adopted by other British philosophers. According to this motivational theory, people do those things that
give pleasure and avoid those that cause pain. "Nothing can act of itself as a
motive but the ideas of pleasure or pain," wrote Bentham in 1779.[33] It was
this simple idea that Edward L. Thorndike (1874–1949) made central to his
psychology of learning.

Thorndike's famous dissertation on *Animal Intelligence* is a classic in the
history of psychology.[34] His most widely quoted experiment dealt with cats
confined in a puzzle or problem box. A hungry cat was in a closed box or
cage, and the food (a morsel of fish) was placed outside. The cat would open a
door to the cage by pulling a loop of string hanging inside. A cat usually
went through a long process of moving and jumping around and clawing the
sides of the cage before it pulled the loop of string opening the door. On
succeeding tests in the cage, the cats took shorter times to pull the string.
The improvement, however, was irregular and gradual. Even after several
experiences opening the door, the animals on a certain trial would still spend
considerable time in random behavior before pulling the string. Careful
analysis of this and similar experiments led Thorndike to conclude that the
cats' "learning" to pull the string did not involve an intelligent understanding of a relationship between string pulling and door opening. The process of
learning was instead a gradual "stamping in" of the stimulus-response
connection between seeing the string and pulling it.

Historically, these studies marked a radical innovation in experimental
psychology. Years before Ivan P. Pavlov's experiments, Thorndike was
carefully observing animal behavior under controlled conditions. Moreover,
in his concern with the gradual strengthening of stimulus-response bonds,
Thorndike had entered into the traditional controversy over animal problem-
solving and had given his classic answer: animals "learned" by neither
instinct nor reasoning, but rather by a gradual "stamping in" of the correct
response.

Thorndike's explanation of learning was theoretically based on neural
connections between stimulus and response. Some connections were
strengthened, and others were weakened. After successive trials to escape
confinement, including some successful attempts, the animals' unsuccessful
impulses were "stamped out" and the particular impulses leading to success
were "stamped in" by *resulting satisfaction or pleasure.* This last point was
noteworthy, for at this juncture Thorndike's discussion deviated sharply
from a strict physiological interpretation of associationism. A satiated animal
would not try to obtain food outside the cage and apparently would not
"learn." Some motive, such as hunger, was essential for learning.

Thorndike insisted on pleasure or reward as the indispensable determinant in all learning. This postulate was his primary law of learning and
became known as the "law of effect": a modifiable connection is strengthened
when accompanied by a satisfying effect and is weakened when accompanied

by an annoying effect. When pleasure or satisfaction results, connections will tend to be learned better; however, pain or annoyance will tend to prevent learning. Thorndike later modified his law of effect to make a "satisfier" or reward much more important than an "annoyer" or punishment. While reward or pleasure strengthens the connection, Thorndike explained, pain or punishment does not directly weaken it. With this change, then, the modified law of effect simply stated that satisfying consequences served to reinforce situation-response bonds.

Thorndike consistently preferred the broader connotation of the word *situation* to the more restricted term *stimulus*. In general, the "connection" was made with a *total* "state of affairs influencing the man," not with a particular thing or happening.[35] Thorndike's preference reflected a contemporary interest in psychology with the *total* behavior of an organism. Called *functionalism,* this system was more concerned with how people behave or function than with an analysis or a description of abstract elements.

Thorndike also formulated two other primary laws of learning: the *law of exercise* and the *law of readiness,* which were corollaries of his famous law of effect.[36] The law of exercise stated that a modifiable connection between a situation and response will be strengthened when it is used and will be weakened when it is not used. The more frequent and recent the use, the greater will be the learning. The law of readiness stated that when the action system is ready to act, satisfaction will follow action; but failure to act when ready will result in annoyance.

The pleasure-and-pain theory of association was not new, but Thorndike's repeated emphasis through the years helped to keep the issue alive among theorists. Edwin R. Guthrie (1886–1959), for example, rejected the terms *satisfaction* and *annoyance* and held instead to *contiguity of stimulus and response*. Clark L. Hull (1884–1952), on the other hand, accepted Thorndike's connectionist theory.

By 1912 Thorndike had extended his theory of animal intelligence to human learning, which he also explained in terms of specific bonds between situations and responses. He was quite consistent in his approach. Throughout his discussions, there was no deviation from the previously published views. "Human nature does not do something for nothing," he wrote in *Education: A First Book,* published in 1912.

> The satisfyingness and annoyingness of the states of affairs which follow the making of the connection are the chief forces which remodel man's nature. Education makes changes chiefly by rewarding them. The prime law in all human control is to get the man to make the desired response and to be satisfied thereby.
>
> The Law of Effect is the fundamental law of learning and teaching. By it a crab learns to respond to the situation, *two paths,* by taking the one, choice of which has in the past brought food. By it a dog will learn to respond to the situation, *a white box and a black box,* by neglecting the

latter if opening it in the past has been promptly followed by an electric shock. By it animals are taught their tricks; by it babies learn to smile at the sight of the bottle or the kind attendant, and to manipulate spoon and fork; by it the player at billiards or golf improves his game; by it the man of science preserves those ideas that satisfy him by their promise, and discards futile fancies. It is the great weapon of all who wish—in industry, trade, government, religion or education—to change men's responses, either by reinforcing old and adding new ones, or by getting rid of those that are undesirable.[37]

Thorndike's doctrine of connectionism dominated educational psychology in the United States for almost fifty years. Adhering to a basic S-R formula, most connectionists still explain behavior as essentially reactions (R) to situations (S). It is assumed that these S-R connections, which can be either quite broad or very narrow, are the units that determine all behavior. To understand human learning, a connectionist argues, one must develop the principles that will explain not only which connections come into being but also which ones become weaker or stronger or disappear completely. *Learning, then, is viewed not as a matter of training potential and unformed "faculties" of the mind, but rather as a process of forming a series of connections or tendencies between situations and responses.*

With this conception of learning, Thorndike and his followers attacked the various assumptions of faculty psychology, especially the theories of mental discipline and transfer of training. His influential research with Robert S. Woodworth (1869–1962), then of New York University Medical College, was aimed directly at certain ideas underlying the transfer value of the classics and other traditional subjects in American education. "There is no inner necessity for improvement of one function to improve others closely similar to it, due to a subtle transfer of practice effect," concluded Thorndike and Woodworth in 1901. "Improvement in them seems due to definite factors, the operation of which the training may or may not secure.[38] In later years Thorndike became more dubious of the so-called disciplinary value of the classics, asserting that any one study would not result in an improvement of the mind more than any other field. Instead, he declared in 1924, "the intellectual values of studies should be determined largely by the special information, habits, interests, attitudes, and ideals which they demonstrably produce.[39] Transfer of training might take place, but *not* because of the inherent disciplinary value of the classics. Transfer occurs because of a particular method of study or a special content appropriate to the desired activity. In other words, if pupils were to be prepared for a definite goal or activity, they should study those courses that can be shown to lead directly to the desired aims.

Through his publications and courses, Thorndike spread his doctrine across the land, coloring the educational thought of a generation of American teachers. His influence was greatly strengthened by his appointment in 1899 to the faculty of Teachers College, Columbia University, where he remained for forty years.

For the first time in the history of American education, psychological sanction was given for including in the curriculum such courses as the newer social studies and various technical subjects. The first half of the twentieth century witnessed a bitter controversy over the "disciplinary" value of these and other courses. Practically every field was examined by the connectionists, and significant changes resulted in elementary and secondary education. Those who adhered to the traditional theory of a classical schooling faced unrelenting, and increasingly hostile, attacks from Thorndike's followers and other utilitarian forces in the progressivist movement.

The so-called modern associationists have elaborated on Thorndike's earlier ideas and now view behavior as much more complex than might be inferred from the rather simple explanation of situation-response connections. Greater emphasis is being placed on the roles of motivation, insight, problem solving, and reasoning as paths to effective learning. More attention is being given to the processes by which concepts are formed. Nevertheless, despite these changes, modern associationists still find little cause for modifying Thorndike's original emphasis on the law of effect.

Behaviorism

From the beginning, connectionism or modern associationism attributed more significance to the inherited elements in human nature than to the effects of environment. Some connectionists asserted that intelligence was mainly an inherited quality and could be altered very little, if at all, by changes in environment. For instance, Thorndike himself finally came to the conclusion during the 1930s that behavior was more a result of heredity than a product of environment. This issue over heredity and environment came to the forefront in the years following World War I, when a point of view known as "behaviorism" was advanced.

Behaviorism, when it flourished during the 1920s, was an extreme form of connectionism. The behaviorists were not concerned with mental activity, but only with overt, observable behavior. As early as 1913 John B. Watson (1878–1958), at Johns Hopkins University, was arguing that physical explanations would be sufficient to explain all human behavior. "Certainly the position I advocate is weak enough at present and can be attacked from many standpoints. Yet when all this is admitted I still feel that the considerations which I have urged should have a wide influence upon the type of psychology which is to be developed in the future," Watson declared. "What we need to do is start work upon psychology, making *behavior,* not *consciousness,* the objective point of our attack."[40]

Watson rejected the classical distinction between mind and body and tried to build an objective psychology. Like Thorndike, he concentrated on learning as a major psychological topic. Watson's main contribution to the history of American education was his intensive study of objective behavior.

At the heart of Watson's conception of learning was the process of conditioning. Referring to the animal experiments of Pavlov, Watson asserted that the conditioned reflex is essential to all learning. Pavlov had discovered that the presentation of food to a dog would bring forth a response marked by an increase in salivary flow. Then he controlled the conditions by ringing a bell every time the food was given to the dog. Pavlov discovered that he could produce the salivary flow in the dog merely by ringing the bell, although the original stimulus of the food was not present. Thus the secondary stimulus (the bell) became so closely associated with the primary stimulus (the food) that the secondary stimulus could call forth the original response or reflex. The response had thus been associated or *conditioned* to a new stimulus.

Watson believed that this form of conditioning through associated stimuli is the basic process of all behavior and learning. He denied that people are born with specific mental abilities or predispositions. A human being inherits his or her body and certain stimulus-response connections called "reflexes." These reflexes, Watson declared, constitute the total behavioral repertoire that human beings inherit. Only through the process of conditioning, first described by Pavlov, can people develop new S-R connections and *learn* new responses to various situations. "Give me a dozen healthy infants, well-formed, and my own specified world to bring them up in," wrote Watson in 1925, "and I'll guarantee to take any one at random and train him to become any type of specialist I might select—doctor, lawyer, artist, merchant-chief and, yes, even beggar-man and thief, regardless of his talents, penchants, tendencies, abilities, vocations, and race of his ancestors."[41] Thus, according to Watson, differences in personality and ability are merely differences in learned behavior.

Like Watson, B. F. Skinner (1904–1990) also tried to develop an objective psychology. Skinner earned his doctorate in psychology from Harvard in 1931, and after teaching in the Midwest, he joined the Harvard faculty in 1948. Although Skinner built his system independently and never studied under Thorndike, there are some interesting similarities between the two psychologists: both are connectionists who deemphasize psychological theory, stress reinforcement as a major factor in the learning process, and exhibit an unusual interest in the classroom situation.

In *The Behavior of Organisms* (1938), Skinner defines his terminology and advances some fundamental behaviorist theories. He maintains that most behavior is *operant* behavior (emitted by the organism), rather than *respondent* behavior (elicited in response to certain stimuli), which Watson assumed to be the basis of all learning. Examples of operant responses are screaming, running, playing, walking, hitting, pushing, and so on. Skinner places primary emphasis on such operant responses (simply called "operants"). Instead of talking about Thorndike's situation-response connections, Skinner discusses the rates at which certain operants are emitted under controlled conditions.

Skinner presented some fascinating demonstrations of the *shaping* of operant behavior, showing before student audiences how a variety of behaviors can be molded through the powers of reinforcement: for example, by an almost mechanical application of certain principles of reinforcement, he trained pigeons to play a miniature version of Ping-Pong and rats to perform certain complex types of behavior. Skinner's research, in fact, was conducted almost entirely within the so-called Skinner box (simply an apparatus containing a manipulandum and a device for delivering reinforcers). But his applied psychology of learning was not restricted entirely to mere tricks of animal training.

Skinner approaches classroom learning in the same way that he treats any other situation in which certain operant behavior (usually verbal behavior, in this case) is to be shaped. Although he was not the first to suggest the use of teaching machines, he has given this type of instruction much theoretical support. The important component of the teaching machine is the program, a series of items through which the student gradually progresses until the material is mastered or learned. Skinner believes that immediate reinforcement—knowing at once, for instance, the correct answer to a question or test item programmed in the machine—constitutes the best possible situation for learning.

Skinner went much farther than Watson in the successful application of his behaviorist views. Both approaches caused a great furor during the years when they were first advanced, and they have precipitated much controversy. Vigorously opposed to what he considered to be any vague, theoretical explanation of human learning, Skinner, for example, refused in his own system to consider the physiological factors *inside* an organism that might make possible all the complex learnings of which people (and even certain lower forms of animal life) are capable. Such extreme environmentalism on the part of the behaviorist has repelled a number of psychologists, who have become more and more intrigued by certain cognitive interpretations of learning.

Early Cognitive Interpretations

In the 1920s a very different group of psychologists strongly objected to the whole doctrine of connectionism or modern associationism. Sometimes called "field" psychologists, this group began to argue that every situation of learning is a total "field" that includes the surrounding situation. Every kind of experience has a structure that dominates the field. Therefore, the argument continued, it is artificial to analyze any situation into its specific elements; this results in an atomistic approach that neglects the total character of the situation. According to the "field" psychologists, behavior can be viewed properly only when the whole organism of an individual and the whole situation surrounding the individual are viewed as significant parts of the total learning process.

The leaders of this rebellion were three German psychologists: Max Wertheimer (1880–1943), Kurt Koffka (1886–1941), and Wolfgang Köhler (1887–1967), who were in sufficient agreement to be grouped together as Gestalt psychologists. Each eventually moved to the United States and devoted much time in this country to the development and refinement of his psychological position. Wertheimer, in particular, challenged the connectionist approach to learning. He criticized the analytical methods of connectionism and behaviorism and argued that learning does not arise from a response to a specific situation. Instead, Wertheimer pointed out, learning occurs as the individual sees the whole configuration (or Gestalt)[42] in a situation and changes his behavior in line with the pervading character of the situation. According to this conception, the learner does not respond mechanically through specific reflexes; the learner is a whole organism and responds as a whole.

Here, then, was a new interpretation of learning, a dynamic approach spearheaded by an intellectual movement in German psychology.

The Gestalt psychologists have been greatly interested in cognition and problems of perception. While Thorndike and Watson analyzed behavior into components and examined the S-R connections, Wertheimer and his colleagues studied unified wholes in consciousness. The important thing to the Gestalt psychologist is what the individual immediately *sees* as a unified whole. To the human eye, for example, a tornado *is* a tornado not because of the gaseous elements in it, but because of the approaching configuration of swirling air. The total *structure* is significant, not the mass of separate details that make up the Gestalt. Even human thoughts are considered whole perceptions, not mental images bound together by an associative process.

These and other elements of the perceptive process have tremendous implications for human learning. The Gestalt approach, for example, has been applied to reading skills: learning to read by whole sentences and whole words is considered more meaningful than building up one letter after another. The main emphasis in this cognitive interpretation is on *whole* systems in which the parts are interrelated in such a way that meaning and understanding are more clearly inferred from the Gestalt than from the separate parts alone.

Another important cognitive factor in Gestalt theory is learning by *insight*. A learner who develops insight into a problem sees, often quite suddenly, the whole situation in a new way with a clearer perception of logical relationships. Material grasped and understood through insightful learning is less likely to be forgotten and is more quickly transferred to new situations.

Some of the most ingenious experiments on insightful learning ever performed were carried out by Köhler during World War I.[43] On the eve of the war, Köhler was appointed director of an anthropoid research station maintained by the Prussian Academy of Sciences at Tenerife in the Canary Islands. He went to Tenerife in 1913 and proceeded to test the Thorndike hypothesis that animal learning was based solely on trial and error and on the "stamping-in" of correct responses. Köhler had ample time for a thorough study. Marooned in the islands at the outbreak of hostilities, he remained at Tenerife until 1920.

For his experiments Köhler used nine chimpanzees (two of which soon died). He tried to show that chimpanzees, which probably represent the most intelligent group of the subhuman animals, reach solutions all at once by a process of insight or integration. Köhler presented a series of simple problems in which the animal had to discover a way of reaching a suspended banana by placing boxes beneath it and climbing up on them or by fitting sticks together that would make it possible to reach the fruit. The bananas were displayed out of reach and could be obtained only by using techniques presumably new in the chimpanzee's experience. All the necessary elements of a solution were visible to the chimpanzee, which was not the case with Thorndike's animals. According to Köhler, the chimpanzees perceived the total situation and displayed *insight* in solving the problem. They did not try blindly every possible response. Their behavior, Köhler explained, displayed much goal-directed activity. The top performance of all was the solution of the jointed-stick problem by Sultan, the most intelligent of the nine animals. In other words, Köhler concluded, "the chimpanzees manifest intelligent behaviour of the general kind familiar in human beings."[44]

Köhler found that the problems were sometimes solved suddenly after a period of time during which the chimpanzee was not actually trying to reach the banana. He believed that the animal, having failed to obtain the fruit, sat and thought about the problem and then suddenly perceived a solution. Of course, gradual learning by trial and error can also be interpreted as partial steps toward insightful learning. But Köhler so arranged his problems that the chimpanzee could see at once the essential elements of a solution. All that was necessary was for these elements to be appropriately organized into a Gestalt. The animals perceived the relationship between the boxes or sticks and the bananas and, according to Köhler, responded to an integrated system of clues all at once, not to a series of separate clues one by one.

Pavlov, upon hearing of Köhler's studies, objected, asserting that Köhler had not controlled the past conditioning history of the chimpanzees.

He believed that "sudden" insight without prior conditioning was impossible. Recent studies of animal behavior suggest that Pavlov may have been correct. It appears that "insight" depends to a large extent on previously learned habits and associations.

In later years Wertheimer became concerned with insightful learning in children and adults and related Gestalt principles more specifically to human learning.[45] Repetition and drill are useless, Wertheimer believed, unless the learner perceives, within a compact pattern, not only the problem as an integrated whole but also the means to a solution. For Wertheimer, the principal aim of education is to develop in the learner a greater understanding of whole Gestalten. Such understanding not only requires a clearer perception of the problem to be solved but also calls for some imaginative thinking in discovering the ways in which the means lead to the end.

The value of insightful learning, developed through reflective thinking and creative problem solving, cannot be overemphasized in a free society. The years since 1919 have witnessed a number of psychological studies of the learning process, and some of the most interesting experiments in the United States have been extended variations on the Gestalt theme.[46] Research is revealing information about conceptual structures of new breadth and power.[47] This stress on cognition as a dynamic phase of human learning is the most important contribution of Gestalt theory to American education.

FOR DISCUSSION AND CRITICAL THOUGHT

1. Some students believe that Montessori's idea of "sense education" is closely related to Pestalozzi's concept of "sense realism" and Dewey's stress on "learn by doing." Do you agree? Explain.
2. Johann Heinrich Pestalozzi, John Dewey, and Maria Montessori worked for a better world for all children. In brief, their goals were to reform society through education. In what ways do Pestalozzi's, Dewey's, and Montessori's ideas coincide with, or stand in opposition to, your own approach to education?
3. Read chapter 7, "Piaget and Montessori," of David Elkind, *Children and Adolescents: Interpretive Essays on Jean Piaget* (Oxford University Press, 1970). Compare and contrast Piaget's and Montessori's theories, and discuss their important contributions to the history of educational thought.
4. Discuss some important implications for educators of Howard Gardner's theory of multiple intelligences.
5. Assess Edward L. Thorndike's contribution to educational psychology.

NOTES

1. Theories of faculty psychology are actually rooted in ancient history. See Walter B. Kolesnik, *Mental Discipline in Modern Education* (Madison: University of Wisconsin Press, 1958), pp. 89–112.

2. William James, *The Principles of Psychology* (New York: Henry Holt, 1908; originally published in 1890), 1:240. Italics in original.

3. Ibid., chap. 9, "The Stream of Thought," pp. 224–290.

4. Edward L. Thorndike, *Educational Psychology*. (New York: Teachers College, Columbia University, 1913), "The Original Nature of Man," 1:2.

5. Ibid., 1:281. Italics in original.

6. Ibid., 1:4.

7. See Edwin G. Boring, *A History of Experimental Psychology* (2nd ed.; New York: Appleton-Century-Crofts, 1950), pp. 323–24, 520. A. A. Roback, however, gives 1881 and 1883, respectively, as dates for the founding of Hall's and Wundt's laboratories. (A. A. Roback, *History of American Psychology* [New York: Library Publishers, 1952], p. 129.) William James contests the priority of both Hall and Wundt, claiming that he established at Harvard in 1874–1875 or 1876 a psychological laboratory that Hall described as nothing more than a "tiny room under the stairway of Agassiz Museum."

8. G. Stanley Hall, *Life and Confessions of a Psychologist* (New York: D. Appleton, 1923), pp. 357, 360.

9. G. Stanley Hall, "The Contents of Children's Minds," *Princeton Review* 11 (May 1883): 249–272.

10. G. Stanley Hall, *Adolescence: Its Psychology and Its Relations to Physiology, Anthropology, Sociology, Sex, Crime, Religion and Education*, 2 vols. (New York and London: D. Appleton, 1916; originally published in 1904).

11. John Amos Comenius, *The Great Didactic*, trans. and ed. M. W. Keatinge (London: Adam & Charles Black, 1907), pt. 2, "Text," chaps. 13, 14, 17, and 18. According to Comenius, *"Nature knits everything together in continuous combination"* (p. 152, italics in original); and "Order, which is the dominating principle in the art of teaching all things to all men, should be, and can be, borrowed from no other source but the operations of nature" (p. 100).

12. G. Stanley Hall, "The Ideal School as Based on Child Study," *Forum* 32 (September 1901): 24–39. See also G. E. Partridge, *Genetic Philosophy of Education: An Epitome of the Published Educational Writings of President G. Stanley Hall of Clark University* (New York: Sturgis & Walton, 1912), p. 96.

13. G. Stanley Hall, "Child-Study and Its Relation to Education," *Forum* 29 (August 1900): 700.

14. Note, for example, Ellen Key's *The Century of the Child* (New York and London: Putnam, 1909).

15. Arnold L. Gesell et al., *An Atlas of Infant Behavior: A Systematic Delineation of the Forms and Early Growth of Human Behavior Patterns*, 2 vols. (New Haven, Conn.: Yale University Press, 1934).

16. See, for example, Arnold Gesell and Catherine S. Amatruda, *Developmental*

Diagnosis: Normal and Abnormal Child Development–Clinical Methods and Practical Applications (New York: Paul B. Hoeber, 1941).

17. David Elkind, *Children and Adolescents: Interpretive Essays on Jean Piaget* (New York: Oxford University Press, 1970), p. 151.

18. This conception runs through most of Piaget's early research. See Jean Piaget, *The Language and Thought of the Child,* trans. Marjorie Gabain (New York: Humanities Press, 1959; first published in 1926). Indicative of Piaget's more recent interest is *The Origins of Intelligence in the Child,* trans. Margaret Cook (New York: International Universities Press, 1952; published in 1936). For a critique of Piaget's work, see John H. Flavell, *The Developmental Psychology of Jean Piaget* (Princeton, N.J.: Van Nostrand, 1963), pp. 405–446.

19. See especially Jean Piaget, *The Child's Conception of the World,* trans. Joan and Andrew Tomlinson (New York: Humanities Press, 1951; first published in 1929).

20. See, for example, William Kessen and Clementina Kuhlmann, eds., *Thought in the Young Child:* Report of a Conference on Intellective Development with particular attention to the work of Jean Piaget, *Monographs of the Society for Research in Child Development 27,* no. 2 (Serial No. 83) (Lafayette, Ind.: Child Development Publications, 1962), pp. 41–61.

21. After widespread publicity and some initial success, the Montessori method virtually disappeared from the United States. "Her American fame was truly meteoric," writes Robert H. Beck, "lasting from 1909 to 1915." According to Beck, "the extinction of Dr. Montessori's public and professional appeal in the United States" was due primarily to the resistance and criticisms of William Heard Kilpatrick and other followers of John Dewey. "For the first time in modern history of American public education," continues Beck, "a genuine lay enthusiasm had been engendered but died in the face of professional opposition." Robert H. Beck, "Kilpatrick's Critique of Montessori's Method and Theory," *Studies in Philosophy and Education* 1 (November 1961): 153, 162. Sol Cohen, supporting this view, remarks, "Progressive Education left little room for any system not espousing the tenets of its faith; by the mid-twenties scarcely a trace of Montessori remained in this country." Sal Cohen, "Maria Montessori: Priestess or Pedagogue?" *Teacher's College Record* 71 (December 1969): 313. For a summary of other views, see John J. McDermott's "Introduction" to Maria Montessori, *Spontaneous Activity in Education* (1917) (New York: Schocken Books, 1965), pp. xi–xxvi.

22. Maria Montessori, *The Montessori Method: Scientific Pedagogy as Applied to Child Education in "The Children's Houses" with Additions and Revisions by the Author,* trans. Anne E. George (New York: Frederick A. Stokes, 1912), p. 33. Italics in original.

23. The lectures she delivered at the University of Rome at this time were later published in 1909. The English translation appeared in 1913 under the title *Pedagogical Anthropology,* trans. Frederic Taber Cooper (New York: Frederick A. Stokes, 1913). This virtually unknown work is indispensable for a full understanding of Montessori's ideas.

24. Ibid., p. 19.

25. Montessori, *Montessori Method,* pp. 48, 49, 52. Italics in original.

26. See Maria Montessori, *Spontaneous Activity in Education: The Advanced Montessori Method,* trans. Florence Simmonds (New York: Frederick A. Stokes, 1917), chap. 8, "Intelligence," pp. 195–240.

27. See Montessori, *Montessori Method,* chap. 18, "Language in Childhood," pp. 310–325.

28. "It is all so interesting to [the children that] they cannot stop to be bored or naughty," noted Dorothy Canfield Fisher in 1911. "The freedom accorded them is absolute, the only rule being that they must not hurt or annoy others." Fisher spent the winter of 1910–1911 at the Casa dei Bambini in Rome. The children in the Casa, she remarked, "are by far the most briskly energetic Romans in the city." See her book, *A Montessori Mother* (New York: Henry Holt, 1912). Her quoted statements are on p. 30.

29. Montessori, *Pedagogical Anthropology,* pp. 20, 34.

30. Sir Francis Galton, *Hereditary Genius: An Inquiry into Its Laws and Consequences* (London: Macmillan, 1914; originally published in 1869).

31. See Howard Gardner, *Frames of Mind: The Theory of Multiple Intelligences* (New York: Basic Books, 1983), chapters 5–10.

32. Marie Winn, "New Views of Human Intelligence," *New York Times Magazine,* part 2, 29 April 1990, p. 28.

33. For a provocative discussion of Bentham's associationist principle, see John Bowring, ed., *The Works of Jeremy Bentham* (New York: Russell & Russell, 1962), vol. 1, sect. 2, "The Greatest-Happiness Principle and Its Application to Morals and Legislation," by John Hill Burton, pp. 17–36.

34. Edward L. Thorndike, *Animal Intelligence: An Experimental Study of the Associative Processes in Animals,* Psychological Monograph *Supplement 2,* no. 4 (New York, 1898).

35. Thorndike, *Educational Psychology,* 1:1. See also Edward L. Thorndike, *The Elements of Psychology* (2nd ed.; New York: A. G. Seiler, 1922), p. 205.

36. Thorndike elaborated on these "laws" in considerable detail. See his *Educational Psychology,* vol. 2., *The Psychology of Learning,* pp. 1–16.

37. Edward L. Thorndike, *Education: A First Book* (New York: Macmillan, 1912), pp. 96–97. Italics in original. See also Edward L. Thorndike, *Human Learning,* Messenger Lectures, Cornell University, Fifth Series, 1928–1929 (New York and London: Century 1931).

38. Edward L. Thorndike and Robert S. Woodworth, "The Influence of Improvement in One Mental Function upon the Efficiency of Other Functions, II. The Estimation of Magnitudes," *Psychological Review* 8 (July 1901): 386. See also in vol. 8 of *Psychological Review* two additional reports by Thorndike and Woodworth: "The Influence of Improvement in One Mental Function upon the Efficiency of Other Functions (I.)," pp. 247–261; and "The Influence of Improvement in One Mental Function upon the Efficiency of Other Functions, III. Functions Involving Attention, Observation and Discrimination," pp. 553–564.

39. Edward L. Thorndike, "Mental Discipline in High School Studies," *Journal of Educational Psychology* 15 (February 1924): 98.

40. John B. Watson, "Psychology as the Behaviorist Views It," *Psychological Review* 20 (March 1913): 176–176. Italics in original.

41. John B. Watson, *Behaviorism* (2nd ed.: New York: People's Institute, 1925), p. 82. See also John B. Watson, *Psychology from the Standpoint of a Behaviorist* (Philadelphia and London: J. B. Lippincott, 1919).

42. There is no English word equivalent to "gestalt"; the nearest English translation is "pattern" or "configuration."

43. Wolfgang Köhler's German reports first appeared in 1917 and in an English translation entitled *The Mentality of Apes,* trans. Ella Winter (2nd rev. ed.; New York: Harcourt, Brace, 1925). The German title in translation is actually *Intelligence Tests on Anthropoid Apes (Intelligenzprüfungen an Menschenaffen).*

44. Köhler, *The Mentality of Apes,* p. 275.

45. See Max Wertheimer, *Productive Thinking,* ed. Michael Wertheimer (enlarged ed.; New York: Harper & Bros., 1959).

46. For a modified Gestalt approach, with some important implications for human learning, see, for example, Edward C. Tolman, *Purposive Behavior in Animals and Men* (New York: Century, 1932). More recently, a special kind of field psychology became influential in the United States. Developed by Kurt Lewin and called "topological psychology," this approach is similar to the classical Gestalt psychology in holding that the overall field or pattern of events determines experience. It differs from Gestalt psychology, however, in making greater use of drive or motive and in stressing behavior more than experience. See Kurt Lewin, *A Dynamic Theory of Personality: Selected Paper,* trans. Donald K. Adams and Karl E. Zener (New York and London: McGraw-Hill, 1935); and *Principles of Topological Psychology,* trans. Fritz and Grace M. Heider (New York: McGraw-Hill, 1936).

47. See pp. 279–281.

PART THREE

Education in
Modern Society
1919 to the Present

CHAPTER 9

Continuing Struggles for Equality of Educational Opportunity

Education, like all society's prime needs, changes as society changes.

> Report of the Harvard Committee, *General Education in a Free Society*, 1945

Only the United States still has buffers between itself and the anxieties of our age: buffers of time, of distance, of natural wealth, of national ingenuity, of a stubborn tradition of hope.

> ARTHUR M. SCHLESINGER, JR.,
> *The Vital Center: The Politics of Freedom*, 1949

The welfare of children has to be our highest priority. Not only are they our future security, but their dreams and ideals can provide a much-needed renaissance of spirit in what is becoming an aging, tired, and disillusioned society. In the end the only thing we have is our young people. If we fail them, all else is in vain.

> ALAN PIFER, "Perceptions of Children and Youth," 1978

As we have listened for centuries to the voices of men and the theories of development that their experience informs, so we have come more recently to notice not only the silence of women but the difficulty in hearing what they say when they speak.

> CAROL GILLIGAN, *In a Different Voice:*
> *Psychological Theory and Women's Development*, 1982

One of the striking themes in American history has been the closing gap between human aspirations and educational opportunities. Efforts toward this ideal have been vigorous and deep rooted. The most conspicuous examples are the demands of women for equality and the quest of black Americans for freedom and civil rights.

THE TEMPO OF CULTURAL CHANGE

The Twenties

The 1920s—the "roaring twenties," the "jazz age," the "prohibition era"— was a colorful period marked by glaring contradictions between shallow manifestations of happiness and prosperity and strong undercurrents from unsolved social and economic problems. In the mainstream of American history, the decade stood out in sharp and vivid contrast, as though it were cut off from the social patterns either preceding or following it. The progressive era had witnessed sweeping reforms and an idealism culminating in President Woodrow Wilson's crusade to save the world for democracy; the debacle of the Great Depression was followed by a broadened responsibility for social welfare under the New Deal. From the end of World War I to 1929, however, the voices of social protest were drowned out, or in some instances brushed aside as un-American, by a business-oriented civilization spending and buying with feverish intensity.

To question the beneficent workings of the free-enterprise system during the 1920s was unthinkable. The temper of the times and a host of legal precedents combined to support a hegemony of business leadership. Everyone seemed under the spell of a booming stock market—General Electric rose to 396, Radio Corporation reached 505, Montgomery Ward hit 466, in a frenzy of speculation—and as long as the nation prospered, people believed unquestioningly in capitalism. There emerged an almost mystical belief in the business creed as a supreme way of life. "Among the nations of the earth today America stands for one idea: *Business,*" boasted one commentator in a typical article of the 1920s. "What is the finest game? Business. The soundest science? Business. The truest art? Business. The fullest education? Business. The fairest opportunity? Business. The cleanest philanthropy? Business. The sanest religion? Business."[1]

"Fordism"

The automobile was not even mentioned in the census of 1900, when there were only 144 miles of paved roads and about 8,000 vehicles in the United States. Expensive and virtually hand-made, it was first driven for pleasure by wealthy owners. In at least one state, a driver in 1900 had to advertise a projected trip one week in advance to give ample warning for pedestrians to clear out of the way!

Around the turn of the century, Henry Ford, a skilled mechanic from Detroit, began to convert this costly machine into a lighter, less expensive model that many people could afford to own. A business genius, Ford shrewdly foresaw the impact of the automobile on the social and business life of the nation. His first step was to standardize and simplify the manufacturing process. In 1909, at the age of forty-six he announced that he would produce only one model—the Model T—with the same chassis for all machines. "Any customer can have a car painted any color that he wants so long as it is black," Ford remarked.[2] His assembly-line system astonished the world. Assigning to his workers simple tasks repeated over and over again by the same individual, he reduced in a startling way all the skill formerly commanded during the intricate production stages.

Ford emerged as the industrial titan of the new motor age. His then fantastic combination of policies created cars for millions. Residents of "Middletown," for example, considered an automobile to be more important than home ownership, electric lights, a telephone, plumbing fixtures, and in some cases even food.[3] Both praised and condemned by Americans and Europeans, "Fordism" astounded the world by its great success. In numerous and profoundly significant ways, Henry Ford was transforming capitalism from a system of exploitation and large profits for the few to a system of mass consumption and increased purchasing power for all.

By 1929, there were an estimated 20 million automobiles in use on dirt or newly paved roads. This figure alone was an important manifestation of the twentieth-century revolution in transportation. The airplane, the radio, and the motion picture were other visible symbols of a mechanized era.

Automobile manufacturing, in particular, was the key to industrial prosperity. It absorbed immense quantities of steel, rubber, copper, and other products. Three companies accounted for 90 percent of the auto industry, and by the close of the decade, General Motors was earning more than $200 million annually. Never before had industrial expansion reported such fantastic gains and profits.

The prevailing wealth, however, did not touch all segments of society. Overlooked, for example, was the poverty of coal miners, southern share croppers, and poorly paid factory workers. During the 1920s, the gap between the wealthy and the poor was indeed extreme. In 1929, before the stock market crash, only 2.3 percent of all families in the United States earned incomes of over $10,000 a year; about 60 percent had incomes of less than $2,000, which, at the 1929 price level, was categorized by the Brookings Institution as the borderline of poverty.

But prices were rising and the market was soaring. The times were obviously prosperous, however superficial the mirage of a stock market boom. From the vantage point of President Calvin Coolidge and business leaders, most of the people were happy.

This prosperity and contentment did not conceal completely some of the pessimism and inner conflicts in American culture. Sinclair Lewis's *Main Street* (1920), with its portrayal of life in "Gopher Prairie," brilliantly satirized the growing conformity in society, with its trend toward national standardization spurred on by radio broadcasting, billboard advertising, and mass production. In many ways, *Babbitt* (1922) was a harsher portrait, pointing up the hypocrisy and cant of certain middle-class mores that dictated an average businessman's life. Meanwhile, F. Scott Fitzgerald's disillusioned revolt in *This Side of Paradise* (1920), *The Great Gatsby* (1925), and other stories revealed a contemporary scene of hopelessness and despair, a cynical picture of American youth, the "lost generation" of the "roaring twenties." Fitzgerald's sense of disillusionment was shared by others who, like Ernest Hemingway, fled to Europe in despair to escape from what they perceived as a barren intellectual climate in American society during the 1920s.

EXPANDING EDUCATIONAL OPPORTUNITIES FOR WOMEN

Perhaps the most significant manifestation of the changing social conditions of twentieth-century life was a new image of the American woman. Her position in society was no longer being constrained by a pattern of mores developed on the premise that a woman's place was solely in the home.

Historical Antecedents

The discrimination against women in any public capacity was deeply rooted in American culture. Custom had long decreed their social role: a young lady's only aspiration was marriage and a family of her own.

During the eighteenth and early nineteenth centuries, this tradition was strongly reinforced by barriers and laws that sharply restricted a woman's social position in a man's world. A wife's legal status was definitely inferior to that of her husband. For example, she was not permitted to vote; the control of her property passed at the time of marriage to her husband; the responsibility for the children of a marriage was vested by law solely in the father; and the husband was usually held accountable by law for the conduct of his wife. A husband could even control the destiny of his children through a will, despite his widow's wishes. In colonial America and in most of the states up to the Civil War, the legal code for court decisions was simple and unequivocal: a married woman, according to English common law, suffered "civil death." She had no legal entity apart from her husband—"her new self," "her superior, her companion, her master."[4]

In frontier society, the management of domestic affairs—revolving for the most part around pregnancy, childbirth, and the care of babies—left little time for a wife of normal strength to pursue activities outside the home. No matter what a woman's position in society, children were usually born to her in regular succession. Births almost always occurred in the home, with no more than the care provided by a midwife or a neighbor. The infant mortality rate was pathetically high. However superior their longevity record amid the rigors and demands of life, women were still considered innately more delicate than men. This deep-seated prejudice only served to strengthen other prevailing notions. In the isolated security of the home, a woman's function was to bear children, to instill in the offspring moral and spiritual values of a Christian society, and to manage the tasks of a large household. For those women with any time to spare, there were very few available jobs away from the home; furthermore, as a good wife, a woman was not expected to engage in any intellectual pursuits or carry on any outside work. There was, in fact, a prevalent notion that women were intellectually inferior to men and that their mental "faculties" were simply not worth training anyway.

Not everyone, of course, shared this prejudiced view. In an essay expressing some *Thoughts upon Female Education* (1787), Benjamin Rush favored a more advanced training for women. If the success of a republic depends on the ability of men to discharge their political responsibilities, Rush argued, then mothers must be enlightened enough to teach their own sons history, geography, and grammar. Horace Mann and Henry Barnard also advocated a broader education for young women. Their ideas, however, were atypical in an age espousing the opinion that "women in general have feebler minds than men."[5]

Capability in homemaking tasks was a primary expectation for girls in colonial society and dictated for decades the dominant type of training pursued by young ladies. Domestic knowledge was obtained from mothers, or in the case of indentured servants, from the mistresses. The girls learned to read and write in the dame schools and occasionally in the reading and writing schools. In the beginning, girls were rigidly excluded from the town schools of New England; however, toward the end of the eighteenth century a few communities began to permit girls to attend the Latin grammar schools in the early mornings and late afternoons when the boys had already been taught and had left the classroom. In the more privileged families, first in the eighteenth-century South and later in New England, girls received private instruction in dancing and the social graces and in French and music. The more tolerant attitudes of Quaker and Moravian settlers led to greater educational opportunities for girls, particularly in the lower schools of some of the Middle Colonies.

A "secondary education" was rarely, if ever, available to colonial girls. In 1684, for example, the Hopkins School of New Haven decreed that *"all girls be excluded as improper and inconsistent with such a grammar school as ye low injoines and as is the Designe of this settlement."*[6] During the early decades of the nineteenth century the wealthier classes sent their daughters to the "female seminaries" or academies that usually operated preparatory departments with instruction in reading and writing. In the sparsely settled areas on the frontier where separate academies could not be maintained, the headmasters occasionally admitted both boys and girls. Most of the cheaper, privately sponsored seminaries were poorly equipped and staffed; others were costly and scattered over wide areas. Even in the academies and seminaries, girls were permitted to receive no more than an elementary schooling. Susan B. Anthony complained that none of her male instructors would teach her long division. Women were expected to be, she remarked, "mere kitchen maids, without a particle of information" in their heads.[7] Not until the end of the eighteenth century did anyone dare propose seriously that women should be educated in skills beyond an elementary level.

If the feeling toward a secondary education for girls was essentially negative, the attitude toward women's collegiate education was far more antagonistic. Occasionally a young lady prepared herself for admission to college. In 1783, for example, a twelve-year-old girl passed the entrance examination to Yale—"fully qualified, except in regard to sex"—but was denied admission.[8] Before the 1830s not a college or university in the United States had opened its doors to women, and every approach to the professions was restricted to men.

Toward a New Intellectual Outlook

Several forces militated strongly against the traditional conception of a woman's social role. Perhaps most significant in terms of its ultimate impact on popular views was a changing intellectual climate in American life. "Whilst you are proclaiming peace and good-will to men, emancipating all nations, you insist upon retaining an absolute power over wives," complained Abigail Adams in 1776 in a letter to her husband, John, who was then serving in the Continental Congress. "But you must remember, . . . we have it in our power, not only to free ourselves, but to subdue our masters, and, without violence, throw both your natural and legal authority at our feet "[9]

The life of Abigail Smith Adams (1744–1818) is an example of the struggle that women had to overcome to survive, and, in her case, to gain knowledge and share ideas during the eighteenth century. The daughter of a minister from Weymouth, Massachusetts, Abigail Smith married John Adams, the first vice president and second president of the United States, in 1764. During their long and happy marriage, Abigail became a spokeswoman for women's rights and education. John Adams's successful career as a politician and diplomat was due in no small part to Abigail, whose informal correspondences with influential and national leaders during the colonial era discussed subjects ranging from race relations and foreign relations to the shaping of the new government. Of the two thousand letters and correspondences she wrote during her lifetime, most were sent to her husband, who valued her opinion and urged her to express it to him. Abigail's exposure to the important issues and the discussion of them in her home led her to make the following comments concerning the independence of women:

> I long to hear that you have declared an independency *{sic}*—and by the way in the new Code of Laws which I suppose will be necessary for you to make I desire you would Remember the Ladies and be more generous and favourable to them than your ancestors. Do not put such unlimited power into the hands of the Husbands. Remember all Men would be tyrants if they could. If particular care and attention is not paid to the Ladies we are determined to foment a Rebellion, and will not hold ourselves bound by any Laws in which we have no voice, or Representation."[10]

Few women of Abigail's generation had her unique opportunity to develop and verbalize opinions on so many important eighteenth century issues (for example, patriotism, liberty, and independence).

In *Vindication of the Rights of Woman* (1792), Mary Wollstonecraft (1759–1797) argued that women's nature was the same as men's—free, independent, and rational—and that "like men, women's first duty is to themselves as rational creatures." She insisted that women "must have a civil existence in the state, married or single." Wollstonecraft believed that education would improve women's character and position, and she argued specifically for coeducation and a system of public, or "national" schools for all social classes.[11] Her writings were widely circulated in the 1790s when a lively debate on women's education was beginning. The publication of the *Vindication* and the conviction and clarity of Wollstonecraft's arguments helped to build some favorable support for improving education for women. However, the general framework of her position—especially her egalitarianism and her belief in the importance of a public role for American women—was not well received during the late eighteenth century.

In a nineteenth-century world of flux and change, in a society espousing the dignity of man and upholding the worth of the individual, demands for political equality became logical arguments in the humanitarian mainstream. Editorials appearing in the highly influential ladies' magazines and egalitarian ideas voiced from the lyceum platform contributed immeasurably to the success of the feminist crusades.[12]

The suffrage issue attracted attention long before the Civil War; but the attainment of the ballot by illiterate freedmen spurred the reformers on with zeal and renewed vigor. At the end of the war, however, women were still without the political rights of citizenship, although a few states had given them the right to control property. With the adoption of the Fourteenth Amendment, the word "male" was inserted in the federal Constitution for the first time. American feminists openly expressed amazement and anger that Congress should be willing to extend the right to vote to two million illiterate African American men while denying the ballot to women. Surely a woman was as fit to vote as an ex-slave, the intrepid reformers exclaimed. If free men had political rights and privileges, why not free women, too?

The "emancipation of women" became a rallying cry for a massive drive for education and political equality. Led by Elizabeth Cady Stanton and Susan B. Anthony and supported by a host of professional reformers, the suffragists voiced new ideas of women's education, including the right to enter such professions as medicine, law, and the ministry. A college open to women, argued Catharine Beecher, should prepare for several professions and educate its students to be independent.[13] Equal educational opportunity, in fact, became a symbol of the whole movement. In the eyes of the feminist leaders, education would open the door to possible leadership and pave the way toward political equality. This in turn would lead to the larger goal of the suffrage movement: recognition of a woman's abilities and rights as a human being. In 1869 the Territory of Wyoming conferred the suffrage on women; by 1911 six western states accepted the idea completely. Finally, after a long and militant struggle, including mass demonstrations and women pickets in front of the White House, the Nineteenth Amendment was added to the Constitution in 1920.

In advancing new concepts of women's education, the feminist movement enlisted the support of some able reformers. The female seminaries founded by Emma Willard at Troy, New York, in 1821, by Catharine Beecher at Hartford, Connecticut, in 1827, and by Mary Lyon in South Hadley, Massachusetts, in 1836 set important precedents. Outstanding were the efforts of Emma Willard (1787–1870) and Mary Lyon (1797–1849), whose ideas had a permanent influence on women's education in the United States.

Emma Willard

Born in Berlin, Connecticut, Emma Willard was an enthusiastic and highly gifted educator. In 1821 she opened the Troy (New York) Female Seminary (now the Emma Willard School), the first endowed school in the United States for the education of girls. Her novel and provocative ideas, obviously in advance of the times, revealed a clear grasp of some important pedagogical principles.

Willard believed strongly that students should be broadly educated in a wide range of subjects. Every year from 1821 to 1838, during the time when she was principal, the Troy Seminary expanded and strengthened its curriculum. New courses were added in mathematics, history, geography, and science. "Why should we be kept in ignorance of the great machinery of nature?" she asked in her famous "Address." "If mothers were acquainted with [natural] science, they would communicate very many of its principles to their children in early youth."[14] Through its advanced work in mathematics and science, Troy soon earned a national reputation and matched the courses offered to men on the collegiate level. Willard introduced the study of physiology in an era when the very mention of the human body by ladies was considered vulgar. "Mothers visiting a class at the Seminary in the early thirties were so shocked at the sight of a pupil drawing a heart, arteries and veins on a blackboard to explain the circulation of the blood that they left the room in shame and dismay," wrote Willard's biographer. "To preserve the modesty of the girls and spare them too frequent agitation, heavy paper was pasted over the pages in the textbooks which depicted the human body.[15] From 1847 to 1859, when the physical sciences were being taught almost completely by a textbook method, the instructor at Troy was teaching the girls chemistry by means of experiments performed through class demonstrations and carried out by the students themselves in the laboratory. By the middle of the nineteenth century Troy was one of the finest girls' schools in the nation.

In her counseling approach with the students, Willard displayed a rare insight into personality development. She devised a plan of student self-government and placed the primary responsibility for discipline on the student body. She offered frequent words of encouragement to the girls, especially to those with personal or academic problems, and tried to bring out in her daily discussions an individual's strong character traits. Long after Willard's retirement, former students remembered her and came back to Troy from far and near to visit, to seek counsel, or just to reminisce.

Willard urged her students to enter teaching as a career. During her seventeen years as principal of Troy Seminary, she loaned about $75,000 to needy girls who wanted to prepare for teaching. Only about half were ever able to repay their debt. Recognizing the inadequacy of these loans, she was probably the first administrator of a woman's institution to point out the necessity of private endowments for scholarships and other educational purposes. Each girl who graduated from Troy received a signed certificate from Emma Willard, confirming the student's qualifications for teaching. Long before the opening of the first public normal schools, Troy prepared about two hundred teachers for the common schools. To increase prestige and command higher teachers' salaries for her trained graduates, Willard even established in 1837 an alumnae organization called the Willard Association for the Mutual Improvement of Female Teachers. It was probably the first organization to bring the issue of salaries before the taxpaying public.

When she retired from Troy the following year, Willard returned to Connecticut and continued to work for educational reform. She traveled from school to school, presenting model lessons in geography and arithmetic and helping teachers to improve their own instructional techniques. At one point in her travels, she so aroused the housewives concerning the needs of the common schools that the women organized a Female Common School Association that agitated effectively for school improvement. In 1846, driving her own stagecoach and accompanied by a former Troy student, she embarked on an eight-thousand-mile journey through the West and the South, urging local women wherever she stopped to organize and work for better schools. A striking personality, obviously poised and persuasive, Willard won friends easily and influenced hundreds of local townspeople with her strong arguments. When she died at the age of eighty-three, she was widely recognized by both men and women as a powerful educational leader.

Mary Lyon

Like Emma Willard, Mary Lyon established some historic precedents in women's education. An ardent Calvinist, imbued with an evangelical faith, Lyon was intensely studious and had an extraordinary memory. "She is all intellect," remarked one of her own teachers. "She does not know that she has a body to care for."[16] Brusque and careless, unconcerned with social amenities, she worked long and hard, going incessantly from door to door soliciting funds for her seminary and missionary work. She was a very ambitious person, with an indomitable and fiery will. During her early years, all her strength and drive were channeled toward one all-consuming purpose: obtaining a better schooling for girls like herself who wanted desperately to learn more about everything but could not afford to pay for a higher education. "My heart has so yearned over the adult female youth in the common walks of life, that it has sometimes seemed as if there was a fire shut up in my bones." she confided in a letter written in 1834 to a friend.[17] More than anything else, Mary Lyon wanted to make an education available to capable girls from all social classes.

But her dream encompassed more than just another seminary: Mount Holyoke would build a rigid program far more advanced than that envisaged by Emma Willard. It would prepare girls for careers other than teaching and would offer courses comparable in scope and depth to those taught in the best academies for men.

Like Emma Willard, Mary Lyon was shrewd enough to recognize the need for a self-perpetuating board and an adequate financial endowment if her proposed school was ever to attain any measure of stability. In 1834, after much preliminary work, she told a group of ministers and businessmen that a new educational institution for young women would be a sound and profitable investment. She even persuaded them to solicit an estimated $27,000 needed to build the school! However, because of public apathy and a growing financial skepticism before the grim panic of 1837, the trustees could not raise the money. In unladylike fashion, Lyon herself broke all propriety and in 1834 went out into the countryside pleading for financial support.

While the colorful and nonconforming Grimké sisters were touring western Massachusetts, denouncing slavery and preaching radical feminism, Mary Lyon was riding in her carriage or sleigh alone through the same territory, soliciting funds for a girls' seminary. She stopped at every farmhouse to argue and beg for money; occasionally in her zeal and determination, she refused to remove her foot from the wheel of a farmer's wagon until he had promised to donate at least part of his crop to the seminary being constructed in South Hadley, Massachusetts. Such unconventional behavior startled both men and women and brought ridicule and condemnation from the conservative elements in the community. "What do I that is wrong?" she replied angrily to those who criticized her action. "I am doing a great work."[18]

In 1837 Mary Lyon's school finally opened its doors. Only a seminary, Mount Holyoke did not attain full collegiate status until 1893; yet few historians seem to refute the institution's claim as the oldest women's college in the United States.[19]

When the first freshmen and their parents arrived in South Hadley in November 1837, no one at the seminary was really prepared to begin. "We are in glorious confusion now, but we hope for better order soon," explained one of the deacons to the startled parents as he hammered noisily at the matting on the floor.[20] That night the trustees' wives washed the dishes in the kitchen, while Mary Lyon happily talked with the parents in the dining room.

A "mother superior" to some, an "absolute monarch" to others, Mary Lyon emphasized discipline, duty, and devotion. She laid down a set of rules for general behavior that included 106 alphabetized items, all of which were strictly enforced. Each girl was required to report her own infractions in daily confessionals—a practice that later evoked much criticism. Even the nearby Amherst College boys, who visited the Mount Holyoke ladies occasionally, "rang the bell in great terror, for fear of Lyon and the assistant dragonesses."[21] In the 1840s, of course, the regulations at Mount Holyoke were no more severe than those that prevailed in the men's colleges; the male lists, in fact, were often longer and more detailed. If the girls were required to sit silently and erect at the tables and refrain from whispering in the corridors, the boys were not allowed to strike their instructors and bring pistols into the classrooms.

In later years Mary Lyon tried to infuse her school with an evangelical spirit. At times she seemed to view her seminary more as a missionary training ground than as an institution of learning. There was, for example, an "annual Pentecost" at the seminary, when the "professed Christians" tried to "convert" other students. "[I] found myself an inmate, of the *Mt. Holyoke Convent,*" exclaimed one student in a letter to friends in 1845, "where I expect to be a *Nun* 40 long weeks!"[22] Everyone in the school attended daily devotional sermons which Lyon herself delivered. The intensity of her earlier drive for women's education narrowed considerably before her death in 1849 and became a fierce religious crusade: she communicated frequently with foreign missionaries, inviting them to Mount Holyoke whenever possible. She personally solicited funds for religious work from the students, faculty, and surrounding community. (She donated about half of her own annual salary of two hundred dollars to the missionaries.) Not unexpectedly, a number of students turned away from teaching in the common schools and embarked instead on missionary work abroad. From 1837 to 1849, during only twelve years as administrator, Mary Lyon created in the seminary so completely her own image that Mount Holyoke College was for decades viewed merely as a religious symbol of its devout founder.

Regardless of its impact on the career choices of the girls, Lyon's missionary zeal did not detract in any way from the intellectual goal of the seminary. Her initial policies established some fundamental principles that greatly enhanced Mount Holyoke's academic prestige. She insisted, first of all, on firm standards for admission, both in terms of age and academic preparation. No girl under sixteen was to be accepted, and a system of entrance examinations was begun. These regulations, which were similar to those of the best academies, reflected Lyon's staunch determination to *select* students on the bases of maturity and intellectual ability.

Far more significant was Mount Holyoke's proposed three-year course of studies, instead of the typical two-year seminary program. "The design is to give a solid, extensive, and well-balanced English education . . . ," explained Mary Lyon, "which will prepare ladies to be *educators* of children and youth, rather than to fit them to be mere teachers, as the term has been technically applied."[23] She had no intention of teaching "domestic work" to the girls. "That should be done by the mothers at home," asserted Lyon.

The strong academic content of the curriculum departed sharply from tradition. After passing the entrance examinations, first-year students enrolled in English, rhetoric, geography, ancient and modern history, botany, politics, Euclid, and human physiology. The following year the girls continued English and botany and then began algebra, history, and natural and intellectual philosophy. The senior program included chemistry, astronomy, geology, ecclesiastical history, Christianity, logic, rhetoric, moral philoso-

phy, analogy, and natural theology. "They are very thorough here," wrote
one of the first students in a letter to her family, "more so than I expected.
They will make us get our lessons and get them well."[24]

It was indeed a rigid course of study. Some feared that girls could never
survive such an ordeal. One preacher, for example, protested that a young
lady

> will die in the process. . . . The poor thing . . . must be on the strain all
> the school hours, study in the evening till her eyes ache, her brain whirls,
> her spine yields and gives way, and she comes through the process of
> education, enervated, feeble, without courage or vigor, elasticity or
> strength. Alas! must we crowd education upon our daughters, and, for
> the sake of having them "intellectual," make them puny, nervous, and
> their whole earthly existence a struggle between life and death?[25]

With its solid academic program and rising admission standards,
Mount Holyoke demonstrated to the skeptics an impressive record of success
and encouraged others to follow in the same path. Vassar opened in 1865 in
Poughkeepsie, New York, with a full collegiate program and 330 students,
who came from as far away as California. "It occurred to me that woman,
having received from her Creator the same intellectual constitution as man,
has the same right as man to intellectual culture and development," declared
Matthew Vassar, an English-born businessman who had made a fortune
brewing and selling ale and beer.[26] A decade later, Wellesley, near Boston,
opened its doors. Both colleges struggled for years with poorly prepared
students and without sufficient endowments. In 1875 Smith College opened
at Northampton, Massachusetts, with only fourteen freshmen. In its admission policy, Smith demanded every year adequate preparation, regardless of
numbers. The beginnings of Radcliffe College go back to 1879, when the
Harvard "Annex" offered its first courses for women. By the time that Bryn
Mawr was founded near Philadelphia in 1885, enough girls were being
prepared for college work that the earlier battles for quality and high
standards demanded from the beginning by Mount Holyoke would not have
to be fought again.

New Ways of Social Life

New modes of American life during the nineteenth century also helped to
expand traditional conceptions concerning the status and education of wom-
en. In the westward migrations, frontier society encouraged a certain egalitarianism and challenged old views of propriety. Women might be inferior
by law, but in a struggling society they shared with men the pathos and
hardships of survival. No wife could work merely within the confines of a

home: those widowed from Indian wars, for instance, carried on a husband's business or started anew in a different venture. Social customs were easily defied and broken by diligent women forced to choose between work and starvation. Such a different way of life, requiring from wives and daughters resourcefulness and great courage, soon earned from all an increased respect for women's ingenuity and abilities.

Thus, it was no coincidence that the first coeducational colleges appeared in the West. In 1837, Oberlin College in Ohio enrolled four women and began the first experiment in coeducation at the college level. Women were also allowed to enroll with men at Antioch College in 1853, and five years later coeducation was permitted at the State University of Iowa.

Meanwhile, the growing demand for teachers to staff the common schools was opening up a whole new vocational area for women. Until the 1830s almost all teachers were men. However, as men turned more to the factories and the open frontier, women began to enter teaching and soon crowded into the newly established normal schools.

During the nineteenth century, teaching became one of the few socially accepted occupations for women. Regardless of their narrow curricula, the booming normal schools nevertheless gave women a new and better chance for intellectual development and special training. The tuition-free normal schools, in fact, catered exclusively to women. The nation's first state normal school, for example, which opened at Lexington, Massachusetts, in July 1839, restricted admission to women and usually enrolled orphans, widows, and daughters from lower socioeconomic groups. Attracting women to teaching was "not designed to make a class of *celibates*," remarked Sarah Josepha Hale, editor of *Godey's Lady's Book,* in 1852. Women were simply better teachers, she declared, "and can afford to teach for one-half or even less, the salary which men would ask."[27] Women did indeed teach for much less: in 1835, for example, "female teachers" in Pennsylvania worked for nine dollars a month, which was considerably less than the wages paid to men. As girls flocked to the expanding normal schools in growing numbers, this trend continued unabated, discouraging men from teacher preparation and staffing the nation's elementary schools almost exclusively with women.[28]

Developments since World War I

After winning the right to vote in 1920, women began to behave differently in society and to demand for themselves the same privileges that men enjoyed. More opportunities for work outside the home created for women a new sense of self-confidence and independence. The introduction of the telephone and the typewriter, for example, had opened the way for new work opportunities in firms and offices for clerks, typists, and stenographers. A job often meant a temporary occupation before marriage, but women were entering the business and professional world in greater numbers. This broader participation in the economic life of the community paralleled reassertions of feminist equality in every phase of social activity.

A freer way of life, characteristic of the prevailing mood after World War I, undermined traditional manners and morals. It was an era of social rebellion, of novelty and experimentation in moral conduct. Scenes from motion pictures and misunderstood excerpts from Sigmund Freud's writing, which were widely publicized in the United States, contributed to a rising vogue in sex. There was a more relaxed attitude toward divorce and even a changed outlook toward traditional marital responsibilities and roles. A Colorado judge, for instance, shocked conservatives by his legal proposal for "companionate" and "trial" marriages. Fannie Hurst, in a widely reprinted article, revealed in 1923 that she and her husband had found a mutually satisfactory arrangement for improving "a monogamous marriage." "I have talked about this thing to women," the famous novelist told a reporter from the *New York Times.* "I have talked it from the platform. I believe that marriage can be happy, but I am also convinced that the old pattern cannot be made to fit all."[29] There was a sharp increase in drinking and cigarette smoking by both sexes. Women invaded the smoke-filled club cars of trains and mingled freely with men in the "speakeasies" (usually well-guarded restaurants serving liquor) and the new cocktail bars.

Feminism, in brief, had entered a new and dynamic phase, altering in conspicuous ways all the Victorian conventions concerning deportment and dress. Changing fashions, in particular, reflected the new assertions of feminist equality. Noteworthy was the popular vogue of bobbed hair, long-waisted dresses, and knee-length skirts. Slacks and sport clothes were also indicative of a new and more relaxed social code.

Women continued to enter the working force in growing numbers. In 1900 only half of the adult American women had ever been employed outside the home. After World War II, one-third of the women over fourteen were working, and almost all had been in the labor force at one time or another. A modern counterpart, perhaps, of the Lowell Textile Mills of the 1830s was the booming airlines of the 1960s; on one of the largest jet lines, most of the young stewardesses worked for about two years and then left to be married. At mid-century, in fact, only about 7 percent of all American women did not marry.

By 1975 this picture had changed radically. Two of every five women in the twenty- to twenty-four age bracket were not yet married, and this proportion rose to about half in 1990. Although they were postponing marriage longer, few women remained single through their adult lives. In 1988 an estimated 56.8 percent of American women were at least once married, 43.4 percent were widowed or divorced, and 65.2 percent were single. One of the most significant trends was the sharp increase of families headed by women.

By the late 1980s women had become a strong political force. In the United States as a whole, women outnumber men. In 1987 there were 124.9 million women compared to 118.9 million men. (By the year 2010 the projected total female population will be 144.2 million compared to 138.3 million men.) In 1985 women owned over 50 percent of the nation's wealth (more than half of all bonds and about half of the cash and corporate stock). In fact, according to the United States Internal Revenue Service, there were more female millionaires than male, and female millionaires actually outnumbered male millionaires in ranking based on total net worth.

One of the acute problems confronting women who hold jobs outside the home is the unavailability of domestic and child-care help. In two-career families husbands share housework and child-rearing responsibilities. Alice Rossi suggests the establishment of a network of professionally managed child-care centers. With trained staff and adequate facilities, these centers should operate on a full-time, year-round schedule.[30]

The changing status of American women is reflected in the life-styles of those who complete advanced degree programs. By 1900 very few women had succeeded in completing a graduate program leading to one of the professions. Those who accomplished this nineteenth-century feat in an exclusively man's world usually affected masculine clothes and mannerisms and did not marry. By mid-century the mores had changed considerably. Most of the women with a Ph.D. degree from Radcliffe College, for example, were not only married; many were "career-mothers," happy and successful, working (part-time or full-time) in areas for which they were trained.[31]

The relatively small number of American women who do earn a Ph.D. degree are successful in highly diverse fields: working in the professions, for instance, are nuclear physicists, Sanskrit scholars, musicians, astronomers, cancer research workers, economists, and foreign affairs officers. Most women with graduate degrees are somehow managing to combine both marriage and a career. The individual problem, thorny and complex at first, seems to revolve around the possibilities of suitable part-time work during the years when children in the family are young and an opportunity to resume a career outside the home when the family is most secure. "Precious little attention has been given to designing educational opportunities to meet the needs of married women," declared Mary Bunting, former president of Radcliffe College. "Rather, we have assumed that if she marries early she is not interested in continuing her education. The possibility that the choice could be a question of timing rather than goals has not received serious attention."[32]

While more women are turning to the professions, many are still not being educated in line with their potential abilities. In November 1960 the Radcliffe Institute for Independent Study was established to assist qualified women to continue creative or scholarly work. The unique features of the

Radcliffe Institute are its emphasis on individual study and its support of part-time research or creative work through fellowships for women who wish to refine or redirect their specialized talents. The University of Kansas City Project for Continuing Education of Women was begun in the fall of 1961. An interesting aspect of the Kansas City project is the research forum, which provides an interchange of ideas among scholars, educators, and women in the community. A center for continuing education was also established in the early 1960s at Sarah Lawrence College. "A few years ago, the opportunity for mature women to continue their education on a basis compatible with their family obligations was a dream," declared Antonia Chayes, who was a technical secretary for the President's Commission on the Status of Women. "Now, in community after community, continuing education for women, especially for those blessed with a certain degree of prior education and worldly comfort, is on its way to becoming part of the American way of life."[33] By 1987 women accounted for nearly 53.5 percent of all students enrolled in higher education.

American women are entering or reentering the labor force and seeking challenging positions. They are demanding equality of the sexes in employment policies, promotions, and salary levels, and calling for a more equitable distribution of men and women in the occupational system. Revising the sex ratio within occupations, women leaders argue, means changing the sex-typing of occupations long before young people make career decisions. Under pressures from women's organizations, some educators and textbook writers and publishers are trying to eradicate sex-role stereotypes during the formative years of elementary schooling when impressions and experiences mold a child's self-image and life expectations.

A New Paradigm of Thought in Human Psychology: Carol Gilligan's Theory of Women's Development

In her book *In a Different Voice: Psychological Theory and Women's Development*, Carol Gilligan presents a new theory of women's development and suggests that traditional theories of human moral development, developed primarily by men and based almost exclusively on the experiences of boys and men, are not able to describe the developmental process of females. Because of the use of these traditional theoretical paradigms, girls and women are often labeled as deviant and are viewed at a lower state or level in their developmental process when compared to their male counterparts. The important point is that the male experience has been defined as the norm: there has been only one way to view human development, and if an individual did not fit that model, then he or she was judged to be deviant. Gilligan concludes that while the male developmental process is based on independence and separation, the female developmental process is based on intimacy and relationships. As a result, men and women view the world from different perspectives. Gilligan's point of view is not that one perception is superior to the other, but simply that differences do exist and they need to be recognized and celebrated.

Due to the changing roles of both women and men, Gilligan's work represents an area of study that is needed to help women better understand the challenges and contradictions that may be present in their lives. Her work also represents a foundation from which to begin the process of reforming education so that all children will feel empowered and validated, not just male children or children who happen to fit into the traditional framework of child development. She has paved the way for future research into the distinct differences between men and women, asserting that those differences do not signify inequality; they simply indicate that we are different in some fundamental ways that are based on gender. According to Gilligan, we need new ways of looking at gender that will foster a better understanding of the human condition and celebrate the inherent differences among human beings. The aim of Gilligan's research was to find a new way to view gender that would include the experiences of everyone.

We should have a much better understanding of men and women if we do not try to make people believe that there is a single definition of human experience. We should allow differences to exist and should focus on diversity. "By positing instead two different modes, we arrive at a more complex rendition of human experience which sees the truth of separation and attachment in the lives of women and men and recognizes how these truths are carried by different modes of language and thought."[34]

By 1990, Carol Gilligan had extended her research from adult women and older adolescents to young girls. As a result, she is questioning some of her earlier ideas of female development and trying to redefine what she believes happens to women during adolescence. "Our work suggests that adolescence is a time of repression for girls," Gilligan explained.

During the early 1980s, Gilligan and her colleagues began several projects designed to connect their study of women to that of young girls. First, they interviewed older teenagers at the Emma Willard School in Troy, New York. By 1985 they had begun another project at the Laurel School, a private school in Cleveland, in which the researchers followed girls aged six through eighteen over a five-year period. This was the first time they had interviewed girls younger than eleven. According to Gilligan, adolescent girls enter Western culture and struggle to resist the loss of their "voice." They internalize the image of the "perfect girl"—one who is controlled, calm, quiet, and cooperative.

The public school, according to Gilligan, plays a key role in perpetuating this image. American girls move from an environment in which most teachers are female (the elementary school, where role models are women) to the secondary school, where role models are usually men and the curriculum is subject-centered. Secondary schools in the United States reflect the values of Western culture—ideas about boys—and educate mainly for autonomy. The emphasis is on subject matter, where schools do not encourage or reward relationships. Some teenage girls resist the loss of their childhood "voice" by becoming rebels. Others silence their voices and settle for idealized relationships, fearing that speaking up will anger their peers. They go underground, according to Gilligan, where the resistance becomes psychological.

Adolescent girls soon distinguish between what they say in public and what they really know. This struggle of teenage girls is not new; however, Gilligan's interpretation views the teenage struggle as a time of repression, not a struggle for autonomy. Gilligan's discovery of the struggle of teenage girls to resist the loss of their "voice" is thought provoking and has led to new questions that, she says, represent a major change in her research. "We have begun to focus more explicitly on intervention."

The development of women is not just a progression; according to Gilligan, it is a recovery of voices that went underground. We must encourage young girls and teenagers to listen to their own voices and the voices of others and to become comfortable exploring what they want to say in public. "What can we do," asks Gilligan, "to sustain resistance in teenage girls?" We must treat girls as authorities about their own experiences and encourage them to speak out in powerful ways that encourage and strengthen autonomy.[35]

Affirmative Action

The federal courts did not simply say what states and educational officials could *not* do in the struggle for equality of opportunity; they moved decisively and positively to tell officials and school boards what they *must* do to eliminate discrimination in school systems and promote equality of educational opportunity. States and school boards were ordered to take "affirmative action" against segregation and prejudice.

Amendments to the Civil Rights Act of 1964 and Title IX of the education amendments of 1972 (which went into effect in 1975) specifically applied to affirmative action to benefit women. Title IX, proposed by Representative Edith Green of Oregon, applied to all public school systems and most postsecondary institutions: "No person in the United States shall, on the basis of sex, be excluded from participation in, be denied the benefits of, or be subjected to discrimination under any program or activity receiving federal financial assistance."

There was considerable controversy over the guidelines issued by the Department of Health, Education, and Welfare regarding what the law meant for such single-sex activities as participation in athletic programs and

what is meant concerning special facilities for sports, fraternities, and so-
rorities. Problems arose throughout the nation concerning all kinds of sex
discrimination against women, ranging from glaring discrepancies in salary
schedules and the small number of administrative positions held by women
to more subtle, and potentially more serious, sexist biases portraying the
traditional role model of young girls and women in school textbooks. The
National Education Association and women's groups such as the National
Organization for Women argued that the law should force school committees
to examine and censor textbooks for any sexist materials. Some publishers
protested, claiming that their First Amendment rights to freedom of the
press were being violated by censorship rules and laws.

The women's movement was most active in institutions of higher
learning that sponsored courses and research in women's studies and continued to offer programs for adult women interested in careers and creative
individual development. In 1977, for the first time in American history,
more women than men were enrolled in U.S. colleges and universities.
Nevertheless, these advances seemed too late and too little to those seriously
concerned with equal rights for women in the broad spectrum of social
affairs: property rights; roles in family life; the job market; inheritance
rights; and access to high-level positions in the professions, government,
business, labor, and politics. By 1980 the Equal Rights Amendment (ERA)
to the U.S Constitution had still not been ratified by fifteen states; ratification by at least three more states was needed for adoption. The original
deadline for the Amendment's adoption, March 22, 1979, was extended by
Congress to June 30, 1982.[36] When the Equal Rights Amendment failed to
win adoption in 1982, feminist leaders were bitterly disappointed and vowed
to continue their efforts in the future.

PROGRESS TOWARD
AN AMERICAN IDEAL

The contemporary social scene has witnessed extensions and strong reassertions of the quest for educational equality. The most dramatic upsurge has
been in the area of race relations.

The Civil Rights Movement

For almost a century after the Civil War, a pattern of separate schools for
African American people was widespread, even outside the South. De facto
segregation, through school districting, existed and continues to exist in
many sections of the nation. In 1896 the U.S. Supreme Court upheld a law
in Louisiana that sanctioned "separate but equal" accommodations in railroad
trains. "Separate" facilities and services for African Americans and for white

people in transportation, public welfare, and education were ruled constitutional, provided these public facilities and services were "equal."[37] This decision, affirming the "separate but equal" doctrine, provided a legal basis for dual school systems during the first half of the twentieth century. Until World War II, in fact, there was little open resistance in African American communities to the "separate but equal" doctrine as applied to public education, to segregation through dual school systems in the South, and to de facto segregation in the North.

The war itself, by erasing segregation in the armed forces and providing new experiences in Europe and the Far East, gave some African American soldiers a broadened outlook on race relations. After the war many who returned went North, not back to their southern homes. The movement of African Americans from the South to the North, in fact, accelerated sharply during the 1950s. By 1960 this population shift had turned into an exodus as African American families uprooted and moved to New York City, Washington, D.C., Philadelphia, Detroit, and Chicago. In the North African American people expected—but did not always obtain—a newer dimension of life.

One power, however, that the northern African American citizen did receive was the right to vote. Of all forms of racial discrimination, the most serious was preventing qualified African American citizens in the South from exercising this right. If a person was thus deprived in the white South, he had the ballot in the North and began to use it. African Americans in the North quickly emerged as a new and potent force on the political horizon. For Americans everywhere, this new power only pointed out in more vivid terms a sharpening contrast between the old and the new, between a segregated South and a freer status in the North.

With a sense of mobility and an increase in political power, African American people also began to demand equality of educational opportunities. "Education has a symbolic significance in the Negro world," wrote Gunnar Myrdal, the Swedish social economist, whose perceptive analysis of the United States' "dilemma" won wide acclaim. For the African American, educational opportunity means personal improvement and progress. In addition, Myrdal explained: *"The long-range effect of the rising level of education in the Negro people goes in the direction of nourishing and strengthening the Negro protest."*[38] These and other changes, then, tended to break down traditional patterns of race relations and to underscore a deepening crisis in American society.

A new approach to the racial problem was dramatized by a series of laws and judicial events in which the U.S. Supreme Court played a leading role. The issue was approached on several legal fronts. First, in several decisions the Court struck down the denials of due process of law in certain southern states. Second, the Court refused to sanction segregation in publicly operated conveyances. Third, the Court also refused to sanction private contracts excluding African Americans from access to certain residential zones; such contracts, considered to be a violation of the Fourteenth Amendment, no longer had any legal validity.

Finally, on May 17, 1954, the U.S. Supreme Court, reversing its decision of 1896, rejected completely the "separate but equal" doctrine. During a period when the Court seemed to speak on important issues with multiple and divided voices, the justices were surprisingly united and brief: the Court brushed aside abruptly and swiftly the "separate but equal" doctrine with the elementary proposition that what was separate was never really equal. To segregate African American children "from others of similar age and qualifications solely because of their race," declared Chief Justice Earl Warren, speaking for the Court, "generates a feeling of inferiority as to their status in the community that may affect their hearts and minds in a way unlikely ever to be undone." The Court rules that segregation in local public schools on the basis of race or color alone deprived the individual of equal protection of the law as guaranteed by the Fourteenth Amendment. "We conclude that in the field of public education the doctrine of 'separate but equal' has no place," Chief Justice Warren continued. "Separate educational facilities are inherently unequal."[39] The Court followed this decision with another ruling on May 31, 1955, emphasizing that desegregation must proceed with "all deliberate speed." The government had assumed a new and important role with far-reaching implications.

This reversal, of course, did not bring a sudden end to segregated schools, for judicial decisions alone do not change public attitudes. In the wake of the Court's rulings, there followed over a decade of struggle and turmoil. The dialogue over race relations has expressed emotion and reason, virulent hate and heartfelt joy. For the first time, large numbers of African American citizens from every walk of life began to challenge a white-oriented paternalism, to threaten through new tactics some of the strongest mores of southern life. Reverend Martin Luther King, Jr., began preaching the idea of nonviolence and massive resistance to segregation. Following his lead, African American citizens used the economic boycott, the "sit-in," and the mass demonstration. They resorted to political campaigns, launched orderly marches to local schools, and even embarked on a grand crusade to the nation's capital.

At the same time James Baldwin, through his essays and novels, was revealing some of the psychological undercurrents of racial inferiority: above all, the agony and bitterness of African Americans, their innermost feelings, their will to achieve. "This is your home, my friend, do not be driven from it," Baldwin told his nephew in 1963. "Great men have done great things here, and will again, we can make America what America must become. It will be hard, James, but you come from sturdy, peasant stock, men who picked cotton and dammed rivers and built railroads, and, in the teeth of the most terrifying odds, achieved an unassailable and monumental dignity."[40] A long-time resident of Paris, Baldwin returned to the United States in 1957 and entered the civil rights crusade. Until his death in 1987, he was widely recognized as the United States's leading African American novelist.

The struggle reached a climax in 1964 with the passage of the Civil Rights Act, one of the most controversial laws ever enacted by Congress. Among its lengthy provisions, the act seeks "to enforce the constitutional right to vote" and to prevent discrimination in employment and public accommodations. The Twenty-fourth Amendment to the Constitution went into effect on January 23, 1964, erasing the poll tax as a barrier to voting in federal elections. The following year Congress passed, and President Lyndon B. Johnson signed on August 6, the Voting Rights Act of 1965.

The School Busing Controversy

Following the United States Supreme Court's desegregation ruling of 1954, decisions flowed from federal courts at every level, striking down one barrier after another to the commingling of racially different children in the public schools. Prince Edward County (Virginia), for example, closed its public schools to avoid integration and then made tuition payments to private schools established for white children. The Court ordered the county to stop the payments and reopen its schools. In 1968 the Court ruled that local school boards are obligated to develop "workable" desegregation plans. And a year later the Court decreed that a federal judge can order integration of the school staff.[41] Thus, in less than two decades, a social revolution had been wrought, especially in those southern states that had long maintained dual school systems.

When the *Brown* decision of 1954 was implemented in northern cities, where racially segregated neighborhoods had led to de facto (actual) as contrasted with de jure (legal) school segregation, a key question arose: if racially segregated schools were "inherently unequal," despite similarities in what the Court termed "tangible factors" (buildings, teachers, textbooks, libraries, and supplies), to what extent did equalization, as defined in the *Brown* decision, require racial integration? To what extent would the Court require the redrawing of school-district boundaries, the combining of urban and suburban school districts, and the extensive transportation of large numbers of students from one district to another? The underlying issue, of course, revolved around Court-ordered school busing: would the Supreme Court require that students of separate public schools in multischool districts be mixed racially in proportions equivalent to the composition of the district's total student population?

On April 20, 1971, a crowd gathered outside the United States Supreme Court building in Washington, D.C. The atmosphere was charged with emotion. Tension erupted when a clerk announced to the spectators

that the Court had unanimously upheld the busing of students as a legitimate tool for achieving school desegregation.[42]

In *Swann* v. *Charlotte-Mecklenburg Board of Education,* the U.S. Supreme
Court decided that mandatory racial mixing of school children was constitutional. Between the *Brown* decision of 1954 and the *Swann* case of 1971, local
school authorities and the courts had proceeded slowly (not, as decreed by the
Court, "with all deliberate speed"), and had exercised considerable discretion
in carrying out the Court's order. The *Swann* case became a landmark
decision because the Court defined in precise terms the obligations of school
authorities and local districts in implementing the *Brown* decision. The
Swann decision even suggested several permissible methods or "corrective
measures" within "the broad remedial powers of a court": "drastic gerryman-
dering of school districts and attendance zones," for example, and "pairing,
'clustering' or 'grouping' schools with attendance assignments made deliberately to accomplish the transfer of white students to formerly all-Negro
schools" which "may be on opposite ends of the city." The Court urged, in
any event, that "the greatest possible degree of actual desegregation" be
achieved. Before the *Swann* decision of 1971, the U.S. Supreme Court had
not dealt with such intricate details of school desegregation.

The most significant aspect of the *Swann* decision was the Court's
support of busing as a tool for desegregating public schools. In *Charlotte-
Mecklenburg* the remedial plan required a massive, long-distance transportation program: students residing closest to inner-city schools were to be
assigned to suburban schools; students residing closest to suburban schools
were to be assigned to inner-city schools. Thus the neighborhood-school
concept, a principal argument against busing, was substantially weakened by
the final Court decree. Although the U.S. Supreme Court did not outlaw
"schools all or predominantly of one race in a district of mixed population,"
it did create conditions that would make such schools difficult to maintain.
The Court implied that patterns of neighborhood schools, long cherished in
some communities, must be abandoned if the local school board failed to
guarantee racially mixed schools for children living in minority sections. The
Supreme Court's ruling foreshadowed the end of de facto segregation in both
the North and the South.

A court-ordered busing issue caused deep conflicts of law and conscience. Antibusing groups tried and failed to muster congressional support
for a constitutional amendment. Even President Richard M. Nixon, who was
responsible for enforcing Supreme Court decisions, declared his opposition to
"the busing of our nation's school children to achieve a racial balance." On
August 30, 1971, ten school buses were dynamited and burned in Pontiac,
Michigan; when schools opened the following week, five women chained
themselves to a gate at the bus terminal to prevent the buses from leaving.
Opposition mounted in many urban school systems, including Boston,

Massachusetts, and Louisville, Kentucky, where emotional outbursts in 1975 generated rallies, boycotts, and more violence. Meanwhile, forced busing or the threat of it accelerated the flight of middle-class white families to the suburbs, leaving the inner cities increasingly nonwhite and creating what some educators termed "urban *apartheid*."

These developments raised a series of questions to which there were no simple answers: Would court-ordered busing improve the quality of education for white pupils and disadvantaged African American children? Are there viable alternatives? "It is ludicrous to attempt to mandate an integrated society," declared James S. Coleman in 1975. "Integration must come through other means."[43]

By the mid-1970s, on the eve of the nation's Bicentennial, concerned parents and citizens wondered whether forced busing would really advance the civil rights cause. Many feared that opposition to court-ordered busing would be used as a pretext to abandon the principle of desegregation itself. Others argued for a greater commitment to public schooling for inner-city youngsters with low self-esteem. Educators and parents seemed to agree that forced busing was futile unless it could be shown to benefit all children.

Perhaps efforts toward racial harmony beyond the classroom would help to ease the tensions that make school desegregation such a volatile issue. A community that rejects prejudice and hate will have public schools that are less racist and biased. A culture in which humane values are held dear will witness more humane classrooms.

FOR DISCUSSION AND CRITICAL THOUGHT

1. How did the westward movement affect the role of women and their changing status in American culture?
2. What societal changes during the twentieth century facilitated the move toward equal opportunity in education?
3. Comment critically on Carol Gilligan's new paradigm of thought in human psychology. What are some serious implications for classroom teachers of Gilligan's research on women's development?
4. According to Carol Gilligan, "adolescence is a time of repression for girls." Explain. Do you agree? Comment critically.
5. Lyon and Willard were real trailblazers in the struggle for equal opportunity. Cite others who have helped pave the way for young women.
6. Supporters of the Equal Rights Amendment argued that when you "open the gates for one group, you open the gates for all." Comment.
7. What were the major civil rights issues in the United States after World War II?

8. Can you envision a community that has rejected prejudice and hate resulting in a public school system that is less racist and biased? Comment critically.

NOTES

1. Edward Earl Purinton, "Big Ideas from Big Business: Try Them Out for Yourself!" *Independent* 105 (16 April 1921): 395. Italics in original.

2. Quoted in Frederick Lewis Allen, *The Big Change: America Transforms Itself, 1900–1950* (New York: Bantam Books, 1961; originally published in 1952 by Harper & Bros.), p. 98.

3. Robert S. and Helen M. Lynd, *Middletown: A Study in Contemporary American Culture* (New York: Harcourt, Brace, 1929). The Lynds lived in "Middletown" from January 1924 to June 1925, to gather data for their sociological study of "a typical American city."

4. Arthur W. Calhoun, *A Social History of the American Family* (New York: Barnes and Noble, 1960; originally published in 1981), vol. 2, *From Independence through the Civil War*, p. 95; and Eleanor Flexner, *Century of Struggle: The Women's Rights Movement in the United States* (Cambridge, Mass.: Harvard University Press, 1959), p. 8.

5. *Godey's Lady's Book* 45 (September 1852), as quoted in Eleanor W. Thompson, *Education for Ladies, 1830–1860: Ideas on Education in Magazines for Women* (New York: King's Crown Press, 1947), p. 39.

6. Henry Steele Commager, ed., *Living Ideas in America* (new ed.; New York and Evanston: Harper & Row, 1964), editorial note, p. 563. Italics in original.

7. Calhoun, *A Social History of the American Family*, 2:88.

8. Thomas Woody, *A History of Women's Education in the United States* (New York and Lancaster, Pa.: Science Press, 1929), 2:137.

9. Letter dated 7 May 1776, from Abigail Adams to John Adams, as reprinted in Charles F. Adams, ed., *Familiar Letters of John Adams and His Wife Abigail Adams, During the Revolution, with a Memoir of Mrs. Adams* (New York: Hurd & Houghton, 1876), p. 169.

10. This statement is one of Abigail's most famous quotes. "Remember the Ladies" became a political slogan of the twentieth century. Letters dated March 16 and 31, 1776, from Abigail Adams to John Adams as reprinted in the *Adams Family Correspondence*, ed. L. H. Butterfield (Cambridge, Mass.: Harvard University Press, The Belknap Press, 1963–1973), vol. I, pp. 359, 370.

11. See Mary Wollstonecraft, *A Vindication of the Rights of Woman, with Strictures on Political and Moral Subjects* (New York: Norton, 1967; first published in 1792); and *Thoughts on the Education of Daughters, with Reflections on Female Conduct in the More Important Duties of Life* (New York: Garland Publishing, 1974; first published in 1787).

12. See Thompson, *Education for Ladies, 1830–1860*, pp. 32–43.

13. Woody, *A History of Women's Education*, 2:436. Beecher's views toward women's education changed through the years. At first, she disapproved of women

entering business and industry and insisted that they be prepared for teaching and home management. See Willystine Goodsell, ed., *Pioneers of Women's Education in the United States: Emma Willard, Catharine Beecher and Mary Lyon* (New York: McGraw-Hill, 1931), pp. 167–168, 189–190.

14. Emma Willard, *An Address to the Public; Particularly to the Members of the Legislature of New York, proposing a Plan for Improving Female Education* (Middlebury, Vt.: Printed by J. W. Copeland, 1819), pp. 3–60.

15. Alma Lutz, *Emma Willard: Daughter of Democracy* (Boston and New York: Houghton Mifflin, 1929), p. 181.

16. Goodsell, ed., *Pioneers of Women's Education,* p. 232.

17. Mary Lyon to Hannah White, 26 February 1834, as reprinted in Flexner, *Century of Struggle,* p. 33.

18. Quoted in *The Power of Christian Benevolence Illustrated in the Life and Labors of Mary Lyon,* comp. Edward Hitchcock et al. (Northampton, Mass.: Hopkins, Bridgman; and also Philadelphia: Thomas, Cowperthwait, 1852), pp. 244–245.

19. Some, however, contend that the first venture into women's collegiate education was launched at the Georgia Female College at Macon, chartered in 1836 and opened three years later.

20. Quoted in Beth B. Gilchrist, *The Life of Mary Lyon* (Boston and New York: Houghton Mifflin, 1910), p. 259.

21. William Gardiner Hamond, *Remembrance of Amherst: An Undergraduate's Diary 1846–1848,* ed. George F. Whicher (New York: Columbia University Press, 1946), p. 108.

22. Lucy P. Putnam to Col. and Mrs. Nathaniel Clarke, South Hadley, 11 October 1845, as reprinted in Arthur C. Cole, *A Hundred Years of Mount Holyoke College: The Evolution of an Educational Ideal* (New Haven: Yale University Press, 1940), notation 34, p. 358. Italics in original.

23. Mary Lyon, "Principles and Design of the Mount Holyoke Female Seminary" (1837), as reprinted in *Power of Christian Benevolence,* comp. Hitchcock et al., p. 295. Italics in original.

24. Nancy S. Everett to her family, South Hadley, 26 November 1837, as reprinted in Cole, *A Hundred Years of Mount Holyoke College,* p. 43.

25. Quoted in Woody, *A History of Women's Education,* 2:154–155.

26. This quotation from Matthew Vassar's first address to the Board of Trustees of Vassar College on 26 February 1861, appears in several sources. It is reprinted, for instance, as a section heading in *The Magnificent Enterprise: A Chronicle of Vassar College,* comp. Dorothy A. Plum and George B. Dowell and ed. Constance D. Ellis (Poughkeepsie, N.Y.: Vassar College, 1961), p. 5.

27. Quoted in Thompson, *Education for Ladies, 1830–1860,* pp. 97–99. Italics in original.

28. Men have made few inroads in the field. Over a century later, only 11.9 percent of all teachers in American elementary schools were men. ("Growth and Change in U.S. Education," *Phi Delta Kappan* 47 [December 1965]: 235).

29. Rose C. Feld, "Eight Years after a Novel Marriage: Fannie Hurst Gives an Accounting of Her Much-Discussed Experiment in Matrimony," *New York Times,* Sunday, 9 December 1923, sec. 4, p. 1, col. 1.

30. Alice S. Rossi, "Equality Between the Sexes: An Immodest Proposal," in *The Woman in America,* ed. Robert Jay Lifton (Boston, Mass.: Beacon Press, 1967), pp. 122–124.
31. Radcliffe College, *Graduate Education for Women: The Radcliffe Ph.D.* (Cambridge, Mass.: Harvard University Press, 1956), chap. 5, "The Ph.D. and Marriage," pp. 52–75.
32. Quoted in *Education and a Woman's Life,* ed. Lawrence S. Dennis (Washington, D.C.: American Council on Education, 1963; Proceedings of the Itasca Conference on the Continuing Education of Women, Itasca State Park, Minnesota), p. 53.
33. Antonia Handler Chayes, "When Walls Come Tumbling Down: New Jobs for Women," *Radcliffe Quarterly* 49 (November 1965): 5.
34. Carol Gilligan, *In a Different Voice: Psychological Theory and Women's Development* (Cambridge: Mass.: Harvard University Press, 1982), pp. 173–174.
35. *Chronicle of Higher Education,* 23 May 1990, pp. A6–A8.
36. C. Walter Berns, "Breaking the Rules: Congress and the ERA," *Atlantic Monthly* 243 (May 1979): 66–67.
37. *Plessy* v. *Ferguson,* 1963 U.S. 537 (1896).
38. Gunnar Myrdal, *An American Dilemma: The Negro Problem and Modern Democracy* (20th Anniversary ed.: New York and Evanston: Harper & Row, 1962; originally published in 1944), pp. 879, 881. Italics in original.
39. *Brown* v. *Board of Education of Topeka et al.,* 347 U.S. 483 (1954).
40. James Baldwin, *The Fire Next Time* (New York: Dial Press, 1963), "My Dungeon Shook: Letter to My Nephew on the One Hundredth Anniversary of the Emancipation," p. 24.
41. *Griffin* v. *Prince Edward County School Board,* 377 U.S. 218 (1964); *Green* v. *New Kent County School Board,* 391 U.S. 430 (1968); and *United States* v. *Montgomery County {Alabama} Board of Education,* 395 U.S. 225 (1969).
42. *Swann* v. *Charlotte-Mecklenburg Board of Education,* 402 U.S. 1 (1971).
43. *Time* 106 (23 June 1975): 60.

CHAPTER 10

The Impact of the Business Creed

The political function of the schools is to teach Americanism, meaning not merely political and patriotic dogma, but the habits necessary to American life.

DENIS W. BROGAN, *The American Character*, 1944

The business man dominates American civilization. His function is to organize American society that he has the freest possible run of profitable adventure. To do this he must organize the symbolism of that society so that there are no vital obstacles to the performance of his function.

HAROLD J. LASKI, *The American Democracy*, 1948

Of all the institutions shaping human life in the world today, none is more influential than business.

M. J. RATHBONE, "What Kind of Managers for Tomorrow's World?," an address delivered at Pace College in New York City, 19 January 1965

It is traditional in the business world that a corporation is only as good as the people it employs. Similarly, our schools can be no better than the teachers who staff them.

Committee for Economic Development, *Investing in Our Children: Business and the Public Schools*, 1985

THE DEPRESSION DECADE

In October 1929 came the collapse in the American market that ushered in the Great Depression. The effects of the crash were immediate and far-reaching. Prices dropped sharply; factories cut production or closed forever;

247

real-estate values declined; new construction stopped; banks failed; and farms, formerly mortgaged passed into the hands of insurance companies. Values in all parts of the nation's economy tumbled.

The public schools, in particular, shared in the effects of this general economic collapse. Educational opportunities in the schools were drastically curtailed because of sharp reductions in school revenues. In one month, for instance, 770 schools closed, leaving no provision for the education of 175,000 children. Tuition was charged in some communities, and those pupils who were unable to pay were excluded from attending a public school. Teachers' salaries were cut after 1929 until at least one in four by 1933 was receiving annual wages of less than $750.[1]

Not since the panic of 1873 had the economy shifted so suddenly from high prosperity to such deep depression. The shock of economic failure, followed by the New Deal invective and the accusations of exploitation and corruption, rocked the business world to its foundations. The great losses and ensuing social turmoil undermined popular faith in a free-enterprise system and constituted the most formidable challenge to the business community in American history. The ultimate response of business leaders to this challenge was of great significance, for it marked the beginning of a new, and profoundly different, relationship between the business community and the public schools.

Social Climate

The atmosphere of the 1930s differed sharply from the business-dominated mood of the 1920s. Plagued and harassed by unemployment and dwindling incomes, by want and hardship, Americans in the 1930s turned again to social and economic issues, to a reappraisal of familiar concepts. "We are facing a new era," wrote Louis Adamic in 1932. "This is a time of transition and profound frustration, of agony and decay."[2]

There was a proliferation of ideas and movements potentially dangerous to the status quo. Communism, for example, lured its hundreds in 1934 and 1935, and Huey Long's "Share Our Wealth" movement attracted its hundreds of thousands. Dr. Francis Townsend and Father Coughlin, advocating among other things social security and nationalization of banking resources, appealed to throngs of followers. "Technocracy" was also widely discussed as a method of bringing about a planned utopia under the direction of the engineers.[3]

New concepts also emerged from the "Keynesian Revolution."[4] According to Keynes, "the outstanding faults of the economic society in which we live are its failure to provide for full employment and its arbitrary and inequitable distribution of wealth and incomes." Keynes made economic stability at full employment a function of politics. He provided an elaborate justification for a wide range of governmental activities that would influence the distribution of economic rewards so as to benefit lower socioeconomic groups. "A somewhat comprehensive socialisation of investment will prove the only means of securing an approximation to full employment," wrote Keynes.[5] Small wonder that in this period of flux, business leaders wanted desperately to control the instrumentalities of government.

Popular articles, motion pictures, and stories of all kinds dramatized the privations and fears which many people were experiencing. In one of the most widely read novels of the period, John Steinbeck grimly described the depression scenes of drought and hunger, of human grief, and aroused the social conscience of a nation. For Americans everywhere, *The Grapes of Wrath*—a powerful story of the Joad family and the migration of the "Okies" from the dustbowl of the Southwest to a promised security elsewhere—was a frightening indictment, an image of despair and degradation. "There is a crime here that goes beyond denunciation. There is a sorrow here that weeping cannot symbolize. There is a failure here that topples all our success," wrote Steinbeck. "In the eyes of the people there is the failure; in the eyes of the hungry there is a growing wrath. In the souls of the people the grapes of wrath are filling and growing heavy, growing heavy for the vintage."[6]

John Dos Passos, another writer of the depression years, also painted a devastating portrait in *U.S.A.* (published as a trilogy in 1937). His unusual style and characterizations were incisive and unrelenting, cutting with scorn and bitterness into the ambitions, the greed, and the passions that Dos Passos saw and despised in a business world. "U.S.A. is a set of bigmouthed officials with too many bank accounts," he wrote. "U.S.A. is a lot of men buried in their uniforms in Arlington Cemetery."[7]

With far greater emotional power, Thomas Wolfe seemed to voice all the doubts and questionings of an uprooted generation as he wrote, "lost, lost, forever lost." Inchoate and autobiographical, *Look Homeward, Angel* (1929) evoked with poetic beauty humankind's concern with the fundamental issue of insecurity in a society of shifting values. In four tremendous novels, with a bold and penetrating style, Wolfe unleashed his innermost thoughts and feelings, filling page after page with fury, exultation, and despair.

No other American novelist has described with such rich, precise details some of life's utter simplicities: the forest and the good earth, the destiny of the common people, the flow "of time and the river." Like Walt Whitman's *Leaves of Grass* (1855), Wolfe's tone, both lyric and epic, is vibrant with the spirit of the United States itself. Whitman had celebrated in stirring verse the glory of the democratic dream. Wolfe, too, had unbounded faith in democracy: from the very beginning the greatness of the United States was his principal theme. Wolfe came to identify completely with his native land and to seek increasingly his own fulfillment in its history and destiny. "I will know this country when I am through as I know the palm of my hand," he remarked at twenty-three, "and I will put it on paper and make it true and beautiful."[8]

Born in 1900, Wolfe was a young southern writer in a small town, alienated at times from the very section to which he was so intensely drawn. He grew up in the 1920s and witnessed everywhere the incongruities of wealth and poverty. In his bitterest rhetoric he denounced the blatant materialism, the selfishness and greed, which he saw and loathed: "O Lost!" he cried in lyrical anguish. "I believe that we are lost here in America"; but, he continued: "I believe we shall be found."

Wolfe never lost faith. Unlike those who fled or turned away during the depression days, Wolfe believed profoundly in the nation's fortitude and the eventual realization of a dream—"America's everlasting, living dream," he called it. This hope for a better tomorrow was, in fact, the symbolic image of his own short life. "I think the true discovery of America is before us," he wrote shortly before his untimely death at the age of thirty-seven.

> I think the true fulfillment of our spirit, of our people, of our mighty and immortal land, is yet to come. I think the true discovery of our own democracy is still before us. And I think that all these things are certain as the morning, as inevitable as noon. . . . This glorious assurance is not only our living hope, but our dream to be accomplished.[9]

Despite the depression gloom of others, Wolfe found in America's heritage fresh sources of inspiration and courage for a changing and turbulent world. So different from Dos Passos's moral defeatism, his prose carried forth a compelling faith, an idea, and revealed one man's lifelong search through crises for deeper understandings.

Political Crosscurrents

After 1929 the whole structure of a business-oriented civilization threatened to crumble in the face of bitter public resentment over the alleged failure of the free-enterprise system. Those who mocked openly at "rugged individualism" and "natural economic law" were supported by New Deal followers and returned to office again and again. In President Franklin D. Roosevelt's speeches, the major domestic enemy was that "minority in business and industry"—those "unscrupulous moneychangers" and that "resplendent economic autocracy"—who stole "the liver of great national constitutional ideals to serve discredited special interests" and who sought "to carry the property and the interests entrusted to them into the areas of partisan politics."[10] Official investigations quickly sketched in some of the details of this harsh image.[11] It was an ominous picture that began to emerge—a picture of private power organized on a scale and in a manner threatening free institutions. Never before had business leaders faced such a political threat: the moral and social fabric of their way of life, built and sustained through past eras of prosperity, seemed to dissolve almost overnight.

At first, the business community responded to the New Deal with pleas for retrenchment and with old ideas that sought to restore constitutional faith by legal exhortation. But the political crosscurrents of the 1930s soon made it clear that traditional arguments would not suffice.

The record peacetime appropriations of federal funds, with large expenditures in new fields, kindled resentment among economy-minded businessmen and brought about quick demands for retrenchment in all governmental functions. This economy drive during the early depression years did not bypass expenditures for the public schools. The activities of organized business that had any relation to public education were concerned with reducing school revenues. The *Nation's Business,* for example, declared editorially in 1932 that "the growth of education cost in this country is startling." The editor quoted data, furnished by Merwin K. Hart, president of the New York State Economic Council, which pointed to the lower teacher-pupil ratio and to the increased expenditures for teachers' salaries and school buildings and equipment. "Our states and cities have still to learn that they cannot always justify spending by the desirability of the thing to be bought; and waste in education is as evil as waste in garbage removal," wrote the editor.[12]

While the National Chamber moved forward in its economy drives, leading business spokesmen reacted sharply to the political ideology of the New Deal and financed a number of organizations strongly opposed to social reform. The American Liberty League, the Sentinels of the Republic, the Crusaders, and the Southern Committee to Uphold the Constitution were business favorites. However the temper of the times presented issues and problems with which the smaller organizations could not cope. After 1934 publicity was increasingly focused on the activities of the newly founded American Liberty League.[13]

The Liberty League symbolized business opposition to the New Deal. Among its founders and chief financial supporters were representatives of the Du Pont, General Motors, United States Steel, and Morgan interests, and on its national executive committee were such names as Sewell L. Avery of Montgomery Ward and J. Howard Pew, president of the Sun Oil Company. The National Association of Manufacturers and the National Chamber were among the important business and industrial organizations supporting the league's principles.

The political ideas of the Liberty League were more than campaign oratory: they reflected traditional fears of popular power and deep-rooted convictions about the sanctity of existing arrangements for the protection of business interests.[14] In this sense, the first response of organized business to the challenge of the Great Depression stood in striking contrast to New Deal aims. It also marked a departure from an earlier tradition that had made social reform an indispensable tool of American politics.

THE GENESIS OF THE
FREE-ENTERPRISE CAMPAIGN

A Historic Policy Change

Concern with public enlightenment, which had been manifest in some business circles since the muckraking era, mounted in intensity during the 1930s. Business leaders were astonished and perturbed by the landslide New Deal victory in 1936. The decision of the United States Supreme Court on April 12, 1937, validating the National Labor Relations Act and upholding its application to manufacturing concerns, marked another serious defeat for the business community. More than any other New Deal measure, the so-called Wagner Act, which guaranteed employees the right to organize and bargain collectively through representatives of their own choosing, seemed to strike directly at the Liberty League's concept of Americanism. Businessmen repeatedly denounced the measure as "class legislation," threatening the "prerogatives of management" and the "sacred right of property." If the business community could no longer rely on the Supreme Court to check the New Deal, was it not essential that business interests go beyond Congress and the President directly to the American people? An increasing number of business spokesmen appeared to think so. By 1937 organized business was changing its tactics and beginning to reevaluate its traditional methods of "public education."

The idea of "selling free enterprise" on a nationwide scale evolved slowly in different quarters. Publishers, public-relations counsels, and corporative officials were among the first to see the necessity for "telling the story of business" to the American people. "The public must be enlightened if it is to be influenced in favor of business," explained a New York publisher. "Be more *articulate*," he told businessmen, and "narrate the fascinating tales" of your success. "Force the minds of public opinion back into the mold of Americanism."[15] Bronson Batchelor, a prominent public-relations counsel, suggested that business leaders develop "a completely new ideology" and disseminate that creed directly to the people. "Education of the public," he declared, is "necessary to the preservation of the enterprise system."[16] More specific was the advice of S. Wells Utley, president of Detroit Steel Castings Company, who warned businessmen that the magnitude of their political problem required more than any halfway attempt at solution. He urged the National Association of Manufacturers to plan and launch a nationwide campaign to tell everyone that the free-enterprise system is the only basis for American prosperity and success.[17]

"You will note especially that this is not a hit-or-miss program," Robert Lund, chairman of the NAM Board of Directors, remarked to business leaders in 1935. "It is skillfully integrated so as to gradually blanket every media for the dissemination of educational material, and then after the medium is created, that it pounds its message home with relentless determination." This will not be "a spectacular campaign," Lund continued. "There is no beating of drums, no attempt to create a turbulent hysteria. This campaign is based on the theory that it is the constant dripping of water that wears away the stone."[18]

Toward the end of the 1930s, *Harper's Magazine* published a revealing three-part article entitled "Business Finds Its Voice."[19] Overburdened with the everyday tasks of producing and distributing economic goods, businessmen had begun at last to speak out and "sell ideas" to the American people.[20] The overall campaign, according to the *Harper's* series, was involving every segment of the business community; it would, moreover, encompass "the whole public"; and, in the eyes of business officials, it has "no foreseeable conclusion." In 1939, the editors of *Fortune* displayed, in reduced size, thirteen illustrated advertisements portraying the business community's theme that "free enterprise is the American way of life." This method is "INDUSTRY'S MOST FAMILIAR TOOL," *Fortune* declared. "These advertisements aim at the emotions with well-practiced skill, but their whole purpose is to sell ideas and sentiments, not products."[21]

Manifestations of this effort during the late 1930s were widespread. NAM, for example, repeated the "way of life" theme over and over again in 1938 through such slogans as "2 Billion People *Envy* You!" and "What Is Good for Industry Is Good for You," which were posted on 45,000 billboards going up along the nation's expanding highway systems. "American Family Robinson," a radio program that sought to demonstrate the importance of free enterprise to the American people, was sent by NAM every week in record form, free of charge, to 273 stations throughout the United States.[22] *Young America,* a weekly newspaper, urged the business community *"to tell its message to boys and girls,"* because "youthful minds in the formative stage are more receptive to your message." The idea was repeated by public-relations counsels, who advised businessmen to tell the story of free enterprise "with all the imagination and art of which modern advertising is capable. It should be told just as continuously as the people are told that Ivory Soap floats or that children cry for Castoria."[23]

"The New Deal has wrought better than it knows, or would like to believe," *Fortune* remarked editorially in 1940. "For the business community today is nothing like what it was in 1929, or 1933, or even 1937. An entirely new spirit is in the air."[24] Two months later in St. Paul, Minnesota, this optimism characterized a preconvention dinner for Republican leaders. In a keynote address Wendell L. Willkie pointed to "a resurgence of hope" in the business community. "For a time," Willkie reminded the audience, "we were submerged in defeat, shaken by fear and victimized by despair." Today, he continued, businessmen can hold up their heads again and look forward to the future.[25] By the end of the depression decade, public-relations counsels were leading the way as businessmen clustered under the free-enterprise banner and sallied forth in every direction to tell their story to the American people.

THE FREE-ENTERPRISE CAMPAIGN
AND THE TEXTBOOK CONTROVERSY

A Clash of Organized Interests

The general uncertainty wrought by the most severe depression in American history was reflected in the writings of social-science educators. Some textbook authors during the 1930s switched from a glorification of the free-enterprise system to a more critical appraisal of the American tradition. This trend could hardly contribute to the security of a business world struggling for political survival. Such a critical approach appearing in school textbooks was soon viewed with alarm by business leaders who were spending time and large sums of money in a campaign to perpetuate the idea that "free enterprise *is* the American way of life."

By the end of the decade several social-science textbooks were being condemned by the American Legion, the Advertising Federation of America, and the New York State Economic Council.[26] In particular, the books written by Harold Rugg, at Teachers College, Columbia University, were most frequently denounced. In a few communities public book burnings were celebrated over the banning of Rugg's textbooks from public-school systems. The attacks increased as the controversy turned into a veritable crusade to eliminate certain textbooks from the public schools.

While the textbook controversy continued to rage, the free-enterprise campaign was gaining momentum. In August 1940 the National Association of Manufacturers announced that its "Mobilization Activities" on behalf of the free-enterprise system were bearing results. Inaugurated in spring of 1940, with over 6,830 "sentinels," this NAM unit was active in over 16,000 assignments in 1,338 communities throughout the country.[27] "This leaves only one major field yet to be pushed to peak effort—stimulation of a fuller understanding of private enterprise among educators," NAM declared. "With the schools resuming sessions in the fall, important educational assignments will be released all over the country, in conjunction with an intensive follow-up drive on previously assigned projects."

The tenor of these new "educational assignments" was revealed three months later. On November 14, 1940, in an address before three thousand leaders of the nation's oil industry, NAM President H. W. Prentis, Jr., charged that "creeping collectivism" had invaded the public schools through social-science textbooks that undermined youth's faith in the free-enterprise system. "For a generation now our free institutions and the heroes of the American republic have been derided and debunked by a host of puny iconoclasts, who destroy since they cannot build," exclaimed Prentis.[28] The following day the National Chamber's Committee on Education met in Washington to discuss ways of advancing "pro-American doctrines" in the public schools. Prentis, chairman of the board of Armstrong Cork Company and also a member of this committee, had rushed from Chicago to Washington in time to participate in the Chamber's discussions. He briefly reviewed before the committee the main points of his Chicago address. Disturbed by Prentis's charges, the members discussed the importance of indoctrinating young people in the basic principles of America's form of government and of modifying certain tendencies of educators "to dwell upon the weak spots" in the free-enterprise system.[29]

The Robey Investigation

On December 10, 1940, business leaders announced to the press that NAM was financing a specific program in "public education."[30] The purpose of the program, according to the press release, was to "encourage educators to seek a better understanding of the private enterprise system so that this institution can be explained to students more effectively as an indispensable concept of the American way of life." Local businessmen "in every community" were being urged to find ways "by which the concept of private enterprise and the details of its operation may be taught in the schools." It was also revealed in the same announcement that NAM was assuming an active role in the textbook controversy.

Ralph W. Robey, assistant professor of banking at Columbia University, had been commissioned by NAM "to abstract textbooks in the field of history, civics, sociology and economics in general use in the public-school systems of the country."[31] These abstracts would then be sent to each business man to be used for "preliminary analysis" before taking action in local communities on "any book which, on the basis of the abstracts, seems to him to be of questionable merit." NAM leaders claimed that the abstracts would "involve no appraisal of any kind."[32] As far as NAM was concerned, public attention was supposed to be centered on a delineation (by means of selected quotations) of the economic and political philosophy of each textbook author. NAM obviously did not expect the interest to be focused on Robey's personal views.[33]

With three assistants Robey prepared in a period of three months 563 abstracts of secondary-school social-science textbooks. In aggregate, the abstracts totaled more than twelve hundred pages of single-spaced typescript containing over five hundred thousand words. Each abstract began with a general paragraph that first indicated the grade level for which the book was intended. This was followed by a brief outline of the subject matter of the book and a summarization of the table of contents or a copy of the unit titles into which the book was divided. Next, the quotations from the textbook were presented. Finally, the position of the author as indicated on the title page of the book along with the copyright and reprint dates, were given. The latter were the only indications of how extensively the book had been used. Included in the 563 abstracts were textbooks by such authors as James Truslow Adams, Charles A. Beard, Henry Steele Commager, David S. Muzzey, Harold Rugg, and Edgar B. Wesley. As soon as Robey and his assistants had completed their assignments, NAM planned to make the abstracts available to businessmen in local communities throughout the United States.[34]

Unfortunately for NAM's plan, Robey held a press interview at his home on February 21, 1941, and discussed his findings with Benjamin Fine,[35] then a reporter for the *New York Times,* which obligingly gave the story front-page coverage. It was a personal interview that, according to NAM officials, was not authorized. Robey expressed his own beliefs, which, he said did not necessarily represent NAM's views. According to Fine's report of the interview, Robey "painted a picture that indicated a growing skepticism and ultra-critical attitude on the part of many students and teachers." In fact, Robey was reported to have claimed that "a 'substantial proportion' " of the textbooks currently used by seven million pupils in the nation's secondary schools displayed "a lack of scholarly competence" and held "in derision or contempt the system of private enterprise."[36] Excerpts from several abstracts were reprinted in the *New York Times*, and textbooks by leading scholars and educators were given unfavorable publicity. Although NAM officially disavowed Robey's statements to the press, business leaders apparently did not disagree entirely with Robey's personal opinions concerning the books and their authors.[37]

Robey's remarks to the press startled some observers. Indeed, a publicity-conscious NAM had unwittingly shattered its hoped-for image: all the kindling resentment from textbook crusades of other organizations during the late 1930s was visited upon organized business. It is doubtful if NAM or any other special-interest group had ever before been subjected to such bitter condemnation.

Educators were openly critical of the whole plan. I. L. Kandel, for example, wondered whether teachers should be disturbed or flattered by this interest of the National Association of Manufacturers in the public schools.[38] "The fear that the schools may exercise a subversive influence on the minds of the younger generation through the use of certain text-books in history, civics, sociology and economics is a real tribute to their effectiveness," Kandel remarked. He facetiously suggested that some enterprising teachers obtain copies of all the abstracts and use them instead of unabridged books. "Is it possible that the association was alarmed at the prospect of the emergence of a generation that can discover, analyze and solve problems which to-day puzzle most experts?" asked Kandel. Alexander J. Stoddard, then superintendent of schools in Philadelphia and chairman of the Educational Policies Commission, strongly objected to the Robey Investigation. "By innuendo and endless repetition, which cover up the lack of real evidence, the American people are being asked to suspect that their schools, their teachers, their youth and their textbooks are disloyal and subversive," Stoddard declared.[39] Ned H. Dearborn, speaking for the American Committee for Democracy and Intellectual Freedom, voiced what many educators considered to be the most serious issue raised by the Robey Investigation, declaring:

> There are unfortunately people who believe that the process of education is one of indoctrinating students rather than of helping them to form sound judgments of their own. We assert on the contrary that our traditional liberties have a substantive value, that they must be cherished in times of crisis even more than in less troubled times, and that it is in the school that our youth must be trained to think freely and soberly and to understand and experience the meaning of these liberties and the institution in which they operate.[40]

Misuse of the NAM abstracts, Dearborn warned, will endanger the United States's heritage of freedom.

Regardless of NAM's official stand concerning Robey's press statements, there were disquieting new reports as to how the abstracts were actually being used by educators and laypersons. For example, on February 26, 1941, John E. Wade, acting superintendent of schools in New York City, ordered a formal investigation of all city-adopted social-science textbooks that had been abstracted by Robey and his assistants. Two months later, the American Legion adopted a recommendation of its Americanism Committee, publicly listing several social-science textbooks that had been included in the Robey Investigation as "not suitable for use in our schools since they oppose the American tradition."[41] As the summer of 1941 approached, the textbook controversy showed no signs of abatement.

NEW PRESSURES AND PRIORITIES

World War II

The Japanese blow at Pearl Harbor on December 7, 1941, came as a shock to the American people. The surprise attack upon American soil, along with the danger of invasion of the continental United States itself, diverted public attention from the political debates and partisan quarrels that had raged on the national scene for almost a decade. The *Chicago Tribune,* for instance, became abruptly silent in its criticism of the Roosevelt administration in Washington and quickly adopted a theme of "our country, right or wrong." Herbert Hoover and Alfred M. Landon, together with minority leaders in Congress, pledged their support to the all-out war effort. Through Philip Murray and William Green, organized labor also promised full cooperation and, with business, agreed that industrial disputes in essential fields would be kept to a minimum. Almost overnight Americans became united in the conviction that they must eliminate the totalitarian threat. This unity led to a mobilization program unparalleled in world history. Industry, on a round-the-clock schedule, began turning out equipment—ammunition, tanks, and planes—on a gigantic scale. By 1942 the United States had girded itself with full military regalia and was making a supreme effort to ensure national survival.

At the beginning of the war, the business community suddenly began to evince unusual interest in the public schools, particularly in alleviating some of the financial dilemmas confronting local boards of education. Slowly at first, but with increasing tempo during the mid-1940s, prominent businessmen courted educators in a large-scale campaign to counteract the unfavorable publicity engendered by the Robey Investigation to perpetuate the idea that "free enterprise *is* the American way of life."[42]

This important policy change in public relations ushered in a new era for American education. The attitudes of the business community toward the public schools gradually changed from the apathetic, almost hostile, feeling displayed during the early 1930s to a new and different interest. By V-J Day (Allied victory over Japan—August 15, 1945), the National Chamber, the National Association of Manufacturers, the Committee for Economic Development, and the Advertising Council had begun to donate time, talent, and money in nationwide drives for increased local support of the public schools. Such unprecedented action on the part of organized business was the most significant outcome of the free-enterprise campaign.

The Dissemination of the Free-Enterprise Creed

Since World War II, organized business has given top priority to its free-enterprise drives, employing and training new personnel, firmly establishing education departments, divisions, and committees, and allotting additional funds for a gigantic program in "public education." The Chamber of Commerce of the United States has concentrated its efforts on "selling free enterprise" to teachers through "Business-Education Days" ("B-E Days"), while the National Association of Manufacturers has disseminated materials aimed primarily at influencing American youth. The overall campaign is the most elaborate and costly public-relations project in American history.

The National Chamber is the largest and most conspicuous voice for organized business. Its members speak with great forthrightness on those issues where American business as a whole has a common interest. "We believe that we can convince you that Free Enterprise is in the public interest and is entitled to be sold as one of our Fundamental Freedoms," declared a chamber leader before an assembly of thirty-three hundred Minneapolis teachers on B-E Day in 1950. "Let's form a selling partnership right now—we businessmen and you teachers. Working together, we can help keep the United States the free and happy country we want it to be for the youngsters in your classrooms."[43] Success of the chamber's work in the free-enterprise campaign is reflected in the enthusiastic response from educators, who have eagerly made B-E Day an annual event.[44]

The National Association of Manufacturers has long been the most articulate voice for the business community. Founded in 1895 in Cincinnati, Ohio, by a small group of businessmen, NAM's membership by the end of World War II had grown to more than twenty thousand companies located in every state and industrial center in the country. This postwar membership included every major company and most of the smaller ones in the United States. The New York headquarters, the Washington office, the five divisional offices, and the twelve regional offices are strategically located across the nation.[45] With an immense public-relations program and forceful representatives, NAM is a zealous and powerful organization. Its members have great local influence.

All in all, NAM has developed a program in "public education" that is so comprehensive that it reaches into every segment of American society. Nationally, and through its twelve regional offices, NAM uses every technique of mass media in a broad-scale program "to achieve public understanding of how the American enterprise system works for the benefit of everyone." For example, NAM motion pictures (called "think pieces" by staff producers) are distributed to business groups, community organizations, and schools and are viewed annually by about three-and-one-half million persons at over forty thousand showings. The *American Business System* is currently the most widely promoted NAM motion picture series. Described by NAM in 1966 as "an educational film series on economics," this production comprises ten half-hour motion pictures, which are distributed on a nominal rental fee basis by Indiana University and included in the "Programmed Learning" text series *Encyclopedia Britannica*. *Industry on Parade,* a weekly newsreel circulated by the NAM Film Bureau in New York, is the oldest continuing television show in the United States. Slide films, charts, and videocassettes are also prepared and presented every year at hundreds of NAM-sponsored meetings with local business, civic, and educational leaders.

More than five million booklets and brochures, written and continuously revised by NAM staff editors in New York, are mailed annually to businesspeople, educators and students, and the general public. In 1956, for instance, 1,837,435 pieces of NAM literature went to American schools and colleges. And during the early 1960s almost four million sets of *Industry and the American Economy* (an eleven-booklet series) were sent to students and teachers across the country. Finally, an elaborate program entitled "How Our Business System Operates," first used by business leaders after World War II in employee-training programs, has been adopted by NAM for disseminating the free-enterprise creed on the widest possible scale to American schools.[46]

Commentary

The launching of the free-enterprise campaign toward the end of the 1930s marked a significant turning point in business-education relationships. Deeply disturbed by New Deal victories and beset by adverse publicity, the business community sought desperately for a way to rebuild its reputation, to perpetuate its image of the American way of life. By the end of World War II, business leaders had made a strategic switch in policy: defensive opposition to the New Deal had shifted to a major offensive to "sell free enterprise" to the nation's schools.

Thus organized business—a powerful interest group in American society—is spending large sums of money in a two-pronged drive to influence pupils, teachers, and principals. One cannot fail to observe the avidity and strength with which organized business has aligned itself with the public schools and the corresponding eagerness with which the professional educator has helped to seal this new bond. This development raises a serious question that must not be obscured in a free society: what is the *primary* responsibility of a public-school official?

In the United States, a professional educator should attempt to meet the challenge of any interested, if not always sound, social expression toward the public schools. American education reflects the democratic tenet that those citizens concerned with the public schools should have some voice in the areas of policy making and control. At least in a theoretical sense, the ideal has evolved into the following pattern: the interests of parents and various associations of the American people at large are represented through their voluntary groups and community affiliations; the general public interest is represented through federal and state units and through local boards of education; and finally, the professional interest is represented through classroom teachers and educational administrators. These elements, of course, are not coequal in power, but each is recognized as having a legitimate role to perform. If one of these three forces should exert excessive pressure or usurp control, the balance would be upset and the democratic ideal destroyed. The supreme task confronting a professional leader is one of balancing the various expressions of popular interest toward the schools with the basic purposes of American education.[47]

The task is not easy in a democracy. Open disagreement is not only expected and encouraged; it is, in fact, a healthy sign among free men and women. Public-school officials are, and will continue to be, bombarded by requests and demands from individuals, voluntary associations, and local agencies outside the schools.[48] Some groups are organized on a national level, are strongly entrenched, and are well financed.

These social forces in any form become ominous indeed if they result in pressures (or intimidations) to teach a particular theory of economics or to inculcate a special kind of "Americanism." An economic system is usually transitory, whatever its age or presumed respectability. A nation that elects to stand or fall on the success or failure of any one system—indeed, a society that would tie its whole way of life to only one institution—is embarking on a precarious and fateful course.

The contribution of education to America's highest purposes and ideals is so fundamental and so precious that the schools must be accorded the maximum of freedom and stability. Peter Drucker contends that "the autonomous enterprise and the autonomous plant community are the firmest basis on which a free society could be built."[49] One might well paraphrase his argument by insisting that a free society *first* requires excellent school systems, responsive but not subservient to the public will. Fortunately, the control of the public school is set apart from other processes of government in the United States. This historic policy assumes that education, in a democracy, should be placed above and beyond partisan control. It recognizes that individuals or groups may be temporarily tyrannical and destructive of the basic goals of American education. The legal structure is designed to enable the school to discharge its functions fearlessly and effectively, regardless of the crosscurrents in pressures and purposes so characteristic of a free nation.

FOR DISCUSSION AND CRITICAL THOUGHT

1. Discuss the impact of the Great Depression of the 1930s on public schooling in the United States.
2. How did the textbook controversy of the 1930s reflect the attitudes of society? How did it affect the public schools? Are there any similarities between the Robey Investigation and the current textbook approval procedures in some states? Comment critically.

3. According to some critics, public schooling in the United States attempts to do everything for everybody. What external forces have pressured adjustments in educational policy during the twentieth century? Why is the public school especially vulnerable to external forces?

4. Some people believe that the public schools have a responsibility to educate young people for the world of business. Does the business community also have a responsibility to the local educational system? What do you think is the ideal relationship between business and education? Explain.

5. The public schools and universities have increasingly turned to the business community for ways to improve the educational system. In what ways can business help the public schools and higher education? What kind of local partnerships should be created between business and education?

6. Discuss other special interest groups whose relation to the public schools may raise serious questions.

NOTES

1. See National Education Association, The Joint Commission on the Emergency in Education, "The Schools and the Depression: A State by State Review" (Washington, D.C.: National Education Association, Research Division, May 1933).

2. Louis Adamic, "The Collapse of Organized Labor: Is the A.F. of L. on Its Deathbed?" *Harper's Magazine* 164 (January 1932): 178.

3. See J. George Frederick, ed., *For and Against Technocracy: A Symposium* (New York: Business Bourse, 1933); and Stuart Chase, *Technocracy: An Interpretation*, John Day Pamphlets No. 19 (New York: John Day, 1933).

4. Robert Lawrence Klein, *The Keynesian Revolution* (New York: Macmillan, 1947), pp. 165–87. See also Dudley Dillard, *The Economics of John Maynard Keynes: The Theory of a Monetary Economy* (New York: Prentice-Hall, 1948). For varied appraisals of Keynesian doctrine, see Seymour E. Harris, ed., *The New Economics: Keynes' Influence on Theory and Public Policy* (New York: Knopf, 1947).

5. John Maynard Keynes, *The General Theory of Employment, Interest and Money* (New York: Harcourt, Brace & World, 1936), pp. 372, 378.

6. John Steinbeck, *The Grapes of Wrath* (New York: Viking Press, 1939), p. 311.

7. John Dos Passos, *U.S.A.* (Boston: Houghton Mifflin, 1937), Foreword, p. vii. Copyright by John Dos Passos. Reprinted by permission of the author.

8. Letter dated April 1923 to his mother as reprinted in Thomas Wolfe, *You Can't Go Home Again* (New York: Harper & Bros. [published posthumously in 1940]), p. xviii.

9. Wolfe, *You Can't Go Home Again*, "Credo," p. 741.

10. These accusations recur in President Roosevelt's public papers. The particular quotations are from his "Annual Message to the Congress. January 3, 1936,"

The Public Papers and Addresses of Franklin D. Roosevelt, with a Special Introduction and Explanatory Notes by President Roosevelt (New York: Random House, 1938), 4:14, 16.

11. Temporary National Economic Committee, *Investigation of Concentration of Economic Power* (Monographs 1–43; Washington, D.C.: Government Printing Office, 1940–1941). See also *Final Report and Recommendations of the Temporary National Economic Committee* (Transmitted to the Congress of the United States pursuant to Public Resolution 113, 75th Congress; Washington, D.C.: Government Printing Office, 1941); U.S. Congress, Senate, *Munitions Industry*, Hearings before a Special Committee to Investigate the Munitions Industry, pursuant to S. Res. 206, 73d Cong. (Washington, D.C.: Government Printing Office, 1934–1937); and U.S. Congress, Senate, Committee on Education and Labor, *Violations of Free Speech and Rights of Labor*, Hearings pursuant to S. Res. 266, 74th Cong., before a subcommittee of the Committee on Education and Labor, 75th, 76th Congresses (Washington, D.C.: Government Printing Office, 1937–1939).

12. "The Growing Cost of Education," *Nation's Business* 20 (March 1932): 15. *Nation's Business* is the official organ of the Chamber of Commerce of the United States (cited hereafter as the National Chamber).

13. See George Wolfskill, *The Revolt of the Conservatives; A History of the American Liberty League, 1934–1940* (Boston: Houghton Mifflin, 1962).

14. The ideas of the American Liberty League are recorded in miscellaneous pamphlets, papers, and reports distributed to the public between 1934 and 1938. Perusal of this material reveals not only a common frame of reference uniting different spokesmen but also a unanimity of opinion on basic issues. The interesting feature is the manner in which the lawyers combined sharp attacks on their political enemies with oversimplified statements from secondary-school civics textbooks.

15. Humphrey B. Neill, *The Untold Stories of Business: Wherein is Surveyed the Power of Books in Business and Likewise Described are Certain Methods and Tactics for Planning and Writing Books about Business* (New York and Chicago: Kingsport Press, 1937), pp. x, 7–13. Italics in original.

16. Bronson Batchelor, *Profitable Public Relations* (New York and London: Harper & Bros., 1938), p. 54.

17. S. Wells Utley, *The Industrialist and Politics* (New York: National Association of Manufacturers [1935]; an address before the Fortieth Annual Congress of American Industry, 5 December 1935, in New York City.)

18. National Association of Manufacturers, "Proceedings of the Fortieth Annual Convention of the Congress of American Industry Held on 4–5 December 1935, at the Hotel Commodore in New York City" (New York: The Association, n.d.), pp. 25–26.

19. S. H. Walker and Paul Sklar, "Business Finds Its Voice," *Harper's Magazine* 176 (January 1938): 113–123; ibid. 176 (February 1938): 317–329; ibid. 176 (March 1938): 428–440. At the same time, Harper & Bros. also published these three articles, with the same title, in book form.

20. As the editors of *Fortune* wrote the following year: "Businessmen of all sorts and conditions began to reflect that public relations might not after all be the name

of sissified perfume, but might well be the label on the bottle of the very elixir that they most urgently needed." See "The Public Is Not Damned," *Fortune* 19 (March 1939): 83.

21. *Fortune* 19 (March 1939): 88.

22. The diversified public-relations campaign of the National Association of Manufacturers cost $750,000 in 1937 alone. Three years later NAM was spending annually $1,600,000 for "staff work and public information." *New York Times,* 11 December 1940, p. 29, col. 8.

23. S. H. Walker and Paul Sklar, *Business Finds Its Voice: Management's Efforts to Sell the Business Idea to the Public* (New York and London: Harper & Bros., 1938), pp. 6, 22. Italics in original.

24. "Business-and-Government," *Fortune* 21 (March 1940): 38.

25. Wendell L. Willkie, "Address, Pre-Convention Dinner, Republican Leaders, St. Paul, Minnesota, 11 May 1940," *Free Enterprise: The Philosophy of Wendell L. Willkie as Found in His Speeches, Messages and Other Papers* (Washington, D.C.: National Home Library Foundation, 1940), p. 65.

26. See, for instance, O. K. Armstrong, "Treason in the Textbooks," *American Legion Magazine* 29 (September 1940): 8–9ff.; Hamilton Hicks, "Ours to Reason Why," ibid. 30 (May 1941): 5–7ff.; "The Battle of the Books," ibid. 29 (November, 1940): 68; R. Worth Shumaker, "No 'New Order' For Our Schools," ibid. 30 (April 1941): 5ff.; Alfred T. Falk, *Does Advertising Harm or Benefit Consumers?* (New York: Advertising Federation of America, 1939); Alfred T. Falk, *The Rugg Technique of Indoctrination* (New York: Advertising Federation of America, n.d.); and Merwin K. Hart, "Let's Discuss This on Its Merits," *Frontiers of Democracy* 7 (15 December 1940): 82–87.

27. Apparently the "sentinels" were dedicated to explaining and advocating the free-enterprise system. (*News Letter* 7 [9 August 1940]: 3. The *News Letter* was issued irregularly by NAM from 20 April 1934 to 11 July 1942. The name of the publication was changed to NAM *News* on 18 July 1942.)

28. H. W. Prentis, Jr. "The Citadels of National Defense" (Address before the Annual Convention of the American Petroleum Institute in Chicago on 14 November 1940), *Vital Speeches of the Day* 7 (15 December 1940): 145. (The *New York Times* gave Prentis's speech considerable publicity [15 November 1940, p. 11, cols. 1 and 2].)

29. Chamber of Commerce of the United States, Committee on Education, "Minutes of the Meeting of 15 November 1940, Held at the National Chamber Headquarters" (Washington, D.C.: The Chamber, 1940), pp. 1–4.

30. *New York Times,* 11 December 1940, p. 29, col. 8. See also "The NAM to Judge School Textbooks in the Social Studies," *School and Society* 52 (21 December 1940): 651.

31. Actually, Robey had contracted with NAM on 6 October 1940, to make the abstracts. (Typewritten letter dated 31 December 1940, from Ralph West Robey, Room 3335, RCA Building, New York, to Mr. Walter B. Weisenburger, Executive Vice-President of the National Association of Manufacturers, 14 W. 49th St., New York City [NAM Library, New York City].)

32. In fact, this claim was repeated in a note that later appeared at the top of every abstract: "THIS ABSTRACT has been prepared by a group of educators of

diverse economic and social viewpoints, and seeks only to ILLUSTRATE the book's attitude toward America's political and economic institutions. It makes no APPRAISAL of that attitude, nor does it express any conclusions about the desirability of the book as a schoolroom text."

33. Robey's political opinions were a matter of record. See Ralph W. Robey, *Roosevelt versus Recovery* (New York and London: Harper & Bros., 1934), which sheds some light on Robey's own economic and political ideas. President Roosevelt's initial program, wrote Robey, was a "series of hidden-ball plays" (p. 56). See especially chaps. 5, "Madness," 6, "Waste," and 8, "Subterfuge."

34. NAM published the abstracts and, beginning 1 March 1941, sent ten copies, free of charge, to anyone who requested them. Additional abstracts cost three cents, up to a maximum charge of five dollars. This policy remained in effect until the end of World War II. Original typescripts of the abstracts and related documents are on file in the NAM Library in New York City.

35. Fine was a close friend of Clyde R. Miller, a professor at Teachers College, Columbia University, and director of the Institute of Propaganda Analysis, which was denouncing NAM "propaganda." See "NAM Textbook Survey Arouses Storm," *Publishers' Weekly* 139 (1 March 1941): 1024.

36. *New York Times,* 22 February 1941, p. 1, col. 4; p. 6, cols. 3–7.

37. See, for example, the critique in *Newsweek* 17 (13 January 1941): 56. At this time *Newsweek* was owned by Malcolm Muir, an influential NAM member. A few months after Robey's press interview with Benjamin Fine of the *New York Times,* H. W. Prentis, Jr., then chairman of the NAM Board of Directors, reiterated before a regional NAM meeting some of Robey's personal remarks. (H. W. Prentis Jr., "The Shape of Things to Come" [Address before the Regional Meeting of the National Association of Manufacturers in Philadelphia on 28 April 1941], *Vital Speeches of the Day* 7 [1 June 1941]: 497–501.) Ralph W. Robey joined the permanent staff of NAM and was later appointed chief economist and made a NAM vice president.

38. I. L. Kandel, "Subversive or Ridiculous?" *School and Society* 53 (18 January 1941): 82–83. For other views, see Carl G. Miller, "The Social Science Textbook Investigation," *Education* 61 (April 1941): 507–8; and Maurice T. Price, "Open Letter to the NAM," *School and Society* 53 (9 April 1941): 510.

39. *New York Times,* 27 February 1941, p. 21, col. 8.

40. Ibid., 23 February 1941, p. 1, col. 1; p. 47, col. 3.

41. Ibid., 26 February 1941, p. 23, col. 1; ibid., 3 May 1941, p. 21, col. 1.

42. Just how desperately business leaders worked to promote a closer relationship with educators is revealed in numerous speeches and articles that appeared in journals, pamphlets, and newsletters published by NAM and the National Chamber during and after World War II. See, in particular, the following: National Association of Manufacturers: *News Letter; NAM NEWS; Trends in Education-Industry Cooperation;* and *Trends in Church, Education and Industry Cooperation.* Chamber of Commerce of the United States: *Washington Review, Business Action, News and Cues,* and the *Nation's Business.* Because this material was primarily written by and for the business community, these sources are of unusual importance in shedding some light on the changing attitudes of businessmen toward the public schools.

43. Donald C. Dayton, "Business, Education Have Vital Stake in Future America" (Address before 3,300 Teachers at the "Business-Education Day" Mass Meeting on 25 October 1950, in the Minneapolis Auditorium), *Greater Minneapolis* 2 (November 1950): 23.

44. By the mid-1960s, thousands of teachers had visited business establishments everywhere. For detailed figures, see the National Chamber's published "Progress Reports" entitled *Leadership and Service,* which appear annually.

45. The five divisional offices are in Detroit, New York City, Chicago, Atlanta, and Palo Alto (California). The twelve regional offices are in Detroit, Pittsburgh, New York City, Boston, Ardmore (Pennsylvania), Chicago, St. Louis, Atlanta, Houston, Palo Alto, Portland (Oregon), and Los Angeles. According to NAM, this decentralization multiplies the Association's effectiveness in "public education." See, among numerous other pamphlets and booklets published by NAM, the following brochure: *NAM Serves You and the Nation* . . . (New York: NAM, n.d.). The periods are in the original title and do not indicate an omission.

46. Even this list could be greatly extended, for the NAM Education Division sends freely to educators and civic leaders throughout the nation a steady stream of materials and program suggestions.

47. The goals of American education have been carefully defined through the years by the Educational Policies Commission. For an important statement by the Commission, see *The Central Purpose of American Education* (Washington, D.C.: National Education Association, 1961). For a provocative discussion of educational purpose, see Lawrence A. Cremin, *The Genius of American Education,* Horace Mann Lecture for 1965 (Pittsburgh, Pa.: University of Pittsburgh Press, 1965).

48. For a revealing analysis of some of the pressures to which superintendents of schools are repeatedly subjected, see Neal Gross, *Who Runs Our Schools?* (New York: Wiley, 1958). Gross lists businessmen as "the second most frequently mentioned group that superintendents described as doing 'most to block public education' in their communities." "Local Government Officials" are listed first (pp. 19–23).

49. Peter F. Drucker, *The New Society: The Anatomy of Industrial Order* (New York and Evanston: Harper & Row Torchbook, 1962), p. 337.

CHAPTER 11

The American School
in Transition

That education should be regulated by law and should be an affair of state is not to be denied, but what should be the character of this public education, and how young persons should be educated, are questions which remain to be considered.

ARISTOTLE, *Politics*

The basic cleavage which runs through our beliefs and values comes to light when we try to determine what we shall teach and how we shall teach it.

ALEXANDER MEIKLEJOHN, *Education between Two Worlds,* 1942

The key to effective education rests with unleashing the productive potential that is already present in the schools and their personnel. It rests with granting them the autonomy to do what they do best. . . . The more autonomous, the less subject to bureaucratic constraint—the more likely they are to have effective organizations.

JOHN E. CHUBB and TERRY M. MOE, *Politics, Markets and America's Schools,* 1990

TRANSFORMATION OF
THE SECONDARY SCHOOL

Conflicting Goals

At the beginning of the twentieth century the public high school was becoming involved in a conflict of goals that gradually assumed an urgency relatively new to the secondary scene. High schools were being confronted with a twofold responsibility: preparation for students who were going to college and programs for those youth for whom high school was to be the last point in formal education.

Traditionally, education above the elementary-school level was viewed as the preparation of a relatively select number of youth for entrance into higher studies leading ultimately to professions. The college-preparatory function had been stated over and over again. However, not all youth wanted to enroll in a college-preparatory curriculum; some hoped to obtain from a secondary schooling a terminal education that would prepare them for a vocation or a specialized skill. When secondary education was quite limited and catered only to a small percentage of the population, the issue was not pressing. When high schools became public and began to expand greatly around the turn of the century, the picture changed radically and the basic conflict over purpose came quickly to the forefront.

It is significant to note, for example, that from 1910 to 1930 enrollment in the public schools increased from about 18 million to 25 million, and total expenditures for education rose from $426,250,000 to $2,317,000,000. The gains were greatest at the secondary-school level, where enrollments increased about 400 percent. In the following two decades, under the impact first of the Great Depression and then of World War II, public-school attendance declined somewhat; but in the 1950s enrollments spiraled upward again. This upward trend was reversed toward the end of the 1970s, when enrollments in the public schools decreased sharply due to a declining birth rate (see pp. 357–358).

Charles W. Eliot (1834–1926) and the Committee of Ten

The report of the Committee of Ten on Secondary School Studies, appointed in 1892, brought into focus the key issue.[1] The idea for the committee was sparked by a movement within the National Education Association to make college-entrance requirements more uniform. But no one seems to know how the ten members were actually selected. Under the chairmanship of Charles W. Eliot, the committee included five college presidents and one professor, two headmasters of private secondary schools, one principal of a public high school, and the United States Commissioner of Education.[2] The unbalanced membership stirred up an early storm of protest: the absence of a woman on the committee, for example, was deplored by feminists, who pointed to the dominance of women teachers and the increasing number of girls in the public high schools.[3] President Eliot was by far the most influential member of the Committee of Ten. As chairman, he wrote the Committee's *Report* and exerted strong leadership and initiative. There is little doubt that the final draft reflected to a large extent Eliot's own educational views. Oscar Robinson, a member of the Ten, wondered, for instance, if the Committee's *Report* should really be called "Dr. Eliot's report."[4]

Charles W. Eliot was a controversial figure in educational history. He spent his early years on Boston's famed Beacon Hill and went to the Boston Latin School. He attended Harvard and was graduated at the top of his class in 1853. Five years later he joined the Harvard faculty as an assistant professor of mathematics and chemistry. In 1869, after a two-year tour in Europe and a brief appointment in chemistry at the then new Massachusetts Institute of Technology, he moved up at the age of thirty-five to the presidency of Harvard. He accepted Harvard's offer only after the corporation compelled a disgruntled board of overseers to reconsider its first vote of disapproval.

Eliot's forty years as president witnessed some remarkable changes at Harvard: an upgrading and extension of the professional and graduate schools, a deemphasis of the classical studies, and the introduction of the elective system. With Dean Langdell in the law school, he pioneered with a new approach to legal study. In the medical school, he improved the curriculum, raised standards, and helped to initiate medical reforms elsewhere. In short, under Eliot's leadership Harvard was transformed from a small college into a leading institute that would eventually surpass all other American universities in the strength of its graduate programs.

Not unexpectedly, Eliot, a brilliant young chemist, sought to expand the technical and scientific areas. This he accomplished by instituting the elective system. Despite bitter opposition from members of his own faculty and from other college presidents, he drastically reduced the number of prescribed classical courses. When he dropped Greek as a Harvard entrance requirement, the overseers demanded his removal. "How is it?" asked a staff member during a meeting soon after Eliot assumed office, "that this Faculty has gone on for eighty years, managing its own affairs and doing it well,. . .and now within *three or four months* it is proposed to change all our modes of carrying on the school—it seems very extraordinary, and I should like to know how it happens." Eliot rose to the floor and responded without hesitation. "I can answer Dr. _____ 's question very easily. There is a new President."[5]

Eliot had great faith in academic freedom and welcomed open debates among those who disagreed with him on any matter. "Discussions in faculty were untrammeled," recalled one biographer, "and no man's career was ever injured because he opposed the President in matters of policy and opinion."[6] Tall and austere, Eliot was seemingly impatient, often abrupt. He wasted few words and came quickly to the point. His short remarks and speeches did not endear him to his own contemporaries or to historians.[7]

Year after year, under Eliot's leadership, the number of required courses at Harvard was reduced and electives were added. By 1894 the only prescribed subjects in the curriculum were rhetoric and a foreign language; three years later even the foreign-language requirement was abolished. At the same time, with the adoption of the elective principle new studies entered the curriculum, and Harvard's faculty increased from sixty members in 1869 to six hundred by the close of Eliot's administration in 1909. Equally significant in quantitative terms was the tremendous rise in Harvard's endowment from $2.5 million in 1869 to over $20 million in 1909.

The introduction of the elective system generated some heated arguments in academic circles. On one occasion President James McCosh of Princeton, who was skeptical of the whole idea, met Eliot in a public debate on the issue. A strong advocate of the classics, McCosh in 1885 openly ridiculed the so-called mental monstrosities enrolled at Harvard who, he charged, could not swallow solid intellectual food and dabbled instead in art, music, and French plays. Yale was even more determined to maintain the traditional disciplines and under President Noah Porter took a firm stand against the encroaching "heresies" of Eliot and his followers. The main arguments against the elective principle were strong: the system did not require a common core of basic knowledge and could not prevent a student from pursuing an exclusively vocational-type training.

But Princeton and Yale were exceptions to a prevailing trend, and by the turn of the century Eliot's view was dominant. Most of the large universities had followed Harvard, and even Princeton and Yale had begun moving slowly toward Eliot's position. In 1901, for instance, students at thirty-four leading colleges and universities could elect more than 70 percent of their courses. Not until the 1930s did the pendulum swing back toward requiring a general education in American colleges and universities. The depression decade, in particular, was marked by a noteworthy return of prescribed courses.

Thus, by the 1890s Eliot was widely known as a powerful reformer of higher education. He was an active member of the National Education Association, and his addresses before NEA departments were earning him a reputation as an avid reformer of the "lower schools" as well.

Despite his preoccupation with Harvard's programs, Eliot had given some thought to public education.[8] He believed, first of all, in uniformity of educational standards and teaching methods. He insisted on rigidly high standards for everyone. Eliot also favored introducing electives into public elementary schools, starting at the fifth grade, with greater freedom of choice as pupils advanced through high school; after the age of fifteen, students would enroll in programs built almost entirely on the elective principle. In Eliot's view, these ideas were perfectly compatible: the aim was to diversify the curriculum without lowering standards, regardless of pupil abilities. The courses in individual programs would vary, but evaluative criteria and methods of instruction should remain the same.

Eliot was a firm believer in "mental discipline," which he thought resulted from studying subjects in which one was thoroughly interested, instead of working in areas where there was no inclination to learn. Children of various abilities, Eliot maintained, would achieve more by studying *elected* subjects picked individually on the bases of intrinsic joy and human ability. The only common denominator essential for all, according to Eliot, was effective use of the English language.[9]

Eliot's advocacy of the elective principle in public education was dismissed by some as a utopian thought divorced from the realities of schooling the masses in a democracy. Eliot, however, remained firm in his conviction and would not change his view. He held consistently in public speeches to the idea of freedom of choice by the individual student. By the time the Committee of Ten met in 1892, Eliot had become a familiar voice in American education.

The Committee of Ten was confronted with a confused situation devoid of any clear-cut policy on the secondary level for preparing students either for college or for a specialized skill. To begin with, the public high schools in the 1890s could not keep pace with an expanding population. Classrooms and trained teachers were scarce, and standards were correspondingly low. Furthermore, as Sizer points out, only a small number of eligible youth were actually attending any school at all around the turn of the century.[10] The newly arrived immigrants, for instance, usually destitute and thus heavily dependent on earnings from child labor, were quite successful in dodging the compulsory elementary-school regulations and could not even contemplate a secondary education. Most of the pupils who were enrolled in the high schools did not plan to attend college and were not studying the traditional preparatory courses. Even more significant, most of them dropped out before the twelfth grade. Surprising, perhaps, was the fact that over half of the students in public high schools in the 1890s were girls with limited career aspirations. In short, as Eliot put it, there was "a wide gap" in the United States' educational ladder between the elementary schools and the colleges.[11] Meanwhile, the colleges, through a maze of rigid admission requirements, were exerting increasing pressures on the public high schools to maintain "disciplinary"-type subjects in the curriculum.[12]

Oddly enough, in the light of these revealing facts, the Committee of Ten asserted that the secondary school was a terminal instead of a college-preparatory institution for the majority of its students and then proceeded to recommend a whole series of courses oriented toward a college-preparatory program. The basic assumption was that those studies that best trained a student for college admission also best prepared an individual for life. The committee, adhering to Eliot's view of "mental discipline," recommended that every subject be taught the same way, whether in preparation for college or as a part of a terminal program. The tradition of faculty psychology was dominant.

In an effort to cope with one of the problems of mass education, the committee adopted the principle of "equivalents": a subject on an approved list was deemed just as acceptable as another if it were studied for an equal length of time. Later the term "unit" or "credit" was used to designate a certain number of class hours of work. This procedure was soon followed in high schools and colleges, which began measuring educational programs in terms of units or credits. The unit or credit system, in fact, became so firmly entrenched after 1900 that an "education" was viewed almost solely in quantitative terms.

The whole system of "equivalents" has had a deleterious impact on American education. For pupils and teachers alike a formal education was soon equated with a mechanical procedure (or race) to acquire units or credits, usually without regard for *what* was actually *learned* in courses. Eventually this routine accumulation of a certain number of credit hours, prerequisite to the awarding of diplomas or degrees, became the most widely accepted criterion of a secondary or college education.

The important report of the Committee of Ten, controlled by Eliot's ideas and the conservative spirit of higher education at the turn of the century, determined the course of the American secondary school for at least a generation. The principal conception of a secondary education was still based on the European pattern, that is, a school designed for relatively few students who were destined to go on to college.

Developments after World War I

Since World War I, American high schools have become increasingly concerned with education for all youth, instead of only for those who could profit from a traditional form of secondary education in the European manner. Those who argued for a continuation of a classical curriculum, on grounds of "mental discipline," found themselves confronted more and more by others who favored a more diversified secondary program that sought to prepare all youth for effective participation in a democratic society. Stimulated by advances in educational psychology and augmented by a growing population in the United States, this broader concept has gained increasing acceptance.

A fundamental shift in aims was first signaled in 1918 by the Commission on Reorganization of Secondary Education in its famous *Seven Cardinal Principles of Secondary Education:* health, command of fundamental processes, worthy home membership, vocational efficiency, civic participation, worthwhile use of leisure time, and ethical character. Only one of the seven was directly related to preparation for college: a command of fundamental processes. The other six were more concerned with the social functions of education. Almost all the significant statements on secondary education published since 1918 have stressed this same theme: for example, *Issues and Functions of Secondary Education,* issued in 1933 by NEA's Department of

Secondary School Principals, and *The Purposes of Education in American Democracy* (1938) and *Education for All American Youth* (1944), prepared by the Educational Policies Commission. Each statement is predicated on beliefs that emphasize practical and social competencies deemed important in democratic living.

Have the secondary schools been too optimistic about meeting the nonintellectual needs of American youth, about accomplishing the *total* task of citizenship education in a free society? The depreciation (or omission) of intellectual goals has been bitterly deplored in commentaries on American secondary education. After all, so the critics argue, an educational climate in which intellectual development and the pursuit of excellence are fostered is more stimulating and challenging—and, for some teachers, threatening. A faculty without scholarly depth is not likely to encourage a respect for excellence in the classrooms. While a few critics still contend that intellectual development is the only legitimate goal of a public high school, others have urged repeatedly that intellectual objectives at least be given greater priority. Recognition of this aim finally came from the Educational Policies Commission in 1961 in a statement that "the central purpose of American education" is to develop in students the ability to think. "The society which best develops the rational potentials of its people, along with their intuitive and aesthetic capabilities, will have the best chance of flourishing in the future," declared the commission. "To help every person develop those powers is therefore a profoundly important objective and one which increases in importance with the passage of time."[13]

Efforts to adapt secondary education to all youth led to important revisions in the high-school curriculum. As enrollments in high schools increased at unprecedented rates, control of secondary education by the precollege curriculum gradually lessened. There was considerable growth not only in the number of courses but also in the range and type of subjects offered. These curriculum changes were accelerated, too, by the publicity surrounding Thorndike and Woodworth's research on transfer of training.[14] The so-called nonacademic studies, such as the fine and practical arts, home economics, and commercial and business courses, were expanded.

In fact, a contrast in clientele underscores sharply the great change that was taking place. In 1900 only about 10 percent of all American youth of high-school age were attending secondary schools, and 75 percent of the high-school graduates were entering colleges. By mid-century about 85 percent of youth of high-school age were actually attending secondary schools, and over half of these were classified as terminal students.

This transformation of the secondary school rekindled some old controversies and ignited a host of new ones. Alarmed at these changes, college instructors and officials, for example, complained that the functional-type programs were having an adverse effect on the intellectual student. Many decried the increase of commercial and vocational courses, charging that the public high school was abandoning its proper academic role. A serious attempt to answer these and other charges was the famous Eight-Year Study, launched in 1933 under the auspices of the Progressive Education Association.

The Eight-Year Study

Overshadowed by World War II, the published results of the Eight-Year Study should be carefully reviewed, for the investigation was a significant development in the history of American education.[15] Thirty secondary schools (one school withdrew in 1936) and over three hundred colleges participated in the experiment.

The investigators wanted to determine how successfully the graduates of the thirty schools performed in college. The colleges agreed to waive formal admissions requirements for students successfully completing a program at one of these high schools. Not all the thirty schools were alike: far from it, according to Paul B. Diederich, a member of the evaluation team. The participating schools included public and private institutions, ranging "in educational policy from conservative to radical." The thirty schools, in fact, were intended to be "a representative cross-section of American secondary schools" offering college-preparatory programs.[16] The evaluative procedure was to identify 1,475 pairs of college students, each consisting of a graduate from one of the thirty experimental schools and a comparable graduate from some other high school, matched as closely as possible on items of age, sex, race, scholastic-aptitude scores, vocational and other interests, and home and community background.

From 1933 until the twenty-nine schools submitted their final report in 1940, the teachers and principals were largely free to make any curricular changes they desired. "Those were exciting days in 1932, 1933, and 1934 when the Thirty Schools were planning and inaugurating their new work," Wilfred Aiken, director of the study, recalled. "Principals, teachers, and students were caught up in the spirit of adventure and exploration." Not everyone, of course, shared this initial enthusiasm. As Aiken wrote: "To some college professors 'Progressive Education now had enough rope to hang itself'; and to some parents the Study was a source of uneasiness and dissatisfaction."[17]

The final evaluation team, in comparing the 1,475 matched pairs, concluded that graduates of the twenty-nine schools: (1) earned a slightly higher total grade average; (2) earned higher grade averages in all fields except in foreign language; (3) received slightly more academic honors during each of the four years; (4) possessed more intellectual curiosity and drive and seemed to be more precise, systematic, and objective in their thinking; (5) demonstrated a higher degree of resourcefulness in coping with new situations; (6) approached the solution of adjustment problems more effectively; (7) participated more frequently in organized student groups except religious and "service" activities; (8) earned a higher percentage of nonacademic honors during each college year; and (9) demonstrated a more active interest in national and foreign affairs. Furthermore, according to the report, "the graduates of the most experimental schools were strikingly more successful than their matches."[18] As Diedrich summarized: "Graduates of the Thirty Schools did as well as the comparison group in every measure of scholastic competence, and in many aspects of development which are more important than marks, they did better."[19] In short, what really mattered in the long run was the *quality* of work completed and the kind of education the students received.

Did the Eight-Year Study produce any lasting change in American education? Apparently not, according to Frederick L. Redefer, who was executive secretary of the Progressive Education Association during the period when the study was being conducted. The results of the experiment were another battle casualty of World War II.[20]

New Tensions

The twentieth-century United States has undergone a remarkable transformation. The relatively stable and less complex routine of yesterday has given way to the faster pace of an urban-industrial setting fraught with uncertainties and emotional imbalance. Of profound significance is a vast extension of knowledge, the basis for a new technological society, which has affected in startling ways some basic patterns of human relationships.[21]

The educational problems wrought by these and other rapid changes have threatened to be overwhelming. To help in a very important way, guidance counselors were added to high-school staffs and were soon compelled to extend their original sphere of responsibility. In the beginning, guidance was vocational and narrowly academic in scope. After World War II, the guidance function was viewed in a new and broader context. Profiting from insights gleaned through mental-hygiene studies, guidance specialists began to expand their programs in order to cope with issues and problems in almost every area of human growth and development. For example, exceptional youth, whatever the reason for their divergence from the norm, are receiving more attention than ever before in the nation's high schools.

The modern secondary school, in fact, has been called upon to play an increasingly larger role in the education of American youth. In some communities the public high school has assumed to an amazing extent almost all the responsibilities of personal development—individual and social tasks at one time performed by the family and the church or synagogue.

These developments illustrate dramatically that the aims of the American high school have changed substantially since the days of the Latin grammar school. Unique in the history of education in the United States is the emergence of a dominant conception that all boys and girls should have an opportunity to attend together a *comprehensive* secondary school. In local communities across the nation, a public high school offering parallel curricula under one roof has become the standard type of secondary education.

Obviously, though, not everyone is satisfied with this outcome. The years since the end of World War II have witnessed an intensification of an old conflict: postwar debates over "life adjustment education" as contrasted with the academic curriculum strike a familiar note and are continuations of a long controversy.[22] There are still those who believe that the secondary schools are overly concerned with the college-preparatory function and are shirking a responsibility to the majority of students who desire and need a different kind of education from that required for college admission. At the other extreme are those who still adhere to the European ideal of a secondary education and argue that many youth attending high school should not be there; consequently, it is charged, standards of scholarship are being lowered. Believing that the primary purpose of a secondary education should continue to be college-preparatory, these critics are disturbed and vexed by the presence of a majority of high-school youth who do not plan to attend college.

The dialogue was not new; but the social and political problems of the 1970s, the 1980s, and the 1990s have added an unusual sense of urgency to the educational scene. Automation and computers, for example, have eliminated lower-level occupations and displaced large numbers of workers, making retraining imperative. U.S. Supreme Court decisions, barring racial segregation and prohibiting Bible reading in the public schools, have drawn increased attention to educational issues. The urgency began in the 1950s when Russian space achievements jarred a free nation from complacency and made Americans acutely aware of the vital need for quality school systems.

The launching of *Sputnik I* in the fall of 1957 released a deluge of harsh attacks on American high schools. The Soviet Union's success in placing in orbit the first manmade satellite ignited smoldering criticisms of influential individuals and interest groups who had repeatedly accused the public high schools of weakening academic standards. Some critics even suggested that American secondary schools reverse a twentieth-century trend in the direction of diversified curricula and revert to a program similar to that which prevailed about two hundred years ago.

There is a paradox in the suggestion that high schools return to a curriculum of the past, since the avowed purpose of such a proposal is to uplift the academic standing of American education. In the first place, there is no evidence that the quality of education in the secondary school of yesterday was superior to that of today. Second, the whole idea is based on the false assumption that the Latin grammar school and the nineteenth-century academy afforded boys and some girls a liberal education superior to that of the present high school. The offerings during the colonial period were meager indeed when compared to a typical college-preparatory curriculum in a modern comprehensive high school.[23]

Americans should be guided by the well-established principle that equality of educational opportunity in a free society requires differentiation, not uniformity. The United States is a highly diversified nation and needs for its continued progress the contributions of many types of abilities.

The First Conant Report

The specific recommendations of the first Conant Report, which received nationwide publicity in 1959, provoked some serious discussions of these and related high-school issues.[24] Unlike earlier critiques, this report was a constructive appraisal of some of the problems that continue to plague local attempts to improve the quality of secondary education. In urging the elimination of the small high schools, for example, Conant was realistic and blunt: unless a secondary school has a graduating class of at least a hundred students, that school is too small to offer diversified curricula to meet the needs of its pupils and the requirements of the nation. "Geography may sometimes be legitimate justification for a small high school, but all too often it is merely an excuse," Conant wrote. "Human nature—not geography—offers the real explanation.[25] There is little doubt that Conant's strong recommendations accelerated the trend toward school-district consolidation. "Imaginative leadership, shrewd political thinking, and a willingness to offer 'an alluring carrot,' " Conant remarked, are often persuasive "incentives" in facilitating district reorganization. On other issues, Conant was equally firm and to the point: the citizen's first obligation to the public schools is to support them; his second duty is to select an intelligent and devoted board of education. These board members, Conant continued, should be competent enough to establish school policies and should have enough sense to leave administrative matters where they legitimately belong—under the jurisdiction of the professional staff.

THE EDUCATIONAL REFORM MOVEMENT

The late 1950s and the early 1960s witnessed the emergence of a remarkable series of educational innovations. These changes sought to reshape on a national scale the total content of the curriculum and to introduce, at the same time, a new set of methodologies. "Indeed, to the outside observer, it must seem as if we were preparing to embark upon a permanent revolution in education," wrote Jerome Bruner, one of the reform leaders, in 1962. "And I think we are entering just such a period."[26]

The reform movement was powered by several closely related forces. The innovations were, first, strongly augmented by the work of academic scholars in colleges and universities. Not only did these men and women introduce new knowledge into the curricula but, more important, each also sought to reorganize the conceptual structure of a discipline for presentation to boys and girls. Some of the questions these scholars tried to answer were old: For example, what knowledge is of most worth? Which methodology is likely to encourage the individual to continue to learn after leaving school? Second, the projects were generously supported from funds that came primarily from federal sources, pointing up sharply a growing federal involvement in education in all areas and at all levels. Third, this reform effort, like some others in the past, began more as a counterthrust against alleged errors or evils. As a protest movement, it drew its leadership from a disarray of potentially powerful elements: college professors and academicians, for example, who blamed the public schools for what they perceived as weak standards and outdated subject matter; certain professional educators who saw in the currents of change opportunities to cut loose from the so-called life-adjustment aims of the past and to restructure the schools toward new and broader goals; influential parents who accused the schools of failing to do all that they *should* or *could* do for their children; and finally, discouraged African American citizens who viewed an education dominated by the neighborhood school concept as a major deterrent to social integration. The overall drive was one massive attempt to reformulate at every level *what* knowledge should be learned in American schools and *how* it should be taught.[27]

Ferment in the Subject Areas

The largest effort of the reform movement was directed toward introducing new content into the subject areas of the school curriculum. In a space age, this is not unusual, for there is a continuing need to bring curricula up to date with new knowledge. There is, in brief, more to learn than ever before. This gigantic effort, however, was aimed toward more than clearing out obsolete material; the innovators were trying to revamp and restock the total academic content of the school program. In 1962, according to one report, there were at least forty-two studies or projects under way.[28]

Certainly, as Goodlad points out, not all the nation's 24,000 public secondary and 85,000 public elementary schools were affected by the reform efforts.[29] Rural areas, in particular, remained virtually untouched by the innovators' work. Research and curricular studies in the social sciences and the humanities, long overlooked in favor of mathematics and the physical sciences, were also needed. Still, when viewed with a clear perspective, the innovations as a whole represented a search for more meaningful content and improved methods. The results from studies in certain disciplines sometimes affected all other areas of the curriculum. New procedural techniques and the use of new media, for example, which were integral to most projects, often became widely adopted by-products of the reform movement.

In devising and proposing new curricula for the nation's schools, most of the scholars shunned professional specialists and leaders. In some fields, such as human development and learning, this led to fruitless research and wasted time in seeking answers to old questions that educators had already explored. Problems in education as a professional enterprise were simply not the primary concern of most scholars.

If the reform movement was to affect permanently the mainstream of American thought, then it was imperative that the contributions of all participants—scholars in academic areas, classroom teachers, and professional educators—be unified and closely coordinated on some permanent basis. Failure to arouse enthusiasm among most classroom teachers, for instance, would lead to a resounding defeat for the whole movement. For this reason, some innovators spent considerable time and effort reeducating elementary- and secondary-school teachers.

The aims and scope of the curricular projects varied greatly. Some encompassed an entire field (for example, mathematics, science, or modern foreign languages); others were limited to the study of only one subject area (for example, biology, chemistry, or physics). Some scholars prepared broad recommendations as guides to textbook authors and school supervisors; others wrote scientific syllabi for the use of classroom teachers. Not all the innovators agreed, even among themselves, on any specific goals. In fact, some intradisciplinary battles were waged over the very rationale supporting certain proposals.[30]

One important similarity, however, characterized almost all innovations: a search for unifying principles and concepts in a body of knowledge and a simultaneous attempt to inculcate a special way of thinking and method of inquiry. The many programs in the reform movement not only introduced new knowledge into the curriculum but also tried to change the conceptual *structure* of knowledge for teaching and learning purposes.

Toward New Cognitive Structures

The term *structure* refers to the parts of a substance or body and the ways in which these parts are interrelated. Set theory, for example, is a conceptual structure frequently employed in elementary education to teach children arithmetical and algebraic concepts; it is used, in brief, as a pedagogical tool for arranging or reorganizing mathematical ideas previously presented as independent and discrete elements. The thesis is that conceptual organizations of greater scope and power will lead to deeper understandings and facilitate a clearer perception of mathematical thinking and ideas.

It is significant to note that this argument is only a hypothesis concerning the relationship between the structure of cognitive stimuli and the relative depth and transferability of cognitive learning. It is also important to remember that knowing the structure of one object does not automatically connote an understanding of its constituent parts. The structure of a curriculum, for instance, refers to the various subjects and their vertical and horizontal arrangements; but knowing this does not necessarily include an understanding of the structure of individual disciplines that make up the curriculum. A discipline is also amenable to structural analysis.[31] Failure to understand clearly this differentiation could lead to erroneous assumptions and needless points of contention between scholars and professional leaders.

An attempt to define more clearly the structure of knowledge began to attract serious attention during the early 1960s. A "Seminar on the Disciplines," convened by the National Education Association in June 1961, discussed "those fundamental ideas and methods of inquiry from selected fields of study which should be in the mainstream of the instructional program of the public schools."[32] Jerome Bruner's *The Process of Education* (1960), widely publicized through notices and reviews, also drew sharp attention to the concept of structure and its implications for learning.[33]

Influenced by the work of Piaget, Bruner and his associates proposed that learning in the classroom be structured to stimulate cognitive behavior—that is, intuitive thinking and learning by discovery. This methodology, in turn, should encourage the student to formulate basic concepts and principles with minimal or no help.

> Mastery of the fundamental idea of a field involves not only the grasping of general principles, but also the development of an attitude toward learning and inquiry, toward guessing and hunches, toward the possibility of solving problems on one's own. . . . To instill such attitudes by teaching requires something more than the mere presentation of fundamental ideas. Just what it takes to bring off such teaching is something on which a great deal of research is needed, but it would seem that an important ingredient is a sense of excitement about discovery—discovery of regularities of previously unrecognized relations and similarities between ideas, with a resulting sense of self-confidence in one's abilities.[34]

This was only one hypothesis; Bruner and his colleagues postulated others. They also proposed, for example, a possible key to successful teaching and learning: organize the subject matter and utilize the learner's cognitive processes in a way that captures both the spirit and thought characteristic of an academic discipline.

> Intellectual activity anywhere is the same, whether at the frontier of knowledge or in a third-grade classroom. What a scientist does at his desk or in his laboratory, what a literary critic does in reading a poem, are of the same order as what anybody else does when he is engaged in like activities—if he is to achieve understanding. The difference is in degree, not in kind. The schoolboy learning physics *is* a physicist, and it is easier for him to learn physics behaving like a physicist than doing something else.[35]

The pedagogy, then, seemed clear: instead of studying *about* a field of knowledge, learn instead its structure and its inherent methodology. It was this fundamental approach that intrigued the innovators.

Using this approach in a classroom situation is fraught with endless difficulties. A thorny problem, for instance, concerns the relative effectiveness of cognitive structures and principles. It is unlikely that *one* system of organization will be effective for *all* learners. Other issues also call for additional study and research: for example, the student might learn to hypothesize, which is basic to skillful problem solving, but does "learning by discovery" produce an organized and sufficiently detailed knowledge of course content and depth?[36] For a beleaguered classroom teacher, the innovators may have opened Pandora's box!

Bruner and his colleagues also raised some provocative questions concerning the sequence of cognitive learning. Their "hypothesis that any subject can be taught effectively in some intellectually honest form to any child at any stage of development" was widely quoted.[37] There is little doubt that some teachers in recent years have underestimated the ability of certain children to learn meaningfully more advanced knowledge. The issue for Bruner and the innovators was not *when* to introduce complex material; the problem was *how* to help pupils learn *more* complex subject matter at any grade level. However, one should not move from Bruner's dictum to the absurd position that *every* discipline must be taught in *each* of the twelve grades. Certainly Bruner himself never meant to convey such an impression.[38]

Proposed Changes in School Organization

An important outgrowth of the reform movement was some interesting plans to reorganize American schools vertically into "multigraded" or "nongraded" classes and horizontally into "team teaching" or cooperative instructional arrangements.

As the term implies, nongrading is an organizational scheme is which grade labels have been removed from some or all classes. An entire school might be nongraded; or, within one school, there might be a nongraded primary or intermediate unit. This is obviously an old concept, reminiscent, in some ways, of the ungraded school that still exists in a few sections of the rural United States, but is slowly disappearing under pressures for school-district consolidation. Nongrading, then, is simply a vertical plan of school organization.[39] It might reflect a philosophical commitment on the part of teachers willing to work within such a framework, but transforming the organizational structure of any school does not automatically change a faculty's approach to teaching and learning.

The rationale supporting a nongraded plan is that progress becomes more closely related to each individual's abilities. Theoretically, at least, a slow learner can progress without some of the pressures often found in a traditionally graded school, and an academically talented pupil can move with a faster pace from basic to more advanced work. For educators committed to pedagogy based on "maturation" and "readiness," these factors are viewed as crucial advantages of a nongraded arrangement.[40]

The switch from a graded to a nongraded organization is not likely to be a smooth transition. Grade-level expectations are deeply entrenched in American educational thought.[41] An innovator armed with this concept needs abundant courage, skill, and community support in order to effect a permanent change.

Some schools that had experimented successfully with nongrading began to combine this vertical plan with "team teaching," which also deviated from a conventional pattern. In general, team teaching involves a redeployment of staff into closer working relationships for the joint instruction of the same group of students. This requires a fundamental shift in traditional teaching roles and procedures (for example, team leaders, cooperating teachers, and instructional aides) and a regrouping of students into more flexible divisions (for example, large sections, small discussion groups, and individual study arrangements). The nature and quality of these teaching configurations vary greatly.

Team teaching, as a concept in school organization, was popularized during the early years of the reform movement.[42] In 1957 Harvard University, working with the town of Lexington, Massachusetts, initiated the Franklin School Project, making Franklin the first elementary school in the United States completely converted to team teaching.[43] This cooperation between Harvard and Lexington led to a School and University Program for Research and Development, supported largely by the Fund for the Advancement of Education. Similar types of programs were established elsewhere: the Claremont (California) Graduate School Team Teaching Program, for example, covered eight school districts involving about 7,000 students and 250 "team leaders," and the Wisconsin School Improvement Program (based at the University of Wisconsin) launched team-teaching projects in several communities. Meanwhile, the National Education Association was predicting that three of every ten school districts in the United States would have team-teaching projects in operation by the mid-1960s.[44]

Much of this enthusiasm stemmed from a widely publicized report issued by a Committee on Staff Utilization, appointed in 1955 by the National Association of Secondary-School Principals.[45] J. Lloyd Trump, the committee's spokesman and secretary, prepared and wrote the final report, although Trump stated that he alone did not deserve all the credit. Judging from his subsequent speeches and writings, there seemed to be little doubt, however, that Trump formulated the basic plan, with team teaching as an organizing principle.

The Trump Plan, in fact, revolved around a greatly expanded concept of team teaching. For example, Trump recommended that about 40 percent of the students' time be scheduled in large sections, 20 percent of time in seminars or small groups, and 40 percent of time in independent study. To implement this plan, school facilities would have to be constructed or substantially remodeled in line with a team concept. A few of Trump's costliest recommendations obviously called for some imaginative institutional planning. For groups of 125 to 135 students, for instance, large rooms, electronically equipped with all types of audiovisual aids, were required. Carrels, with built-in recording and listening apparatus, were also suggested for individual study.

These and other institutional changes were encouraged by liberal grants from the Educational Facilities Laboratories, Inc., established by the Ford Foundation in 1958. "In the future we hope our schoolhouses will be flexible enough to permit change," remarked Harold B. Gores, director of the laboratories. "As education changes, the schoolhouse must not stand in the way of the program, the teacher and the children."[46] Through January 1966, the Foundation had given the Laboratories $19.5 million, over a third of which had already gone toward 392 grants to educational institutions in forty-seven states.

During the early 1960s, enthusiasm for the Trump Plan was widespread; interest, in fact, was so intense that professional meetings preassigned to other topics often shifted spontaneously to Trump's report and explanatory notes that were being distributed by the National Association of Secondary-School Principals. During the mid-1960s, new buildings designed in line with Trump's version of team teaching opened in several communities, including Wayland, Massachusetts; Greenwich, Connecticut; Huntington, New York; Racine, Wisconsin; and Carson City, Michigan. Never before in the history of American education had an idea moved so swiftly from one man's blueprint to such widespread adoption.

THE CONTINUING DEBATE: STRUGGLES
TO IMPROVE PUBLIC EDUCATION

The Drive to Establish
Alternative Educational Systems

For over a generation educational critics have sought reform within the context of the public school. Criticisms are frequently voiced over matters of curriculum, educational methodology, or school organization. By the late 1960s however, arguments began to shift toward sweeping redefinitions of the goals and functions of public schooling in the United States. During the 1970s, the critics moved from protest to action through important strategies for change.

A popular strategy was to circumvent the political and institutional constraints of existing public school systems and provide new environments for learning. Such "free schools" were either completely autonomous or existed through special arrangements with larger school systems. They were founded by parents and teachers in community experiments and focused on teaching-learning patterns that released boys and girls from adult, professional controls.[47]

Another tactic was the development of an innovative subsystem within the traditional school district. Proponents of such programs hoped that the creation of an experimental pattern would encourage change in the larger institution. An example of this approach was the Parkway Program in Philadelphia, adopted in 1969 by the city's Board of Education. The project was called a "School Without Walls," a new "venture in public education."[48]

The most radical of all proposed reforms called for the abolition of public schools and the total "deschooling" of society. Ivan Illich is a widely publicized proponent of deschooling who strongly opposes all institutional intervention in education, including governmental support of public schools. "Gradually the idea grew that schooling was a necessary means of becoming a useful member of society," wrote Illich in 1969. "It is the task of this generation to bury that myth."[49] Here the call is not for alternatives of a different character; the demand is for no formal schooling at all.

There are important parallels between the drive to establish alternative schools in the 1970s and the progressive education movement of the 1890s. Both began as protests against the alleged formalism, narrowness, and inequities of the public school, and both adhered to dominant child-centered concepts. There are also striking contrasts between the two movements. The radical element in the alternative school drive was much more sweeping in its demands. In the progressive movement, no reformer wanted to eliminate the public schools completely. Perhaps the most significant difference between the two movements was the absence of a philosophic base for the alternative school drive. There were few profound questions raised about the process of education, and the reformers were unwilling to turn to the history of Western civilization for ideas. An enormous amount of energy in the alternative schools was spent repeating the trials and errors of past innovators and progressive teachers.

A Nation at Risk

By the 1980s, several national commissions had reported on the perceived ills of education in the United States.[50] A major report on education presented in 1983 was that of the National Committee on Excellence in Education, chaired by David Gardner, president of the University of California. "If an unfriendly power had attempted to impose on America the mediocre educational performance that exists today, we might well have viewed it as an act of war. . . . We have, in effect, been committing an act of unthinking, unilateral educational disarmament." *A Nation at Risk: The Imperative for Educational Reform* warns that "a rising tide of mediocrity" threatens to engulf our schools and nation. Through the media this report and other publications pushed nationwide concern for public schooling to the center of state and national debate and controversy. By the mid-1980s, more than two hundred important state commissions were formed to improve public education.

The state and national reports of the 1980s continue a progression of reform proposals that date back to the report of the Committee of Ten in 1893. The reform-oriented reports of the 1980s argued that change is necessary to improve education in the United States. However, most of the proposals focused on mechanical solutions imposed from the top that should be implemented without delay.

A Nation at Risk stressed the urgency that characterized other reports and summarized the problems that necessitated reform. Credited with the most influence and urgency, the report, however, did not offer a model of schooling likely to lead to basic changes and quality education. There was no discussion of pedagogy and of the most promising instructional methodologies. In fact, *A Nation at Risk* stressed more of what already exists— more required subjects, more homework, higher teacher salaries, and a longer school year. However, more of the same is not necessarily an improvement of the educational experience. *A Nation at Risk* tried to patch the present system in ways not likely to lead to fundamental reform.

As society changes, curriculum planners must use the best knowledge and technology in the field of education and benefit from lessons learned from the past. For example, the reform movement of the late 1950s and 1960s was marked by new curricula, technology, and organization—an era of innovation that argued for many changes. Committees and commissions undertook curriculum development projects in almost all subject areas, often supported by foundations and the federal government. Nevertheless, despite the reform proposals that produced the "new math" and emphasized science and "discovery learning," most schools remained virtually unchanged. The schools, in fact, were expected to accomplish so many tasks at once that they could not do the job very well for an extended period of time.

The American people need to transform the present system of public schooling into a new and comprehensive model for the future—a different, more flexible structure that will encourage creativity and the maximum development of human potential. The challenge is to modernize the schools and transform public education from an outmoded system based on a nineteenth- and twentieth-century model to one appropriate for the twenty-first century.

Commentary

Now, more than ever before, the challenge of swiftly moving events calls for a reassertion, and a thoughtful consideration on the part of all citizens, of the general goals of public education in a democracy. The first battle in the public-school movement was waged to provide a free education for all youth. The current challenge confronting the American people is really a concomitant of that initial effort: to improve public education in order that every person has a chance for human self-fulfillment. Educators, in turn, must reassure local citizens that all students will at least acquire by graduation the basic concepts and skills that encourage intelligent and responsible action in American life.

Fundamental issues should be explored in greater depth. The growing dropout or "push-out" problem is complex and requires imaginative thought and action on the part of all citizens. In 1970, for instance, almost two million children from seven to seventeen years of age were not enrolled in any school. Careful examination of the census data revealed that most of the children had been "excluded" from public school. "It is as if many school officials have decided that certain groups of children are beyond their responsibility and are expendable," reported the Children's Defense Fund in 1974. "Not only do they exclude these children, they frequently do so arbitrarily, discriminatorily, and with impunity."[51]

Other issues reflect deeper problems in American culture. For example, the growing use of alcohol and drugs in schools and the shocking suicide rate among teenagers are serious problems that demand intelligent thought and prompt action.

Searching questions must be answered. Will the American people consistently improve the quality of public schooling for *all* boys and girls? Can a public high school inculcate in youth a necessary respect for academic excellence and, at the same time and in the same school, fulfill the dreams and aspirations of a conglomerate student body with widely varying abilities and talents? According to a timely analysis of educational goals, the United

States must do this and more, for a free society has no choice: "We must seek excellence in a context of concern for all."[52] Certainly any response that overlooks the democratic heritage of the United States would be untenable.

The public schools in a democracy cannot be closed with the assurance or even the hope that certain oppressive features attributed to the schools will thereby disappear from American culture. Many schools will and must change but not simply in response to charges of oppressiveness or threats to "deschool" society. Without viable alternatives, deschooling would, in fact, be disastrous for large numbers of American children in the culture of poverty.

These issues and questions, then, pose some basic dilemmas for the modern United States, and there are no quick and easy solutions. A nation so dedicated to the ambitious principle of compulsory education for all should reexamine seriously from time to time the nature and scope of this historic commitment.

FOR DISCUSSION AND CRITICAL THOUGHT

1. Discuss the impact of the Committee of Ten on the development of the secondary-school curriculum.
2. For over a century female teachers have dominated primary-school teaching in the United States. Does gender play a role in teacher effectiveness? Comment critically.
3. Note the Jeffersonian dictum that a free nation must have a literate citizenry. Is there a viable alternative to public schooling in a free society? Explain.
4. Comment critically on the relevance of Jerome Bruner's theory of "structure" for curriculum development in your own field of study.
5. React critically to David Gardner's remark from *A Nation at Risk* (1983) that "a rising tide of mediocrity" threatens the strength and security of the United States.
6. Discuss the social and political contexts for the national reports of the early 1980s.

NOTES

1. National Education Association, *Report of the Committee on Secondary School Studies Appointed at the Meeting of the National Education Association, July 9, 1892, with the Reports of the Conferences arranged by this Committee and held December 28–30, 1892,* U.S. Bureau of Education, Document No. 205 (Washington, D.C.: Government Printing Office, 1893).

2. Charles W. Eliot, president of Harvard, Chairman; James B. Angell, president of the University of Michigan; James M. Taylor, president of Vassar College; James H. Baker, president of the University of Colorado; Richard H. Jesse, president of the University of Missouri; Henry C. King of Oberlin College; John Tetlow, headmaster of the Girls' High School and the Girls' Latin School of Boston; James C. Mackenzie, headmaster of the Lawrenceville (New Jersey) School; Oscar D. Robinson, principal of the Albany (New York) High School; and William T. Harris, U.S. Commissioner of Education.

3. In fact, according to Krug, "practically everything about the Committee of Ten has been controversial." Edward A. Krug, *The Shaping of the American High School* (New York: Harper & Row, 1964), p. 39.

4. Oscar D. Robinson, "The Work of the Committee of Ten," *The School Review* 2 (June 1984): 366. Robinson, however, qualified his remark by pointing out that Eliot compromised on a number of points—"perhaps no one so much as he [Eliot]—in the various compromises reached."

5. This scene, with the exact quotations, is described by Dr. Oliver Wendell Holmes in a letter dated 3 April 1870, which Dr. Holmes wrote to John Lothrop Motley. The letter is reprinted in John T. Morse, Jr., ed., *Life and Letters of Oliver Wendell Holmes* (Boston and New York: Houghton Mifflin, 1896), 2:188. Italics in original.

6. William A. Neilson, ed., *Charles W. Eliot: The Man and His Beliefs* (New York and London: Harper & Bros., 1926), I, "Biographical Study" (by William A. Neilson), p. xvii.

7. According to Sizer, "No one today reads Eliot; his influence remains rather in the kinds of colleges and secondary schools he had a hand in shaping." Theodore R. Sizer, *Secondary Schools at the Turn of the Century* (New Haven and London: Yale University Press, 1964), p. 78.

8. For Eliot's ideas, see his own "Essays and Addresses" in *Educational Reform: Essays and Addresses* (New York: Century, 1901); and Neilson, ed. *Charles W. Eliot: The Man and His Beliefs,* I, "Education," pp. 1–239. For a discussion of Eliot's philosophy of education, see Edward A. Krug, ed., *Charles W. Eliot and Popular Education,* Classics in Education No. 8 (New York: Teachers College Press, Columbia University, 1961), "Introduction," pp. 1–28.

9. Actions, of course, mean more than words. Sizer, after studying Eliot's recommendation to the Chelsea (Mass.) school committee in 1884 for a four-year curriculum, notes that by the time Eliot had concluded his proposal for course *constants,* very little flexibility remained in the curriculum for *electives.* "If Eliot had his way," states Sizer, "all students—whether preparing for college or not—would have the same education." Sizer, *Secondary Schools at the Turn of the Century,* p. 81.

10. Ibid., pp. 39–54.

11. Charles W. Eliot, "The Gap Between the Elementary Schools and the Colleges," National Education Association, *Journal of Proceedings and Addresses Held at St. Paul, Minnesota* (1890), p. 522.

12. In any event, pupil *discipline* in the schools was quite firm—controlled, in fact, like "a machine" with "cast-iron rules" and "arbitrary enactments," according to Eliot. (Charles W. Eliot, "Undesirable and Desirable Uniformity in Schools"

[Address Before the National Education Association in Saratoga on 12 July 1892] in Eliot, *Educational Reform: Essays and Addresses,* p. 285.)

13. Educational Policies Commission, *Central Purpose of American Education* (1961), p. 11.

14. See pp. 206–207.

15. The story of this experiment, which ended in 1940, was recorded in a series of five volumes entitled "Adventure in American Education," which were published by Harper & Bros. in 1942 (vol. 5 appeared in 1943): Wilford M. Aiken, *The Story of the Eight-Year Study with Conclusions and Recommendations* (vol. 1): H. H. Giles et al., *Exploring the Curriculum: The Work of the Thirty Schools from the Viewpoint of Curriculum Consultants* (vol. 2); Eugene R. Smith et al., *Appraising and Recording Student Progress* (vol. 3); Dean Chamberlin et al., *Did They Succeed in College? The Follow-up Study of the Graduates of the Thirty Schools* (vol. 4); and *Thirty Schools Tell Their Story* (vol. 5).

16. *Thirty Schools Tell Their Story,* "Introduction,"by Paul B. Diederich, p. xviii.

17. Aiken, *The Story of the Eight-Year Study*, pp. 23–25.

18. Chamberlin et al., *Did They Succeed in College?* pp. 207–9.

19. *Thirty Schools Tell Their Story,* "Introduction," by Paul B. Diederich, p. v.

20. For a provocative commentary in retrospect, see Frederick L. Rederfer, "The Eight-Year Study. . . . After Eight Years," *Progressive Education* 28 (November 1950): 33–36. (The periods are in the original title and do not indicate an omission.) See also Redefer's extended survey entitled "The Eight-Year Study— Eight Years Later" (Ph. D. dissertation, Teachers College, Columbia University, 1952).

21. See pp. 370–378.

22. C. Winfield Scott et al., eds., *The Great Debate: Our Schools in Crisis* (Englewood Cliffs, N.J.: Prentice-Hall, 1959). See also Mary Anne Raywid, *The Ax-Grinders: Critics of Our Public Schools* (New York: Macmillan, 1962); and Jack Nelson and Gene Roberts Jr., *The Censors and the Schools* (Boston: Little, Brown, 1963).

23. In fact, according to Elmer E. Brown, the only courses required for admission to the leading American colleges before 1800 were Latin, Greek, and arithmetic. See Elmer Ellsworth Brown, *The Making of Our Middle Schools: An Account of the Development of Secondary Education in the United States* (3rd ed.; New York: Longmans, Green, 1910), p. 231.

24. James B. Conant, *The American High School Today: A First Report to Interested Citizens* (New York: McGraw-Hill, 1959).

25. Ibid., p. 84.

26. Jerome Bruner, "Introduction: The New Educational Technology," *American Behavioral Scientist* 6 (November 1962): 5.

27. An avalanche of materials poured forth from reform enthusiasts and proponents for change. For some direction through this miscellaneous mass of articles, pamphlets, and books, consult *The Education Index.* The disturbing element in all the literature was a dearth of carefully controlled research.

28. Dorothy M. Fraser, *Current Curriculum Studies in Academic Subjects: A Working Paper Prepared for the Project on the Instructional Program of the Public Schools* (Washington, D.C.: National Educational Association, June 1962). "Since new

studies begin almost every month," remarked Fraser in her foreword, "this book will be out of date even before it appears in print." For other overviews, written in most cases by the scholars themselves, see Robert W. Heath, ed., *New Curricula* (New York and Evanston: Harper & Row, 1964). For more concise summaries, see John I. Goodlad, *School Curriculum Reform in the United States* (New York: Fund for the Advancement of Education, March 1964).

29. Goodlad, *School Curriculum Reform in the United States,* p. 10.
30. See Benjamin DeMott, "The Math Wars," in Heath, ed., *New Curricula,* pp. 54–67; and Harry Schwartz, "New Math Fears It Is Growing Old," *New York Times,* 20 February 1966, p. 92, col. 1.
31. See G. W. Ford and Lawrence Pugno, eds., *The Structure of Knowledge and the Curriculum* (Chicago: Rand McNally, 1964).
32. *The Scholars Look at the Schools: A Report of the Disciplines Seminar* (Working Paper prepared for the Project on the Instructional Program of the Public Schools) (Washington, D.C.: National Education Association, February 1962), pp. 1–2.
33. Jerome S. Bruner, *The Process of Education* (Cambridge, Mass.: Harvard University Press, 1960), chap. 2, "The Importance of Structure," pp. 17–32.
34. Ibid., p. 20.
35. Ibid., p. 14. Italics in original. Reprinted by permission of the publishers.
36. David Ausubel has critically analyzed some of the claims advanced in support of learning by inquiry and discovery. He shows that some of the arguments advanced have not yet been supported by research evidence. His critique of Bruner's position is devastating. For summaries of Ausubel's opposing views, see his own "Introduction" to part I and his three articles in Richard C. Anderson and David P. Ausubel, eds., *Readings in the Psychology of Cognition* (New York: Holt, Rinehart & Winston, 1965), pp. 3–17, 58–75, and 87–115.
37. Bruner, *The Process of Education,* p. 33.
38. See Jerome S. Bruner, *Toward a Theory of Instruction* (Cambridge, Mass.: Harvard University Press, 1966).
39. John I. Goodlad and Robert H. Anderson, *The Nongraded Elementary School* (rev. ed.; New York: Harcourt, Brace & World, 1963; reissued by Teachers College Press in 1987), p. 59.
40. For another variation of the traditional scheme, with a novel approach to the organization of subject areas in the elementary school, see George D. Stoddard, *The Dual Progress Plan: A New Philosophy and Program in Elementary Education* (New York: Harper & Bros., 1961).
41. Anderson and Goodlad recognize this, but Brown did not. See Goodlad and Anderson, *The Nongraded Elementary School,* especially chap. 9, pp. 203–26; and B. Frank Brown, *The Nongraded High School* (Englewood Cliffs, N.J.: Prentice-Hall, 1963), especially chap. 1, pp. 27–40, and chap. 11, pp. 203–16.
42. A classification for the term "team teaching" did not appear in *The Education Index* until 1957. For a collection of commentaries, see Judson T. Shaplin and Henry F. Olds., Jr., eds., *Team Teaching* (New York and Evanston: Harper & Row, 1964).
43. For a view of the Project, written by two innovators who helped to launch it, see Medill Bair and Richard G. Woodward, *Team Teaching in Action* (Boston: Houghton Mifflin, 1964), passim.

44. National Education Association, Project on Instruction, *The Principals Look at the Schools: A Status Study of Selected Instructional Practices* (Washington, D.C.: NEA, April 1962), p. 18.

45. J. Lloyd Trump and Dorsey Baynham, *Focus on Change: Guide to Better Schools* (Chicago: Rand McNally, 1961). Publication of this report (frequently cited as the "Trump Plan") was financed by the Fund for the Advancement of Education.

46. *New York Times,* 12 January 1966, p. 48C, col. 6.

47. The movement gained momentum through the widely publicized and reprinted writings of A. S. Neill, John Holt, Jonathan Kozol, Herbert Kohl, James Herndon, and George Dennison. See A. S. Neil, *Summerhill* (New York: Hart, 1960); John Holt, *How Children Fail* (New York: Pitman, 1964), *How Children Learn* (New York: Pitman, 1967), and *Freedom and Beyond* (New York: Dutton, 1972); Jonathan Kozol, *Death at an Early Age* (Boston: Houghton Mifflin, 1967); Herbert Kohl, *36 Children* (New York: New American Library, 1967); James Herndon, *The Way It Spozed To Be* (New York: Simon & Schuster, 1968); and George Dennison, *The Lives of Children* (New York: Random House, 1969).

48. John Bremer and Michael von Moschzisker, *The School Without Walls: Philadelphia's Parkway Program* (New York: Holt, Reinhart & Winston, 1971).

49. Ivan D. Illich, *Celebration of Awareness: A Call for Institutional Revolution* (New York: Doubleday, 1969, 1970), p. 123. See also Illich's *Deschooling Society* (New York: Harper & Row, 1971); and Everett Reimer, *School Is Dead* (New York: Doubleday Anchor Books, 1971).

50. Among the most noteworthy reports were the following: Mortimer J. Adler, *The Paideia Proposal* (Macmillan, 1982); Ernest L. Boyer, *High School: A Report on Secondary Education in America* (Harper & Row, 1983); John I. Goodlad, *A Place Called School: Prospects for the Future* (McGraw-Hill, 1984); and Theodore R. Sizer, *Horace's Compromise: The Dilemma of the American High School* (Houghton Mifflin, 1984).

51. Children's Defense Fund, *Children Out of School in America* (Cambridge, Mass.: Children's Defense Fund of the Washington Research Project, 1974), p. 4.

52. Rockefeller Brothers Fund, *Prospect for America: The Rockefeller Panel Reports* (New York: Doubleday, 1961), Report 5, "The Pursuit of Excellence: Education and the Future of America" (published originally on 26 June 1958), p. 362. See also Harry S. Broudy, et al., *Democracy and Excellence in American Secondary Education* (Chicago: Rand McNally, 1964); and John W. Gardner, *Excellence: Can We Be Equal and Excellent Too?* (New York: Norton, 1984; rev. ed.).

CHAPTER 12

Crosscurrents in Higher Education

If we mean to recapture our momentum and press forward as a nation, we can not afford to respond to short-term fiscal problems by restricting educational opportunities and diluting the talents of the very people on whom our future progress ultimately depends.

DEREK C. BOK, "The President's Report,"
Harvard University Gazette, March 1982

Make no mistake about it: there is in this country a crisis of confidence in the public schools and the teachers who are so widely blamed for the poor state of the schools.

HARRY JUDGE, *American Graduate Schools of Education:
A View from Abroad*, 1982

We all stand together on the threshold of a potentially historic rededication of our collective democratic belief in the importance of education and in our respect for those who deliver it. We seek the reform of teaching in ways to make it a genuine profession, a profession charged with no less than the shaping of human beings. The stakes are high.

JONAS F. SOLTIS, *Reforming Teacher Education:
The Impact of the Holmes Group Report*, 1987

THE EXPANSION OF
HIGHER EDUCATION

Developments in higher education have been closely related to the main currents in American political and social history. Certainly conditions shift from time to time, and the colleges and universities, reflecting the demands of each age, have adapted their programs to the changing social order. The remarkable rise of the United States' modern universities, for example, coincided with the emergence of Darwinism, and curricular revisions and faculty appointments (and dismissals) quite naturally reflected the post–Civil War ferment in evolutionary thought.

American colleges and universities have also perpetuated a conception of liberal learning that differentiates higher education from other forms of schooling. Through an endless search for the whole truth, higher education, at least in an ideal sense, is bound by a tradition of profound scholarship that seeks to clarify and expand humankind's cultural heritage.

The Pioneer Statesmen

The extraordinary growth and expansion of higher education after the Civil War stemmed in large part from the statesmanship of a small group of university presidents and from the massive financial resources these leaders were able to tap. These men were often skilled administrators with great philosophical breadth. Most notable was President Eliot of Harvard. Much older, but also fully responsive to the currents of the age, was Frederick A. P. Barnard, president after 1864 at Columbia. Equally prominent were such newly appointed presidents as James McCosh of Princeton (1868), Andrew Dickson White, first president of Cornell (1868), James Burrill Angell of Michigan (1871), Noah Porter of Yale (1871), John Bascom of Wisconsin (1874), and Daniel Coit Gilman, first president of Johns Hopkins (1875). Critical of their own narrow training, these leaders were also familiar with European developments. According to a prevailing custom of American scholars, most of them had studied or traveled abroad, and all except McCosh (a Scot from the University of Edinburgh) had been educated in New England. Their aim, however, was not to copy European patterns or to preserve New England traditions; they sought instead to adapt an evolving system of higher education to a changing society.

The reorganization of Tulane in 1884 and the opening of Chicago and Stanford, both in the early 1890s, were other manifestations of the remarkable growth and expansion of higher education in the United States. In 1870, for example, 67,350 men plus a small number of women were enrolled in American colleges and universities; two decades later this figure had risen to 156,756; by 1910 the total enrollment in higher education had reached 355,215. This acceleration paralleled the tremendous growth in the secondary schools, which were sending a large percentage of their students to the colleges and universities. So swift, indeed, were the great changes in higher education in the decades following Appomattox that Woodrow Wilson urged his colleagues and the nation in 1896 to hold on to past ideals and values. "We have broken with the past and have come into a new world," declared Wilson, then professor of jurisprudence and political economy at Princeton.

> Can any one wonder, then, that I ask for the old drill, the old memory of times gone by, the old schooling in precedent and tradition, the old keeping of faith with the past, as a preparation for leadership in days of social change? We have not given science too big a place in our education; but we have made a perilous mistake in giving it too great a preponderance in method in every branch of study. We must make the humanities human again; must recall what manner of men we are; must turn back once more to the region of practicable ideals.[1]

By the close of the century, American higher education had entered another age: the period of the college had passed, and a new era of the multipurpose university was beginning.[2]

In contrast to the eighteenth- and early nineteenth-century colleges, the emerging universities were too large to be overly concerned with any single sectarian purpose. The new-style university presidents were astute and experienced men of affairs. They encouraged the scientific discoveries of the age by welcoming into the curricula new knowledge, which included at this time Darwin's theory of evolution. Although these men were not antidenominational, they did tend to foster those elements of academic life that deemphasized sectarianism in higher education.

During his early years at Cornell, for example, President Andrew Dickson White took a firm stand on academic freedom and became embroiled in some bitter controversies with the local pastors, who accused him and the faculty of being "atheistic" and "demoniac." At the time, the Cornell students, in a satirical vein, added fuel to the lively discussions by forming in 1873 a "YMHA" ("Young Men's Heathen Association"). When Felix Adler was appointed professor of Hebrew literature and history the following year, a ludicrous and confusion-ridden situation developed, attracting widespread and potentially dangerous (for Adler) publicity.[3] Young, handsome, and highly gifted, Adler quickly became the most popular lecturer on campus, especially among the Ithaca ladies. Finally, after a hectic two-year appointment, he was "quietly dropped" by the trustees. He returned to New York City, where, happily, he became famous for his work with the Ethical Culture Society.

Basic to the growth and expansion of higher education after 1865 were the donations of millions of dollars by philanthropists. Before the Civil War the largest gift to Columbia was $20,000. The famous Yale Report of 1828 mentioned that the total contributions received by the college since its founding amounted to less than $300,000 from all sources. The highest gift to Princeton during an alumni drive in the 1830s was a donation of $5,000. In 1831 Stephen Girard's bequest of $2 million to found a boys' school in Philadelphia was so unusual that Girard was branded an eccentric.

This picture, however, changed after the Civil War. Enormous gifts not only became a general trend in American philanthropy; they were also expected and zealously sought by university administrators. New universities were sometimes endowed by a single philanthropist. In 1865, for example, Ezra Cornell, who made a fortune from investments in Western Union Telegraph Company, donated $500,000 to found a university in Ithaca, New York. Similarly, in 1873, Cornelius Vanderbilt, the railroad magnate, endowed Vanderbilt University in Nashville, Tennessee.

Three years later Johns Hopkins University opened in Baltimore because a wealthy Quaker merchant and railroad director had donated investments valued at the then unprecedented sum of $3,500,000. Before Hopkins died in December 1873, he had bequeathed the principal part of his massive fortune for the establishment of both a university and a hospital. The university was ready for graduate students in 1876, but the hospital was not opened until 1889. By the fall of 1893, a medical school was organized and also prepared to begin.

Johns Hopkins's bequest in the 1870s led to a new and different type of American university. At the very time President Eliot was launching his elective system at Harvard, President Daniel Coit Gilman was beginning another educational experiment in Baltimore.[4] Gilman, unrestricted concerning the type of institution to be built with Hopkins's money, proposed a university modeled after the European pattern. Instead of starting with the traditional college as the basis for an evolving university, Gilman wanted to begin by appointing a faculty of scholars—"a strong staff of young men"— who would then develop a graduate center of research. Gilman, in fact, was completely free to do whatever he thought necessary to attract the ablest scholars and to create for them a university atmosphere in the European sense of the term. An adequate library, foremost in Gilman's plan, was to be developed first; next, the professional schools and graduate divisions would be added as funds became available; and, finally, as an appendage (if, indeed, at all), an undergraduate college would be built later. "I see no advantage,"

Gilman remarked, "in our attempting to maintain the traditional four-year class system of the American colleges."[5]

Although he did not recommend the admission of women, Gilman did propose that a separate women's college, linked with Johns Hopkins and similar to Girton College at Cambridge University, be established. Largely through the efforts of a feminist benefactor, women were finally admitted to Johns Hopkins for graduate study in 1907.

Gilman's proposal aimed toward a broad foundation for graduate training. "The object of the university is to develop character—to make men," Gilman declared.

> It misses its aim if it produces learned pedants, or simple artisans, or cunning sophists, or pretentious practitioners. Its purport is not so much to impart knowledge to the pupils, as to whet the appetite, exhibit methods, develop powers, strengthen judgment, and invigorate the intellectual and moral forces. It should prepare for the service of society a class of students who will be wise, thoughtful, and progressive guides in whatever department of work or thought they may be engaged.

Gilman hoped that this new type of university, founded with the profits from private enterprise and freed from church or state control, would have a unique opportunity for the pursuit of truth and the discovery of new knowledge. "If we would maintain a university, great freedom must be allowed both teachers and scholars," he insisted.

> This involves freedom of methods to be employed by the instructors on the one hand, and, on the other, freedom of courses to be selected by the students. But this freedom is based on laws, two of which cannot be too distinctly or too often enunciated. A law which should govern the admission of pupils is this, that before they win this privilege they must have been matured, by the long preparatory discipline of superior teachers, and by the systematic, laborious, and persistent pursuit of fundamental knowledge; and a second law, which should govern the work of professors, is this, that, with unselfish devotion to the discovery and advancement of truth and righteousness, they renounce all other preferment, so that, like the greatest of all teachers, they may promote the good of mankind.[6]

With a decade after its opening in 1876, Johns Hopkins University was being recognized as the most notable institution of its kind in the United States.

With a doctoral program and a faculty drawn primarily from Europe, Gilman's experiment produced some of the nation's ablest intellectual leaders. When the newly established state universities in the West also began emphasizing the importance of research, American scholars no longer had to go to Europe to pursue advanced work. In 1850, according to President Ira Remsen, Gilman's successor at Johns Hopkins, there were only eight graduate students in the entire United States; twenty-five years later this number had increased to 399; and by the turn of the century, there were 5,668 students enrolled in American graduate schools. The new Ph.D. degree, copied from the German model, was becoming a goal of every young scholar.

The Emphasis on Research

This growing emphasis on research, introduced by Gilman at Johns Hopkins, was a concomitant of the whole university idea. Without research the endeavors of a graduate-oriented institution would be severely limited. There would be little or no pursuit of the whole truth which the excitement of research encourages.

Research, with its necessary adjunct, publication, became guiding criteria for faculty tenure and promotion. By 1900, for example, those professors at the University of Pennsylvania who focused their time and energy on teaching instead of research were advised in writing to seek appointments elsewhere.[7] The prestige of the academic world was being reserved for those whose eminence was known, not through excellence in teaching, but rather from the quality (and quantity) of their articles and books. This new cycle in academic life overshadowed the importance of teaching in higher education and led to the founding of learned societies, the issuing of scholarly journals, and the rapid professionalization of American scholarship.

In 1877 Johns Hopkins University launched the *American Journal of Mathematics,* followed by a long line of Hopkins journals in such areas as biology, chemistry, philology, and psychology. When Hopkins required in 1888 that all doctoral dissertations be published, the Johns Hopkins University Press became a full-scale operation, marking another first of its kind in the United States. By the turn of the century, the University of Chicago Press was turning out annually over one hundred thousand copies of journals in such diverse fields as astrophysics, classics, geology, Hebrew, political economy, sociology, and theology. The journals of the newly formed learned societies also provided major outlets for the publication of monographs and research findings.

Such pioneer societies as the American Academy of Arts and Sciences (1780) and the American Association for the Advancement of Science (1848) were general organizations and comprehensive in scope; the new scholars, however, were research specialists and tended to group according to fields of learning. The American Philological Association appeared first in 1869, followed by the organization of the American Chemical Society (1877), the Modern Language Association (1883), the American Historical Association

(1884), the American Economic Association (1885), the American Mathematical Society (1888), the Geological Society of America (1888), the American Psychological Association (1892), the American Philosophical Association (1901), and the American Sociological Society (1905). (The highly specialized interests of scholars were even finding expression in such subdivided interest groups as the American Society for Church History [1888] and the American Irish Historical Association [1897].) The founding of the American Association of University Professors in 1915, designed to promote higher standards of teaching and research and to protect academic freedom, was another indication of the growing professionalization of scholarship in the United States.

One result of this flurry of organization, research, and publication has been to narrow a scholar's interest down to the investigation of minutiae. While the learned societies have stimulated many worthwhile endeavors and have helped to eliminate the isolation of scholars, the growing specialization of research has also tended to fragment the disciplines and to separate learning from the wider context in which the meaningful discovery of knowledge occurs.

But one must not minimize the function of distinguished research in a university; neither should one overlook the contributions some scholars have made to the advancement and security of American society. Research has indeed become a matter of grave national concern. The difficult challenge confronting a university scholar is one of meeting successfully two demands: the imperative for teaching excellence and the sustaining and equally important necessity for research of lasting value.

This challenge poses a serious dilemma for American higher education. With the tremendous growth of federal and philanthropic support, research has obviously become an enticing alternative in any choice of teaching *or* research. Scholars in growing numbers are involved in gigantic research projects; some maintain university connections on nominal bases only, while pursuing time-consuming projects that involve frequent travel to distant places. The trend is toward large-scale research (supported by immense grants) at so-called centers, operated by teams of scholars and other personnel. A net result, of course, has been to deemphasize even further the teaching function of university scholars. It does not follow, however, that a greater stress on research necessarily detracts from teaching effectiveness; on the contrary, not only should a scholar's research advance the frontiers of knowledge but ideally it should also result in a stronger command of a special teaching field. The current irony is that the most gifted scholar is frequently being moved, voluntarily or not, away from the college classroom where his or her contribution is so vitally needed.

There is also a trend toward the support of utilitarian scholarship that stresses some problem-solving type of project. Historians, for instance, have privately admitted "dressing up" research proposals with certain "gimmicks" in order to obtain grants.[8] This has raised the far more serious question of outside "control" over the nature and direction of research—an issue that is being discussed behind the scenes by scholars and university officials.

According to Donald Kennedy, president of Stanford University, good teaching was too often undervalued. "It is time for us to reaffirm that education—that is, teaching in all its forms—is the primary task, and that our society will judge us in the long run on how well we do it," Kennedy said in a speech in 1990. Too many courses were taught by temporary faculty members who were undercompensated and unappreciated and who had strong teaching records—junior faculty who "fail at the tenure lines too often." Kennedy stated that Stanford University, renowned as a research university, should be superb at both teaching *and* research. He asserted that academic officials at Stanford were developing a strategy to elevate the status of teaching.[9]

Foundation Philanthropy
and Corporate Support
Foundation subsidies and corporate gifts have indeed brought unusual strength to organized research. Immense funds are being granted to higher education for research purposes.

The 1950s and 1960s in particular, witnessed new activity in philanthropic enterprise. The mammoth Ford Foundation, the largest philanthropic organization in American history, launched its colossal grant-giving programs after World War II. Created by the foundation in 1951 to handle its educational donations, the Fund for the Advancement of Education stimulated a variety of innovations. While other organizations also made contributions to American colleges and universities, donations from the Fund overshadowed all other philanthropy. About 90 percent of all funds granted by the Ford Foundation went to universities, colleges, schools, and community organizations in the United States. In fact, $744 million went to proposals in education at all levels during the 1950s. In 1965 alone, a total of $164.5 million was committed to new educational projects. With assets valued at almost $6 billion still in its accounts in 1990, the Ford Foundation's support of research in the decades ahead promises some noteworthy developments.

As was previously noted, the public image of organized business and industry has changed markedly since the early 1930s. Attitudes of suspicion and open hostility have gradually given way to new feelings of respect for business leadership and responsibility. This shift was due in large part to the enormous success of the costly free-enterprise campaign. Nowhere was this victory more clearly evident than in the close business-education cooperation that emerged after World War II.

One of the most significant manifestations of this new era of cooperation and goodwill has been the generous financial assistance given to higher
education by big business. In February 1957, Frank W. Abrams, who was
chairman of the board of Standard Oil Company of New Jersey from 1946 to
1953, estimated that corporate support of higher education by the end of
1956 had reached $100 million a year. This figure agreed with a survey
conducted by the Council for Financial Aid to Education, Inc., a nonprofit
organization established in 1953 by businesspeople and educators to encourage greater financial support of American colleges and universities. A pioneer
in the postwar movement of corporate aid to higher education, Abrams
believed that corporations had certain responsibilities of citizenship just as do
individuals. For example, argued Abrams in 1957, "if individuals are under
obligation to support their school systems, why not corporations?"[10] Irving
S. Olds of United States Steel, Alfred P. Sloan of General Motors, Clarence
B. Randall of Inland Steel, and Eugene Holman of Standard Oil Company of
New Jersey were voicing the same idea. "Social responsibility is no longer an
ideal to be hoped for in business circles," wrote Randall, "but a working
philosophy that is widely practiced."[11] The whole idea of corporate assistance
to higher education was being widely urged by business spokespersons as a
necessary step toward a creative free society.[12] By 1988–1989 total corporate
aid to private colleges and universities amounted to $791 million, while
public institutions of higher education received $855 million in corporate
gifts.

The Land-Grant Concept

A major factor in the rise of state universities in the United States was the
generous gifts of land made by the federal government to the states under the
terms of the historic Land-Grant Act of 1862, sponsored by Congressman
Justin S. Morrill of Vermont. In return for a land subsidy equal to thirty
thousand acres for each representative and senator in its congressional delega-
tion, a state was to establish within five years at least one college that,
"without excluding other scientific and classical studies, and including
military tactics," would "teach such branches of learning as are related to
agriculture and the mechanic arts."[13] The Morrill Act also provided that
should any of the land granted to the states be sold, the principal had to be
reserved as a perpetual endowment and only the interest used. However, 10
percent of the land-grant fund might be spent for the purchase of experimental farms or a college site. Any depletion in the fund would have to be filled
by the states through legislative appropriations. "The fundamental idea,"
explained Morrill in 1888, "was to offer an opportunity in every State for a
liberal and larger education to larger numbers, not merely to those destined
to sedentary professions, but to those much needing higher instruction for
the world's business, for industrial pursuits and professions of life."[14]

Justin Morrill was a self-educated Vermonter who believed strongly in utilitarian training for the common person. His intent was to democratize higher education so that anyone who wanted a "practical" college course would have an opportunity to pursue it. "Being myself the son of a hardfisted blacksmith, ..." he declared, "I could not overlook mechanics in any measure intended to aid the industrial classes in the procurement of an education that might exalt their usefulness."[15] Morrill's proposal was the first successful attempt in American higher education to combine a strictly vocational-type curriculum with programs in the liberal arts.[16]

The Morrill Act initiated an epoch-making policy of federal aid to education, not only in the West but also in the older states. Under the terms of the measure, the proceeds from the sale of 17,430,000 acres were turned over to the land-grant colleges and state universities. Ultimately this amounted to a total of $7,545,405. A glaring defect in the original law was Congress's failure to specify a minimum price per acre below which the land could not be sold; finally, in 1889, an amendment set a $10 minimum per acre. In the meantime, before the amendment was passed, the average yield per acre was only $1.65. Lands in Rhode Island were sold for as little as $.41 per acre. The highest return per acre in any state was attained in New York, where the price reached $6.73. This variation in price was due more to the careless manner in which the transactions were handled than to the actual value of the lands.

Those land-grant colleges that did not benefit substantially under the original measure were aided by another Morrill Act passed in 1890. Through implementation of a "matching dollars" concept, the second act provided appropriations annually and stimulated the state legislatures to do the same. No grant was to be made to a state that denied admission to its land-grant college because of an applicant's race; however, such an education could be provided in "separate but equal" institutions. Also, in contrast with the law of 1862, the Second Morrill Act specified in greater detail the exact subject areas for which the annual federal grants could be used. Any state that failed to adhere to such federal criteria would not receive a monetary grant. This "matching dollars" idea has remained a strong federal principle. Additional support to the land-grant colleges was also provided by the Nelson Amendment of 1907 and the Bankhead-Jones Act of 1935.

Not only did the Morrill Act of 1862 lead to the creation of new land-grant colleges but the funds made available under the terms of the act were often used to strengthen the older universities as well. Some states added the funds to preexisting university endowments. In New York, for example, the land-grant funds were used constructively toward the development of Cornell University. In those states where no tax-supported university had been established, the land-grant college became the state's first experiment in public higher education. Some used the grant to found single state universities, while other states preferred to establish separate colleges of agriculture and engineering. After a state had accepted a college or university as a financial responsibility, the legislature usually continued to support the institution through regular appropriations. Thus the Morrill Acts not only laid the foundation for a new type of curriculum at government expense but also provided powerful incentives for greatly extended state programs of higher education.

THE IMPROVEMENT OF PROFESSIONAL EDUCATION

Perhaps the most significant transformation in higher education occurred in the professional areas of medicine, law, and teaching. By modern criteria, professional education prior to the twentieth century was sadly deficient. For decades professional preparation was mainly under an apprenticeship system. The emphasis was strictly empirical, with little or no systematic rationale for strengthening professional skills. Even in the more formal type of training offered in the first professional schools, the orientation was usually brief and of poor quality.

Before the Civil War, medical education, in particular, was plagued by low standards, the influence of profit-making institutions, and rudimentary equipment. Schools were devoid of laboratory facilities and hospital affiliations. There were no admission requirements: all a person had to do in order to enroll in a medical school was simply to register his name and pay a fee. Tuition was paid directly to the instructors, most of whom were practicing doctors. Even at Harvard, which had one of the best medical schools in the nation, a student was required to take only two lecture courses for a winter term that was not quite four months in length; then he was awarded an M.D. degree, if his total medical experience amounted to three years and if he passed a brief oral test. As late as 1870, written examinations were not given at Harvard because the students could not express themselves coherently. Many, in fact, "could barely read and write."[17]

It was this lax state of affairs that President Eliot denounced soon after assuming the presidency of Harvard in 1869. In his first annual report, he assailed the low standards in medicine, labeling the medical school the poorest one in the university and demanding a "thorough reformation" of "the whole system of medical education in this country." Supported by Dr. Oliver Wendell Holmes, Eliot insisted that medical students attend the university for a three-year period, with classes closely related to laboratory and clinical experience. Students were also required to pass annual written examinations before being allowed to progress in the three-year sequence, and to pass all subjects before being awarded degrees. Eliot turned the whole system "over like a flapjack," remarked Dr. Holmes in 1871. "There never was such a *bouleversement* as that in our Medical Faculty."[18]

Despite Eliot's enthusiasm and vigorous leadership, his progressive ideas on medical education spread very slowly. Not until 1893, for example, when the Johns Hopkins University Medical School opened, was the practice of requiring a bachelor's degree for admission even begun. A general upgrading of medical education was delayed until after the turn of the century.

In 1904, according to a survey conducted by the newly reorganized American Medical Association (AMA), there were at least 166 "medical schools" in the United States. The following year AMA established a Council on Medical Education to investigate the entire situation and to recommend some criteria for medical training. Meanwhile, complaints and condemnations of medical practices continued to mount. One physician, for example, reported to the American Academy of Medicine that the profession was filled with "a vast number of incompetents, large numbers of moral degenerates; crowds of pure tradesmen, blatant demagogues; hospitals organized and conducted to the damage of profession, patient, and people."[19] Finally, in 1910, the publication of the revealing and highly influential Flexner Report, financed by the Carnegie Foundation for the Advancement of Teaching, produced the first large-scale reformation of United States medical schools. [20]

Abraham Flexner's scathing report on medical education is a landmark in the history of professional education. His proposed changes, coincident with the progressive movement, drew strong support from the same reformers who were already rebelling against exploitation and graft.[21] Using the "unexcelled" and "practically ideal" medical facilities of Johns Hopkins University as models, Flexner critically examined the condition of other medical schools in the nation. His shocking assessment soon instituted some long-overdue reforms. Flexner, in fact, proposed that all except thirty-one of the then existing medical schools in the United States be abolished. A number of schools were actually eliminated, and some of the better ones were strengthened.

Flexner's findings underscored over and over again that medical research and teaching desperately needed strong financial support. Published at a fortuitous time, his revelations in 1910 deeply interested John D. Rockefeller and the members of the General Education Board that administered Rockefeller's philanthropic grants. Rockefeller, in fact, had already established in 1901 an Institute for Medical Research in New York City. In 1912, Frederick T. Gates, one of Rockefeller's closest associates, communicated with Flexner, who was completing another project on medical education in Germany and France.

"I have read your 'Bulletin Number Four' from beginning to end. It is not only a criticism; it is also a program," Gates remarked.

"It was intended, Mr. Gates, to be both," replied Flexner, "for you will remember that it contains two maps: one showing the location and number of medical schools in America today; the other showing what, in my judgment, would suffice if medical schools were properly endowed and conducted."[22]

From this and subsequent conferences between Flexner and Gates evolved a quick and masterful plan to upgrade medical education in the United States. Gates was a man of action who wasted few words on preliminary details. "He had imagination, daring, and an intuitive sense of educational strategy," Flexner recalled. "He had no patience with small things unless he could foresee an important and large outcome." First of all, Johns Hopkins University ("the one ideal medical school in America," Flexner told Gates) was to be transformed into a leading institution to stand as both stimulus and model for improving other centers. At the same time, Rockefeller's millions would also be used to subsidize "full-time" medical staff salaries. This would help to eliminate what Flexner considered to be a major root of medical education's ills: the professional tradition of dividing time, money, and loyalties between outside practices and clinical teaching. So demanding, in fact, were Flexner and Gates on this point that the General Education Board required institutional recipients to sign contracts stating that this requirement of "full-time" service would be followed. (The policy was eventually changed, however, after some heated exchanges between university officials and physicians.)

Spurred on by Gates, Rockefeller donated to the General Education Board millions of dollars earmarked for medical education and research. From 1919 to 1921, for example, he gave to the board $45 million specifically for this purpose. The funds were used to improve medical education at leading universities across the nation. Millions were donated to Hopkins, Vanderbilt, Yale, the University of Chicago, and Washington University in St. Louis. In 1929, surveying the status of American medical education, the General Education Board was undoubtedly satisfied with the tremendous gains wrought by its donations: deciding to end the project, the members noted that the board's donations had literally primed the pump, reaping in philanthropic support approximately $100 million for medical education and research in the United States. By the end of the 1920s, the number of medical schools had been reduced to seventy-four, all of which were now subject to periodic inspection by the American Medical Association. Within an amazingly short period of time after Flexner's report and Rockefeller's philanthropy, the United States' vastly improved medical schools were moving forward to front-rank positions among the finest centers in the world.

Also noteworthy were the efforts to revise American legal education. Here again the leadership stemmed from Harvard, where in 1870 President

Eliot encouraged a small faculty of law to elect as their new dean Christopher C. Langdell. The total faculty, including Langdell, consisted of only four professors, who taught a total of 165 students. At the time, the method of legal study in the United States was nothing more than a system of learning by rote certain principles from a textbook. Influenced by Blackstone's *Commentaries on the Laws of England,* most law instructors before 1870 viewed their subject as a self-contained body of precepts, as a code of fixed rules, sustained by authority and stable for indefinite periods of time.

Dean Langdell proceeded from a fundamentally different conception. He treated the rules of law pragmatically, not as eternal principles, but rather as tentative hypotheses advanced to govern changing patterns of social behavior. He believed that law, like science, was inductive and that the method of legal training was like the method of science. A good scientist studies the sources; so, too, should a good lawyer study directly the sources of law. For Langdell, these sources were the printed cases of the appellate courts. These cases a student should study inductively; then, and only then, would he truly grasp *and be able to apply* basic legal principles.

Langdell and his colleague Oliver Wendell Holmes, Jr., appointed to the U.S. Supreme Court in 1902, were among the first to advance such an evolutionary interpretation of law. "I am certain from my own experience that Mr. Langdell is right," Holmes declared.

> I am certain that when your object is not to make a bouquet of the law for the public, nor prune and graft it by legislation, but to plant its roots where they will grow, in minds devoted henceforth to that one end, there is no way to be compared to Mr. Langdell's way. Why, look at it simply in the light of human nature. Does not a man remember a concrete instance more vividly than a general principle? And is not a principle more exactly and intimately grasped as the unexpressed major premise of the half-dozen examples which mark its extent and its limits than it can be in any abstract form of words? Expressed or unexpressed, is it not better known when you have studied embryology and lines of its growth than when you merely see it lying dead before you on the printed page?[23]

Such a relativist legal view, challenging the historical doctrine of natural law, contained some startling implications. If law evolved in relation to the changing needs of people and society, why should the present generation be denied a role in creating customs and mores? The answers to such a question could destroy the past absolutism expressed in natural law and even challenge the practice of judicial decision by legal precedent. The philosophical cleavage between the old and the new was sharp and explosive in Langdell's day; the clash continues on varied themes even to the present time.[24]

Langdell and Holmes were influenced by the philosophical ideas of the post–Civil War era. William James and Charles Peirce, for instance, were formulating their theories of pragmatism. James, Peirce, and Holmes were friends and members of the Metaphysical Club, a Boston philosophical society founded about 1870 to discuss some of the broad issues of the day. Langdell, Holmes, James, and Peirce were well-known figures in Cambridge when the Harvard faculties were a very small community of scholars. Developments in science and, above all, the ideas of Charles Darwin and Thomas Huxley were provocative topics, stimulating some lively debates and striking deep roots into American and European legal thought.

Strongly supported by President Eliot, Dean Langdell introduced the case method of legal study. Langdell assumed that law was worthy of teaching on the university level; if not, he wrote, legal training should be obtained, as in the past, through apprenticeships. Instead of memorizing a compendium of established rules and principles from texts and lectures, students would now be required to uncover and apply for themselves the rules of law that had evolved from judicial decisions. To master certain principles was only one aspect of legal training, Langdell insisted; "to apply them with constant facility and certainty to the ever-tangled skein of human affairs, is what constitutes a true lawyer."[25] Langdell's primary aim was to convert the study of law into an inductive analysis of outstanding cases.

There is little doubt that Langdell's method strengthened legal education. While it may have deemphasized some of the theoretical aspects of Anglo-American law, it did transform the passivity of textbook memorization into a serious methodology congruent with the realities of legal practice. By 1880, the Harvard Law School was using the case method exclusively. In subsequent decades, Langdell's method was also adopted by practically every other reputable law school in the nation.

During the very decades when the case method was reshaping legal pedagogy, the rationale that supported Langdell's approach was gradually weakened by the swiftly moving forces of social change. The case method was ideally suited to the courtroom business of the post–Civil War lawyer. Until the 1890s, law was chiefly a matter of courtroom interplays, of cases involving small businesses and personal clients. However, with the growth of corporations the foci shifted from the small practitioner to the metropolitan lawyer, from the courtroom attorney to the urban law firm and the highly paid business counsel. This transition was sharply accelerated by the rise of organized labor and the emergence of an immense federal hierarchy. Thus the case method, dealing almost exclusively with appellate decisions, became inadequate as an educational instrument for legal training. To see perceptively through the corporate maze and to deal with the legal intricacies of big business and labor, the law student needed, for example, a much broader understanding of the social milieu in which legal decisions evolved.

Legal pedagogy, responding to these shifts in focus, slowly changed. In a number of law schools, for instance, the legal realism of the corporate age was reflected in a greater emphasis on cases *and materials* that students began memorizing in a manner surprisingly reminiscent of pre-Langdell methodology. The current cross fire between law professors and practicing attorneys concerning the nature and direction of legal education is not unlike some of the heated controversies still being waged over the professional education of American teachers.

DEVELOPMENTS IN
TEACHER EDUCATION

Toward a Concept in Professionalization

An important key to professional improvement is the ability of a profession to regulate itself. State examining officials, associations of professional schools, and national professional organizations have all worked diligently in recent years to upgrade professional standards. The forceful AMA and the American Bar Association (ABA), for example, have long had special councils or committees charged with the responsibility for recommending requirements for admission into the ranks. Both organizations wield tremendous influence through powers of professional self-regulation.

Educators have learned, too, that public-school teaching must also possess strong powers of self-regulation in order to measure up completely to the criteria of a profession. This includes, specifically, a firm control over standards for admission into, or exclusion from, the teaching profession.

If teaching has not attained the professional strength characteristic of the AMA or the ABA, it is certainly not because teachers and administrators have refused to band together in groups. In fact, classroom teachers and educational administrators are typically "joiners." There are over five thousand local education associations in the United States; in addition, all fifty states have teachers' associations affiliated with the National Education Association (NEA), the largest professional organization in the world. Formed originally in 1857 as the National Teachers Association, and chartered by Congress in 1906, NEA today has a huge staff and a highly complex structure.[26] Through the Educational Policies Commission, one of its most important agencies, NEA has assumed a leadership role in American education since the 1930s.

An important development in the politics of public schooling was the gradual transformation of the NEA from an organization controlled by school administrators into a militant teachers' union. During the early 1960s, the NEA began using effectively the strike and collective bargaining that were successful tools of the influential local groups of the American Federation of

Teachers (AFT). Formed in 1916 as an AFL affiliate, AFT is another organization in the politics of education that is relatively small when compared to the NEA. By 1989 the AFT had about 680,000 members compared to NEA's total of 1,600,800. The AFT, however, has worked steadily to increase its membership by appealing to teachers in metropolitan areas. By 1989 NEA had increased its membership to over 1.9 million. Membership went up in all categories and increased 100,000 in one year, according to NEA officials. This increased membership combined with the growing militancy of NEA marked a different era in the historic relationship between teacher's groups and administrators of public education in the United States.

Fundamental to the development of teaching as a profession is a period of formal preparation that all professions require for fully qualified practitioners. Not only has the amount of preservice preparation for teaching been increased since the early days of the normal school; the content and quality of teacher education have also been vastly upgraded. Those who still cling to notions that an elementary schoolteacher requires less preparation than a secondary schoolteacher or that scholarly depth alone is sufficient to teaching in a modern high school are simply not informed.

Teaching success is contingent on a number of complex factors. Possession or attainment of the following constitutes a minimum preparation: (1) a cluster of positive personality components that every successful teacher possesses to some degree; (2) a broad background of general education deemed important for all citizens; (3) a specialization in depth in all subject areas that are to be taught; and (4) a range of professional competencies and skills necessarily acquired *before* admission into the ranks. Recognizing that this preparation demands an extended period of formal study and laboratory work, some state officials and local school boards now require that a beginning teacher also have a master's degree or at least a year of postgraduate training before receiving an initial appointment.

The conception of teaching as a profession was reinforced during the 1950s and early 1960s by a large-scale movement to improve teacher education and to raise standards for admission into the ranks. One factor that helped to create this climate for change was the heightening controversy over the professional preparation of teachers. The comments still range all the way from tones of disparagement and bitter scorn to constructive suggestions from a responsible citizenry.[27]

Perhaps the most widely publicized critique of all was James B. Conant's *The Education of American Teachers* (1963), which a few reviewers compared to Flexner's 1910 report on medical education. There was one similarity: both Flexner's report and Conant's work were subsidized by the Carnegie Foundation for the Advancement of Teaching. In the eyes of some educators, that was the only resemblance between the two studies. Conant's most controversial point was his proposal for almost complete institutional freedom and responsibility for developing programs in teacher education and for licensing candidates.[28] Professional educators in general were critical, pointing out, for instance, that Conant's recommendations actually raised more questions than they answered.[29]

Every profession is guided (or controlled) by a centrally organized group whose members seek to provide a unity of goals and direction. In medical education, this group is recognized as the AMA; in legal education, the ABA. In teacher education some believe that this power is now held by the National Council for Accreditation of Teacher Education (NCATE).

Beginning in 1923, accreditation of teacher education on a nationwide basis was first performed by the American Association of Teachers Colleges. In 1948 this organization merged with two other groups and formed the American Association of Colleges for Teacher Education (AACTE). By mid-century, of approximately 1,200 institutions involved in teacher education, only 246 had been accredited by the AACTE. With a small membership, AACTE's influence was severely limited and its policies and standards virtually impotent. In 1954 a newly established and more broadly based NCATE took over the task of accrediting all teacher-preparatory institutions in the United States.

Almost from the very beginning, there has been great turmoil surrounding the work of NCATE. Early opposition originated in colleges fearful of NCATE's structure. More highly publicized controversies have arisen from those colleges and universities denied accreditation by NCATE. The withholding of full accreditation from Carleton College and the University of Wisconsin, for example, stirred an angry debate in academic and professional circles.

Nevertheless, despite unfavorable publicity and bitter antagonisms, NCATE has continued to grow in professional stature. It seeks to improve teacher education through the "adoption of standards and continuing development of policies and procedures for accreditation."[30] On March 31, 1966, the National Commission on Accrediting officially recognized NCATE as "the sole agency" to accredit all teacher-education programs in American colleges and universities.

Regardless of one's philosophical stand, there is little doubt among enlightened practitioners and laypersons that the successful functioning of national accreditation might indeed be the most potent force yet devised for improving the professional preparation of American teachers.

The Carnegie Commission Report of 1986

A noteworthy plan to change teaching "from an occupation into a profession" was presented in *A Nation Prepared: Teachers for the 21st Century*, a 140-page report released in May 1986 by the Carnegie Forum on Education and the Economy. Created in January 1985 by the Carnegie Corporation, the forum tried to explore links between economic growth and the quality of the nation's schools. The report was drafted by a fourteen-member task force chaired by Lewis M. Branscomb, chief scientist and vice president of International Business Machines, Inc.[31] The final report charged that, as currently structured, American public schools are not prepared to provide workers for a growing technological society.

The task force report proposed the establishment of the first nationwide system of certifying elementary and secondary teachers. A new National Board for Professional Teaching Standards, scheduled to begin work by June 1987, would give practicing teachers, instead of state boards of education, primary responsibility for establishing standards of their own profession and determining who meets them. According to the Carnegie plan, prospective teachers could still be authorized to teach in public schools through current licensing procedures and would not be obligated to obtain credentials from the board. However, the Carnegie task force expressed hope that local school boards would give preference to board-certified teachers in hiring, salaries, and promotions. The new system would introduce a concept of differentiated credentials—a teaching certificate for beginning teachers and an advanced teaching certificate for those who demonstrated exceptional skills. This would replace or supplement the single license that previously existed in each state. "The goal is to put teaching on a par with law, medicine and other fields where members of the profession take responsibility for setting and maintaining high standards," declared David A. Hamburg, president of the Carnegie Corporation.

There were other significant changes proposed by the task force toward restructuring the nation's schools. "We do not believe the educational system needs repairing," asserted the task force. "We believe it must be rebuilt to match the drastic change needed in our economy if we are to prepare our children for productive lives in the 21st century." As a start, declaring that "four years of college education is not enough time to master the subjects to be taught and acquire the skills to teach them," the report called for the elimination of undergraduate programs in education and the transfer of formal training to the graduate level.

The new degree would be designed to "set a standard for the professional preparation of teachers." The task force did not clarify how long such a degree program would take, nor did it explain the content; the program, the task force wrote, would be "clinical" in nature. One possible model, for example, would include course work during the summer and paid "internships" and "residencies" in which students would work in laboratory schools under the supervision of excellent teachers in a procedure similar to the way medical students obtain clinical training in teaching hospitals.

The task force also suggested a new category of "lead teachers" selected from recommended experienced teachers in a school. In addition to teaching and supervision, some of these "lead teachers" would be requested to supervise beginning teachers and provide leadership in curriculum development. The task force argued that a full-time professional teacher should be considered a "manager" of many resources, such as paraprofessionals, retirees with expertise in subject matter, parent volunteers, and interns.

According to the task force, the current hierarchical system of managing schools would gradually be replaced by a partnership common in other professions. "Just as law firms are run by lawyers, so schools should be run by teachers," declared Marc S. Tucker, executive director. "Lead teachers" might choose to manage their school as a group with one person designated as a "managing teacher," or they might prefer to hire a nonteaching administrator. According to the suggested plan, the "lead teachers," while exercising some autonomy, would be responsible to the local school board to reach specified goals of student performance. "If they do well, the entire school staff might be rewarded, possibly by financial bonuses; if they do poorly, the school district should find new leaders." The task force noted that substantial increases in teacher salaries would be required to compete with other professions for capable people. "It should be obvious that this plan calls for teacher-compensation systems that will represent a significant departure from current practice for almost every school district in the nation." According to Bernard R. Gifford, dean of the school of education at the University of California at Berkeley, the Carnegie Commission Report of 1986 "is a powerful synthesis of the best ideas that stand some chance of improving public education." Added Governor Thomas H. Kean of New Jersey, a task force member: "All state policy leaders are going to have to react to this report."

The Holmes Group Report of 1986

Another significant attempt to reform teacher education in the United States is the Holmes Group Report entitled *Tomorrow's Teachers,* which appeared in 1986 shortly before the Carnegie Commission Report.[32]

A small group of education deans concerned with the quality of education in the United States conducted a series of meetings in 1983. From these meetings over a period of three years evolved the Holmes Group, which proposed a plan for a consortium and outlined a set of goals. The institutions whose deans are members of the Holmes Group are considered leading research institutions in their respective states and regions. The Holmes Group established five major goals for the reform of teacher education: (1) to make the education of teachers intellectually sound; (2) to recognize differences in knowledge, skill, and commitment among teachers; (3) to create honest standards of entry into the profession of teaching; (4) to connect schools of education with schools in the community; and (5) to make schools better places in which teachers can learn and work.

Both the Carnegie and the Holmes reports recommend abolishing undergraduate teacher preparation, a recommendation that led to much controversy and debate. The Holmes Group is especially critical of the bachelor's degree in education, especially for elementary school teachers. "These teachers are certified to teach all things to all children," the deans declare. "But few of them know much about anything, because they are required to know a little of everything. No wonder so many pupils arrive in high school so weak in so many subjects."

Both groups also view high-quality liberal arts education as an essential step toward the improvement of professional education for teachers. Both groups are also concerned with the qualities prospective teacher candidates must possess. The Holmes Group, for example, is especially blunt: "Competent teachers . . . possess broad and deep understanding of children, the subjects they teach, the nature of learning and schooling, and the world around them. They exemplify the critical thinking they strive to develop in students, combining tough-minded instruction with a penchant for inquiry."

The two reports have proposed little that is new: the issues have been debated repeatedly in professional journals and at national conferences. However, the publication of two reports in one year by two professionally important groups is especially noteworthy in the recent history of American education. Both have focused on key issues in public education and have brought the issues through the media into open debate.

ISSUES AND TRENDS

The issues that perplexed the nineteenth-century university presidents have increased in complexity and scope with the added stresses and strains of a swiftly changing and more affluent social order. The sprawling "multi-university" of the 1960s, 1970s, 1980s, and 1990s, for instance, with its unsolved problems, would stagger the imagination of even the most creative and talented educational statesperson. The priorities of national security forced leading universities to divert a large part of their resources and staff into military and space-age research, while cold-war tensions and conflicts posed new threats to academic freedom.

"With faculty in orbit, students out looking for their lost identity and administrators out setting off dynamite under foundation vaults—who is taking care?" asked James A. Perkins, president of Cornell University, in a lecture delivered in November 1965. The university president, answered Perkins. Any suggestion of a coalition of administrative officers, faculty members, and students leading a large university is absurd, he declared. The function of leadership, Perkins insisted, cannot be divided among such disparate elements of a giant enterprise. The university president of today has to be the key decision maker, a leader striving for academic consensus as a necessary shield against student dissension or outside interference.[33] Certainly not everyone would concur with Perkins regarding his conception of academic leadership, but his widely publicized views did draw attention to some of the heavy demands placed on a university president.

During the decades following World War II, almost every college and university in the United States faced a flood of highly qualified applicants in unprecedented requests for higher education. By 1960, for example, 3.6 million American students were actually enrolled in college and university degree programs. One factor, of course, was a general population upsurge, with a greatly increased secondary-school student body seeking postgraduate training. In 1940 about 34 percent of all high-school graduates were going to college. In 1965 college enrollments soared to 5.9 million students, which included by then 54 percent of the total high-school graduating classes in the nation. This trend was sharply reversed in the 1970s under the impact of growing inflation and a declining birthrate.[34]

Growth of the Junior or Community College

A recent development in higher education is the movement to establish junior colleges. The first public junior college was founded in Joliet, Illinois, in 1902. Five years later California passed a law permitting local school boards to offer for high-school graduates courses similar to those prescribed during the first two years of college. After World War I, the idea spread to other states. California, with the fastest population growth of the fifty states, has remained unquestionably a leader in the junior-college movement. Although variations exist in course offerings and patterns of financial support, the trend is toward publicly supported institutions, sometimes called "community colleges."

Most junior colleges have shifted their initial emphases from standard college offerings to more vocational-type curricula closely related to the needs of terminal students. Some, in fact, are building their total programs almost exclusively on a concept of adult education and are becoming cultural centers for the supporting communities.[35]

Junior-college enrollments have climbed steadily. By mid-century, 505 junior colleges were registering about 13 percent of the total enrollment in higher education. By 1987, according to the National Center for Education Statistics (NCES), about 4,776,222 students were enrolled in two-year junior colleges.

Organizational Changes

The overwhelming demand for higher education in the 1960s not only accelerated the junior-college movement but also led to the creation of some new and in some ways distinctly different institutions and programs.[36] From 1961 to 1965, in fact, a total of 146 new colleges and universities were founded in the United States.

Monteith College of Wayne State University in Detroit, for example, was an experimental attempt to develop a small autonomous college, with its own faculty and student body, *within* a larger university. The first steps toward implementing the Monteith idea were taken by a university committee in 1957. The following year, the Ford Foundation allocated to Wayne State University $725,000 to complete the planning stage and to help launch a totally new college. In September 1959 Monteith opened with a freshman class of 314 and a projected growth not to exceed 1,200. The small enrollment is similar to that of Wayne State, which draws its student body mainly from metropolitan Detroit and surrounding areas. Monteith students complete most of their work in the college and at the same time use the library and laboratory resources offered by the university. From its inception, Monteith has sought to maintain this "small-college atmosphere on a large university campus."[37] A strong supporting force seems to be the Monteith Center, which is a focal point for informal meetings and discussions. The center helps to give the Monteith commuting students a sense of identification and to fuse an otherwise disparate group into a small college unit.

Other examples of this attempt to operate a small, separate college in a larger campus environment were Justin S. Morrill College at Michigan State University in East Lansing, New College at Hofstra University on Long Island, New York, and the several residential colleges established at the University of California at Santa Cruz and at the University of the Pacific at Stockton, California. Classes were small, and tutorial instruction was planned as an integral part of the college programs. Each of these institutions enrolled from 250 to 1,200 students and like Monteith was patterned along the lines of an autonomous college-within-a-university framework.

For years a number of institutions have been offering instruction in college residence halls, usually by tutorial work or through resident faculty or visiting lecturers. Most of these programs were extracurricular and did not include regular course offerings. A noteworthy trend was to extend this concept beyond the informal arrangement by transforming typical residence halls into complete, self-contained centers of higher learning.

Michigan State University, for example, constructed eight coeducational "living-learning units." Approximately 1,200 students were housed in each unit, with men occupying one wing and women another. Each unit also contained twenty-four to thirty faculty offices and six to eight classrooms and laboratories. Grouped in complexes of three or four contiguous units, the residence halls shared such facilities as the library, auditoriums, multipurpose rooms, and conference areas.

The "House Plan" at Stephens College in Columbia, Missouri, was even more inclusive: four basic courses in general education were taught at Searcy Hall to which about one hundred first-year students were assigned. The plan involved five faculty members who participated completely and had no other responsibilities in the college. Four taught the courses, and one served as a residence hall counselor. With an office in the dormitory, each faculty member served as an adviser to one-fifth of the students.

A new "learning center" at Stephens College also attracted nationwide attention during the 1960s. Called the James Madison Wood Quadrangle, the center was actually a complex of four electronically equipped buildings grouped near a four-story "resources library." Included in the complex were a fine-arts center, a science hall, a multipurpose auditorium, a modern theater, an art gallery, an educational media workshop, a language laboratory, and several classrooms, study carrels, and faculty offices. The unusual feature of the quadrangle was a master communications system that disseminated information to any part of the campus. Programming, in fact, could originate, and be received, from almost anywhere in the college. The Florida Atlantic University at Boca Raton also developed an electronic center to serve as a core unit for the total instructional program.

Meanwhile, Oklahoma Christian College (OCC) at Oklahoma City opened the first completely electronic educational center in the United States. Each of OCC's 652 students was assigned to a small, separate study booth linked to a central computer. With over 700 booths ready for use, the college was installing 150 more annually until a planned capacity of over one thousand was reached.

In 1966 all students at Oklahoma Christian adhered to prearranged programs of tape-recorded lectures in required and elected courses from such fields as religion, English, literature, biology, mathematics, speech, German, music, art, typing, and shorthand. A student was expected to supplement an audio program with a workbook prepared by the same OCC instructor presenting the taped lecture. Consulting a mimeographed list of 136 recordings, a student simply flipped the switch on a cubicle 3½ by 4 feet, adjusted a headset, dialed a three-digit code number, and listened to a fifty-minute lecture via one of forty-six playback machines which operated daily from early morning until late at night.

Educators and businesspeople were just beginning to recognize the potential that this new power held for American schools and colleges. At educational conferences across the nation, there was a pervasive method of innovation and reform as these new technological developments in teaching and learning elicited widespread interest.

Student Unrest
Beneath the surface, however, all was not serene. An explosive dispute began over a seemingly minor incident at the University of California in Berkeley.

In September 1964 a campus official ordered students to remove their literature from tables on a strip of sidewalk near the university's main gate. Often used by student activists, the strip appeared to be off campus, and university restrictions on political activity were not applied to the area. On October 1, campus police arrested Jack Weinberg, a graduate student and active member of the Congress for Racial Equality (CORE). Students blocked the police car and would not allow it to move. The administration finally acquiesced and made an agreement that students hailed as a victory.

At the end of November, just when the dispute appeared settled, the university's Board of Regents summoned four student leaders to answer charges that they had committed acts of violence during the October demonstration. On December 1, in an ultimatum, the student leaders gave the regents twenty-four hours to drop their charges. When the regents failed to answer, students surrounded Sproul Hall, the administration building.

Mario Savio, twenty-four years of age and a student of philosophy, climbed to the top of a police car and spoke to an estimated six thousand spectators. He denounced the university as a machine that treats students like raw material. "It becomes odious, so we must put our bodies against the gears, against the wheels . . . and make the machine stop until we're freed." His address sparked the rise of the Free Speech Movement (FSM), and Savio became its popular spokesman. [38]

While folk singer Joan Baez sang "We Shall Overcome," about one thousand people marched into Sproul Hall and organized a "free university" inside the building. The police arrested 814 persons; when 590 were released on bail, members of the faculty arrived and took most of them home. On December 3, a student strike occurred, and more than half the university's classes did not meet. On December 7, President Clark Kerr addressed approximately eighteen thousand people in the outdoor Greek Theater.

The following day the faculty convened and after a long debate broadcast to students listening outside the auditorium, voted to place no restrictions on free speech. On March 8, 1965, the administration and faculty appointed a "Select Committee on Education" under the chairmanship of Professor Charles Muscatine of the English Department. [39] The FSM appeared to be the victor, but in the end, no one really won. The chancellor and President Kerr were forced to leave, and the new university administration did not please the campus militants.

There were several explanations for the rise of the Free Speech Movement, and no one is certain as to the exact cause. In retrospect, the regents' attempted reprisal was probably a tactical error. "Freedom of speech on campus must be fully protected, not only from attacks from without but also from within. This is fundamental," declared Clark Kerr, recalling the events of 1964. [40] Student unrest was not a new phenomenon. Some of the rights that students were demanding at Berkeley were freedoms others had already demanded and won elsewhere. Certainly the civil rights movement encouraged college students in the United States to take deliberate action against repression.

Many observers blamed the University of California whose structure was so large that it confused and perhaps alienated both students and faculty. The disorder was aggravated by the university's slow, complex decision-making process, which allowed one administrator to overrule another. The university, of course, survived the turmoil, but its reputation for academic excellence was severely tarnished.

After 1965, campus disturbances at Berkeley continued and spread, and Governor Ronald Reagan of California cut the university's budget requests, harassed campus officials, and antagonized students. Many distinguished professors resigned, and Berkeley became the symbol of student power. The uproar continued through the late 1960s, with major disturbances at Cornell University, San Francisco State College, Columbia University, and in 1970, at Kent State University. The college campus, declared student leaders, had become a sanctuary from the political and social realities of the outside world.

During the 1960s, opposition to the Vietnam War was intense among students in colleges and universities. Increasingly violent demonstrations were mounted against the war. Police and the National Guard were called in to quell the disorders, which culminated in the tragic deaths of four students in 1970 at Kent State University when they were fired on by National Guard troops.

The unrest slackened as the United States withdrew from the war, but the turmoil raised the classic issue of academic freedom. In Western civilization the concept probably had its first champion in Socrates, who, dedicated to the belief that the pursuit of truth has no boundaries, died rather than renounce this ideal. For American colleges and universities, academic freedom is inseparable from the larger concept of intellectual liberty in a republic. Incessantly the question arises: in the interest of social stability, how much difference of opinion is desirable, how much heterodoxy is permissible?

The U.S. Supreme Court and
Affirmative Action in Higher Education

One of the most difficult problems in the recent history of higher education is that of "reverse discrimination," which surfaced in 1971. After the University of Washington Law School refused to admit a white applicant, he charged that he was denied admission because of the preferential treatment and the reservation of places for less qualified minority students. Marco

DeFunis, Jr., claimed that this constituted denial to him of the equal protection of the laws under the Fourteenth Amendment.[41]

A lower court ordered DeFunis's admission to the law school, but the Washington Supreme Court reversed the lower court. In April 1974, the U.S. Supreme Court declared the case moot on the grounds that regardless of its decision, the student would graduate in June, having completed the law school program while the courts were arguing the case. A minority of four justices protested that the constitutional issues should have been decided. Justice William Brennan, for example, predicted that the legal issues posed by *DeFunis* would soon confront the Court again: "Few constitutional questions in recent history have stirred as much debate, and they will not soon disappear. They must inevitably return to the federal courts and ultimately again to this Court."

Among those watching the *DeFunis* case closely was Allan Bakke, who was planning to file suit to gain entry to the University of California Medical School at Davis, on grounds similar to those advanced by Marco DeFunis. When the U.S. Supreme Court agreed to hear the case, *Bakke* became the successor case to *DeFunis* that Justice Brennan had anticipated.

Few Supreme Court cases in American history attracted the attention of the public as did *Regents of the University of California* v. *Bakke.*[42] During the months before the decision, the case was often compared to *Brown* v. *Board of Education,*[43] the landmark decision in which the Court declared that segregation in public schools deprived minority schoolchildren of equal protection of the laws guaranteed them by the Fourteenth Amendment to the U.S. Constitution.[44] *Bakke* became a rallying point for individuals and organizations who hoped the Court would legally resolve controversial issues on which there appeared to be no national consensus. The decision announced by the Supreme Court on June 28, 1978, tried to determine when voluntary measures intended to remedy the present effects of past race-conscious actions may actually take race into account.

The most noteworthy, and most confusing, aspect of the *Bakke* decision was its lack of unanimity. No single opinion represented the views of a majority of the Court. Six separate opinions were published, two of which were supported by four justices each. The crucial vote was cast by Justice Lewis Powell, whose separate opinion agreed in part with certain points of the two major opinions, although Powell used a different reason to reach his conclusions.

This split among the justices on the Court led to one 5–4 majority that found the "affirmative action" program at the University of California at Davis illegal and ordered Allan Bakke admitted to its medical school. By another 5–4 majority, the Court held that some forms of race-conscious admissions procedures are constitutional. Although these conclusions were supported by five justices, none of the justices' reasoning was accepted by more than four. Consequently, it was not possible to predict how the Supreme Court would decide when it was presented with different facts in similar cases.

The facts of the *Bakke* case were essential to an understanding of the final decision. The medical school at the University of California at Davis opened in 1968 with an entering class of fifty students. The procedures of the Admissions Committee for the first year resulted in an entering class with no Mexican-Americans, no American Indians, and no blacks. During the following two years, the faculty tried to develop a special admissions program to permit the participation of minority students. The size of the entering class was doubled in 1971, and sixteen of the one hundred places were reserved for disadvantaged applicants selected by a special Admissions Committee. In practice, "disadvantaged" candidates meant minority applicants.

Allan Bakke, a white male, applied to the Davis Medical School for admission in 1973 and again in 1974. He was rejected both times. Bakke brought suit in a California state court, contending that minority candidates with lower grade averages and test scores were admitted under the school's special program. He asserted that he had been discriminated against because of his race when he was not allowed to compete for the sixteen reserved seats and argued that the school's special two-track admissions system violated the equal protection clause of the Fourteenth Amendment to the U.S. Constitution, a similar clause in the California Constitution, and Title VI of the Civil Rights Act of 1964.[45] The California Supreme Court affirmed the lower court's ruling that the two-track admissions program did indeed violate the federal Constitution and ordered the medical school to admit Bakke.

Before the case was argued in the U.S. Supreme Court, hundreds of graduate schools, civil rights groups, and other organizations filed over sixty *amicus curiae* briefs.[46] Several briefs argued that facts favorable to minority groups were not being presented by either Bakke or the university, and stated that the case should be returned to the California courts so that more facts could be ascertained. These briefs notwithstanding, the Supreme Court went ahead with the case and issued its opinion on June 28, 1978.

Justice John Paul Stevens, joined in his opinion by Justice Potter Stewart, Justice William Rehnquist, and Chief Justice Warren Burger, ruled that the Davis Medical School had violated Title VI. These four justices interpreted Title VI to mean that race cannot be the basis for excluding anyone from participation in a federally funded program. Because the medical school had admitted that Bakke was excluded because of his race, these justices voted to order the medical school to admit Bakke. However, Justice Stevens did not elaborate, stating that it was "perfectly clear that the question whether race can ever be used as a factor in an admissions decision is not an issue in this case, and the discussion of that issue is inappropriate."

Another group of four justices, William Brennan, Byron White,

Thurgood Marshall, and Harry Blackmun (referred to as the Brennan group) voted to reverse the entire lower court decision. They believed that both Title VI and the Fourteenth Amendment would permit the university to take voluntary race-conscious steps, even granting numerically based racial preferences, whenever the program was designed to remedy the effects of past discrimination. These four justices did not consider it important, for this purpose, whether or not the university had previously discriminated. The Brennan group would uphold race-conscious remedies as long as there is reason to believe that minorities are still handicapped by past discrimination.

Justice Lewis Powell did not align himself with either bloc of justices. In one instance, he agreed with Justice Stevens that the admission program violated Title VI. On another point, he agreed with the Brennan group in concluding that race may properly be considered in several circumstances under the Fourteenth Amendment. Thus, both these propositions have the support of five justices. Nevertheless, Justice Powell's opinion is the only reasoning that explains the final result. He speaks for himself when he explains the rationale for his support of both conclusions.

Under both the Fourteenth Amendment and Title VI, the Supreme Court has upheld the use of race-conscious affirmative action remedies where there has been a judicial finding of discrimination. Moreover, a majority of the Court would uphold affirmative action in instances in which a legislative body or administration agency has concluded that it is necessary to remedy identified discrimination. The four members of the Brennan group would also permit race-conscious affirmative action whenever it is designed to remedy the lingering effects of past discrimination against minorities.

Justice Powell took a more limited approach. He felt that race-conscious action taken to help minorities must be viewed as skeptically as the courts have traditionally viewed actions that disadvantage minorities and restrict their opportunities. He listed only three circumstances in which he would uphold the Davis Medical School's use of racial classifications in admissions without governmental findings of discrimination. First, if grading systems or standardized tests were shown to be biased, the school could perhaps consider the racial or ethnic background of its applicants in order to rectify the test's bias and place all applicants on an equal footing. Second, the medical school could consider the race of its applicants if it could demonstrate that it must admit more students of certain racial or ethnic groups in order to produce enough doctors to deliver adequate health care to certain racial or ethnic communities. Justice Powell stated that the regents at the University of California at Davis had failed to produce evidence supportive of either of these purposes.

Finally, Justice Powell would uphold the use of race-conscious criteria in a university admissions program in order to promote student diversity in a university setting. Justice Powell found this aim attractive in the light of the

First Amendment's historic protection of academic freedom. However, he asserted that the Davis Medical School's two-track system was not a suitable means toward the final goal of achieving real diversity. Citing examples from undergraduate admissions programs of Harvard and Princeton, Justice Powell explained that the academic variety valued by the First Amendment seeks not only racial or ethnic diversity but also diversity of talent, geographic region, interest, and background. In his opinion, the Davis Medical School's "special admissions" program, by focusing *solely* on ethnic diversity, would hinder rather than further attainment of genuine diversity.[47]

According to Justice Powell, an admissions program that would meet constitutional requirements must be "flexible enough to consider all pertinent elements of diversity in light of the particular qualifications of each applicant, and to place them on the same footing for consideration, although not necessarily according them the same weight."

The *Bakke* case was more than a legal issue, more than a matter of constitutional rights. It symbolized a conflict of basic values. We must not miss, writes Paul Freund, "the significance of the *Bakke* case. Its real meaning is that we are dealing with a complex problem whose outer contours can be drawn by judges but whose resolution lies within a wide spectrum of moral and practical choices to be made by ourselves, choices that must consider not only individual rights but the health of the society within which those rights are asserted."[48]

The major issue confronting the Supreme Court in *Bakke* was a contemporary and pressing controversy concerning what means could be used to hasten the equalization of opportunities for minority students. Some citizens urged that a positive race-conscious policy based on minority-group membership—*affirmative action*—offered the most effective means. Others maintained that the heart of legal and desirable policy was the race-free treatment of individuals by the same or comparable standards. What made the *Bakke* case a national dilemma and potentially a landmark case was that it had to come to grips with this issue and ultimately to favor one means more than the other.

Several *amicus curiae* briefs submitted on behalf of Allan Bakke posed the central question: "Does the Equal Protection Clause, held to protect blacks from discrimination in state university admissions, also protect whites?"[49] Put another way: "May a state, consistently with the commands of the Fourteenth Amendment, exclude an applicant from one of its Medical Schools solely on the ground of the applicant's race?[50]

And the University of California argument opened with these statements:

The outcome of this controversy will decide for future decades whether blacks, Chicanos, and other insular minorities are to have meaningful access to higher education and real opportunities to enter the learned professions, or are to be penalized indefinitely by the disadvantages flowing from previous pervasive discrimination. . . . There is, literally, no substitute for the use of race as a factor in admissions if professional schools are to admit more than an isolated few applicants from minority groups long subjected to hostile and pervasive discrimination.[51]

FOR DISCUSSION AND CRITICAL THOUGHT

1. Affirmative action and open-admission policies of colleges and universities have received some recent criticisms. How can minorities and disadvantaged youth be encouraged to seek a college education?
2. Compare and contrast the recommendations of the Carnegie Commission and the Holmes Group reports of 1986. Comment critically on what you consider to be the most significant recommendations for the improvement of the teaching profession.
3. What social and political changes led to the enactment of the Morrill Land-Grant Acts of 1862 and 1890? What was the significance of the Land-Grant concept in the development of state universities?
4. Read George P. Kennan's *Democracy and the Student Left* (Little, Brown, 1968). How do you account for the contrast between the radical attitudes and actions of college students in the 1960s and the conservative mood during the 1980s?
5. Minorities are declining rapidly as a percentage of the teaching force and as a percentage of the college population. These trends are happening at precisely the same time that the minority enrollment in our schools is rising. What strategies should be implemented to increase the number of minority teachers?

NOTES

1. Woodrow Wilson, "Princeton in the Nation's Service," *Forum* 22 (December 1896): 465.
2. See Richard Hofstadter and C. DeWitt Hardy, *The Development and Scope of Higher Education in the United States* (New York: Columbia University Press, 1952), "The Age of the College" and "The Age of the University," by Richard Hofstadter, pp. 3–56.
3. Morris Bishop, *A History of Cornell* (Ithaca, N.Y.: Cornell University Press, 1962), pp. 190–93.
4. For a discussion of Gilman's career, see Francesco Cordasco, *Daniel Coit Gilman and the Protean Ph.D.: The Shaping of American Graduate Education* (Leiden, Netherlands: E. J. Brill, 1960).

5. Daniel Coit Gilman, *University Problems in the United States* (New York: Century, 1898), "The Johns Hopkins University in Its Beginning" (Inaugural address delivered in Baltimore on 22 February 1876), p. 33.

6. Ibid., pp. 19–20, 33.

7. Richard H. Shryock, *The University of Pennsylvania Faculty: A Study in American Higher Education* (Philadelphia: University of Pennsylvania Press, 1959), p. 35.

8. Merle Curti and Roderick Nash, *Philanthropy in the Shaping of American Higher Education* (New Brunswick, N.J.: Rutgers University Press, 1965), p. 236.

9. *Chronicle of Higher Education* 36 (18 April 1990): A13.

10. National Citizens Council for Better Schools, *Better Schools: Spotlight Report* 3 (February 1957): 3.

11. Clarence B. Randall, *Freedom's Faith* (Boston: Little, Brown, 1953), p. 39.

12. For a look at the new image which corporate leadership was seeking to portray before the public, see "SR's Businessman of the Year: Joseph C. Wilson [of Xerox Corporation], Finder and Seeker," *Saturday Review* 49 (8 January 1966): 72–75ff.

13. Sections of this act are reprinted in Richard Hofstadter and Wilson Smith, eds. *American Higher Education: A Documentary History* (Chicago: University of Chicago Press, 1961), vol. 2, document 2, "The Morrill Act, 1862," pp. 568–569.

14. Justin S. Morrill, *State Aid to the U.S. Land-Grant Colleges* (Address on behalf of the University of Vermont and the State Agricultural College, delivered in the Hall of Representatives at Montpelier, 10 October 1888) (Montpelier, Vt: Argus and Patriot Printing House, 1888), p. 11. See also Justin S. Morrill, *The Land-Grant Colleges* (Address delivered at the Eighty-ninth Commencement of the University of Vermont and State Agricultural College, 28 June 1893) (Burlington, Vt: Free Press Association, 1893).

15. Quoted in Allan Nevins, *The Origins of the Land-Grant Colleges and State Universities: A Brief Account of the Morrill Act of 1862 and Its Results* (Washington, D.C.: Civil War Centennial Commission, 1962), p. 4.

16. Edward D. Eddy, Jr., *Colleges for Our Land and Time: The Land-Grant Idea in American Education* (New York: Harper & Bros., 1956), p. 38.

17. This critical assessment of early medical training was made by President Charles W. Eliot in one of his addresses. See Eliot, *Educational Reform: Essays and Addresses,* "Medical Education of the Future" (Address before the Medical Society of the State of New York, 28 January 1896), p. 344. For a historical review of early practices in American medical schools, see Abraham Flexner, *Medical Education in the United States and Canada: A Report to the Carnegie Foundation for the Advancement of Teaching,* Bulletin No. 4 (New York: Carnegie Foundation, 1910), pp. 3–19.

18. Letter dated 22 December 1871, from Oliver Wendell Holmes to John Lothrop Motley, as reprinted in Morse, ed., *Life and Letters of Oliver Wendell Holmes,* 2:190.

19. Richard H. Shryock, *American Medical Research: Past and Present* (New York: Commonwealth Fund, 1947), p. 117.

20. Flexner, *Medical Education in the United States and Canada*, chap. 3, "The Actual Basis of Medical Education," pp. 28–51, was probably the most influential part of the Report.

21. See pp. 146–150.
22. This conversation, and other behind-the-scenes developments, are presented in *Abraham Flexner: An Autobiography* (New York: Simon & Schuster, 1960; a revision, brought up to date, of Flexner's *I Remember* [1940]). The particular quotations are on p. 109.
23. Oliver Wendell Holmes, Jr., *Collected Legal Papers* (New York: Harcourt, Brace, 1921), "The Use of Law Schools" (Oration before the Harvard Law School Association in Cambridge, Mass., 5 November 1886), pp. 44–65.
24. For an interesting commentary, see James B. Conant, *Two Modes of Thought: My Encounters with Science and Education* (New York: Trident Press, 1964), chap. 3, "The Education of Lawyers and Business Executives," pp. 46–65.
25. Christopher C. Langdell, *A Selection of Cases on the Law of Contracts, with a Summary of the Topics Covered by the Cases, Prepared for Use as a Text-Book in Harvard Law School* (2nd ed.; Boston: Little, Brown, 1879), p. viii.
26. For a glimpse into this structural maze, see the latest *NEA Handbook for Local, State, and National Associations,* which is issued annually in August by the National Education Association.
27. For a close-up of the battle, with some suggestions for a truce, see G. K. Hodenfield and T. M. Stinnett, *The Education of Teachers* (Englewood Cliffs, N.J.: Prentice-Hall, 1961).
28. See James B. Conant, *The Education of American Teachers* (New York: McGraw-Hill, 1963), especially chap. 4, "The Redirection of Public Authority," pp. 56-72.
29. See, for example, Donald W. Robinson: "Education's Flexner Report?" *Phi Delta Kappan* 45 (June 1964): 426–32.
30. National Council for Accreditation of Teacher Education, "Constitution" (as amended October 1965), Art. I, Sec. C.
31. The members of the task force on teaching as a profession were: Lewis M. Branscomb, chairman; Alan K. Campbell, vice chairman of the board and executive vice president, ARA Services, Philadelphia; Mary Hatwood Futrell, president, National Education Association, Washington, D.C.; John W. Gardner, writer and consultant, Washington, D.C.; Fred W. Hechinger, president, New York Times Company Foundation, New York; Bill Honig, superintendent of public instruction, State of California, Sacramento; James B. Hunt, lawyer, Pyner & Spruill, Raleigh, N.C.; Vera Katz, speaker, Oregon House of Representatives, Salem, Oregon; Thomas H. Kean, governor, State of New Jersey, Trenton; Judith E. Lanier, dean, College of Education, Michigan State University, East Lansing, Michigan; Arturo Madrid, president, The Tomas Rivera Center, Claremont, California; Shirley M. Malcolm, program head, Office of Opportunities in Science, American Association for the Advancement of Science, Washington, D.C.; Ruth E. Randall, commissioner of education, State of Minnesota, St. Paul; and Albert Shanker, president, American Federation of Teachers, Washington, D.C. According to task force members, Marc S. Tucker, executive director of the Carnegie Forum on Education and the Economy, was the principal author of the report.
32. *Tomorrow's Teachers: A Report of the Holmes Group* (East Lansing, Mich.: Holmes Group, Inc., 1986).

33. *New York Times,* 7 November 1965, p. E11, cols. 1–6. For the complete text of this lecture, see James A. Perkins, "The Search for Internal Coherence," *The University in Transition* (Princeton, N.J.: Princeton University Press, 1966), pp. 31–59.

34. See pp. 357–358.

35. See pp. 358–359.

36. The best overview is Samuel Baskin, ed., *Higher Education: Some Newer Developments* (New York: McGraw-Hill, 1965), chap. 1, "The New Colleges," pp. 1–26, by Lewis B. Mayhew; and chap. 6, "Providing the Conditions for Learning: The 'New' Media," pp. 128–152, by C. R. Carpenter and L. P. Greenhill.

37. "Monteith College: A Report to the President" (Detroit, Mich.: Monteith College, December 1963), "Summary and Conclusion," p. 3.

38. Later, when Savio expressed his views in public, over three hundred television and news reporters surrounded him and gave the FSM national publicity. For a clear description of the events during this period, see William L. O'Neill, *Coming Apart: An Informal History of America in the 1960s* (New York: Quadrangle Books, 1971), pp. 275–305.

39. The central issues raised by the committee were focal points of renewed deliberations. See Select Committee on Education, *Education at Berkeley* (Berkeley: University of California Press, 1966; usually referred to as the Muscatine Report).

40. Clark, Kerr, "What We Might Learn from the Climacteric," *Daedalus* 104 (Winter 1975): 2.

41. *De Funis* v. *Odegaard,* 40 S. Ct. Rpts. Law. Ed. 2^d.

42. 483 U.S. 265 (1978).

43. 347 U.S. 483 (1954).

44. See pp. 240–241.

45. Title VI prohibits the federal government from giving financial aid to any person who discriminates on the basis of race, color, or national origin.

46. Such briefs are filed in order to provide information to the Court by interested groups that have no legal right to become parties to a lawsuit. The Latin phrase means "friend of the court."

47. 483 U.S. 265 (1978).

48. Paul Freund, "Bakke: The Choices That Remain," *New York Times,* 9 July 1978, p. E17.

49. *Amicus* brief, Petition for Writ of Certiorari, U.S. Supreme Court, *Bakke,* Committee on Academic Nondiscrimination and Integrity, p. 5.

50. *Amicus* brief, California Supreme Court, *Bakke,* Anti-Defamation League of the B'nai B'rith, p. 2.

51. Brief for the Petitioner, *Regents of the University of California* v. *Allan Bakke,* Supreme Court, October Term, 1977, No. 76–811, 13–14.

CHAPTER 13

Contemporary Issues and Problems

Laws and institutions no matter how efficient and well-arranged must be reformed or abolished if they are unjust.

JOHN RAWLS, *A Theory of Justice,* 1971

Every child—gifted, normal and handicapped—has a fundamental right to educational opportunity. . . . Justice delayed is justice denied. The Federal Government must now take firm leadership to guarantee the rights of the handicapped.

HUBERT H. HUMPHREY, remarks
to the U.S. Senate, January 20, 1972

The culture of poverty cuts across regional, rural-urban, and even national boundaries.

OSCAR LEWIS, *Five Families: Mexican Case Studies
in the Culture of Poverty,* 1959

In our quest for higher standards and superior academic performance we seem to have forgotten that schools cannot be excellent as long as there are groups of children who are not well-served by them. In short, we cannot have educational excellence until we have educational equality.

JEANNIE OAKES, *Keeping Track:
How Schools Structure Inequality,* 1985

THE CONTINUING STRUGGLE
FOR EQUALITY OF OPPORTUNITY

The Sixties

The 1960s witnessed a reassertion of equality as a goal in American society. The meaning of equality and the means of achieving it became central topics of debate. "Each person possesses an inviolability founded on justice that even the welfare of society as a whole cannot override," declared John Rawls in a powerful treatise entitled *Justice as Fairness.*[1] Such arguments did not result immediately in a reduction of inequality, but the principal reform thrust was clearly evident in educational and social action.

This concern for equality was closely related to a sharp upswing in all forms of citizen participation: demonstrations, protest pickets, and "public interest" lobbying drives. There was a strong movement for human rights and a pervasive criticism of those who held great wealth or power. Such ideas and struggles—the spirit of equality, outbursts of protest, exposés of inequities—were deep in the democratic tradition. Like the themes of Jacksonian Democracy and the Progressive era, the issues of the 1960s commanded a passionate intensity of purpose.

A striking source of new national power in the 1960s was the public media—television networks, major news magazines, and leading newspapers such as the *New York Times* and the *Washington Post.* Indeed, during the late 1960s and early 1970s, the media played a dominant role in domestic discord and helped to bring about what no other social institution had previously done: the involuntary resignation of a U.S. President who had been elected, less than two years before, by an overwhelming popular majority.

Television, in particular, had a revolutionary impact on society. One cannot overemphasize its influence in portraying some of the harsher realities of life: social evils and injustices, brutality and violence, chaos and disorder. During the 1960s, for example, "CBS Evening News" provided graphic television coverage of the Vietnam War, displaying, among other atrocities, "American soldiers lopping off Viet Cong ears."[2] On Saturday, November 23, 1963, the day after the assassination of President John F. Kennedy, Americans spent about ten hours watching television.

Perhaps the deepest impressions of the mass media were made on people in the inner-city ghettos and in rural poverty areas where television, for the first time, offered a glimpse of the sharp contrasts in daily existence. Stories, programs, and advertisements instantly showed an affluent way of life beyond easy reach. For the rural and the urban disadvantaged, for children growing up in the culture of poverty, hopelessness and apathy slowly turned to frustration and rage. The United States must restore the "authenticity and validity of the American dream," warned Max Lerner in 1969. Each child must feel a sense of identity and worth, dignity and pride. Each person must have "equal access to equal life chances, so that every unequally born youngster gets the chance to develop his unequal ability to the fullest."[3]

The cherished belief that American public schools provide boys and girls with equal opportunity was challenged during the late 1960s by a combination of educational research, legal decisions, and widespread social action. Civil rights leaders, reform lawyers, and black citizens argued strongly that the expression "equal educational opportunity" was meaningless for a large number of schoolchildren in the United States. The early 1970s witnessed a sharpening debate as continued efforts to equalize educational opportunity met growing skepticism over whether public schooling contributes to equality in the first place.

The Coleman Report

Significant evidence concerning the limited effectiveness of the public schools was continued in James S. Coleman's research report entitled *Equality of Educational Opportunity* (1966).[4] The Coleman Report concluded that the quality of a school's physical facilities had little or no relationship to the achievement levels of a typical student, while the social class of the student's peers had a significant effect on his mathematics and reading scores.

> One implication stands out above all: That schools bring little influence to bear on a child's achievement that is independent of his background and general social context; and that this very lack of an independent effect means that the inequalities imposed on children by their home, neighborhood, and peer environment are carried along to become the inequalities with which they confront adult life at the end of school.[5]

The report stated that individual achievement was dependent on a school's social composition and, furthermore, that a student was influenced by his or her classmates' social class, background, and aspirations rather than by their race. This implied, for instance, that a black child from a poor family would not profit from attending a public school with poor white children, but that he or she would benefit from attending school with middle-class children, black or white. The Coleman Report's 737 pages of text, tables, and graphs contain other conclusions that challenge traditional beliefs about what contributes to effective education.

Coleman's research report was largely statistical and contained few recommendations. Nevertheless, his findings brought about a fundamental change in public policy. According to Coleman, equality of educational opportunity, reflected in equal facilities and services, yields unequal educational attainment. Differences in academic achievement, which were already evident in the first grade, appeared to mount as children moved up the educational ladder.

Those leaders who accepted Coleman's interpretation were increasingly resistant to spending additional funds for public schools. Daniel P. Moynihan, for example, who was counselor to President Richard M. Nixon during the early years of the President's first administration, agreed with Coleman's conclusions. In fact, argued Moynihan in 1972, the United States may be spending too much for its public schools, since "money doesn't seem to matter that much in terms of what happens to students." School expenditures have no real impact on student achievement, because additional money is simply absorbed into higher salaries for teachers in the system.[6]

At the same time, in a massive study entitled *Inequality,* Christopher Jencks and his staff at Harvard University raised questions concerning the relationship between schooling and earning power and contended that there was little connection between the two. Subtitled "A Reassessment of the Effect of Family and Schooling" on economic and social success in the United States, Jencks's book concluded that (1) educational opportunity is unequally distributed in the United States; (2) inequalities in educational attainment would persist even if qualitative differences between elementary and secondary schools were erased ("schools serve primarily to legitimize inequality"); and (3) neither educational opportunity nor attainment is responsible for economic and social success in adult life. Instead, argued Jencks, success is due to such factors as "chance" or luck and subtle, unmeasured differences in "character traits" and on-the-job competencies. In short, better schools would neither eliminate nor reduce economic and social inequalities in the United States. To solve those larger problems, "we will have to establish political control over the economic institutions that shape our society. This is what other countries usually call socialism."[7]

Jencks's study touched on several controversial issues and stirred a nationwide debate. Some commentators charged that the interpretations presented in *Inequality* reflected the political convictions of the author instead of an objective analysis of the data. Others warned that the studies Jencks had cited in his book actually indicated a more direct relationship between public schooling and adult success than Jencks had really allowed. Surely much of the dissonance stemmed from conflicting definitions of "equality" and serious disagreements regarding the public school's responsibility for achieving it.[8]

Educating Handicapped Persons:
The Legal Mandates

The *Brown* decision of 1954 became a legal basis for other civil rights legislation.[9] It gave civil rights activists a powerful tool for persuading Congress to enact antidiscrimination legislation. It encouraged "right-to-education" cases and helped establish rights for handicapped persons.

Although the federal Constitution does not refer to public schooling, the principles of equal protection and due process under the Fifth and Fourteenth amendments have an important impact on public education, which is clearly exemplified in the right-to-education cases. If you substitute "handicapped" for "Negro" and "nonhandicapped" for "white" wherever those words appear in the *Brown* case, you can see why the decision is central to the education of the handicapped and how the Fourteenth Amendment can become a constitutional basis for the right of the handicapped to be schooled. For example, any state-required or state-sanctioned segregation based solely on an individual's unalterable characteristic (race, sex, or handicap) is generally deemed unconstitutional.

Two widely publicized and precedent-setting right-to-education cases occurred in Pennsylvania and the District of Columbia in the early 1970s. As a result of judicial intervention and a growing legislative mandate, it is now illegal for any public school to deny an education to a child with behavioral problems, an inability to learn, or a physical or mental handicap.

In January 1971, the Pennsylvania Association for Retarded Children, (PARC, now referred to as the Pennsylvania Association for Retarded Citizens) brought suit against the Commonwealth of Pennsylvania for the alleged failure of the state to provide school-age retarded children with access to a free public education. In addition to PARC, the plaintiffs included fourteen mentally retarded school-age children, who represented themselves and "all others similarly situated." The defendants included the state board of education, the state secretaries of education and public welfare, and thirteen school districts, representing the class of all school districts in Pennsylvania. The suit, heard by a three-judge panel in the U.S. District Court of the Eastern District of Pennsylvania, questioned state policy and practices that excluded, denied, or postponed free access to public education opportunities for school-age mentally retarded children who could profit from such schooling.

An October 1971 injunction, consent agreement, and order resolved the suit. The order decreed that the state could not apply any policy that would deny, postpone, or terminate mentally retarded children from access to a publicly supported education, including a public school program, tuition maintenance, and homebound instruction. Moreover, by September 1972, all retarded children from six to twenty-one years of age were entitled to a publicly supported education. As the court stated:

> Expert testimony in this action indicates that all mentally retarded
> persons are capable of benefiting from a program of education and
> training; but the greatest number of retarded persons, given such educa-
> tion and training, are capable of achieving self-sufficiency, and the
> remaining few with such education and training, are capable of achieving
> some degree of self-care; that the earlier such education and training
> begins, the more thoroughly a mentally retarded person can benefit at
> any point in his life and development from a program of education and
> training.[10]

PARC and subsequent cases were persuasive in establishing the principle that
every child, no matter how different he or she is from others, has the right to
an education. In brief, public schools must provide appropriate education for
literally all children, either in the schools' buildings or by arrangement with
other community agencies.

Thus *PARC* established a broad concept of public education. The
appropriate function of the public schools was decided judicially to include
equipping children with "life skills." This notion goes far beyond the aim of
transmitting academic or intellectual skills. The court emphasized the en-
hancement of individual development as the critical aim of public education.
The court favored placing exceptional children in regular classes for their
schooling, with referrals to special schools and classes requiring extraordinary
justification. This least restrictive alternative was supported in subsequent
cases. Unless there is clear evidence that an alternative setting is advan-
tageous, the child must be schooled in the regular classroom.

This concept of least restrictive environment is often referred to as
"mainstreaming." Effectively complying with due process requirements
means designing educational programs that meet the individual needs of
each child. The process is supposed to ensure that handicapped children
receive their education in the least restrictive setting. It assumes that
alternative settings exist in which a child can be placed: the usual or regular
school environment with nonhandicapped peers; more restrictive settings
such as special classes on a part-time or full-time basis; special schools; or
residential institutions, which are most restrictive. From a legal point of
view, the concept of least restrictive alternative means that if, as a matter of
public policy, an individual is removed from a normal situation into one that
is restrictive, this is a limitation of the individual's liberty. For example,
placement in a special class instead of a regular class deprives the student of
some freedom and is therefore "restrictive." Adherence to due process in
placement decisions means that for each child, regardless of the severity of
his or her handicap, the schools must suggest a placement in the most
normal setting possible.

Following the *PARC* case, a more impressive federal decision was announced in 1972 in the District of Columbia. In *Mills* v. *Board of Education* the parents of seven district children brought a class-action suit on behalf of all out-of-school handicapped children against the district board of education, the Department of Human Resources, and the mayor for failure to provide all children with a publicly supported education. The plaintiff children ranged in age from seven to sixteen and were noted by the public schools to have problems that led to a denial of their opportunity for a public education: hyperactive behavior, slight brain damage, epilepsy combined with mental retardation, and mental retardation combined with an orthopedic handicap. At issue was the manner in which the children were excluded from the public school programs. "Plaintiff children merely have been labeled as behavior problems, emotionally disturbed or hyperactive."[11] In addition, it was charged that "the procedures by which plaintiffs were excluded or suspended from public school are arbitrary and do not conform to the due process requirements of the Fifth Amendment. Plaintiffs are excluded and suspended without notification as to a hearing, the nature of offense or status, any alternative or interim publicly supported education . . ."

In December 1971, the court issued an order that by January 3, 1972, (1) the children be provided with a publicly supported education and (2) the defendants provide the court with a list of every child of school age not receiving a publicly supported education. When the defendants failed to comply with the order, the plaintiffs on January 21, 1972, filed a motion for implementation of the judgment.

The important judicial precedent stemming from *PARC* and *Mills* was that all school-age children, regardless of the severity of their handicaps, were entitled to a free public education. These decisions revealed the intention of the courts that handicapped children were to have equal access to all public school curricula and activities—academic, vocational, and extracurricular—available to their nonhandicapped peers. This mandate was reaffirmed in 1975 when Public Law 94–142 became law.[12]

P.L. 94–142 was originally introduced in the U.S. Senate on May 16, 1972. The Senate Subcommittee on the Handicapped held long hearings on its provisions in New Jersey, Massachusetts, South Carolina, Minnesota, Pennsylvania, and Washington, D.C. Over one hundred witnesses, representing parents, legislators, and educators, appeared before the subcommittee. A landmark in the extension of educational rights to handicapped children, P.L. 94–142 was signed into law by President Gerald Ford on November 28, 1975. Many judicial principles—the right to education, least restrictive alternative, individualized programming, and due process—are embodied in the law.

P.L. 94–142 is a detailed and comprehensive blueprint for federal participation in special educational programs at state and local levels. It proposes a substantial escalation of federal funding for special education programs. To qualify for funding, states have to comply with a broad set of standards on assessment and planning for individual children. Parents must be involved in planning and other procedures. Perhaps the most controversial provisions of P.L. 94–142 are those that encourage "mainstreaming" the handicapped with nonhandicapped children and that mandate the preparation of a specific program for each child. The law requires that an Individualized Educational Program (IEP) be developed and maintained for each handicapped child. The public schools were given two years (until October 1977) to prepare for the law's requirements. Full compliance with the demand for a "free appropriate public education" had to be made "not later than September 1, 1978."

A related piece of legislation is the Rehabilitation Act, which became law in 1973 (P.L. 93–112). A statement of social policy that guarantees individual rights, this act adds the category of handicapped to the previously protected categories of race and sex. It specifically excludes using a handicapping condition as a basis for a negative decision in employment, schooling, and the broader activities of society. The nondiscriminatory proposals became the final section of the act, which stated in part:

> No otherwise qualified handicapped individual in the U.S., as defined in Section 7(6), shall solely, by reason of his handicap, be excluded from participation in, be denied the benefits of, or be subjected to discrimination under any program or activity receiving federal financial assistance.[13]

This final section of P.L. 93–112 plus the provisions of P.L. 94–142 so significantly affect the education of handicapped persons that they overshadow all related federal laws.

Legal Issues: The Drive to Reform School Finance

Efforts to equalize educational opportunity were closely related to continuing attempts to change long-established patterns of school finance in the United States. The property tax has increasingly come under attack as an unfair method of supporting public education. Some low-income districts raise less money from property taxes than they need, although the tax rate in these districts is sometimes quite high. The higher rate produces less money because the total property value is low. On the other hand, more affluent school districts can raise more funds and provide better educational services and programs; the suburbs of Chicago and New York City, for example, spend more than twice as much per pupil as the inner cities appropriate. Thus the tax system for allocating educational resources leads to glaring financial inequities.

On August 30, 1971, the California Supreme Court ruled in the case of *Serrano* v. *Priest* that the use of the property tax to support the state's public schools was unconstitutional. The *Serrano* case tried to show that the traditional method of school finance, based largely on the property tax, is unlawful because it classifies students on the basis of their collective affluence and makes the quality of a child's schooling contingent on the resources of the school district and "upon the pocketbook of his parents." The court declared that such a system of financing schools discriminated against children in low-income school districts and thus violated the equal protection guarantee of the Fourteenth Amendment to the United States Constitution. "We are convinced that the distinctive and priceless function of education in our society warrants, indeed compels, our treating it as a 'fundamental interest,' " the court declared. The decision stated that the level of spending for an individual's public schooling should not depend on the financial status of one's family or the wealth of the school district.[14]

The widely publicized *Serrano* decision established a new legal framework for reforming school finance, and a number of similar cases in other states quickly following the California precedent. The most important case was decided on December 23, 1971, by a three-judge panel of the United States District Court for the Western District of Texas. In *Rodriquez* v. *San Antonio Independent School District* the judges decided, as in the *Serrano* case, that the method of financing elementary and secondary education in Texas violated the Fourteenth Amendment. The court granted state officials two years in which to devise a new plan that would reallocate school funds. Such a plan was to assure that the educational opportunities of students, as measured by expenditures per pupil, would no longer be contingent on local district wealth, as measured by the value of locally taxable property per student. The Texas Board of Education voted to appeal this decision to the U.S. Supreme Court.

On March 21, 1973, the U.S. Supreme Court decided the *Rodriquez* case and, by a narrow margin of one vote, supported the constitutionality of the existing system of school finance in Texas.[15] In the majority decision the judges argued that they could not identify a disadvantaged class. The system of school finance in Texas does not discriminate against a class of people whose incomes are beneath a designated poverty level. Low-income people live in both rich and poor districts. Therefore, argued the Court, no group is *completely* excluded from the benefits of public education because of poverty. The existence of relative deprivation, defined as differences in expenditures among school districts, is not sufficient to identify a disadvantaged class. The Court asserted that the Equal Protection Clause of the Fourteenth Amendment does not require absolute equality under the law.

Concerning the question of interference with a fundamental right, the Court argued that the federal Constitution does not explicitly guarantee the right to education. The importance of a service, argued the judges, does not establish its status as a fundamental right (similar, for example, to the right to vote) that is guaranteed under the U.S. Constitution.

The basic constitutional brief used by lawyers in the *Rodriquez* case was similar to the one developed earlier in *Serrano,* which was not appealed to the U.S. Supreme Court. Thus, when the Court rejected arguments based on the Equal Protection Clause, including such concepts as "fundamental right" and "fundamental societal interest," it also nullified that part of the *Serrano* case based on the Fourteenth Amendment. Nevertheless, in the struggle for equal educational opportunity, other legal challenges are certain to arise as reform lawyers study carefully the *Serrano* and *Rodriquez* decisions.

By the time the U.S. Supreme Court handed down its decision in the *Rodriquez* case, the imbalance of educational opportunity had become an issue of deep national concern. Community involvement in the public schools took a new and dramatic turn as black parents in the inner cities demanded, and sometimes obtained, a major role in determining educational policy. The call for action was also sounded by another group—Native Americans.

Education of Native Americans

Native Americans have been less vocal in their demands for a controlling voice in schools that educate their children. To begin with, their position differs from that of other minority groups. They have been less united, and they are primarily rural peoples. Nevertheless, their demands are no less urgent than those of other groups, and their claims have a special appeal in the light of a sordid record of past relationships to mainstream America.

Their numbers are small: Native Americans account for no more than one-half of one percent of the total population in the United States. In 1988 there were approximately 1.7 million Native Americans. About 786,000 still remained on three hundred reservations located in thirty states, and about 614,000 were living among the general population, mainly in the cities. The largest tribal group, with 16 million acres of land, was the Navahos, who numbered about 170,000.

The reservations are poverty stricken. Most Native Americans live in leaky adobe huts, brush shelters, tin-roofed shacks, and even abandoned automobiles. Over 60 percent still transport their own drinking water, often from contaminated sources more than a mile away. In a world hidden from public view, Native Americans are generally ignored by neighboring whites, who for three centuries have tried, and failed, to "Americanize," or acculturate, what was considered a small group of uneducated savages. Most white people are still puzzled and chagrined when they refuse to conform to "civilization."

Native American cultures have been deeply and deliberately eroded, yet they persist. Despite unremitting pressures toward submission, Native

Americans show no signs of disappearing or relenting. Alienation and hostility increase, while the population grows.[16]

On the reservations, families suffer from disease and dietary deficiency. Welfare services are inadequate (many exist on the brink of starvation), and housing is a national scandal (over two-thirds of all dwellings inhabited by Native Americans are substandard). Infant mortality after the first month of life is the highest in the United States, and the average life span is forty-four years.

The world of the Native American is dominated by the Bureau of Indian Affairs (BIA), which operates 77 boarding schools scattered across the nation and 147 day schools situated on or near reservations.[17] Most of the schools located off the reservations are secondary schools with boarding facilities, and almost all the elementary schools (both day and boarding) are located on reservations.

Located on or off the reservation, the BIA school is clearly set apart from the population it serves. In a compound surrounded by a fence, it is a noticeable enclave of federal property, and the life of the staff is quite distinct from that of the local people. The school is sometimes called a "compound culture" because staff members socialize with one another instead of with the Indian community.

Two-thirds of all children entering BIA schools have little or no skill or fluency in the English language. The challenge posed by this fact alone threatens to be overwhelming. There are about three hundred languages in use, and over half the Native American youth between the ages of six and eighteen use their native tongue.

The BIA educational system is plagued by unsolved problems: out-of-date textbooks and materials, insufficient funds for innovation, inadequate physical facilities, and an overburdened and sometimes insensitive teaching staff who arrive on the reservation knowing little about the children they are scheduled to teach. Staff orientation sessions concentrate on housing, salary, and fringe benefits, paying scant attention to Indian cultural values or to issues that teachers confront in relating to pupils who speak no English and have different backgrounds from their instructors (only about 1 percent of elementary teachers on the reservations are Native Americans). Although empathy and rapport are serious needs, the complexities and problems of cross-cultural education are largely neglected.

The BIA has tried to transfer responsibility for educating Indian children to local school districts by entering into contracts with the states. By the early 1970s, in fact, over half of all Native Americans in school were in public schools, attending classes with other boys and girls. Two-thirds of the remaining children, or about 35,000 youngsters, were being sent to boarding schools. BIA day schools served 16,000 children, or about 14 percent of all Native Americans in school.

Attending a public school often places the Native American child at a socioeconomic disadvantage, especially in areas with a long history of antipathy toward the Native American population. For these pupils the public schools are usually a greater distance from home than the BIA day schools, and occasionally the nearby federally supervised BIA school is superior to the local public school in size and facilities. Native Americans are urging that BIA school transfers be curtailed, unless approval is obtained in advance from parents and the local group.

In the classroom the meanings and values of the Native American world are generally overlooked. Pupils are taught little or nothing about their history and tribal life. Almost every action is perceived by children and youth as an expression of the white man's disdain for the Native American way of life. The possibility that Native Americans might require different programs to help them function more successfully in their subcultures or that Native American parents might desire another type of education for their children is rarely considered. On the Navaho reservation, for instance, BIA schools are called *"Washingdoon bi oltka"* (Washington's schools), and distant boarding schools or public schools off the reservation are referred to as *"Beliganna bi oltaka"* (little white man's school).[18]

By the late 1960s over 16,000 Native American children of school age were not attending any school at all. The dropout rate was twice the national average: one of every five males had less than five years of schooling. In addition, Native American boys and girls were scoring consistently lower than white children at every grade level in verbal and nonverbal skills. The longer the Native American child remained in school, the further behind he or she lagged.

The profile of adult Native Americans is characterized by a median education substantially lower than that found among any other ethnic or racial group that has not recently immigrated into the United States. In 1981, for example, few Native American adults had attended college and only 57 percent had a high school diploma or its equivalent. Moreover, one-third of all adult Native Americans were dissatisfied with the education they had received. More than three-fourths of them would have liked to have had more education. In addition, two-thirds of the adult Indian population felt that they had received an inappropriate education for the kinds of occupations and lives they wanted to lead.[19]

Equally serious, and with far greater implications, was the fact that Native American youth were learning to reject their own heritage. In some cases this rejection has caused deep despair and led to identity confusion. Suicides among Native American teenagers are three times the national rate, and on some reservations the suicide rate reaches ten times the national average. "Cynicism and despair are rife," declared LaDonna Harris, an Oklahoma Comanche leader.[20] Apathy and alienation, despondency and despair—these and other factors pose a real threat to racial survival.

Too often acculturation is viewed as a narrow, one-way process. While

Native American children and youth are being taught about life in the modern United States, other pupils and teachers might also learn something from projects on Native American cultures: for example, a respect for the beauty of nature, the value of group identity, and the age-old struggle of people for self-determination over their own destiny. As one Native American leader explained: "The question is not how you can Americanize us but how we can Americanize you. The first thing we want to teach you is that, in the American way of life, each man has respect for his brother's vision." Still proud and defiant, Native American leaders today are struggling to conserve an ancient and priceless heritage.

Three centuries of social engineering have underscored the point that no policy or program in Native American education can succeed without the commitment of the people themselves. Almost every critic of Native American education has stressed the need for reforming the BIA, which is a bureau within the United States Department of the Interior. A recent proposal for fundamental change suggested the creation of a federal commission to assume control of Native American education, with a firm mandate to transfer this control to Indian communities within five years. The most cogent recommendations call for national policies of educational excellence and flexible procedures that permit and encourage tribal governments to manage their own schools.

The Indian Education Act of 1972

Clearly the federal government's paternalistic approach toward Native American education had disastrous effects. This was made clear through a study initiated in 1967 by a Special Subcommittee on Indian Education, which called the condition of Native American education a "national disgrace." What was the status of the first Americans during the 1970s? They were the last Americans educationally, economically, socially, and politically. Native Americans' national income was 75 percent below the national average. Their children slipped further behind the longer they remained in school— that is, if they stayed in school. The dropout or "push-out" rate for Native American children was twice the national average. Something needed to be done to remedy the plight of Native Americans.

In response to the alarming facts presented in the subcommittee report entitled *Indian Education: A National Tragedy—A National Challenge,* the Indian Education Act (IEA) was enacted in 1972. The IEA reflected a new direction in the government's treatment of the Indians. More than ever, the United States was recognizing Native Americans' right to self-determination. While continuing to honor the treaties that specified giving federal assistance to the tribes, the government also began to recognize Native Americans as a unique people and has asked for increased participation in federally funded education programs for all Native Americans. This attitude of self-determination was welcomed and considered long overdue by the nation's tribes.

Specifically, the IEA encouraged the government's desire for increased Native American participation in their own education by "requiring that all projects funded under the act must be organized and implemented with the cooperation of tribes, parents, teachers, and students." The IEA indicated a national attempt to deal more fairly with Native Americans for a number of reasons. First, responsibility for administering the IEA programs was no longer placed with the BIA. Many Native Americans distrusted the BIA, which was accused of not representing their best interests. Second, the IEA programs were open to all Native Americans, regardless of whether they lived on a reservation or in a city, or whether their tribe was terminated or federally recognized. The IEA's broader definition provided opportunity for most Native Americans from preschool age to adulthood to participate in one or more of its programs.

In 1978 the IEA was amended (Public Law 95–561) to focus on "culturally related academic needs" of Native American children, to include tribally operated schools, and to give parent committees more power and structure. In addition, the government established training programs aimed at producing more Native American teachers, administrators, and other educational personnel. Part D of the act established the Office of Indian Education (OIE), which was responsible for administering the IEA. Part D established a fifteen-member Indian/Native Alaskan National Advisory Council on Indian Education (NACIE), which was responsible for advising and evaluating government programs affecting Indian education. In general, the amendments served to broaden the scope of the act, allowing for greater Native American control of the IEA-funded programs.

With the IEA, the federal government established a different course for dealing with Native Americans. Through the IEA the government indicated its respect for their rights to control their own destiny. This policy of self-determination, which the IEA underscored with its emphasis on educational programs run by and for Native Americans, began during the administration of President Lyndon B. Johnson and continued through the administrations of Presidents Ronald Reagan and George Bush.

There are a few exemplary programs that illustrate this important principle of self-government. The Indian Arts and Crafts School at Santa Fe, for example, recognizes the cultural heritage of its students. At the Rough Rock Demonstration School in northern Arizona, instruction in Navaho language and culture is an integral part of the curriculum, and the school is supervised by an all-Navaho school board. The Navaho Community College at Many Farms, Arizona, is also developing a curriculum that is more relevant to the needs of Native American students. These experimental institutions are among the first tribal-run schools established in the United

States. Although problems of understanding and commitment remain, such attempts to involve the Native American community in the management of its own schools offer hope for more effective educational programs in the future.

By the early 1970s Native American involvement in political and educational affairs was on the upsurge. There were meetings of the National Indian Youth Council, the National Congress of American Indians, the American Indian Leadership Conference, and the National Indian Education Conference; small Red Power organizations were being formed on college campuses. Rivalry for leadership was intense, especially between the National Indian Youth Council (NIYC) and the National Congress of American Indians (NCAI), two of the most influential organizations. The NIYC was founded in 1961 and has a growing membership of individual Indian students who call themselves "the younger generation"; according to its constitution, the NIYC works on behalf of "all Indians" toward achieving "a greater Indian America." On the other hand, the NCAI, founded in 1944, emphasizes tribal strength and solidarity and tends to coalesce around issues affecting member tribes. Among important figures on the national scene are Gerald One Feather, who helped to organize the American Indian Leadership Conference; Ernie Stevens, director of the California Intertribal Council; and Vine Deloria, Jr., former executive director of the NCAI.[21] Militant policies of activism and self-interest are shattering old myths of the powerless and vanishing American Indian.

Indians were granted full citizenship status in 1924, and they are free to leave the reservations whenever they wish. However, those who do leave and reside elsewhere do not benefit from some Indian-aid programs.

Since the end of World War II, hundreds of reservation Indians, along with other rural Americans, have migrated to urban centers. During the 1980s, about one-third of the Indian population lived in cities. Some traveled on their own, searching for jobs; others moved through urban relocation programs designed by the federal government to facilitate transfers from reservation life to urban employment. In the inner city, these newly arrived citizens joined the ranks of the culturally disadvantaged.

Asian Americans

As political turmoil increased in Southeast Asia during the 1970s, immigration to the United States from Indochina increased. The Immigration Act of 1965, which ended fifty years of restriction based on race, permitted large-scale immigration by Asians, who by 1986 represented about 40 percent of all newcomers to the United States. By 2010 the Asian immigrant population in the United States is expected to double.

The term Asian American includes a range of cultures and languages. It covers about twenty nationalities, including Japanese, Chinese, Filipinos, and refugees from Southeast Asia who fled persecution and imprisonment after the withdrawal of the United States from Vietnam in 1975. The largest group of Asian immigrants were the Vietnamese, who by 1983 numbered about 400,000. There were also large immigrant groups of Cambodians, Thais, and Laotians.

The extraordinary record of success achieved by Asian-American youth has astonished many citizens. At Harvard University, the Massachusetts Institute of Technology, and the Juilliard School of Music, for example, Asian American students have compiled an amazing record of achievement. In 1985, former President Ronald Reagan called them "our exemplars of hope and inspiration." This phenomenal success has prompted researchers to try to discover the reasons behind such levels of excellence in science and music. So far there is little agreement on possible causes.

Some attribute the success of Asian American youth to a traditional reverence for learning and the strong support of family. Often compared to Jews, many Asian Americans appear to share certain values and modes of acculturation. Some characteristics are familiar and similar: a deep belief in the importance of education and a high level of filial respect. Asian students are instilled with a serious attitude toward education and are expected to turn to their teachers, especially male teachers, for information, guidance, and authority. Most Asian Americans regard education as the best path to success and achievement. Many students have well-educated parents who can provide learning toys, computers, and a superior education.

Others believe that the Confucian ethic is the most powerful determinant of behavior among Asian American youth. In Confucianism, one can never repay one's parents—a family orientation that makes people work for the honor of the family, not for themselves. The Confucian ethic is very compelling and sometimes results in a self-motivated push for overachievement. Success seems to be linked to basic values: hard work and educational achievement are top priorities in Asian American families. Researchers are discovering that Asian American parents are able to instill in their children a much greater motivation to work harder. Some Asian American students spend over five hours more per week on homework than do white or African American teenagers.

Demographic studies indicate that Asians are the most upwardly mobile group in the United States. They are new immigrants with dreams of seeking the best opportunity for their children. In the eyes of most Asian American parents, the path to success and human self-fulfillment is through education.

Parental push can also have a negative result and cause social problems for youngsters trying to adjust to a new and different culture. Intense pressure has led to mental illness and even suicide attempts. Some Asian American students experience feelings of deep guilt when not studying intensely and often. Thus for some the price of survival has been extreme stress.

There needs to be a greater appreciation and a clearer understanding of the contributions of culturally different immigrants to a pluralistic society. Through well-designed cross-cultural studies, some educational issues might be clarified. For example, the adjustment of the Asian child's cognitive learning skills to an American classroom warrants more attention by educators. There is a need for more studies involving cognitive-style patterns and instructional methodologies. Second-language acquisition and successful instructional approaches to English as a second language are also areas that require more research.

Bilingual Education

The Teacher Corps, a special title of the Higher Education Act of 1965, was instituted to encourage colleges and universities to offer special preparation to student teachers in disadvantaged areas. After their training, these teachers would instruct students in areas with large concentrations of low-income families.[22] Six years after the law was passed, 60 percent of Teacher Corps interns came from nonwhite ethnic minorities; by 1976, the Teacher Corps was promoting bilingual and multicultural education and cultural pluralism.[23]

The Elementary and Secondary Education Act of 1965 was amended in 1968 with Title VII, leading to the Bilingual Education Act. This act offered federal aid to local school districts to help them meet the needs of children of "limited English-speaking ability." The act stressed the need for instruction in English, and indeed the 1970 census reported that about 33 million people (about 16 percent of the total U.S. population) spoke a primary language other than English.

Some controversy has surrounded the purpose of bilingual education programs: should the programs be transitional, assisting students to a better use of the English language, or should they be designed to allow students to maintain a bilingual facility throughout life? By the mid-1970s the U.S. Office of Education estimated that federally aided language programs existed in forty-one states; they served about 165,000 children in sixty-eight languages, of which forty were Native American languages.

In *Lau* v. *Nichols* the U.S. Supreme Court decided in 1974 that a school system's failure to provide language instruction for children whose primary language was not English denied those children an equal opportunity to participate in public schooling, which was a violation of the Civil Rights Act of 1964. In San Francisco, children of Chinese ancestry brought a class-action suit to force the public schools to design unique programs for them. Justice William O. Douglas spoke for the Court in asserting that California must take affirmative action to enable Chinese-speaking children to profit from their school experience; merely providing the same textbooks and curricula to all children was not considered equality of treatment.[24]

During the early 1980s proponents and critics disagreed vehemently concerning the successes and failures of bilingual education. By 1986 there was a major controversy over how public schools should educate boys and girls with "limited English-speaking ability." Then–Secretary of Education William J. Bennett ignited a national debate when he termed bilingual education a "failure" and argued in 1985 for a major policy change in bilingual efforts. "The responsibility of the Federal government must be to help ensure that local school boards succeed in teaching non-English-speaking students English," Bennett declared. "We need a common language. In the United States this language is English."[25]

California voted to declare English the state's official language in the public schools; and there were bills introduced in Congress to designate English as the official language of the United States. With the birth rates of Hispanic and other ethnic groups served by bilingual programs running higher than those of English-speaking whites, the problems underscored by the controversy over bilingual education are likely to increase.[26]

MEETING THE NEEDS
OF A POPULATION IN FLUX

Demographic Changes

In 1986 the population of the United States was about 240 million people, of whom 21 percent (or about 50 million) were Asian, Hispanic, and black. According to various projections of the federal government, one out of every three Americans will be non-Caucasian soon after the beginning of the twenty-first century. Thus the nation's racial composition was changing in significant ways. The population of the United States was expected to increase to about 265 million by the year 2020, and much of the population growth was expected to be among minority segments of society. In fact, by 2020, one in three children will come from a minority group—Hispanic Americans, African Americans, Asian Americans, and others.

In 1980, about 27 percent of public school students were non-Caucasian, an increase of 6 percent from 1970. By 1988 a majority of urban public school students were minorities. Most of the minority student population was concentrated in a section of the United States that began in New York, moving southward down the Atlantic Coast, and then westward to California. As expected, Hispanic enrollment was highest in California, Arizona, New Mexico, and Texas; black enrollment was highest in Georgia,

Alabama, South Carolina, Mississippi, and the District of Columbia. In the nation's largest school systems, the majority of students were minorities. In Texas, for example, almost half the students enrolled (about 46 percent) were Hispanic and African American; and most of the enrollment in California's elementary schools were from minority groups.

A primary concern of Hispanic leaders is the large number of Hispanic school dropouts, and African American leaders are especially concerned with the decline in the college enrollment of African American high-school graduates. The dropout or "push-out" situation was especially tragic because it indicated a massive waste of human potential, certain to add to Latino and African American poverty in the future.

Equally significant is the aging of America. In 1983, for the first time in American history, the number of people in the United States over age sixty-five surpassed the number of teenagers—a figure that will remain unchanged as the United States enters the twenty-first century. At the turn of the century, the median age will be thirty-six; soon after the year 2030, it will be over forty. Also important are predictions concerning life expectancy. In 1986 one of every ten Americans was sixty-five or older; by the year 2030, one of every five Americans will be over sixty-five. In 1986, about 30 people a day were reaching one hundred; by 2030 about 280 a day will live beyond age one hundred. As the older segment of the population increases in size, it will also grow in political influence. By 1986 the number of eligible voters sixty-five and older outnumbered those voters aged eighteen to twenty-four. Some educators were concerned that older citizens without children, worried about the rising costs of health care, will be less willing to help support the growing costs of public schooling.

Also noteworthy are radical changes in the structure of the American family. The so-called traditional American family—a working father, a housewife at home, and two or three school-age children—was disappearing. During the 1980s married couples with children have no longer been the norm. Family styles have been more varied than ever before in American history. Of 80 million households, about 20 million have consisted of Americans living alone. And, equally important, almost 10 million have been households of women raising children alone.

The rapid growth of households headed by single females has led to a concurrent increase in the number of poverty-stricken families. Since 1980, two of every three families headed by single Hispanic and single African American females have lived in poverty. A large percentage of American children have been growing up in environments that endangered their maturation and development; and the number of "at-risk" children entering the public school has been increasing. By the year 2000 many of these children will be parents, unable to earn a living and fulfill the obligations of adults; they may see their own children lost to drugs and destitution.

The way a nation treats its children reveals the kind of future its citizens can envision. The willingness of a nation to relegate so many of these poorly fed and poorly housed children to the role of outcasts in a wealthy society may come back to haunt its citizens. In 1990, of the 33 million poor Americans, 13 million were children, and 500,000 of these children were homeless. According to the Children's Defense Fund, the United States ranks twentieth worldwide in infant-survival rates—behind Canada, Japan, Ireland, and Australia. During the 1980s, some 2 million children were dropped from school-lunch programs, and 80 percent of children eligible for Head Start never received an opportunity to participate. For the first time since the Great Depression, homeless children were begging in the streets of major cities. By the late 1980s, about half the occupants of homeless shelters in New York City were children, usually only six years of age.

In the future, more children will enter school with an array of "risk" factors that will impede or threaten their health or environment. Shocking numbers of these children have not been inoculated, and whooping cough and tuberculosis, once considered archaic diseases, might reach epidemic proportions among children in poverty. An increasing proportion of young people will come from broken families in which the family members themselves lack education. Most will be nonwhite, poor, and with little proficiency in English. On the average, African American and Hispanic children will continue to score far below white children on standardized tests.

An increasing percentage of American women have been choosing to have children later or not at all. By 1985 there were 24 million married couples with children compared with 26 million childless couples. The largest increase in first births was to women aged thirty to thirty-four. Most women who decided to have children were combining motherhood and an occupation. By 1986, about seven out of ten women between the ages of seventeen and forty-four were in the work force. Moreover, women were returning to work much sooner after giving birth, often within one year.

The incidence of divorce and the number of children under age eighteen living in single-parent households have also increased dramatically. For example, in 1986, more than 50 percent of African American children lived with one parent compared to 16 percent of all white children and 25 percent of all Hispanic children. Large numbers of children who grow up in single-parent households (often headed by single females) have mothers who did not complete high school and who are unemployed. During the mid-1980s, almost half of all young women who dropped out of school did so because of pregnancy or marriage. The cycle is heritable and tragic: teenage mothers tend to give birth to children who also become teenage parents. About 20 percent of premature babies born in the United States are born to teenagers and grow up less healthy, with more poorly developed immune systems than other babies, and later exhibit learning difficulties.

The American Family in Crisis

The changing values and attitudes of American society during the latter part of the twentieth century have had a profound impact on families and schools struggling to cope with a rapidly changing social order. To understand more clearly some of the important changes American families are experiencing, it is necessary to examine those broader aspects of society that directly affect family life.

An important force is the push of many middle-class individuals to achieve materialistic wealth; these people value success and strive for higher status. To attain these goals, they have been willing to change the character of their family units. Women are entering the work force in greater numbers than ever before. Family attitudes toward childbearing have changed drastically, as couples are limiting the number of children they have, or electing not to have any. The children of working mothers must be entrusted to day-care centers or sometimes become latch-key children, lacking in parental support and guidance.

For whatever reasons, the divorce rate by 1990 was at an all-time high, resulting in many single-parent homes. The problems of child care and nurturing faced by single parents are even more daunting than those that are shared by both parents.

Such difficulties are even greater for parents in the lower socioeconomic levels, married or single. With adequate housing in the United States becoming more expensive and less available, many poorer families are forced to live in housing projects or even to join the growing numbers of the homeless. Some estimates suggest that by the year 2000 one child in four will be poor and probably homeless.

Not only are children being deprived of their parents' time because both are working; more parents of all economic levels are opting for self-pursuits, seeking health and recreational activities, and spending less time with their children. Such self-directed pursuits allow less time for child rearing or the development of extended family ties. Many parents are willing to share their child-rearing responsibilities with others, especially the public schools.

More and more, the decline of the family unit is depriving children of personal guidance and intimate interaction with caring adults. The result of these weakened connections to parents and extended families is often children with fewer socialization skills and disabling self-concepts. Some children, teenagers, and even young parents have substituted tragic strategies to compensate for personal needs no longer met by family bonding, leading to increased drug addiction, the epidemic of acquired immune deficiency syndrome (AIDS), and family violence and abuse. Among children, greater incidences of learning disabilities are appearing, caused to some extent by parental abuse and the use of drugs.

This decline of family values has serious consequences for both society at large and the public schools. Some schools are compensating by accepting more responsibility for child rearing and nurturing—for example, opening day-care centers for infants and toddlers, providing services for latch-key children through an extended school day, and staffing human resource centers that deal with sexual awareness, social ills, and infectious diseases. However, research suggests that strong families are one of the best assurances of public school success. Establishing an ongoing positive community-parental involvement plan that fosters strong ties between families and schools is probably one of the most effective long-range strategies that any school can adopt to have a positive impact on the lives of children.

The Culture of Poverty:
Educating Children of the Poor

The technology that created material advantages in American life has by-passed growing numbers of those who are trapped in poverty and insulated against economic advancement. As their condition deteriorates, this impoverished minority is becoming increasingly resentful and desperate, dangerously alienated from an affluent society that seems to function so easily without them. Now clustered in urban ghettos, with little upward mobility, these racial or ethnic groups are forming a distant subculture of poverty.

This large subculture is composed of reservation Native Americans, Appalachian Mountain farmers, rural southern African Americans, landless Puerto Ricans, Mexican immigrants, and others who have uprooted their families and moved to the cities. Most are newcomers searching for elusive advantages, fleeing from frustrations of the past. Poverty forces them to live in low-rent, deteriorating neighborhoods where absentee landlords fail to keep the buildings in good repair. As the whole area becomes more and more depressed, garbage piles up, sewage drains clog, and rats and vermin move in with the tenants. "Tomorrow," the slum dwellers say, "we will return to the farm." The record shows, however, that they seldom do. Some try to build a new set of hopes; for others, time has shown the futility of aspirations and dreams. All are trapped in the social disorganization of slum conditions, which poses different and more intensified problems of adjustment. Their predicament is compounded by class and racial prejudice. Thus those who migrate from rural communities to the inner city find all too often that the move not only fails to relieve their plight, but leads instead to situations of chronic dependence from which they are unable to establish a meaningful new life.

By 1990, some 5 million American children under the age of six— about one out of every four—were in families living below the poverty line. About 23 percent, more than double the number of adults, were living in poverty. In fact, young children were the poorest of any group in American society. Their future was indeed grim. According to former U.S. Secretary of Education Lauro Cavazos, by the year 2000 as many as one-third of the nation's children will be disadvantaged and at risk. "We have children in the barrios, the ghettos, the hills and hollows of this country who are so deprived, so isolated, so ill-fed, ill-housed and ill-treated, they don't know how to function in society," exclaimed President Keith Geiger at the NEA Representative Assembly in 1990. *"Somebody must take responsibility for these children."*[27]

Poverty and ignorance usually go hand in hand. There is, in fact, a heritable cycle of despair in the culture of poverty—from poverty to ignorance and back again to poverty—that perpetuates the problems of the uneducated and unskilled from generation to generation. Early in life children from the culture of poverty are usually typed as "slow" or "dull" because of relatively poor scores on standardized achievement and intelligence tests; they are then shunted into programs that do not offer them a way out of their home surroundings. Frustrated and disillusioned, these boys and girls become school dropouts and pass on their negative attitudes to succeeding generations who are then caught in the same unfortunate cycle. "When you talk about the real underclass, then you are talking about blacks, Hispanics, and Appalachian whites and Native Americans," declared Paul Yzaguirre, president of the National Council of *La Raza* (see pages 351–352), in 1986. "With those populations, poverty seems to be permanent."[28]

Migrant Children

This cycle is not limited to the urban slums. Migrant children are trapped in similar situations. Every year almost 200,000 children move with their parents across the croplands of the nation, harvesting as they go. Deprived of cultural experiences that contribute to academic success, unwelcomed in communities and schools, these children seem destined for failure.

There are approximately 2 million migrant workers who derive a meager living from seasonal crop harvesting. Because of their temporary residence status, these families are usually ineligible for public assistance and other legal benefits. Many are illiterate, and most are educationally retarded. Burdened by poverty and disease, with annual incomes of about $800 per family, migrants are among the poorest people in the United States.

Migrant children (sometimes as young as four years of age) work in the fields beside other members of the family. School attendance and child labor laws are difficult to enforce with this rootless population. Fathers need every able member to help supply an income, and as a result the children's schooling is irregular and constantly interrupted. Even worse, each year about 500 migrant children are maimed from working in the fields with their parents.

Mexican Americans

The history of Mexican Americans dates to the original Indian and Spanish settlers of the American Southwest. In 1848 after the treaty of Guadalupe Hidalgo, which ended the Mexican War, Mexico ceded to the United States vast territories that included California, Arizona, New Mexico, and Texas. For more than a century after the treaty, many of the first families of the region and the Mexican immigrants who followed them worked on ranches and in construction gangs and in the fields and the mines, mostly as menial laborers. A small number rose to middle-class status as merchants, doctors, or lawyers. Many fought bravely on foreign soil for the United States; even so, they were rarely accepted as Americans.

All in all, Mexican Americans are victims of the typical poverty syndrome. The second largest minority in the United States is among the most educationally, socially, and economically disadvantaged groups. During the 1970s, about 25 percent of Mexican Americans were living below the poverty line, compared to 33 percent for African Americans and 10 percent for Anglos. In 1978, for example, according to the U.S. Bureau of the Census, over 9 percent of Mexican American families had incomes of less than $4,000, compared to 5 percent of non-Hispanic families. By 1981, over 32 million people—one of every seven Americans—were living below the poverty line of $7,250 a year for a family of three.

Even those Mexican Americans who had jobs worked at the bottom of the wage scale: 75 percent were unskilled factory or service laborers or farm laborers. Furthermore, according to a report of the United States Commission on Civil Rights, out of every 100 Mexican Americans who enter first grade only 60 graduate from high school, compared to 37 for blacks and 86 for Anglos. The proportion of Mexican Americans reading below grade level was generally twice as large as that of Anglos, and Mexican Americans repeated grades at a rate of 16 percent compared to 6 percent for Anglos. To these heavy burdens have been added the result of frequent prejudice against the culture and language of Spanish-speaking peoples. All in all, Mexican Americans share with other minorities a full circle of political and social deprivations: high unemployment, low income, inferior schooling, and bad housing.

As with other ethnic groups, some people assume that the low socioeconomic status and the school failure of Mexican Americans are the natural consequences of racial and cultural inferiority. These prejudicial assumptions have deep roots and continue to persist. Educators have long recognized that Chicano school enrollment and academic achievement are substantially lower than for other groups and that the dropout (or "push-out") rate is alarmingly high. Other social indicators are also depressing: high rates of unemployment, poor housing, low political participation.

By the 1980s Mexican Americans were the second largest minority in the United States, after African Americans, with a population estimated at 8.7 million and growing twice as fast as the general population. The majority live in California and four southwestern states (Arizona, Colorado, New Mexico, and Texas), although there is also a sizeable, and growing, dispersion throughout the nation. Large Mexican American communities are scattered across the United States, especially in the large cities of the Midwest.

Unlike other national groups, Mexicans continue legal and illegal immigration at a lively pace. There will be an estimated 45 million more Mexicans in the year 2000 than there were in the early 1980s, and for many, survival means migrating to the United States. Food, clothing, housing, and jobs are increasingly in short supply for the masses in Mexico. Unemployment runs around 50 percent. Even worse is the rapid growth of the Mexican population. By the year 2000, Mexico will have 100 million people, and unless jobs are found for new workers, large numbers will head north to the United States.

Before 1986, propelled by a worsening economic crisis in Mexico, thousands of illegal immigrants slipped across the two-thousand-mile boundary every day, alone or aided by smugglers who charged up to $1,200 a head for rides to Chicago or other cities. In January 1983, for example, 88,811 aliens were caught along the border. However, according to the Border Patrol's estimate, only one in three was being caught. The flow of illegal aliens from Mexico was unprecedented in American history. Most of the Mexicans who sneaked into the United States were lured by minimum-wage jobs that paid six times the rate in Mexico because of the devaluation of the peso. The complications and problems stemming from the great increase in the illegal migration of Mexicans into the United States were enormous. The surge occurred at a time of the highest American unemployment in four decades. Those who urged tighter immigration laws argued that American workers were displaced by aliens who entered the nation illegally. Hispanic groups reported that jobs taken by aliens were the type Americans did not want—as busboys, day laborers, and workers in garment sweatshops paying less than the minimum wage.

Finally, after much debate, the U.S. Congress approved a landmark immigration bill on October 17, 1986. The Immigration Reform and Control Act of 1986 marked a historic change in American immigration policy. The act prohibited the hiring of illegal aliens and offered amnesty or legal status to millions of illegal aliens who had resided continuously in the United States since before January 1, 1982. The ban applied to all employers, who would be required to ask all job applicants for documents to confirm that they were either citizens or aliens authorized to work in the United States.

The Immigration Reform and Control Act of 1986 altered in significant ways the future context of immigration to the United States. There was little doubt that the primary reason for its enactment was the large number of unauthorized or illegal immigrants in the United States. The media and the general public had exerted pressure on the government to do something about the problem. There was the widespread view that the routine violation of the nation's immigration laws had persisted too long and must be reversed—hence the word *control* in the new law's title.

Thousands of alien children are enrolled in schools of Los Angeles, Chicago, and New York. Mexican American children suffer not only the general discrimination and inadequacies of a rural school in a castelike community social structure but also the additional handicap of migrancy. Many children travel from area to area working the fields and are not in school at all.

Some educators, trying to explain the failure in school of Mexican-American children, rely heavily on a theory of cultural deprivation. The problem is perceived to be in the socialization of the home and neighborhood, and it is assumed that the behavior of the child must be changed, not the school or society. Field research seems to support the view that some educators, especially in the more conservative areas of the Southwest, believe that Chicano children are innately inferior—inferior because they are so obviously Mexican. Inherent in this belief is the prejudicial view that Mexicans are culturally, if not racially, inferior. The "inadequacies" of the Mexican American culture and home become the Mexican American child's educational "needs." Unfortunately, the characteristics usually ascribed to Chicano children correspond frequently to the widely accepted stereotype in the Southwest of "Mexicans" in general—noncooperative, lackadaisical, and lazy.

A small number of educators decry the cultural determinist approach, and suggest instead a structural environmentalist perspective. They believe that social, economic, and educational conditions are reasons for the Mexican Americans' low school achievement. They argue that school policies and practices retard learning and encourage culture conflict, emotional distress, and eventually school dropouts. These educators blame the school because of its inability to adjust realistically to the needs of culturally different groups: there is nothing deficient about the Mexican American child; the school simply does not capitalize on positive elements. Tracking and other school practices isolate Mexican American children, reinforce racist stereotypes, and gradually discourage Mexican American success. These educators argue that Mexican American children are not culturally deprived and urge instead that teachers view the Mexican American background as rich and significant. It is possible for educators to modify the school social climate, eliminate racism, and help Mexican Americans to make positive contributions.

During the late 1960s and early 1970s the Chicano, or *La Raza* movement, played an important role in bringing about some school reforms. *La Raza* was a loosely organized political movement with many different objectives. It advocated some of the Great Society goals of former President Lyndon Johnson and sought cultural pluralism and bilingual education. It drew much strength from the disaffected Mexican American community in urban areas. *La Raza* tactics included boycotts and confrontation in widely publicized militant efforts to implement educational change. Leaders demanded an equal or dominant voice in educational decision making. All in all, the Chicano or *La Raza* movement became a vital force for equal educational opportunity and in eliminating flagrant discrimination.

Radical political tactics in the *La Raza* movement were slowly replaced by special-interest actions. The Mexican-American Legal Defense and Education Fund (MALDEF), which was formed in 1968, has waged a sustained effort to combat discrimination in jobs, housing, public services, and education. For the most part, MALDEF has supported bilingual education and pushed civil rights and equal opportunity cases that show promise of establishing new legal principles beneficial to Mexican Americans nationally. Organizations of women have advocated changes in line with their own special interests. The tactics are less militant and tend to work for change within the system, using traditional organizational approaches. The late 1970s and early 1980s witnessed growing demands for better and specially prepared teachers, increased demands for more Chicano educators, and above all, a heavy stress on bilingual and cross-cultural education. MALDEF has chalked up an impressive record in civil rights test cases. For example, in 1974 MALDEF participated in a U.S. Supreme Court case *(Lau* v. *Nichols)* that dealt with non-English-speaking Chinese American students and had significant implications for Spanish-speaking communities throughout the nation.

All in all, the Chicano movement made important contributions to school reform. For the first time, the history, culture, and tradition of the Mexican American minority entered into the curriculum in a meaningful way. However, with massive cutbacks in federal and state financial funding, fewer programs based on cultural and linguistic pluralism are being implemented. By the mid-1980s, the socioeconomic plight of the Mexican American group remained relatively unchanged, and Mexican American school achievement was in the same low position relative to other ethnic groups. Some discriminatory policies were modified, but few were radically changed or completely eliminated.

Deeply rooted prejudices along with inherent assumptions of Mexican American cultural inferiority are barriers to educational reform. By 1990 the Mexican American in some communities remained politically underrepresented, economically disadvantaged, and poorly educated.

The "New Immigrants" of the 1980s

During the 1980s, the United States again became a nation of immigrants. Not since the years of immigration before World War I have so many newcomers tried to enter this country. Each year during the 1980s an estimated six hundred thousand immigrants and refugees were legally admitted into the United States, and a large number of others entered and remained without legal status, some overstaying their visas or clandestinely crossing the border. Apparently the attraction of the United States remained as strong as ever, along with the accompanying ambivalence and even alarm that many native-born Americans expressed toward the new arrivals. However, unlike the older flows of immigrants, the immigrants of the 1980s were drawn not from Europe but largely from the developing nations of the Third World, especially from Latin America and Asia. The heterogeneous mix of the earlier European waves pales in comparison to the diversity of the 1980s. These immigrants came in jetliners, by boat, on foot, and in the trunks of automobiles. Entrepreneurs and refugees, manual laborers and polished professionals, illiterate peasants and some of the most talented people in the United States—all helped to reshape the fabric of American culture.

The newcomers were different from the immigrants at the turn of the century. They reflected in their origins and motives the powerful forces that helped to forge a different world order during the second half of the twentieth century. And the United States that accepted them is not the same America that processed the "huddled masses" through Ellis Island. Thus the theories that explained the acculturation of the earlier immigrants do not illuminate the nature of the "new immigrants of the 1980s." What has been the impact of post–World War II immigration on American culture? What were the hopes and dreams of the many national groups that became, with or without hyphens, the newest American citizens? By 1990, historians were just beginning to catch glimpses of the extraordinary human drama of the new immigrants in a contemporary context. The true-life stories were just as riveting, but the circumstances and the people were different from the earlier influx of immigrants from southern and eastern Europe.

The Culturally Disadvantaged

In an educational context, the term "disadvantaged" refers to children from the culture of poverty. This does not imply that other cultural groups escape similar hardships; it merely means that the social ills restricting growth and development tend to be concentrated within the culture of the poor. The term is relative, and the label may change—for instance, the culturally different, the economically restricted—but the problems remain. Recognizing that these children have a subculture of their own, sociologists point out that they are not "culturally deprived." However, in the urban milieu of the twentieth-century United States, they are indeed culturally disadvantaged.

Not only are the culturally disadvantaged not ready for the public school, but the schools, by and large, are not ready for them. Upon entering the structured classroom, an individual from the culture of poverty moves into a totally different world, one that reflects the wider society outside, a world that evaluates the disadvantaged child in terms that serve only to reinforce a negative self-concept. Poverty is a stigma that some schools unwittingly see as a sign of personal unworthiness.

Poverty, then, has a subtle, crushing dimension. To be poor is to be stigmatized by American society, for an individual's worth is often equated with financial ability—with the amount of money one earns, the car one owns, the clothes and other material things one can afford to buy. In the eyes of some people, the disadvantaged child, lacking financial worth, also lacks personal worth. It is a tragedy of immense proportions that so many children from the culture of poverty willingly accept society's value definitions and view themselves as failures.

The culturally disadvantaged are alienated from the value structure that the public school seeks to cultivate because these children lack the resources and perceptions to maintain norms acceptable in a dominant middle-class society. This middle-class society is shaped by such values as aggressive competition, economic self-sufficiency, success striving, and social adjustment. These values, which deeply influence American teachers, require conformity in the classroom and the wider world outside. On the other hand, values in the culture of poverty reflect a different way of life, in which demands and expectations are often completely different from those considered important in the public school. Thus the problem of educating the culturally disadvantaged is made more complex by a value clash between the culture of poverty and the larger middle-class society that determines the life-styles of the majority of the population.

An important effort toward easing the tensions of this value clash has been to foster in young people from the culture of poverty a predisposition toward schooling that is deemed necessary for success. During the 1960s, $10 billion was invested in compensatory programs designed to improve the educational achievement of the disadvantaged. These projects ranged from preschool through the college level and varied from extra-guidance services to experimental curricula. Perhaps the most ambitious efforts were preschool projects such as Head Start and Follow Through, and the "open admissions" programs in higher education.

The Issue of Compensatory Education

The federally financed project Head Start tried to provide preschool experiences for culturally disadvantaged children. The program was initiated in 1965 under the Economic Opportunity Act, a key measure in the federal government's "war on poverty." In 1969 responsibility for Head Start was shifted from the Office of Economic Opportunity to the Department of Health, Education, and Welfare.

Children in Head Start ranged in age from three to six years and usually came from families whose annual income was less than $3,000. The goal was to help "the child of poverty" start "his school career on more equal terms with his more fortunate classmates." The class included about fifteen pupils led by a teacher who was assisted by several aides. Enrollment in Head Start was voluntary, of course. An effort was made to offer a range of experiences: for example, new school tasks that children could successfully complete, play activities for the group, and planned excursions to nearby places of interest.

The approach was essentially compensatory: the entire project was predicated on the belief that deprivation in the early years of life produces a basic retardation that is difficult or impossible to overcome later in life.[29] When Head Start appeared inadequate, project Follow Through was begun in 1968 in an attempt to maintain the progress attributed to the preschool experience.

One outcome of Head Start and similar compensatory programs has been to attract nonprofessional personnel to work as aides in the public schools. Project Head Start, in particular, captured the imagination of many people who, in the past, seemed unconcerned about children from the culture of poverty.

Some educators and psychologists are questioning the entire rationale for compensatory programs such as Head Start. Arthur R. Jensen, for example, argues that the major premises underlying compensatory efforts should be reexamined.[30] In a widely publicized monograph, Jensen states that preschool compensatory programs are misdirected in their choice of goals and practices.

A nationwide controversy has centered around Jensen's assertion that African Americans as a racial group, when compared with Caucasians or Orientals, score poorly on that aspect of general intelligence that involves abstract reasoning and problem solving. He states that this ability (which Jensen equates with the ability measured by standardized intelligence tests) is inherited—in short, is simply a matter of genes and brain structure. Therefore, argues Jensen, no amount of compensatory education or forced exposure to middle-class values will improve this aspect of general intelligence. Jensen is quick to point out that the constellation of abilities termed "intelligence" (which is measured by means of "intelligence tests") is only part of the whole spectrum of human abilities. It has been singled out from "the total galaxy of mental abilities" as being important in American culture because of the structure of our "traditional system of formal education" and the job tasks with which this system is coordinated.

Jensen examines the whole *"concept of the IQ: how it came to be what it is; what it 'really' is; what makes it vary from one individual to another; what can change it, and by what amount."*[31] The most important environmental factors affecting "intelligence," he writes, occur during the prenatal stage and the first year of life. He argues that the Intelligence Quotient (IQ) is determined more by genetic than by environmental forces.

For young children, declares Jensen, changes in IQ produced by compensatory programs are very small. He suggests that the "heritability"[32] of intelligence is very high and that genetic traits are more important than environmental factors in producing differences in the IQ. Social class and racial differences in intelligence cannot be accounted for by variations in environment; these differences, concludes Jensen, must be attributed to genetic factors. Needless to say, there is a dearth of conclusive evidence on several points raised by Jensen, and the controversy sparked by his comments continues unabated.[33]

"Open Admissions" Programs in Higher Education

Theoretically an open-admissions policy means that anyone has a right to *begin* a college education after obtaining a secondary-school diploma. Between the beginning and the end, however, policies vary, and colleges actually have great power to encourage or block a student's progress. On this point there has been much controversy surrounding the whole idea.

The open-admissions movement raises some fundamental issues concerning the purposes and functions of higher education in a democracy. Some view open admissions as a political move toward greater equality, a "poverty interrupter," a mechanism for the redistribution of income. The policy does, in fact, lead to the admission of large numbers of students from disadvantaged backgrounds, and many enter college unprepared for advanced courses. For that reason, argue the advocates, the college should use its resources to assist and sustain these students during their years of study. Critics counter this argument by pointing to the need to uphold academic standards and the intellectual tradition of the institution. These issues are likely to spark a continuing controversy as increased pressures from low-income groups are brought to bear upon public institutions.

After intense pressures from African American and Hispanic citizens, the City University of New York (CUNY) initiated an open-admissions program in September 1970, which permitted graduates of the city's high schools, regardless of grades, to enter one of the institution's undergraduate colleges. Because CUNY is one of the largest systems of higher education in the nation, the experiment was watched closely by other colleges and universities. Despite initial disorder, the program at CUNY has challenged some traditional assumptions. The freshman class increased from 6,000 to more than 15,000 students, and the *New York Times* published a confidential CUNY report that revealed 51 percent of these new students required some remedial work in mathematics and reading. Nevertheless, by 1975 many students who had entered the university under the open-admissions policy were striving with academic success and remaining at CUNY through the end of their programs.

In 1975 a grave fiscal crisis at CUNY threatened the survival of the open-admissions concept. Because of New York City's financial difficulties, CUNY faced a retrenchment of more than $50 million. "There are national implications to the [fiscal] battle over [open admissions at] CUNY," declared Michael Harrington. "If this experiment is abandoned, people will . . . cite CUNY to prove that the masses are just too stupid to be taught serious subjects."[34]

The Fiscal Crisis of the 1970s

CUNY, of course, was not alone. Retrenchment policies at colleges and universities across the land produced similar fears and warnings. By the end of 1971, libraries were closing early, part-time and lower-level faculty and staff were being dismissed, and academic programs were being drastically curtailed. Colleges and universities left vacant faculty positions unfilled, and all departments were asked to curtail spending and trim their budgets.

The Carnegie Commission on Higher Education, in an extensive report on the fiscal crisis, disclosed that 540 of the 2,300 institutions of higher learning in the United States were experiencing financial difficulties in the early 1970s and another 1,000 were on the brink of bankruptcy. Columbia University revealed a deficit of $15 million. Stanford University disclosed a six-year plan with a budget reduction of $6 million extending over that period. Even Harvard University, with an endowment of more than $1 billion, was experiencing fiscal problems. "Education in the United States— primary, secondary, and higher education—is in grave trouble," concluded the commission.[35]

The crisis affected public and private schools and colleges across the nation. New York City, for example, struggled to keep its parochial schools open, and several local school districts in California went bankrupt. The number of school budget defeats in local communities increased sharply, as taxpayers, troubled by the high cost of living, resisted demands for educational expenditures.

In 1973, for the first time in twenty-eight years, the total enrollment in American schools and colleges actually declined. This reversal of the upward trend was caused by a drop in elementary-school enrollments.

The fiscal crisis occurred after a decade of expansion and relative affluence. Too many institutions, according to the Carnegie report, were overextended and undercapitalized. In addition, one should not overlook the deep impact of spiraling inflation, and the combined effects of the Vietnam

War on the federal budget and of student unrest on state spending. At all levels of education, the gradual loss of federal and state support created a wide gap between income and expenditures.

By the mid-1970s the crisis worsened, causing a serious erosion in academic quality and educational opportunity. School districts operated on austerity budgets, and many systems cut the school calendar to save on rising fuel and maintenance costs. Little or no money was available for guidance counselors and special programs. Virtually all colleges and universities registered deficits, as research funds were eliminated and the costs of educating students continued to soar. In sharp contrast to the mid-1960s, the pressure disappeared from the college admissions scene, and several colleges reported available space for qualified applicants. University trustees raised fees and tuition charges and questioned everything from the nature of tenure to the needs of libraries. It was even suggested, for instance, that the University of California at Berkeley sell its rare book collection and use the money to meet present expenses. Schools, colleges, and universities facing bankruptcy were not likely to experiment in such programs as Head Start and open admissions and to reach out for impoverished young people.

Lifelong Learning: The Growth of Continuing Education Programs

Somewhat ironically, without much debate and publicity, colleges and universities have for decades implemented an open-admissions policy through continuing education programs developed for local citizens. President Charles Van Hise of the University of Wisconsin organized the first general extension program in 1906. "The boundaries of the campus should be coterminous with the boundaries of the state," he said. During subsequent decades, there were increased efforts in land-grant colleges and state universities to disseminate knowledge and technical information to farmers and their families. Success in this endeavor led to the development of general extension programs for nonfarming adults in small towns and villages and in urban centers located away from the main campus. After World War I, universities opened "evening colleges" that offered adult-education courses for university credit.

The original concept gradually expanded into a full-scale movement, with vast numbers of older adults engaged in lifelong learning. By 1981, more than 21 million persons seventeen years of age and older participated in adult education activities, according to the National Center for Education Statistics.

In 1986, for example, researchers at Pennsylvania State University invented a "talking computer," the first computer-learning program designed for adults who read below the fourth-grade level or who are totally illiterate. The computer "talks" to students and teaches them about one thousand survival words that might appear on insurance forms or job applications, such as "occupation," "spouse," and "address." According to a research associate at Pennsylvania State University's Institute for the Study of Adult Literacy, who developed the lesson plans, the talking computer is helpful to students because it is patient and does not make value judgments. Using a voice synthesizer, with sound and bright orange letters, the computer encourages the adult learners with "good job" or "wonderful" for correct responses and "sorry, try again" for mistakes. The computer never says "you're wrong"—something the research associates say the adults have heard too frequently in the past. There is also an element of status for the learners who like to say, "I'm working on a computer. No one," the adult learners say, "asks you what you are doing with it." The computer program fosters feelings of self-esteem when adults begin to think, "If I can use this computer, I can learn to read. I can do anything." In 1986, the Department of Education estimated that almost 13 percent of all American adults were illiterate; of people in their early twenties, almost 6 percent read below the fourth-grade level and 5 percent could not complete a job application or total entries on a bank deposit slip. By 1990 it was estimated that over 23 million adults in the United States were functionally illiterate.

Programs in continuing education were almost endless in diversity and design. Adjunct faculty were drawn from industries and professions in the surrounding community, and students frequently participated in the development of curricula. Sometimes centers with a focus on the contemporary scene (for example, environmental studies and urban problems) were created to meet a local need. By the mid-1980s it was estimated that over 13 percent of the total adult population was enrolled in continuing education programs. The full potential of continuing education for social change and individual self-fulfillment was just beginning to unfold. The full potential of continuing education for social change and individual self-fulfillment was just beginning to unfold.

By the closing decades of the twentieth century, American society was witnessing extensions and strong reassertions of the quest for equality of opportunity. Noteworthy examples included a new image of the American woman and a growing respect for the achievements of black citizens. Demands for more humane and meaningful educational experiences were on the upsurge among Mexican Americans, Puerto Ricans, Asian Americans, and American Indians.

In its broadest sense, this quest for the fulfillment of individual potentialities is a continuing manifestation of national purpose. The quest springs from the United States' heritage, from a nation's deepest commitments. It helps to explain the educational efforts to eliminate ignorance and poverty in the United States and to combat misery and frustration in other lands. It helps to account for the enthusiasm with which American reformers have plunged into crusades for social betterment.

Eleanor Roosevelt and the Universal Declaration of Human Rights

An enthusiastic reformer with great self-control, Eleanor Roosevelt (1884–1962) was able to reach out and touch the world in profoundly compassionate ways. Although committed to the tradition of women as primarily responsible to family, she herself personified the strength of the free and independent woman. Both by will and by destiny, she became one of the most important female reformers of the twentieth century.

After President Franklin D. Roosevelt died in April 1945, President Harry S. Truman nominated Eleanor Roosevelt as a United States delegate to the United Nations. At the United Nations she argued, debated, and lobbied for the development of a document on human rights that would embody standards that civilized humankind would accept as sacred and inalienable. Finally on December 10, 1948, the Universal Declaration of Human Rights, basically shaped by Eleanor Roosevelt, passed the General Assembly. Delegates rose in a standing ovation to the woman who more than anyone else had emerged to symbolize the basic cause of human rights. The cause of world peace and efforts to help the victims of war quickly became central to Eleanor Roosevelt's efforts. In moving speeches that vividly portrayed the suffering wrought by war, she tried to educate the United States to its postwar responsibilities.

Throughout the 1950s Eleanor Roosevelt remained an important public figure, attracting the attention of millions by her statements. She argued vigorously for civil rights, became one of the most outspoken supporters of Israel, and fought forcefully against the "witchhunts" of McCarthyism.

Her last official position was to chair President John F. Kennedy's Commission on the Status of Women, to which she was appointed in 1961. More than anyone else of her generation, Eleanor Roosevelt symbolized the freedom and political independence that were central themes to the feminist movement. She had not been a militant feminist; but on the issue of women's equality as in so many other areas, Eleanor Roosevelt frequently affirmed the inalienable right of the human spirit to grow and seek fulfillment. Reared amidst anti-Semitic and racist attitudes, she transcended her past and became a staunch champion of minority rights and human freedom.

As she entered her seventies, Eleanor Roosevelt had emerged as first lady of the world. She traveled to Japan, India, and the Soviet Union and talked about the best that was in the United States. She participated in the activities of the Commission on the Status of Women until August 1962, testifying in April before a congressional hearing on the needs for equal pay laws. In November of that year she died at her home in New York City from tuberculosis. Despite personal disappointments and deep tragedy, she had helped millions of less fortunate people to experience a sense of hope and human self-fulfillment.

To allow for equality of opportunity is to work toward fulfilling human aspirations, to give concrete meaning to the whole concept of human dignity. Success or failure in this task is of crucial importance to the United States. "We in this country, in this generation, are, by destiny rather than choice, the watchmen on the walls of world freedom," wrote President Kennedy in an undelivered speech released to the press just before his tragic assassination.[36] No other nation has yet succeeded in measuring up fully to the high ideal that the United States has set for itself; only a free society would ever attempt such an arduous and noble venture.

FOR DISCUSSION AND CRITICAL THOUGHT

1. Discuss some of the social forces that are bringing about great changes in the American family.
2. Examine the key legal cases related to "mainstreaming" and the education of the handicapped. What important elements and practices should a school demonstrate in implementing the concept of equal access for the handicapped?
3. Are "open-admissions" programs in higher education a reflection of the right of any secondary-school graduate to pursue a college education, or are such programs really a marketing opportunity for colleges to maintain enrollment in an era of declining high-school graduates? Explain.
4. Eleanor Roosevelt, as a crusader for human rights, is often overlooked in American educational history. How do you account for this omission? Cite other American reformers who have plunged into crusades for social improvements and the fulfillment of human aspirations.
5. What do you consider to be the most important purpose of public education in the United States today? Discuss the dichotomy between your ideal goal and the current realities in American schooling and culture.
6. What types of issues and problems should educators address in order to accommodate in the public schools the growing numbers of nonwhite and minority students? What successful programs have been implemented to help minorities in American schools?
7. How do you account for the unusual record of academic success achieved by young Asian Americans? An unanswered question is whether Asian

American youth will maintain their record of achievement as they become more assimilated into the larger society. Comment critically on possible barriers to future success.

NOTES

1. John Rawls, *A Theory of Justice* (Cambridge, Mass.: Harvard University Press, 1971), "Justice as Fairness" (1958), p. 3.
2. William Manchester, *The Glory and the Dream: A Narrative History of America, 1932–1972* (Boston: Little, Brown, 1974), p. 1228.
3. Max Lerner, "Colleges and the Urban Crisis" (Address before the annual conference of the American College Testing Program in May 1969), as reprinted in Fred F. Harcleroad, ed., *Issues of the Seventies* (San Francisco: Jossey-Bass, 1970), p. 35.
4. James S. Coleman et al., *Equality of Educational Opportunity*, Superintendent of Documents Catalog No. FS5. 238:38001 (Washington, D.C.: Government Printing Office, 1966). This publication is generally referred to as the Coleman Report.
5. Ibid., p. 325.
6. Daniel P. Moynihan, "Equalizing Education: In Whose Benefit?" *Public Interest* 29 (Fall 1972): 71, 74–75.
7. Christopher Jencks et al., *Inequality: A Reassessment of the Effect of Family and Schooling in America* (New York: Basic Books, 1972). The quoted words and statements are on pages 135, 192, and 265.
8. See Donald M. Levine and Mary Jo Bane, ed., *The "Inequality" Controversy: Schooling and Distributive Justice* (New York: Basic Books, 1975).
9. See pp. 240–241.
10. *Pennsylvania Association for Retarded Children* v. *Commonwealth of Pennsylvania*, 343 F. Supp. 279 (E.D. Pa., 1972), Consent Agreement.
11. *Mills* v. *Board of Education of the District of Columbia*, 348 F. Supp. 866 (D.D.C., 1972).
12. U.S. Congress, Public Law 94–142, Education for All Handicapped Children Act (1975).
13. Public Law 93–112, Vocational Rehabilitation Act (1973), Section 504.
14. *Serrano* v. *Priest*, California Supreme Court, 96 *California Reporter* 601–626 (1971).
15. *San Antonio Independent School District* v. *Rodriquez*, 36 Law. Ed. 2^d 16 (1973). The case was actually argued on 12 October 1972. In the meantime, between October 1972 and March 1973, there was widespread discussion in state legislatures over how to change tax structures.
16. Contrary to popular belief, the Indian population is multiplying rapidly. In 1970, for instance, the growth rate of the Indian population on reservations was 3.3 percent per year, which is three times the growth rate for the national population at large. In 1988 an estimated 1.7 million Indians were living in the United States.

17. In 1970 most of the 224 schools in the BIA system were located in Alaska, Arizona, New Mexico, North Dakota, and South Dakota, where there are the greatest concentrations of Indians. Other BIA schools were located in California, Florida, Iowa, Kansas, Louisiana, Mississippi, Montana, Nevada, North Carolina, Oklahoma, Oregon, and Utah.

18. The distance from home is sometimes very great indeed. In 1969 Indian children from Alaska were shipped 6,000 miles from home to attend a poorly equipped BIA boarding school in Chemawa, Oregon. This practice is obviously disliked by Indian parents. The Navaho Tribal Council, for example, passed a resolution recommending that adequate schools be built on or near the reservation so that children could be educated close to their families.

19. Rodney L. Brod and John M. McQuiston, "American Indian Adult Education and Literacy: The First National Survey," *Journal of American Indian Education* 22 (January 1983): 1–16.

20. *New York Times*, 1 February 1970, p. 41, col. 5.

21. Deloria, a Standing Rock Sioux and diligent student of law, is among the most outspoken of the new young leadership. See his books, *Custer Died for Your Sins: An Indian Manifesto* (New York: Macmillan, 1969); and *We Talk, You Listen: New Tribes, New Turf* (New York: Macmillan, 1970).

22. See p. 367.

23. See the special issue of the *Journal of Teacher Education* 26 (Summer 1975): 101–154.

24. *Lau* v. *Nichols*, 94 S.Ct. 786 (1974).

25. *New York Times*, 26 September 1985, p. B9.

26. For a balanced discussion of the controversy, see Edward B. Fiske, "One Language or Two?" *New York Times*, 10 November 1985, section 12, pp. 1, 45.

27. *Higher Education Advocate* 7 (9 August 1990): 2. Italics in original.

28. *Education Week*, 14 May 1986, p. 26.

29. For a critique of project Head Start, see Frank Riessman, "The New Pre-School Mythology: Child-Centered Radicalism," *American Child* (Spring 1966): 19–21. The Westinghouse Learning Corporation/Ohio University evaluation of Head Start has generated much controversy. See Victor G. Cicirelli et al., *The Impact of Head Start: An Evaluation of the Effects of Head Start on Children's Cognitive and Affective Development* (Washington, D.C.: Office of Economic Opportunity, 12 June 1969; the report of a study conducted by Westinghouse Learning Corporation and Ohio University under contract B89-4536 dated 20 June 1968, with the Office of Economic Opportunity).

30. Arthur R. Jensen, "How Much Can We Boost IQ and Scholastic Achievement?" *Harvard Educational Review* 39 (Winter 1969): 1–123. Recognized as a leading educational psychologist, Dr. Jensen concluded his research for this study at the University of California at Berkeley. It was published on 15 February 1969, and is one of the longest and most controversial articles ever to appear in an educational journal.

31. Ibid., p. 5. Italics in original.

32. Heritability is a technical term in genetics. It is used as a statistical tool for assessing the degree to which individual differences (in a trait like intelligence) can be accounted for by genetic factors.

33. Note, for instance, the responses by six psychologists and one geneticist to Jensen's conclusions in the *Harvard Educational Review* 39 (Spring 1969): 273–347. See also Jensen's reaction to their criticisms: "Reducing the Heredity-Environment Uncertainty: A Reply," *Harvard Educational Review* 39 (Summer 1969): 449–83. Some nationwide reactions to Jensen's conclusions are reported in Lee Edson, "*jensenism, n.* The theory that I.Q. is largely determined by genes," *New York Times Magazine,* 31 August 1969, pp. 10–11ff.

34. Michael Harrington, "Keep Open Admissions Open," *New York Times Magazine,* 2 November 1975, pp. 16–17ff. CUNY's experiment with open admissions ended because New York City ran out of funds to support the policy. See Theodore L. Gross, "How to Kill a College: The Private Papers of a Campus Dean," *Saturday Review* 5 (4 February 1978): 13–20.

35. *Priorities for Action: Final Report of the Carnegie Commission on Higher Education* (New York: McGraw-Hill, 1973), p. 3.

36. John F. Kennedy, *The Burden and the Glory,* ed. Allan Nevins (New York: Harper & Row, 1964), "Undelivered Speech for the Dallas Citizens Council, the Dallas Assembly and the Graduate Research Center of the Southwest in Dallas" (released to the press at noon, Central Standard Time, 22 November 1963), p. 277.

CHAPTER 14

Approaching the Twenty-first Century

Behind it all, of course, is the knowledge explosion. There is no more dramatic demonstration of its impact than the fact that the present "half-life" of many engineers is just ten years. Half of the material they'll need to know ten years from now is not available to them today.

C. PETER McCOLOUGH, "Educate or Erode," remarks before
the Los Angeles Society of Financial Analysts, June 1965

I believe that robots with human intelligence will be common within fifty years.

HANS P. MORAVEC, *Mind Children: The Future
of Robot and Human Intelligence,* 1988

In our still profound ignorance, who can prescribe the right path to take?

ANTHONY G. OETTINGER, *Run, Computer, Run:
The Mythology of Educational Innovation,* 1969

THE GROWTH OF FEDERAL INFLUENCE AND POWER

During the 1960s, the massive nature of the federal government's commitment to the reform movement was reflected in the unprecedented millions of dollars spent annually for projects at all levels. The National Science Foundation, established in 1950 by the National Science Foundation Act, is a tax-supported federal agency designed to promote education and basic research in the sciences. Under the provisions of the National Defense Education Act

(NDEA) of 1958, the United States Office of Education (USOE) sponsored research and innovations in science, mathematics, modern foreign languages, and guidance. The NDEA program also permitted the federal government to finance training programs for teachers, to purchase equipment, to establish research centers, and to experiment with new educational methods or techniques. In 1962 the USOE launched a new program for supporting centers in English and social studies that would attempt to improve curriculum and instruction in these subject areas. In 1964 Congress extended the National Defense Education Act for a period of three years and expanded Title III of the act to include funds for improving instruction in reading, English, geography, history, and civics. The greatly increased number of full-time positions required in state departments of education to administer these new programs and projects was a vivid indication of the rising federal involvement in education; in Tennessee, for example, eighty-five new professional jobs in the state department of education were filled from 1955 to 1964 to handle almost exclusively federally financed programs.

At the same time, enrollments in the public schools spiraled upward: about 25 million in 1950, 36 million in 1960, and 50 million in 1970. However, due to a declining birth rate, this trend changed dramatically toward the end of the 1970s. According to the National Center for Education Statistics, one of the sharpest drops in school enrollment occurred in the fall of 1979 when 41.5 million pupils entered public elementary and secondary schools, a decrease of 1,069,000 or 2.5 percent from the previous year.

In 1965 the first session of the Eighty-ninth Congress established a record of legislative action in education unparalleled in American history. "This has been the fabulous 89th Congress," remarked President Lyndon B. Johnson shortly before the session adjourned.[1] In some ways Congress exceeded even the president's requests. The Elementary and Secondary Education Act of 1965 (Public Law 89–10 [1965]) authorized for the first time funds for general use (with certain stipulations) in elementary and secondary schools. A major obstacle that had blocked this type of federal aid in the past—the issue of also permitting assistance to nonpublic schools—was overcome by providing financial assistance directly to nonpublic school students and not to the institutions these boys and girls attended. With authorizations totaling over $1.3 billion, this act contained five "Titles," with provisions of great significance for the future of American education. Most of the authorization—over $1 billion, in fact—pertained to Title I, which provides assistance in the form of grants ("basic" and "special incentives") for programs designed to meet the needs of "educationally deprived" children from low-income families. Pupils attending public or private elementary and secondary schools were eligible for financial help. In areas with high concentrations of "disadvantaged" children, public-school officials could use the funds for a variety of special services in which these children participated.

Another measure, also of far-reaching significance, was the Higher Education Act of 1965 (Public Law 89–329 [1965]), which carried a first-year authorization of $841.4 million. For the first time, this bill approved funds for "federal scholarships" (termed "Educational Opportunity Grants"). Repeated efforts in the past to establish similar programs had failed. Among its many noteworthy features, this act authorized low-interest, government-insured loans to qualified students and established a National Teacher Corps (although no funds were appropriated) to supply experienced personnel to poverty-stricken communities. Congress also enacted a tremendous amount of other basic legislation affecting education in all areas.

On September 27, 1979, Congress approved legislation establishing a new cabinet-level Department of Education, which would be administered by a secretary of education appointed by the president. The new department was allocated an initial budget of about $14.1 billion and would begin with about 17,400 employees. Most of the education programs in the new department came from the Department of Health, Education, and Welfare, which Congress renamed the Department of Health and Human Services.

The willingness of the federal government to assume educational leadership and such a large share of the financial support of education has brought into sharp focus a recurring issue: who is responsible for shaping educational policy?

Traditionally, the responsibility belongs to the states and the local school districts. Of the two, the state has the basic legal responsibility. The legislature in most states is required by the state constitution to establish and maintain a system of public education. The fact that this obligation has been discharged by creating local school units does not absolve the state of its legal duty. Most states, in fact, have developed vigorous roles in this working relationship. Minimum criteria for maintaining public schools, including the licensing or certifying of teachers, have been established; and state departments of education have long been responsible for enforcing these standards. Some state departments, with highly competent and responsible officials, have exercised strong leadership in working for school improvements. In discharging these responsibilities, the states have been historically and legally free from federal interference.

The balance of power in education shifted fundamentally during the 1960s. Congressional action probably made 1965 a pivotal date in federal-state relationships. The first session of the Eighty-ninth Congress, according to former President Johnson, would "go down in history as 'The Education Congress.' "[2] And so it may: The Education Congress accelerated some important changes in the historic roles of the state and federal governments. After 1965 decisions affecting the expenditure and disbursement of billions of dollars were made by a greatly augmented U.S. Office of Education.[3] While the tradition of federal participation is old, this increased federal aid was considered necessary because of the greater tax-collecting powers of the federal government.

In July 1965, John W. Gardner, president of the Carnegie Corporation, was selected by President Johnson for the cabinet post of secretary of health, education, and welfare. At the same time, the president promoted Francis Keppel (1916–1990), U.S. commissioner of education, to a new post of assistant secretary for education. Keppel's persuasive leadership during his three years as commissioner was a major factor in strengthening the USOE and in obtaining favorable congressional action on reform legislation in education. In December 1965, Harold Howe II, a Yale alumnus and former superintendent of the Scarsdale (New York) public schools, was named U.S. commissioner of education. During the mid-1960s the combined talents and skills of Gardner, Keppel, and Howe greatly enhanced the status and prestige of the USOE. "The innovators," wrote Fred M. Hechinger in 1966, were "in command."[4]

Power in education is, of course, "shared" by the federal government and the state and local agencies. The American Association of School Administrators calls this arrangement a "partnership," with the federal government assuming a major policy-making role.[5] During the early 1970s, President Richard M. Nixon's retrenchment policies sharply curtailed expenditures at all levels and accentuated this growing federal influence and power in shaping educational policy.

There were strong indications in the mid-1960s that some states and local units were eager and willing to play a much larger role in this "emerging public school partnership." The crux of the issue was highlighted in the fall of 1965 when several hundred local and state leaders convened in Kansas City, Missouri, to endorse a Compact for Education.[6] The compact would become a legal reality with its ratification by the legislatures of at least ten states. On February 18, 1966, when New Mexico and Rhode Island became the ninth and tenth states to join, the compact officially began operations.

Under this historic arrangement, an Educational Commission of the States was formed. The commission is designed for nationwide action: its maximum size is 350 members (seven representatives from each participating state). The commission meets annually as a policy-making group. A steering committee, with delegated powers to act between annual meetings, implements the commission's policies.[7]

The ultimate success of the compact is contingent to a large extent on the quality of its constituent leadership. The steering committee, for example, consists of thirty members, ten of whom must be governors (no substitutes or "proxy" voting will be allowed). Five members of the committee are legislators and the additional fifteen are professional staff members and laypersons involved in education.

The whole idea of a compact for education is not new. Conant, in fact, had proposed in 1964 that such an instrument be created in order to cope with the growing complexities of educational problems and issues.[8] But this may be more than even Conant had expected. A successful compact for education organized on such an all-encompassing basis holds tremendous potential for wielding a powerful force in American education.

Former President Ronald Reagan's "New Federalism"

In 1980 former President Ronald Reagan promised the American people a renewed faith, pride, and confidence in the United States as a world power. The President's vision of the nation was based on less government and more individual enterprise. On February 18, 1981, four weeks after his first inauguration, President Reagan presented Congress with his agenda for economic growth: a budget reform plan to reduce the rate of federal spending; and several proposals to reduce personal income taxes by 10 percent a year over three years and to create employment by accelerating depreciation for business investment in plant and equipment. To President Reagan, a better America would require a greater national defense program, a stronger economy, and less involvement of the federal government in local and state affairs. The central tenets of the President's "New Federalism" were (1) a belief that the best government is government "closest to the people"; (2) an assumption that states and local governments are able and willing to assume the responsibilities previously held by the federal government; and (3) a strong conviction that the administration of federal programs had become too complex and overly intrusive and specific.

As a result, retrenchment occurred in federal domestic policies, and social programs were given the deepest federal cuts. The irony of President Reagan's New Federalism was that the federal government might have been expected to give higher priority to human resource programs (for example, child welfare, education, nutrition, and social services) as a way of reducing poverty and welfare dependency; instead these were the very programs in which the Reagan administration proposed the deepest cuts in federal spending.

Thus President Reagan's New Federalism during the 1980s underscored a major shift in national priorities and signaled the withdrawal of federal responsibility in the creation and implementation of educational policy. This was a notable departure from the historic role of the federal government in national educational policy. The New Federalism of the Reagan years represented the most serious effort to change the course of United States economic policy since the New Deal.

Critics of the New Federalism claimed that the President's policies were an effort to help the wealthy make more money at the expense of the rest of society. While the critics admitted that the President's tax reductions gave tax advantages to all classes of citizens, they frequently pointed out that the largest benefits went to people with high incomes and to large corporations. In fact, during the 1980s, the gap between wealthy and poor citizens had widened so much that the richest 1 percent received almost as much of the nation's total income after taxes as the lowest 40 percent. While the rich obtained tax breaks, the critics exclaimed, assistance to the poor was being cut. The Reagan counterargument was that the program cuts were intended primarily to eliminate fraud and waste and that many people on welfare should not need public assistance and should become economically self-sufficient. Allowing them to stay on welfare, argued President Reagan, simply encouraged their dependence on public funds and did little to eliminate the causes of poverty. Nevertheless, critics of the budget cuts in federal social programs pointed out that the real victims of the New Federalism were frequently children of the poor who were deprived of adequate nutrition and other basic necessities.

ADVANCES IN TECHNOLOGY

Developments in technology since World War II have proceeded at an accelerated pace. Commercial television, for example, was only a small industry after the war. In a relatively brief period of time, from 1946 to 1966, over 90 percent of all American homes had acquired television sets. Audiences increased from only a few thousand in the late 1940s to over fifty million, viewing special attractions, in 1966. Television, in brief, became an integral part of American culture during the course of only two decades. Antennae towering above rooftops in small communities are a more familiar landscape feature today than tall chimneys or church spires.

With three commercial networks and a national educational TV system transmitting videotapes and films, nationwide television in the mid-1960s symbolized an immense technological advancement in modern communication. In August 1965 a National Center for School and College Television (NCSCT), with headquarters at Indiana University, was established with a two-year grant of $1,104,652 from the U.S. Office of Education. NCSCT served as a central source of information about TV and its applications to education. Its primary aim was to acquire, and distribute throughout the United States, TV materials for classroom use. By January 1966, there were 114 local educational television (ETV) stations on the air with a potential viewing audience of 130 million. Increased facilities for in-school telecasts made it possible for two of every three pupils in the nation to view television in classroom during school hours.

By 1990 television sets had been installed in almost all American homes and the medium had demonstrated an impressive ability to participate in formal instruction. The enormous success of such programs as *Sesame Street* and *The Electric Company*, for example, has clearly shown television's ability to teach and entertain at the same time. Without credit or compulsion, these and other popular programs on ETV have continued to attract learners of all ages.

Similar expansions occurred in other media. The use of electronic computers, for example, led to some ingenious ways of storing, classifying, recording, retrieving, and displaying vast amounts of information and materials. In its computer-based laboratories at Santa Monica, California, System Development Corporation, a nonprofit organization involved in educational research, built an elaborate program that permits students to query a computer in dialogue style by typing freely constructed questions that the computer answers almost instantaneously with printed responses from materials in its memory. International Business Machines, Inc. (IBM), a leader in the computer field, developed for the Central Intelligence Agency a data-storage system that retrieves information instantly through the use of coded symbols. Project GASP (Generalized Academic Simulation Programs) at the Massachusetts Institute of Technology (MIT) used an IBM 7094 computer to simulate the institute (its faculties, students, curricula, and facilities), register students, and build all of MIT's course schedules with speed, economy, and no conflicts. By 1965, four secondary schools had also experimented with Project GASP in building complex master schedules and in assigning students to individual class sections.[9] At the University of Illinois, Project PLATO (Programed Logic for Automated Teaching Operation) used a computer network of slides, television screen, and student response panels for teaching groups simultaneously, while still permitting individuals to work on the same material separately. And in 1966 in Columbia City, Maryland (near Washington, D.C.), a new community was planned with a built-in system of computer communications. A proposed coaxial cable network would link over ten thousand homes to a single computer center. Under the Columbia plan, for instance, students might use a home television set and a keyboard unit for receiving homework fed by the computer, while parents, without leaving home, could play chess or bridge with other residents.

Communications satellites, also using television, might eventually provide on a global scale an instantaneous exchange of information and cultural contacts among civilized nations of the world. The successful launching of Telstar II on May 7, 1963, for example, opened up possibilities so fantastic that even Francis Bacon or Jules Verne might have dismissed the idea if it had ever occurred to them.

Meanwhile, the technological search for new ideas and devices continued with vigor and speed. The Raytheon Company, an electronics corporation, bought D.C. Heath and Company, a textbook publishing firm in Boston; IBM purchased Science Research Associates; and Xerox Corporation acquired American Education Publications and Wesleyan University Press, Inc. Soon after its acquisitions, Xerox placed a large advertisement in the editorial section of the *New York Times,* soliciting applications from qualified personnel to fill five vacancies. "Xerox can put anyone who can educate and write in a position to reach almost half the youth of America—every week," stated the advertisement in bold type. "The important thing is that you are as vigorously sympathetic to the innovative tasks that education must perform as we are."[10]

These developments were quickly followed by a press release on January 11, 1966, that Radio Corporation of America (RCA) would purchase Random House, Inc., one of the nation's largest book publishers. This merger agreement with RCA, explained Bennett Cerf of Random House, reflects our "conviction that publishing and electronics are natural partners for the incredible expansion immediately ahead for every phase of education." Future RCA–Random House plans called for the development and distribution of "new electronic equipment and systems for handling all types of printed information."[11]

Each month witnessed a proliferation of potential learning resources: from airborne television instruction, automated teaching programs, and language laboratories to "telemation," audio-visumatic systems, and new computers adapted to self-instruction. Indicative of the changing times was the publication in 1966 of a textbook with the imposing title *Cybernetic Principles of Learning and Educational Design.* "Cybernetic theory views the individual as a feedback system," explained the authors, "which generates its own activities in order to detect and control specific stimulus characteristics of the environment."[12]

These advances were changing profoundly educational procedures and techniques long hallowed by custom and tradition. Yet, oddly enough, few voices of dissent were heard over the loud chorus of acclaim for the superiority of the new media. While the innovators hailed the inventions, only a small number of Americans began to perceive some of the wider issues raised by the onslaught of technological change and the impact of automation on teaching and learning. Had sufficient thoughtful inquiry preceded the adoption of large-scale technological programs? In what ways would these developments affect the interpersonal relationships between teachers and pupils? In an age of mass conformity, would the "electronic revolution" depersonalize even further the very core of the teaching-learning process? With a rising anonymity in urban life, all the issues were by no means settled.

CONTEMPORARY DEVELOPMENTS IN COMPUTER TECHNOLOGY

Due to swiftly moving developments in microprocessor technology, the cost and size of computers have been reduced even as their computing power and applications have expanded. One result is a proliferation of electronic games—Pac-Man, Space Invaders, and the like—that people play. Another important outcome, with greater long-term significance, is the growing use of computers in education.

Low-cost microcomputers (called personal computers) have created new interest in student use of computers in schools. In 1981, for example, about one-half of the nation's school districts provided its students with access to at least one microcomputer or computer terminal, according to the National Center for Education Statistics. About one of every four public schools had at least one microcomputer or computer terminal for instructional use by students. This represented one-half of all secondary schools and 14 percent of all elementary schools in the nation. In 1982, about 96,000 microcomputers were used solely for educational purposes; three years later this figure tripled. In 1983, for example, at Carnegie-Mellon University in Pittsburgh, Pennsylvania, about 75 percent of the student body of 5,500 students used the time-sharing computer system every day. In addition, there were about one thousand computer workstations available on campus, and most faculty members and administrators had terminals in their offices or at home. Carnegie-Mellon planned to equip every student and each staff and faculty member with a personal computer.

Indeed, computers and other microelectronic devices have literally transformed the entire field of communications. Now machines can ingest, store, manipulate, and transfer vast amounts of information. For example, in less than a millionth of a second the vast computer of an international airline can simultaneously accept 800 booking inquiries and search its 50 million memory units for appropriate replies. In another split second the requested information is flashed up on 800 separate monitors, which are hundreds of miles apart. Such is the enormous power of the modern mainframe computer.

In essence the computer is a high-speed calculator with an electronic memory. Instructions (the program) are fed in using computer languages imprinted on magnetic tape or electronic disks. This then reaches a control unit that converts it into a series of stepwise arithmetical operations, which are performed by the arithmetical logic unit. To complete its work, it may draw on information stored in a read-only memory unit or transfer data to a random access memory unit for use later on in the calculation. The final result is then "translated" into mathematical symbols, numerals, letters, or graphics, and either printed out on paper or displayed on a separate monitor.

The first electronic computers, such as the ENIAC (Electronic Numerical Integrator and Calculator) built in 1945, were huge machines equipped with more than 18,000 thermionic valves. Each computer occupied 1,500 square feet of floor space. The thermionic valves were supposed to permit the flow of an electric current that corresponded to a particular number. The valves were plugged in manually to program the computer, which could then complete 5,000 calculations a second.

The "brain" of the computer is housed in a silicon chip. The larger a computer, the more chips it has, and the bigger and better its memory and calculating power. Because of the silicon chip, computers are now so ubiquitous that they are used in some way by about 40 percent of the total work force of the Western world.

The power of the computer for scientific and educational change could never have been envisaged by Charles Babbage, British inventor and "father" of the computer. In 1834, Babbage sketched the first plans for an engine that, with the aid of a memory stored on punched cards, would work as a calculating machine. This punched card idea (with the holes read by feelers) was used by U.S. statistician Herman Hollerith for analyzing the results of the 1890 Census.

For the next half-century few real advancements were made in computer science. However, experiments in the 1930s used machines with mechanical parts driven by electrical input to make calculations. Much more important was the incorporation of thermionic valves into calculating machines. These were used to permit the passage of electric currents generated to be equivalent to numerals. Banks of valves, plugged in by hand, were necessary to accomplish even simple arithmetic.

During the 1940s additional developments included the invention of the binary code—the representation of numbers in sequences of 0 and 1—which meant that the valves would be operated simply by transmitting or not transmitting current, and by advances in the design of memory stores. When computers entered the business community as payroll calculators during the 1950s, their everyday applications became more obvious. However, the invention of the transistor during the 1960s launched a second generation of computers.

By using transistors in place of valves to conduct electricity, computers became smaller, cheaper, and more reliant. Indeed, so fast was the progress in electronics that by the mid-1960s, a third generation of computers was invented—this time using silicon chips in place of transistors. Soon millions of calculations and memorizations could be made on a thin slice of silicon only a quarter-inch (5 mm) square.

Personal microcomputers are now available at increasingly low prices. At the other end of the spectrum, industry's largest computers have "bubble" memories made of garnet that can store a million bits of information.

Indeed, the computer is changing the whole tenor of American society. Without computers, units such as the Jet Propulsion Laboratory at the National Aeronautics and Space Administration (NASA) could not exist. The many mathematical calculations required to propel people and machines into space and keep them in orbit are so complex that only a computer can complete them in a realistic time period, and it is the speed of computer calculation that also puts space flight within the bounds of safety: as crafts orbit through space, or when emergencies occur, only computers can make the correcting sums fast enough to ensure the accurate in-flight responses.

The visual display screen is vital to many computer tasks. For example, in the manufacture of drugs the configuration of a possible new formulation is shown on the screen. To determine this solution, the computer is fed information about an enormous range of existing drugs and their actions, both good and bad, on the human body. To investigate further, scientists can interact with the computer by feeding additional instructions and data through a control panel. Thus the power of the computer remains unchanged—the quality of the program fed in by a human operator.

Since the late 1970s, computers have become a familiar part of everyday life. Wage slips are computerized; many households own an electronic calculator or a personal microcomputer; children play with electronic toys. Home systems built around microcomputers are becoming commonplace. Data stored on flexible "floppy" discs, and shown on visual display units, are becoming indispensable aids for business, education, security, and even shopping—computer links with stores and banks allow "remote control" purchase without cash changing hands. The fantastic surge of development in computer science during the 1970s and 1980s will surely continue in the future.

The crucial central technology in computers is a silicon integrated circuit (SIC). SIC is the heart of the microelectronic industry. At the present time a SIC is produced by cutting an extremely thin slice of silicon from a single huge crystal. On this semiconducting substrate, circuitry is produced on a microscopic scale. Researchers in Japan, Europe, and the United States are currently seeking to improve the basic processing power of SICs or even to replace them with different types of logic circuitry. The research will truly spawn competing systems during the next decade. One element to enter commercial computer production is the obvious one of compressing more and more components into each square millimeter of silicon surface—"ultrahigh" level integrations. Photoreduction has been developed to the point where circuitry patterns less than three microns ($\frac{3}{1000}$ mm) across the commercial norm, and packings of submicron dimensions are already being produced in the laboratory. However, wavelength considerations mean that this is the theoretical limit to lithography using light. In the future, electron beams or x-ray sources, both with shorter wavelength characteristics than visible light, will certainly be used to achieve circuit printing of even greater density. When such developments are commercially available, the single memory chip that now contains about 64,000 memory elements may contain more than a million elements.

More revolutionary options will develop commercially before the end of the twentieth century. For example, during the late 1970s IBM was interested in "Josephson junction" technology. Such junctions in microcircuits depended for their operation on the property of some materials to become superconducting at temperatures close to absolute zero ($-273°C$). In 1979, IBM demonstrated that, in laboratory conditions with enormous cooling equipment to generate the necessary low temperatures, Josephson circuits could be made to operate ten times faster than SIC systems. Foreign computer companies, such as Fujitsu in Japan, were experimenting to learn whether semiconductors other than single crystal silicon-gallium arsenide, for example, might produce advantages in operating speed.

In 1986 new IBM software made a widely used programming language for artificial intelligence application available to users of System/370-based computers. The software offering, LISP/VM, could help customers create, modify, run, and update applications as diverse as robotics and "expert systems." LISP/VM was part of a large demonstration of advanced IBM artificial intelligence projects presented at a technical conference in Austin, Texas. In another demonstration, YES/MVS, an experimental expert system designed to assist operators in keeping large computer complexes running smoothly, was also exhibited. Other IBM projects displayed at this time included a system that enabled computers to manipulate abstract symbols and relationships.

Information transfer over long distances can take place between computers via telephone networks. An alternate system for transmitting digital information uses electronically modulated light signals sent along glass or silica fibers of hairlike fineness. Digital information from the first computer is converted into visual form by modulating a semiconductor laser or light-emitting diode. The optical signals are then transmitted along the inside of the fiber and reconverted into digital form in the second computer. The advantages of these fiber optic signals over other systems include increased security, low basic material costs, light flexible cables, and low signal loss per unit of cable length. Such advantages make it extremely likely that gossamer-fine optic cableways, laid next to roads or railway tracks, or slotted inside power transmission cables, will be as common as copper cables by the year 2000.

Meanwhile, in Japan during the 1980s there was a huge subsidized effort for reaching the so-called fifth-generation level of computing power. The aim of this work has been to produce computers that duplicate the human powers of hearing and vision, thus opening up the possibility of direct communication between people and the machines they have created. Even more fantastic is the fact that these fifth-generation machines will have the ability of "creative thought." Concepts and programming would be revolutionized, and software in such computers would use human "fuzzy" or open-ended logic. Thus the great breakthrough to artificial intelligence (AI), the last area that hovers before computer scientists, will no doubt come before the end of the twentieth century.

Peering into the twenty-first century, scientists expect extraordinary changes in the home, the classroom, and the workplace. New scientific breakthroughs will encourage machines to perform more tasks that the human brain has traditionally done. In laboratories around the world, scientists working at computer keyboards are creating electronic versions of biological entities—ants, microbes, proteins—that resemble their biological counterparts in striking ways. During the process, these computer scientists are focusing on issues that touch some of biology's most intriguing myster-ies: How did life emerge from nonlife? How did nature create order from chaos? The scientists who are working on "artificial life" want the life-forms to create themselves, to emerge from nonliving components.

No one yet claims to have created true artificial life, but some are coming very close in astonishing ways. Christopher Langton, a scientist at New Mexico's Los Alamos National Laboratory, coined the term *artificial life*. In the mid-1980s he was working on programs known as cellular automata, when he noticed a loop-shaped figure that would reproduce itself spontaneously. During the early 1990s, many researchers were exploring the origins of artificial life-forms on computer screens. For example, at Bellcore, the research affiliate of Bell telephone companies, David Ackley made graphical representations of little creatures with humanoid faces that roamed through a computer-simulated world evading predators, consuming re-sources, and multiplying like rabbits. Scientists are currently exploring possible users for self-replicating, adaptive machines—for example, cleaning up toxic wastes, or exploring outer space. However, there is the danger that such machines might multiply uncontrollably, similar to the viruses that, inadvertently or maliciously, have disrupted vast computer networks.

As the twenty-first century approaches, computers that at one time only remembered data will make more decisions. Machines that tell physicians today what symptoms the patients have may soon be recommending surgery. Other computers will design buildings after questioning buyers about their preferences. Increasingly, human thought processes and even values are being programmed into computers. People will talk directly to computers without pushing buttons; and the computer will respond. Computers are already vital parts of such household devices as television sets, stereo equipment, telephones, and thermostats. Scientists envision audiovisual encyclopedias that combine pictures, sound, and text. Students, for example, will select Beethoven on the computer screen and then read the text, watch a short film, and even hear the symphonies.

More people will work at home by computer, allowing them to earn a living and remain close to their families. Computers will also allow remote schooling; classes will be conducted by computers in homes, vacation resorts, and hospitals with actual teachers located in distant places. However, few predict that computer learning will ever replace face-to-face contact between student and teacher.

Technological advances may make their most profound impact on genetic engineering, in which DNA—the genetic blueprint of life—can be altered. In agriculture, scientists predict larger trees, increased grain yields, and even square tomatoes easily packaged with much less water content. It will be possible to breed cows the size of elephants that produce 40 percent more milk. "We are very near to the time when virtually no essential human function, physical or mental, will lack an artificial counterpart." It will be, argues Hans Moravec, "a postbiological world dominated by self-improving, thinking machines—a population consisting of unfettered mind children."[13]

Yet these and other technological advances could be rendered meaningless by other visions of the future—uncontrolled population growth, energy and food shortages, and environmental disasters or nuclear war. Some scientists worry that genetic engineering, for example, could lead to tragic mistakes—for instance, new killer bees or gypsy moths that escape from laboratories and create havoc. There are also fears that unemployment will lead to unrest, bitterness, and growing depression, as robots cause increasing joblessness among people. It was estimated that the number of robots performing blue-collar jobs will increase from 3,000 in 1981 to 40,000 by 1990. Thus the same technology that makes life more comfortable might create problems unprecedented in human history.

FOR DISCUSSION AND CRITICAL THOUGHT

1. During the twentieth century the responsibility for public schooling in the United States has become progressively more centralized. What are some serious implications of this trend? What might be the results today of a stronger federal commitment to public schooling?

2. In what way did the Elementary and Secondary Education Act of 1965 affect public schooling?
3. Read Alvin Toffler's *The Third Wave* (New York: Bantam Books, 1981). Do you share Toffler's hope and enthusiasm for the new "information society"? Comment critically.
4. Discuss some important implications of advances in computer technology for public schooling and higher education in the United States.
5. From the vantage point of 1991, contrast the decade of the 1980s with the dreams and aspirations of the 1960s.
6. What do you consider to be the most pressing problem for American education as we approach the twenty-first century?

NOTES

1. Quoted in National Education Association, *NEA Reporter* 4 (19 November 1965): 5.
2. Quoted in *The Federal Government and Public Schools* (Washington, D.C.: American Association of School Administrators, 1965), p. 7.
3. For a recent study, see Harry Kursh, *The United States Office of Education: A Century of Service* (Philadelphia: Chilton Books, 1965).
4. Fred M. Hechinger, "New Guard Leads National Effort toward Reforms," *New York Times,* 12 January 1966, p. 45C, col. 8.
5. See *The Federal Government and Public Schools* (1965), chap. 6, "The Emerging Public School Partnership," pp. 58–68.
6. A copy of the Compact is reprinted in the American Association of University Professors, *AAUP Bulletin* 51 (December 1965): 440–446.
7. With national headquarters in Denver, Colorado, the Commission publishes *Compact,* a bimonthly magazine of articles on educational issues.
8. James B. Conant, *Shaping Educational Policy* (New York: McGraw-Hill, 1964), pp. 123–124.
9. The four schools were Cohasset High School in Cohasset, Massachusetts; Pascack Hills High School in Montvale, New Jersey; Ridgewood High School in Norridge, Illinois; and Wayland High School in Wayland, Massachusetts. See *School Scheduling by Computer: The Story of GASP* (New York: Educational Facilities Laboratories, 1964), pp. 8–17.
10. *New York Times,* 16 January 1966, Sec. 4, p. 8E, cols. 6–7.
11. Ibid., p. 14E, col. 1. See also ibid., 6 February 1966, Sec. 3, p. 1F, col. 8; p. 14, col. 3.
12. Karl U. Smith and Margaret Foltz Smith, *Cybernetic Principles of Learning and Educational Design* (New York: Holt, Rinehart & Winston, 1966), pp. vii–viii.
13. Hans Moravec, *Mind Children: The Future of Robot and Human Intelligence* (Cambridge, Mass.: Harvard University Press, 1988), pp. 2, 5.

Bibliographical Essay: Guides to Further Readings

This book is based on primary-source materials, monographs and other secondary publications, and my own research (mostly unpublished). A wide range of collateral source material is available in my documentary history, *Educational Ideas in America* (David McKay, 1969). A well-organized guide to several major tools for locating information or researching topics in education is Marda Woodbury, *A Guide to Sources of Educational Information* (2nd ed.; Information Resources Press, 1982). See also chapter 7, "Doing History: Two Examples," of Robert R. Sherman, ed., *Understanding History of Education* (2nd ed., rev.; Schenkman Publishing Co., 1984).

Because of the broad scope of my work, I have necessarily limited my suggestions for further readings, chapter by chapter, to highly selective sources that are still readily available. Representative rather than definitive, these titles should be of interest to the general reader and inquiring student. The notes and index also provide guides to studies on specific topics.

CHAPTER 1: THE COLONIAL TRADITION

Louis B. Wright, *The Cultural Life of the American Colonies, 1607–1763* (Harper & Row, 1957, also available as a Harper Torchbook), is a general survey of the whole period. Daniel J. Boorstin, *The Americans: The Colonial Experience* (Random House, 1985); Bernard Bailyn, *The Ideological Origins of the American Revolution* (Belknap-Harvard University Press, 1967); and Henry Steele Commager, "The Revolution as a World Ideal," *Saturday Review* 3 (13 December 1975): 13–14ff., are provocative interpretations of colonial thought and action. James H. Merrell, *The Indians' New World* (Institute of Early American History and Culture; University of North Carolina Press,

1989), argues that historians have failed to integrate American Indians into the mainstream of colonial history; scholars should recognize not only the tragic side of the Indian experience but also the marvelous ways in which the Indians have survived and constructed a whole new world for themselves.

For the transmission of European ideas to colonial America, see Edward Eggleston, *The Transit of Civilization from England to America in the Seventeenth Century* (D. Appleton, 1901; reissued in 1961 by Beacon Press). In chapter 3 of *The Formative Years, 1607–1763* (Hill & Wang, 1964), Clarence L. Ver Steeg analyzes some cultural forces from England that profoundly affected life in the New World. De Crèvecoeur's *Letters from an American Farmer* (published originally in 1782 and now available in several modern editions) presents a fascinating picture of colonial diversity. Part I of Max Sevelle, ed., *The Colonial Origins of American Thought* (D. Van Nostrand, 1964), is a useful summary.

The historical roots of town life are examined in Page Smith, *As a City Upon a Hill: The Town in American History* (Knopf, 1966). Carl Bridenbaugh dispels some historical fallacies in *Myths and Realities: Societies of the Colonial South* (Louisiana State University Press, 1952). Significant, too, are Bridenbaugh's two studies of urban institutions: *Cities in the Wilderness: The First Century of Urban Life in America, 1625–1724* (Ronald Press, 1938), and *Cities in Revolt: Urban Life in America, 1743–1776* (Knopf, 1955).

Indispensable for an understanding of Puritan thought are Perry Miller's three intensive works: *Orthodoxy in Massachusetts, 1630–1650* (Harvard University Press, 1933; 2nd ed., Beacon Press, 1959); *The New England Mind: The Seventeenth Century* (Macmillan, 1939); and *The New England Mind: From Colony to Province* (Harvard University Press, 1953). Herbert W. Schneider, *The Puritan Mind* (Henry Holt, 1930), and chapters 1 and 2 of Loren Baritz, *City on a Hill: A History of Ideas and Myths in America* (Wiley, 1964) are also useful. Edmund S. Morgan, *The Puritan Dilemma: The Story of John Winthrop* (Little, Brown, 1958), and Robert Middlekauff, *The Mathers: Three Generations of Puritan Intellectuals, 1596–1728* (Oxford University Press, 1971), are excellent biographies.

CHAPTER 2: EDUCATION IN THE SEVENTEENTH AND EIGHTEENTH CENTURIES

For a comprehensive overview, see Lawrence A. Cremin, *American Education: The Colonial Experience, 1607–1783* (Harper & Row, 1970). Bernard Bailyn's helpful "Bibliographical Essay" in *Education in the Forming of American Society: Needs and Opportunities for Study* (University of North Carolina Press, 1960; reissued in 1972 in a Norton paperbound edition), contains an extensive list of pertinent titles.

For the European background of the colonial family, see part 3 of Philippe Ariès, *Centuries of Childhood: A Social History of Family Life*, trans. Robert Baldick (Vintage Books, 1965; originally published in France in 1960). Ross W. Beales, Jr., "In Search of the Historical Child: Miniature Adulthood and Youth in Colonial New England," in Ray Hiner and Joseph M. Hawes, eds., *Growing Up in America: Children in Historical Perspective* (University of Illinois Press, 1985) challenges the traditional belief that Americans in colonial New England viewed children as "miniature adults." Edmund S. Morgan, *The Puritan Family: Religion and Domestic Relations in Seventeenth-Century New England* (Harper & Row, 1966, rev., Torchbook Edition), is a scholarly account. Peter Laslett challenges some traditional views in chapter 1, "The History of the Family," of *Household and Family in Past Time*, ed. Peter Laslett and Richard Wall (Cambridge University Press, 1972). Some useful information is also available in volume 1 of Arthur W. Calhoun's disjointed *A Social History of the American Family* (Barnes & Noble, 1960; originally published in 1917).

Marcus Wilson Jernegan, *Laboring and Dependent Classes in Colonial America, 1607–1783* (Frederick Ungar, 1960; originally published in 1931), is an important study of colonial apprenticeship. Jackson Turner Main, *The Social Structure of Revolutionary America* (Princeton University Press, 1965), explores the relationships between socioeconomic status and educational opportunity during the colonial period. Samuel Eliot Morison, *The Intellectual Life of Colonial New England* (2nd ed.; New York University Press, 1965; originally published as *The Puritan Pronaos*), is a highly sympathetic treatment of Puritan accomplishments. More objective is Robert Middlekauff's scholarly *Ancients and Axioms: Secondary Education in Eighteenth-Century New England*, Yale Historical Publications *Miscellany* 77 (Yale University Press, 1963). Also significant are Samuel Eliot Morison's monumental *The Founding of Harvard College* (Harvard University Press, 1935) and *Harvard College in the Seventeenth Century*, 2 vols. (Harvard University Press, 1936).

CHAPTER 3: AGE OF THE ENLIGHTENMENT: THE IMPACT OF SECULAR THOUGHT

The European background of the American Enlightenment is vividly portrayed in Alfred Cobban, ed., *The Eighteenth Century: Europe in the Age of the Enlightenment* (McGraw-Hill, 1969). Peter Gay, *The Enlightenment: An Interpretation*, 2 vols. (Knopf, 1966–1969), is a brilliant synthesis. Carl L. Becker, *The Heavenly City of the Eighteenth-Century Philosophers* (Yale University Press, 1932; reissued in 1959 as a Yale paperbound), should be supplemented by Raymond O. Rockwood, ed., *Carl Becker's Heavenly City Revisited*

(Cornell University Press, 1958). Chapter 3 of Jack Rochford Vrooman, *René Descartes: A Biography* (Putnam, 1970), discusses "A Revolution in Thought."

S. S. Laurie's clearly organized "Lectures" entitled *Studies in the History of Educational Opinion from the Renaissance* (Frank Cass [London], 1968; originally published in 1903) present an overview of the European Enlightenment, with specific reference to educational ideas. James L. Axtell, ed., *The Educational Writings of John Locke: A Critical Edition with Introduction and Notes* (Cambridge University Press, 1968), contains important background information.

Indicative of a renewed interest in Pestalozzi's ideas are Michael Heafford, *Pestalozzi: His Thought and Its Relevance Today* (Methuen, 1967); Gerald Lee Gutek, *Pestalozzi and Education* (Random House, 1968); Lewis Flint Anderson, *Pestalozzi* (Greenwood Press, 1974; originally published in 1931); and Hugh C. Black, "Pestalozzi and the Education of the Disadvantaged," *Educational Forum* 33 (May 1969): 511–21. Will S. Monroe's pioneer study, *History of the Pestalozzian Movement in the United States* (C.W. Bardeen, 1907), long out of print, was made available in 1969 in a xerographed publication from University Microfilms. Thomas A. Barlow, *Pestalozzi and American Education* (Estes Press, University of Colorado Libraries, 1978), is a good overview. Gerald Lee Gutek, *Joseph Neef: The Americanization of Pestalozzianism* (University of Alabama Press, 1978), discusses the early influence of the Pestalozzian movement on American education, especially the work of Joseph Neef, "who was its first promoter in the United States." The best biography is Kate Silber's *Pestalozzi: The Man and His Work* (Schocken Books; originally published in 1960).

Chapter 5 of Merle Curti, *The Growth of American Thought* (3rd ed.; Harper & Row, 1964), is an excellent introduction to the American Enlightenment. For pertinent selections by Franklin and Jefferson, see parts 1 and 3 of Adrienne Koch, ed., *The American Enlightenment: The Shaping of the American Experiment and a Free Society* (Braziller, 1965). Also important are several essays, written between 1786 and 1799 by Benjamin Rush, Noah Webster, Robert Coram, Samuel Knox, and others, which are available in Frederick Rudolph, ed., *Essays on Education in the Early Republic* (Belknap-Harvard University Press, 1965).

One of the most informative biographies of Franklin is Ronald W. Clark, *Benjamin Franklin: A Biography* (Random House, 1983). Other useful studies are Carl Van Doren, *Benjamin Franklin* (Viking Press, 1938; also available as a Viking paperbound reprint), and Verner W. Crane, *Benjamin Franklin and a Rising People* (Little, Brown, 1954). Merrill D. Peterson, *The Jefferson Image in the American Mind* (Oxford University Press, 1960), discusses some changing conceptions of Jeffersonianism in American thought. Robert D. Heslep, *Thomas Jefferson and Education* (Random House, 1969), is a brief overview of Jefferson's contributions. Robert M. Healey, *Jefferson on Religion in Public Education* (Yale University Press, 1962), examines another dimension of Jefferson's influence. Garry Wills, *Inventing America: Jefferson's Declaration of Independence* (Doubleday, 1978), is a scholarly inquiry into "the real meaning" of the document. For a fascinating account of the long political struggle to enact Thomas Jefferson's Virginia Statute of Religious Liberty (finally approved by the Virginia Assembly on January 16, 1786), see part 1 of William Lee Miller, *The First Liberty: Religion and the American Republic* (Knopf, 1985); Jefferson's original text of the bill is reprinted on pp. 357–358.

Ruth Miller Elson, *Guardians of Tradition: American Schoolbooks of the Nineteenth Century* (University of Nebraska Press, 1964), is a good overview. For a fascinating account of the "Blue-Back Speller" during Noah Webster's lifetime, see E. Jennifer Monagham, *A Common Heritage: Noah Webster's Blueback Speller* (Shoe String Press, Archon Books, 1983). Theodore Sizer discusses the academy movement in his introduction to *The Age of the Academies* (Teachers College, Columbia University, 1964). Chapter 10 of Frederick S. Rudolph, *The American College and University: A History* (Vintage Books, 1965; originally published in 1962), presents the *Dartmouth College* case in its social context.

CHAPTER 4:
THE COMMON SCHOOL MOVEMENT

For background information see Kenneth M. Stampp, ed., *The Causes of the Civil War* (Prentice-Hall, 1959, a Spectrum Book); parts 1 and 2 of Leon Litwack, ed., *The American Labor Movement* (Prentice-Hall, 1962, a Spectrum Book); Henry Steele Commager, ed., *The Era of Reform, 1830–1860* (D. Van Nostrand, 1960); David Brion Davis, ed., *Ante-bellum Reform* (Harper & Row, 1967); part 4 of Daniel J. Boorstin, *The Americans: The National Experience* (Random House, 1965); and Carl Bode, *The American Lyceum: Town Meeting of the Mind* (Oxford University Press, 1956). Constance McL. Green, *Eli Whitney and the Birth of American Technology* (Little, Brown, 1956), also contains useful background material. The sources in part 2 of Oscar Handlin, ed., *This Was America: True Accounts of People and Places, Manners and Customs, as Recorded by European Travelers to the Western Shore in the Eighteenth, Nineteenth, and Twentieth Centuries* (Harvard University Press, 1949), convey some vivid impressions through the eyes of the immigrants themselves. Clement Eaton, *The Mind of the Old South* (Louisiana State University Press, 1964), is important and well documented. James Mellon, ed., *Bullwhip Days: The Slaves Remember* (Weidenfeld & Nicolson, 1988), based on a project in oral history during the 1930s, underscores the harsh racism and immense cruelty of the slave system.

The African American's struggle for freedom during the antebellum period is vividly portrayed in chapter 6, "The Meaning of Harriet Tubman," by Otey Scruggs in Carol V. R. George, ed., *"Remember the Ladies": New Perspectives on Women in American History* (essays in honor of Nelson Manfred Blake; Syracuse University Press, 1975). Sarah Hopkins Bradford, *Harriet Tubman: The Moses of Her People* (Peter Smith, 1981; originally published in 1869 and 1886 by Mrs. Bradford) is an early, sympathetic biography. For a critical commentary on Harriet Jacobs, "Incidents in the Life of a Slave Girl," one of the few autobiographical works written by a slave woman, see part I of Mary Helen Washington, *Invented Lives: Narratives of Black Women, 1860–1960* (Anchor Press, Doubleday, 1987).

For discussions of Ralph Waldo Emerson's contributions to the history of educational thought, see Howard Mumford Jones, *Emerson on Education* (Teachers College Press, 1966), and Lewis Leary, *Ralph Waldo Emerson: An Interpretative Essay* (Twayne Publishers, 1980).

An excellent overview of nineteenth-century education, emphasizing the growing importance of newspapers, voluntary associations, and systems of schooling is Lawrence A. Cremin, *American Education: The National Experience, 1783–1876* (Harper & Row, 1980). For a succinct overview of America's rural educational heritage, with some vivid photographs of actual "country schools," see Andrew Gulliford, *America's Country Schools* (The Preservation Press, National Trust for Historical Preservation, 1984). Note especially the bibliography on pp. 277–286. Chapter 2 of Carl F. Kaestle, *Pillars of the Republic: Common Schools and American Society, 1780–1860* (Hill and Wang, 1983), is a vivid overview of rural education from 1830 to 1860.

Jonathan Messerli, *Horace Mann: A Biography* (Knopf, 1972), is a critical overview of Mann's life and career. See also Lawrence A. Cremin, ed., *The Republic and the School: Horace Mann on the Education of Free Men* (Teachers College Press, 1957); chapters 2, 3, and 4 of Merle Curti, *The Social Ideas of American Educators, with New Chapter on the Last Twenty-five Years* (Littlefield, Adams, 1959; originally published in 1935); and John S. Brubacher, *Henry Barnard on Education* (Russell and Russell, 1965; originally published in 1931). Mann's twelve annual *Reports* were reprinted in complete facsimile editions by the National Education Association during the 1940s and 1950s.

Michael B. Katz, *The Irony of Early School Reform: Educational Innovation in Mid-Nineteenth Century Massachusetts* (Harvard University Press, 1968), is a critical reinterpretation of the educational reform movement. See also chapters 2, "Alternative Models for American Education," and 5, "The Politics of Educational History," of Michael B. Katz, *Reconstructing American Education* (Harvard University Press, 1987), which are useful summaries of the revisionist stance. Part I, "An Aristocracy of Character, 1820–1890," in David

B. Tyack and Elizabeth Hansot, *Managers of Virtue: Public School Leadership in America, 1820–1980* (Basic Books, 1982) also provides fresh insight into the common school movement of the nineteenth century. See also part 2, "From Village School to Urban System: Bureaucratization in the Nineteenth Century," of David B. Tyack, *The One Best System: A History of American Urban Education* (Harvard University Press, 1974), and Joel Spring, *The American School, 1642–1990: Varieties of Historical Interpretation of the Foundations and Development of American Education* (2nd ed.; New York: Longman, 1990).

CHAPTER 5: EVOLVING PATTERNS OF EDUCATIONAL THOUGHT

A helpful overview of the controversial Reconstruction period are chapters 31 through 39 of J. G. Randall and David Donald, *The Civil War and Reconstruction* (2nd ed.; Heath, 1961). Donald's rewriting of the late Professor Randall's original work leans heavily toward the "revisionist" interpretation that recasts the African Americans in more favorable roles. John Hope Franklin, *Reconstruction: After the Civil War* (University of Chicago Press, 1961), is a widely acclaimed "revisionist" study which, in Franklin's own words, "rests much more on the author's interpretation of sources already known to most students of the period than on the discovery and use of new materials" (p. 232).

Theodore Rosengarten, *All God's Dangers: The Life of Nate Shaw* (Knopf, 1974), is a remarkable autobiography derived from oral history. C. Vann Woodward, *The Strange Career of Jim Crow* (3rd rev. ed.; Oxford University Press, 1974), probes with insight and deep understanding into the racial dilemma. Horace Mann Bond, *Negro Education in Alabama: A Study in Cotton and Steel* (Atheneum, 1969; originally published in 1939), is a carefully documented thesis that traces the influence of socioeconomic forces on black education in Alabama from 1865 to 1930. Earl E. Thorpe, *The Mind of the Negro: An Intellectual History of Afro-Americans* (Ortlieb Press [Baton Rouge, La.], 1961), is an ambitious study that leaves unanswered a number of provocative questions. Earle H. West, "The Peabody Education Fund and Negro Education, 1867–1880," *History of Education Quarterly* 6 (Summer 1966): 3–21, contains a critical evaluation of Barnas Sears's educational policies. George A. Dillingham, *The Foundation of the Peabody Tradition* (University Press of America, 1989), discusses the contributions of the Peabody Education Fund during the late nineteenth century and focuses on the work of the George Peabody College to improve Southern education.

For extensive writings by and about Booker T. Washington, see the *Booker T. Washington Papers*, 11 vols., Louis R. Harlan et al., eds. (University of Illinois Press, 1972–1981). The most controversial period in Washington's life is discussed in Louis R. Harlan, *Booker T. Washington: The Wizard of Tuskegee, 1901–1915* (Oxford University Press, 1983), a work of outstanding scholarship. Samuel R. Spencer, Jr., *Booker T. Washington and the Negro's Place in American Life* (Little, Brown, 1955), is a readable biography. For a critique of Washington's views, see chapter 7 of August Meier, *Negro Thought in America, 1880–1915: Racial Ideologies in the Age of Booker T. Washington* (University of Michigan Press, 1963). Meyer Weinberg, ed., *W.E.B. DuBois: A Reader* (Harper & Row, 1970), is a useful collection. Chapter 7 of John Milton Cooper, Jr., *Walter Hines Page: The Southerner as American, 1855–1918* (University of North Carolina Press, 1977), discusses Page's involvement with the Southern Education Board and other philanthropic agencies.

The material on industrial enterprise after the Civil War is extensive, but the educational ideology of business leaders is ignored in most of the studies. For a concise overview of industrial progress, see part 3 of Louis M. Hacker, *The Triumph of American Capitalism: The Development of Forces in American History to the End of the Nineteenth Century* (Columbia University Press, 1940). Dale Fetherling, *Mother Jones, the Miner's Angel* (Southern Illinois University Press, 1974) is a sympathetic portrayal of Mary Harris Jones's life and work. See also Philip S. Fones, ed., *Mother Jones Speaks: Collected Writings and Speeches* (Monad Press for the Anchor Foundation, 1983).

The best summary of the business creed as reflected in the words and deeds of educational leaders during this period is chapter 6 of Curti, *Social Ideas of American Educators*. The same area is briefly covered from a different vantage point in chapter 1 of Raymond E. Callahan, *Education and the Cult of Efficiency: A Study of the Social Forces That Have Shaped the Administration of the Public Schools* (University of Chicago Press, 1962, a Phoenix Edition). Sol Cohen highlights some important issues in "The Industrial Education Movement, 1906–17," *American Quarterly* 20 (Spring 1968): 95–110.

CHAPTER 6: TOWARD A NEW PEDAGOGY

The only useful source on the drive to Americanize the immigrant is Morris Isaiah Berger, "The Settlement, the Immigrant and the Public School: A Study of the Influence of the Settlement Movement and the New Migration upon Public Education, 1890–1924" (Ph.D. dissertation, Columbia University, 1956, available from University Microfilms in a xerographed publication). The various changes in U.S. immigration laws during the twentieth century, especially after 1965, are discussed in the "Introduction: Reopening the Doors," of Thomas Kessner and Betty Boyd Caroli, *Today's Immigrants,*

Their Stories: A New Look at the Newest Americans (Oxford University Press, 1981), pp. 3–30. Bernard J. Weiss, ed., *American Education and the European Immigrant* (University of Illinois Press, 1982), contains some thought-provoking essays that focus on the late nineteenth and early twentieth centuries when the influx of immigrants coincided with efforts to equate education with public schooling. Nathan Glazer, ed., *Clamor at the Gates: The New American Immigration* (San Francisco: Institute for Contemporary Studies, 1985), examines immigration patterns during the 1970s and early 1980s and discusses some of the contemporary problems associated with assimilation and integration. Alejandro Portes and Rubén G. Rumbaut, *Immigrant America: A Portrait* (University of California Press, 1990), describes the immigrants of the 1980s, overwhelmingly from the developing nations of the Third World, especially from Latin America and Asia, who have struggled to survive and adjust to life in the United States.

For a biographical overview highlighting Addams's broad philosophy of education, see Ellen Condliffe Lagemann, ed., *Jane Addams on Education* (Teachers College Press, 1985), pp. 1–39. Based on unpublished manuscripts, *Jane Addams: A Biography* (D. Appleton-Century Company, 1935), was written by Jane Addams's nephew, James Weber Linn, with Addams' approval and assistance. The annotated bibliography in Marshall W. Fishwick et al., eds., *Illustrious Americans: Jane Addams* (Silver Burdett, 1968), is useful and informative. See also Emily Cooper Johnson, ed., *Jane Addams: A Centennial Reader* (Macmillan, 1960). Helen L. Horowitz, "Varieties of Cultural Experience in Jane Addams' Chicago," *History of Education Quarterly* 14 (Spring 1974): 69–86, describes the settlement house movement in Chicago during the 1890s. Chapter 10 of Mary Jo Deegan, *Jane Addams and the Men on the Chicago School, 1892–1918* (Transaction, 1988), discusses the lifelong friendship between Jane Addams and John Dewey and their mutual influence.

There is, of course, no substitute for reading the original sources. Some excellent selections appear in Otis Pease, ed., *The Progressive Years: The Spirit and Achievement of American Reform* (Braziller, 1962). Lawrence A. Cremin, *The Transformation of the School: Progressivism in American Education, 1876–1957* (Knopf, 1961; also available as a Vintage Book), is not only an important study of the progressive movement; Cremin's conception is so broad that the work is also a history of American education for the chronological period the author covers. Patricia A. Graham, *Progressive Education: From Arcady to Academe* (Teachers College Press, 1967), traces the rise and fall of the Progressive Education Association from 1919 to 1955. See also Claude A. Bowers, *The Progressive Educator and the Depression: The Radical Years* (Random House, 1969). Chapter 5 of Richard Hofstadter, *The Age of Reform: From Bryan to F.D.R.* (Knopf, 1955), discusses "The Progressive Impulse" with penetrating insight. William O'Neill, *The Progressive Years: America*

Comes of Age (Dodd, Mead, 1975), views the Progressive era "more as an age of modernization than of reform." For some recent critiques of the muckraking movement, see part 5 of Herbert Shapiro, ed., *The Muckrakers and American Society* (Heath, 1968).

Stow Persons, ed., *Evolutionary Thought in America* (Yale University Press, 1950), is a useful collection of articles on a variety of topics excluding pedagogy. Richard Hofstadter, *Social Darwinism in American Thought* (Beacon Press, 1955; originally published in 1944), evaluates social thought derived from evolutionary theory. Chapter 22 of Curti, *Growth of American Thought*, is an excellent discussion of evolutionary influences upon society. See also chapter 14 of Rush, Welter, *Popular Education and Democratic Thought in America* (Columbia University Press, 1962).

CHAPTER 7: BUILDING A PHILOSOPHY OF EDUCATION

There is no better way to gain a clear understanding of Herbart's and Froebel's educational ideas than by reading their own writings. Some representative passages are reprinted in Robert Ulich, ed., *Three Thousand Years of Educational Wisdom: Selections from Great Documents* (2nd ed.; Harvard University Press, 1965). An excellent summary of Herbartianism appears in Harold B. Dunkel, *Herbart and Education* (Random House, 1969). The ideological roots of the kindergarten movement are discussed in chapter 2 of Marvin Lazerson, *Origins of the Urban School: Public Education in Massachusetts, 1870–1915* (Harvard University Press, 1971).

Chapters 9 and 11 of Curti, *Social Ideas of American Educators*, are useful summaries of Harris's and Parker's theories and accomplishments. Kurt F. Leidecker, *Yankee Teacher: The Life of William Torrey Harris* (Philosophical Library, 1946), is a sympathetic study. Franklin Parker, "Francis Wayland Parker, 1837–1902," *Paedagogica Historica* 1 (1961): 120–133, contains a six-page bibliography including the locations of important manuscript materials. See also Jack K. Campbell, *Colonel Francis W. Parker: The Children's Crusader* (Teachers College Press, 1967), for more information about Colonel Parker's life and career.

Herbert M. Kliebart, *The Struggle for the American Curriculum: 1893–1958* (Routledge and Kegan Paul, 1986) describes the curriculum of the Dewey School at the University of Chicago in the 1890s. George Dykhuizen, *The Life and Mind of John Dewey* (Southern Illinois University Press, 1973), provides valuable insight into Dewey's long career and recreates the activism that characterized Dewey's life after his so-called retirement in 1930. For thought-provoking discussions of Dewey's basic principles and values relevant to education in a democracy, see Gary Bullert, *The Politics of John Dewey*

(Prometheus Books, 1983). William A. Paringer, *John Dewey and the Paradox of Liberal Reform* (State University of New York Press, 1990), is a critique of the progressive tradition and Dewey's key ideas.

Approaching John Dewey's voluminous bibliography for the first time is difficult and hazardous. Articles and books by and *about* Dewey fill several library shelves. Duplications abound, for there are numerous reprintings and collections of Deweyan literature. The only sensible suggestion is to begin with Dewey's major educational writings to which I have already referred in the chapter and then proceed to Milton Halsey Thomas' indispensable *John Dewey: A Centennial Bibliography* (University of Chicago Press, 1962). A never-ceasing task is separating the useful material from the diatribes.

CHAPTER 8: THE INFLUENCE OF EDUCATIONAL PSYCHOLOGY

For a historical background to some current controversies, see Walter B. Kolesnik, *Mental Discipline in Modern Education* (University of Wisconsin Press, 1958). Geraldine Joncich's "Essay on Sources" in *The Sane Positivist: A Biography of Edward L. Thorndike* (Wesleyan University Press, 1968) is a valuable guide to pertinent material. Chapters 12 and 13 of Curti, *Social Ideas of American Educators*, contain some original and provocative insights into Hall's and James's ideologies. Also informative is chapter 7 (Edwin G. Boring, "The Influence of Evolutionary Theory upon American Psychological Thought") of Persons, ed., *Evolutionary Thought in America*. B. F. Skinner's stance is explained by himself in volume 5 of Edwin G. Boring and Gardner Lindzey, eds., *A History of Psychology in Autobiography* (Appleton-Century-Crofts, 1967), pp. 387–412. On changing views of human intelligence, especially the MI theory, see Howard Gardner, *Frames of Mind: The Theory of Multiple Intelligences* (Basic Books, 1983); and Tina Blythe and Howard Gardner, "A School for All Intelligences," *Educational Leadership* 47 (April 1990): 33–37.

Piaget's insights are in growing vogue among American psychologists and educators, and a flood of translations and explications has appeared. Piaget-oriented researchers are following up his leads. See, for example, David Elkind, *Children and Adolescents: Interpretive Essays on Jean Piaget* (Oxford University Press, 1970); and Irving E. Sigel and Frank H. Cooper, eds., *Logical Thinking in Children: Research Based on Piaget's Theory* (Holt, Rinehart & Winston, 1968). Part 3 of John H. Flavell, *The Developmental Psychology of Jean Piaget* (D. Van Nostrand, 1963), is a stimulating critique. Barry J. Wadsworth, *Piaget for the Classroom Teacher* (Longman, 1978), is a useful study that helps to translate Piagetian theory into practice. Chapter 4, "Experiments with Children: The Discovery of Developmental Stages," of

Jean-Claude Bringuier, *Conversations with Jean Piaget*, trans. Basia Miller
Gulati (University of Chicago Press, 1980), pp. 23–35, clarifies some of
Piaget's important cognitive research. Jean-Claude Brief, *Beyond Piaget: A
Philosophical Psychology* (Teachers College Press, 1983), is a critical interpreta-
tion of Piaget's genetic epistemology.

There is now considerable material on the Montessori method, but so
far no one has shed more light on Maria Montessori's ideas than she did
herself in her own books. Mario M. Montessori, Jr., general director of the
Association Montessori Internationale (AMI) in Amsterdam, is expected to
perpetuate the work of his grandmother; from AMI headquarters, information and instructions are disseminated to countries where the Montessori
movement and its disciples are still active. However, much of the original
spirit of the Montessori pedagogy seems to have disappeared with the death
of its founder in 1952.

The only way to gain an understanding of the Montessori method is to
peruse the original writings. Although some of the first English translations
of Dr. Montessori's works are currently out of print, all are available through
interlibrary loan or in reissued editions: *The Montessori Method*, trans. Anne
E. George (Frederick A. Stokes, 1912); *Pedagogical Anthropology*, trans.
Frederic Taber Cooper (Frederick A. Stokes, 1913); *Dr. Montessori's Own
Handbook* (Frederick A. Stokes, 1914); *The Secret of Childhood*, trans. Barbara
Barclay Carter (Longmans, Green, 1916); *The Advanced Montessori Method:
Spontaneous Activity in Education*, trans. Florence Simmonds (Frederick A.
Stokes, 1917); and *The Absorbent Mind*, trans. Claude A. Claremont (Holt,
Rinehart & Winston, 1967).

Also helpful to Americans are Maria Montessori's remarks before the
International Congress on Education in Oakland, California, on 16–27
August 1915. These were published in the National Education Association,
Journal of Proceedings and Addresses (1915) in the form of four short talks: "My
System of Education," pp. 64–73; "Education in Relation to the Imagina-
tion of the Little Child," pp. 661–667; "The Organization of Intellectual
Work in School," pp. 717–722; and "The Mother and the Child," pp.
1121–1130.

Some psychoanalytic theories are discussed in part 2 of Benjamin B.
Wolman, *Contemporary Theories and Systems in Psychology* (Harper & Bros.,
1960). One of the most striking chapters in recent intellectual history ("The
Migration of Psychoanalysis: Its Impact on American Psychology" by Marie
Jahoda) is told in chapter 9 of Donald Fleming and Bernard Bailyn, eds., *The
Intellectual Migration: Europe and America, 1930–1960* (Belknap-Harvard
University Press, 1969), pp. 420–445. Chapter 24 of Gardner Murphy,
Historical Introduction to Modern Psychology (rev. ed.; Harcourt, Brace, 1949),
is an excellent overview of Alfred Binet's work.

Chapters 5, 8, and 9 of John F. Travers, *Learning: Analysis and Applica-*

tion (David McKay, 1965), are concise and scholarly introductions. Chapters 21 through 24 of Edwin G. Boring, *A History of Experimental Psychology* (2nd ed.; Appleton-Century-Crofts, 1950), contain information about American developments, Gestalt psychology, and behaviorist theories. See also chapters 2, 7, and 8 of Ernest R. Hilgard, *Theories of Learning* (2nd ed.; Appleton-Century-Crofts, 1956), and chapters 3, 5, and 8 of Robert S. Woodworth and Mary R. Sheehan, *Contemporary Schools of Psychology* (3rd ed.; Ronald Press, 1964).

CHAPTER 9: CONTINUING STRUGGLES FOR EQUALITY OF EDUCATIONAL OPPORTUNITY

Business leadership before the Great Depression is discussed in chapter 15 of Cochran and Miller, *Age of Enterprise*. The selections in George E. Mowry, ed., *The Twenties: Fords, Flappers & Fanatics* (Prentice-Hall, 1963, a Spectrum Book) recapture the mood of the period. Arthur S. Link, "What Happened to the Progressive Movement in the 1920s?" *American Historical Review* 64 (July 1959): 833–851, is a provocative reinterpretation of events following World War I.

A thought-provoking analysis of the woman suffrage movement, written by a female historian and a male political scientist, is Anne Firor Scott and Andrew MacKay Scott, *One Half the People: The Fight for Woman Suffrage* (Lippincott, 1975; reprinted in 1982 by the University of Illinois Press); the noteworthy bibliographical essay, pp. 171–174, is concise, up-to-date, and very useful. For a partially annotated bibliography of the women's rights movement, see Albert Krichmar et al., *The Women's Rights Movement in the U.S., 1848–1970: A Bibliography and Sourcebook* (Scarecrow Press, 1972); the section on "education," pp. 203–226, is especially noteworthy. For a critical reappraisal of the woman suffrage movement, with excellent commentaries by Ellen Carol DuBois and Gerta Lerner, see *Elizabeth Cady Stanton and Susan B. Anthony: Correspondence, Writings, Speeches* (Schocken Books, 1981). A good overview covering the period from the mid-nineteenth century to 1967 is William L. O'Neill, *Everyone Was Brave: The Rise and Fall of Feminism in America* (Quadrangle Books, 1969). See also David Tyack and Elizabeth Hansot, *Learning Together: A History of Coeducation in American Public Schools* (Yale University Press, 1990). Lynn D. Gordon, *Gender and Higher Education in the Progressive Era* (Yale University Press, 1990), focuses on the generation of women who attended American colleges from 1890 to 1920.

Ellen Condliffe Lagemann, "Looking at Gender: Women's History," John Hardin Best, ed., *Historical Inquiry in Education: A Research Agenda* (American Educational Research Association, 1983), pp. 251–264, is a thought-provoking essay that focuses on some research needs of women's history. An excellent introductory essay on women's history is Esther Katz and Anita Rapone, "American Women and Domestic Culture: An Approach to Women's History," from *Women's Experience in America: An Historical Anthology* (Transaction Books, 1980). For harsh critiques on the historians' and publishers' past neglect of women's lives and accomplishments in American history, see Berenice A. Carroll, *Liberating Women's History: Theoretical and Critical Essays* (University of Illinois Press, 1976).

For a long list of references dealing with the lives and education of colonial women, see Eugenie A. Leonard et al., *The American Woman in Colonial and Revolutionary Times: 1565–1800* (originally published in 1962 by the University of Pennsylvania Press; reissued in 1975 by the Greenwood Press). Section VII, "The Education of Colonial Women," outlines some sexist attitudes and educational practices in colonial America. Phyllis Lee Levin, *Abigail Adams* (St. Martin's Press, 1987), is an excellent biography that contains an extensive list of manuscript and published sources. See also Paul C. Nagel, *The Adams Women, Abigail and Louisa Adams, Their Sisters and Daughters* (Oxford University Press, 1987), which provides an intimate view of how women lived and what they thought between 1750 and 1850. The section on "Education" in Barbara Haber, *Women in America: A Guide to Books, 1963–1975* (G. K. Hall, 1978) contains an annotated bibliography of educational material that tries to redress the sexism in children's textbooks and literature. For a selection of audiovisual materials focusing on the lives and accomplishments of outstanding women, see *Films by and/or about Women* (Women's History Research Center, 1972).

In *In a Different Voice: Psychological Theory and Women's Development* (Harvard University Press, 1982), Carol Gilligan underscores the human strengths of women and tries to reshape the psychological view of the female personality. See also Carol Gilligan et al., eds., *Mapping the Moral Domain: A Contribution of Women's Thinking to Psychological Theory and Education* (Harvard University Press, 1988). For a discussion of Gilligan's work, see Francine Prose, "Confident at 11, Confused at 16," *New York Times Magazine*, 7 February 1990, pp. 22ff. A special edition, "Women's Influence on Education," in the *History of Education Quarterly* 19 (Spring 1979), and two special issues addressing women and education in the *Harvard Educational Review* 49 (November 1979) and 50 (February 1980), contain some noteworthy essays that cover a wide range of issues.

The original writings of the feminist educators seldom passed through more than one edition. Outside of a few notable research centers (the Arthur and Elizabeth Schlesinger Library on the History of Women in America at Radcliffe College and the Sophia Smith Collection at Smith College, for example), the sources are not readily accessible. Thus the reprintings in Willystine Goodsell, ed., *Pioneers of Women's Education in the United States:*

Emma Willard, Catharine Beecher and Mary Lyon (McGraw-Hill, 1931), are indispensable. Some of Mary Lyon's manuscripts, in fact, were lost in a fire. Luckily, several of her letters and papers are reprinted in *The Power of Christian Benevolence Illustrated in the Life and Labors of Mary Lyon*, comp. Edward Hitchcock and others (Hopkins, Bridgman [Northampton, Mass.], 1852). This important source is often referred to as the "Hitchcock Memoir of Mary Lyon." Excerpts from some of Mary Lyon's papers also appear in Eleanor Flexner, *Century of Struggle: The Women's Rights Movement in the United States* (Harvard University Press, 1959), and Arthur C. Cole, *A Hundred Years of Mount Holyoke College: The Evolution of an Educational Ideal* (Yale University Press, 1940). An up-to-date biography drawing heavily on manuscript materials in the Mount Holyoke College Archives is Elizabeth Alden Green, *Mary Lyon and Mount Holyoke: Opening the Gates* (University Press of New England, 1979). In *In the Company of Educated Women: A History of Women and Higher Education in America* (Yale University Press, 1985), Barbara Miller Solomon discusses the experience of women in higher education since the beginning of the nineteenth century and shows through skillful analysis and some lively anecdotes that the behavior of college women yesterday and today reflects the conventions of their times.

Sylvia Ann Hewlett, *A Lesser Life: The Myth of Women's Liberation in America* (Morrow, 1986), argues persuasively for adequate support systems, including, for example, affordable day-care facilities and improved maternity benefits that working women and their children so desperately need. Lenore J. Weitzman, *The Divorce Revolution: The Unexpected Social and Economic Consequences for Women and Children in America* (The Free Press, 1985), is a well-documented study of the impact of the no-fault divorce laws of the 1970s, which have led to an inadequate child support system and created a new social "underclass" of divorced women. "Women Working: Toward a New Society" (1976) and "Perceptions of Childhood and Youth" (1978) of *Philanthropy in an Age of Transition: The Essays of Alan Pifer* (Carnegie Corporation Foundation Center, 1984), a collection originally published in the Carnegie Corporation's Annual Reports from 1970 to 1982, are powerful pleas for enlightened public and private policies to assure the health and well-being of American children in the light of growing numbers of working mothers and dramatic changes in family life. "No nation," writes Alan Pifer, "can afford to neglect its children."

It is difficult to select representative titles from the extensive literature on race relations; too many articles and books are merely impassioned pleas espousing one point of view. Perhaps the best introduction is the essays on "The Negro American" in *Daedalus* 94 (Fall 1965). Also provocative and well balanced is the collection of commentaries and essays entitled *Equal Educational Opportunity* (Harvard University Press, 1969; originally published in 1968 in the *Harvard Educational Review*). Some changing patterns of thought are summarized by C. Vann Woodward in *The Strange Career of Jim Crow*. In addition, see Woodward's *The Burden of Southern History* (Louisiana State University Press, 1960). The rise of black militancy is discussed in chapter 4 of Christopher Lasch, *The Agony of the American Left* (Knopf, 1969). For the legal background, see some of the relevant material in David Fellman, ed., *The Supreme Court and Education* (rev. ed.; Teachers College Press, 1969); Arthur E. Wise, *Rich Schools, Poor Schools: The Promise of Equal Educational Opportunity* (University of Chicago Press, 1968); and LeRoy J. Peterson et al., *The Law and Public School Operation* (Harper & Row, 1969). Gary Orfield and William L. Taylor, *Racial Segregation: Two Policy Views* (Ford Foundation, 1979), argue for stronger efforts and leadership on the part of the federal government in carrying out its antidiscrimination responsibilities. Chapter 6, "Black American Adolescents," of Jewelle Taylor Gibbs et al., *Children of Color: Psychological Interventions with Minority Youth* (Jossey-Bass, 1990), highlights a major tragedy in contemporary United States: the multiple risk factors for black youth, who have experienced long-term psychological impairments exacerbated by discrimination and intense poverty.

Richard Kluger, *Simple Justice: The History of Brown v. Board of Education and Black America's Struggle for Equality* (Knopf, 1975), is a comprehensive study, focusing on the major issues stemming from the historic Supreme Court decision on 17 May 1954. The aftermath of the *Brown* decision is vividly described in Stephen B. Oates, *Let the Trumpet Sound: The Life of Martin Luther King, Jr.* (Harper & Row, 1982). Chapter 22, "The March on Washington," of Taylor Branch, *Parting the Waters: America in the King Years, 1954–1963* (Simon and Schuster, 1988), focuses on Martin Luther King's passionate "I have a dream" speech in 1963 at the foot of the Lincoln Memorial. Neil V. Sullivan, *Bound for Freedom: An Educator's Adventures in Prince Edward County, Virginia* (Little, Brown, 1965), is one more vivid episode in the black people's continuing quest for educational equality. Mary King, *Freedom Song: A Personal Story of the 1960s Civil Rights Movement* (William Morrow, 1987), provides a fascinating overview of the civil rights struggle from the perspective of an active participant.

The emotional debate over court-ordered busing led to vitriolic outbursts in newspaper editorials and popular magazines. For a balanced overview, see Nicolaus Mills, ed., *The Great School Bus Controversy* (Teachers College Press, 1973). See also J. Anthony Lukas, *Common Ground: A Turbulent Decade in the Lives of Three American Families* (Knopf, 1985), a Pulitzer Prize-winning account of the tragic events in Boston in the mid-1970s when court-ordered busing was imposed to facilitate the desegregation of the public schools. "This is a work of non-fiction," writes Lukas. "Nothing has been disguised or embellished." For an unusual perspective on court-ordered busing, written from a positive point of view, see Lee A. Daniels, "In

Defense of Busing," *New York Times Magazine* (17 April 1983), pp. 34–35ff. Chapter 9, "Strategies for Multicultural Education," of Donna M. Gollnick and Philip C. Chinn, *Multicultural Education in a Pluralistic Society* (3rd ed.; Merrill, 1990), focuses on building a positive school climate and developing critical thinking skills.

CHAPTER 10: THE IMPACT OF THE BUSINESS CREED

Studies of the depression decade are extensive. Frederick Lewis Allen, *Since Yesterday: The Nineteen-Thirties in America, September 3, 1929–September 3, 1939* (Harper & Bros., 1940); Caroline Bird, *The Invisible Scar* (David McKay, 1966); and Cabell Phillips, *From the Crash to the Blitz: 1929–1939* (Macmillan, 1969), provided vivid overviews, while David A. Shannon, ed., *The Great Depression* (Prentice-Hall, 1960, a Spectrum Book), sketches in some of the grim details with contemporary impressions. David H. Donald, *Look Homeward: A Life of Thomas Wolfe* (Ballantine Books, 1987), is an excellent biography that portrays Wolfe's unhappy life, his career as a novelist, and the times in which he lived. Joseph Alsop, *FDR, 1882–1945: A Centenary Remembrance* (Viking Press, 1982), portrays the beginning of the New Deal and its accomplishments in the 1930s and underscores Eleanor Roosevelt's role as first lady and her assistance to Franklin, who was crippled by polio; Eleanor went everywhere, including the coal mines, and wrote a newspaper column, "My Day." Chapter 9 of J. D. Glover, *The Attack on Big Business* (Graduate School of Business Administration, Harvard University, 1954), is a "Critique of the Critics." The only extended account of the rise of the Liberty League is George Wolfskill, *The Revolt of the Conservatives; A History of the American Liberty League, 1934–1940* (Houghton Mifflin, 1962). For an excellent commentary on the league's activities, see Frederick Rudolph, "The American Liberty League, 1934–1940," *American Historical Review* 56 (October 1950): 19–33.

Extensive use was made of primary source materials from the Washington office of the Chamber of Commerce of the United States and from the Library of the National Association of Manufacturers in New York City.

After plowing through the accusations and rebuttals surrounding the Roboy Investigation, the reader quickly discovers that there is never a satisfactory substitute for a perusal of the actual documents. Few studies have been made of this interesting episode.

For a clearer understanding of business attitudes toward the schools, pertinent editorials in the *Nation's Business* are important. The following publications also contain useful information:

From the Chamber of Commerce of the United States:
Washington Review (vol. 1, 1933–vol. 11, 1944). This publication was superseded by *Business Action* (vol. 1, 25 March 1944–vol. 8, no. 41, 21 December 1951) and then by *Washington Report* (vol. 1, no. 1, 28 December 1951–vol. 5, 1956). *News and Cues* (February 1947–November 1955).

From the National Association of Manufacturers:
News Letter (vol. 1, no. 1, 20 April 1934–vol. 9, no. 28, 11 July 1942 [issued irregularly]), superseded by *NAM NEWS* and then in 1964 by *NAM REPORTS*. *Trends in Education-Industry* Cooperation (September 1944–May 1946 [published irregularly]). *Trends in Church, Education and Industry Cooperation* (September 1949–December 1951 [numbered irregularly]).

Marsha Levine and Roberta Trachtman, eds., *American Business and the Public School: Case Studies of Corporate Involvement in Public Education* (Teachers College, 1988), discusses seven case studies of business involvement in the public schools and describes some patterns of working relationships during the 1980s. For graphic illustrations of the business community's efforts to "sell free enterprise" to students and teachers, see Sheila Harty, *Hucksters in the Classroom: A Review of Industry Propaganda in Schools* (Center for Study of Responsive Law, 1979). In chapters 2 and 11 of *The Makers of Public Policy: American Power Groups and Their Ideologies* (McGraw-Hill, 1965), R. Joseph Monsen, Jr., and Mark W. Cannon summarize the business creed and comment on "how American democracy really works."

In a provocative essay, "Business with a Social Conscience," *New York Times Book Review*, 18 January 1970, pp. 8–9ff., Arjay Miller, former president of Ford Motor Company, argues that business "cannot meet today's problems working alone." Committee for Economic Development, *Investing in Our Children: Business and the Public Schools* (Committee for Economic Development, Research and Policy Committee, 1985), is a strong policy statement that calls for "effective partnerships" between business and the nation's schools "to develop workable reforms and to implement them in a coherent and consistent manner." In "What Ideas Are Safe?" from *Freedom and Order* (Braziller, 1966), Henry Steele Commager presents the classic case for freedom of thought and inquiry.

CHAPTER 11: THE AMERICAN SCHOOL IN TRANSITION

Part 3 of Daniel Tanner and Laurel N. Tanner, *History of the School Curriculum* (Macmillan, 1990), discusses some of the conflicts that have shaped the curriculum since the 1930s. For a thought-provoking study of "equality and excellence" in secondary education, see Jeannie Oakes, *Keeping Track: How Schools Structure Inequality* (Yale University Press, 1985). Excerpts from some important documents appear in Frederick M. Raubinger et al., eds., *The Development of Secondary Education* (Macmillan, 1969). The best study of the Committee of Ten is Theodore R. Sizer, *Secondary Schools at the Turn of the Century* (Yale University Press, 1964). Edward A. Krug, *The Shaping of the American High School* (1:1880–1920, Harper & Row, 1964; and 2:1920–1941, University of Wisconsin Press, 1972), is also an important and well-documented history. For the genesis of the Eight-Year Study, see chapter 7 of Cremin, *The Transformation of the School*. *Children Out of School in America* (Report of the Children's Defense Fund of the Washington Research Project, Cambridge, Mass., 1974), contains startling statistics on the dropout (or "push-out") problem.

Chapter 2, "New Curriculum, Old Issues" of Marvin Lazerson et al., *An Education of Value: The Purposes and Practices of Schools* (Cambridge University Press, 1985), is a critique of the curriculum reform movement of the late 1950s and early 1960s. Association for Supervision and Curriculum Development, *Content of the Curriculum* (1988 ASCD Yearbook; ed. Ronald S. Brandt), focuses on new developments and contemporary trends in the various subjects of the curriculum.

In *Toward a Theory of Instruction* (Harvard University Press, 1966), and *Beyond the Information Given: Studies in the Psychology of Knowing*, selected and ed. by Jeremy M. Anglin (Norton, 1973), Jerome S. Bruner elaborates upon some of his previously published views. Chapter 7 of David P. Ausubel, *The Psychology of Meaningful Verbal Learning* (Grune & Stratton, 1963), is a critique of learning by inquiry and discovery.

Other writings of significance include John I. Goodlad and Robert H. Anderson. *The Nongraded Elementary School* (rev. ed.; Harcourt, Brace & World, 1963; reissued in 1987 by Teachers College Press); Judson T. Shaplin and Henry F. Olds, Jr., eds. *Team Teaching* (Harper & Row, 1964); J. Lloyd Trump and Dorsey Baynham, *Focus on Change: Guide to Better Schools* (Rand McNally, 1961); and Gerald Grant, *The World We Created at Hamilton High* (Harvard University Press, 1988). Ronald and Beatrice Gross, eds., *Radical School Reform* (Simon & Schuster, 1969), and Charles E. Silberman, *Crisis in the Classroom: The Remaking of American Education* (Random House, 1970), are harsh critiques of conventional schools and styles of teaching. Jeannie Oakes and Martin Lipton, *Making the Best of Schools: A Handbook for Parents, Teachers, and Policymakers* (Yale University Press, 1990), offers important strategies for school improvement. Chapter 1, "The Teaching Face: An Historical Perspective" by Kenneth G. O'Bryan in *Children and the Faces of Television: Teaching, Violence, Selling*, Edward L. Palmer and M. A. Dorr, eds. (Academic Press, 1980), is an excellent overview of ETV's growth and impact.

For a description of some alternative high school programs, see Timothy W. Young, *Public Alternative Education: Options and Choice for Today's Schools* (Teachers College Press, 1990). Allen Graubard, *Free the Children: Radical Reform and the Free School Movement* (Pantheon Books, 1972), traces the development of the "outside-the-system" schools. See also Bonnie Barrett Stretch, "The Rise of the 'Free School,' " *Saturday Review* 53 (20 June 1970): 76–79ff.; Jonathan Kozol, *Free Schools* (Houghton Mifflin, 1972); and John I. Goodlad et al., *The Conventional and the Alternative in Education* (McCutchan, 1975). For a discussion of "the largest alternative to public schooling in the United States," see Thomas C. Hunt and Norlene M. Kunkel, "Catholic Schools: The Nation's Largest Alternative School System," in James C. Carper and Thomas C. Hunt, eds., *Religious Schooling in America* (Religious Education Press, 1984).

On the deschooling controversy, see Ivan Illich, "De-Schooling: A Working Paper for Discussion," printed in *De-Schooling/De-Conditioning* (Portola Institute [Menlo Park, Calif.], 1971), pp. 1–6; Ivan Illich, *Deschooling Society* (Harper & Row Harrow Book, 1971); Joel H. Spring, *Education and the Rise of the Corporate State* (Beacon Press, 1972); chapter 7 (Joel Spring, "Deschooling as a Form of Social Revolution") of Clarence J. Karier et al., *Roots of Crisis* (Rand McNally, 1973); Everett Reimer, *School is Dead* (Doubleday Anchor Books, 1971); and Martin Carnoy, ed., *Schooling in a Corporate Society: The Political Economy of Education in America* (2nd ed.; David McKay, 1975). These works should be read in conjunction with Robin Barrow, *Radical Education: A Critique of Freeschooling and Deschooling* (Wiley, 1978); and Diane Ravitch, *The Revisionists Revised: A Critique of the Radical Attack on the Schools* (Basic Books, 1977). An excellent guide is John Ohliger, *Bibliography of Comments on the Illich-Reimer Deschooling Theses* (ERIC Clearing House on Teacher Education, document SP 007 833, April 1974). For a short biography of Ivan Illich, see Francine du Plessix Gray, *Divine Disobedience: Profiles in Catholic Radicalism* (Knopf, 1970), pp. 273–322. Chapter 5 of Henry A. Giroux, *Ideology, Culture and the Process of Schooling* (Temple University Press, 1981), discusses "Paulo Freire's Approach to Radical Educational Theory and Practice." "If one looks closely at Freire's efforts," writes Giroux, "I think one will find specific themes and practices that will help to enrich and broaden radical pedagogy in North America."

Tracy Kidder, *Among Schoolchildren* (Houghton Mifflin, 1989), a dispassionate look at the day-to-day work of a female elementary school teacher and her children in a predominantly Hispanic neighborhood, would have been enriched with a prescription for school reform. Chapter 3, "School Reformation Studies: Past and Present" in Mario D. Fantini, *Regaining Excellence in Education* (Merrill, 1986), places the school reform reports of the 1980s in historical perspective. See also Joseph Murphy, ed., *The Educational Reform Movement of the 1980s: Perspectives and Cases* (McCutchan Publishing Co., 1990), which assesses the impact of the reform movement on the schools. In a scathing critique of American high schools, David Pierpont Gardner et al., *A Nation at Risk: The Imperative for Educational Reform* (Government Printing Office, 1983; report of the National Commission on Excellence in Education) calls for an "upgrading" or reform of the secondary-school curriculum. See also Mortimer J. Adler, *The Paideia Proposal* (Macmillan, 1982); Ernest L. Boyer, *High School: A Report on Secondary Education in America* (Harper & Row, 1983); John I. Goodlad, *A Place Called School: Prospects for the Future* (McGraw-Hill, 1984); Theodore R. Sizer, *Horace's Compromise: The Dilemma of the American High School* (Houghton Mifflin, 1984); Robert L. Hampel, *The Last Little Citadel: American High Schools since 1940* (Houghton Mifflin, 1986); and Arthur G. Powell, et al., *The Shopping Mall High School: Winners and Losers in the Educational Marketplace* (Houghton Mifflin, 1985). Marilyn Clayton Felt, *Improving Our Schools: Thirty-Three Studies That Inform Local Action* (Education Development Center, 1985), summarizes some major studies on public high schools during the early 1980s, identifies common problems, and recommends action for school improvement. William J. Johnston, ed., *Education on Trial: Strategies for the Future* (ICS Press, 1985), suggests some important strategies for reform.

CHAPTER 12: CROSSCURRENTS IN HIGHER EDUCATION

For a lively discussion of the various social forces affecting the goals of higher education, see Burton Blatt, *In and Out of the University: Essays on Higher and Special Education* (University Park Press, 1982). Richard Hofstadter and Wilson Smith, eds., *American Higher Education: A Documentary History*, 2 vols. (University of Chicago Press, 1961), is a valuable source book. On the elective controversy, consult chapter 14 of Rudolph, *The American College and University*, and chapter 6 of John S. Brubacher and Willis Rudy, *Higher Education in Transition: An American History, 1636–1956* (Harper & Bros., 1958). Eliot states his own position on a number of issues in *A Turning Point in Higher Education: The Inaugural Address of Charles William Eliot as President of Harvard College, October 19, 1869* (Harvard University Press, 1969).

Studies of special significance are George P. Schmidt, *The Liberal Arts College: A Chapter in American Cultural History* (Rutgers University Press, 1957); Edward D. Eddy, Jr., *Colleges for Our Land and Time: The Land Grant Idea in American Education* (Harper & Bros., 1956); Alan Nevins, *The State Universities and Democracy* (University of Illinois Press, 1962); Laurence R. Veysey, *The Emergence of the American University* (University of Chicago Press, 1965); Frederick S. Rudolph, *Curriculum: A History of the American Undergraduate Course of Study Since 1636* (Jossey-Bass, 1977); Merle Curti and Roderick Nash, *Philanthropy in the Shaping of American Higher Education*

(Rutgers University Press, 1965); Ellen Condliffe Lagemann, *Private Power for the Public Good: A History of the Carnegie Foundation for the Advancement of Teaching* (Wesleyan University Press, 1983); and Edgar B. Wesley, *NEA: The First Hundred Years: The Building of the Teaching Profession* (Harper & Row, 1957).

For a general critique of American schools, with a focus on graduate education, note especially Section 2 of Carl R. Rogers, *Freedom to Learn for the 80's* (Merrill, 1983; 2nd ed.). For a constructive, up-to-date critique of professional training in American schools of education, see Harry Judge, *American Graduate Schools of Education: A View from Abroad* (Ford Foundation, 1982). *Abraham Flexner: An Autobiography* (Simon & Schuster, 1960; a revision, brought up to date, of Flexner's *I Remember* [1940]) is a revealing self-portrait that contains valuable information on the improvement of professional education. M. Ludmerer, *Learning to Heal: The Development of American Medical Education* (Basic Books, 1985) covers the period from 1870 to 1920 and tells the fascinating story of how the United States has achieved world leadership in medical education. See also William G. Rothstein, *American Medical Schools and the Practice of Medicine: A History* (Oxford University Press, 1987), and Steven C. Wheatley, *The Politics of Philanthropy: Abraham Flexner and Medical Education* (University of Wisconsin Press, 1988).

Michael W. Kirst, *Who Controls Our Schools?* (Freeman, 1984), places in historical perspective some of the twentieth-century issues confronting the public school as a social institution—financial support, curriculum priorities, and the professionalization of teaching. John I. Goodlad, *Teachers for Our Nation's Schools* (Jossey-Bass, 1990), examines some of the obstacles to successful teacher education programs and suggests strategies for effective change. *Tomorrow's Teachers: A Report of the Holmes Group* (Holmes Group, 1986), and Carnegie Forum on Education and the Economy, *A Nation Prepared: Teachers for the 21st Century* (Carnegie Forum on Education and the Economy, 1986), propose some major strategies aimed at transforming the education of American teachers and the entire profession of teaching. Jonas S. Soltis, ed., *Reforming Teacher Education: The Impact of the Holmes Group Report* (Teachers College Press, 1987), discusses the implications of *Tomorrow's Teachers* for schooling in the United States and abroad.

In Sterling M. McMurrin, ed., *On the Meaning of the University* (University of Utah Press, 1976), John W. Gardner, "The Individual and Society," discusses one of the central roles of the modern university—to preserve "a society that has at its core a respect for the dignity and worth of the individual, a society that pursues fulfillment and growth for the individual." The changing conceptions of university leadership are reviewed in Joseph K. Kauffman, *At the Pleasure of the Board: The Service of the College and University President* (American Council on Education, 1980). Chapter 2 of Harold

Taylor, *On Education and Freedom* (Abelard-Schuman, 1954), is a provocative essay, "The College President." See also Nathan M. Pusey, *The Age of the Scholar: Observations on Education in a Troubled Decade* (Harper & Row Torchbook, 1963; originally published by the Harvard University Press); James A. Perkins, *The University in Transition* (Princeton University Press, 1966); Robert F. Goheen, *The Human Nature of a University* (Princeton University Press, 1969); Kingman Brewster et al., *Educating for the Twenty-first Century* (University of Illinois Press, 1969); and Derek Bok, *Universities and the Future of America* (Duke University Press, 1990). Richard Berendzen, *Is My Armor Straight? A Year in the Life of a University President* (Adler and Adler, 1986), describes the continuing pressures on a university president during the 1980s.

Allan Bloom, *The Closing of the American Mind: How Higher Education Has Failed Democracy and Impoverished the Souls of Today's Students* (Simon and Schuster, 1987), is a harsh critique of higher education in the 1980s, arguing that universities no longer teach "great ideas"; instead, argues Bloom, colleges have become "job-factories" offering an array of unrelated disciplines. See also Page Smith, *Killing the Spirit: Higher Education in America* (Viking, 1990), which discusses, among other timely issues, the heavy emphasis of research over teaching and the neglect of undergraduate instruction at leading universities.

Student unrest during the 1960s is discussed in a number of studies and reports. Consult, for example, Seymour M. Lipset and Sheldon S. Wolin, eds., *The Berkeley Student Revolt* (Doubleday Anchor, 1965), and the Select Committee on Education, *Education at Berkeley* (University of California Press, 1966, commonly known as the Muscatine Report). Arthur W. Chickering, *Education and Identity* (Jossey-Bass, 1969), and Ronald G. Corwin, *Education in Crisis* (Wiley, 1974), raise some crucial academic questions. In Philip G. Altback and Robert O. Berdahl, *Higher Education in American Society* (Prometheus Books, 1981), Walter P. Metzger, "Academic Freedom in Delocalized Academic Institutions," argues that the current theory of academic freedom needs to be redefined in the light of new social forces.

Studies of special interest also include U.S. President's Commission on Campus Unrest, *The Report of the President's Commission on Campus Unrest* (Government Printing Office, [1970]); chapter 7, "A Special Analysis of Student Protests," of Harold L. Hodgkinson, *Institutions in Transition: A Profile of Change in Higher Education* (McGraw-Hill, 1971); chapter 9, "Organized Student Power," of Leon D. Epstein, *Governing the University: The Campus and the Public Interest* (Jossey-Bass, 1974); and chapter 5, "Protest," of Alain Touraine, *The Academic System in American Society* (McGraw-Hill, 1974). "The Lament of the Individual" in Bernard Bailyn et al., *The Great Republic: A History of the American People* (2nd ed., Heath, 1981), pp. 903–907, underscores the "noisy rebellion" of the 1960s and focuses on the critical problems of the individual in modern society: "a dehumanizing bureaucracy," and "the individual's feelings of loneliness."

Allan P. Sindler, *Bakke, DeFunis, and Minority Admissions: The Quest for Equal Opportunity* (Longman, 1978), is an excellent overview of key issues. Barry R. Gross, ed., *Reverse Discrimination* (Prometheus Books, 1977), offers a useful bibliography on affirmative action issues. U.S. Commission on Civil Rights, *Toward an Understanding of Bakke* (Government Printing Office, 1979; Clearinghouse Publication 58), contains a complete reprint of the Supreme Court decision. See also Mary W. Gray, "The Tragic Legacy of the Supreme Court's 1978 Bakke Ruling Is That Affirmative Action Has Been Ineffectual Ever Since," *Chronicle of Higher Education*, Section 2 (29 June 1988), p. B1. Chapter 11, "Applying Liberal Equality: Compensatory Programs," of Kenneth A. Strike, *Educational Policy and the Just Society* (University of Illinois Press, 1982), is a critical discussion of Head Start and Affirmative Action programs, especially the controversial *Bakke* case.

CHAPTER 13: CONTEMPORARY ISSUES AND PROBLEMS

Two historical overviews of the United States during the 1960s are William Manchester, *The Glory and the Dream: A Narrative History of America, 1932–1972* (Little, Brown, 1974), and William L. O'Neill, *Coming Apart: An Informal History of America in the 1960s* (Quadrangle Books, 1971). See also Todd Gitlin, *The Sixties: Years of Hope, Days of Rage* (Bantam Books, 1987), and Richard N. Goodwin, *Remembering America: A Voice from the Sixties* (Little, Brown and Co., 1988). John Rawls, *A Theory of Justice* (Harvard University Press, 1971), defines justice largely in terms of "equality" and individual rights. Susan Littwin, *The Postponed Generation: Why American Youth are Growing up Later* (Morrow, 1986) is a vivid portrait of the "children of the children of the Sixties," a floundering generation, a group struggling to cope with diminished expectations.

John E. Chubb and Terry M. Moe, *Politics, Markets, and America's Schools* (Brookings Institution, 1990), argue that serious problems in American public education are linked to the policies and practices of bureaucratic institutions (i.e., school boards, superintendents' offices) that deny schools the autonomy they need to be academically successful. John W. Gardner, *Excellence: Can We Be Equal and Excellent Too?* (Norton, 1984; rev. ed.), discusses the conditions that enhance "excellence" in a democracy and raises some thought-provoking questions concerning the whole concept of equality in a free nation. For a discussion of the Coleman Report, see Christopher Jencks, "A Reappraisal of the Most Controversial Educational Document of Our Time," *New York Times Magazine* part 1, 10 August 1969, pp. 12–13ff.

James S. Coleman responds to some of the criticisms in "The Concept of Equality of Educational Opportunity" (reprinted from the Winter 1968 issue of the *Harvard Educational Review*), and "A Brief Summary of the Coleman Report" (published for the first time), in Harvard Educational Review Editorial Board, *Equal Educational Opportunity* (1969): 9–24, 253–259; see also the following articles that appear in this same compendium: Samuel Bowles, "Towards Equality of Educational Opportunity?," pp. 115–125; Gerald Lesser and Susan S. Stodolsky, "Equal Opportunity for Maximum Development," pp. 126–138; and Kenneth B. Clark, "Alternative Public School Systems," pp. 173–186. Ivan Illich, *Gender* (Pantheon Books, 1982), calls the contemporary movement toward equality a "myth," and points to the "overwhelming" economic discrimination against women.

The diversity of American family life, the impact of churches and synagogues, and the growing influence of newspapers, radio, and television during the twentieth century are discussed in Chapter 11 of Lawrence A. Cremin, *American Education: The Metropolitan Experience, 1876–1980* (Harper & Row, 1988). Based on a five-year study, Robert N. Bellah et al., *Habits of the Heart: Individualism and Commitment in American Life* (University of California Press, 1985), analyzes a major moral dilemma of contemporary society: the conflict between a nation's urgent need for community and commitment and the fierce individualism of the American people. Christopher Jencks et al., *Who Gets Ahead? The Determinants of Economic Success in America* (Basic Books, 1979), supplements Jencks' *Inequality: A Reassessment of the Effects of Family and Schooling in America* (Basic Books, 1972; also available in a Harper Colophon Edition). Both studies should be read in conjunction with the critiques reprinted in Donald M. Levine and Mary Jo Bane, eds., *The "Inequality" Controversy: Schooling and Distributive Justice* (Basic Books, 1975).

Chapter 1 of Kenneth Keniston, *All Our Children: The American Family under Pressure* (Harcourt Brace Jovanovich, 1977), is an excellent discussion of some major changes in the American family structure. Brigitte Berger, "The Fourth R: The Repatriation of the School," in John H. Bunzel, ed., *Challenge to American Schools: The Case for Values and Standards* (Oxford University Press, 1985), argues that the role of the middle-class family in the education of their children has been misunderstood and misinterpreted. Chapter 4, "Restructuring Family Life," by Frances Smalls Caple, in Elizabeth A. Mulroy (ed.), *Women as Single Parents: Confronting Institutional Barriers in the Courts, the Workplace, and the Housing Market* (Auburn House, 1988), discusses some of the stresses and unmet needs of single-parent families.

Jeffrey J. Zettel and Alan Abelson, "Right to a Free Appropriate Public Education," in chapter 8 of the National Society for the Study of Education's *Yearbook* 77 (1978): 188–216, discusses the changing concept of equal educational opportunity in the United States. Richard A. Johnson et al., *Handicapped Youth and the Mainstream Educator* (University of Minnesota Press, 1975), presents diverse points of view concerning "mainstreaming" children with special needs. James L. Paul et al., *Mainstreaming: A Practical Guide* (Syracuse University Press, 1977), focuses on some of the issues and problems in implementing the mainstreaming concept. See also Frederick J. Weintraub et al., eds., *Public Policy and the Education of Exceptional Children* (Council for Exceptional Children, 1976). Reed Martin, *Educating Handicapped Children: The Legal Mandate* (Research Press, 1979), defines some key words and phrases in recent public laws and court cases, especially P.L. 94–142. Chapters 1 and 2 of Maynard Reynolds and Jack Birch, *Teaching Exceptional Children in All America's Schools* (Council for Exceptional Children, 1977), are a good overview of forces leading to the enactment of P.L. 94–142. See also Alan Abelson and Jeffrey Zettel, "The End of the Quiet Revolution: The Education for all Handicapped Children Act of 1975," *Exceptional Children* 44 (October 1977): 114–127; and H. Rutherford Turnbull and Ann Turnbull, *Free Appropriate Public Education: Law and Implementation* (Love Publishing, 1978). Chapter 1, "Historical Perspectives," of Cecil D. Mercer, *Children and Adolescents with Learning Disabilities* (Merrill, 1979), is an extensive overview. Chapter 15 of Gerald Wallace and James A. McLoughlin, *Learning Disabilities; Concepts and Characteristics* (2nd ed.; Merrill, 1979), underscores some contemporary issues.

Estelle Fuchs and Robert J. Havighurst, *To Live on This Earth: American Indian Education* (Doubleday Anchor, 1972), and Margaret Szasz, *Education and the American Indian: The Road to Self-Determination, 1928–1973* (University of New Mexico Press, 1974), are based heavily on field work and interviews with tribal leaders. William T. Hagan, *American Indians* (University of Chicago Press, 1961), is a scholarly work that tells briefly the story of conflict and cultural annihilation. Estelle Fuchs, "American Indian Education: Time to Redeem an Old Promise," *Saturday Review* 53 (24 January 1970): 54–57ff., also provides helpful background information.

Alice Marriott and Carol K. Rachlin, *American Epic: The Story of the American Indian* (Putnam, 1969), is a sympathetic portrayal of hardship and accomplishment. Chapter 10, "Indian Women in Fancy and Fact," of Christine Bolt, *American Indian Policy and American Reform: Case Studies of the Campaign to Assimilate the American Indians* (Allen & Unwin, 1987), examines the status of Native American women and depicts their roles in family, work, and religion. Frank Waters, *Book of the Hopi* (Viking, 1963; also available as a Ballantine Paperback), reveals the mythology and world views of a famous cliff-dwelling tribe in northern Arizona. The value conflicts faced by Hopi children are explained in Laura Thompson, *Culture in Crisis* (Harper & Row, 1950). Ruth M. Underhill, *The Navajos* (University of Oklahoma Press, 1956), is a useful history of the "Earth People" (as the Navahos call themselves), written by a former employee of the U.S. Indian Service who spent thirteen years studying the United States' largest Indian tribe.

Vine Deloria, Jr., *Custer Died for Your Sins: An Indian Manifesto* (Macmillan, 1969), calls for a new system of law that operates within the framework of Indian tribalism. For the genesis of the Red Power movement, see chapter 19 of Stan Steiner, *The New Indians* (Harper & Row, 1968; also available as a Delta Book). On the new militant mood, see, in addition, "The Angry American Indian: Starting Down the Protest Trail," *Time* 95 (9 February 1970): 14–20: Vine Deloria, Jr., "This Country Was a Lot Better Off When the Indians Were Running It," *New York Times Magazine*, 8 March 1970, pp. 32–33ff; and Howell Raines, "American Indians: Struggling for Power and Identity," *New York Times Magazine*, 11 February 1979, pp. 21–24ff.

For thought-provoking discussions of some of the successes and problems of the Asian Americans, see Fox Butterfield, "Why Asians Are Going to the Head of the Class," *New York Times Education Supplement*, 3 August 1986, pp. 18–23; David A. Bell, "The Triumph of Asian-Americans," *New Republic* 193 (15–22 July 1985): 24–26; chapter 9, "Asian Americans: From Pariahs to Paragons," by Peter I. Rose, in Nathan Glazer, ed. *Clamor at the Gates: The New American Immigration* (San Francisco: Institute for Contemporary Studies, 1985); Anna Quindlen, "The Drive to Excel," *New York Times Magazine*, 22 February 1987, section 6, pp. 32–39; and E. Gareth Hoachlander and Cynthia L. Brown, "Asians in Higher Education: Conflicts over Admissions," *Thought & Action* 5 (Fall 1989): 5–20.

On bilingual education, consult Theodore Andersson and Mildred Boyer, *Bilingual Schooling in the United States*, 2 vols. (Government Printing Office, 1970); and Francesco Cordasco, *Bilingual Schooling in the United States: A Sourcebook for Educational Personnel* (McGraw-Hill, 1976). The relation of bilingual education to the civil rights movement is discussed in chapter 18, "Politicization and the Schools: The Case of Bilingual Education," of Diane Ravitch, *The Schools We Deserve: Reflections on the Educational Crisis of Our Times* (Basic Books, 1985). "Who is La Raza?" by Armando M. Rodriquez, in Wayne Moquin and Charles Van Doren, eds., *A Documentary History of the Mexican-Americans* (Praeger, 1971), pp. 383–386, underscores the importance of cultural pluralism and bilingual education. Noting the language and cultural biases of I.Q. tests, George I. Sánchez, "Bilingualism and Mental Measures: A Word of Caution" in Carol A. Hernandez et al., eds., *Chicanos: Social and Psychological Perspectives* (2nd ed.; Mosby, 1976), focuses on some key issues relative to the use of standardized intelligence tests in bilingual minority groups. In a poignant autobiography, Richard Rodriquez, *Hunger of Memory: The Education of Richard Rodriquez* (David R. Godine, 1981), views the issues from an unusual perspective and questions the traditional arguments supporting bilingualism and affirmative action in higher education.

Chapter 8, "The Bilingual Instruction Model," in Ricardo L. Garcia, *Teaching in a Pluralistic Society: Concepts, Models, Strategies* (Harper & Row, 1982), is a clear and concise overview of research on bilingual education, with a thought-provoking discussion of some critical issues in bilingualism.

For statistical reports on demographic changes in the United States, see a special issue entitled "Here They Come, Ready or Not," of *Education Week*, 14 May 1986, pp. 13–40.

Starting with Michael Harrington's *The Other America: Poverty in the United States* (Macmillan, 1962), a spate of books presaged the recent concern with poverty. Traveling among migrant workers, African American citizens, and Native Americans in the United States, Jacob Holdt, *American Pictures: A Personal Journey through the American Underclass* (Copenhagen, Denmark: American Pictures Foundation, 1985), presents a powerful, disturbing portrait of courage, dignity, and intense poverty. Edgar May, *The Wasted Americans: Cost of Our Welfare Dilemma* (Harper & Row, 1964), points to the tragic plight of "the shadow children." The same theme is explored by Robert Coles, *Children of Crisis: A Study of Courage and Fear* (Atlantic–Little, Brown, 1967), which paints a grim picture of poverty and human suffering in the South. See also volumes 4 and 5 of Robert Coles, *Children of Crisis: Eskimos, Chicanos, Indians* (Atlantic–Little, Brown, 1977), and *Privileged Ones: The Well-Off and the Rich in America* (Atlantic–Little, Brown, 1977). Frank Riessman, *Strategies Against Poverty* (Random House, 1969), discusses some programs aimed at removing or reducing the poverty syndrome. Jonathan Kozol, *Rachel and Her Children: Homeless Families in America* (Crown, 1988) focuses on the mothers and their children who are in temporary shelters of New York City's "welfare hotels," a tragic picture of homeless families and children "at risk." Sally Reed and R. Craig Sautter, "Children of Poverty: The Status of 12 Million Young Americans," *Phi Delta Kappan* 71 (June 1990): K1–K12, present a timely report, revealing that "the nation's children are worse off than ever, 25 years after America first declared war on poverty." "The mind-boggling statistics paint a dreadful picture of what life in this nation is like for far too many children. The result is frightening."

By 1991 numerous organizations and educational groups were focusing on the problems and welfare of children in the United States. Most noteworthy is the Children's Defense Fund (CDF), a private, nonprofit child-advocacy organization that disseminates extensive information and research publications. For a list of current materials, contact the CDF at 122 C Street, N.W., Washington, DC, 20001.

For comparative studies, see Oscar Lewis's *Five Families: Mexican Case Studies in the Culture of Poverty* (Basic Books, 1959), and *The Children of Sánchez: Autobiography of a Mexican Family* (Random House, 1961); both are important anthropological field works, carried out with compassion and insight and reported in humanistic, face-to-face dialogues. In another book entitled *A Study of Slum Culture: Backgrounds for La Vida* (Random House, 1968), Oscar Lewis compares the life styles of low-income Puerto Rican families from the slums of San Juan with their relatives who have emigrated to New York City.

Robert Benjamin, *Making Schools Work: A Reporter's Journey through Some of America's Most Remarkable Classrooms* (Continuum, 1981), shows some interesting alternatives that work—many within urban public school systems for the poor in which children of the urban poor are enthusiastically learning. Mario D. Fantini and Gerald Weinstein, *The Disadvantaged: Challenge to Education* (Harper & Row, 1968), discuss "the hidden curriculum" that children from the culture of poverty learn outside the formal classroom. For a comprehensive report, with extended commentaries and critiques, see *Project Head Start: A Legacy of the War on Poverty*, Edward Zigler and Jeanette Valentine, eds. (Free Press, 1979).

For a useful guide to published and unpublished sources, focusing on the contemporary scene and including a vast range of 668 separate items, see Barbara J. Robinson and J. Cordell Robinson, comp., *The Mexican American: A Critical Guide to Research Aids* (JAI Press, 1980). For brief histories of the second largest minority group in American society, see Harold J. Alford, *The Proud Peoples: The Heritage and Culture of Spanish-Speaking Peoples in the United States* (David McKay, 1972); Joan W. Moore, *Mexican Americans* (2nd ed.; Prentice-Hall, 1976); and Julian Samora and Patricia Vandel Simon, *A History of the Mexican American People* (University of Notre Dame Press, 1977). "Selected Documentary Films" are listed in Stan Steiner, *The Mexican Americans* (Minority Rights Group, February 1979; Report No. 39), pp. 18–19. Written in a journalistic style, Stan Steiner's *La Raza: The Mexican Americans* (Harper & Row, 1970), focuses on some fascinating episodes in the Mexican-American experience in the United States.

The complications and problems stemming from the great increase in the illegal migration of Mexicans into the United States are analyzed in Paul R. Ehrich et al., *The Golden Door: International Migration, Mexico and the United States* (Ballantine Books, 1979). On the experiences of Mexican Americans in a migrant camp in the Midwest, see Bret Williams, "Migrants on the Prairie: Untangling Everyday Life," in Stanley A. West and June Macklin, eds., *The Chicano Experience* (Westview Press, 1979), pp. 83–106. For a range of contemporary articles dealing with issues on the mental health of Mexican Americans, see part 3 of Augustin Baron, Jr., *Explorations in Chicano Psychology* (Praeger, 1981), and part 4 of Joe L. Martinez, Jr., ed., *Chicano Psychology* (Academic Press, 1977).

Using an interdisciplinary approach, chapter 7, "The Education Gap," of Leo Grebler et al., *The Mexican-American People: The Nation's Second Largest Minority* (Free Press, 1970), pp. 142–79, focuses on the low attainment in formal schooling. Chapter 4, "Education: The Equal Opportunity Myth," of Tony Castro, *Chicano Power: The Emergence of Mexican America* (Dutton, *Saturday Review Press*, 1974) highlights the Mexican-American's struggle for better schooling. See also Gilbert G. Gonzalez, *Chicano Education in the Era of Segregation* (Balch Institute Press, 1990), which portrays another chapter in the continuing struggle for justice and equal opportunity. For an overview of the Chicano movement, with some timely selections from the protest literature, see Gilberto Lopez y Rivas, *The Chicanos: Life and Struggles of the Mexican Minority in the United States with Readings* (Monthly Review Press, 1973), translated and edited by Elizabeth Martinez and Gilberto Lopez y Rivas.

Jerome Karabel, "Perspectives on Open Admissions," from *Universal Higher Education*, ed. Logan Wilson (American Council on Education, 1972), is a thought-provoking essay. For a case history of "open admissions" at CUNY, see Theodore L. Gross, "How to Kill a College: The Private Papers of a Campus Dean," *Saturday Review* 5 (4 February 1978): 13–20. The final recommendations of the Carnegie Commission on Higher Education are summarized in chapter 12 of *Priorities for Action: Final Report of the Carnegie Commission on Higher Education* (McGraw-Hill, 1973).

Malcolm S. Knowles, *A History of the Adult Education Movement in the United States* (R. E. Krieger, 1977), contains useful background information. See also Harold W. Stubblefield, *Towards a History of Adult Education in America: The Search for a Unifying Principle* (Routledge, 1988). For an overview of trends in continuing education, with a focus on the adult learner and adult learning programs, see Peter Jarvis, *Adult and Continuing Education: Theory and Practice* (Nichols, 1983). The entire issue of the Harvard Graduate School of Education *Alumni Bulletin*, 32 (Summer 1989), 1–16, which focuses on the increasing concern over adult literacy, is a good introduction to a critical problem of the 1980s and 1990s.

The best biography to shed light on Eleanor Roosevelt's work after Franklin's death is Joseph P. Lash's *Eleanor: The Years Alone* (Norton, 1972). Several manuscript collections at the Schlesinger Library, Radcliffe College, bear directly on Eleanor Roosevelt's life and work. J. William T. Youngs, *Eleanor Roosevelt: A Personal and Public Life* (Little, Brown, 1984), is a moving description of Eleanor Roosevelt's growing sensitivity to the hardship and misery of millions of men, women, and children during a period of vast economic and social changes.

CHAPTER 14: APPROACHING THE TWENTY-FIRST CENTURY

Phillip C. Schlechty, *Schools for the 21st Century: Leadership Imperatives for Educational Reform* (Jossey-Bass, 1990), suggests new strategies to make schools more responsive to the needs of children. *Harvard Educational Review* editorial board, *Education in Crisis: The Impact of the New Federalism* (1983), examines some of the funding changes and cutbacks experienced on the state and local school levels during the 1980s and discusses some of the long-term effects of the "New Federalism." Beryl A. Radin and Willis D. Hawley, *The Politics of Federal Reorganization: Creating the Department of Education* (Pergamon Books, 1988), describes the battle to give cabinet status to the federal role in education.

James R. Beniger, *The Control Revolution: The Technological and Economic Origins of the Information Society* (Harvard University Press, 1986), is a thought-provoking discussion of society's growing dependence on new information technology. Chapter 7, "Advantages and Disadvantages of Computers in Education," in Alfred Bork, *Personal Computers for Education* (Harper & Row, 1985), is a concise and balanced discussion. In *Run, Computer, Run: The Mythology of Educational Innovation* (Harvard University Press, 1969), Anthony G. Oettinger takes a critical look at the uses (and misuses) of the educational hardware and argues that instructional technology "is being forcefed, oversold, and prematurely applied." For insightful discussions of the technological boom in microcomputers, see "Colleges Struggling to Cope With the Computer Age," *Chronicle of Higher Education* 26 (30 March 1983): 1, 10; and "Big I.B.M. Has Done It Again," *New York Times*, 132 (27 March 1983), section 3, pp. 1, 28. The impact of computer technology on colleges and universities is discussed in Jack Magarrell, "Microcomputers Proliferate on College Campuses," *Chronicle of Higher Education*, 26 (6 April 1983): 9.

For a fascinating discussion of research to develop artificial intelligence, see William Stockton, "Creating Computers that Think," *New York Times Magazine*, December 7, 1980, pp. 41, 182–87. Hans Moravec, *Mind Children: The Future of Robot and Human Intelligence* (Harvard University Press, 1988), presents an astonishing view of the future in which the line between biological and artificial intelligence disappears with the emergence of "the intelligent robot, a machine that can think and act as a human, however inhuman it may be in physical or mental detail." In *Mindstorms: Children, Computers, and Powerful Ideas* (Basic Books, 1980), Seymour Papert discusses his research at the Artificial Intelligence Laboratory at the Massachusetts Institute of Technology, where children master the powerful technology of computers and explore some of the deepest ideas in science and mathematics. Theodore Roszak, *Cult of Information: Folklore of Computers and the True Art of Thinking* (Pantheon, 1986), is a harsh critique of the new "data merchants" (the "hackers and hucksters") and the development of "fifth generation" computers that simulate human reasoning. Chapter 6, "Artificial Intelligence: The Expert Tool," of Howard Gardner, *The Mind's New Science: A History of the Cognitive Revolution* (Basic Books, 1985), explores some critical issues surrounding the famous Dartmouth College meeting of 1956 on artificial intelligence, at which ten young scholars discussed the possibilities of producing computer programs that could "behave" or "think" intelligently. See also Chapter 1, "Can a Computer Have a Mind?" of Roger Penrose, *The Emperor's New Mind: Concerning Computers, Minds, and the Laws of Physics* (Oxford University Press, 1989). Chapter 4, "The Promise of the Computer," of Larry Cuban, *Teachers and Machines: The Classroom Use of Technology Since 1920* (Teachers College Press, 1986), questions some basic assumptions regarding the use of microcomputers in public school classrooms.

Christopher Lasch, *The Minimal Self: Psychic Survival in Troubled Times* (Norton, 1984), expresses a pessimistic outlook on the future, in which "people have lost confidence. . . . In the nuclear age, survival has become an issue of overriding importance." Chapter 7, "Children and the Nuclear Bomb," of Robert Coles, *The Moral Life of Children* (Atlantic Monthly Press, 1986), explores children's fears about death from nuclear war.

Index

Abbott, Edward, 127
Abrams, Frank W., 300
Academies, 64–67
Acculturation, 337–338
Ackley, David, 377
Act of 1642, 36
Act of 1647, 37
Adamic, Louis, 248
Adams, Abigail Smith, 224–225,
    244 *n*. 10
Adams, Charles Francis, Jr., 168–169
Adams, John, 24, 225
Addams, Jane, 144, 145, 147–149, 174
Adler, Felix, 148–149, 294–295
Adolescence
    psychology of, 191
    as time of repression for girls, 236, 237
Adult education, 358–360
Advertisements, for 18th-century private
    schools, 63–64
Advertising Federation of America, 254
Affirmative action
    to benefit education of women,
        237–238
    in higher education, 317–322
African Americans. *See also* Slave system
    civil rights movement for, 238–241
    in colonial period, 19
    demographic information of, 343–345
    equal educational opportunities for,
        328. *See also* Equal opportunity
    IQ controversy regarding, 355–356
    movement to disfranchise, 120–121
    in post-Civil War period, 119–120,
        238–239
    poverty among, 347, 348
    public education for, 57, 124–127
    respect for achievements of, 359
    segregation of, 238–240, 318
    voting rights for, 226, 239

Age of Enlightenment. *See* Enlightenment
    period
Age of Reason (Paine), 51
Agriculture
    in colonial South, 5, 8–10
    impact of cotton cultivation
        on Southern, 76–78
Aiken, Wilfred, 274
Alcohol use, 286
Alternative schools
    drive to establish, 284
    and progressive education of 1990s, 285
American Academy of Arts and Sciences,
    297
American Association for the Advancement
    of Science, 297
American Association of Colleges
    for Teacher Education (AACTE), 309
American Association of School
    Administrators, 268
American Association of Teachers Colleges,
    309
American Association of University
    Professors, 298
American Bar Association (ABA), 307,
    309
American Business System, 259
American Chemical Society, 297
American Committee for Democracy
    and Intellectual Freedom, 257
American Economic Association, 298
American Federation of Teachers (AFT),
    307–308
American Historical Association, 297–298
American Indian Leadership Conference,
    340
American Indians. *See* Native Americans
American Industries magazine, 135
American Institute of Instruction, 90
American Irish Historical Society, 298

413